WORLD RELIGIONS TODAY

WORLD RELIGIONS TODAY

Fifth Edition

JOHN L. ESPOSITO
Georgetown University

DARRELL J. FASCHING
University of South Florida

TODD T. LEWIS
College of the Holy Cross

New York   Oxford
OXFORD UNIVERSITY PRESS

Oxford University Press is a department of the University of Oxford. It furthers the University's
objective of excellence in research, scholarship, and education by publishing worldwide.

Oxford   New York
Auckland   Cape Town   Dar es Salaam   Hong Kong   Karachi
Kuala Lumpur   Madrid   Melbourne   Mexico City   Nairobi
New Delhi   Shanghai   Taipei   Toronto

With offices in
Argentina   Austria   Brazil   Chile   Czech Republic   France   Greece
Guatemala   Hungary   Italy   Japan   Poland   Portugal   Singapore
South Korea   Switzerland   Thailand   Turkey   Ukraine   Vietnam

For titles covered by Section 112 of the US Higher Education Opportunity Act,
please visit www.oup.com/us/he for the latest information about
pricing and alternate formats.

Published by Oxford University Press
198 Madison Avenue, New York, NY 10016
www.oup.com

Library of Congress Cataloging-in-Publication Data

Esposito, John L.
    World religions today / John L. Esposito, Georgetown University; Darrell J. Fasching, University of
South Florida; Todd T. Lewis, College of the Holy Cross.—Fifth edition.
        pages cm
    ISBN 978-0-19-999959-0
    1. Religions—Textbooks.   I. Fasching, Darrell J., 1944–   II. Lewis, Todd, 1952–   III. Title.
    BL80.3.E88 2014
    200—dc23
                                                                                    2014008987

Printing number: 9 8 7 6 5 4 3 2 1
Printed in the United States of America on acid-free paper

For Jean Esposito and Melissa and Nathan Lewis,
and in memory of Harold and Lillian Gushin

BRIEF CONTENTS

CONTENTS

Chapter 4   CHRISTIAN DIVERSITY AND THE ROAD TO MODERNITY   147

Chapter 7   BUDDHISM: PATHS TOWARD NIRVANA   399

Chapter 9   GLOBALIZATION: FROM NEW TO NEW AGE RELIGIONS

PREFACE

Religion is unquestionably a dynamic spiritual and political force in the world today. Around the globe religious experiences and beliefs profoundly change individual lives even as they influence politics and play a powerful role in international affairs. This fifth edition of *World Religions Today* addresses this reality with an introductory volume for college and university students.

Although this is a multiauthored text, with each author taking primary responsibility for different chapters (John Esposito: Islam; Darrell Fasching: Judaism, Christianity, and New Age Religions and Globalization; and Todd Lewis: Hinduism, Buddhism, East Asian Religions, and Indigenous Religions), it has truly been a collaborative project from start to finish. Throughout the entire process we shared and commented on each other's material.

World Religions Today grew out of our several decades of experience in teaching world religions. It is a product of our conviction that, for our students to understand the daily news accounts of religions in our global situation, they need more than just the ancient foundations of the world's religions. Textbooks on world religions have too often tended to emphasize historical origins and doctrinal developments, focusing on the past and giving short shrift to the "modern" world. Many stressed a textual, theological/philosophical, or legal approach, one that gave insufficient attention to the modern alterations of these traditions. Most gave little attention to their social institutions or their connections to political power. As a result, students came away with a maximum appreciation for the origins and development of the classical traditions but a minimum awareness of the continued dynamism and relevance of religious traditions today. So, despite the growing visibility and impact of a global religious resurgence and of the unprecedented globalization of all world religions, most textbooks have not quite caught up. *World Religions Today* began with our commitment to address this situation.

World Religions Today, Fifth Edition, continues our hallmark approach of using historical coverage of religious traditions as a framework to help students understand how faiths have evolved to the present day. Indeed, we open most chapters with an "Encounter with Modernity." These encounters illustrate the tension between the premodern religious views and the modern/postmodern world. Each chapter then returns to the origins of the tradition to trace the path that led to this confrontation with "modernity." We attempt to show not only how each tradition has been changed by its encounter with modernity but also how each religion in turn has influenced the contemporary world.

NEW TO THE FIFTH EDITION

The book's major theme and chapter structure have been retained from the earlier editions, though they have been updated and revised. We have also updated chapter content to reflect recent events at the time of writing. In response to reviewer suggestions, we have included the following new content:

- NEW marginal definitions of Key Terms help students understand each term within its immediate context.
- EXPANDED coverage of Zoroastrianism (Chapter 4), Baha'i (Chapter 9), and Jehovah's Witnesses (Chapter 9)

FEATURES

Each chapter is enriched by a wide variety of thematic and special-topic boxes that explore particular ideas or practices in some depth. It is our hope that these lively and interesting boxes are seen as an integral part of the text, allowing students to imagine how religion today is among the most colorful, lively, and striking of human endeavors.

- "Gender Focus" boxes present additional information, beyond that in the regular text, about different practices by believers of different sexes.
- "Rituals and Rites" boxes describe the ritual practices of believers, often with a focus on ways these rites have changed over time.
- "Contrasting Religious Visions" boxes compare the beliefs of two significant adherents of a faith who each see the demands of their religion calling believers in very different directions in the modern age. These demonstrate that, no matter what religion we are examining, that very same religious tradition can be used to promote both peacemaking and conflict.
- "Teachings of Religious Wisdom" boxes offer some of the primary texts and formal teachings of different religions.
- "Tales of Spiritual Transformation" offer descriptions of religious experiences in the believers' own words.

SUPPLEMENTARY MATERIALS

For the instructor: Supplementary materials are available on the Oxford University Press **Ancillary Resource Center (ARC)**, a convenient, instructor-focused single destination for resources to accompany your text. Accessed online through individual user accounts, the ARC provides instructors with access to up-to-date ancillaries at any time while guaranteeing the security of grade-significant resources. In addition, it allows OUP to keep instructors informed when new content becomes available. Available on the ARC:

- The **Instructor's Manual**, which includes the following:

  Chapter summaries
  Chapter goals
  Key terms with definitions
  Lecture outlines
  Suggested web links and other resources

- A **Computerized Test Bank**, including 40 fill-in-the-blank, 40 multiple-choice, 40 true/false, and 12 essay/discussion questions per chapter
- **Lecture outlines** as PowerPoint®-based slides

A link to the ARC is available on the **Companion Website** (www.oup.com/us /esposito).

For the student: The **Companion Website** (www.oup.com/us/esposito) includes the following student resources:

- Chapter goals
- Flashcards of key terms
- Suggested web links and other resources
- Self-quizzes, containing 20 fill-in-the-blank, 20 multiple-choice, 20 true/false, and 6 essay/discussion questions per chapter, selected from the Test Bank in the ARC

The Instructor's Manual and Computerized Test Bank, as well as the student material from the Companion Website, is also available in **Learning Management System Cartridges**, in a fully downloadable format for instructors using a learning management system in their courses.

Dashboard by Oxford University Press delivers a wealth of activities and assessments for *World Religions Today* in an intuitive, text-specific, integrated learning system. The *World Religions Today* Dashboard site includes the following:

- Chapter goals
- One "Level 1" and one "Level 2" quiz per chapter, each containing 15 multiple-choice and 5 true/false questions, some of which are taken from the Test Bank in the ARC. All Dashboard quiz questions are **automatically graded** and linked to the chapter goals

- A complete glossary of key terms
- Flashcards of key terms for each chapter

Access to Dashboard can be packaged with the text at a discount, stocked separately by your college bookstore, or purchased directly at www.oup.com/us/dashboard. For details, please contact your Oxford University Press representative or call 800-445-9714.

ACKNOWLEDGMENTS

This fifth edition of *World Religions Today* has been substantially revised in light of the valuable comments we continue to receive from colleagues across the country who have used it and in light of our own subsequent experiences and reflections. We offer special thanks to the following professors and to the other, anonymous, reviewers. This edition is much stronger because of their thoughtful comments:

Todd M. Brenneman, University of Central Florida
Robert Brown, James Madison University
David Kitts, Carson-Newman University
Peter David Lee, Columbia College—California
Robin L. Owens, Mount St. Mary's College
Linda Pittman, College of William and Mary
Paul Schneider, University of South Florida
Caleb Simmons, University of Mississippi
Phillip Spivey, University of Central Arkansas
Mlen-Too Wesley, Penn State University
Mark Whitters, Eastern Michigan University
Simon A. Wood, University of Nebraska—Lincoln

Thanks also to the reviewers of the previous editions for their lasting input on the work: Constantina Rhodes Bailly, Eckerd College; Herbert Berg, University of North Carolina–Wilmington; Sheila Briggs, University of Southern California; Terry L. Burden, University of Louisville; Dexter E. Callender Jr., University of Miami; David Capes, Houston Baptist University; James E. Deitrick, University of Central Arkansas; Sergey Dolgopolski, University of Kansas; Joan Earley, State University of New York at Albany; James Egge, Eastern Michigan University; John Farina, George Mason University; Debora Y. Fonteneau, Savannah State University; Liora Gubkin, California State University–Bakersfield; William David Hart, University of North Carolina–Greensboro; William Hutchins, Appalachian State University; Father Brad Karelius, Saddleback Community College; Sandra T. Keating, Providence College; Mohammad Hassan Khalil, University of Illinois;

Louis Komjathy, University of San Diego; Ian Maclean, James Madison University; Sean McCloud, University of North Carolina at Charlotte; Tim Murphy, University of Alabama; Nancy Nahra, Champlain College; Jason Neelis, University of Florida; Patrick Nnoromele, Eastern Kentucky University; Catherine Orsborn, University of Denver; Andrew Pavelich, University of Houston–Downtown; Kris Pratt, Spartanburg Methodist College; Rick Rogers, Eastern Michigan University; Barry R. Sang, Catawba College; Brooke Schedneck, Arizona State University; D. Neil Schmid, North Carolina State University; Martha Ann Selby, University of Texas at Austin; Theresa S. Smith, Indiana University of Pennsylvania; Yushau Sodiq, Texas Christian University; Bruce Sullivan, Northern Arizona University; Aaron J. Hahn Tapper, University of San Francisco; James H. Thrall, International College–University of Bridgeport; Eglute Trinkauske, Nazareth College; Peter Umoh, University of Bridgeport; Hugh B. Urban, Ohio State University; Anne Vallely, University of Ottawa; Andrew Christian Van Gorder, Baylor University; Glenn Wallis, University of Georgia; Tammie Wanta, University of North Carolina at Charlotte; Catherine Wessinger, Loyola University New Orleans.

We have been fortunate to work with an excellent, supportive, and creative team at Oxford University Press, led by Robert Miller, Executive Editor in Oxford's Higher Education Group. Senior Production Editor Barbara Mathieu, Editorial Assistants Kaitlin Coats and Emily Krupin, and Senior Development Editor Meg Botteon have been extraordinarily supportive throughout the writing process. Our thanks also to Robin Tuthill, who prepared the student and instructor support materials for the first four editions of the book, and to Kate Kelley, who updated them for this fifth edition.

John L. Esposito
Darrell J. Fasching
Todd T. Lewis

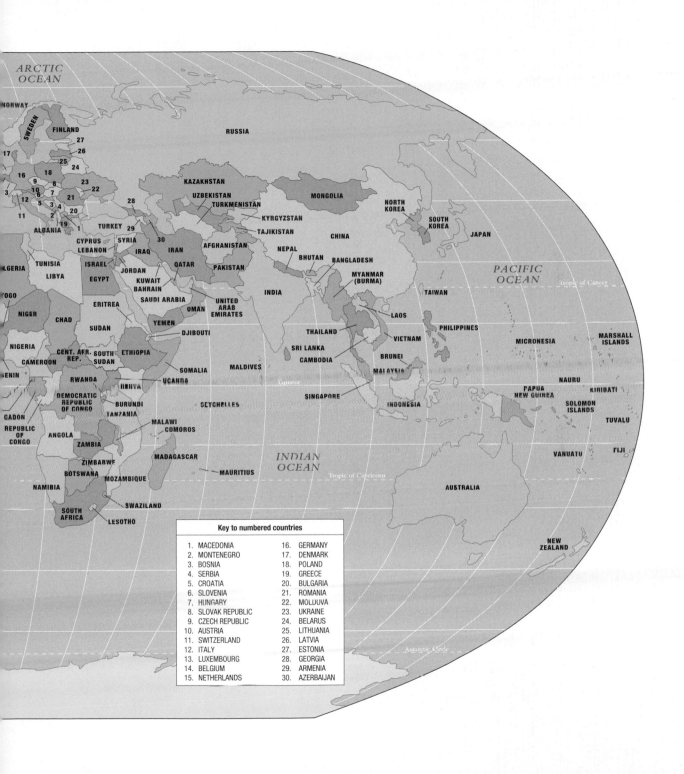

ARCTIC OCEAN

NORWAY
SWEDEN
FINLAND
RUSSIA

27
26
17
25
24
16 18
9 8 23 22
3 10 6 7 28
12 5 3 4 21
11 2 20
19 1
ALBANIA
TURKEY 29
CYPRUS SYRIA 30
LEBANON IRAQ IRAN
ISRAEL JORDAN
EGYPT KUWAIT
BAHRAIN
SAUDI ARABIA
OMAN
YEMEN
DJIBOUTI

KAZAKHSTAN
UZBEKISTAN
TURKMENISTAN
KYRGYZSTAN
TAJIKISTAN
AFGHANISTAN
PAKISTAN
NEPAL BHUTAN
BANGLADESH
INDIA

MONGOLIA
CHINA

NORTH KOREA
SOUTH KOREA
JAPAN

PACIFIC OCEAN
Tropic of Cancer

MYANMAR (BURMA)
LAOS
THAILAND
VIETNAM
CAMBODIA
TAIWAN
PHILIPPINES

MARSHALL ISLANDS

UNITED ARAB EMIRATES

ALGERIA
TUNISIA
LIBYA
TOGO
NIGER
CHAD
NIGERIA
CAMEROON
CENT. AFR. REP.
SOUTH SUDAN
SUDAN
ERITREA
ETHIOPIA
SOMALIA
UGANDA
RWANDA
KENYA
BURUNDI
TANZANIA
DEMOCRATIC REPUBLIC OF CONGO
GABON
REPUBLIC OF CONGO
ANGOLA
ZAMBIA
MALAWI
COMOROS
ZIMBABWE
MADAGASCAR
MOZAMBIQUE
BOTSWANA
MAURITIUS
NAMIBIA
SWAZILAND
SOUTH AFRICA
LESOTHO

BENIN

MALDIVES
SRI LANKA
SINGAPORE
BRUNEI
MALAYSIA
INDONESIA

SEYCHELLES
Equator

INDIAN OCEAN

NAURU
KIRIBATI
PAPUA NEW GUINEA
SOLOMON ISLANDS
TUVALU
VANUATU
FIJI

MICRONESIA

Tropic of Capricorn

AUSTRALIA

NEW ZEALAND

Antarctic Circle

Key to numbered countries

1.	MACEDONIA	16.	GERMANY
2.	MONTENEGRO	17.	DENMARK
3.	BOSNIA	18.	POLAND
4.	SERBIA	19.	GREECE
5.	CROATIA	20.	BULGARIA
6.	SLOVENIA	21.	ROMANIA
7.	HUNGARY	22.	MOLDOVA
8.	SLOVAK REPUBLIC	23.	UKRAINE
9.	CZECH REPUBLIC	24.	BELARUS
10.	AUSTRIA	25.	LITHUANIA
11.	SWITZERLAND	26.	LATVIA
12.	ITALY	27.	ESTONIA
13.	LUXEMBOURG	28.	GEORGIA
14.	BELGIUM	29.	ARMENIA
15.	NETHERLANDS	30.	AZERBAIJAN

WORLD RELIGIONS TODAY

INTRODUCTION

Globalization: World Religions in Everyone's Hometown

1

I n an age of globalization, human events reach through time and around the world to transform our personal, social, and political lives. In 2008 the citizens of the United States elected their first African American president, Barack Obama. This would not have been possible without the civil rights movement of nonviolent protest against racial injustice led by a black Baptist minister, Dr. Martin Luther King Jr. Fifty-some years earlier King's movement brought racial equality and equal voting rights to the United States. Likewise, Dr. King's commitment to bringing about racial equality through the use of nonviolent protest would not have been imaginable without the civil rights revolution brought about in the British empire a generation earlier. In South Africa and then India this revolution was led by the great Hindu religious teacher of nonviolence, Mohandas K. Gandhi. Dr. King took Gandhi as his model and learned about nonviolence by studying Gandhi's teachings. America has never been the same since.

In 1950 a black president would have been unimaginable. Then the United States was considered a white Protestant nation whose majority was just beginning to grudgingly accept Catholics and Jews as equal citizens. At that time race still deeply divided America. In many parts of the country, black citizens were forbidden to share the same water fountain or use the same bathrooms as whites. In 1960 the startling news was that John F. Kennedy had been elected the first Catholic president of the United States. Then in 1964 the landmark Civil Rights Act was passed by Congress not long after President Kennedy's assassination.

Just as important as the Civil Rights Act of 1964 was the Immigration Act of 1965, signed by President Lyndon Johnson. This act abolished the immigration system set up in 1924 and modified in 1952. The earlier system heavily favored immigration from

3

Europe and severely restricted immigration from other parts of the world, especially Asia. The 1965 legislation dramatically changed the face of America. According to government figures, in 1950 about 3.6 percent of immigrants were from Asia; by the year 2000, more than 30 percent were. In the fall of 2010 the news headlines reported that for the first time there were no Protestants on the Supreme Court and with the 2012 national election, the governor of one southern state is now of Hindu descent and another is of Sikh descent. All of this indicates that the process of globalization that began in earnest after World War II is profoundly transforming American culture.

In the 1950s, if you walked down the streets of almost any city in the United States, you would have expected to find churches, both Catholic and Protestant, and Jewish synagogues. When people thought about religious diversity, it was limited largely to Protestants, Catholics, and Jews. In the twenty-first century the situation is dramatically different. Almost daily the newspapers take note of new religious members of the community—announcing such events as a meditation retreat at a Korean Zen center in the suburbs of Providence, Rhode Island; the opening of an Islamic mosque in St. Louis, Missouri; or the dedication of a Hindu temple in Tampa, Florida.

Figure 1.1, compiled by Todd Lewis from PEW Foundation reports, census data, and other studies, offers a very rough approximation of the number of adherents of the various religions found in the world today, and their numbers in relation to each other. There is no reliable exact count available or even possible for many reasons: the lack of surveys utilizing the same criteria; disagreements about what is a branch of a world religion and what is a "new religion"; and the lack of any census/survey data from the world's two most populous nations, India and China. Existing surveys that summarize religious identity on a global level are extremely problematic due to these issues of definition, limited global scope, and affiliation.

Central to any survey data is the assumption that a person can be listed under one variable and be only that; but such an exclusive choice of one and only one religion does not very well capture the reality of world religions today. (For this reason, the estimated percentages assigned to each tradition in Figure 1.1 exceed 100%.) Even among those professing to be monotheists, there are now many hyphenated identities (such as Buddhist Jew, Zen Christian, or agnostic Yoga devotee). Singular identity is even more problematic to represent the religious reality for most people in Asia and across the various indigenous peoples across the world, where many follow more than one tradition. As we discuss elsewhere in this textbook, there are many native religions blended with Christianity, or Buddhism, or the ancestor veneration practices rooted in Confucian tradition; in other words, individuals can adhere to two or more traditions and feel no need or compulsion to choose just one. In East Asia, individuals typically follow the "diffuse religious tradition," a mixture founded on Confucianism, with elements of Daoism, Buddhism, and often shamanism. If we listed those in the world who believe in and resort to spirit mediums (shamans, oracles, etc.), it is possible that their total number (from Hindus, Buddhists, East Asians, and indigenous peoples) would be greater than those counted in the largest organized religion, Christianity. And those now following one of the world's "new religions" embrace a new tradition that combines elements from the major world religions with one or more others such

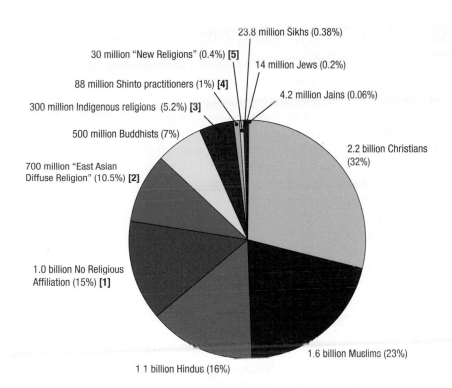

23.8 million Sikhs (0.38%)

30 million "New Religions" (0.4%) **[5]**

88 million Shinto practitioners (1%) **[4]**

300 million Indigenous religions (5.2%) **[3]**

500 million Buddhists (7%)

700 million "East Asian Diffuse Religion" (10.5%) **[2]**

1.0 billion No Religious Affiliation (15%) **[1]**

14 million Jews (0.2%)

4.2 million Jains (0.06%)

2.2 billion Christians (32%)

1.6 billion Muslims (23%)

1.1 billion Hindus (16%)

Figure 1.1 The world's major religions (percentage of global population).

Notes:

[1] Includes atheists, agnostics, and people who do not self-identify with any particular religion in surveys. Studies have also revealed that many of the "religiously unaffiliated" do have some religious beliefs. Some of the religiously unaffiliated, for example, do express belief in God or a higher power, a view shared, for example, by 7% of Chinese unaffiliated adults, 30% of French unaffiliated adults, and 68% of unaffiliated U.S. adults. Some of the unaffiliated also engage in certain kinds of religious practices. For example, 7% of unaffiliated adults in France and 27% of those in the United States say they attend religious services at least once a year.

[2] A combination of Confucian, Daoist, and local religious devotions. This figure was estimated based on a Chinese government statistic indicating that 44% of adults reported that they had worshiped at a graveside or tomb in the survey year.

[3] Practice various folk or traditional religions, including African traditional religions, Indian tribal traditions, Native American religions, and Australian aboriginal religions.

[4] This number for adherents to Shinto in Japan is based on recent surveys that have shown that 80% of Japanese register their newborn children at a Shinto shrine, and that roughly the same number visit these temples on New Year's Day and other major traditional holidays.

[5] The formation of new religions has been a key hallmark of global religious life since 1750, and it has been recorded on every continent. Some have come and gone (such as the "Shakers" in Colonial America); some have arisen and command the loyalty of few until today; most have arisen and spread in a particular region; a few have become global in membership.

as ancestral cults, martial arts, and new Western philosophies or psychologies. It is easy for demographers to give a false certainty to the pluralistic and fluid boundaries of the world's religions today.

Why Study World Religions?

In the emerging global economy, most neighborhoods, workplaces, and schools reflect this diversity as well. The beliefs and practices of world religions have become part of the mosaic of American society. *Karma* has become part of the American vocabulary, Hindu visualization practices are used in sports training, and Buddhist meditation techniques have been adopted in programs of stress management. No matter where we live today, it is more and more likely that our next-door neighbors are ethnically, politically, and, yes, even religiously diverse—coming from many parts of the globe (see Map 1.1). To understand other religions is no longer an "elective" activity that one might do just because it is interesting. Today understanding diverse religions is a necessity because it is now about understanding our neighbors. If we do not understand each other, our misunderstandings may well lead to prejudice, conflict, and even violence.

The academic study of religion is one of the newest disciplines in the modern university. Its beginnings go back to the emergence of the social sciences in the nineteenth century, with the appearance of such fields as anthropology, sociology, and comparative linguistics. One of the great founding fathers of this study was the Indologist Max Muller (1825–1900), who argued that "the person who knows only one religion understands none."[1] It is only by studying the diverse expressions of religion throughout history and across cultures that we come to understand its unity and diversity.

Prior to the 1960s, in the United States, for instance, one could not have studied religions comparatively in secular and state universities. Only religious colleges and universities offered courses on religion, and these were typically on the teachings of their own denominations. If other religions came up for discussion it was usually to point out their "erroneous teachings." Then in the 1960s departments of religious studies began to appear in nonreligious colleges and secular state universities. Responding to the new diversity brought on by globalization, these departments began to offer courses on Asian traditions such as Hinduism and Buddhism, on Islam and comparative religions. What they attempted was completely new in history: They sought to empathetically understand the diverse religious traditions of the world in an objective manner.

The academic study of religion requires a new way of looking at the religion of others. It requires the courage and compassion to sympathetically understand the diverse worldviews of others and the willingness to learn from each. Its goal is not to show one religion is right and all others wrong but rather to show what humans have found compelling in each and how each tradition has shaped history. The task in the study of world religions today is to overcome stereotypes and glimpse the wisdom found in each of these traditions. To judge another's religion without understanding it and what it means to its members is to "prejudge" them—that is the meaning of the word *prejudice*. When encountering beliefs and practices we do not understand, it is

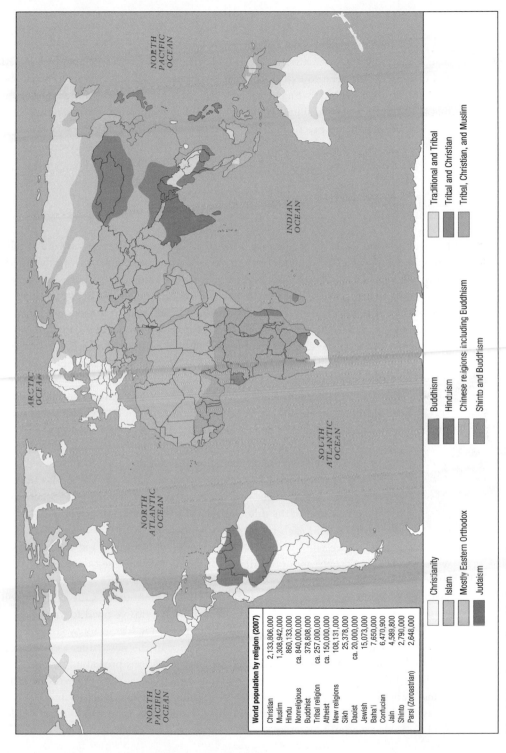

World population by religion (2007)	
Christian	2,133,806,000
Muslim	1,308,942,000
Hindu	860,133,000
Nonreligious	ca. 840,000,000
Buddhist	378,808,000
Tribal religion	ca. 257,000,000
Atheist	ca. 150,000,000
New religions	108,131,000
Sikh	25,378,000
Daoist	ca. 20,000,000
Jewish	15,073,000
Baha'i	7,650,000
Confucian	6,470,900
Jain	4,589,800
Shinto	2,790,000
Parsi (Zoroastrian)	2,648,000

Christianity
Islam
Mostly Eastern Orthodox
Judaism

Buddhism
Hinduism
Chinese religions including Buddhism
Shinto and Buddhism

Traditional and Tribal
Tribal and Christian
Tribal, Christian, and Muslim

Map 1.1 Distribution of world religions today

In surveying world religions today, we shall not be able to cover everything that could be said about them. Our selection will be governed primarily by the following question: What do we need to know about the past to understand the role of religion in the world we live in today?

easy to fall into the trap of ridiculing them, saying, "How can anyone possibly believe that?" Certainly each of us wants to be understood and respected, not stereotyped and dismissed. We need to extend that same courtesy to all others as well. So in the academic study of religion we agree to "bracket" our preconceptions and prejudices—that is, put them aside and simply try to understand and appreciate the meaning others find in their beliefs and practices.

Our Task

In this book we focus on the diverse ways in which human beings have been religious in the past and are religious today. Indeed, the last decades of the twentieth century brought a global religious resurgence, a development that defied countless predictions that the irresistible secularization of civilization would lead to the disappearance of religion. Religions, it was thought, are tied to ancient premodern worldviews, and these would inevitably be replaced by a worldview based on modern science. Indeed, the clash of traditional religions with contemporary scientific and secular society is a major concern of this textbook. Awareness of this conflict is essential if we are to understand the interactions between religions and cultures in the world today. We will begin every chapter not with a discussion of the origins and early history of each religious tradition, but with examples of a major controversy or significant tension each religion faces in the world today.

We describe our present time as one in transition between "modernity" and a new "postmodern" era of globalization that is emerging. To understand what is "new" about our situation, we will have to understand the premodern period of the different religious traditions and how the premodern worldview of each relates to and contrasts with the modern period. In particular, we will have to compare the premodern period in each tradition with the changes brought about by an era that began with the rise of modern science after 1500 and declined after World War II. In surveying world religions today, we shall not be able to cover everything that could be said about them. Our selection will be governed primarily by the following question: What do we need to know about the past to understand the role of religion in the world we live in today? In order to understand many of the conflicts that we read about in the newspaper or watch on cable news, we need to understand how religious traditions profoundly shaped the world to be the way it is today. Since religious beliefs are at the center of the individual's core values, and because religious communities are major actors in our world today, studying world religions provides crucial insights for understanding our world. And to do that we must begin by introducing some basic concepts.

With the Space Age, awareness that all humans share life in a global village has come to the religions and cultures of the earth.

Understanding Religious Experience and Its Formative Elements

Wherever we find religious practice, as we shall come to see, we will find certain key elements:

> The Experience of Sacredness
> Myth or Symbolic Story (typically embodied in sacred writing or *scripture* and expressed in a system of *beliefs*)
> Ritual
> Community
> Morality
> Religious Leaders/Experts

religion: the sense of being tied or bound by sacred obligations to powers believed to govern our destiny

Let us begin with a working definition of the term **religion**. Suppose we have a time machine and can transport ourselves back to the city of Rome in the first century. Why are we interested in that time and place? The word *religion* has its roots in Latin, the language of the Romans, so understanding how the Romans defined the concept helps us understand our topic.

Imagine yourself now walking down a street in Rome in the first century CE. You approach a small group of people on a street corner and ask them: "What religion are you?" They look at you strangely. They understand the individual words you have spoken, but they don't normally put those words together as you have done. Some give you blank stares, while others just look puzzled. Frustrated, you try rephrasing your question: "Are you religious?" Suddenly their faces light up and they smile and say, "Of course, but who isn't?"

By its wording, the original question assumes that *religion* is a noun applied to distinct social bodies in the world, such that you can be a member of one only if you are not a member of another. So the question seeks to find out the distinct religious group to which you belong. This way of understanding religion naturally arises among monotheists, who by definition have chosen one god and excluded all others. However, such an exclusiveness was foreign to antiquity. In rephrasing the original question as "Are you religious?" you are no longer treating *religion* as a noun, describing something you join. Instead, you are treating it as an adjective, describing an attitude toward the human condition—a way of seeing, acting, and experiencing all things. In most times and places throughout history, religion and culture were like two sides of the same coin. Therefore people did not think of their practices as "a religion"—a separate reality they had to choose over and against another. Today in Japan, for instance, it is possible to practice Buddhism, Daoism, Confucianism, and Shintoism all at the same time. This seems odd from the monotheistic perspective of Western religions, where one can be, for instance, a Muslim or a Christian or a Jew but not two or more at the same time. And yet, paradoxically, Jews, Christians, and Muslims all claim to worship the same God.

In first-century Rome, with very few exceptions, people didn't belong to a religion in any exclusive sense. They were, however, religious. Our first-century respondents would probably continue the discussion you had started something like this: "Being religious is simply a matter of common sense. I respect all those powers that govern my destiny. Therefore I worship all the gods and goddesses. It would be stupid not to. If I must go to war I want the god of war on my side. So I would perform the correct ritual sacrifices before going into battle. And when I looked for someone to marry, I petitioned the goddess of love to help me. And needless to say, when I plant my crops every spring, I do everything possible to ensure that the goddess of fertility and the gods of wind and rain are on my side. I am not a complete idiot. To ignore or antagonize the gods would be stupid."

The Sacred

What does our discussion with the ancient Romans about "religion" tell us? It tells us that religion is about what people hold sacred, what matters more than anything else to them—namely, their destiny individually and collectively. For the ancient Romans, and nearly all other human beings in all places and all times throughout history, religion has been about power and meaning in relation to human destiny. Although its exact root is uncertain, the word *religion* is probably derived from the Latin *religare*, which literally means "to tie or bind" and has the connotation of "acting with care." It expresses our sense of being "tied and bound" by relations of obligation to whatever powers we believe govern our destiny—whether these powers be natural or supernatural, personal or impersonal, one or many.

Ancient peoples everywhere believed that the powers governing their destiny were the forces of nature. Why? Because nature was experienced as that awesome collection of powers that surround and, at times, overwhelm human beings. On the one hand, nature provides life and all its necessities (food, clothing, shelter, etc.); but on the other hand, nature may turn on people, destroying them quite capriciously through earthquakes, storms, floods, and so on. Therefore the forces of nature evoke in human beings the ambivalent feeling of both fascination and dread. Rudolf Otto (1869–1937), a pioneer in the comparative study of religions, argued that the presence of these two ambivalent emotions is a sure sign that one is in the presence of the sacred. They are a defining mark of religious experience across cultures. They are the emotions that are elicited by the uncanny experience of being in the presence of that power or powers one believes have the ability to determine whether one lives or dies and, beyond that, how well one lives.

Religion as a form of human experience and behavior, therefore, is not just about purely "spiritual" things. Nor can the study of religion in global perspective be defined only by gods or God. People's religiousness over the millennia and around the earth has proven to be as diverse as the forms of power they believe govern human destiny. These powers have ranged from gods as forces of nature to the unseen ancestral spirits or spirits associated with sacred places, to more impersonal sacred forces or energies; or finally the mysterious power(s) that govern history (including the seemingly secular powers associated with wealth and politics that get treated as if "sacred"). Hence, whatever powers we believe govern our destiny will elicit a religious response from us and inspire us to wish "to tie or bind" ourselves to these powers in relations of ritual obligation. Thus tied or bound, we will act respectfully and carefully in relation to these powers, to ensure that they will be on our side.

How do we know what our obligations to these powers are? Throughout history this knowledge has been passed down from one generation to the next through myth and ritual.

Myth, Scripture, and Beliefs

Our word **myth** comes from the Greek *mythos*, which means "story." Myth, we could say, is a symbolic story about the origins of the world and destiny of human beings; myth "ties and binds" human beings in relations of obligation to whatever powers they believe ultimately govern their destiny and explains what these powers expect of them. Unlike the contemporary English use of *myth* to indicate an untrue story or a misunderstanding based on ignorance, in every religious tradition, myths

myth: symbolic story about the origins and destiny of human beings and their world

A Shinto priest and believers purify their bodies in icy water for the New Year's ceremony at the Teppozu Shrine in Tokyo.

convey the deepest and most profound truths about life. These truths are expressed through grand stories of creation and destiny rather than in abstract theories. After the invention of writing (about 3000 BCE), these stories came to be written down, creating what we now call the "scriptures" of the various religions. Because these scriptures tell the stories about the power or powers that govern human destiny, they have been treated as sacred scriptures and passed on from one generation to the next.

The fact that the word used to designate these great religious stories, *myth*, came to be understood in modern contemporary language as meaning a "false story" reveals one of the most challenging tasks facing anyone trying to understand religious language. That challenge is understanding the symbolic nature of much of religious language. To understand a religious story literally can often lead to misunderstanding its meaning and so make it seem false. For example, in Western biblical tradition, the Psalms say "God is my shepherd," just as Buddhist scriptures refer to their founder, the Buddha, as "a bull of a man." We know such statements are not meant literally: God is not literally a shepherd, nor is the Buddha literally a bull.

To live well, have many descendants, and live a long life—these are three great treasures in Chinese culture. A Chinese woman prays for prosperity, posterity, and longevity at a Buddhist temple on the island of Lantau.

To speak like this is to speak metaphorically, that is, to use things that are more familiar to help explain what is less familiar, a reality that is mysterious or even beyond human language. Shepherds and bulls we can see and know something about, but God or a Buddha is a little more mysterious. A person who says "God is our shepherd" has expressed the thought that God is like a shepherd, in the sense that God watches over and cares for persons in the same way a shepherd tends his sheep. Similarly, "Buddha was a bull of a man" expresses the conviction that the man who achieved enlightenment was a strong and powerful enlightened man. These metaphors both assert that the Buddha and God are realities that can always be relied upon.

Not all religious experiences are theistic, reflecting belief in one or more gods. Theravada Buddhists in ancient India refused to use the Hindu words roughly equivalent to the English word *God* to describe their religious understanding. Instead they spoke of the emptiness and inadequacy of all spoken metaphors to explain their goal, the blissful state of *nirvana* (see Chapter 7). And yet they too used metaphors to try to help people understand what they had experienced as the "blowing out of the flame of desire," which leads to liberation from all suffering.

In fact, the word *God*, which is so central to the Abrahamic religious traditions (Judaism, Christianity, Islam), is just one of many diverse terms used in different religions and cultures across the world to designate the **ultimate reality**, that which is the highest in value and meaning for the group. This class of terms includes not only the personal God of Western theism but also the impersonal Brahman of Hinduism, the transpersonal nirvana of Buddhism, and the impersonal power of the *Dao* at work in all things that is central to Chinese religions. At the same time one can find some parallels to Western personalistic theism in Asia, too: D'ien (Heaven) and Shang Di (Lord of Heaven) in China; incarnations of Brahman in gods such as Shiva and Krishna in devotional schools of Hinduism; and the cosmic Buddhas and bodhisattvas to whom Mahayana Buddhists pray for help.

ultimate reality: that which has the highest value and meaning to a group

All these expressions for what is truly ultimate and meaningful may in fact refer to different ultimate realities—or perhaps different people use language unique to their own cultures and times to point to what may ultimately be the same reality. Here lies the challenge, mystery, and fascination of studying the religions of the world: Do differences in religious terminology reflect experiences of different realities? Or are they different expressions of or ways of describing the same reality? Because religious metaphors come out of particular historical and cultural times and places and because they are symbolic forms of expression, to understand the religious languages and messages of different religious traditions requires that we put ourselves in the time and place of their origins and use our **sympathetic imagination** to understand the metaphors used.

sympathetic imagination: empathy; necessary to understand the religious languages and messages of different times and places

If religious language is primarily symbolic, where do these metaphors and symbolic expressions come from? To answer this question requires putting yourself imaginatively in the following situation: Think of a beautiful warm summer evening. The sky is clear, and millions of stars are shining brightly. The evening is so breathtaking that you decide to go for a walk in the rolling hills just outside the city. As you walk, you are suddenly in the grip of an experience so overwhelming that it cannot be expressed in words. After a short time, which seems in retrospect like an eternity, you return to your normal consciousness and wander back to the city, where you run into some friends at the local cafe. You order a latte and then you say to them, "You'll never guess what happened to me tonight. I had the most incredible experience, so incredible it defies description." Yet paradoxically, your friends immediately ask, "What was it like?" With that question, we have entered the realm of metaphor and symbolic language.

Your friends are asking you to describe what you have just said is indescribable. To answer at all, you must draw analogies to things they already know about. So you might say that the experience was like being in the presence of a shepherd who really cares for his flock. At least you might say that if you and your friends were nomads familiar with the raising of sheep, like the people of ancient Israel. Roughly a thousand years before the start of the Common Era, however, the people stopped being nomads and settled into a fixed territory under the rule of a king. Although many continued to raise sheep, they started speaking of God as a king who protects his subjects. In this way different cultures and different generations have each contributed to the rich variety of metaphors used to illuminate the mystery and meaning of human existence.

Religious language, as symbolic language, can take one of two forms: analogy or negation. The metaphors just quoted ("God is my shepherd" and "God is my rock") are examples of the way of analogy (***via analogia***). In these metaphors, we use familiar words to create an analogy that describes something less familiar. However, there is another form of religious language, the way of negation (***via negativa***). This way of speaking religiously proceeds not by asserting what God or ultimate reality is (or is like) but by saying what it is not. This approach is very typical of mystical traditions. The Muslim mystic declares that Allah is "nothing," stating that Allah (God) is beyond (i.e., transcends) or is different from anything in our material universe and experience. Allah is not this thing and not that thing. Allah is in fact no "thing" at all. Being beyond all finite things and thus **transcendent**, Allah must be said to be no-thing.

In general, Western monotheism has emphasized the way of analogy by saying that there is one God who is like humans, able to "know" and to "love," but in a superior fashion. Thus, God is described as all-knowing, all-loving, or all-powerful. By contrast, Buddhism, of all the religions, has emphasized most strongly the way of negation, insisting that what is most valuable or true cannot be either named or imaged. Yet both ways are found in all traditions. Some Jewish, Christian, and Muslim mystics have referred to God as a "Nothingness," even as some Hindus have referred to the ultimate reality as a cosmic person (*purusha*) rather than an impersonal power (Brahman). Moreover, we should note that these two ways are not really in conflict, for the way of analogy itself implies the way of negation. That is, every time we say God is *like* some thing, we are at the same time saying God is not literally that thing. Every analogy implies a negation.

Our discussion of religious language should help us to appreciate just how challenging and at times confusing it can be to study and compare various religious traditions. Just as religious communities and religious traditions from different parts of the world use different metaphors and symbols, they also mix the way of analogy and the way of negation in varying degrees. Therefore, two different traditions sometimes talk about the same human experience in ways that seem to be totally contradictory. For example, it may seem that a Jewish theist and a Theravada Buddhist hold diametrically opposed religious beliefs, for Jews believe in a personal God who created the universe and Theravada Buddhists do not. Yet, when we look more closely at Jewish beliefs, we discover that Jews believe that God can be neither named nor imaged, even as Theravada Buddhists believe that ultimate truth is beyond all names and images. And yet, in both traditions, experiencing the nameless is said to make one more human or compassionate, not less.

After learning about the traditions covered in this book, you might conclude that perhaps theistic and nontheistic religious experiences are really not far apart. However, it is also possible that they might be seen as truly different. To pursue this great human

via analogia: a way of explaining spiritual reality by using analogies from particular finite qualities and characteristics

via negativa: a way of explaining spiritual reality by negating all finite qualities and characteristics

transcendent: beyond all finite things

question, we must begin by "bracketing" or withholding judgment and simply try to understand how stories and rituals shape people's lives—their views, values, and behavior. Perhaps the real measure of comparison should be how people live their lives rather than the apparently diverse images and concepts they hold. If both Jews and Buddhists, for example, are led by their religious experiences and beliefs to express compassion for those who suffer or are in need, then clearly the two faiths are similar in that very important respect.

Ritual

Like myths, **ritual** actions "tie and bind" the individual and the community to the sacred. Such actions often involve the symbolic reenactment of the stories that are passed on from one generation to the next. Typically myth and ritual are closely tied to the major festivals or holy days of a religious tradition and illuminate the meaning of human destiny in relation to sacred powers. By celebrating a cycle of festivals spread throughout the year, people come to dwell in the stories that tell them who they are, where they came from, and where they are going.

ritual: actions that link the individual and the community to each other, through the sacred

Carefully choreographed religious rituals recall important events in the history of each faith: the "Night Journey" of the Prophet Muhammad, the enlightenment of the Buddha, the birthday of Confucius. In other rituals, the faithful donate gifts to the supernatural beings to whom they ascribe a power to profoundly affect their lives. Still other rituals require circumcision, tattoos, or burn marks to set the believers off from nonbelievers, fostering in-group solidarity. The consumption of certain foods as part of some rituals suggests that the believer can acquire the "same essence" as the **divine** through ingestion, as in the Christian communion, Hindu puja, or tribal eating of a totemic animal to affirm common identity.

divine: highest spiritual reality

We should not assume that rituals only communicate ideas or beliefs. Religions are not confined to doctrines regarding the sacred. Rather, they include many *careful acts* that, in their own right, *tie and bind* people to each other and to cosmic meaning. Being religious thus entails taking decisive action at times, abstaining from certain acts at others—offering, for instance, precious gifts to supernatural beings, making pilgrimages to sacred places, or engaging in meditation or other disciplined spiritual practices.

For many believers, acting in the prescribed manner, called **orthopraxy** (correct practice), is more important than **orthodoxy** (correct belief)—acceptance of the often intricate doctrines set forth in texts and formulated by scholars. Performing the five daily Muslim prayers, visiting a Buddhist or Hindu temple to offer flowers on the full moon day, cleaning a Chinese family's ancestral grave during the spring festival, or being baptized as a Christian—all these acts are as central to "being religious" as is adopting beliefs or doctrines defined as orthodox.

orthopraxy: practice of "right actions" as prescribed by sacred traditions

orthodoxy: acceptance of "right beliefs" based on sacred texts as formulated by religious authorities

The great annual festivals in the world's religions give devotees a break from the profane time of normal working life, times for special rituals, for fasts or feasting, and periods of rest and reflection on the fundamental truths. These events also reinforce important ties with family and fellow devotees. The need to orchestrate such crucial ritual actions also leads followers to create the religious institutions that come to occupy central places in their societies.

Community and Morality

Myth and ritual express the communal nature of human experience and shape unique communities to foster the way of life that emerges out of their religious experiences. So Buddhists form sanghas, Jews form synagogues, Christians form churches, Muslims form ummahs, and so on.

We live in communities of shared language—we share stories and we share a way of life. Religion not only ties us to the sacred powers we believe govern our destiny; it also binds us to each other. Consequently, in most religious traditions, ritual and **morality** have been closely intertwined. "Right" is often defined by "rite"—the ritual patterns of behavior that keep life sacred. Morality is an inherent dimension of religious experience, for religion not only concerns sacred powers but also describes the way of life the powers require and make possible.

morality: right action

A Tlingit shaman performing a healing ceremony.

The sacred—what matters most to a given community—provides the ground for the moral experience of the virtuous life, a yardstick for measuring the rightness of any human action. The blueprint for what is just or moral is expressed in myth and ritual. Take, for example, the Jewish festival of Yom Kippur. This is the occasion at the beginning of a new year for each person to repent, to seek and offer forgiveness for the ways each has harmed others; each person also resolves to live more compassionately and justly in the new year.

This is just one example of how a religious tradition shapes morality. Even the most secular and seemingly nonreligious morality, insofar as it treats anything as sacred, can be understood as having a religious dimension. In the self-proclaimed atheist nation of the former Soviet Union, a major world power rivaling the United States in the decades after World War II, May Day was a great national festival celebrating the Russian revolution of 1917 and the founding of an atheistic state. At this celebration, the values of the way of life in the USSR were held up as sacred—worth living for and worth dying for. Although not connected in any way to the world's religions, this festival served a profound religious purpose: It told Soviet citizens that their individual lives were important and that they were tied and bound into a great historical drama that would inevitably lead to a communist society in which all would be equal.

Once we realize that religion is about what people hold sacred and the way of life that is called for by such beliefs, then it makes sense to say that all morality has a religious dimension, because every morality is grounded in religious experience, namely in the experience of what is held sacred (i.e., what matters most) in a given community. In this sense even the morality of atheists or others who may not think of themselves as religious can be said to have a religious dimension—to the degree that certain values are held sacred. Such an observation still leaves open the philosophical question of the degree to which a tradition's sacred morality is truly ethical, for ethics is the questioning of sacred moralities, asking whether what people customarily say is good or virtuous really is good or virtuous.

Religious Leaders/Experts

In every religion we will find interpretive and ritual specialists: the shamans, priests, ministers, monks, scholars, and teachers who mediate between the sacred power(s) and the community by explaining the myths and performing the rituals. The world's oldest religious specialist is the shaman, a man or woman who goes into a trance to leave his or her body to go to the spirit realm and communicate with sacred ancestors and supernatural beings (spirits, gods, demons, ghosts). Practitioners of this art (also called *mediums*

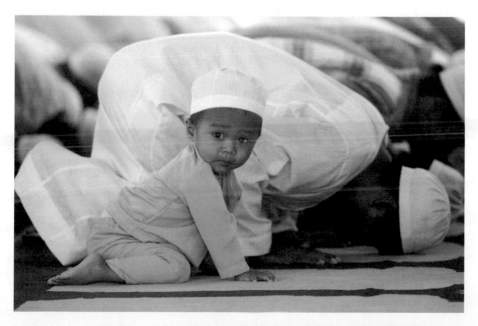

A two-year-old Muslim boy, living in predominantly Catholic East Timor, prays alongside his father at a mosque in Dili.

or *oracles*) are depicted on cave walls across Eurasia from the Neolithic period 25,000 years ago. Shamans still exist in many parts of the world, not only among the remaining indigenous peoples but also within the great world religions (see Chapter 2).

Since the invention of writing in 3000 BCE, the great world religions have relied on written materials and on scholars who have learned to write and read and thereby interpret the sacred texts. These keepers of the sacred writings translate their meanings for the great majority of rank-and-file followers, most of whom, until the modern era, were illiterate. The Confucian masters, the Muslim ulama, and the Hindu brahmin are examples of this religious specialist. And then there are those who specialize in being spiritual teachers, such as the Hindu guru, the Jewish rabbi, or the Sufi Muslim shaykh. Although we can point to interesting comparative patterns among religious rituals and between religious teachers, it is also true to say that each tradition can and must be known by its own unique set of religious practitioners and institutions.

The Great Religious Stories of the World

Since the beginning of the human race, people have told stories. We human beings are not just storytellers, we are "storydwellers." We live in our stories and make sense of the world through them. Even our understanding of what is good and evil, right and wrong, is shaped by the kind of story we see ourselves in and the role we see ourselves playing in that story. Although religious stories need not only be about gods and other spiritual beings, most of the earliest stories that have shaped human religious life have been.

While specific religious stories are indeed unique and diverse, we can group religious stories into four main types, each of which presents a symbolic story of the origins and destiny of human beings and the challenges they face in striving to realize their sacred destiny. These four main types of sacred story are:

the myths of nature
the myths of harmony
the myths of liberation
the myths of history (see Figure 1.2)

The Myths of Nature

If one goes back far enough into the history of any society, the earliest religious stories, found everywhere, are myths of nature. These are stories about the powers of nature that govern human destiny, which portray them as either personal beings (gods, spirits, and sacred ancestors) or impersonal powers. Such religions tend to see time as cyclical, always returning to the moment just before and after creation. Just as winter and death are followed by spring and new life, starting the earthly cycles all over again, time is an endless loop. Myth and ritual are the means to erase the distance between "now" and the time of origins, "in the beginning," when the gods or ancestral spirits first created the world fresh and new. In such stories one key problem of life is time. Time is the enemy. Time brings decay. It inevitably brings sickness, decline, and death. The ideal in human life is to return to the newness of life at the beginning of creation, before time began.

The means for bringing about this return is the recitation of the myths and the performance of rituals reenacting creation. Hunter-gatherer stories emphasize the fertility of the earth, the relations with animals and plants, the need for the ritual renewal of life in harmony with the seasons, and the role the tribe plays in maintaining the eternal cosmic order. In many of these societies, a shaman is the spiritual leader; as will be seen in the next chapter, the shaman's trance journeys restore harmony between the human community, spirits, and the forces of nature.

China and the Myths of Harmony

In China the great cosmic story that emerged was that of the Dao (sometimes rendered Tao). The universal Dao, which all beings share, is the source of harmony in the universe at work but hidden in all the forces of nature. One's true self is knowable only in relation to the Dao. All of creation works through combinations of complementary opposites of *yin* and *yang*, of dark and light, of earth and heaven, of female and male. Yin and yang are never polar opposites; rather, each flows into the other with no absolute division, the way day flows into night and night into day. There is a little day in every night, a little male in every female (and vice versa). The ideal for human life, then, is balance and harmony. The great problem of existence is the disharmony that occurs when the elements of society and/or the universe are out of balance.

To restore balance, two different religions emerged in China: Both Daoism and Confucianism sought to bring harmony between heaven and earth, self and society. These two traditions offered very different means to overcome the problem and realize the ideal. Daoist sages urged humans to seek harmony with the rhythms of nature through cultivating *wu-wei*, the art of "not doing," or not interfering with the natural flow of life. Out of that harmony, the harmony of society would flow spontaneously. By contrast, the Confucian sages urged humans to establish harmony in society through the practice of *li*, the ritual observance of obligations attached to one's station in society. They taught that people can be in harmony with the rhythms of the universe only when individuals know their place (as child, parent, citizen), cultivate their character, and sacrifice their self-interest for the good of the whole society.

India and the Myths of Liberation

In India, life was also seen in relationship to the cycles and rhythms of nature, and its ancient priests enacted careful, powerful rituals to control the gods behind all cosmic activity. But in India these worldly rhythms and concerns were ultimately to be

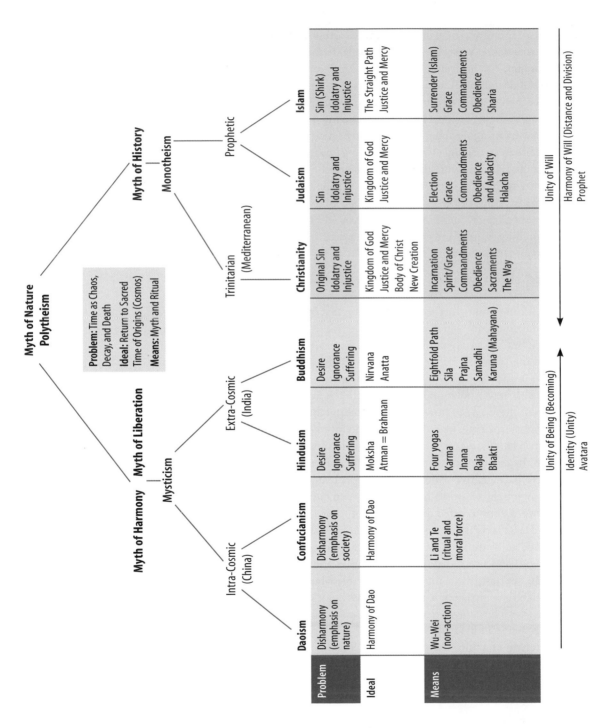

Figure 1.2 The world's religions in perspective.

escaped, not affirmed. Human existence was seen as distorted by delusion and suffering, not because there is nothing good about life but because no matter how good it is, it is transient and always ends in old age, sickness, and death. The problem of life is human entrapment in an endless cycle of suffering and rebirth; the highest goal was to overcome these bonds. The ultimate goal of all the great religions originating there is to destroy the illusions fostered by our selfish desires, for only when these are mastered can humans be freed from the wheel of death and rebirth (*samsara*). In that moment of liberation or enlightenment, one will come to realize the ultimate reality and find blissful union with it.

For most Hindus, the true self (*atman*) is merged with the eternal Brahman in either the personal or impersonal form. Buddhism offers the possibility of removing selfish attachments and realizing complete enlightenment within the suffering and impermanence of life, achieving the indescribable and transpersonal reality called *nirvana*.

Hinduism and Buddhism developed a variety of means, called yogas, for achieving release from samsara. These range widely, from disciplined ritual activity and the selfless performance of one's duties, to seeking spiritual knowledge through meditation, or cultivating selfless devotion toward a particular god.

Hindu women pay homage to the god of the sun during the Chat Puja festival on the banks of the Hooghly River in the eastern Indian city of Calcutta. Thousands of Hindu devotees reached the riverside at sunset and will spend the night praying.

The Middle East and the Myths of History

The myths of nature, of harmony, and of liberation use the human experience of the rhythms and cycles of nature as the basis for religious metaphors and symbolic language expressed in sacred stories. In the myths of history, by contrast, it is not nature but history that comprises the realm of human experience from which the metaphors for religious experience are primarily drawn. While all religions communicate their traditions by telling stories, only the religions of the Middle East, beginning with Judaism, make "story" itself the central metaphor of religious expression. Unlike the eternally cyclical rhythms of nature, stories have a beginning and an end. Ancient Judaism conceived of the cosmos as a great unfolding story told by a great divine storyteller (God): In the beginning God spoke, the world was created, and the story of revelation began.

Three versions of this story of revelation arose in the Middle East—first the Judaic, then the Christian, and finally the Islamic. For each of these, human beings are considered human by virtue of being children of the one God who created all things. All three traditions tell the myth of Adam and Eve as the first human beings, and venerate the patriarch Abraham, whom each considers to be the true model of faith and obedience to divine revelation. In all three, the problem of life is viewed as "sin"—failing to follow God's laws, a combination of idolatry and human selfishness that leads to injustice. The ideal goal of life is for humans to be in harmony with the will of God, whereupon peace and justice will reign and death will be overcome. The means for bringing this about are obedience to the will of God but also even debate

All that remains of the great temple in Jerusalem, destroyed by the Romans in 70 BCE, is the Western Wall. It is considered to be the holiest of sites where observant Jews come to pray.

with God (Judaism), acceptance of divine grace or aid through the incarnation of God (Christianity), and submission to the will of God (Islam). Although each of the three Abrahamic religions has its own story of the cosmos full of many trials, triumphs, and tragedies, each tells of the human-divine story having a happy ending, though only for faithful believers. In contrast to the myths of nature, harmony, and liberation, traditions founded on myths of history regard time not as the enemy but as the vehicle for encountering the ultimate reality, which is God, for eternity. The goal is not to escape time by returning to the beginning through ritual, nor rising above time in mystical ecstasy, but of meeting the one God in time and making a journey with God through time. Time for the faithful is promising, and the future is ultimately hopeful.

Religious Diversity and Historical Change: The Structure of This Book

Each of the great religious traditions addressed the problem of mortality. In India and China the ultimate answer was essentially mystical: All find their true identity through inner transformation, achieving union or harmony with the same ultimate reality (whether Brahman or the Dao) or, in the case of Buddhism, experiencing the same ultimate destiny of nirvana. In the Middle East, the answer was not primarily mystical but apocalyptic—the union with God at the end of time, which leads to the resurrection of the dead and eternal life.

Each of these traditions speaks to the problem of morality as well, by helping the individual to get beyond the self-centeredness that came with urban individualism and to grasp the essential unity and interdependence of all human beings. And each sought to provide life with meaning by depicting individuals and communities as participating in a great cosmic story that gives drama and purpose to human life. These were stories that were not made absurd by death; rather, their purpose was to show individuals a way to overcome the finality of death.

Finally, we need to qualify our statements about the unity and diversity of religions. When we stand back at a great distance we can use the four types of myth or story—those of nature, harmony, liberation, and history—to classify the various religions. As we get closer, we discover that each of these stories has variations expressing internal differences in doctrine and in practice. Those familiar with Christianity need only recall how many different kinds of Christianity there are. There is such a great difference between church rituals conducted by contemplative Quakers, enthusiastic Southern Baptists, and the more formal rituals of Anglicans that it is hard to believe they are all examples of the same religion. In fact, this range of diversity is true of every religious tradition.

In the chapters to come we will be examining how human beings struggle to continue the religiousness of their ancestors in a radically different, fast-changing, and globalizing world. We will see how Western civilization gave birth to modernity and, through its colonial expansion, spread its religious and cultural influence around the world, disrupting premodern religious cultures everywhere. By *colonialism* we mean the political, social, cultural, and economic domination of one society by another. Colonialism is as old as civilization and is part of the story of virtually all religions and civilizations, East and West. But after 1492, modern Western colonialism came closest to achieving global domination. Propelled by European colonialism, Christianity became the first faith to spread globally, forcing every religion to reckon with its beliefs, its practices, and its critiques of non-Christians.

We will also describe how colonialism, in turn, provoked postcolonial reactions that have divided those in each religious tradition into three groups:

fundamentalist: one who rejects aspects of modernity and wants to return to the perceived foundational purity of an ancestral sacred social/political order, or way of life

1. **Fundamentalists**, who reject important aspects of modernity and want to go back to what they perceive as the purity of an "authentic" social/political order manifested in the sacred way of life of their ancestors.
2. Modernists, who seek an accommodation of their religious tradition to the insights of science and the social and political realities of modern life.
3. Postmodernists, who, while rejecting the dominance of science and Western modernity, seek to go forward into a new situation that affirms the role of religion in public life in a way that embraces religious diversity and is open to change in their religious tradition in this regard.

While some fundamentalists reject everything modern, most accept modern technology while rejecting changes suggested by the sciences that would call into question the fundamentalists' religious worldview. Earlier we spoke of "orthodoxy" as "right belief," and while many fundamentalists would consider themselves orthodox, not all who call themselves orthodox would consider themselves fundamentalists. Very often orthodox movements will interpret their scriptures allegorically or symbolically, while fundamentalists tend to interpret their scriptures literally. For instance, an orthodox Christian might interpret the seven days of creation as symbolic periods of undetermined length. A fundamentalist, however, would be inclined to say, "No, we are talking about creating the world literally in seven 24-hour periods of time, so scientific accounts of the origin and development of the universe over millennia are false."

Among modernists and postmodernists, most argue that some parts of the religious tradition must change. What is distinctive about the modernist end of the spectrum is the view that the human understanding of religious truth and practice is subject to historical change and development, a notion that fundamentalists find abhorrent, even blasphemous.

As Figure 1.3 indicates, religions are not monolithic. And they should not be studied as vague, disembodied abstractions but as vibrant multifaceted phenomena embraced by real people. Humans are different, too, and born with different talents and shaped by varying experiences; they are diverse in how they engage with their surroundings. The template of the bell curve (Figure 1.3) is useful to display the universal pattern of the range of beliefs that humans adopt in adhering to a given world religion. Although impossible to graph with exactitude in each case, the effort to understand

Total Commitment/   Committed   Professes Belief   Vague on Doctrines   Indifferent to Teachings
Ultra Elite   Observant Believer   Usual Attendance   Occasional Attendance   Very Rare Attendance

how religion exists for the elite, the average believer, and the hardly observant is a valuable exercise. The vertical axis plots the percentage of believers; the horizontal axis is a measure of belief vitality and ritual attendance. On the left side are the elite who have complete commitment and lifestyle to the highest religious ideals. They are "all in." Examples include the Tibetan Buddhist nun doing a three-year cave meditation retreat, and the Hindu holy man or Daoist monk who has turned the remainder of life into a religious pilgrimage. On the far right are those who are indifferent to doctrine or who disbelieve. (Yes, their presence is also universal; the records of skeptics and dis-believers are as ancient as those of believers.) In learning about world religions, being attentive to this variance guides our efforts to explain how world religions captured the imagination and elicited the loyalty of believers in every society. Here are also clues about how religion has brought out the best and worst of humanity in history.

Our treatment of the history of each tradition in each chapter will be organized as follows:

- Overview
- Encounter with Modernity
- Premodern
- Modern
- Postmodern
- Conclusion

The overview at the start of each chapter introduces the basic worldview of the religious tradition. The section that follows, "Encounter with Modernity," describes a particular moment in which premodern religious traditions clashed with the mod-ern worldview and explains the diverse responses that emerged from that encounter. Next, each chapter will shift back to the *premodern* period and begin to trace the origins and development of the tradition, to better explain why modernity represents a chal-lenge to it. This period is accounted for in two phases—a *formative period*, which traces the origins of the traditions, and a *classical period*, which explains its fully developed premodern beliefs, rituals, and institutions.

The section on *modernity* traces the diverse fundamentalist and modernist responses that developed in each tradition as it was challenged and threatened by Western colonial-ism and its modern scientific/technological worldview. This is followed by a *postmodern* section, in which we survey the most recent reactions to the adaptations each tradition has made to the modern world. These reactions tend to be postcolonial attempts (in most regions, after 1945) to reclaim religious and cultural identities that existed before the advent of modern Western colonialism. In this way we show why the world, with all its possibilities for coexistence and conflict, is the way it is today. The *conclusion* to each chapter addresses the implications of this history for the future of each tradition.

Historical Overview: From Premodern to Postmodern

The structure of this book revolves around two great transitions in human history that we are positing:

Premodern to Modern
Modern to Postmodern

The first began with urbanization, and the second begins with globalization.

From about 8000 BCE the domestication of plants and animals made village life possible. Acquisition of agricultural skill then allowed the development of the first great cities, from approximately 3000 BCE, bringing about a great transformation in human experience. Urban life drew people together out of different social groups, each with a different culture. In the earliest indigenous human groups, everyone lived close to the rhythms of nature, in extended families or clans that shared a common way of life and lived by the same myths and rituals. In the cities people came together from different groups, bringing with them different stories, different rituals, and different family identities.

The complexities and new possibilities of urban life led to the specialization of labor. Whereas in small-scale indigenous societies everyone shared the hunting and gathering or simple agriculture, in the cities the agricultural surplus created by peasant farmers made it possible for some to engage in diverse occupations such as carpentry, blacksmithing, and record keeping. Society became more complex and differentiated into classes (peasants, craftsmen, noblemen, priests, etc.). In a parallel fashion, elaborate and detailed new mythologies emerged in the cities, assigning special powers and tasks to each of the many gods and spirits of the different tribes now embraced as the gods of the city.

These changes fundamentally transformed the economies and cultures of the new urban centers. The human situation evolved. In the indigenous group, identity was collective because everybody shared the same stories and hunting and gathering activities. The cities, by contrast, were communities of strangers. People did not automatically share a collective sense of identity. Urban life enhanced awareness of how one person differed from another.

The loss of collective sense of identity and the emergence of large, impersonal, and often-brutal urban city-states in Egypt, India, China, and Mesopotamia led to growing populations for whom the experience of the world was marked by suffering and cruelty. Populated by strangers and ruled by emperors, kings, or Pharaohs considered divine or representatives of the gods, these new city-states eventually faced a threefold crisis.

First, tribal collective identity was experienced as eternal—the tribe never dies. However, under the impact of urban individuation humans began to think of themselves as individuals, and death suddenly loomed as a personal problem even as life seemed more cruel and uncertain. With the greater development of individual self-awareness, death presented people with a new and unsettling problem: What happens to my (individual) "self" when I die?

Second, urban life created the new problems of law and morality. In the isolated indigenous group the right thing to do was prescribed by ritual, and the same rites were known and respected by all. In cities, people from a variety of religious traditions lived together; yet as individuals, each looked out for his or her own good, if necessary at the expense of others. Thus in the cities law emerged to set the minimum order necessary to sustain human life, and it became necessary to develop a system of ethics to persuade people to live up to even higher ideals.

Third, the situation evoked a crisis of meaning. Can life really have any meaning if it is filled with injustice and ends in meaningless death? The first written expression of this great question appeared in the ancient Near East at the beginning of the urban period (ca. 3000–1500 BCE) and is known as the *Epic of Gilgamesh*.

The great world religions emerged in the three great centers of civilization in the ancient world—China, India, and the Middle East—as their founders and prophets responded to critical questions about the meaning of life, mortality, and morality. Between 800 BCE and 600 CE all developed their classical expressions, dividing much of the world among them (see Map 1.2) in the context of the formation of great empires that united peoples of various tribes and city-states into larger political entities. These new political orders created a need for a more inclusive understanding of human identity. Sages and prophets arose who redefined the meaning of being human in terms beyond the boundaries of the tribe and the city-state, seeing a higher unity to reality beyond the many local gods and spirits. In China, for example, all humans were said to share in common the *Dao* (the hidden power of harmony that governs the universe), and the effect of a truly humane ruler was believed to radiate outward to ensure social harmony. In India, for Hindus it was the reality of *Brahman* (the universal, impersonal, eternal spirit that is the source of all things), and for Buddhists, the universal causality of interdependent becoming. In the Middle East, Judaism, Christianity, and later Islam each developed as religious traditions that emphasized that they were children of the one God who created all things. Biblical figures such as Abraham, Moses, Jesus, and Muhammad emphasized that their community had a special covenant with God. These ideas about the meaning of the divine-human relationship remain central to the world's great religions.

Map 1.2 Distribution of world religions circa 1500 CE.

Theravada Buddhism
Tibetan Buddhism
Hinduism
Hindu-Buddhism
Mahayana Buddhism mixed with Confucianism and Daoism
Mahayana Buddhism mixed with Confucianism, Daoism, and Shinto
Islam
Catholic Christianity
Russian Orthodoxy

NORTH AMERICA
Algonkin
Sioux
Cheyenne
Kiowa
Iroquois
MESOAMERICA
SOUTH AMERICA
Cuzco
Inca Cultural Influence

PACIFIC OCEAN
ATLANTIC OCEAN
PACIFIC OCEAN

WESTERN EUROPE
Bergen
Stockholm
London
Cologne
Paris
Geneva
Venice
Naples
Marseilles
Barcelona
Rome
Cordova
Tangier
Algiers
Fez
Tripoli
Tunis

RUSSIA
Novgorod
Moscow

OTTOMAN EMPIRE
Baghdad
Jerusalem
Mecca
Alexandria
ARABIA
SAFAVID EMPIRE
Isfahan

MUGHAL EMPIRE
TIBET
INDIA
Delhi

CHINESE MING EMPIRE
Beijing

JAPAN

Hanoi
Rangoon
Ayutthaya
Vijaya
Phnom Penh
Malacca
Bantam
SUMATRA
JAVA
BORNEO
CELEBES
Macassar
MINDANAO
NEW GUINEA

AUSTRALIA
Aborigines

NEW ZEALAND
Maoris

SONGHAY
GHANA
Timbuktu
Jenne
MALI
MOSSI STATES
HAUSA STATES
WADAI
DARFUR
Agadez
Goa
KANEM-BORNU
BAGIRMI
FUNJ
Dongola
AFRICA
ETHIOPIA
ADAL
Mogadishu
Mombasa
spread of Bantu tribes
GREAT ZIMBABWE
Great Zimbabwe
Sofala

0   2000 miles
0   2000 kilometers

28

Today the secularizing influences of modernization and the unprecedented international migration are transforming the ancient geographic division of the world's religions. Before we can move on to explore the struggle of peoples everywhere to continue the religiousness of their ancestors in today's very different world, we need to be clear about the terms **premodern**, **modern**, and **postmodern**.

In general, premodern history around the globe describes a wide range of cultures in which religion played the decisive role in explaining and ordering life. In premodern societies, religion provided the most certain knowledge one could have of the world, and consequently religious authority played a central role in each culture's social, political, and economic ordering of public life. In this respect, all premodern cultures have more in common with each other than with modern **secular** (i.e., nonreligious) culture. With the advances in science that gathered steam in the eighteenth century, the scientific worldview spread globally and, for many, came to replace religion as the most certain form of knowledge. The modern period is marked by a tendency for individuals to view religion as a matter of personal faith or opinion. Gradually most areas of public life were secularized. That is, religious doctrines and officials no longer played central roles in politics, economics, or public education. The most dramatic institutional expression of this change in the West was the emergence of the separation of church and state. The secular state was the expression of "modern" reality—politics governed a society's public life, and religion was a private matter for individuals and their families. From the end of the nineteenth century up until the early 1970s, many scholars even predicted the end of religion and a coming nonreligious, or *secular*, stage in world history.

Every premodern society saw the universe through explicitly religious eyes and pronounced its vision of life sacred. Since all premodern societies were dominated by the influence of religious authority, they all understood and ordered their worlds through religious myths and rituals that had been passed down for many generations. Modern culture, by contrast, tends to emphasize the centrality of rational and empirical science. And, as we shall see in Chapter 4, the scientific worldview brought with it certain distinctive features, especially the tendency to reject the premodern past and to regard its beliefs and traditions as irrational and superstitious. In addition, history was understood as representing inevitable progress toward an ideal future, and the knowledge that would bring about this glorious future could be had only through science, with its "objective view" of the world, finally ending the centuries of human hatred and bloodshed caused by religions.

While much more can and will be said in the remaining chapters about this premodern/modern contrast, we have at least suggested that the contrast between premodern and modern is dramatic and clear. But a word needs to be said about our use of the third term in this sequence, the *postmodern* situation. According to the postmodernist thinker Jean-François Lyotard, this era is characterized by the collapse of all the grand, all-encompassing sacred stories through which human beings interpreted life in their respective cultures.[2] In ancient societies, these **metanarratives** (to use Lyotard's term) were the religious myths of the four types

premodern: civilization in which there is no separation between a dominant religion and society

modern: civilization that separates its citizens' lives into public and private spheres, restricting religion to private life

postmodern: society typified by accepting public diversity in both religious beliefs and social practices

secular: sociologically used to mean "nonreligious"

metanarrative: grand cosmic and/ or historical story accepted by majority of a society as expressing its beliefs about its origins, destiny, and sacred identity we have described; the notion that they were true for all times and places went virtually unquestioned. In modern culture the primary metanarrative has been the story of history as progress driven by science and technology. However, the globalization of religious and cultural interaction that began in the twentieth century has tended to relativize them all, to see each as a historical construction, and regard none as ultimately, universally true. Significantly, this includes the modern myth of inevitable scientific progress.

In the premodern world a single grand narrative or religious worldview was typically experienced as true, valuable, and meaningful by the overwhelming majority of people. It is this kind of metanarrative that has collapsed for many in our day. For Lyotard, "postmodern" is more a style of thinking than a stage of history. It is a decentered style of thinking that invites pluralism and rejects imposing a single truth on all. In our postmodern world a new type of metanarrative is arising globally, an anti-metanarrative accepting the reality of religious and cultural pluralism. In this anti-metanarrative, no single story is all-encompassing for all people in a given culture—especially as a global culture emerges and practitioners of the world's religions are found in everyone's hometown. The grand stories of the world religions have thereby become miniaturized and globalized. Everyone has his or her own stories, knowing full well that other people in one's neighborhood and around the world live by other stories.

The very creation of textbooks on world religions encourages just such a postmodern awareness. In this situation the adherents of each religious tradition have to deal with diversity within their own traditions as well as diversity among religious traditions. All, but especially those who follow the great missionary faiths—Christianity, Islam, Buddhism—are challenged to explain how it is that the world continues in this ever-multiplying religious pluralism and why their own understanding of ultimate reality (God, Allah, Brahman, Buddha nature, Dao, etc.) has not led all the world into their own path.

An adult pilgrim is baptized in the Jordan River, Israel.

We also suggest that there is a strong correlation between the postmodern challenge to modernity and the postcolonial challenge to colonialism. A postcolonial era typically begins with a rejection of the modern Western historical metanarrative of scientific-technological progress and in this way opens the door to postmodern awareness and critiques. However, that door swings two ways: some seek a return to premodern fundamental notions of religious truth and practice, insisting that there is only one true religious story and way of life; others embrace the postmodern situation and seek to accommodate the reality of diversity. What these fundamentalisms and postmodern pluralisms have in common is a rejection of the modern strategy of privatizing religion. Both insist that religion ought to play a role in influencing not only private but also public life. But fundamentalists advocate accomplishing this by returning to an absolute religious metanarrative and work to impose a political order that should shape public life for everyone; postmodernists (as we use the term) accept a plurality of narratives, recognizing the public benefits of embracing religious pluralism in an age of globalization.

We use the contrast between *modern* and *postmodern* to describe not a philosophy or an existing historical period but, rather, a newly emerging historical trend. A postmodern trend deserves to be called "new" because it challenges the assumptions of modernity without simply reverting to premodern views of reality. In particular, postmodern pluralism challenges modern "science" as the single form of objective knowledge about the world and also the modern practice of privatizing religion. Today, all the world's religions are caught up in the struggle between their premodern, modern, and possible postmodern interpretations.

Because Christianity is the dominant religion of Western civilization, the civilization that produced modernization, it went through the trauma of accommodation to modernity first. Being the first, it had the luxury of embracing modernization in slower stages than those religions that did not encounter modernization until it had attained a more developed form. Therefore Chapter 4, on Christianity, will have to tell two stories. One is an outline of the intellectual and social history of the West that resulted in modernization, and the other is the story of the role that Christianity played in that history, both in promoting modernization and in resisting it.

Some have charged that modernization is a form of Western cultural and perhaps even religious imperialism that has been forced on other cultures. However, modernization and secularization challenge all sacred traditions and identities, including those of Western religions. As we shall see in the remaining chapters of this book, the patterns of modernization's impact on diverse religions and cultures are quite variable, as are the responses elicited. Modernization did not have an impact on all religions simultaneously, nor did all react in exactly the same way, although there are striking similarities. Therefore, we should not expect all religions and societies to exhibit exactly the same patterns and responses.

The Modern/Postmodern Transition: Colonialism, the Socialist Challenge, and the End of Modernity

In the nineteenth century the synergy of Western science, economics (capitalism), and technology fostered among the dominant European nations, especially England and France, a thirst for building colonial empires. These colonial ambitions were paralleled in the modern period by those of only one Asian nation—Japan. By 1914 most of the world was under the domination of Western European culture.

Geographically the Russians and the British controlled about a third of the globe. In terms of population, the British Empire controlled about a fifth of the human race—nearly 400 million people—while France controlled over 50 million colonial subjects (see Map 1.3).

Colonial dominance and paternalism (the British spoke of "the white man's burden" and the French of their "mission to civilize") was accompanied by the spread of science, technology, and capitalism, which proved traumatic to indigenous cultures and their religious traditions. The impressive achievements of Western civilization often prompted an initial phase of emulation of Western ways by elites, leading them to embrace modernization and secularization. Almost inevitably, however, there was a religious and political backlash, seen in struggles for national liberation as indigenous peoples sought to reclaim their independence and autonomy and to reaffirm the value of their original ways of life. This backlash often included a resurgence of religious influence as a force in anticolonial struggles. Most independence movements readily adopted a key element of Western civilization—nationalism—in their attempts to resist foreign occupation and to protect their religious and cultural identities by resisting exploitation.

Many of these movements paradoxically struck an alliance with socialism, the philosophical and political movement that arose in the nineteenth century in Europe among the new urban working class as a protest against the poverty and social dislocation created by early capitalism and the Industrial Revolution. Socialism was itself a modernist movement, sustained by a vision of scientific progress, yet it also championed premodern values of community against the rampant individualism of modern capitalism. In Karl Marx's formulation of "scientific socialism," it became an international movement that had an impact on world history as profound as that of any world religion. Indeed, as religious societies around the globe revolted against European imperialism, most experimented with some form of socialism as a modern way of protesting and of dialing back modernity itself. The twentieth century produced examples around the world of Jewish, Christian, Islamic, Hindu, Buddhist, and neo-Confucian forms of socialism. In its secular form socialism or communism became the dominant element in Russian culture, spreading throughout Eastern Europe and across Asia like a new missionary religion, most prominently "converting" China, the largest country of Asia, by 1949.

Consistent with the myth of modernity, the German socialist Karl Marx (1818–83) saw history as progressively unfolding in three stages. He defined these stages in terms of a class theory of society that went from primitive communism (tribal societies), in which all were equal; through the rise of complex urban civilizations, which gave birth to societies ruled by bureaucracies, pitting privileged classes against the masses; to a final stage of history in which society would once more be communistic. In this last age all were again to be equal—for all complex, class-defined institutions would wither away, and people would live together in spontaneous harmony. As many who have studied Marx and his followers have suggested, this vision takes the biblical myth of history, culminating in the appearance of the messianic age, and recasts it in secular form as the coming to earth of a classless society in an earthly paradise.

Map 1.3 Missions and colonialism.

Marx secularized the biblical myth of history by replacing the will of God as the directing force of history with what he maintained were "scientific" laws of social development that guide the progressive unfolding of history. Marx believed that capitalism depended on a large class of urban workers, who, once they were gathered together in the industrial cities of the modern world, would organize, creating an international workers union that would lead a worldwide revolution. This revolution would result in the replacement of capitalist societies, based on hereditary wealth and privileges, with a new, classless society of freedom, equality, and social justice for all.

Socialism represents an ambivalent rejection of a modern scientific world dominated by an economic system, capitalism, that seemed to make the rich richer and the poor poorer. It claimed to be "modern," "secular," and "scientific." Yet Marxism, unlike capitalism, retained much of the religious and ethical power of biblical tradition, with its emphasis on justice for the poor, the widow, the orphan, and the stranger as the final outcome of history.

While socialism provided a vehicle to protest the impact of modernity on society, two world wars decisively undermined belief in inevitable progress toward greater scientific understanding, prosperity, and benevolent coexistence. World War I (1914–18) and World War II (1939–45) were the great wars of modern technology that shattered this myth. Science and technology, which had been viewed as the engines of progress, had become, as well, the means of unprecedented destruction. The utopian dream of technological progress ended as a nightmare in August 1945, when newly invented atomic bombs were dropped on the Japanese cities of Hiroshima and Nagasaki.

The use of nuclear weapons brought World War II to an end, only to usher in a "cold war" between the Soviet Union and the United States. Throughout the second half of the twentieth century, an armed standoff between these two superpowers threatened to plunge the whole human race into a third and final war of thermonuclear annihilation. The makers of the modern myth of progress had failed to foresee that a technology that increases efficiency can be applied not only to the improvement of public health and the production of less expensive consumer goods, but also to the invention of weapons of mass destruction. Indeed, since World War II progress in the means of destroying large numbers of humans has been staggering. It took the Nazis six years to kill 6 million Jews and others in their death camps. Today, nuclear war could destroy virtually the whole human race in a few days.

Finally, it is important to note that World War I and especially World War II not only called into question the "scientific age of progress" but also brought an end to the modern age of empires. The twentieth century saw the withdrawal of European powers from the Middle East, South Asia, Southeast Asia, East Asia, and Africa. European colonial powers left behind independent nation-states whose rulers were unelected. Many of these new political entities had arbitrarily drawn boundaries. Often, moreover, people were divided without regard to ethnic identity or religious communities, and the legacy of exploitative colonial practices was economic poverty.

Postmodern Trends in a Postcolonial World

In the modern period the social authority of religion was undermined by the new scientific rationalists, whose descriptions of reality, they believed, explained how the world "really is," in contrast to the fanciful myths of religions. The postmodern world begins with the further loss of innocence, as many have argued that not only religious knowledge but also scientific knowledge is relative in important ways. That is, science too is an imaginative interpretation of the world based on faith (faith in the intelligibility of the world) and cannot offer the final truth about reality. Of course, many today dispute this understanding of science. Nevertheless, these arguments are similar to the arguments between premodern religious philosophers (defending religion) and the new secular scientists (challenging religion) at the beginning of the modern period. No matter who is ultimately correct, the very existence of such disputes suggests that the postmodern situation is one in which unquestioning faith in science, which characterized the modern era, no longer exists.

From the perspective of postmodernists, all knowledge is relative, including religious and scientific knowledge. Postmodern trends seem to promote cultural and ethical relativism. Some rejoice in this, arguing that it means the end of all the absolutes that have been used to justify violence by some against others. Still others are afraid that total relativism will lead to the end of civilization and the beginning of a new barbarism—that once we have relativized the absolute distinction between good and evil, we will plunge into an ethical void in which any atrocity can be justified.

Thus for individuals living in the postmodern period, scientific knowledge now competes on equal intellectual footing with religious knowledge. They are equally relative and equally subject to criticism by those who reject their main precepts. Therefore the position that scientific secularism is a source of public and certain knowledge, while religious knowledge is mere private opinion, no longer seems as valid as it once did. Consequently, the appearance of postmodern trends has been accompanied by a resurgence of religion in the public realm—a resurgence whose diverse forms are responses to both the threat and promise of postmodernity.

In the new, postmodern civilization, another stage in the history of religions has emerged, one in which the world religions encounter each other as they spread via **globalization**. Until the modern period the great world religions had largely divided the globe among them, with some modest overlap. But in the postmodern world, more and more, all the world's religions have members in every country or society. Just as Christians had migrated to every city in the world by 1850, today Hindus, Buddhists, and Muslims are now found in significant numbers in all large American and European cities and increasingly in smaller ones. Today, anyone using the Internet can take in a live web-cam view in major temples, shrines, churches, mosques, and monasteries from around the world; devotees can offer prayers, order rituals, or make monetary offerings through their websites. This is globalization.

globalization:
in terms of world religions, the idea that all the world's religions have members in almost every country or society; technology affords access to all key religious sites and practices

Conclusion: We Are All Heretics in Our Postmodern Situation

In the premodern period, people, for the most part, acquired their religious identities because of where they were born. In the postmodern world, however, every individual is faced with what sociologist Peter Berger calls "the heretical imperative."[3] *Heretic* comes from an ancient Greek word that means "to choose." In our postmodern world every religious person becomes a **heretic**, that is, one who is no longer simply born into a given religion or identity but must choose it, even if it is only to retain the identity offered by the circumstances of his or her birth.

In this world of "heretics," all the world's religions, each of which originated to provide a universal answer to the questions of human identity, have been forced to take account of the others. Today global media allow distant viewers to experience the positives and negatives, both exemplary and scandalous actions, of individuals acting in the name of their religions as never before. Around the globe, religious adherents and skeptics come face to face with their own particularism amid the undeniable reality of the world's enduring diverse faiths.

Until postmodern trends set in, other people's religions could be readily dismissed in a series of negative stereotypes. When people of diverse religions are neighbors, this option is both more difficult and more dangerous. To the degree that stereotyping and discrimination persist, they promote prejudice, conflict, and violence. The alternative is to develop new understandings of the relation between world religions and the societies around the world—one that allows the peoples of the earth to follow their respective faith traditions, including nonbelief, yet also share their wisdom with each other in an atmosphere of mutual respect and understanding. This alternative—to appreciate what we have in common as well as to acknowledge our distinctive differences—has been explored brilliantly by two of the great religious figures of the twentieth century, Mohandas K. Gandhi and Martin Luther King Jr. Each spiritual leader "passed over" from his native religion and culture to the religious world of the other and came back enriched by that second tradition without having abandoned his own. You are invited to embark on a similar journey through the study of the world's religions today.

heretic: from the ancient Greek term for "one who chooses," used to communicate the postmodern idea that there is no longer a single center of "taken-for-granted commonly shared truth" in society and so everyone has no choice but to choose his or her beliefs

"Modernity multiplies choices. . . . The modern individual is faced not just with the opportunity but with the necessity to make choices as to his beliefs. This fact constitutes the heretical imperative."

—Peter Berger

Discussion Questions

1. Define religion in terms of its six characteristics—sacred, myth, ritual, community, morality, and religious leaders—and explain the possible relations among them.

2. What do the authors mean when they argue that all morality is religious, even that of atheists?

3. In what way does religious language complicate the question of whether there is agreement or disagreement among religions on various issues? Describe in terms of the *via analogia* and the *via negativa*, giving examples of each.

4. Explain the four types of religious story and give a historical example of each.

5. Why did urbanization lead to the emergence of the great world religions? That is, what new urban problems did these religions address?

6. What is colonialism, and what is its significance for religions and cultures in the modern period?

7. How are the terms *premodern*, *modern*, and *postmodern* being used in this text, and how are they related to modern colonialism?

8. According to the authors, modernization privatizes religion, whereas in premodern and postmodern religious movements religion plays a public role in society but in different ways. Explain.

9. Explain Marxist socialism, and tell why it was an attractive option to religious movements protesting modernity.

10. How might you justify the statement that both postmodernist and fundamentalist religious movements are examples of Peter Berger's "heretical imperative"?

Key Terms

divine	myth	secular
fundamentalist	orthodoxy	sympathetic
globalization	orthopraxy	imagination
heretic	postmodern	transcendent
metanarrative	premodern	ultimate reality
modern	religion	*via analogia*
moral	ritual	*via negativa*

Notes

1. F. Max Muller, *Lectures on the Origin and Growth of Religion as Illustrated by the Religions of India* (London: Longmans Green, 1880), p. 218.
2. Jean-François Lyotard, *The Postmodern Condition: A Report on Knowledge* (Minneapolis: University of Minnesota Press, 1984).
3. Peter Berger, *The Heretical Imperative* (New York: Doubleday, 1979), p. 60.

INDIGENOUS RELIGIONS

2

Overview

Across all the earth's inhabited continents today are thousands of different *indigenous peoples*, ethnic groups whose ties to their lands go back a millennium or much longer. Some have migrated to new homelands and changed their ways of life in recent centuries; others have been relocated in recent generations to "reservations" within modern states; still others (in growing numbers) live in two worlds, moving between life in their modern countries and their native group. Indigenous peoples today defy easy characterization: In remote Highland New Guinea, the village headman wears only a penis sheath as he performs a ritual to protect his home. More typical is a Kayapo chief in the Amazon rain forest who one day dresses in little more than body paint and on another wears western clothes. A visitor to a Lakota ceremonial leader in the North American Plains would find him in blue jeans, western-style shirt, and a Stetson hat.

All surviving indigenous peoples (or *first peoples*) have been affected by the modern world and its trade, technologies, or communications. The cultural traditions and religious lives of all these peoples have been altered, often dramatically, by outsiders encroaching on their lands, exposing them to new diseases, and imposing laws to take their lands and assimilate them into the majority citizenry. Around the world and over recent centuries, hundreds of indigenous groups have succumbed or been assimilated, their religions like their languages forever gone.

The religious traditions discussed in this chapter are different from those of the great world religions covered in the other chapters of this book. Yet these indigenous peoples and their religions remain a noteworthy part of the world's religious landscape today, despite their small populations. Few possess literary texts or great temples. Yet these independent, ethnic, and land-bounded religions are themselves worthy of study; they also help us understand the general phenomenon of humanity as a religious species. The treatment of indigenous peoples by the great world religions gives us important insights about the latter's role in the historical expansion of early states and modern nations; and we can see beliefs and practices of the world's indigenous religions being assimilated into the new religions forming across the globe today.

This chapter will begin by looking back to prehistory to understand the long history of some of the common worldviews, religious roles, and ritual practices evident among early *Homo sapiens*. We will then examine case studies of the world's last living hunter-gatherers and simple agriculturalists to sample indigenous religions across the globe today. The world's surviving indigenous religions would best be represented, due to their richness and diversity, by a series of chapters devoted to each one. The scope of this textbook precludes this; however, the short, introductory treatment here inevitably requires making generalizations and relies on somewhat arbitrary but representative case studies. Beyond conveying an awareness of the spiritual vitality and the neglected histories of these extraordinary indigenous traditions, we want to show that understanding religions today is enriched by seeing how all humanity, even in isolated nonliterate groups, has always been "religious."

Origins of *Homo religiosus*: Prehistory

At some point around a hundred thousand years ago, *Homo sapiens* emerged from a 4-million-year process of hominid evolution to become the animal who speaks, makes tools, buries its dead, and thinks symbolically. Long before agriculture and urbanization, the first *Homo sapiens* lived in hunter-gatherer societies. By studying their artifacts as well as the small-scale societies that still subsist in this mode of life, we can imagine what their existence was like. We know our ancestors lived and ate well, yet without the material possessions and conveniences we now consider to be essential. We know they made efforts to communicate with the spirits of their ancestors and with animals. Most likely, they regularly sought assistance from these spirits through trance and altered states of consciousness, which may have been the origins of religion.

Just as the core meanings of modern English words can be discovered by looking up their origins in Latin or Greek history, our appreciation of world religions can be enriched by understanding the origins of religion itself, by comparing the archaeological record with the customs of well-studied modern indigenous peoples.

Although the earliest humans used language, writing had not yet been invented. Consequently, these societies had oral cultures in which everything that was known

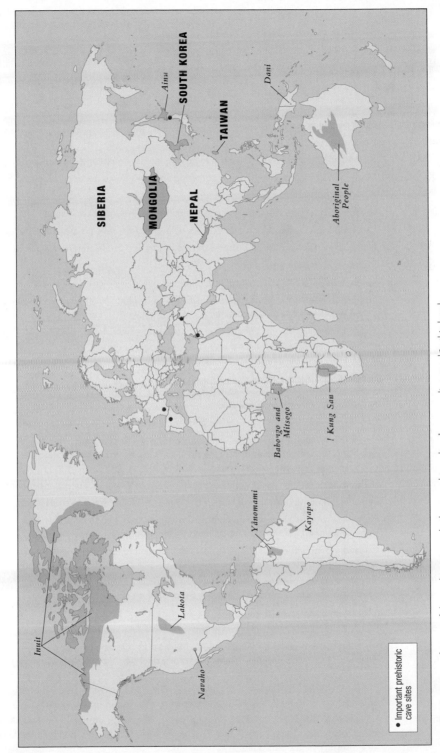

Map 2.1 Locations of some of the prehistoric and ethnographic cultural groups discussed in this book.

SIBERIA

MONGOLIA

NEPAL

SOUTH KOREA

TAIWAN

Ainu

Dani

Aboriginal People

Baborgo and Mitsogo

! Kung San

Yãnomami

Kayapo

Inuit

Lakota

Navaho

• Important prehistoric
  cave sites

Timeline

2 million	Early hominids use the first stone tools
½ mill	Fire domesticated
100,000	*Homo sapiens*: Neanderthals and another line present evidence of ritual burial
40,000 BCE	Modern man biologically; hunting-gathering societies found across Africa and Eurasia
	Humans just "another animal" on earth
30,000	Human language and symbolic thought reach new level of advancement
15,000	Human burials across Africa and Eurasia with offerings, reflecting afterlife belief
10,000	*Homo sapiens* from Siberia disperse across North and South America via Bering Strait
9,000	Domestication of sheep/goats
7,000	Beginnings of settled agriculture, first cities
5,000	Earliest archaeological evidence of Australian aboriginal belief connected with the Rainbow Serpent, perhaps the oldest continuing belief in the world
2,000	Major states arise on the Yellow River, China; Indus River, India; Babylon on Tigris-Euphrates; Nile in Egypt
800 BCE–200 CE	Axial Age, era of lasting formulations of social-spiritual teachings defining ethical modes of human existence in cities
100 BCE	States expanding into wilderness frontiers; Axial Age traditions legitimate expansion, assimilation of indigenous peoples
1400	Growing populations in Americas live in hierarchically organized chiefdoms or small kingdoms
1492 CE	Columbus reaches America. He writes that the native peoples encountered "are the best people in the world and above all the gentlest." His record is nonetheless filled with accounts of enslavement, murder, and rape.
1492–1600	Europeans make first contact with native peoples of Western Hemisphere continents
	Introduction of the horse alters human ecology across the "New World"
	Peoples having no natural immunological defenses to Eurasian microbes succumb to diseases in great numbers; 90 percent mortality in many settlements
	Christian missionaries travel on the networks of exploration and empire, making Christianity the world's first global religion
1546	The "New Laws" barring enslavement of indigenous peoples were repealed; "New World" colonists form societies and economies dependent on slave labor
1606	Earliest recorded contact between Europeans and Australian Aborigines
1616	Smallpox epidemic decimates native tribes in New England region
1709	A slave market erected on Wall Street in New York; African Americans and Native American men, women, and children are daily declared the property of the highest cash bidder
1716	Alamo Mission in San Antonio is authorized by the viceroy of Mexico. The mission becomes an educational center for Native Americans who converted to Christianity.
1808–1811	Tecumseh, chief of the Shawnees, organizes a defensive confederacy of Northwest frontier tribes, attempting to make the Ohio River a permanent boundary between the United States and indigenous peoples' land
1811	William Henry Harrison, governor of Ohio, leads the ferocious Battle of Tippecanoe, which destroys Tecumseh's town as well as the remnants of Tecumseh's indigenous confederacy

1830	Indian Removal Act passed; over next ten years U.S. government forcibly removes thousands of indigenous peoples west of the Mississippi
1838	"Trail of Tears": Native Americans force-marched by U.S. military to settle in Oklahoma
1850–1875	Hunting by American colonists leads to near extermination of buffalo herds, undermining Plains Indians' survival
1871	1871 Indian Appropriation Act specifies that no tribe thereafter would be recognized as an independent nation
1876	Colonel George Custer leads army attack on assembled native tribes and all 250 soldiers are killed. Afterward, U.S. Army orders troops "to attack and kill every male Indian over twelve years of age."
1888	The White Australia Policy articulated
1889–1890	Wovoka, the Paiute spiritual leader, has vision and spreads message of the Ghost Dance
1890	Massacre of Sioux at Wounded Knee, South Dakota
1910	Bwiti, a West Central African religion, is founded among the forest-dwelling Babongo and Mitsogo people of Gabon and the Fang people of Gabon and Cameroon
1918	Native American Church founded in Oklahoma, combining use of peyote with Christian beliefs of morality and self-respect. Church prohibits alcohol, requires monogamy and family responsibility, and promotes hard work.
1920	Santo Daime, a syncretistic religion based on ceremonial ayahuasca (called daime) ingestion, is begun in western Brazil by Raimundo Irineu Serra
1930	Stalin begins Soviet repression of shamans in Siberia and in their satellite, Outer Mongolia, that lasts until 1989
1950	People's Republic of China labels shamanism a "superstition" and represses spirit mediums across China
1951	Australian government formally adopts assimilation policy toward aboriginal peoples
1961	União do Vegetal, a syncretistic religion based on the use of ayahuasca and elements of folk Christianity, shamanism, and ancient Incan soul traditions, is founded by Jose Porto Velho
1975	The Australian Senate acknowledges prior ownership of country by aboriginal people and seeks compensation for their dispossession. The World Council of Indigenous People is founded.
1978	Religious Freedom Act promises to "protect and preserve" for Native Americans "freedom to believe, express, and exercise" traditional religions, "including but not limited to access to sites, use and possession of sacred objects, and the freedom to worship through ceremonial and traditional rites"
1989	Kayapo people joined by international indigenous group rights advocates to protest dam project at Altamira
1992	Australian High Court rules that native title to land has not been extinguished, rejecting 200-year-old settler claims that aboriginal lands were *terra nullius*, "no one's land"
2004	Smithsonian Institution's National Museum of the American Indian opens in Washington, DC
2008	Australian and Canadian governments issue formal apologies to aboriginal peoples for policies detrimental to integrity of lives, including forcibly sending children to Christian boarding schools
2013	Kayapo clans oppose new Amazon basin dam project on the Xingu River that will flood tribal lands

was known only because someone remembered it. And memories were made readily accessible because they were expressed in stories—stories of sacred ancestors, spirit beings, and heroes. Not recorded in written texts, these stories were kept alive in song and dance.

Moreover, time and space were not cold abstractions but were reckoned according to ancestral myths and sacred experiences. Religion likely began at sites where people believed the powers that govern the universe first manifested themselves. Whether in sacred groves, on riverbanks, or on mountaintops, human beings experienced such places of revelation as "centers of the world" (*axes mundi*). Indeed, in the indigenous religions, most everything is spiritually alive, a collective of living entities to which people must relate. The trees, the mountains, the rivers, special stones, animals, and, of course, humans are said to have souls or spirits that give them life, or *animate* them. Anthropologists once used the term **animism** to describe a worldview in which a measure of conscious life is attributed to these entities.

Each of the thousands of indigenous peoples have (or had) a unique **cosmogony**, or account of the world's origins and its essential powers. Because in most cosmogonies the group telling the story was a part of the everlasting cycle of nature's rhythms, the group is assumed to be an integral part of the cosmos. Everything in premodern indigenous group life reinforced a collective sense of common identity: All shared the same occupations (hunting and gathering, simple agriculture), the same myths, and the same rituals; and all were integral to the group. As a result, a person's identity was deeply embedded in the collective identity and fate of the group. The group lives on and the individual can stay connected to it, even after his or her own death.

This collective worldview is radically different from the extreme individualism and social fragmentation that is common today. In the following chapters on the world's great religions, we will show how each in its own way pushed humanity, at least in part, out of the collective community mind-set and toward greater individualism. Comprehending the features of indigenous religions will make it clear how the world religions have some of the basic features of the earliest religious traditions, yet also how they have simultaneously reinterpreted and transposed them as the details of human existence have changed.

Our human nature endows us with certain qualities that underlie the most basic expressions of religion. These include a propensity for repetitive behaviors (ritual), a virtually unique cognitive ability to create meaning (symbols, ritual acts), the enhancement of survival by identification with land or territory (sacred space), and a strong mother-offspring bond (devotion).

Archaeologists have ascertained that about 30,000 years ago humans—who are distinct from hominids because they possessed the same physiology and cognitive capacity as we do—established themselves across Eurasia. They wove cloth for clothes, used finely wrought fishhooks, constructed boats that crossed large bodies of water, and were experts in subsistence wherever they lived, from the tropics up to the edge of the Ice Age glaciers. The record of human life indicates that in every society over the last 100,000 years, a progressive complexity in the mastery of tools

animism: belief in an inner soul that gives life and identity to living things and emphasizes rituals in which humans interact with other souls

cosmogony: mythological account of the world's creation

The Limitations of the Term *Animism*

The term *animism*, though still in widespread use, is rooted in a problematic distinction in earlier scholarship. An *animist* was said to see the world as inhabited by a host of souls (*anima*) that are embodied in a variety of life-forms. By applying the term only to indigenous peoples, who usually worship a polytheistic pantheon, early scholars tried to create the basis for a distinction between them and peoples adhering to the major monotheistic religions. (Tylor and others saw monotheism as a superior form of religion that emerged among animist peoples, in conformity to the accounts of the Jews in the Hebrew Bible.) But does belief in souls truly separate humanity's religious belief systems and its thousands of believers? All three Abrahamic faiths hold that human beings possess souls (anima), as do traditional Indian and Chinese religions. In that sense, most world religions are animist. Furthermore, even the monotheistic religions hold that a multitude of nonhuman "souls" inhabit the world alongside human beings: angels, ghosts, *jinn*, demons, and so on. A second limitation with the term *animism* as a blanket term is that it also masks the large array of very different conceptions of "soul" recorded in human religious history, including peoples (e.g., the early Chinese) who believed that human bodies are inhabited by two or more souls.

was accompanied by the development of language ability and the unmistakable presence of religion.

The universality of religion in human societies even led Mircea Eliade, a pioneering scholar of comparative religions, to call our species **Homo religiosus**, or "religious humanity." In fact, now as well as from the earliest days of the modern species, religion has been at the center of human culture, reshaping social life. Thus, we can say that religion has always been an integral, at times even essential part of humanity's evolutionary path. It supported the success of small hunter-gatherer groups, the domestication of plants and animals, and then reinforced humanity's prodigious efforts to create cities, empires, and superpowers. We now turn to the very beginning of this extraordinary story.

Homo religiosus: religious humanity

Religion's Origins Among Hunter-Gatherers

For 99 percent of our species's history, all human ancestors lived as nomadic hunter-gatherers. However, our world has been transformed in so thoroughgoing a manner that few if any people anywhere on the planet still live in this mode of life.

The earliest *Homo sapiens* existed much like the people we refer to today as belonging to indigenous or *simple subsistence* societies. Small groups of related individuals (usually fewer than fifty) "lived off the land and ocean," moving with the seasons to find wild fruits and nuts and to be close to the animals or fish they hunted for food. Close-knit bonds within these living groups were essential to everyone's survival, with individuals sharing the food and relying on each other for protection. Also typical was a division of labor, with men predominantly the hunters and women the gatherers. Compared to the permanently settled societies that began in recorded human history, most of these societies were (and are) highly egalitarian, with food and wealth shared equally. Scholars have used data from anthropological studies of modern hunter-gatherer groups to reconstruct the usually good lives of early *Homo sapiens* as follows:

> Life lived by our prehistoric ancestors was not characterized by constant depri-
> vation . . . with both men and women contributing substantially to the family,
> the economy, and the social world. . . . Life was rich in human warmth and
> aesthetic experience and offered an enviable balance of work and love, ritual
> and play.[1]

The Kung San of southern Africa, one of the most studied, late-surviving hunter-gatherer groups, are typical. A nomadic people, the Kung utilize simple tools and build temporary houses. An intricate knowledge of their environment is expressed in a language that recognizes 500 species of plants and animals, yielding a diet that consists of 105 different foods. Utter mastery of an environment shared with large predators is typical of such groups. Once scholars gained firsthand knowledge of hunter-gatherers like the Kung, they began to appreciate the highly skilled nature of this mode of life, the clear rationality of the people, and the very sophisticated languages and cultures that had evolved among them. This new and empirical understanding disproved the theories of nineteenth-century social scientists, who had speculated that religion had its origins in the fear and ignorance of humans facing a threatening and incomprehensible world.

Prehistoric cave art: the first shaman. Over fifty examples of animal-human figures like this one suggest that shamanism had its origins in the prehistoric era.

The human capacity for language to create and build culture was almost certainly present by 100,000 BCE among the Neanderthals and those who succeeded them, the *Homo sapiens*. By 30,000 BCE, humans were performing ceremonial burials, painting and carving art, keeping rudimentary records on bone and stone plaques, and crafting elaborate personal adornments. They also made music with flutes and drums.

From this time onward, the human record shows our species constantly adapting and refining their material world, and it was by this time that humans acquired the capacity to think symbolically, almost certainly as a result of their development of more complex languages. We who cannot conceive of complex thought without the medium of language can easily imagine the advantages (in hunting, warfare, etc.) that a leap ahead in linguistic capacity must have given to those early humans.

As we saw in the first chapter, religion is centered on humans establishing and expressing life's ultimate truths. Scientists, therefore, have posited a breakthrough in cognitive ability that changed the destiny of our species forever: "categorizing and naming objects and sensations in the outer and inner worlds, and making associations between resulting mental symbols . . . for only once we create such symbols can we recombine them and ask such questions as 'What if . . . ?' "[2] The simultaneous emergence of modern humans and religion indicates that many "what if" questions were

Issues of Terminology and Imagination: Primitive, Indigenous

Writers who wish to refer to the peoples living in simple subsistence societies, both modern and prehistoric, face a problem of nomenclature. The term *primitive* was once popular, but it falsely suggests a lack of cultural development or factual understanding, since in fact many native peoples have complex languages and mythologies. In choosing the term *indigenous religions*, we are implying that the social and religious lives of a given people are rooted deeply in a given place. This first mode of religious life known in the record of human history is inextricably bound to the life of small groups. The reader should note that we are not equaling modern hunter-gatherers with humans living in this mode of life 30,000 years ago or suggesting that these contemporary groups are "living fossils," since none today live isolated from the developed world and all have distinct histories. The term *indigenous* until recent times referred to peoples living in premodern modes of subsistence, either as hunter-gatherers or utilizing nonmechanical agricultural methods. In growing numbers, indigenous peoples today are quickly learning about the legal systems of modern states and selectively adopting modern technologies in an attempt to preserve their lands, ease the burdens of subsistence, and ensure their culture's adaptation and survival.

aimed at explaining the unseen powers of life, the inner world of personhood, and the ultimate mystery, that of death. Many artifacts of prehistoric religion have been found that reflect human engagement with each of these realms.

Fertility, Childbirth, and Survival

One striking kind of object found across Eurasia in late prehistory is what scientists have called **"Venus" figurines**, small stone sculptures of females with large breasts and hips, often with their genitalia emphasized. To understand these objects, we must enter into the reality of prehistoric human life. Small tribes were doubtless greatly concerned with ensuring the regular birth of healthy children to keep their own group numerous enough for success in subsistence, hunting, and warfare. Further, since at that time all pregnancies and all childbirths were high-risk events and since it was realized that mothers' bountiful lactation helped ensure the survival of newborn children, it is likely that the figurines are related to concerns about birth and the survival of children in small groups. Some scholars therefore interpret the Venus figurines as icons representing a protecting, nurturing "mother goddess." They have speculated that the makers of these objects recognized and revered a special female power that lay behind the mystery of conception and birth; they focused on the miracle of females producing beings from their own bodies and celebrated the ability of women to perpetuate human life.

Added to this evidence of veneration of a mother goddess is another important archaeological find: After 15,000 BCE the dead were uniformly buried in mounds or

"Venus" figurines: prehistoric Eurasian small stone figures with exaggerated female characteristics graves in the fetal position, suggesting that people perceived the earth as a womb from which some sort of new birth was expected. Some have gone further, to conclude that the so-called Venus icons indicate the predominance of hunter-gatherer groups that were dominated by women, who led their groups in harmony with nature. This presumed matriarchal period, in which women had superior status, is said to have ended with the expansion of groups dominated by aggressive warrior males (such as the Indo-Europeans), who adopted settled agriculture and came to rule the new, patriarchal, societies. With little more than figurines and burial practices as evidence, it is difficult to prove or confirm these speculations or to declare their universality.

Religion in Prehistory: The Secret of Early Cave Rituals

Scholars believe that prehistoric hunting group initiation ceremonies were held in underground sanctuaries decorated with carefully rendered images of animals like this early masterpiece of painting from the Chauvet cave in southern France.

In the famous cave paintings of Eurasia, hunted animals such as bison, bear, and deer are rendered with grace and subtlety in a variety of styles. Humans are also shown, some in poses that are still puzzling, challenging us to understand who created the images and the meaning of their context.

Again, we must use our imagination to understand the context and to surmise the place of religion. Caves could be dangerous places, and groups of individuals taking the trouble to go several hundred yards under the earth, traversing narrow, damp, and dark passageways, seem to engage in no ordinary task. Archaeologists surmise that these sites were related to the hunts undertaken by bands of able-bodied men. Hunter-gatherers needed animals for their survival. They hunted to secure the meat essential for their diet, the skins for clothing, and the bones and sinew used for tools and adornment. Some painted cave scenes also indicate that the prehistoric hunt was often dangerous: Wild bison, cave bears, and large cats are shown inflicting lethal injuries on humans.

The hunt required group coordination for success, since tracking, stalking, encircling, and using spears or stones to make kills at close range could not be achieved without coordinated action, individual bravery, and strong group loyalty. A hunting expedition could fail if a single member broke ranks and failed at his station, endangering not only himself and others in the group, but the entire tribe, which was depending on the hunters. Having documented similar rites among modern hunting tribes, scholars view some of the prehistoric caves as ritual theaters for initiating adolescent boys into the ranks of hunters, sites of instruction in hunting lore, killing practices, and ritual. Perhaps it was to these remote sites that elders brought frightened initiates and dramatically staged rituals that revealed the prey the men pursued and established the youths' new identity as adult hunters. Through this initiation ritual, young men bonded with the other adult males with whom they would risk their lives.

Such practices in the service of human survival formed the basis of the first religions according to the definitions we discussed in Chapter 1: They helped *bind* a group critical to the society's success, and they reinforced the human need to *be careful* with regard to the unseen powers surrounding them. The second point is especially

TEACHINGS OF RELIGIOUS WISDOM: The Dreamtime

In this creative era, a host of supernatural beings from an unspecified somewhere arrived and set out to populate and transform the previously flat and featureless Australian landmass. By their activities . . . they created diverse, religiously-charged landforms, richly imprinted with meaning and replete with fauna and flora. During their wanderings and numerous adventures, they established rituals and human institutions. These set in place for all time the various groups, their languages, cultural characteristics, and bound the first humans to a kind of contract. Through obedience to the laws of Dreaming, and the proper and regular performance of rituals, living Aborigines are charged with keeping the whole cosmic system of order going. This occurs under the watchful and caring gaze of the creative beings . . . who monitor human affairs without direct interference, but stay in touch via spirit-being messengers through whom they channel new knowledge and ritual elements into human society. [Humans] remain keenly aware of the proximity and relevance of the spiritual powers to their well-being and future existence. Failure by humans to uphold the human blueprint will cause the inhabitants of the spiritual realm to cut off the flow of power into human society and bring all life to an end. . . . Each succeeding generation is charged with enormous responsibility for society's continuing reproduction.

Source: Robert Tonkinson, "The Mardu Aborigines: On the Road to Somewhere," in George Spindler and Janice E. Stockard, eds. *Globalization and Change in Fifteen Cultures* (Belmont, CA: Thomson, 2007), p. 233.

important if we assume that the elders taught that each animal, like every human being, has an inner spirit or soul, one that must be respected in death and returned to the world or sent on its way back to the animal spirit world or afterlife. We now turn to this topic and trace its frequent presence in a variety of modern indigenous groups.

Indigenous Religious Traditions: Soul Belief and Afterlife

Today thousands of separate native peoples still exist, testimony to the resilience of the human spirit and the power of strong social and cultural bonds. Their religions have been an integral part of their survival, in each case somehow reflecting the group's connection with its lands, identity, modes of subsistence, and historical memory. There are indigenous peoples today who subsist primarily as hunter-gatherers, shifting slash-and-burn agriculturalists, or settled agricultural cultivators, as well as those who have assimilated in various ways into the world's modern states and economies. The traditions of these indigenous groups relating to the sacred, though uniquely grounded in each people's separate historical existence, remain an important part of the story of the world's religions today.

Studies of indigenous peoples reveal extraordinary human diversity, imagination, and religious wisdom. Their myths recount what is sacred to the group: the origins of life, its relations with animals, its connections to landforms, and the origination of the norms governing the members of the group. Indigenous religions convey the breadth of human spiritual experience across earth's diverse natural settings and reveal humanity's seemingly universal inclination for reverence. The religious experiences cultivated among these groups also show the great extent of humanity's experimentation with altered states of consciousness and extremes of bodily endurance. The rituals performed to heal, revere, and express group solidarity reveal the ways our species has conceptualized and faced the dual mysteries of birth and death.

The presence of a human belief in some sort of afterlife emerges from the earliest archaeological records of ceremonial burials. In hundreds of excavations, burial clearly was done to preserve the body and provide it with decoration (colors, jewelry, flowers, animal skulls, or antlers), foods (meat, grain), and tools (spears, sticks). These arrangements suggest that early humans felt that there was a nonmaterial component of the self, an essence that "lived on" after the physical body had perished and decayed. Thus the disposal of human corpses is clearly more than merely functional: Death seems to be likened to sleep, not mere dissolution, and the function of burial seems to be to open a gateway to an afterlife.

We noted at the start of this chapter the common belief that living beings and some inanimate objects possess a special life force which was first labeled by scholars as *animism*. An early and still widely popular articulation of soul belief was made in

"The first thing when we wake up in the morning is to be thankful to the Great Spirit for the Mother Earth: how we live, what it produces, what keeps everything alive."

—Joshua Wetsit, an Assiniboine from Montana

SOURCE: *The Sacred Ways of Knowledge, Sources of Life.*

Awakening the Spirits: A Bullroarer

Bullroarers are powerful ritual tools that convey the bond between living and dead members of scattered aboriginal groups, from those in prehistory up to those still used among native peoples in Australia. A bullroarer is a sphere that has a hole at one end, and when the device is swung around on a string, air passes through, resulting in a booming-whirring sound. The sound waves vibrate at a frequency that affects the human viscera, evoking a strange feeling, one that conveys the presence of sacred time and space.

A bullroarer painted with a serpent motif. Swinging the roarer produces a deep, piercing sound that elicits a feeling of numinosity in ritual participants.

1871 by E. B. Tylor (1831–1917), who argued that religion originated in the universal human perception that there is an invisible soul or intangible spirit inside our visible, tangible bodies. He argued that in all "primitive societies," recognition of a soul shaped similar belief systems across the world.

More recent studies of surviving indigenous religions focus less on belief in vaguely defined souls or spirits and more on the phenomenon of how indigenous peoples actually perceive and establish relations with a range of others, human and nonhuman, through their sensory experience. For them, being religious is not about creeds or texts that need interpreting; instead, people experience an embodied engagement with the environment around them, one in which certain stones, animals, trees, and the dead may "speak" to the living. Here emotions, memory, direct experiences, and altered states of consciousness play a part. Most indigenous people sustain a very close relationship with the natural world, one in which the ecosystem is deeply sensed as alive, as fertile, and in the flow of a larger, ordered cosmos.

In hunter-gatherer societies today, human life is more bound up with the recurring rhythms of nature and group interconnections than is the case today in urban industrial societies. The people live by the rising and the setting of the sun, the phases of the moon, and the seasons of the year. Time is circular. This **circular time** follows the pattern of the celestial and natural world. Human lives, too, revolve like the seasons: from life to death, as from spring to summer, fall to winter and then spring and the returning of new life, ever and again in a circle. In myth and ritual and in contact with their sacred centers of revelation, indigenous peoples feel themselves to be part of the largest rhythms of life. There is flow and a quest for equilibrium with

circular time: awareness, especially in hunter-gatherer societies, that time and life follow the same recurring cycle of time determined by the sun, moon, and the seasons the environment; finding the good life has always meant learning to live with the plants, animals, and spirits that share the indigenous peoples' own world, discerning their motivations and intentions, their love and anger.

This practical and integral relatedness with the natural home world—of hunted animals, essential plants, and surrounding landforms—is realized through the engagement of all their five senses and is guided by myth, mind, and emotions. Resident spirit beings that have souls also have personalities and the faculty of hearing, and many command the ability to speak; indigenous traditions vary, in fact, by the ways these spirit beings speak, their personalities, and the landscapes they occupy through the seasons. The human community's attuning of its senses to these entities through ritual ensures their finding food, avoiding illness, sustaining group harmony, creating healthy children.

All known indigenous peoples have imagined their universe populated by a multitude of supernatural beings that interact with them in life. Many groups believe these ties extend into an afterlife; some assume that souls of the dead reincarnate as humans or other life forms. Relating with spirit beings (or souls) entails making ongoing, reliable connections with them; accordingly, indigenous communities tend to be very careful in performing their communal rituals.

Among most indigenous peoples today, ancestors are in some way still connected with the living; their dreams or visions support the idea that the dead can "return" in nonmaterial form. As we will see, this belief is supported by spirit mediums who serve as dramatic communicators with the dead, who enable a departed soul to speak to the living "from the other side." Although many in the contemporary Euro-American world do not take the content of dreams as seriously as facts derived from "normal waking reality," indigenous peoples today, like most humans before the modern era, regard dreams and visions as very significant sources for understanding the ultimate meanings and purposes of life.

Death is not an ultimate, irrevocable end; in most indigenous societies, it does not imply a final disconnection between the living and the dead. On the contrary, death is an elevation of one's status to that of sacred ancestor. Ancestors, in turn, are venerated as spirits who can help the living by guiding them to the hunting grounds and bringing prey animals their way or by invigorating the wild foods or cultivated crops. By the same token, misfortune in a community may be the fault of the living, who have incited the ancestors' anger and punishment by breaking a moral law or neglecting a ritual. In such situations, harmony between the living, the dead, and all of nature needs to be restored.

Ancestral spirits are seen as custodians of the traditions. They may harm those who flout custom and bless those who are faithful to it. Some scholars, following Tylor, believe that later religions evolved from early animist views of the world and efforts to manage the activities of supernatural spirit-beings. Recent archaeological evidence suggests that the most elaborate burials in late prehistory were conducted to protect the living from the power of malevolent souls. Perhaps powerful ancestral spirits (both the kind and the dangerous) became the world's first gods.

Among the Dani, a simple agricultural group in highland New Guinea, belief that the soul survives into an afterlife profoundly shapes the ways of the living. In their death rituals, the Dani try to direct the soul of a person who has just died to a distant ghost land. Yet many ghosts are thought to return to cause problems, especially if their last rites were not done properly or their death is not avenged in timely fashion. Thus Dani elders take great care when performing funerals, and they maintain small guest houses to accommodate, and pacify, the occasional ghost visitors.

Further, rival Dani villages engage continually in lethal warfare, whose main purpose is for the men to satisfy a newly departed kinsman's spirit by killing someone on the enemy's side. The Dani moral code includes the precept of "a life for a life." Moreover, since losing a kinsman inevitably weakens the collective community and each individual's soul, avenging the loss of the deceased by killing an enemy tribesman is the only means

Burial of children from 20,000 BCE: With the remains are perforated shells and remnants of decorated clothing found in Grottes des Enfantes, France

to restore the vitality of the survivors' souls. In fact, Dani kinship and food production is organized around the central need for supplying the feasts that must be held to mark deaths and celebrate revenge killings. Appeasing ancestral ghosts is always in mind.

The Dani, like the Blackfoot tribe of the Northern Plains of North America, are representative of the many indigenous groups in which shamans are absent or marginal. Lacking a class of priests, every adult learns to perform the most common rituals. But there are in both societies wise religious leaders who are looked to for leading major communal festivals based on their ready knowledge of the intricate rites. Dani religious leaders are thoughtful in hosting the regular visits of ancestral ghosts; the Blackfoot wise men and women religious leaders show care in treating spirits as honored guests, feeding them, making lovely home altars, and assembling the finest medicine bundles for offerings.

Religious tradition pervades the lives of indigenous peoples. If they live in the prescribed ways, which always requires them to show respect for the beings around them (human and nonhuman), members of the group will lead successful lives.

Totemism: Australian Aboriginal Religion

Across the world, anthropologists have noted that many indigenous groups use a symbol, or totem, to establish their fundamental identity, identify proper marriage partners, promote collective solidarity, and regulate relations with outsiders. A **totem** is an

totem: symbol taken from natural world to represent common origin and essence of a social group animal, reptile, insect, or plant that is emblematic of the community and is treated as sacred. The relationship between totems and groups reveals a special circle of kinship and a primal connection between humans and the rest of nature.

Totemism is still found among some Native Americans and is common among the various aboriginal peoples of Australia. To understand this belief system, we can take an example from the latter: Members of the aboriginal kangaroo clan believe that their origins occurred in the **Dreamtime**, when the world as we know it was being created. Their myths inform them that their clan consists of the descendants of their totemic progenitor, the first kangaroo, who created them from her own body

Dreamtime: for Australian Aborigines, the time when the world was created, and which exists in another realm

RITUALS AND RITES: Shamans Across the World

The shaman remains the key religious specialist in many societies today. The term *shaman* (alternatively pronounced "SHAY-man" or "shah-MAN") comes from the Evenk, a group of hunters and reindeer herders in Siberia. The term was adopted for all similar practitioners, however, because early scholars thought that the Siberian shaman tradition had spread across Eurasia and into the Americas, a theory that is doubted today. Four religious figures are central to an understanding of the world's religions: the shaman, the prophet, the sage, and the priest. The first is our concern in this chapter, for

the shaman is still found among peoples on every inhabited continent and in the earliest records of our direct forebears.

Though differing in details of clothing and techniques, shamans are found across the world today: left, a Yanomami shaman in the Amazon; right, a Korean shaman in Seoul.

and essence, established their existence as humans, and then led them to their current home territory, making landforms, including rivers and mountains, and other creatures. Accordingly, the group members ritually decorate their bodies with kangaroo drawings; and before children are considered to be adults, they must learn the distinctive dances and songs recounting the group's totemic kangaroo story. Elder men pass down these secrets to the young men through initiation; they are most protective of the sacred symbols, the polished wood or stone *churinga* that symbolize the totem and are inscribed with the most sacred maps or tales of the founder and other heroes. The group is also protective of its own "songlines," the myths that are sung to trace in detail the progenitor's trail of creation over the land, an oral record giving the group claims to a shared identity and territory.

Harming or eating a kangaroo is almost always forbidden, or **taboo**, to members of the kangaroo clan. The totemic kangaroo spirit that dwells in the home territory is thought to be alive and protective of the group. Elders pray to and invoke it for healing and guidance. Women of the kangaroo clan who want to become pregnant visit the places where the totemic spirits reside, for they believe that conception—via spirit/soul acquisition—cannot occur without exposure to the totem's life force.

There is also a unique and regularly performed ritual that unifies the totemic group. In addition to singing and acting out their myth of origins, all the "kangaroos" in the group, on this one annual occasion, gather to renew their primordial identity and "become one flesh" again. How? By hunting down a kangaroo and ingesting its flesh. These rites are performed to increase the totemic species and give spiritual strength to individuals in the group. Here, again, in the totemic belief system, humans and nature form a spiritual totality: Although the design of the world was fixed once and for all in the Dreamtime, it is the task of humans, through their totemic rites, to maintain and renew this creation.

The French sociologist Émile Durkheim (1858–1917) argued that totemism points to a key feature in all religious life. It is the sacred totem (in our

taboo: action or object that is normally forbidden

Aboriginal men from Arnhemland, Australia, painting their bodies to show their identification with a totemic ancestor.

The art of contemporary Australian Aborigines depicts totemic beings and their role in creation during the "Dreamtime."

example, the kangaroo) that gives the group a singular focus and in so doing really stands for the group itself. For Durkheim, religion is at root about making a group's own identity, survival, and worth sacred by focusing on and identifying with a common symbol. What human groups felt as an unseen but deeply felt sacred force was really, he argued, the cohesive power of group unity. For Durkheim the central purpose of religious myth is to frame society's customs with a long and noble history such that they can be respected as sacred and bring social stability to human life.

Durkheim's influential theory is that whatever else has come to define religious beliefs across the world's human groups, religion's power to bind us together is what established it and keeps it central to human life.

Shamans: "Technicians of the Sacred"

What happens if the group's band of skilled hunters comes home empty-handed after a month? How to respond when debilitating illness marked by fever, chills, and physical weakness afflicts a growing number of villagers? Who can halt or reverse the series of misfortunes befalling a family that has let its ancestral shrine fall into ruins? Only a

spirit medium, or **shaman**, referred to variously also as *medicine man, folk healer, witch doctor*, and so on, can intervene with the unseen powers. These terms taken together designate some of the usual traits attributed to shamans.

Among the many fascinating scenes shown in prehistoric cave art are over fifty images of humans that suggest the depiction of no ordinary person. Two are famous: a bison hovering over a man, with a pole surmounted by a bird, and a human seeming to morph into a composite animal who walks hidden among a large herd of deer. These two ancient paintings may be the first recorded depictions of the shaman, an individual with special powers, whose roles, even 30,000 years ago, may have included healing the souls and bodies of others, dealing with death, and venturing into the realm of the dead. The Kung healers in recent centuries have embellished rock walls with shamanic paintings, and records of similar practices have been found in ancient caves in Europe and Asia. Scholars have posited that the prehistoric shamans are shown discerning the movements of animal herds, guiding the hunters to success, and perhaps recalling the errant souls of the living.

The term *shaman* identifies a religious specialist who mediates between the human community and the usually unseen supernatural beings also populating our world. The role varies across the world: In some indigenous societies they dominate in the group's religious life; in others, the medium remains a marginal, often-distrusted figure resorted to only in dire circumstances, where chiefs, priests, or healers perform the group's ritual and healing functions. And some indigenous societies have no tradition of spirit mediums at all.

The most common shaman's role worldwide is the ability to heal (both literally and metaphorically) through **spirit flight** achieved in trance or an altered state of consciousness; in some indigenous groups, shamans utilize psychotropic drugs found in nature to achieve or aid their otherworldly journey. Shaman healers usually cooperate with spiritual beings and in some places are distinct from **sorcerers**, mediums who manipulate the spirit world and coerce the supernaturals without their consent, often for their own benefit and against community values.

Where found, shamans are ritual specialists, intermediaries who attempt to connect this world to another realm of being that impinges on humanity. By these acts, they knit together the community in the face of the chaos of disease, death, and discord. Many shamans through their spirit flights return to teach their communities, and through trance rituals they demonstrate that the daily, ordinary world is not all there is. A deeper spiritual order enfolds the known, everyday experience of life. In most indigenous societies, the living and the dead, the community and its sacred ancestors, form one great community. Binding it all together, the shaman uses his or her body as a bridge to connect these two worlds. If harmony in an indigenous group has been shattered by troubling ancestral ghosts, only the shaman, who is able to visit both worlds and communicate the needs of one to the other, can restore balance.

Shamans have been found in over a thousand indigenous societies, though details of their practices vary. A commonly held conception in the indigenous religions is that sickness can be due to the loss of an individual's soul, by accident or by theft. In some indigenous societies, people believe that illness can be induced by an enemy's

---

spirit medium/ shaman: person who communicates with deities and spirits through ritually induced trance

spirit flight: shaman's attempt to locate another person's soul in another realm

sorcerers: mediums who manipulate the spirit world, often for their own benefit rather than on behalf of the community inserting a foreign object such as a piece of bone or an insect into a victim's body. The common characteristic of their intervention is to discover this, locate the object, and remove it to cure the afflicted party.

The trance state can be reached by drumming and singing alone, but in global perspective shamans have also discovered a long list of psychotropic agents for altering consciousness to their purposes. Fasting is common, but practices may also involve the inhaling of incense, snuffs, smoke from tobacco or other psychoactive herbs, or the ingesting of mushrooms or potent plant concoctions. The shaman's trance may be marked by bodily fever, loud breathing, protruding eyes, insensitivity to temperature or pain, convulsions, or trembling. In many traditions, the shaman's soul is thought to leave the physical body, free to fly to the heavens, beneath the earth, or under the sea. On these *spirit flights*, or *soul journeys*, shamans attempt to locate another person's lost soul, perhaps because it has wandered off in this world or passed on to the afterlife. Another common belief is that the dead person's soul needs a shaman's assistance to reach the afterlife dwelling place of the clan's ancestors.

tutelary spirit: supernatural agent, often an ancestral spirit, who helps a shaman

Shamans through initiation find connection with a protective spirit, or **tutelary spirit**. This is a supernatural agent, often an ancestral spirit, whose help is required to perform the difficult soul journeys, negotiate with evil spirits, compel a soul to return, or increase the shaman's healing powers. In many tribes, shamans have human helpers who watch over their unconscious bodies during trance states, for they, too, can remain stuck as spirits if their souls cannot return to their bodies.

numinous: human perception of the sacred

The shamanic world is one in which spirits coexist with humans in a layered cosmos, with humans occupying the earth between an upper and a lower world. The spirits are particularly accessible to humans around sacred physical objects or unusual places. As we saw in Chapter 1, each culture regards these locations as being connected to the "center of the world" (*axis mundi*). Most commonly, such sites are actual or symbolic sacred mountains or sacred trees, revered as places of original revelations, intensely alive with spiritual power, or **numinous** presence. Several examples show how shamanic traditions from around the world today share common traits.

Case Study in Healing Trance: Kung San Healers

n/um kausi: shamans of the Kung people

The Kung San of southern Africa believe that the dead go to an afterlife, a "next world" populated by ancestors, one that is similar to this world and is linked closely to the living. Souls that miss the living return to earth as ghosts and try to sicken friends and family members in an effort to hasten their arrival in the next world. The most accomplished Kung shamans (**n/um kausi**) have the ability to enter into a trance during night-long dances, in which everyone joins in ceremonies of rhythmic drumming and singing around a fire. With this group support and social purpose, anthropologists suggest, the Kung shamans activate a natural force within their bodies, the *n/um*, a power that "boils" in and moves up the spine. The body shakes and sweats, and inhalations grow forced and deeper as the shaman slips into a trance state. Thus empowered, the shaman begins to touch the bodies of others to transfer the healing force of the boiling

A Kung healing ceremony. The trancing and healing performed by Kung shamans depends on the community's participating in drumming, singing, and dancing.

n/um into them. Expert healers can also identify and suck out poisons from the bodies of the sick; some may massage the patient with a mixture of the shaman's own sweat and blood. Healers who perceive the ghosts of troublesome ancestors watching the dance outside the community circle may shriek or hurl stones at deities in the shadows who are identified as causing difficulties. The most effective Kung shamans are honored, but they are otherwise typical members of the tribe; most are men.

The most skilled Kung shamans enter into a deep trance state (*kia*) so that their souls can leave the body and journey to the "next world." There they confirm the fate of the dead, investigate causes of sickness, or convey messages between the dead and the living. The spirit flight is a practice attributed to shamans in nearly all indigenous societies, past and present.

The shaman's role is universally regarded as mortally dangerous. The Kung call entering trance "being half-dead" and with great care guard a shaman's physical body while the healer's soul journeys to "the other world." Like many indigenous peoples, the Kung are also careful not to startle sleeping individuals, for fear that souls wandering during sleep will not have time to return to a person who has been awakened suddenly.

Men and women who become shamans in the Kung or other cultures must train through long apprenticeships. But in most groups it is common for shamans to feel that they were chosen for the role by a tutelary spirit, often in spite of their own resistance. Novice shamans must prove their ability by surviving an initiation ordeal that may require fasting and acts of extraordinary physical endurance. Each must demonstrate the capacity for trance, the grace of a tutelary spirit, and evidence of supernormal powers. Many shamans feel that they wear out their bodies by repeatedly undergoing near-death experiences in the course of soul journeys or the ingestion of spirit-infused herbs.

"You dance, dance, dance, dance. Then *n/um* lifts you up in your belly and lifts up in your back, and you start to shiver. In trance, you see everything, because you see what's troubling everybody. . . . Then *n/um* enters every part of your body, right to your feet and even your hair. . . . Then *n/um* makes your thoughts nothing in your head."

—Kinachau, a Kung San healer

SOURCE: Richard Katz, *Boiling Energy: Community Healing Among the Kalahari Kung* (Cambridge, MA: Harvard University Press, 1982).

Modern Native American art of the Ojibway depicting spirit guides in the flight of the shaman.

Case Study: Sioux Vision Quest for a Spirit Ally

Among the Lakota Sioux of North America, young men go to a sacred wilderness region on a *vision quest* in search of a personal protector spirit. After preparatory training, the apprentices fast and purify themselves in a sweat lodge. Then each one ventures out alone into the wilderness. The Lakota believe, as do the Kung, that every human being has the potential for supernatural connection and that all should be encouraged to develop this ability.

Those contacted by strong spirit allies in dreams and those who have vivid visions of the ancestors may go on to become shamans after further training with an elder practitioner. As the Lakota shaman Lame Deer recalled his experience, "All of a sudden I heard the cry of an eagle, loud and above the voices of many other birds. It seemed to say, 'We have been waiting for you. We knew you would come.' "[3] Apprentices learn the techniques of trance, the myths of the tribe, the location of "power places" in the landscape, and other healing arts that involve the use of medicines. Shamans are never the same after initiation; many receive a new name, a new identity, and in the myths they even obtain a new body. Shamans encounter evil spirits that must be tricked, seduced, or killed to complete the healing task. Given these arduous demands, becoming a shaman is often described as a death–and–rebirth experience.

Bear Sacrifice: A Widespread Arctic and Pacific Rim Tradition

We have noted how shamans can serve as mediums who bring the spirits down to earth for "ritual negotiations." An example of this practice is the bear sacrifice, once one of the most widespread rituals in the world and common across the upper Pacific

Rim and the vast circumpolar region from northern Japan to North America. As observed in modern times, shamans carefully manage the sacrificial rituals, offering gifts from humans in exchange for an animal's life. A common belief in hunter-gatherer societies is that animals are actually spirits in disguise who assume animal bodies to interact with humans. This may have been the earliest example of humanity conceptualizing divine incarnation, the embodiment in earthly form of a supernatural being.

Among the Ainu people on Hokkaido Island in northern Japan, spirits that incarnate themselves as animals are called *kamui*. They mostly dwell in an "other world" but can have contact with humans by coming to earth and assuming life in a bear's body. The Ainu conception is that humans and *kamui* are of equal status. Although the latter (when unencumbered by a body) can fly and have magical powers, only humans can give them what they really need and want: precious sake (a wine made from rice) and *inau*, the earth's fragrant willow sticks. In the Ainu understanding, the spirits don animal bodies to acquire their fur as "clothes" to trade, for they can get *inau* and sake from humans. This transaction requires that they be ritually hunted and have their bodies killed to complete the exchange that benefits both parties.

Ainu elders celebrating a Bear Feast. Offerings of food and sake are placed before the dead bear; swords and sacred quivers hang on the altar behind the men. This photograph was taken by the anthropologist Bronislaw Pilsudski (1866–1918), who lived with an Ainu community for several years in the early twentieth century.

The Ainu shaman performs special rituals to attract a spirit in its bear incarnation. Knowing that an exchange has been requested and consenting to it if humans have kept up their part in earlier exchanges, a bear cub leaves trail signs that allow hunters to track and capture it. Villages then raise the specially chosen animal until it becomes fully grown. Afterward, the shaman addresses the bear respectfully, makes the proper offerings, performs a ritual execution, and releases the *kamui* spirit to return to the other world, presumed to be happy with its gifts. The Ainu believe that if the sacred conventions of the exchange are duly observed, the *kamui* just released and other spirits will continue to assume animal form. Thus the shaman ensures that the people will have a continuous supply of meat and shelter.

Shamans Who "Repair the World"

A shaman's expertise can also be effective when a human group acts improperly. The practices of the Inuit (who dwell around the Arctic region) illustrate the shaman's role in "repairing the world." The Inuit believe that the great goddess Takanakapsaluk, Mistress of Sea Animals, lives on the ocean floor and releases whales, seals, fish, and other marine creatures so that they may be killed for human use. But the Inuit believe that when their community performs the ritual improperly or someone breaks a moral taboo, the goddess's hair "becomes soiled" and she burns in anger, holding back all creatures in her domain. The Inuit shaman must then be called for a séance. To follow one account:

> He sits behind a curtain and says again and again, "The way is made ready for me!" after which the audience responds, "Let it be so." Finally from behind the curtain, the shaman cries, "Halala-he-he-he halala-he-he!" Then he drops down a tube, which is believed to lead straight to the bottom of the sea. The shaman's voice can be heard receding further in the depths, and finally it disappears. During the shaman's absence, the audience sits in the darkened house, listening to faint sighing and groaning, while singing songs of past journeys: the shaman's dodging three deadly guard stones, averting the father of the goddess, and getting past a fierce guard dog. Approaching the goddess, the shaman finds her angry, with hair uncombed, filthy, and hanging over her eyes. The creatures of the ocean sit in a pool beside her. The shaman gently turns the goddess toward the animals and a nearby lamp, combing and washing her hair. He then asks why the animals are not coming, and she replies that they are being withheld because the people have eaten forbidden boiled meat and because the women have kept their miscarriages secret, failing to purify their homes afterward. Mollified by praises and promises to make amends, goddess Takanakapsaluk releases the animals and they are swept back into the ocean. The shaman's return is marked by a distant, then louder call of "Plu-a-he-he!" as he finally shakes in his place, gasping for breath. After a silence, he demands,

"The greatest peril in life lies in the fact that human food consists entirely of souls. All these creatures that we have to kill and eat, all we have to strike down to make clothes for ourselves, have souls, souls that do not perish and which must be pacified lest they revenge themselves on us for taking away their bodies."

—Ivaluardjuk, an Inuit healer

SOURCE: *The Sacred Ways of Knowledge, Sources of Life.*

"Your words must rise up," and then the audience members begin to confess their misdeeds. By the end of the séance, there is a mood of optimism.[4]

The Yanomami shamans of the Amazon rain forest also illustrate how mediums repair community life by bringing spirits down to earth. Village leader, curer, and defender against evil spirits, the village shaman (always male) locates and returns the disoriented souls of sick or dying villagers. If others have acted to weaken or steal someone's soul, it is the shaman who must identify both the misdeed and the perpetrators. To be initiated as shaman and to achieve such abilities, an individual must memorize chants, drumming, and struts to attract the support of his special ancestral spirits. The Yanomami shaman must also master the use of the hallucinogenic snuff called *ebene*, made from psychoactive plants that the shaman's own teacher repeatedly blew into the student's nostrils as part of his training. This powerful substance is thought to be a spirit ally that is essential for opening the Yanomami shaman's body to perceive, feel, and contact his tribe's spirit allies.

The Yanomami shaman has the power to conduct the spirits into the human world. The spirits can then be induced to enter the shaman's body and respond to questions about matters of concern, small or great. At times and without invitation, the shaman's mouth may speak the spirit's messages about group origins, life's meaning, or any hidden facts relevant to recent events.

The reliance on psychoactive substances to assist the shaman to achieve altered states of consciousness, as found among the Yanomami, is not universal. Drug-induced trances are limited mostly to groups in the Americas, where the use of the cactus peyote, the vine extract ayahuasca, and plants such as jimson and datura have long been in the shaman's medicine bag. What is universal for shamans across the world, even among

TALES OF SPIRITUAL TRANSFORMATION: The Peyote Ceremony

Divine Communion

From that time, whenever they held peyote meetings, we all attended and . . . one time something happened to me. . . . I was sitting with bowed head, . . . we prayed, . . . then I saw Jesus standing there. . . . I will pray to him, I thought. I stood up and raised my arm. I prayed. I asked for a good life—thanking God who gave me my life. And as the drum was beating, my body shook to the beat. I was unaware of it. I was just very contented. I never knew such pleasure as this. There was a sensation of great

joyousness. Now I was an angel. That is how I saw myself. Because I had wings I was supposed to fly but I could not quite get my feet off the ground. . . . I knew when I ate peyote that they were using something holy. That way is directed toward God. Nothing else on earth is holy, . . . and if someone sees something holy at a peyote meeting, that is really true. I understood that this religion is holy.

—Shirley Etsitty, Native American Church

Source: *The Sacred: Ways of Knowledge, Sources of Life* (Tsaile, AZ: Navajo Community College Press, 1996).

shamans utilizing psychoactive drugs, is reliance on the impact of rapid rhythmic drumming, dancing, chanting, and fasting to induce trance experiences. Thus, the drum or the rattle is a universal symbol of the shaman's extraordinary religious practice.

Indigenous Religions Today

The Cataclysms of Colonialism

A theme that runs throughout this book is the disruptions to life and religious traditions caused by modern European colonialism. For indigenous societies across the planet, this global expansion of invading outsiders and the political dominance they imposed has been disastrous.

This cataclysm has had many facets. Native peoples of the New World and other remote regions were decimated by the diseases of Eurasia, to which they had no natural resistance. Often simultaneously, the disease-bearing outsiders plundered the native people's riches, utilizing horses and superior weapons technology to achieve their aims. In the early colonial era, millions of people in small-scale subsistence societies were killed or enslaved. In countless instances, the outsiders appropriated and transformed the native lands when natural resources were discovered there. Whole peoples were ruthlessly swept aside, and ways of life that had evolved over centuries were cut off. Since religion is closely related to a community's way of life, the epidemics and genocide suffered by the world's indigenous peoples inevitably included the destruction and deformation of ancient religious traditions.

Over time, as the worst cruelties of colonial rule eased, the survivors and their descendants faced stark choices. Would they risk the chaos of migration by retreating into the receding natural frontiers of forests and mountains? Would they acquiesce to a nineteenth-century government's program of forced resettlement on reservations? Or would the best choice be for individuals to go their separate ways, to assimilate with the dominant society and submit to the national laws of others? Whatever the choice, the solidarity and cultural integrity of most of these displaced groups worldwide has weakened over every generation. It has inevitably been the young who have seen the limits of their minority status, rejected the old dialects and religious customs, and responded to the allure of the dominant culture by embracing assimilation.

Exposure to missionary religions and their alien exponents often contributed to the downfall of the indigenous religions. Beliefs and practices of many native peoples elicited much hostility and criticism. Governments in the Americas and Australia forced indigenous children to attend missionary schools, where Christianity was aggressively taught and in which traditional practices were ruthlessly banned. Students who spoke their native languages were subject to punishment. Missionaries viewed shamans as obstacles to the advance of the colonizing powers. Outsiders often accused

"Our church is the world."

—John Emhoolah, Kiowa leader of North America

SOURCE: *The Sacred Ways of Knowledge, Sources of Life.*

the native healers of combining evil with fakery: acting as "servants of the devil" while also being imposters or religious charlatans who exploited their own people. For the Euro-American Christian immigrants, for example, shamanism represented the chaotic wilderness, the shaman a shady character and source of disruptive chaos that threatened the colonial order. Under these circumstances, native peoples in many cases had to hide their drums, medicines, and sacred images. They believed that the only way to preserve their culture was to take it underground.

Other native peoples, however, organized in attempts to restore their place in the world and give new life to their traditions. In North America, shamans rallied to attempt to revitalize native peoples in the nineteenth century through a movement called the **Ghost Dance**. After the decimation of the buffalo by white hunters, which greatly contributed to the destruction of the indigenous way of life on the Great Plains, several elders had the same visionary revelation: Their tutelary spirits announced a way to restore the lost world by bringing back the ancestors and causing the whites to disappear. Native American religious leaders then preached that this could be accomplished if all the people performed a new dance ritual as prescribed by the spirits. Soon this Ghost Dance was practiced with fervor across the Great Plains by those whose kin had died, with the dancers falling unconscious in hopes of experiencing reunion with their deceased relatives. One leader in this movement had this vision of the Ghost Dance recorded:

> All Indians must dance, everywhere, and keep on dancing. Pretty soon in the next spring, the Great Spirit come. . . . The game be thick everywhere. All dead Indians come back and live again. . . . White can't hurt Indian then. Then big flood come like water and all white people die, get drowned. After that, water go away and then nobody but Indians everywhere and game animals of all kinds thick.[5]

The pain of engagement with outsiders is unmistakable in this new religious movement, one that sought to bind a vision of ecological renewal with the restoration of traditional religious consciousness. In 1890 the U.S. Cavalry was ordered to end this nationwide movement by massacring the men, women, and children gathered for a Ghost Dance at Wounded Knee, South Dakota.

By 2014, no indigenous societies remain that have not been exposed to the world of outsiders, with their missionaries, armies, nation-states, corporations, and technologies. Some have even been the targets of genocidal persecution. Most of the Kung people have been relocated onto reservations, forced to give up hunting, and directed to adopt agriculture or simple craft production. The Ainu of northern Japan have suffered land seizures and discrimination and are so stigmatized today that few are willing to profess knowledge of the old traditions and shamanic practices. Native peoples of the Amazon rain forest have been displaced by land-clearing settlers and threatened by multinational mining and oil drilling projects. The history of Native Americans since 1500 is a story of genocide and land taking, made worse by legal discrimination against Native American religious practices. In the twenty-first century, hundreds of

Ghost Dance: nineteenth-century Native American religious revitalization movement led by spirit mediums indigenous languages and religious traditions will decline in use and disappear forever. It is hard for those centered in the dominant world civilization to absorb vicariously the shattering impact of the past centuries on the earth's "first peoples." Many groups today are involved with land ownership disputes with their federal governments, and they call for the return of human remains and the sacred items of their ancestors that were collected by museum curators in the past.

Some indigenous groups that have survived with their cultures most intact are those living far from resources the modernizing world has sought: in the trans–Arctic zone, deep in the rain forests, high in the remotest mountains, or on isolated islands far from the continental landmasses. Others have found successful means of assimilating, with members gaining education and employment outside the group and integrating modern economic life with indigenous tradition. Those groups that have retained autonomy, resisted assimilation, and worked to revitalize their identity show both the near-boundless adaptability of human culture and the deep resilience of the human spirit. An example of this indigenous vitality is in groups like the Kayapo in Brazil, who now use the Internet to share their anti-expropriation strategies and principles of cultural revitalization with other groups across the globe; their experience emphasizes

The Native American Church

In the United States today, over 550 Indian nations are recognized by the U.S. federal government, each with its own history and tribal land and each practicing its own distinct traditional religion. In the last century, there have been successful efforts to draw scattered Native Americans into new religious groups in what scholars have identified as the "pan-Americanization" of indigenous peoples.

The Native American Church is a major example of this phenomenon, one that has had one faction drawn into the orbit of Christianity and another that remains independent. But the two are united in their ceremonial use of the cactus peyote as a communal sacrament. This "melting pot" movement remains controversial among some Native Americans, who criticize how the Native American Church draws tribal members away from their own group's traditions. An additional problem this group encounters is the drug enforcement laws of the U.S. government. Similar indigenous peoples' new religions have started in South America. Two examples are Santo Daime and União do Vegetal; both are syncretistic, influenced by Christian morality and folk religion, and centered on a traditional psychotropic herb, in this case, ayahuasca. Both also have now spread across the globe, attracting nonindigenous devotees from Japan to Europe.

Source: http://www.nativeamericanchurch.net/Native_American_Church/NATIVE_AMERICAN_CHURCH.html

the role of the young as bicultural actors who negotiate with the world outside the indigenous group. They have also harnessed the power of modern video to document infringements on their lands by outsiders and as an effective medium to communicate about group issues and share cultural teachings between Kayapo in separate regions.

Shamans in some indigenous groups were pivotal figures who led groups in facing the crises of modernity. Because traditionally they were entrusted with mediating between spirits and humans, shamans have been the natural choices to act on behalf of the group when the outside world intruded. In the face of repression, many shamans saw confrontation as the only hope for their group, led rebellions, and died in vain defense. Siberian and Mongolian shamans under Soviet rule, for example, retreated to the deep wilderness and continued to practice there.

Religious leaders found other creative responses. Some advocated **syncretism**, in which indigenous religious beliefs and practices were woven together with those of outsiders. In present-day Mexico, for example, shamans have integrated Catholic saints and sacramental theology into healing rites that utilize peyote. Another example of combining elements from different traditions to create a new religion is **Bwiti**, a West Central African religion. Organized in the early twentieth century among the forest-dwelling Babongo and Mitsogo people of Gabon and the Fang people of Gabon and Cameroon, Bwiti incorporates animism, ancestor worship, and Christianity into its belief system. As with the **Native American Church**, a mild hallucinogen plays a role, in this case the root bark of the *Tabernanthe iboga* plant, which is now specially cultivated for its religious purpose. Individuals joining the Bwiti community are taught that iboga induces a rich spiritual experience, one that allows the disciple to be healed and solve problems.

syncretism: combination of elements from different belief systems

Bwiti: west central African syncretic religion

Native American Church: modern religious group uniting native peoples of North America

Religious leaders in the Bwiti movement creatively combine regional and Christian traditions.

The Kayapo of Brazil: Selective Modernity and the Survival of Tradition

Kayapo chiefs act as religious and political leaders, trying to retain control of the land that is essential to the continuation of tradition.

The Kayapo until recent decades killed all intruders on their lands, whether lumberjacks, gold miners, or rubber-tree tappers, and were regarded as the most dangerous natives of the Amazon rain forest. Outsiders made every effort to exterminate the Kayapo, going so far as to fly over them to drop blankets infected with smallpox onto their villages. But in the middle of the twentieth century, Kayapo chiefs changed their relationship with outsiders, and in 1982 they regained ownership and control of most of their indigenous lands, the largest tract held by native peoples in South America. On a limited scale, their leaders have sold rights to cut timber and to allow outsiders to mine for gold, using the substantial rents and taxes collected to sustain and protect their culture.

The Kayapo consider themselves an integral part of the universe, bound to the cycles of the natural year and nature's ongoing rebirth. Returning from their hunts, men sing to the spirits of the game they killed in order for the animal or reptile spirits to remain in the forest. Each species is connected to a distinctive song that begins with the cry of the dead animal. A "center of the world" is located in each village's central plaza, where rituals and public life take place. To go back to the time of mythical origins and stimulate the energy required for life's prosperity and continuance, the Kayapo dance the myths recounting their origins and subsequent incidents, recalling their past to reaffirm their identity and innate vitality.

Kayapo shamans specialize in ritual healing. Their supernatural visions and capacity to contact tribal spirits enable them to perform rites that recall and restore the integrity of the *mekaron*, the soul double; at death they ensure that this soul makes a successful journey to their "village of the dead," located on tribal land, near a mountain range, where it lives an afterlife similar to that in the village of the living.

Now that some of their young men have gained an education and attracted the support of international organizations upholding the rights of native peoples, the Kayapo have secured a firm legal existence in modern Brazil. Their chiefs have acted decisively and creatively to selectively modernize yet preserve their religious traditions. From their taxes on tenant miners, they brought the group into the national cash economy, even going so far as buying airplanes and hiring Brazilian pilots to police their territory. They invested in radios and video equipment for recording group rituals and communicating with other Kayapo across their large territory, all to cultivate their common identity, ritual celebrations, and cultural survival. Traditional lip plugs and body painting remain common in village life, and group hunts keep male and female jungle survival skills honed; yet these have been integrated alongside the adoption of Western medicine, canned foods, and business connections in the global economy (such as supplying Brazilian nut oil to the corporation The Body Shoppe). As material wealth has increased, Kayapo chiefs, by adapting to the possibilities of modern life, have been outspoken in having their group maintain their jungle traditions and resist compromising their sociocultural integrity.

Many indigenous peoples, especially those decimated by disease, forced immigration, or land loss, have been attracted to missionaries of the major world religions seeking to convert them. Governments often cooperated with this goal. In many colonized lands, rituals of the indigenous religions were banned outright. It was also common that marriage was only recognized under national laws if conducted by a Christian priest. Possessing neither wealth, institutional power, nor prestige among the colonial rulers, indigenous peoples in the early contact periods who persisted in their practices were subjected to discrimination, and some states,

Protest against modern states Is a regular fact of life among indigenous peoples in the world today. Struggles to retain control of the land, secure their legal rights, and ensure the education of the young are central to the survival of indigenous religious traditions today. Here, Australian Aborigines demonstrate in Sydney for the restoration of lands annexed from them by the national government.

such as the Soviet Union, imprisoned shamans in psychiatric hospitals. Many studies have found that even after an indigenous people's successful accommodation to a dominant colonial culture, what often survives as its "shamanic tradition" is only fragmentary, reduced to practical applications such as healing services.

In a world turned upside down, one in which the ancestral spirits clearly failed to protect the group or safeguard its territory, radical change was inevitable. Over generations, many shamanic traditions themselves have been diminished or reformulated to match the new life circumstances. Under colonial conditions and until today, cultures that were thriving only a few centuries ago exist only in dimming memory. What has proven the most enduring of these indigenous traditions, even in regions that came to be dominated by one or more world religion, is shamanism.

Shamanism in Modern Asia: Division of Labor Within the World Religions

Shamanism continues to exist as an integral part of the pluralistic religious cultures of Asia. In most settlements across the region, there is a shaman who can enter into the trance state, if called on to heal or to solve practical problems. Such shamanic practice today has been harmonized with the doctrines of the dominant religions and is tolerated by the Hindu, Buddhist, or Islamic religious establishments that are also by now deeply rooted in these areas.

This pattern of coexistence also includes East Asia, where shamans augment popular Confucian beliefs and ancestral rituals, a tradition of pluralistic accommodation there

"Look around. . . . So much of nature has been ruined. Spirits of trees and rocks are displaced and haunt humans because they have nowhere else to go. No wonder the country is a mess."

—Kim Myung, a Korean shaman

SOURCE: *New York Times*, July 7, 2007.

going back to the beginnings of recorded history, as will be discussed in Chapter 8. Here we can say that given the widespread belief in deities inhabiting this earth and in the soul's afterlife destiny, it is not surprising that East Asians still recognize the utility of spirit mediums who attempt to communicate with the dead. Divination has provided answers to such problems as where grandmother's soul might be residing, whether the ghost of a dead child is causing family troubles, or what might be done to gain the favor of a god who could help end a drought. Unhappy spirits (*kuei*) are also thought to cause distress to the living, so here, too, shamans have had an important role in healing the sick.

Typically, a client approaches a spirit medium today because of the suspicion that an illness is due to ghost possession. The medium goes into trance in the sick one's presence and speaks or acts (sometimes writing on a slate or sand-covered board) after having made contact with one or more spirits. The medium's communications are usually interpreted by an assistant, who acts as the intermediary for the family and community members present. For example, contemporary mediums in Taiwan, called *dangki*, become possessed and rapidly write divinely inspired characters in red ink on yellow papers. Sometimes the objects become amulets for their patients; alternatively, they may be burned, whereupon their ashes are mixed with water that is then drunk as medicine. The role of these spirit mediums has, if anything, *increased* with the modernization and rising prosperity of Taiwan. The same phenomenon has been reported in modern Korea as well.

Global Neo-Shamanism: Expropriation by "White Shamans"

Traditional shamanistic practices now appeal to those in the dominant societies who are drawn to the mysteries of life and want to discover them outside the practices and normative worldviews of the major world religions. With their esoteric and primordial qualities, shamanic practices are seen by some in the West as "uncontaminated," the last remaining spiritual frontier on earth. Now growing numbers of adventurers, romantics, and spiritual explorers from urban civilizations across the world seek out shamanic experience as the representative of nearly lost worlds, hoping to recover something of value. Thousands of Euro-Americans each year sign up for tours to Siberia, the Amazon, or the Himalayas to observe and even be initiated by local shamans. A number of Westerners (hence **"white shamans"**) have created global organizations propagating a purported "universal" shamanic tradition, charging high fees for tours, courses, initiations, and healing services, pledging to use some of the proceeds to assist local shamans.

white shamans: westerners who claim to be practitioners in a "universal" shamanic tradition

In indigenous societies, the shaman has a social rather than a personal reason for entering into trance and contacting the spirits, with a primary concern for the community and its well-being. This is an orientation that contrasts sharply with that of the neo-shamans, whose primary interest is in personal development and a self-healing disconnected from any wider community.

Some native peoples regard this development as an attempt by the conquerors to take the last of their possessions, their culture. Well aware of how much their peoples

GENDER FOCUS: Women Healers and Shamans Today

In most hunter-gatherer societies, where there was minimal social hierarchy and only the gendered division of subsistence labor existed, both women and men worked as healers. As indigenous societies became more complex and settled, and adopted forms of pastoralism and simple agriculture, women were subject to greater restrictions, but in some societies they still serve as healers and noted spirit mediums. In most urban communities of China and Japan, shamans are typically regarded as marginal figures of low status, but in South Korea their practices are uniquely honored and sought by people of all faiths. Korean shamans called *mudang* tend to be predominantly women, drawn into the role from one of two backgrounds: troubling personal experiences that led them to initiation; or inheritance of the role

through kinship lines. An estimated 100,000 Korean shamans practice their healing arts today, dealing with life's pragmatic problems. Their séances, called *kut*, are usually held to contact a deity to request economic blessings, healing, restoration of good marital relations, or help in becoming pregnant. The *mudang* enters a trance and then begins to speak with voices attributed to deities. Typically the first statements are complaints of deficiencies in the offerings laid out or about impurity, which Korean supernaturals particularly dislike. When sponsors apologize and promise to do better next time, the divinities usually entertain the sponsor's request(s). A second type of ritual has the most proficient *mudangs* go to the next world with the soul of someone who has recently died or to check the status of a newly departed soul

have lost and ever zealous to guard their traditional secrets, many shamans today distrust the outsiders and doubt their sincerity. Responding to these postmodern possibilities, the indigenous shaman is again mediating between worlds in creative ways. As David Chidester has noted:

> Acting on behalf of a community, even when that community was displaced and dispossessed, shamans developed new religious strategies, not only for preserving archaic techniques of ecstasy, but also for exercising new capacities for memory, concealment, performance, translation, and transformation in negotiating indigenous religious survival under difficult . . . conditions.[6]

Assimilating indigenous animistic and shamanistic traditions into urban-based civilizations goes back to the very beginnings of recorded human history, as we saw in Chapter 1. We will see in subsequent chapters how world religions from antiquity onward performed a central role in the absorption of tribal peoples into states by "converting them" away from their indigenous religions. It will also be seen in the final chapter that the "civil religions" of modern nations have been focused on legitimating the often violent work of assimilating indigenous peoples.

In the next chapters, we can find repeatedly the imprint of indigenous religions, especially soul belief and trance. Soul beliefs remain nearly universal in the great religions, with East Asia's widespread ancestor veneration an important example of archaic practices that still remain compelling and satisfying. Death rites continue to be powerful expressions of religious tradition, and states of altered consciousness are still central to spiritual growth. The metaphor of human life existing on a plane between heaven above and a netherworld below is found in all major world religions. Finally, sacred places that are believed to be at the center of the world (the *axis mundi*) in the early indigenous traditions continue to be revered in the great world religions: Divine revelations occur on mountains (as to Abraham, Moses, Muhammad, and the Daoist sages), and trees connect humans to life's sacred cosmic mysteries (Buddha was enlightened under a tree; Jesus was crucified on a wooden cross). As for the connection with shamans, when examining the lives of the founders of the world religions, prophets as well as sages, we can notice the performance of miracles such as healing the sick and ascending to the heavens on magical flights, in both cases demonstrating the mastery of what began as the chief shamanic arts.

In the last chapter of this book, we will trace further this now-global arc of interaction between indigenous religions, their leaders, shamanism, and "white shamans." We will also see how the shamanic experience of trance, communication with other worlds, and spirit flight have again found their way into the syncretistic practices of many of the "new religions" that have arisen across the world.

Conclusion

For at least the last 30,000 years, humans have evolved primarily through their cultures, not anatomy. Art, religious practices, and complex symbols were all present among modern *Homo sapiens* from the beginning. And all three emerged simultaneously. What should we understand from this circumstance? Religion is an essential element in our species's evolution: It has helped humanity bond more tightly, face the unknown, hunt more effectively, and reconcile with death. Cultural historians see all these factors helping human groups maximize the quality of their diet, which in turn enabled them to better organize, understand, and adapt to their environment as well as to each other. With more free time, there were greater possibilities for individuals to specialize, experiment, and so introduce cultural innovations.

Evidence of religion in prehistory reflects the major concerns of our species as hunter-gatherers. Fertility was important for group survival, the need to hunt for prey was a constant and central fact, and there was ongoing concern to maintain group and gender boundaries. Indigenous religions among early and later hunter-gatherers and early settled cultivators clearly aided group survival.

To the extent a group adopted religious beliefs and practices, that group obtained advantages vis-à-vis other groups. As a force binding communities, as a means of "being careful" about the unseen, and as a decisive factor in helping human groups adapt to their environment, the world's indigenous religions point out the central issues we face in understanding the continuing and universal role of religion in later human life.

Finally, we can also discern the emergence of the first religious specialist, the shaman, who cultivates the universal human capacity for entering altered states of consciousness. Both serving and leading the people, the shaman has given peoples confidence and direction in dealing with the world's unseen forces. Shamanism is still widespread in the world today. Even where one or more of the great world religions has been adopted by a population, shamanic traditions continue to find patrons. In some cases, shamans express concepts associated with one of the now-dominant world religions (e.g., the soul, hell, the force of karma). In other instances, a shamanic cosmos exists side by side with that of a world religion. Today, shamanism is practiced "underground" if there is reason to fear persecution. In most places, however, it is integrated with the dominant world religions.

Discussion Questions

1. What are the problems in knowing and understanding the religions that existed before the development of written language?

2. How might the history of religions be written by a member of an indigenous people?

3. In many hunter-gatherer groups, the people often refer to themselves as "the true people." How might sudden awareness of the existence of other people in itself undermine the cosmos posited in such indigenous religious traditions?

4. Do you think it is valid to generalize from modern hunter-gatherers back into the past to reconstruct the origins of religion? Why or why not?

5. How might a modern shaman explain the endurance of her tradition and the attraction of shamanic practices by those living in modern industrial societies?

6. Some scholars have noted that the practices of modern sports fans in the West often resemble the totemic practices of indigenous peoples. Describe these commonalities in the case of your college or for a professional team such as the Chicago Bears. How do mascots and symbolic practices function to achieve group unity and individual identity?

7. Scholars who have studied tribal peoples now counsel sympathetically imagining indigenous religions as "lived through the body" and involving the entire spectrum of human perception. Explain why this approach has value, given the practices of Kung shamanism.

8. The scholar of comparative religions Joseph Campbell once suggested that the dominant world religions all differed from the indigenous religions by their requiring followers to distance themselves from the powerful personal religious experiences that were routine in many indigenous societies. While you are invited to test this assertion in the following chapters, can you see any problems with traditions that invite everyone to have regular immersions into the sacred as described in this chapter?

9. In 1985, the anthropologist Michael Harner founded the nonprofit Foundation for Shamanic Studies, which seeks to foster "greater respect for the knowledge of indigenous peoples and ultimately help to preserve and dignify this wisdom for future generations." What questions would you have for this organization, given that they also offer workshops to train Western peoples in shamanic practices?

Key Terms

animism	*n/um kausi*	syncretism
Bwiti	Native American	taboo
circular time	Church	totem
cosmogony	numinous	tutelary spirit
Dreamtime	sorcerers	"Venus" figurines
Ghost Dance	spirit flight	"white shamans"
Homo religiosus	spirit medium/shaman	

Suggested Readings

Beck, Peggy, Anna Lee Walters, and Nia Francisco. *The Sacred: Ways of Knowledge, Sources of Life* (Tsaile, AZ: Navajo Community College Press, 1996).

Buyandelger, Manduha, *Tragic Spirits: Shamanism, Memory, and Gender in Contemporary Mongolia.* (Chicago: University of Chicago Press, 2013).

Gardner, Robert. *Gardens of War: Life and Death in the New Guinea Stone Age* (New York: Random House, 1969).

Grim, John. *The Shaman: Patterns of Religious Healing Among the Ojibway Indians* (Norman: University of Oklahoma Press, 1983).

———. *Indigenous Traditions and Ecology: The Interbeing of Cosmology and Community* (Cambridge, MA: Center for the Study of World Religions, 2001).

Harris, Marvin. *Our Kind* (New York: Harper & Row, 1989).

Hayden, Brian. *Shamans, Sorcerers and Saints: A Prehistory of Religion* (Washington, DC: Smithsonian Institution Press, 2004).

Katz, Richard. *Boiling Energy: Community Healing Among the Kalahari Kung* (Cambridge, MA: Harvard University Press, 1982).

Kendall, Laurel. *The Life and Times of a Korean Shaman* (Honolulu: University of Hawaii Press, 1988).

———. *Shamans, Housewives, and Other Restless Spirits* (Honolulu: University of Hawaii Press, 1988).

Lame Deer, and R. Erdoes. *Lame Deer: Seeker of Visions* (New York: Simon & Schuster, 1972).

Lawson, E. Thomas. *Religions of Africa: Traditions in Transformation* (San Francisco: Harper & Row, 1984).

Olupona, Jacob K. *Beyond Primitivism: Indigenous Religious Traditions and Modernity* (New York: Routledge, 2003).

Pfeiffer, J. E. *The Creative Explosion* (New York: Harper & Row, 1982).

Ritchie, Mark. *Spirit of the Rainforest: A Yanomamo Shaman's Story* (New York: Island Lake Press, 1996).

Spindler, George, and Stockard, Janice E., eds. *Globalization and Change in Fifteen Cultures* (Belmont, CA: Thomson, 2007).

Sullivan, Lawrence A., ed. *Native Religions and Cultures of North America: Anthropology of the Sacred* (New York: Continuum, 2003).

Taylor, Timothy. *The Buried Soul: How Humans Invented Death* (Boston: Beacon, 2002).

Vitebsky, Piers. *The Shaman* (New York: Macmillan, 1995).

Notes

1. Marjorie Shostack, *Nisa: Autobiography of a Kung Woman* (New York: Random House, 1982), p. 16.
2. Ian Tattersall, "Once We Were Not Alone," *Scientific American*, January 2000, p. 62.
3. Lame Deer and R. Erdoes, *Lame Deer: Seeker of Visions* (New York: Simon & Schuster, 1972), pp. 136–137.
4. Summarized from Piers Vitebsky, *The Shaman* (New York: Macmillan, 1995), p. 125.
5. Quoted in Sherman Alexie, *The Lone Ranger and Tonto Fistfight in Heaven* (New York: Atlantic Monthly Press, 1993), p. 104.
6. David Chidester, "Colonialism and Shamanism," in Mariko Walter and Eva Fridman, eds., *Shamanism: An Encyclopedia of World Beliefs, Practices, and Culture* (Santa Barbara, CA: ABC Clio, 2004), p. 48.

Additional Resources

Aboriginal Culture (http://www.aboriginalculture.com.au/index.shtml). A detailed site that contains information about traditional Australian Aboriginal Cultures, including material culture, social organization, art, and Aboriginal religion.

African Traditional Religion (http://www.afrikaworld.net/afrel/). A site with essays and links discussing the practices of African tradition religions on the continent and in diaspora.

Foundation for Shamanic Studies (http://www.shamanism.org/). Website by the nonprofit organization dedicated to the preservation of shamanic cultures and spreading their beliefs and practices across the world.

Native Languages of the Americas (http://www.native-languages.org/religion.htm). A website written by Native American scholars and practitioners, with links to other sites on a variety of themes in religion and spiritual culture.

Virtual Religion Index: American Studies (http://virtualreligion.net/vri/america.html). A rich and exhaustive listing of Web resources on every aspect of Native American religious traditions.

THE MANY STORIES OF JUDAISM

Sacred and Secular

3

Overview

Diversity, as we shall see, is an essential characteristic of all religious traditions. In this chapter we seek to understand the diversity of the Jews of yesterday and today. Jews, like all other religious people, are divided on whether diversity is a good thing or a problem. In fact, that issue is a constant theme throughout the various chapters of this book. To appreciate its manifestation in Judaism, we can start by painting a clearer picture of the diversity we are talking about: In a neighborhood in Jerusalem, on a Friday evening as dusk approaches, ultra-Orthodox Jewish men, dressed in black suits and hats, close off their streets and neighborhoods to traffic in strict observance of the rules of the Sabbath as a holy day. The majority of Jerusalem's inhabitants are secular Israelis in modern Western dress who do not consider themselves to be religious Jews. They see themselves as only ethnically Jewish and choose to ignore the Sabbath and most other religious rules. Meanwhile, in a New York City neighborhood, a male rabbi leads the traditional worship at an Orthodox **synagogue**, a role not permitted to women among the Orthodox. Nevertheless, three blocks away a woman rabbi leads her more liberal, Reform congregation in a Friday night prayer service. There is, indeed, great diversity in Judaism today. And while, since the Holocaust, the majority of Jews worldwide

synagogue: community centered on prayer and study of Torah; the building in which the community meets for these activities

77

Israel: Jews as a religious people; also the land and state of Israel

reside either in **Israel** or in the United States, one can still find communities of Jews throughout Europe and scattered throughout the Middle East, Africa, Latin America, and Asia, including India and China.

Behind this modern diversity and the conflicting understandings of how to live a Jewish life that they express lies premodern **Rabbinic** Judaism, which provided the model for Jewish life from about the sixth century CE until the emergence of modern forms of Judaism in the nineteenth century. Indeed, ultra-Orthodox Jews see themselves as preserving premodern Judaism against the onslaught of modern Jewish diversity. Judaism is the smallest of the great world religions; its 14 million adherents comprise .2 percent of the world's population. Yet Jews have had, and continue to have, a major impact on history. Over the millennia, Judaism has been many things to many people in different times and places. Moreover, as we have said, some people today who consider themselves to be Jewish do not identify themselves as religious. Yet secular or ethnic ways of being Jewish, as we shall see, have had profound effects on the Jewish religion and so must be included in our survey to help us understand

Rabbinic: Judaism of the postbiblical premodern period

Judaism Timeline

2000 BCE	The approximate time for the events attributed to Abraham
1280	The time of the events attributed to Moses—Exodus, and Covenant
1240	Conquest of land of Canaan under Joshua
1004–965	King David
721	Fall of northern kingdom of Israel to Assyrians
586	Fall of southern kingdom of Judah to Babylonians
538	Return from Exile
198–167	Maccabean revolt against enforced Hellenization
63	Beginning of rule by Rome
ca. 30 CE	Hillel and Shammai—first of the Tannaim
70	Destruction of the second temple
73	Fall of Zealot fortress at Masada
90	Emergence of the Academy at Yavneh
90–200	Formation of the Mishnah
200–500	Formation of the Gemara
1070	Founding of Talmudic academy by Rashi in Troyes, France
1095	First Crusade—beginnings of pogroms—mass slaughter of Europe's Jews
1306	Jews expelled from France, beginning of pattern repeated throughout Europe
1700–1760	Hasidic leader Israel ben Eliezer, the Ba'al Shem Tov
1729–1786	Moses Mendelssohn, leading figure in Jewish *Haskalah* (Enlightenment) movement/Reform Judaism

the religion of Judaism. We will find great diversity among the Jewish people, but we shall also discover a common thread. That is the task of this chapter.

Jews take as the highest reality the God of creation and history, who revealed himself at Sinai, and they believe that to act in harmony with the will of this God is the highest goal of life. Indeed, the monotheism of both Christianity and Islam is rooted in this most ancient of the three traditions. Christianity and Islam also follow Judaism in seeing the gravest problem in human life as sin—the failure to live in harmony with the will of a God who demands justice and compassion. The ideal of life is living in harmony with the will of God. Sin disrupts that life-giving harmony. In Judaism, one overcomes the problem and realizes the ideal by means of the study and practice of God's teachings or revelation: **Talmud** Torah.

Talmud: the oral Torah and its commentaries written down

In Judaism, each and every human being is free to choose good or evil because each person stands before God in the same relationship that Adam and Eve did. The idea that the sin of the first two human beings, Adam and Eve, was inherited by all descendants, the Christian concept of original sin, does not exist in Judaism (nor in

1808–1888	Samson Raphael Hirsch, leading figure in emergence of Orthodox Judaism
1860–1904	Theodor Herzl, founder of modern Zionism
1917	Balfour Declaration—proposal for Jewish homeland in Palestine endorsed by British government
1933–1945	Rise and fall of Nazi Party; the Holocaust, 6 million Jews murdered
1939–1945	World War II
May 14, 1948	Birth of state of Israel
May 11, 1949	Israel admitted to United Nations
1967	Six-Day War, followed by emergence of Judaism of Holocaust and Redemption
1973	Yom Kippur War, followed by growth of ultra-Orthodox movements
1979	Camp David peace treaty between Egypt and Israel
1980s	*Intifada*: Palestinian uprising and escalation of conflict between Palestinians and Israelis
1993	*Oslo Accord*, developing increased autonomy for Palestinians and the framework for negotiating peace with Israel, followed by continued violence on the part of radicals on both sides who view compromise as betrayal; also, continued tension between secular Israeli Jews and ultra-Orthodox haredim and between Israeli haredim and Conservative and Reform Jews of the Diaspora
1995	Oslo II agreement establishing an independent Palestinian Authority
2002	Israeli construction of a wall of separation between Israel and the territories of the Palestinian Authority; conflict between Israelis and Palestinians continues in the following years

covenant: agreement between God and Israel promising God's protection in exchange for Israel's obedience to God's commandments

halakhah: religious commandments or laws of Talmudic Judaism; God's 613 commandments

mitzvot: God's commandments requiring deeds of loving kindness

Islam). In creating the people Israel, God gave them a gift to tip the balance between good and evil in favor of good. This was the dual Torah, the sacred oral and written teachings concerning God's revelation to his people. In giving Israel the Torah, God established a **covenant** (i.e., a binding agreement) with Israel, making them a holy people and reminding them: "I will be your God and you shall be my people, I will guide and protect you and you will obey my commandments." According to the story of Torah, God set before Israel the choice between life and death and made it possible for the people to choose life. This could be accomplished by following the 613 commandments that are God's law and called *halakhah*, which means "to walk in the way of God." These commandments require deeds of loving kindness, or *mitzvot*, by which the people would embody in their lives the justice and mercy of God as a model for all the world.

It would be misleading, however, to think that this summary sketch of the religious worldview of Judaism would be agreed to by all Jews. In the remainder of this chapter we shall try to understand both the unity and the diversity of Judaism as a religious tradition and the profound impact of the emergence of modernity on its development. We begin by discussing the twentiety-century encounter of Judaism with modernity that gave rise to ultra-Orthodoxy. We then go back to the historical beginnings of Judaism and trace its history, to understand the sources of the diverse threads of contemporary Judaism and the ongoing struggle to define its future. Because our goal is to understand Judaism's encounter with modernity, we shall focus primarily on those aspects that reveal the diversity of Judaism today and show how that diversity developed.

The interior of the Touro Synagogue in Newport, Rhode Island, the oldest synagogue in the United States, consecrated in 1763.

Encounter with Modernity: Modern Judaisms and the Challenge of Ultra-Orthodoxy

Premodern Rabbinic Judaism was a world unto itself. It embraced every aspect of life and offered safe haven from the non-Jewish world that largely rejected it while greatly restricting the role of Jews in the larger society. The modern world, by contrast, seems to offer Jews a new option—the possibility of sharing in its citizenship. Thus all modern forms of Judaism draw a line between the secular (i.e., nonreligious) and the religious and allow Jews to participate in both worlds.

Each modern form of Judaism tries to preserve an essential core of Judaism in a private sphere while allowing Jews to play active "nonreligious" roles in the secular, or public, world around them. For Reform Jews the essential unchanging core of Judaism is its ethics, while all beliefs in supernatural phenomena and all traditional ritualistic requirements can be changed as needed. For Conservative Jews the rituals must remain unchanged, but beliefs about the supernatural can be changed. The Orthodox say that neither beliefs nor rituals are negotiable but still allow that some parts of a Jew's life (secular education, job, etc.) can be carried out in the secular world. The new, late twentieth-century, ultra-Orthodox movements reject even this compromise with the world. They seek to create a Jewish way of life, totally separate from both the modernizing forms of Judaism and the surrounding **gentile** (i.e., non-Jewish) world. They accomplish this for themselves by means of segregation: creating Jewish communities where all of life (the way one dresses, how and where one works, how one spends one's leisure time) is governed by supernatural beliefs and traditional ritual.

gentile: anyone not Jewish

The ultra-Orthodox seek to recapture, as far as possible, the way of premodern Jews. And they hope to see the day (at least in Israel) when all modern forms of Judaism will disappear and their own communities will be the model for the whole of society. The goal of "deprivatizing" Judaism, so that its religious vision can shape all of public life, sets ultra-Orthodox Judaism apart from other modern forms of Judaism. At the same time, ultra-Orthodoxy rejects pluralism, a key characteristic of what some call "postmodernity." Because they fear that pluralism leads to religious and ethical relativism, they rebel against modern religious pluralism, insisting that there is one truth, one way of life to which all Jews must return if they are not to drown in a sea of relativism that will undermine any sense of higher purpose for life. For the ultra-Orthodox there cannot be many ways to keep the covenant—only one way. And that one way is all-encompassing. It does not permit a Jew to parcel out his or her life into separate secular and religious portions. Nor does it permit men and women to redefine their gender roles in new and "liberating" ways. Such redefinitions, they argue, will inevitably lead to moral chaos and the collapse of the family. Although only a minority of the world's Jewish population have opted for ultra-Orthodoxy, this way of being Jewish offers a challenge to Jews the world over to examine the implications of their modern spiritual and political beliefs: Can one be both modern and Jewish without sacrificing the essence of one's religious identity?

The Conflict over Public Life: Religion and Politics in the State of Israel

The conflict created by ultra-Orthodoxy is most obvious in the state of Israel, where public life was shaped initially by secular Jews with a nonreligious socialist-Zionist worldview. **Zionism** is a nineteenth-century Jewish secular political movement that promoted giving Jews their own national homeland. Since the 1990s, at least 80 percent of Israelis have remained secular. However, especially since the mid-1970s, the ultra-Orthodox have formed increasingly influential religious parties that seek to undo this secularity and place the public order under the rule of *halakhah*, the religious commandments or laws of premodern Talmudic Judaism.

Although a minority with considerable diversity and disagreement among themselves, the ultra-Orthodox share in the desire to make the public life of the secular state of Israel more religiously observant. They insist, for example, that all businesses be closed on the Sabbath, and they succeeded in having the Israeli legislature, the Knesset, pass a law requiring that all marriages be performed by Orthodox rabbis. In the eyes of the ultra-Orthodox, their secular, Reform, and Conservative brethren are not really Jews, and Orthodox Jews are not orthodox enough. All non-ultra-Orthodox Jews are urged to repent and return (*teshuvah*) to the true Judaism. Consequently, both Orthodox and ultra-Orthodox Jews have campaigned to amend an Israeli law enacted in 1950, two years after Israel achieved statehood. The act, called "the law of return," assures all post-Holocaust Jews that Israel is their homeland and grants automatic Israeli citizenship to all Jews, born of a Jewish mother, who apply. Orthodox and ultra-Orthodox partisans have repeatedly tried to have the law modified to prevent anyone who has not undergone an Orthodox conversion from being accepted for citizenship.

Religious political movements and religious parties in Israel are too diverse and complex to fully account for here, but we can understand something of the dynamics of their role in Israeli society by looking at representative groups. Beyond favoring segregation and opposing pluralism, the ultra-Orthodox are themselves quite diverse. The spectrum extends from tradition-bound anti-Zionists, such as the Neturei Karta (Guardians of the City), to something quite new, the transformation of modern secular Zionism into religious Zionism with movements like the Gush Emunim (Bloc of the Faithful). In between these extremes stand various compromise movements.

The Neturei Karta emulate a centuries-old way of life that comes out of the traditions of the eastern European **haredim**, or "those of true piety." They and most other ultra-Orthodox movements have their roots in a strand of vigorously anti-Zionist eastern European Orthodoxy, which, unlike most of western European Orthodoxy, made no compromise with modernity. It is because they seek to preserve the way of life of premodern eastern European Judaism that the haredim refuse to permit secular education and modern dress.

Unlike the more modern Reform, Conservative, and Orthodox Jews, the ultra-Orthodox haredim do not live in communities having gentile residents, nor are they willing to mix with modern Jews who do not share their views. Rather, they live in ghetto-like communities typically led by a rabbi revered for his piety and Talmudic skill—communities where the faith is a way of life, untarnished by the compromises with modernity regarded as unavoidable by "modern" Jews. Certain that only the coming of the messiah in God's own time can bring about a true Jewish polity, the haredim reject the state of Israel as secular and profane.

The Gush Emunim, while remaining rigorously ultra-Orthodox in their observance of Jewish law, or *halakhah*, have developed a manner of dress (e.g., jeans, short-sleeved shirts, and skullcaps for the men) that distinguishes them from the haredim, in their wide-brimmed hats and long, black coats. Rather, the Gush identify with the secular Zionists who founded the state of Israel, whom they see as their secular counterparts.

Although the Gush Emunim do not accept the Jewish state in its secular form, they, unlike the Neturei Karta, have firmly endorsed the emergence of the secular state as in accordance with the divine will, seeing it as a step on the way to a genuine (*halakhah*-based) religiously observant Jewish state. Coming into existence early in 1974, the Gush Emunim represent a distinct branch of ultra-Orthodoxy. Unlike the Neturei Karta, they sought to transform secular Zionism— to put this form of nationalism on the correct path by making public life in Israel conform to religious law, or *halakhah*.

While religious Jews make up only about 20 percent of the population in Israel (and despite the anti-Zionist stance of most of them), the various political parties that represent them have managed to play a significant role in Israeli public life, because typically neither of the major secular parties—Labor and Likud—is able to secure enough votes to form a majority government without entering into a coalition with at least some of the religious parties. This state of affairs has given such religious parties bargaining power out of all proportion to their numbers.

Ultra-Orthodoxy as a Form of Fundamentalism

The rise of Ultra-Orthodoxy in Judaism is a part of a larger religious resurgence that has been going on in all religions and cultures around the globe since the mid-1970s. The late 1960s and early 1970s were a time of radical cultural disruption in Western urban secular societies—a time when the youth of the Western world, the children of those who experienced World War II, were rejecting what they described as the emptiness of modern secular culture. In their rejection, large numbers turned to various Eastern and Western religious movements as a way of recovering a sense of meaning and purpose in life. Indeed, the less modern and secular the movement, the more attractive it appeared.

One form that this religious resurgence took was distinctively fundamentalist. What all religious fundamentalist movements have in common is a desire to return to the foundations of belief and action that existed in their respective traditions prior to the coming of modernity. These movements see in contemporary culture, where many view all truth and all values as relative, the decadence of the modern period. So they think that this is a period in which most human beings have lost their way and have ended up in a world without standards and norms.

Much of the new strength of ultra-Orthodoxy is due to significant numbers of new adherents. These are mostly former secular Jews and modern religious Jews whose dissatisfaction with life made them receptive to the ultra-Orthodox movements. These Jews have made a leap of faith out of a world that either did not ask them to give their heart to anything (pure secularism) or asked them to give only a part of their heart (modern religious forms of Judaism). They have chosen a form of Judaism that promises to bring order and meaning to the whole of life, not just to a part of it; that requires a full-time commitment, not just a part-time commitment. They have sought to return to the fundamentals of the Judaism of the **dual Torah**—that is, premodern Rabbinic Judaism.

dual Torah: the scriptures of Rabbinic Judaism, composed of the written Torah (Tanak) and the written formulation of the oral Torah (Talmud)

The fundamentalist movements challenge modern forms of Judaism by refusing to reduce being Jewish to historical heritage, morality, and ethnicity. Ultra-Orthodox Jews attempt to recover what they believe has been lost to modern Judaism, namely, the centrality of God (as a living reality), Torah (as divine revelation), and Israel (as an eternal people). Ultra-Orthodoxy rejects all forms of secular Judaism and the diversity found in Judaism today. The ultra-Orthodox wish to revert to a time when, in their view, there was one truth and one way.

The total immersion in a deliberately premodern way of life represents to the ultra-Orthodox a definitive break with what it views as the decadence of Western civilization. And while the completeness of their immersion experience emulates that of the premodern tradition of Rabbinic Judaism, its self-consciousness does not. These "new" Jews have chosen to engage in an experiment, and in this sense their religion, too, belongs to the range of forms of Judaism of the modern/postmodern period. They, like all other religious persons of the modern era, have no choice but to choose. Their choice is between withdrawal from and involvement with the modern world, either back to what they somewhat romantically view as the "one way" of premodern Judaism or forward into pluralism. To understand the implications of this choice, we must return to the beginnings of premodern Judaism in the biblical period and work our way forward.

Premodern Judaism: The Formative Era (2000 BCE–500 CE)

The Biblical Roots of Judaism

Judaism, along with Christianity and Islam, is shaped by the myth of history, a concept we learned in Chapter 1. Indeed, the myth of history begins with Judaism. Judaism finds its roots in the story of the God who made promises to Abraham and his descendants that were fulfilled centuries later. This happened when the God of Abraham sent Moses to deliver his people from slavery to the Egyptians and lead them into the "land of promise"—the land of Canaan. From these beginnings the story blossomed into the full myth of history, which tells of the God who acts in time (i.e., in history) and leads his people on a journey through time toward a day of final resurrection in which all injustice, suffering, and death will be overcome.

While all religious traditions pass on their vision of reality through stories, story plays a unique role in Jewish religion. All the great religions of the world have told stories that draw on the metaphors of nature to explain religious experience. For instance, the cycles of nature are used to explain the wheel of death and rebirth in the myths of liberation from India and the rhythms of yin and yang in the myths of harmony from the religions of China. Analogies from nature are not absent from Judaism, but there is a clear shift of emphasis from nature to history. That is, if you want to understand who the God of Israel is, you do not look primarily to nature but to history as the story of the people Israel's journey with God through time. (In this chapter, *Israel* refers to the country and "the people Israel" to the biblical people of the Mosaic covenant from which Judaism developed.)

Indeed, for Judaism God is the divine storyteller, and the unfolding of creation in history is God's story. In the beginning God said, "Let there be light," and the story began. And the unfolding story will continue to play out in history until God brings it—after many trials and tribulations—to a happy conclusion at the end of time, when the dead are raised to enjoy a new heaven and a new earth.

In this 1953 painting, *Moses Receiving the Tablets of the Law*, the Russian painter Marc Chagall portrays Moses receiving the Ten Commandments at Sinai. Jews trace the beginnings of Judaism to the covenant made between God and Israel at Sinai.

The Story Begins: One God Above All Others

The religiousness of ancient Israel that gave birth to Judaism developed against the background and influences of two great ancient polytheistic civilizations—Egyptian and Babylonian. Indeed, the names of the two greatest figures of the Torah, "Abraham" and "Moses," are, respectively, Babylonian and Egyptian names. And the biblical stories of both reflect this. Abraham is said to have migrated from Ur in Babylonia down into the land of Canaan, while Moses is born in Egypt, where the descendants of Abraham had migrated, seeking refuge from famine in their own land.

The great sociologist Max Weber (and many scholars since) argued that the beginning of the secularization of Western society began with the ancient Israelite religion that gave birth to Judaism. Although influenced by the religions of the Egyptians and Babylonians, ancient Israelite religion was strikingly different. For the Egyptians and the Babylonians, the world was the sacred embodiment of the gods (i.e., the waters, the land, the sun, etc., were all gods); then biblical religion came along and by the time of the Prophets had declared there is but one God and he is not the world but creator of the world. Therefore the world is secular, and God alone is holy—although the world can be sanctified, or made holy, by serving this God.

The story of the past, as it was imagined by the people Israel, proceeds from the creation of the first man and woman, Adam and Eve, to the near annihilation of humanity, as related in the story of Noah and the flood. Then came the division of humans into many language groups at the tower of Babel, God's call to Abraham to be a father of many nations, and God's promise to give the land of Canaan to the descendants of Abraham (Genesis 15). The story moves on to the migration of the family of Abraham's great-grandson Joseph into Egypt at a time of famine. It relates how the tribes of Israel, Abraham's descendants, became enslaved in Egypt and how God sent Moses to deliver them from slavery.

In the story of the Exodus, God assists Moses by sending down ten plagues on the Egyptians and then parting the waters of the Red Sea to enable the Israelites to escape to the land God gives them, in keeping with a promise made to Abraham (Genesis 15:18–21). According to this story, on the way to this land of promise God brought the people to Mount Sinai, gave the Torah to Moses, and formed a covenant with the people. As the book of Exodus (19:3–6) describes it:

> Moses went up to God, and the Lord called to him from the mountain [Mount Sinai], saying, "Thus shall you say to the house of Jacob, and tell the people of Israel; You have seen what I did to the Egyptians, and how I carried you on eagles' wings, and brought you to myself. Now therefore, if you will obey my voice indeed, and keep my covenant, then you shall be my own treasure among all peoples; for all the earth is mine; And you shall be to me a kingdom of priests, and a holy nation. These are the words which you shall speak to the people of Israel."

This description of the delivery of the covenant at Mount Sinai is a climactic moment in a powerful and dramatic story about a journey that created a holy people—the people Israel. In fact, the Hebrew word for holy (*qadosh*) suggests that to be holy is to be "set apart." So Israel was chosen out of all the nations and set apart to be God's people.

The story goes on to tell how the tribes of Israel wandered in the desert for forty years, entering the land of promise, under the leadership of Joshua only after the death of Moses (see Map 3.1). For the next 200 years they lived on the land

"I am the Lord your God who brought you out of the land of Egypt, the house of bondage: You shall have no other gods beside Me."

—NRSV, Exodus 20:1

Map 3.1 The route of Exodus.

as a loose confederation under military leaders called *judges*. However, as threats of conquest from their neighbors became more frequent, many among the tribes began to demand to have a king like other nations, with a standing army to protect Israel. Some, however, argued that there could be only one king over Israel—the God of Abraham, Isaac, and Jacob. According to the story, God agreed to allow the people to have a king. And so Saul, chosen by God, was anointed with oil by a prophet, as a sign that the first king over Israel had been selected by God, not the people. Indeed, the concept of messiah (*mashiah*) has its beginnings here, for *messiah* means "anointed one," and it was understood that the one so anointed had been chosen to rule over the kingdom of God, the kingdom of Israel (1 Samuel 9:11–11:15).

Saul, however, proved to be a weak king, for he lacked independent authority and had to depend on the cooperation of the tribes, which could be uncertain. It was David, the second king over Israel, who established Israel as a nation. Under David and later his son Solomon, Israel claimed, for a brief time, to be the greatest nation in the Middle East. Stories were told of David's rise to power—how even as a young boy he had saved the tribes by slaying the Philistine giant, Goliath. Indeed, Saul, who had virtually adopted David as a member of the royal family, soon became jealous and turned on him. Forced to flee and fearing for his life, David became a Robin Hood type of figure, leading a private army of loyal followers. When Saul died in battle against the Philistines, David was proclaimed by the people and anointed as their king. Later, the northern tribes, called Israel, visited David and asked him to be their king, too. Soon he would consolidate the monarchy, becoming known as the king of all Israel and Judah.

David used his army to capture Jebus, a Canaanite city, renaming it Jerusalem, or "God's peace." Because Jerusalem had not belonged to any of the tribes of Israel, it gave David a neutral vantage point from which to rule over both Israel and Judah. David made his capital a holy city by bringing to it a sacred object, the gold-covered chest called the Ark of the Covenant, which was believed to contain the stone tablets inscribed with the commandments given at Mount Sinai.

Indeed, during David's reign it is said that God promised David that his heirs would rule Israel into the far distant future (2 Samuel 7:16). After David's death, his son Solomon succeeded him to the throne, and Israel was at the height of its power. It was Solomon who built the first **temple** so that God could dwell in a splendor greater than that of any of the gods of the other nations.

However, after the time of Solomon there was quarreling about the succession to the throne, and for over two centuries Israel (in the north) had one king and Judah (in the south) had another. Soon prophets like Amos and Hosea arose in Israel. The biblical prophets were revered persons believed to know God's will. They reminded the people that since abandoning their nomadic life to become farmers and city dwellers, they had been drifting further and further from the tribal values of the covenant made at Sinai. In the cities the people acted as if they were strangers to each other, and the rich mistreated the poor. The prophets warned that God would punish those who offered sacrifices in the temple while acting unjustly as citizens and neighbors. What God wants most of all, the pious believed, is the sacrifice of a pure heart committed to deeds of justice and compassion.

temple: the place in Jerusalem where the Jews worshiped

"Your house and your Kingdom shall be made sure forever before me; your throne shall be established forever."
—NRSV, 2 Samuel 7:16

The Story Continues with the Prophets—The One God of All

It is with the prophets that Jewish monotheism becomes fully formed, for in the tribal days of the time of Moses, Israel's commitment had been *henotheistic*—that is, to one God above all others. Thus the commandment "I am the Lord your God . . . you shall have no others beside me" did not mean that there were no other gods, only that Israel was forbidden to follow them. God was their tribal God. But after Israel was established as a great nation in the time of David, the prophets forced Israel to see that they did not own God, nor could they renege on the covenant once in the land of promise. The covenant conferred not so much privileges as responsibilities. According to the prophets, Israel's God was the God of all the nations and he would use the other nations, if necessary, to punish Israel for any failure to keep the covenant.

Instructed by the prophets, the people Israel began to think of God in the manner expressed in the book of Genesis—as the creator of all things and all peoples. From the eighth century BCE forward, Israel would become progressively convinced that having "no other gods" required more than loyalty to a tribal deity. It required affirming that there were no other gods. Out of the prophetic experience came the pure and simple creed of Judaism, the **Shema**: "Hear O Israel, the Lord our God, the Lord is one" (Deuteronomy 6:4). This confession is completed by reminding the people to love this God with all their heart, soul, and strength; to pray the *Shema* on arising and retiring; and to bind its words on their hands, foreheads, and doorposts to ensure that the awareness of the one true God might permeate their every thought and action.

The prophets warned the people that if they did not return to the covenant, the God of Israel, Lord of all creation and history, would punish them. And that is exactly how the misfortunes of Israel and Judah came to be interpreted. For in 721 BCE the Assyrians conquered the kingdom of Israel and carried its inhabitants off into slavery. In 621 Judah's King, Josiah, is said to have discovered in the temple what he believed to be the long-lost book of the law (the biblical book of Deuteronomy). These writings echoed the teachings of the prophets about the need to practice justice to please

King David conquered the Canaanite city of Jebus and sanctified it by placing the Ark of the Covenant there. Renamed Jerusalem by David, the city has ever since been holy for Jews.

● *Shema*: in Judaism, the essential confession of monotheistic faith

"Thus says the Lord to his anointed (messiah), to Cyrus, . . . For the sake of my servant Jacob, and Israel my chosen, I call you by your name, I surname you, though you do not know me."

—NRSV, Isaiah 45:1 & 4

God. On this basis Josiah initiated a reform that included a renewal of the covenant and designated the temple in Jerusalem as the only proper site for sacrifices. However, according to the biblical story, the reforms were not observed conscientiously, and God again allowed the people to be punished. In 586 the Babylonians conquered the Assyrians and their territories, destroyed the temple Solomon had built, and carried off the inhabitants of the southern kingdom of Judah into exile and slavery.

As the time of the Babylonian exile approached, another generation of prophets arose—Jeremiah, Ezekiel, and Isaiah—spanning the time of exile and eventual return. These prophets asserted that God was indeed punishing Israel for its failure to keep the covenant, but they added that the punishment would be temporary (to teach them a lesson). As it happened, the Persians soon conquered the Babylonians, and after only fifty years, in 538, the Israelites were permitted to return to the land. This turn of events was due to the benevolent policy of the Persian king, Cyrus. That a pagan king should so favor the Israelites was seen as miraculous, and Cyrus was declared a messiah, that is, one anointed by God to carry out God's will to return his people to their land (Isaiah 45:1–13). Cyrus himself, of course, was not aware of this role attributed to him in the destiny of Israel. Thus we see that even in the biblical period, Judaism was capable of finding religious significance in secular political events.

A model of the city of Jerusalem centered around the temple as it might have looked in 50 BCE.

The Story Becomes One of Exile and Return

When the first wave of exiles returned to the land (520–515 BCE), the leadership was weak and the people lacked a clear direction. It was not until Ezra, a priest, and Nehemiah, a gifted layman, led a second wave of exiles (458 BCE) in a return to the land of Israel that a clear pattern for a postexilic Judaism emerged. These leaders demanded that the people repent: They had married citizens of other nations and sacrificed to other gods, and now they must rededicate themselves to the covenant and repurify themselves as a holy people by separating themselves from their neighbors. It is with this priestly reform that Judaism adopted the experience of exile and return, in which they saw the liberation from slavery in Babylon as a repeat of the liberation from slavery in Egypt. So exile and return became the normative pattern through which to interpret all past and future Jewish experiences. Whenever Jews felt persecuted and exiled they would hope for the day of return—"Next year in Jerusalem" became their cry. In this sense, the experience of exile and return gave birth to Judaism.

In the fourth century BCE, Alexander the Great conquered the ancient world, and after his death in 323 his empire was divided among his generals. For over a century the Ptolemies ruled over Israel (301–198). They were replaced by the Seleucids (198–167), who began a policy of enforced Hellenization, requiring all their conquered peoples to adopt Greek customs and beliefs, including veneration of many gods. The Jews, who refused to abandon their worship of the God of Abraham, Isaac, and Jacob, were severely persecuted for their noncompliance. Thus in the middle of the second century, Judas Maccabaeus and his brothers led a revolt against the cruel Seleucid ruler Antiochus Epiphanes IV. This effort, the Maccabean revolt, was successful in bringing about a status of semi-independence, which lasted into the first century CE. However, in a bid to resist new efforts at control by the Seleucids, the Jews in 63 BCE invited in the Romans to protect them. After the Exile, the temple was rebuilt on a modest scale and then later, between 20 BCE and 60 CE under the domination of Rome, the second temple was rebuilt on a grander scale. It is from the time of Alexander through the time of the Roman Empire that the religion of ancient Israel splintered and developed into a variety of forms of Judaism, each claiming they represented the true practice of faith.

The Historical Roots of Diversity

By the first century the most important of these new Jewish movements were the Sadducees, the Pharisees, the Hellenists, the Samaritans, the Zealots, the Essenes, and the Nazarenes—all of which were engaged in ongoing debate. Today we would be tempted to say the debate was about the right way to be Jewish, but the idea of Judaism as a religion did not yet exist. Rather, the partisans of the first century saw the debate as about an attempt to define how one must live to be the "true Israel," or the true people of God. To understand this debate it is important to remember that at the beginning of the first century there was no official Bible and no set of practices and commitments accepted as normative by all Jews (see Timeline on pp. 78–79). It was only at the end of the first century that the **Tanak**, or Bible of Judaism as we have it today, came into existence, along with Rabbinic Judaism as the normative pattern of Judaism for the next 1,800 years.

Tanak: the written Torah, or Hebrew Bible

Now, let's consider each of these movements in a little more detail. The Sadducees came from the wealthy upper class, were associated with the temple tradition that was exclusive to Jerusalem, and saw their task as keeping peace with Rome. They accepted only the five books of Moses as sacred scripture and insisted on literal adherence to the written Torah.

The Pharisees were teachers associated with the synagogues (houses of study and prayer) found in every city and village; they accepted not only the books of Moses but also the historical and wisdom writings and those of the prophets. Both the Jewish Bible (Tanak) and the Christian Old Testament are largely derived from the Pharisees' selection of scriptural materials. The Pharisees taught that God revealed himself in the written Torah and through oral traditions that accompanied the giving of the Torah to Moses. Moreover, they insisted that the written word could not be properly interpreted without the oral traditions. In these teachings the Pharisees offered a precursor to the later Rabbinic doctrine of God's revelation through the dual Torah, the oral and the written. Politically, the Pharisees were neither cozy with the Romans nor openly hostile to them.

Jews who were dispersed in the Roman Empire (i.e., outside the protectorate of Palestine) were known as the Jews of the **Diaspora**. The leaders of their synagogues were Hellenistic Jews who used a Greek translation of scriptures that closely corresponded to the Hebrew scriptures of the Pharisees, with some important exceptions. The Hellenists were the great missionaries of Judaism, who used Greek philosophy to explain the meaning of the biblical stories. They were anxious to promote Judaism as a religion that had a place for gentiles, and they adapted Judaism to Greek customs whenever feasible. They successfully encouraged large numbers of gentiles to come and worship the one true God of Israel.

> **Diaspora:** the dispersion of a religious people outside their geographic homeland

Finally, there were sectarian movements like the *Zealots*, the *Samaritans*, the *Essenes*, and the *Nazarenes* (the followers of Jesus of Nazareth). Some, like the Zealots and Essenes, were openly hostile to the gentile world, whereas the Nazarenes, like the Hellenists, were very positive toward gentiles and sought their conversion. Adherents of these movements tended to be apocalyptic, believing that God would bring the world to an end soon and so would send a messiah to judge all human beings and reward the faithful. In the first century there was no single clear definition of *messiah*. A wide variety of speculations emerged, and each sectarian group had its own ideas. Most were expecting a spiritual leader, but some, primarily the Zealots, looked for a military leader able to overthrow the Romans, whose rule in Palestine had become oppressive.

What was typical of these sectarian movements was a strong distrust of the Sadducees, who were viewed as having sold out to the Romans. The Zealots, the most hostile of all, had nothing but contempt for the Sadducees and chose to oppose them directly. If the Sadducees urged, "Don't rock the boat," the Zealots were committed to rocking the boat as often as possible. To this end, they staged random guerrilla attacks against the Roman legions. In the second century a Zealot, Simon bar Kokhba, claimed the title of messiah and was executed by the Romans.

Finally, at least some of the sectarian groups practiced baptismal rites, that is, ritual immersion and purification. Ritual immersion was already a requirement for any gentile convert to Judaism (along with **circumcision** for males). From the first century on, however, some groups insisted that not only gentile converts were to be immersed and purified, but also Jews, if they had strayed from the true path of Judaism as understood by the particular sectarian movement.

> **circumcision:** the cutting of the foreskin as a sign of the covenant of Abraham

Exodus and Exile: Story, History, and Modernity

The difference between premodern and modern is the difference between sacred story (scripture) and secular story (history). Fundamentalists fear the incursion of time and history into their sacred story, whereas modernists welcome it. The biblical writings as we have them are organized to tell a story of God's saving journey with his people. It is, as we have noted, the story of the God who acts in time and leads his people through time toward a final fulfillment. This is a grand story that answers questions of origin and destiny for the Jews as a religious people: Where do we come from? Where are we going? When modern historians read this story, they ask different questions. Primarily they want to know if things really happened as described in the sacred texts. They try to find out by comparing the stories with what else is known about the past through ancient writings, through literary analysis of stylistic changes in the writings, and through archaeological artifacts.

When historians began to read the biblical stories critically, they believed they could identify different layers of historical development in the scriptural writings. It is on this basis that they identified four major layers of historical materials: J and E (Jahwist and Elohist, from two different Hebrew names for God), from the period of the monarchy of David and Solomon (ca. 1000 BCE); D (Deuteronomic, ca. 621 BCE), associated with the prophetically rooted reforms of King Josiah; and P (priestly, ca. 458 BCE), associated with the priestly reforms of Ezra and his administrative successor, Nehemiah. Today biblical scholars do not think that the historical materials can be sorted out quite that neatly, but the recognition of historical layers remains essential to the historical study of biblical writings.

The earliest stories (J and E) seem to have been written down in the courts of David and Solomon to tell the story of how God chose Israel, from humble beginnings, to become a great kingdom. Bringing together diverse ancient tribal narratives, the royal storytellers constructed a larger and more complex story that begins with the creation of the world and ends with the kingdom of Israel under David and Solomon as the greatest nation of the ancient Middle East. It is an unambiguous story of promise and fulfillment. However, the story had to be revised in light of the Babylonian exile. The Priestly revision describes Israel as a people shaped by seemingly broken promises that are unexpectedly fulfilled, at least in part, leading to new hope and new life—a story of exile and return.

If the Exodus was the founding event of the story of Judaism, the Exile was its formative event. As one distinguished scholar of Judaism, Jacob Neusner, has noted, it was the great crisis of exile and the astonishment of return that set the mythic pattern of Judaic thought and experience ever since.[1] The exile and return provided a story pattern through which all past and future events, whether of triumph or of tragedy, could be meaningfully integrated into Jewish identity. "Exile and return" shaped the imagination of all future generations. No longer did Israel think of itself as David did (in 1 Chronicles 22:1–19), as having an unconditionally guaranteed existence. On the contrary, its existence was dependent on its commitment to the covenant.

Therefore, the fall of the second temple at the hands of the Romans in 70 CE was a trauma and a deep blow to those who wholeheartedly believed the story of the God who leads his people through time, but the crisis was not without precedent or without meaning. For although the power of leadership shifted once more, this time from the priests to the teachers (i.e., rabbis), the rabbis immediately reverted to the priestly pattern of explanation, arguing once more that the cause of the present misfortune was that Israel had not kept the covenant faithfully enough. Consequently, although the disasters that befell the first and second temples were two of the most traumatic events in the long history of Judaism, neither destroyed the faith of Jews. On the contrary, in each case Jews came to the conclusion that the loss of the temple was not a sign of God's abandonment but a call to the people Israel to be more fully observant of the covenant. Thus today Jews willingly recall these two disastrous events on the holy day of **Tisha B'Av**, for remembering brings about not despair and hopelessness but repentance and renewal.

Tisha B'Av: day of mourning to commemorate tragedies affecting the people Israel

From Torah to Talmud

The Pharisaic Roots of Rabbinic Judaism

To follow the emergence of Rabbinic, or Talmudic, Judaism, we need to resume our discussion of the various Jewish sects and movements that existed in the first century. Such diversity was brought to an end by the destruction of the temple in 70 CE. Of the movements that had been vying to provide a model for Jewish life, only a few survived, and of these it was the Pharisees who provided new leadership. There were at least three reasons for this.

First, the political neutrality of the Pharisees in the period before the fall of the temple made them appealing to the Romans. Unlike the Zealots, the Pharisees seemed benign in their views of the Roman Empire. So the Roman authorities gave them permission to establish an academy at Yavneh on the coast of present-day Israel. There they began the task of reconstructing Judaism for a new period of exile apart from the land and the temple. Second, the Pharisees were already the leaders of the synagogue tradition and the teachers (rabbis) of the importance of the oral tradition. And finally, the oral tradition the Pharisees had espoused gave them the flexibility to interpret the requirements of Jewish life in changing circumstances. Thus when the temple priesthood disappeared, no new institutions needed to be invented. The Pharisees became the natural leaders by default everywhere in ancient Palestine.

The task of the new leadership was to transpose the priestly model focused on the temple in Jerusalem into a new key—one that would allow the people Israel, like their ancestors in Babylon, to survive as Jews apart from the land and the temple. The solution the Pharisees arrived at was a model in which the people Israel (not just the temple) were holy, and every male head of a Jewish household was in fact a priest, even as the table in every Jewish house was an altar. In this new model, the center of Jewish life shifted from written Torah to the oral tradition, from priest to rabbi, from temple to synagogue, and also from temple altar to family table.

The priestly tradition had insisted that Israel was a holy people, set apart for service to the one true God, and had established elaborate rules of ritual separation to keep the people from blending in with the general population. The Pharisees, drawing on the prophets, insisted that what God wanted more than cultic worship, with its sacrifices, was deeds of loving kindness (*mitzvot*)—that is, acts of justice and mercy. To this end, then, the Pharisees transferred the rituals of separation from the temple cult to a system of ethics. The prophets had issued sweeping demands, in the name of God, for justice and mercy. The Pharisees took these demands and made them the content for the priestly rituals of holiness, working out their application in all the details of everyday life according to the best insights of the oral tradition. Between the second and fifth centuries, Rabbinic Judaism, or the Judaism of the dual Torah, emerged as the insights of the oral tradition were written down and incorporated into what became known as the Talmud. And it was this Talmudic tradition that shaped Jewish life from the sixth century until the advent of Jewish modernizing movements in the nineteenth century.

The heart of the teachings of the Pharisees was that God was a loving personal father who chose Israel and entered into the covenant with them. This is the covenant revealed in the oral and written Torah which teaches that each and every individual who keeps this covenant can live in hope of resurrection from the dead. Although the Pharisees are depicted as legalists in some of the Christian scriptures, historians have shown quite the contrary. What the Pharisees actually taught was that the sacrifices that God wants are deeds of loving kindness rooted in a pure heart, not merely external observance of divine laws.

The Pharisees asked Jews to love God above all and their neighbor as themselves. They insisted that what is hateful to oneself must not be done to one's neighbor. They insisted that humans do not live by bread alone, and therefore one should trust in God rather than worry about tomorrow. They insisted that those who would seek the will of God would find it and that those who humbled themselves would be exalted. All these teachings were adopted by Christianity as well, as we shall see in Chapter 4.

The Rabbis and the Formation of the Talmud

Hillel and Shammai were the two leading rabbis, or teachers of oral tradition, in the first century of the common era (CE). Their influence led to the development of two major schools: the house of Hillel (*Bet Hillel*) and the house of Shammai (*Bet Shammai*). The disputes between Hillel and Shammai, and their schools, eventually became the foundation of the Talmud and set the tone of disputation and dialog that is characteristic of Talmudic Judaism. Both Hillel and Shammai sought to apply the oral Torah tradition to the details of everyday life. In general it is said that Shammai interpreted the demands of Torah more strictly and severely. Hillel tended to be more lenient and compassionate in his decisions. In general, although not always, it is the teachings of Hillel that shaped the emerging Talmudic tradition. And it was the students of Hillel who were the primary shapers of the **Mishnah**—the writings that form the core of the Talmud.

It was the disciples of Hillel and Shammai and their descendants who led the Jews into the Talmudic era. A disciple of Hillel, Johanan ben Zakkai, started the academy at Yavneh. There the first task was to settle one of the key arguments that had been going on in Judaism at the beginning of the century—namely, which writings of the

"If water, which is soft, could hollow out the hard stone, the words of the Torah, which are hard, will certainly make an impression on my soft heart."

—Rabbi Akiva

"Do not unto your neighbor what you would not have him do unto you. This is the whole of the Jewish law. All else are but commentaries."

—Rabbi Hillel

Mishnah: the writings that form the core of the Talmud

The Talmud records the ongoing discussion of Torah by the great rabbinic minds across the ages and is meant to be studied and debated in a communal setting.

tradition to regard as holy and, therefore, as revelations from God. The argument, of course, was settled by default. Since the Pharisees survived to reestablish Judaism, it was the writings they revered that were selected to comprise the canon, the official set of scriptures. Unsurprisingly, the Pharisees did not limit their choices to the Torah, that is, the books attributed to Moses. In addition to the five books called the Pentateuch (Genesis, Exodus, Leviticus, Numbers, Deuteronomy), the Pharisees included the books of the prophets (e.g., Jeremiah and Ezekiel, Amos and Hosea), some historical writings (e.g., First and Second Kings), and also the writings of the wisdom literature (e.g., Proverbs, Ecclesiastes, Job). Thus it was the academy at Yavneh that settled on the books that make up the Bible of Judaism, known as the *Tanak*—an acronym standing for

- Torah (teachings),
- Neviim (prophets), and
- Ketuvim (writings).

In Western culture it has often been thought that to compare the teachings of Judaism and Christianity, all one need do is compare the Tanak, or Hebrew Bible (which Christians call the Old Testament), with the New Testament. Such a view, however, is totally misleading. The Talmud and the New Testament are like two different sets of glasses for reading the Hebrew Bible. Through the Talmud glasses, certain passages seem very clear and easy to read, while other parts are fuzzy and unreadable. And with New Testament glasses, the fuzzy passages become clear, and vice versa. Both Jews and Christians read the Hebrew Bible through the eyes of a further revelation (Talmud and New Testament) that tells them how to read the Hebrew scriptures, including what is valid and what can be dismissed. Thus Jews and Christians who seem to be reading an important body of holy writings in common might just as well be reading two different books—which, in a sense, they are. Consequently, to understand Judaism one must understand the Talmud and the central role it plays in Judaism.

The Talmud and the Torah

With the Jewish people's sacred teachings committed to writing in the written Torah, or Tanak, the **Tannaim** ("those who study") began the paradoxical process of writing down the vast and diffuse teachings of the oral tradition and transforming this material into the oral Torah. The process occurred in two phases.

> **Tannaim:** the generation of sages who created the Mishnah

First, the Tannaim, led by Hillel and Shammai, organized the wisdom of the Jewish oral tradition into categories, or *seders*, covering six areas of everyday life: agriculture, sabbaths and festivals, women and property, civil and criminal law, laws of conduct for cultic ritual and temple, and rules for maintaining cultic purity. Then the discussions of the rabbis recalling the wisdom of the oral Torah on each of these areas were written down. This collection of materials, known as the *Mishnah*, codifies the wisdom of the oral Torah. The Mishnah was intended to show Jews how they could sanctify life (i.e., make it holy) despite their loss of the temple and absence from the land of Israel.

In the second phase of Talmudic formation, the successors to the Tannaim, the *Amoraim* ("those who interpret"), set about developing a commentary on the Mishnah that would link the oral to the written Torah. The result of their work was called the **Gemara**, and these writings in combination with the Mishnah form the Talmud (meaning "learning" or "study" as related to Torah).

> **Gemara:** commentary on the Mishnah, and part of the Talmud

Even though the Talmud (Mishnah and Gemara) is said to have been completed by the sixth century, there is a sense in which the Talmud is never complete. For example, sages in the tradition, the Geonim (eminent scholars), followed up the work of the Amoraim by providing the *Responsa*—further commentaries on the Talmud. These writings constitute answers to requests from Jews throughout the Diaspora for insight and guidance in applying the teachings of the Talmud to the problems of everyday life. The tradition of commentary, which continues from generation to generation, is integral to Judaism, leaving the Talmudic traditions, as an expression of oral Torah, open to continuous development.

Producing the Talmud by writing down the oral Torah surely seems like a self-contradictory task. And yet the genius of the Talmud is in preserving the oral character of the material in written form. To appreciate the uniqueness of the Talmud

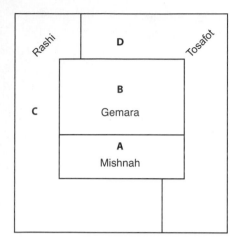

A page of the Talmud.

one really has to look at it and see how its pages are constructed. A typical page is made up of diverse and distinct parts, coexisting on the same piece of paper. These parts express the voices of the rabbis throughout the ages, and teachings about the same subject are juxtaposed on the same page. The Talmud is an ongoing dialog among Jews not only of the same time period but from age to age. At the core of a page you may find statement (A) from the Mishnah of the second century outlining the opposing points of view of Hillel and Shammai on a question of appropriate behavior. Above this text, on the same page, might be a section of the Gemara (B) from a period 200 or 300 years later, relating the Mishnah to relevant passages from the Tanak and to the diverse opinions of the Amoraim, who comment on the meaning of the Mishnah in light of the scriptures and of the opinions of the Tannaim. Typically, as well, there will be a section (C) devoted to the commentary of the greatest of the Rabbinic Talmudic scholars, Rashi. In yet another section (D) will be the commentaries of the students of Rashi from a collection known as the *Tosafot*. Each of these expresses views on the meaning of the passages of the Mishnah in light of the comments of the others and in light of additional commentaries and writings that supplement the tradition. The sections on a given page of the Talmud might span a thousand years or more.

Although Talmudic decisions are made to guide the life of the Jewish community, it would be a mistake to think that the whole point of Talmud study is to reach a conclusion. For Talmudic study is a form of religious ritual whose purpose is nothing less than to bring the student of Torah to experience God through the thrust and parry of argument about the one thing that matters most in life—God's word. That is why it is not unheard of for a debating partner to help an opponent who is stumped for a response by suggesting a line of argument that might be able to refute the point the stronger partner has just made. In this way the Talmud sanctifies doubt and questioning as a medium of religious experience that brings one in touch with God. God is in the questions even more than in the answers. For this reason too, then, the Talmud is never finished as long as there is one more Jew ready to join the debate. It is a tradition of commentary upon commentary that guarantees that the Talmud is always both ancient and ever fresh and new. The Talmud is always about how one is to make the new day holy.

This understanding of Talmudic debate echoes the Torah story that explains how Israel got its name: According to Genesis (32:23–32), one night Jacob wrestled with a stranger who refused to tell his own name but, rather, blessed Jacob and gave him a new name, Israel, meaning "one who has wrestled with God and men and prevailed." As the sun arose, Jacob limped away, convinced that he had "seen God face to face."

So the Torah teaches that Israel is the one God has chosen to wrestle with, and the way of Torah is a wrestling with the God who cannot be named (or, for that matter, imaged). The Torah teaches that the one who wrestles not only with God (and God's Torah) but with other humans (about the meaning of Torah) can prevail. Indeed, to

A page of the Torah in Hebrew, illustrating the use of a pointer called a "yad" (the Hebrew word for "hand") to follow the text.

wrestle with the Torah is to see God face to face, to be transformed and given a new name: Israel, or "wrestler with God." Hence in Rabbinic Judaism there is no higher calling than to wrestle with others over the meaning of God's Torah. This activity is one that includes rather than excludes those who disagree. According to Talmudic tradition, when the rabbis disagree on the observance of *halakhah*, the majority opinion is to prevail for the good of order. Yet it is understood that those in the minority are not necessarily wrong. The Torah is large enough to embrace everyone.

Indeed, the story of the covenant at Sinai, through which God chose Israel, suggests just such a give-and-take relationship. According to the story, the covenant established that day was a *mutual* agreement between two parties, much like a marriage contract that is both a legal arrangement and an expression of mutual love and care. In this covenant the people promise to obey the commandments of God and walk in the way of the Torah, which gives life. And God promises to guide and protect them on their journey through time. Throughout this journey, God and Israel have wrestled with each other—at one moment God is reminding Israel that by their sins the people have strayed from their promise to obey the commandments, and at another moment Israel is reminding God that he appears to have strayed from his promises to guide and protect. Within the bounds of the covenant, each party can be held accountable by the other. It is this covenant that makes Israel *Israel*—that is, the chosen people. For the rabbis, the identity of the Jews lay not in their national or ethnic history, although within the myth or symbolic story of Torah they surely embraced that history. Nor is the people's Jewishness a function of their being, by choice, members of a religion called *Judaism*; in fact, there is no word for *Judaism* in biblical Hebrew!

"The world is suspended in space and has nothing to rest on except the breath of Torah study from the mouths of students—just as a man may keep something up in the air by the blowing of his breath."

—Talmud

Instead, the Jewish identity lies in having been chosen, before all creation, to be God's beloved eternally. The rabbis reminded the people how God had brought them to himself on eagles' wings, to be a holy people (Exodus 19:3–6), set apart to be a witness to the holiness of life. In this "setting apart" lies the ultimate meaning of the rules for **kosher** dining that forbid Jews to eat pork, to mix meat and milk, and so on. Even what one eats and the way one eats should remind the world that life is not meant to be profane and meaningless. Rather, a holy life, one that is set apart, is not one's own but belongs to God. Indeed, every act of one's life, whether in work, in eating, in the bedroom, or in prayer, should be a witness to the One who alone is truly holy and in turn sanctifies all creation.

Torah, in the Talmudic tradition, is a multidimensional word. In its narrowest sense, Torah refers to the Pentateuch, the first five books of the Bible. In a broader sense it refers to the entire Bible, or Tanak. Broader still is its meaning as the dual Torah—that is, Torah plus Talmud. And ultimately Torah is the source and pattern for all creation, for, according to the Talmud, when God created heaven and earth he did it by consulting the Torah, which was already with God in the beginning. Hence the Torah provided the pattern for the right order of the universe, a pattern revealed in the *halakhah*, given through oral and written Torah. It was this understanding of the dual Torah (Torah plus Talmud) that shaped classical Judaism.

Premodern Judaism: The Classical Era (500 CE–1729 CE)

The Premodern Rabbinic World: God, Torah, and Israel

If human beings are not only storytellers but also storydwellers, then the Torah story of the rabbis was a magnificent dwelling indeed. If religion (*religio*) is about being "tied and bound" into the cosmic drama of life by one's story symbolically told (myth) and enacted (ritual), then Torah was, and is, just such a story. The Torah story of the rabbis created the cosmic vision of classical Judaism. It is a story that embraces not only every minute, hour, and day of Rabbinic Jewish life, providing a template to make it holy, but also the whole of time, from the creation of the world to its ultimate messianic redemption.

In the premodern world, the right to live within this story accompanied being born of a Jewish mother (and also those who were converts). While women thus determined Jewish identity, the primary guardians of Rabbinic religious life were men. Males alone had to be confirmed in their religious status through two key rituals: circumcision shortly after birth, and **bar mitzvah**, a ceremony in which they demonstrated their knowledge of the faith as they entered adulthood at age thirteen.

kosher: what is suitable or fit, particularly in reference to Jewish dietary laws

bar mitzvah: rite of passage for Jewish boys to become full members of the religion of Judaism; the **bat mitzvah** is a parallel rite for girls

Observant Jews, like this young man putting on *tefillin*, declare God's oneness by binding the Torah scrolls to their bodies before daily prayer.

The Jews of the Rabbinic age of classical Judaism ate, drank, and slept Torah. The men began the day by dressing in garments with fringes (*tzitzit*) to remind them of the commandments of the covenant (Numbers 15:37–40). Before morning prayer, they wrapped the words of Torah (Deuteronomy 6:4–9) on their arms and foreheads, encased in small leather boxes known as *tefillin*, or phylacteries. Indeed, every act of the day would be couched in prayer. And every Sabbath (the seventh day of the week), all work ceased and eternity pervaded all things as the people both recalled the beginning of creation and contemplated its fulfillment to come in the messianic era at the end of time. No matter what suffering history brought to Israel, on the Sabbath an eternal people dwelled with their eternal God, savoring a foretaste of that messianic day for which all creation was made—when God will be all in all.

The meaning of the Sabbath unfolded in the portion of Torah assigned for every week of the year, organized around a great cycle of festivals. From New Year's, which begins with the story of creation on Rosh Hashanah (literally, "head of the year") and concludes ten days later with stories of divine judgment on Yom Kippur (day of atonement), through Passover (liberation/redemption of the Exodus) to the Feast of Weeks (the giving of the dual Torah and the covenant) to the Feast of Booths (the wandering in the desert, awaiting the fulfillment of the promises) as well as the commemoration of disasters averted (Purim) and not averted (Tisha B'Av), the great story unfolded. The story of Torah stretched out over the lives of Jews from the beginning of the day until the end of the day, from the beginning of the year until the end of the year, from the beginning of their lives until the end of their lives, and from the beginning of time until the end of time. In the Torah story, God and Israel

RITUALS AND RITES: Rituals of the Life Cycle

Rituals marking the important transitions in the life of the individual can be found in all religious traditions. In Judaism these are the *Bris* or *Brit milah*, the bar and bat mitzvah, and the rituals for marriage, and death.

Bris or Brit Milah

In accordance with the teachings of the Torah (Genesis 17:10–14), every male child must be circumcised when he is eight days old, as a sign of the covenant between God and his people. This ceremony is known as the *Bris* or *Brit milah* (derived from the Hebrew for "covenant" and for "circumcision"). During this ritual the child is named and the foreskin of his penis is cut off as an external sign of the covenant. This ritual ties and binds every male child's life to the eternal covenant between God and his people, renewing that covenant with each generation, child by child.

Bar and Bat Mitzvah

When a boy reaches the age of adulthood, thirteen, he is eligible to become a bar mitzvah (son of the commandments, or covenant); to this end, he is expected to demonstrate the ability to carry out his responsibilities in maintaining the religious life of the community. After intense training by his rabbi in the study of Hebrew and of Torah and Talmud, the young man is called forth at a synagogue service to recite the blessing that precedes the reading of the Torah. Then he reads the Torah portion for the week and then a portion of scripture from the Prophets. He may also be asked to comment on the meaning of the passages. By doing this the boy shows that he is able to function as a full member of the religious community. Once he has completed this ceremony he is considered to be an adult, qualified to form part of the *minyan* (ten adult males) required for any Jewish worship service. With the appearance of the Conservative and Reform Jewish communities the ritual has been extended to include young women as well. For them the ritual is called the bat mitzvah (daughter of the commandments, or covenant).

Marriage

A Jewish wedding takes place under a *huppah*, a sort of grand prayer shawl stretched over four poles that can be said to symbolize the heavens and God's creation, even as the bride and groom stand in the place of Adam and Eve, the first man and woman created by God. In the marriage ceremony, prayers and blessings sanctify the union of a man and a woman by binding them to each other and to the story of Israel's relation to God, from creation through exiles and tribulations to joyous redemption in the new Zion. Before entering under the canopy, the man places the veil over the bride's face. Under the canopy the marriage contract (*ketubah*) is witnessed, the couple are betrothed and married with an exchange of rings, and the words "Behold, you are sanctified to me by this ring in accord with the tradition of Moses and Israel" are followed by seven blessings said over a cup of wine. It is customary, at the end of the ceremony, for the groom to step on and break a glass, symbolizing the fall of the second temple. Great festivity and celebration follow.

Death

Jewish death rites are very simple. A person facing death is encouraged to say a prayer of confession, asking for forgiveness of sins and healing if possible. The prayer continues by asking that the person's death, if it is to come now, serve as atonement for all his or her sins. The prayer ends with requests ("Grant me a share in the world to come" and "Protect my beloved family") and commits the person's soul into the hands of God. Burial takes place on the day of death or the day after, without embalming. The community places the body in the ground with prayers binding the soul of the deceased to the Eternal One. The immediate family of mourners remains at home for seven days and will continue to recite memorial prayers (kaddish) for eleven months and thereafter on the anniversary of the death.

dwelled—sometimes in harmony and sometimes wrestling with each other—but always within a drama that gave life meaning in spite of the brutal incursions of the profane world that surrounded and rejected the Jews.

The genius of this Talmudic Judaism was that instead of totally rejecting the messianic apocalypticism of the biblical period, it transformed it, replacing political Zionism with an apolitical spiritual Zionism. The rabbis argued that Israel had been seduced by the Zealots into trying to force the coming of the messianic era by their own political activity. The truth is, the rabbis argued, that only God can initiate the messianic era, and God will bring the age of exile to an end and restore to Israel the land of promise only when all Israel is fully observant of *halakhah*. This view prevailed throughout the Middle Ages and was not seriously challenged until the coming of modern secular Zionism in the nineteenth and twentieth centuries.

The Medieval Journey of Judaism

Medieval Judaism reveals the precarious situation of the Jews in a world dominated by the new religion of Christianity. With the emergence of the Holy Roman Empire in 800 CE, at first Jews were more or less tolerated. By the late Middle Ages, however, this toleration gave way to persecution, except in Spain. There, for a brief period in the twelfth and thirteenth centuries CE known as the "Golden Age," Jews were welcome and Judaism flourished.

Discrimination Against Jews in the Early Middle Ages

Dwelling in the great cosmic story of Torah, the people Israel survived their journey through the medieval world of persecutions and expulsions. Their unity was then splintered by the Jewish Enlightenment in the nineteenth century and nearly shattered by the Holocaust in the twentieth century. That journey is a tale of tragic precedents for the Holocaust; and yet it is also a story of amazing spiritual endurance and creativity that enriched and expanded the house of Torah in which Israel dwelled—especially through the contributions of Kabbalistic mysticism and Hasidic piety.

The situation of the Jews deteriorated with the decline of the Roman Empire and the rise of Christianity. While Jews in Palestine, the land of Israel, were under the colonial rule of the Romans in the first four centuries, they enjoyed a unique protected status as a legal religion, despite their refusal to worship the gods of the official state cult. However, when the emperors and the empire became Christian in 380, the colonial domination of the Jews became more severe, and Jews eventually lost most of the legal protection they had enjoyed under the Romans. That domination did not really end until the establishment of the state of Israel in the twentieth century. The view that Christians had superseded or replaced the Jews as God's "chosen people" led to what in later centuries would be called "the Jewish problem"—namely, the continuing existence of Jews. Jews came to be seen as an "obstinate" and "stiff-necked" people who refused to acknowledge the truth of Christianity and convert (or, in later modern secular culture, refused to give up their Jewishness and assimilate).

RITUALS AND RITES

Major Festivals: The Days of Awe and Passover

All religions also have annual rituals that mark important events from the religious stories that shape their identity. After the Sabbath, which sets the rhythm of Jewish religious life, the Jewish New Year (Rosh Hashanah and Yom Kippur) and Passover are the most prominent of the Jewish holy days or festivals. Unlike Passover, which is focused on the home and family, Rosh Hashanah and Yom Kippur are days of communal prayer spent in the synagogue.

Rosh Hashanah and Yom Kippur

The new year begins for Jews with the Rosh Hashanah synagogue service, during which the story of creation is retold and people are reminded that God is deciding who will and who will not be written in the book of life for another year, even as he will decide the fate of nations and of the whole world. So the new year raises questions of life and death and calls for self-examination. The process ends ten days later, on Yom Kippur, a day of total fasting and repentance. When Yom Kippur ends at sunset and the fast is broken, penitents consider themselves to be both cleansed and prepared to face the new year. The solemnity of Yom Kippur is intended to fill worshippers with the appropriate awe and respect for the Lord God of the universe who governs the destiny of all.

Passover

Passover, or *Pesach*, recalls God's deliverance of the tribes of Israel from slavery in Egypt (Exodus 1–15). Passover is celebrated in the home, usually with the extended family and friends. The Passover *aggadah* is an order of service that retells the story of the liberation from Egypt with extensive commentary from the sages of the Talmud. The male head of the household presides at this retelling, which is done around the dining table, but members of the family are invited to

participate, individually and collectively, in the recitation. Prominence is given to the youngest child, who must ask four key questions, the first of which is: "Why is this night different from all other nights?" In this way the story is passed on from generation to generation. As the story is retold, certain symbolic foods are eaten to remind everyone of the events that led and still lead to liberation from slavery for every Jew.

This festival is also called the feast of unleavened bread (*matzah*), for the story indicated that only bread without yeast was used at the time of the original event, since the tribes left in a hurry and did not have time to make leavened bread. To prepare for Passover all leavened bread must be removed from the premises and all utensils cleaned. Special foods used in the Seder service include wine to celebrate the joy of deliverance; bitter herbs (e.g., horseradish) to recall the bitterness of oppression

To be rescued from peril is an experience that can transform the identity of a person or of a people. The Passover meal is a ritual meal, celebrated annually, to recall God's liberation of the tribes of Israel from slavery in Egypt. A Jewish family celebrates this great story of deliverance.

by the Egyptians; saltwater to recall the tears of the tribes in slavery; celery or parsley as a sign of spring, life, and hope; one roasted or boiled egg and a roasted shank bone to recall both the destruction of the temple and Israel's redemption at the Red Sea by the "outstretched arm" of God; and a mixture of apples, walnuts, and spices, called Haroset, to recall the mortar used by Israelite slaves in building the Egyptian cities. After the symbolic foods are consumed during the telling of the story, a full family meal of celebration is eaten, and the meal concludes with further prayers and recitations from the Passover *aggadah*. During the Passover meal it is said that ordinary time is suspended and every Jew becomes part of the liberating event and so can say, "This day I too have been liberated from slavery."

Minor Festivals

In addition to the major festivals, a variety of other festivals are celebrated through the year, including the following.

Sukkot and Simchat Torah

Five days after Yom Kippur, the Festival of Booths is celebrated. Temporary dwellings (a wooden frame covered with branches) are constructed outdoors where Jews will eat their meals and may even sleep. The dwellings are to remind Jews of their journey through the wilderness to the land of promise, during which they had no permanent shelter. Sukkot is followed by Simchat Torah or the festival of "Rejoicing in the Torah." The last words of Torah (the end of the Book of Deuteronomy) are read, followed by the reading of the opening words of the first book of Torah, Genesis. This symbolizes the bringing of the year of "reading through the Torah" to an end and starting the

cycle over for a new year. This is a festival of joyous celebration that includes a ritual "dancing with the Torah."

Purim

Jewish history is filled with many incidents of persecution. This joyous festival commemorates an occasion in Jewish history where an attempted Persian persecution is thwarted. The festival celebrates the tale of the book of Esther. Esther is a pretty young Jewish woman who is raised by her cousin Mordecai. She becomes one of the wives of the king of Persia, who does not know that she is Jewish. Moreover, she becomes the favorite of the king. The sinister Haman, an adviser to the king, turns the king against the Jews and seeks to exterminate them. However, Esther goes to the king and exposes Haman and his lies. As a result she wins the king's support, the Jews are saved, and Haman and his sons are executed.

Hanukkah

This is an eight-day festival of light, celebrated in the dead of winter and symbolizing the light of hope. It commemorates the reopening of the Temple in Jerusalem reclaimed from the Syrian persecutors in a Jewish revolt led by the Maccabean brothers. The temple was cleansed, and the temple menorah or candle stand needed to be relighted. However, there was only enough olive oil to burn for one day. Miraculously, the oil lasted eight days, until further oil could be supplied, keeping the fire and hope in God's love and protection alive. Today the festival is observed by lighting a special menorah that has nine branches—one to use to light each of the other eight over the successive eight days of the festival, during which family members often give each other gifts.

The First Crusade ended with the violent retaking of Jerusalem from the Muslims in 1099.

The Carolingian Era of Tolerance

For a while in Europe, under the Frankish Carolingian kings, who founded the Holy Roman Empire (800 CE), the life of Jews improved. Jews enjoyed high positions in the courts and in the professions and experienced new opportunities for wealth. And while Jews were not considered full citizens, they prospered under so-called diplomas of protection from the king's court. They became "the king's Jews." This practice was a benefit as long as Jews were favored by the king. However, in later periods the arrangement resulted in sudden reversals of fortune whenever a king (or Holy Roman Emperor) found it convenient to rescind his protection.

Centuries of Persecution and Pogrom

In the late Middle Ages, Jewish life became truly precarious in Europe. The tide turned against Jews with the launching of the First Crusade by Pope Urban II in 1095. The announced reason for the Crusades was to free Jerusalem and all of the Holy Land from the Muslims, who had taken Jerusalem in 638. In Islam as in Christianity and Judaism, Jerusalem is a holy city.

A plenary indulgence, or guarantee of forgiveness of sins and entry into heaven, was promised by the Pope to anyone who participated in the Crusades. However, as the armies raised for this purpose passed through the cities and towns of Europe on their way to rid the Holy Land of infidels (i.e., the Muslims), they decided to use the opportunity to purge the Christian world of its other "enemy" as well.

The Christian armies passing through the Rhine Valley offered Jews the choice of conversion or death. Many responded by committing suicide; many others were massacred. Few converted. The pattern of persecution and violence against Jews continued in the centuries that followed. In 1251 the Fourth Lateran Council of the Catholic Church adopted a practice first used by Muslims in eleventh-century Egypt, that of forcing Jews to wear distinctive dress. Also at this time, the Jews were forced to live in segregated quarters called *ghettos*. To the pattern of discrimination and violence was added the periodic practice of expulsion. In 1306, in a single day, all the Jews of France were arrested and ordered to be out of the country within a month. Other countries followed suit, driving the majority of Europe's Jews into eastern Europe. In 1348, as the Black Death swept across the Continent, Jews were blamed and made the scapegoats, and the Jews of many communities were executed. In Strasbourg, in the year 1349, for instance, 200 Jews were burned alive in a cemetery on the Sabbath.

The Protestant Reformation, initiated in 1517, seemed to be characterized by a more positive attitude toward Judaism. At first, Martin Luther wrote favorably of the Jews. But toward the end of his life, the German religious leader realized that Jews were no more receptive to his interpretation of the Gospel than to the Catholic interpretation. Thereafter, Luther turned viciously anti-Judaic, advocating the abuse of Jews and the burning of synagogues. Nevertheless, the aftermath of the Reformation in the sixteenth and seventeenth centuries left Christians too busy fighting each other to make the Jews a central concern. This distraction, as well as a modification of ghettos that put Jews under lock and key at night, served to reduce the violence Jews experienced at the hands of Christians.

However, at the same time, as the Jewish population of eastern Europe grew by leaps and bounds as a consequence of the expulsions from western Europe, new waves of violence broke out against Jews in eastern Europe. Between 1648 and 1658, in organized massacres called *pogroms*, over 700 Jewish communities were destroyed. Jewish deaths numbered in the hundreds of thousands. Fueling this violence in Europe was an ethos of Jew hatred that expressed itself in the rationalization that "the Jews are our misfortune" and helped prepare the way for the Holocaust.

The Jews of Italy offer a striking exception to this history of persecution: On the whole, they fared much better than the rest of European Jewry. Rome is the only major city of Europe from which Jews were never expelled. And unlike those in the rest of Europe, the Jews of Rome experienced no punitive taxes, were free to select their occupations, and were not forbidden by law to marry Christians. Nor were Jews persecuted in Italy during the Crusades and the years of the Black Death.

There were a number of reasons for this paradoxical thread in the religious history of Europe. For example, since usury was an allowable occupation for Christian financiers in Italy, Jews were not singled out for resentment as "money lenders." But perhaps the most influential factor was the relation between the popes and the Jews.

It was widely believed by medieval Christians that the gentile followers of Jesus had replaced the Jews as God's chosen people. To explain away "the Jewish problem"— why God nevertheless permitted Jews to continue to exist—the popes, from the sixth century on, turned to a theory developed by St. Augustine, the so-called "negative witness theory." According to this theory, it was God's will for Jews to wander the earth without a home, their unhappy existence functioning as a "negative witness" that proved the superiority and truth of Christianity. Consequently, the popes preached that God had rejected the Jews while, at the same time, paradoxically, acting as the legal protectors and guardians of the original chosen people, insisting that they not be physically harmed.

Although the negative witness theory shaped papal strategy for dealing with "the Jewish problem" in medieval Christendom, during the Renaissance some popes took a less biased view. Pope Sixtus IV (1471–84), for example, commissioned a Latin translation of the Kabbalah. Later Pope Clement VII sought to develop a common translation of the Old Testament by Jewish and Christian scholars, and he suspended the persecution by the Spanish Inquisition of Jews who had been forcibly baptized in Spain.

From the Golden Age in Spain to the Spanish Inquisition

In the midst of this violent history stands the Golden Age of Spain as an extraordinary interlude, when Jews were welcomed as allies against the Muslims in the portions of Spain that had been reconquered by Christians. For a time in the twelfth and early thirteenth centuries, Jews were encouraged to settle in the reconquered territories and were given unusual freedom both socially and politically, achieving important roles in the royal court and in the professions. It was a period of unprecedented intellectual exchange between the great scholars of Judaism, Islam, and Christianity.

The period came to an end in the mid-thirteenth century as a Christian backlash developed. Christians suddenly became alarmed at the growing number of Jews in high places. This fear of a "Jewish takeover" led to a new period of persecution, violence, and forced conversions, culminating in the Spanish Inquisition. Between 1480 and 1492 some 13,000 Jews, most of whom had been forcibly baptized as Christians, were condemned as **Marranos**—Jews masquerading as Christians while practicing their Judaism in secret. Many were tortured and burned at the stake. The Jews were expelled from Spain in 1492 (see Map 3.2).

Two Great Medieval Scholars: Rashi and Maimonides

The period of the late Middle Ages produced two of the greatest scholars in the history of Judaism: Rabbi Solomon ben Isaac (1040–1105), otherwise known as Rashi, and Moses ben Maimon (1135–1204), otherwise known as Maimonides. Rashi's commentaries on the Gemara of the Babylonian Talmud, which appeared in the first

Marranos: Jews of Spain who, although forced by the Inquisition to convert to Christianity, continued to practice Judaism in secret

"If there is no peace, then there is really nothing, because peace is the equivalent of all other blessings put together."

—Rashi

printed edition of the Talmud and have been in all editions since, are considered to form an essential component of the work. Rashi is hailed as the most unsurpassable teacher of Torah in the history of Talmudic Judaism. He founded an influential Talmudic academy in Troyes, France.

Maimonides, known as Rambam (for Rabbi Moses Ben Maimon), is famous for his philosophical writings, in which he uses Aristotelian concepts to explain Jewish teaching. His *Guide of the Perplexed* is well known today, and for over three centuries his compendium of Talmudic law, the *Mishnah Torah*, was the most influential guide to *halakhah* in Judaism. Although Judaism is not a religion that emphasizes *dogma* (right belief) as the test of true faith, Maimonides is credited with giving Judaism a creedal statement known as the *Thirteen Articles of Faith* (which are found on the website for this book; www.oup.com/us/esposito).

Kabbalah—Jewish Mysticism

Judaism, like all religions, has a mystical dimension. Not only in Judaism, but in the other two monotheistic traditions of Christianity and Islam, mystics have generally been viewed with an element of mistrust because mystical experience is direct and immediate and so tends to undermine traditional lines of religious authority. The mystic finds God without the guidance of either a priest or a teacher (rabbi). Moreover, the mystic often speaks of God in ways that are unconventional and sometimes seem contradictory to the nature of prophetic monotheism.

In the monotheistic traditions mysticism expresses itself in two dramatically different forms—the mysticism of love and union (the divine-human marriage) and the mysticism of identity. The place of the mystic in monotheism has always been especially ambivalent for the mystics of identity. The mystics of identity sometimes seem to say they are not just in union with God but *are* God. Whenever mystics speak in this way they are in danger of being accused of confusing themselves with God and claiming to be God. Any such representation would be heretical and blasphemous in all three biblical religions, hence would be unacceptable by any of them. And yet, despite this seemingly ever-present danger, each of the monotheistic religions has chosen to maintain an uneasy peace with its mystics, neither denying the importance and validity of mysticism nor suppressing its practice.

Although Jewish mysticism goes back to the ancient world and also reflects the influences of Neoplatonism and Gnosticism, it did not become a decisive influence in Judaism until the explicit emergence of **Kabbalah** in the late medieval period. Kabbalism sought to explain the mystery of good and evil in the universe precisely at a time of intensifying persecution and pogroms. Jews could not help but seek an understanding of God that could sustain them through a new period of suffering.

The most important Kabbalistic work is the **Zohar** (Book of Splendor). According to Kabbalistic teaching, there was a time when God manifested himself in the world, allowing his *Shekinah* ("divine presence") to be perceived in all things. However,

> "I believe with perfect faith that the Creator, blessed be Your name, is not a body, and that You are free from all the accidents of matter, and that You have not any form whatsoever."
>
> —Maimonides' Third Principle of Faith

Kabbalah: Jewish mystical tradition

Zohar: "Book of Splendor," the most important Kabbalistic work

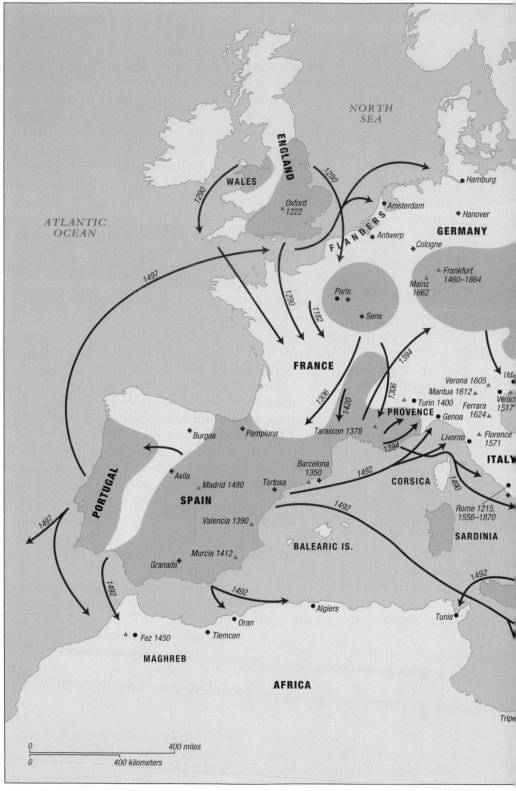

Map 3.2 Jews in Christian Europe.

Areas of Jewish communities

→ Expulsions, with date
● Major centers of resettlement
▲ Main ghettos, with date established
◆ Centers of disputations between Jews and Christians

BALTIC
SEA

LITHUANIA

1495
1495
1495

1445

● Grodno
● Bialystok

1096–1192

POLAND
SILESIA

● Pinsk
● Brest-Litovsk

● Chernigov

● Kharkow

1012

▲ Posen *pre-1532*

● Lódź
● Kalisz
Radom

● Lublin

● Luck
● Zhitomir

1016

1016

3reslau
1266

Kazimierz 1494

1248

1159

Lemberg

1350

Cracow

▲ Tarnopol

que
3

1348

▲ Vienna *1570*

1421

Kishlnev ●

USTRIA

Buda ▲
1279

1349–1360

1016

BLACK
SEA

● Trebizond

HUNGARY

● Nicopolis

● Spalato

● Cattaro

● Adrianople

▲◆● Constantinople
late 11th century

● Salonica

OTTOMAN EMPIRE

1016

● Naples

● Corfu

● Smyrna

ermo
12

Patras
1532

NCILY

Modon
pro-1461

▲ Rhodes
1310–1522

CYPRUS

● Damascus

● Safed

CRETE

● Jerusalem

MEDITERRANEAN SEA

● Alexandria

Cairo ●

because of the fall of Adam, evil entered the world and the divine presence has been exiled from its unity with God as the infinite (*En Sof*). Humans were created for *devekut* ("communion") with God, but this relationship was destroyed by Adam's sin and must be reestablished through mystical contemplation (*kavanah*) of the divine through prayer and the devout performance of the requirements of *halakhah*. The reunion of all with the infinite will bring about nothing less than the ingathering of all Jews from exile in the messianic kingdom to come.

The Kabbalistic tradition comprises a profound mystical variation on the theme of exile and return. It can be seen as a powerful religious response to the overwhelming tragedy of persecution and expulsion that marked Jewish life in Europe in the late Middle Ages and beyond. It explained the age of darkness in which Jews lived in exile and offered them a hope of transcending that darkness with a future ingathering of all Jews.

Hasidism

Hasidism: form of Judaism strongly rooted in mysticism

The mystical impulse of Kabbalism was given further embodiment in the Hasidic movement. **Hasidism** really came into its own in eastern Europe at the beginning of the eighteenth century largely in response to the pogroms endemic to the region. A *hasid* is a pious one, whose life is marked by great devotion. With Hasidism, piety took on a new intensity of meaning.

The Hasidic movement emerged in Poland with the activities of Israel ben Eliezer, who was called *the Besht* by his followers. This title was a shortened form of Ba'al Shem Tov, or "Master of the Good Name," where the "good name" was understood to be the name of God. The Besht was an ecstatic healer who worked miracles using magic, amulets, and spells. He taught that joy is the appropriate response to the world no matter how much suffering Jews experience.

In fact, although Hasidism emerged in an era of pogrom and immense suffering in eastern Europe, the Hasidim say there is no greater sin than melancholy, or sadness (*atzut*). Indeed they argue that sadness, which stems from ignorance of the pervasive presence of God in all things, is the root of all sin. According to the Besht, God hides himself in his creation. Therefore, there is no distance between God and humanity for those who have the eyes to see. And once you do see, there can be no sadness but only *simhah*—deep, pervasive, passionate joy and celebration.

The Besht was a charismatic figure whose followers hung on his every word and gesture. Their prayer circles were characterized by ecstatic singing and dancing, and they looked forward to deeply moving spiritual talks by the Besht around the Sabbath dinner table. The Besht taught that the essence of the way of Torah is to be found in devotion (*kavanah*), burning enthusiasm (*hitlahavut*), and attachment or clinging to God (*devekut*) rather than in study of the Talmud.

Tzaddik: in the Hasidic tradition, a "righteous man"—a religious leader who is as influential as a rabbi is in a traditional Talmudic community

The Besht became a model for the Hasidic notion of the **Tzaddik**, or "righteous man." The Tzaddik's authority in each Hasidic community was every bit as powerful as that of the rabbi in a traditional Talmudic community. For the Hasidim, the

For the Hasidim there is no greater sin than sadness. The proper response to God's presence, hidden everywhere in creation, is joy. One expression of that joy is to dance with the Torah, as this Hasidic man in Jerusalem is doing, accompanied by other male dancers of all ages.

Tzaddik was no ordinary person but one especially chosen by God as a direct link between heaven and earth. He was revered as a savior figure whose holiness was considered so powerful that, like Moses (Exodus 32:11–14), he could intervene on behalf of the faithful and literally change the mind of God. Like the rabbis, the Tzaddik was a religious virtuoso; however, his virtuosity was of mystical piety and devotion, not of Talmudic scholarship. His holiness was said to be spontaneously contagious: Just being near him, the Hasidim could catch his piety as a spark to light their own.

Hasidism garnered an enthusiastic popular following, for it offered even the poor and unlearned a way to move from the periphery into the heart of Judaism as they understood it. One reason for this was that in the early days, Hasidic Judaism rejected the elitism of Rabbinic Judaism, for the rabbis and their students were an intellectual elite, trained as Talmudic experts—something the average Jew could not hope to be. Hasidic Judaism offered ways to reach God other than Talmudic study: namely, devotion and prayer, which were within the reach of every sincere Jew. This path brought into popular practice the deep mystical piety of the Kabbalistic tradition.

What was most extraordinary about Hasidic mysticism was, and is, its communal nature. One cannot achieve this state of joy and selflessness by going off alone to a mountaintop but only by total immersion in the community life of the Hasidim organized around the festive worship made possible by the presence of the Tzaddik. It is this linking of deep mystical spirituality with community life that made Hasidism such a powerful force for renewal. In the nineteenth century, Hasidism moved toward reconciliation with Rabbinic Judaism by incorporating more emphasis on the study of Talmud and was eventually accepted by the rabbis who had originally rejected it.

The Kabbalistic-Hasidic tradition was deeply influenced by ancient Greek philosophy (Neoplatonism and Gnosticism). The success of its integration into the Talmudic tradition through the Hasidic movement demonstrates the extraordinary ability of Judaism to absorb and sanctify the "secular" and non-Jewish while reaffirming the practices of the tradition. This is a pattern we see repeated in the twentieth century, when many of the movements of modern and post-Holocaust Judaism have grown closer together. Judaism, despite inner tensions and conflicts, shows an amazing ability to absorb conflicting movements, which often catalyze transformation and renewal. This should not surprise anyone, for this has been true of Judaism from its very beginnings in the biblical period.

Having surveyed premodern Judaism, we are now in a position to look at the emergence of modern forms and to understand better how they are both like premodern forms of Judaism and different from them.

Judaism and Modernity (1729–1967 CE)

The Emergence of Modern Religious Forms of Judaism

Reform Judaism

From the early days of Rabbinic Judaism, between the second and fifth centuries, until the French Revolution in 1789, Jews in Europe lived as a rejected minority in a world dominated by Christians. With Enlightenment secularization, the categories of human self-understanding underwent radical revision. Enlightened Europeans were secular universalists who defined their humanity not in terms of religious myths, which they believed created divisiveness, but in terms of reason, which they held to be a capacity found universally in human beings. The ideal of this new orientation was to replace the categories of "Jew" and "Christian" with a single category: "rational human being."

For the first time in almost 2,000 years, the dominant culture looked at Jews as rational beings, equal to all other human beings, and Jews were invited to participate as citizens alongside all other individuals in the modern capitalist nation-states (see Map 3.3). This message of inclusion was widely accepted by the Jews of western Europe. It seemed that a new day was dawning. One of the leading Enlightenment scholars of the eighteenth century, Gotthold Lessing (1729–81), a gentile, wrote impassioned works proclaiming the humanity of Jews and of Muslims and arguing for their acceptance in society. Lessing befriended Moses Mendelssohn (1729–86), who became the leading figure in the Jewish Haskalah, or Enlightenment, movement, the eventual source of Reform Judaism, the first "modern" form of Judaism.

Like Hellenistic Judaism in the first century, the Haskalah movement favored partial assimilation into the gentile world, trying to show that in the 1800s, one could be an enlightened citizen of the secular world and a Jew at the same time. This required

Map 3.3 The emancipation of European Jewry, 1789–1918.

the leaders of the Reform movement to answer a question that all modern forms of Judaism (including Orthodoxy) have confronted: How can I be both a Jew and a citizen of a secular state? It had been pointless to ask this question earlier, when secular states did not exist and Christian states offered Jews no possibility of citizenship.

Reform Judaism and all other forms of modern Judaism, however, have had to make a decision about how to relate to the larger secular society. Embracing the Enlightenment ideal of religion within the "limits of reason," the leaders of the Reform movement defined the essence of Judaism as a rational–ethical system rooted

GENDER FOCUS: Women in Judaism

Premodern

Talmudic Judaism shares with the emerging Judaism of the ancient biblical period a common assumption of premodern urban societies, transposed into a monotheistic frame of reference. Specifically, it was long assumed that there is a sacred natural order of the world, revealed by God, in which maleness is the normative pattern for full humanity. Traditionally, this assumption was validated by the second creation story presented in the Bible: Genesis 2:5–3:24 (as opposed to the first version, Genesis 1:1–2:4). Since in the second story God created Adam first and then Eve from the rib of Adam, men were accorded primary responsibility for the order of things, women having been created to help men. Indeed, women (like animals and slaves) are the property of men. A father could sell his daughter as payment for a debt (Exodus 21:7), for instance. Basically, a woman belonged to her father until she was given to the man who married her, to whom she then belonged. Women had no role in the public worship in the temple, but at the same time women were honored as mothers and the mainstay of the family.

The biblical attitude toward women was continued in premodern Rabbinic Judaism. However, during the biblical period certain exceptional women were revered for their wisdom and their gifts of prophecy: Miriam (the sister of Moses), Deborah (one of the judges of Israel), and Huldah (a prophetess during the reign of Josiah). Both Rabbinic and later Hasidic traditions also present models of women who were exceptions, noted for their learning and piety. Beruriah, the wife of Rabbi Meir, was noted for her skill as a Talmudic scholar, and Oudil, the daughter of the Ba'al Shem Tov, was praised for her wisdom and joyous piety. Nevertheless, such women were not the norm. They remained the exception that proved the rule.

Modern

The Enlightenment brought with it a gradual change in the status of women in Western culture, and women have progressively claimed autonomy, that is, control of their own lives. Modern forms of Judaism tend to demythologize traditional Jewish gender roles as inessential historical accretions that may even contradict fundamental insights of Judaism concerning justice and human dignity. Thus, it is probably fair to say that the greatest equality for women has been among the secular forms of Judaism, especially Jewish socialism

in the prophetic-ethical ideal of justice—an ethic that was Judaism's gift to humanity. Like their Hellenistic counterparts, they did not think that this ethic was for Jews alone but rather that Judaism was its source and purest form. This universal rational ethic was the essence of Judaism; all other aspects of Judaism were open to negotiation.

As Reform Judaism developed, it showed a remarkable openness to secular society. For instance, Jews could use the vernacular instead of Hebrew in worship; thus synagogue prayers and sermons could be spoken in the local language (German, French, English, etc.). As the movement developed in the late nineteenth century, it was also prepared to abandon the observance of kosher laws, restricting the foods Jews can eat, and other "historical accretions" as inessential to being Jewish. Indeed, it rejected the Talmud as revelation, seeing it instead as simply a human historical tradition. And it rejected belief in a literal coming of the messiah, replacing it with a belief in a messianic age and Zionism, and among the most secular forms of religious Judaism—Reform first, then Conservative, and least among the Orthodox.

The Declaration of Independence of the State of Israel, drawing on the nation's secular socialist and Zionist roots, asserts complete equality of men and women in social and political rights. The Equal Rights for Women law of 1951 guarantees women the same rights enjoyed by men to own property and to make decisions on behalf of their children. Among the explicitly religious forms of Judaism, the Reform movement has led the way. As early as 1846 a movement to declare women equal appeared in Germany. Nevertheless, the desire of women to become rabbis was not discussed seriously until the 1920s, and it was not until the 1970s that women began to be ordained (although one private ordination is said to have occurred in 1935 in a German Reform congregation)

Today it is not uncommon, in both Reform and Conservative synagogues in America, for a young woman to celebrate her bat mitzvah as a parallel rite to a brother's bar mitzvah. Nor is it unusual for women

Today in both Reform Judaism and Conservative Judaism women are ordained to the rabbinate. Here Barbara Aiello, the first female rabbi in Italy, lights Hanukkah candles.

to read the Torah scrolls at a Sabbath service. And it is even becoming more common for women cantors to chant such services and for women rabbis to conduct them. All of this was unthinkable in premodern Judaism. And it remains unthinkable among the ultra-Orthodox.

that could easily be identified with the goal of the modern age of scientific and rational progress. Finally, it renounced any desire to return to the land of Israel, insisting that Jews were not a people tied to a specific land but a "religious community."

What especially marks the Reform movement as modern is its openness to secular learning and historical consciousness. In premodern Rabbinic Judaism (with such notable exceptions as Maimonides), the only learning worthy of consideration was the study of Torah and Talmud. But among enlightened Jews, secular learning not only was permitted but took precedence. For instance, in deciding what is and what is not essential to Judaism, Reform Judaism argued not from the "revealed will of God," as had premodern Judaism, but from the history of the development of Judaism as a religion. Thus "history" and "Judaism," not "God" and "Torah," became the defining categories. Religious disputes were to be settled primarily by appeal to the developmental history of Judaism. After all, what history reveals, Reform Jews argued, is that Judaism is a religion not of eternal, unchanging truths but of constant change. From their perspective, Reform Judaism is the true Judaism for the modern world and the logical successor, in the authentic unfolding of the historical tradition, to premodern Rabbinic Judaism.

Reform Judaism explained how one could be a Jew and still be part of a larger secular society. Reform Judaism, which initiated the journey of Judaism into the modern world, was the pioneer of all modern Judaisms. For some, Reform Judaism was a model to be emulated with modifications, especially the more secular forms of Judaism—ethnic Judaism, Jewish socialism, and Zionism (to be discussed shortly). Indeed, it would be hard to imagine the secular state of Israel without the path opened up by Reform Judaism. Yet other Jews believed that this was the wrong direction. Indeed, it was only after the bold statements of Reform Judaism that a second form of modern Judaism appeared: Orthodox Judaism, which vigorously rejected the claims of the Reform movement.

Orthodox Judaism

To call Orthodox Judaism a modern form of Judaism may seem contradictory, for orthodoxy claims that it continues the ancient tradition of premodern Rabbinic Judaism. Reform Judaism, of course, also claims to continue the same tradition. Orthodoxy, however, defined continuity in terms of resisting all change, whereas Reform Judaism thought it meant being true to the historical law of constant change. The issue between Reform and Orthodox Jews was whether, as Reform Jews held, God was acting through an ever-changing history, progressing toward an age of messianic freedom, or whether the Orthodox were correct in their view that God revealed himself only in the eternal, unchanging covenant given at Sinai. This reflects the choice modernization puts to all religions—whether to embrace historical change or reject it out of faithfulness to a view of premodern unchanging fundamental truths and practices.

Reform Jews argued for changes that would accommodate the modern world, while the Orthodox want to refuse all accommodation, although they seldom fully achieve this. Orthodox Jews wanted to present their choice of orthodoxy as if it were no choice. But clearly, the very appearance of Reform Judaism meant that one could no longer just be a Jew; one had to choose to be a Jew of a certain kind. In agreeing that it was necessary to choose, Orthodoxy gave evidence that it too was a Judaism of the modern period. From now on, like Reform Judaism, it would have to think of itself as one religious community alongside others. Premodern Rabbinic Jews had no such dilemma, for there was no "Judaism" to choose, only God, Torah, and Israel, the givens of one's birth into the chosen people.

Orthodoxy became, in many ways, the mirror image of Reform Judaism, for mirror images reverse the original that they reflect. Thus if Reform Jews prayed in the vernacular, the Orthodox insisted that all prayers be in Hebrew. If Reform Jews insisted on historical change, the Orthodox insisted on eternal unchanging truth. If Reform Jews decided issues of religious practice on the basis of history, the Orthodox decided them on the basis of the eternal word of God given in the Torah and the

Talmud. If Reform Jews abandoned literal messianic beliefs, the Orthodox reaffirmed them. If Reform Jews dismissed the Talmudic requirements (*halakhah*) as historical accretions, the Orthodox insisted on continued observance of the requirements of the dual Torah (the written Torah and the oral Torah). And if Reform Jews abandoned any ambition to return to the land of Israel, the Orthodox prayed "next year in Jerusalem" while awaiting the deliverance of the messiah.

In western Europe even the Orthodox saw the futility of separating themselves completely from the secular world and allowed that in "inessentials," such as clothing, secular education, and choice of job or career, Jews may be like everyone else. Indeed, Orthodoxy's first great intellectual defender, Samson Raphael Hirsch (1808–88), sought to show that one can live as a Jew in a secular nation-state and remain fully Orthodox. Therefore, above all, what makes Orthodoxy a modern Judaism is that, like Reform Judaism, it divides the world into the religious and the secular, separating religion and politics in a way that allows Orthodox Jews to be both Jews and citizens of a secular nation-state. However, the ultra-Orthodox set out on a path of segregation, challenging the integrationism of Reform Jews and even the minimal accommodation to the "outside world" of the Orthodox. Eastern European haredim tried to shut out modernity altogether, but this meant doing what no premodern Rabbinic Jew had ever had to do—become a sectarian.

Conservative Judaism

Once the lines had been drawn between the first two modern ways of being Jewish, it was perhaps inevitable that a third option would emerge, seeking a compromise. That option was Conservative Judaism. The Orthodox saw Jewish life as the life of an eternal people; Reform Jews saw Jewish life as the life of a historical religious community. Conservative Jews saw Jewish life as the life of a historically ethnic people that included but was not limited to the religious dimension. Conservative Judaism arose among Jews who were deeply committed to the Orthodox way of life yet sympathetic to the "modern" intellectual worldview of Reform Judaism.

The message of the leaders of Conservative Judaism was "Think whatever you like, but do what the law requires." Thus on the question of the relationship to the secular, Conservative Judaism focused on practice rather than belief. This compromise gave Conservative Jews considerable intellectual freedom of interpretation—one could believe or disbelieve any or all elements of the supernatural worldview of premodern Rabbinic Judaism and still be a Jew, as long as one observed Talmudic law in everyday life (although modest compromises in this area were permitted). This position puts the emphasis on orthopraxy (right practice) as opposed to orthodoxy (right belief).

Conservative Judaism fits very well with the pragmatic attitude of modern (especially American) culture. Like Reform Jews, Conservative Jews see Judaism as a historically unfolding religion; but unlike the Reform Jews and more like the Orthodox, the Conservative Jews emphasize an organic continuity. Historical change does not produce abrupt reorientations but gradual development—a development of the unfolding essence of Judaism. And that essence is found not so much in belief as in practice. In this way, Conservative Judaism, like Reform and Orthodox Judaism, sees itself as the logical continuation of the tradition. Conservative Judaism, as the third option, is largely an American phenomenon and is the most widely embraced form of Judaism practiced in America.

Reconstructionism

In addition to the three main strands of modern Judaism there is another movement, known as Reconstructionism, founded in America in the 1930s by Mordecai Kaplan. Kaplan cast his understanding of Judaism in almost completely secular terms drawn from the modern social and historical sciences. Kaplan defined Judaism as the religion of Jewish civilization, where "religion" was understood not in supernatural terms but as the embodiment of the ideals and group identity of a culture. But for that very reason, the practice of the religious rituals of the tradition was an important means of preserving the identity and continuing vitality of Jewish civilization. For Kaplan, Judaism must not be about life beyond death but about improving the individual's life here and now by working for the progress of society. Membership in the Reconstructionist movement is modest, but many of its themes are found in the three main types of secular Judaism that, as we shall see, found the need for religious ritual less compelling.

The Emergence of Secular Forms of Judaism

The dawning of the age of Enlightenment created an optimistic mood among Jews. But that mood did not last, for the promise of inclusion for Jews turned out to be false. The hidden premise of the new offer became apparent in the aftermath of the French Revolution, which had offered full citizenship to Jews. The offer, however, gave *everything to Jews as individuals and nothing to the Jews as a people*. To be a citizen in the new secular society, one had to trade one's religious identity for a secular or nonreligious one.

But even the considerable number of Jews who paid the high price never were accorded the equality that had been promised. The ideals of the Enlightenment were genuine enough, but they quickly crashed on the rocks of the intractability of human prejudice. As more and more Jews were "secularized" in Europe, either abandoning or minimizing their Judaism, they entered into the political and economic life of their respective countries. As they achieved success, a backlash occurred. Throughout Europe, non-Jews began to fear that the Jews were taking over "their" society.

By the end of the nineteenth century a secular, supposedly scientific, definition had come to replace the old religious definition of the Jews. The Jews became defined as a race—an inferior race that had a biologically corrupting influence on society. With the introduction of the language of race, all the old Christian stereotypes of Jews as a rejected people were resurrected in a new guise. Theoretically, at least, the Jews as a religious people could be converted—hence, "the Jewish problem" could be solved.

But race is perceived as a biologically unchangeable fact; people cannot convert from one race to another. Moreover, the advocates of the "scientific" theory of race viewed any attempt at assimilation through intermarriage as racial pollution. In the 1930s the Nazi Party in Germany could begin to exploit this new kind of prejudice against "the Jewish race" to devastating effect.

In the United States, Jews fared better than in Europe. America was forged as a nation of many peoples fleeing religious intolerance in England and on the continent. Anti-Semitism and other forms of religious bigotry were not absent from America's formative history, but Jews in America never experienced pogroms and mass expulsions. American individualism allowed more space for diverse ethnic and religious communal identities.

Jewish immigrants to the United States came in two waves. The first and more modest wave, dating from 1654, consisted of seekers of religious freedom, Jews of Spanish or Portuguese extraction, known as **Sephardic** Jews. The second and much larger wave began in the nineteenth century among the **Ashkenazi**, Jews of eastern Europe who were fleeing persecution and pogrom. By the beginning of World War II, approximately a third of the world's Jews lived in the United States. After World War II, twice as many Jews lived in the United States as in all of Europe.

Sephardic: Jews whose traditions originated in Spain or Portugal

Ashkenazi: Jews whose traditions originated in central and eastern Europe

While Jews in America were being integrated into society, in the late 1800s and early 1900s the Jews of western Europe were once more being persecuted. Most of the Jews of eastern Europe never did sense that they had been invited to join a new Enlightenment order of equality and inclusion. On the contrary, they experienced an increase in persecutions and pogroms. The challenge was to devise a strategy for surviving in societies that were replacing religious anti-Judaism with secular anti-Semitism. And it was among the more fully assimilated and secularized Jews that the new responses emerged, responses that would form a bridge from the modern forms of Judaism (Reform, Orthodox, and Conservative) to the postmodern and postcolonial Judaism of Holocaust and Redemption. These new secular forms of Judaism were Jewish socialism, ethnic (Yiddish) Judaism, and Zionism, each one offering a distinct way of being Jewish. Yet they were capable of combining in interesting and powerful ways that set the stage for the emergence of the Judaism of Holocaust and Redemption.

Jewish Socialism

Some of the strongest currents of Jewish socialism came out of eastern Europe, where secularized Jews saw in socialism another way of resolving the tension between being Jewish and being modern. As noted in Chapter 1, socialism, especially the later "scientific" socialism of Karl Marx, offered an essentially secularized version of the Jewish and Christian myths of history. It was a view of history as a story of exile and return, in which human beings begin in paradise (primitive communism), only to be expelled from the garden into a world of selfishness and sin (class conflict). Socialism, however, promises an eventual transformation into a future global, classless, society in which suffering and injustice will be overcome (including anti-Semitism) and all will live in perfect harmony—a vision very much like that of the messianic kingdom of God. Perhaps this is no coincidence, given that Karl Marx, whose father was a convert to Christianity, was the grandson of a rabbi.

For the many "secularized" Jews of Europe, the socialist story of history offered a new, yet very familiar, framework in which to understand their place in the drama of history. This new secular story gave the Enlightenment-oriented secular Jews a secular way of being Jewish. In this, Jewish socialism adapted the spirit of Reform Judaism, opting for historical development as the key to continuity in Jewish history and for a secular vision of Judaism that favored the prophetic witness of the written Torah (redefined as socialist ethics) over that of the oral Torah traditions of the Talmud. And, like Reform Jews, the Jewish socialists did not need to regard their message as exclusive to Judaism. For them it was enough to see Judaism as the unique contributor of the ideal of social justice to an international ethic for the whole human race. However, unlike their Reform counterparts, Jewish socialists no longer represented themselves as "religious"—for religion belonged to the prescientific age that was passing away.

Who was attracted to this way of being Jewish? In the wake of the Russian Revolution of 1917, socialism was especially attractive to the Jews of Russia and eastern Europe and to the poor Jewish immigrants from these areas who came to the United States. These were Jews who were victims not only of anti-Semitism but also of economic depression and unemployment. The pivotal date for Jewish socialism is usually said to be 1897, the year of the formation of the Bund, or Jewish Worker's Union, in Poland. Many secular Jews joined the socialist movement but rejected all connections with Judaism. They thought of themselves as purely secular, nonreligious persons. Some even vigorously disavowed their Jewish roots, going so far as to contribute to existing currents of anti-Semitism.

Yiddish Ethnic Judaism

Other Jewish socialists, however, wished to retain and affirm their ties to the history of the Jewish people. And so they turned to ethnicity as the key to Jewish identity—an ethnicity that was primarily identified with speaking the Yiddish language.

Even secular Jews who no longer used or knew Hebrew knew Yiddish, the common language of European Jews that developed from about the eleventh century—an amalgam of Hebrew and German. The focus on Yiddish language, and especially Yiddish literature, which often echoes Talmudic and biblical stories, gave secular Jews a way to identify with Judaism without being "religious" and to draw on the wisdom of the tradition.

Yiddish was more than a language. It stood for a way of experiencing and interpreting the world that was still deeply rooted in Judaism. Indeed, ever since the first nation-states emerged in Europe in the seventeenth century, language had been the key to national identity. Through Yiddish, Jews, otherwise dispersed—without a land of their own—sought to sustain their identity as a people in a secular age. As the language of working-class Jews, Yiddish gave Jews a deep sense of "ethnicity," of being bound together in a common historical tradition that offered, as well, a unique identity. That ethnicity could easily be tapped by Jewish socialists to mobilize Jews, that is, to organize them for the workers' revolution that was part of the Marxian scheme of history.

From the end of the nineteenth century until the end of World War II, Jewish socialism was the predominant secular response to modernity among Jews in both Europe and America. But it was not the only response, for there emerged in the nineteenth century another Jewish movement that, in the long run, would be even more influential—Zionism.

The Origins of Zionism

Zionism was born out of disenchantment with modernity and its Enlightenment promises. Unlike Jewish socialism, Zionism did not hold out much hope for a future in which Jews would be accepted as equals in society. In the Zionist view, the only viable solution for Jews in light of the long history of rejection, first by Christendom and then by modern secular society, was to have a state of their own where they could protect themselves.

Theodor Herzl, founder of the Zionist movement to create a Jewish state.

Zion is a biblical term used to refer to the city of David—Jerusalem. The word *Zionism*, coined in 1893, represents a longing virtually as old as Judaism itself: to return from exile, home to Zion. In premodern Rabbinic Judaism, this longing was expressed in a messianic belief that someday God would send a messiah and reestablish a homeland for his people in the land of Israel. For premodern Rabbinic Judaism as well as for much of modern Orthodoxy and ultra-Orthodoxy, the return of Jews to their own land can only be the work of God. Any attempt by Jews to create a Jewish state on their own is presumptuous to the point of blasphemy. Thus when Zionism appeared at the end of the nineteenth century, this secular movement to organize Jews for the creation of a homeland in Palestine was vehemently rejected by the Orthodox and ultra-Orthodox. Reform Jews, having defined themselves as a religious community rather than as a "people," showed little interest in returning to the Middle East. In truth, Zionism did not come into its own until after the Holocaust, when it seemed clear to Jews everywhere that Jews could never count on being accepted as equals in Europe and that the only protection available to them would be in their own homeland—their own state.

A pivotal event in the development of secular (political) Zionism was the Dreyfus affair in France. This trial of a Jewish army officer on charges of treason had a profound

"Distress binds us together and, thus united, we suddenly discover our strength. . . . Let sovereignty be granted us over a portion of the globe large enough to satisfy the rightful requirements of a nation; the rest we shall manage for ourselves."

—Theodor Herzl on Zionism

influence on a young Jewish journalist, Theodor Herzl (1860–1904). The outcome of the trial—conviction of Dreyfus, who was innocent—convinced Herzl that assimilation would never be a feasible option for Jews. In 1896 he wrote *The Jewish State*, in which he rejected assimilation and proposed the creation of a Jewish state. Thus was born a movement that was destined to change the future of Judaism: secular political Zionism. Herzl convened the First Zionist Congress in Basel, Switzerland, in 1897, the same year as the formation of the Jewish socialist Bund in Poland. At this conference the World Zionist Organization was founded. In addition to Palestine, Herzl considered sites for a Jewish homeland in Cyprus. Later, the Sixth Zionist Congress rejected a British offer for a colony in Uganda, then a British protectorate. From that time forward Palestine became the sole option for Zionists. Herzl even wrote a utopian novel, *Altneuland*, imagining a Jewish state in Palestine.

Herzl's Dream and Its Ramifications

Theodor Herzl died in 1904, but not his dream. He left behind a thriving and committed body of political Zionists, the World Zionist Organization. In 1911 this organization began a modest but persistent program of colonizing areas in Palestine, which was then under British colonial control. In 1917, as a result of Zionist efforts, the British foreign secretary, Lord James Balfour, wrote the letter now known as the Balfour Declaration, pledging Britain's support for a Jewish national home in Palestine. France, Italy, and the United States endorsed the idea. One cannot overestimate the tremendous importance of the organizational infrastructure developed in both Jewish socialism (embodied in the Bund) and in Zionism (embodied in the World Zionist Organization). The skills developed in these organizations and transferred to the early

This 1948 poster illustrates a vision of the strength and power of the Israeli Jew, a vision fostered by a Zionist movement prepared to defend the new nation of Israel.

settlements in Palestine, with ongoing support from Jews all over the world, made possible the "sudden" emergence of the state of Israel in 1948 with sponsorship by the United Nations.

Like Reform Judaism, Zionism relied on history and historical change as its link to the premodern traditions of the Jewish people. But unlike Reform Judaism, political Zionism did not think of itself as a religious movement. Therefore, unlike Reform Judaism, Zionism sought continuity in the idea of the Jews as a historical people. Zionists reappropriated the biblical stories of the origins of Israel as part of their story, but the biblical narratives were to serve not as religious stories of God's actions in history but as "secular" stories of the Jewish people's struggles to achieve and preserve their national identity.

Therefore, Zionists retold the stories of origins from a perspective other than that of the premodern Rabbinic tradition of the dual Torah. That tradition had its beginnings in the failure of ancient militant Jewish political messianism (with the defeat of the Zealots) and the success of a political policy of neutrality practiced by the Pharisees. The Zionists reacted to what they perceived as the failure (after almost

2,000 years) of the Rabbinic strategy of accommodation to the surrounding non-Jewish world and to
the more recent Reform strategy of partial assimilation. They were not content to wait to be emancipated by others (whether God or modern gentiles).
They were looking for Jewish heroes who were prepared to emancipate themselves. Thus they retold
the stories of Moses and David as stories of nation
builders and militant revolutionary political leaders.

For the Zionists, the interesting stories were
the marginal ones of the Maccabean revolts of the
second century BCE and those of the Maccabees'
successors, the Zealots, who would rather kill themselves (as they did at Masada in 73 CE) than let the
fight for their land end in surrender. The Zionists
were looking for militant heroes who could serve
as prototypes for a new kind of Jew, one prepared
to fight to the last against all odds. This hero, they
imagined, was the kind of Jew who would reestablish a homeland in Israel.

And yet, while calling for a new kind of Jew,
Zionism was repeating the formative pattern of
Judaism, telling a story of exile and return—a people
who originated in the land of Israel, were forcibly
dispersed for almost 2,000 years, and now sought
to return. Moreover, like Jewish socialism, Zionism
offered secular Jews a powerful secular version of the
goal of history. In the Zionist vision, however, the
Jewish people were not incidental but essential. This
vision recalls the biblical prophecies (Isaiah 65:17–
18) that God will create not only a new heaven and
a new earth but also a new Jerusalem, namely, a reestablished Jewish homeland. All in
all, they made much more comprehensive and creative use of the stories of the biblical
past than did the Yiddish-speaking Jewish socialists.

Like Jewish socialism, Zionism created a new way for secular Jews to be Jewish,
reappropriating the tradition through story, language (which for Zionists was the recovery and reconstruction of Hebrew as a modern language), and social organization.
While before World War II Jewish socialism had more adherents than Zionism, it
was later eclipsed by a Zionism that absorbed and transformed its vision. After the
Holocaust and the destruction of nearly a third of the world's Jews, the validity and
the urgency of the Zionist message seemed self-evident to the overwhelming majority
of Jews, both religious and secular. If they were to survive, Jews must have their own
national homeland.

An aerial view of
Masada, where
first-century Jews who
had resisted Rome
chose suicide rather than
surrender. The defenders
of Masada were an
important symbol of
courage and resistance
to Zionists.

CONTRASTING RELIGIOUS VISIONS

As the following contrasting visions indicate, every religious tradition is capable of generating both visions that encourage peace and understanding and visions that encourage conflict and violence.

Abraham Joshua Heschel, 1907–72

On June 16, 1963, Rabbi Abraham Joshua Heschel sent a telegram to the President of the United States, John F. Kennedy. Heschel and other religious leaders were scheduled to meet with the president the next day to discuss race relations and civil rights in America. The rabbi proposed that the president declare a state of "moral emergency" to aid black Americans. "We forfeit the right to worship God as long as we continue to humiliate negroes. . . . Let religious leaders donate one month's salary toward a fund for negro housing and education. . . . The hour calls for high moral grandeur and spiritual audacity."

Abraham Joshua Heschel, 1907–72, a great Hasidic Jewish scholar and rabbi who marched with Martin Luther King Jr. at Selma and championed the way of nonviolence.

Abraham Joshua Heschel was born in Warsaw, Poland, on January 11, 1907. He was the son of a Hasidic rebbe and a long line of distinguished Hasidic teachers who were deeply steeped in Jewish mysticism. Heschel was a child prodigy. By age fourteen, he had mastered the Talmud and was himself writing Talmudic commentaries. As a young university student he was expelled from Germany by the Nazis and fled back to Poland and then to America, by way of England, shortly before the invasion of Poland. He taught first at Hebrew Union College in Cincinnati and then, for most of his career, at the Jewish Theological Seminary in New York. He is the author of numerous books that have deeply influenced modern Judaism, including *Man Is Not Alone*, *The Sabbath*, *God in Search of Man*, and *Man's Quest for God*.

Heschel's life demonstrates the capacity of Orthodox Judaism to embrace the pluralism of the modern world. As a great Jewish scholar and Hasidic rabbi, Heschel was the leading Jewish voice responding to social injustices in America during the civil rights/Vietnam War era of the 1950s and 1960s. An advocate of nonviolent civil disobedience, Heschel marched with Martin Luther King Jr. from Selma to Montgomery, Alabama, in the spring of 1965 in defense of civil rights for black Americans. "Any god who is mine but not yours, any god concerned with me but not with you," Heschel asserted, is an "idol," or false god. To segregate the races, he insisted, is nothing short of "segregating God."

As a leader of Clergy and Laymen Concerned about Vietnam, the Center for Nonviolent Social Change, and also the Jewish Peace Fellowship, Heschel convinced Dr. King to join the protest against the Vietnam War. To this end, the rabbi introduced the Baptist pastor to the leader of the Vietnamese Buddhist Peace Movement, the monk Thich Nhat Hanh. In this act Heschel showed himself to be a revolutionary not only in his advocacy for social justice for all peoples but in his openness to other religions, working closely with Christians and Buddhists to bring about social justice. Holiness, he insisted, is not to be limited to those of any one religion, not even Judaism. Holiness is defined by the intention of the heart and the righteousness of the deed. To equate God and any one religion is, for Heschel, the essence of idolatry, for God is the all-inclusive reality. The will of God is to be found, he argues, not in uniformity but in diversity. Thus whenever we meet and welcome each other as human beings, sharing a common humanity despite our differences, we encounter the presence of God.

Meir Kahane, 1932–90

Meir Kahane was born in Brooklyn, New York, on August 1, 1932. The son of a rabbi deeply involved in the Zionist movement, he too became a rabbi. In 1968 he founded the JDL, or Jewish Defense League. Kahane was no advocate for nonviolence. On the contrary, he argued that Jews cannot depend on others to defend them and need to learn to protect themselves, using violence if necessary.

Kahane's life illustrates the insistence of ultra-Orthodoxy that there can only be "one way" for all Jews, a way that protects them from pollution by the secular world and all religious diversity. In 1971 he moved to Israel and founded the anti-Arab Kach Party, which called for the forcible removal of all Arabs. This party attracted a strong following among the Gush Emunim and other religious Zionists. In 1984 Kahane was elected to the Knesset, but his party was banned before the next election, in 1988, on the grounds that Kach incited racism. Kahane was assassinated by an Egyptian Muslim radical in New York City on November 5, 1990, after a speech urging all American Jews to return to Israel to protect the land from the Arabs. In the speech he had warned of a coming apocalypse in which the American stock market would collapse, leading to a new holocaust against all Jews who were still in the United States.

Meir Kahane, 1932–90, did not share Rabbi Abraham Joshua Heschel's commitment to nonviolence. His party was banned from the Knesset (the Israeli governing body) in 1984 for inciting racism.

Kahane was an advocate of a messianic Zionism that was violently apocalyptic, expecting the messiah to come soon and lead the Jews in driving all Arabs out of Israel. He rejected the view of some religious Zionists that a secular state might be a stepping-stone to the final appearance of a genuinely religiously Jewish state. Kahane had little patience with the secular state of Israel and saw its secular leaders as the enemies of all religious Jews and hinderers of the creation of a genuine Jewish state. For Kahane, any act that elevated Jews and humiliated Arabs and all other enemies of the Jews was viewed as sanctifying God's name and hastening the coming of the messiah.

In 1994 the Kach Party and its offshoot, Kahane Chai, were designated terrorist organizations by both the Israeli government and the U.S. government. This labeling was largely in response to the 1994 attack on a mosque in Hebron during which a Kach member, Baruch Goldstein, killed thirty-four Muslims. Then, in 1995, another Kahane admirer, Yigal Amir, assassinated the prime minister of Israel, Yitzhak Rabin, to put a stop to his attempts to make peace with the Palestinians. Rabin's willingness to consider compromising with the Palestinians on land issues was viewed as treason by these radical Zionists, and in their eyes this justified his murder. While most Jews remember Kahane as a terrorist, some hold him up as a hero, martyr, and true revolutionary for a militant Zionism that preaches that, by divine command, Israel is for Jews only

Quotations from: Abraham Joshua Heschel, *Moral Grandeur and Spiritual Audacity* (essays edited by Susannah Heschel) (New York: Farrar, Straus and Giroux, 1996).

Some Sabras, secular Jews who led the Zionist movement to create an Israeli state, stand guard over their fields on a kibbutz in Israel in the early days of the new nation.

Zionism shaped a nation and turned a utopian dream into a reality—the state of Israel. Jewish ethnic socialism and Zionism together represented a powerful, if ambivalent, rejection of the modern era and its ideal of assimilation as defined by the Enlightenment. It was the amalgamation of these ways of thinking that made a natural bridge to the Judaism of Holocaust and Redemption, for without the socialist-Zionist revolution, there would be no state of Israel. And without the state of Israel, there would be only Holocaust and no sense of redemption—no sense of rescue from the forces of slavery and death similar to their ancient deliverance from slavery in Egypt into the "promised land."

The new state of Israel became a haven for Jews from around the world, including these Ethiopian schoolchildren.

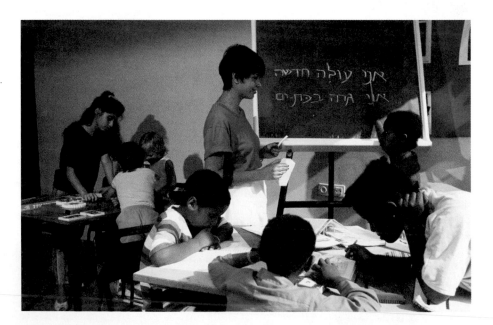

Judaism and Postmodern Trends in a Postcolonial World (1967–)

Challenges to Jewish Faith After the Holocaust

In 1933 Adolf Hitler and the Nazi Party came to power in Germany. By 1939 they had drawn Europe into World War II, a six-year war of expansion that was meant to give additional *Lebensraum* ("living space") to what the Nazis considered to be the superior Aryan race of Germany. Near the end, however, when Germany was losing badly and soldiers and supplies were desperately needed at the front, trains were diverted to the task of transporting Jews to the death camps. Hitler was more desperate to rid the world of Jews than he was to win the war.

The **Holocaust** was a singular event in human history that brought the modern era of progress to an end in mass death. *Holocaust* (which means "burnt sacrifice") is the name given to the attempt by Nazi Germany to eliminate an entire people, the Jews. Unlike the millions of others who died on the battlefronts of World War II, the Jews were not military combatants (see Map 3.4). The Jews of Germany were not enemies of Germany, but citizens. There was no military or territorial advantage to be had by systematically killing them. They were marked for death simply because they existed. Germans, defeated and humiliated in World War I (1914–18) and suffering from extreme economic depression as a result of war reparations, chose not to blame these troubles on the aggressive military actions of their government during the war. Instead, they said, "The Jews are our misfortune"—they are to blame. The Nazis rose to power partly by portraying the Jews as a racial pollutant or a diseased growth on the healthy body of the German people that had to be surgically cut out if the nation was to be restored to health and greatness.

When the Nazi Party came to power, the Jews were stripped of their citizenship and all their legal rights; their homes and businesses were appropriated; and they were herded into boxcars that delivered them to an elaborate system of death camps, where they were either worked to death as slaves or murdered in specially designed gas chambers made to order for mass killings. At the most infamous of the camps, Auschwitz, in Poland, it is estimated that 2 million Jews were executed.

One has to ask: Why the Jews? Blaming a scapegoat for misfortune is not unusual in history, but what induced the Nazis to pick the Jews for this role? The answer takes us back in large part to the story of the beginnings of Christianity (which we will discuss further in Chapter 4). As a Jewish sect that came to be dominated by non-Jews, gentiles saw themselves as having superseded and replaced the Jews as God's chosen people. The establishment of Christianity as the dominant religion of the Roman Empire led to both legal discrimination and popular discrimination that often was expressed in violence against Jews as "the children of the devil"—a people most Christians believed had been rejected by God for their role in the "killing of Jesus, the Son of God."

Holocaust: the attempt by Nazi Germany to exterminate the Jewish people

Map 3.4 The Holocaust.

Moreover the "negative witness" theory suggested by the influential Christian theologian Augustine of Hippo portrayed the Jews as condemned to wander the earth without a home, their misery supposedly offering negative proof of the truth of Christianity. From the time of this early theologian (354–430) forward, through the Middle Ages and into the modern period, Jews were the scapegoats, blamed for whatever misfortunes occurred in Western civilization. Indeed, Hitler played on popular Christian anti-Jewish sentiments to rise to the position of chancellor of Germany. Later, neither the Catholic nor the Protestant churches of Germany officially protested the Nazi treatment of the Jews—only the treatment of Jewish converts to Christianity.

The Nazis rounded up European Jews and sent them to the death camps in boxcars. These Jewish prisoners, some of them children, were photographed at the infamous Auschwitz death camp.

It took more than Christian anti-Judaism to make the Holocaust possible: For instance, the rise of secularism and scientific-bureaucratic forms of social control played an important part. Nevertheless, it is hard to imagine the Holocaust's occurring without the significant contribution of Christian anti-Semitism.

The Holocaust deeply challenges the Jewish faith orientation promoted in the stories of the exodus and exile traditions. If these stories promised a God who would always be with the people of the covenant, guiding and protecting them, then the Holocaust seemed to prove this promise a lie. Many Jews felt that God had failed to keep his promises.

After the Holocaust, some of the most Orthodox of Jews wanted to treat the Holocaust as a tragedy of the same type as the fall of the first and second temples, where these tragedies had been explained as due to a failure to keep the covenant. In fact, they proposed that the best way to remember the Holocaust was to include it in the period of fasting and mourning of Tisha B'Av. But to many other Jews, both secular and religious, this seemed wholly inappropriate. For the main victims of the Holocaust were not the most liberal and secularized Jews but rather the most orthodox and observant population in Jewry, the Jews of eastern Europe. Moreover, for many

Jews the scope of the tragedy was so great that the argument of "failure to keep the covenant" faithfully enough seemed inadequate to explain it.

How does one commemorate such an event? And how, after the Holocaust, could Jews go on believing the promises of God to guide and protect them on their journey through time? Indeed, a major debate is being carried out in contemporary Judaism in which a number of important authors offer suggestions on how Jews should respond to the Holocaust.

One author, Richard Rubenstein, says that God died at Auschwitz, and Jews will have to go on with their stories and their rituals without God. Emil Fackenheim argues that, on the contrary, God is still present in history. He justifies this view by suggesting that it is as if Jews had heard a silent yet commanding voice from Auschwitz, giving them a new commandment, a 614th commandment to be added to the 613 in the Torah. This commandment demands that Jews remain Jewish lest they allow Judaism to die, thus giving Hitler a posthumous victory.

Elie Wiesel, the Nobel Prize–winning author who is himself a survivor of Auschwitz, sees it somewhat differently.[2] Only the Jew knows, says Wiesel, that one can have the *chutzpah* (audacity) to argue with God as long as it is in defense of God's creation—as Abraham argued with God over the fate of the innocent at Sodom (Genesis 18:22–33). Indeed, a Jew has the right to put God on trial and find him guilty of abandoning the Jews during the Holocaust.

Another major Holocaust scholar, Irving Greenberg, argues that after Auschwitz, Jews can only live a "momentary faith"—tossed back and forth between the stories of the Exodus and the stories of the Holocaust. In one moment a Jew might believe in the promises of Sinai, only in the next moment to have them clouded over by memories of the smokestacks of Auschwitz. Like Wiesel, Greenberg argues that Jews

TEACHINGS OF RELIGIOUS WISDOM:
The 614th Commandment

The post-Holocaust Jewish scholar Emil Fackenheim, himself a survivor of the Holocaust, argues that Jews must not give in to despair and abandon their faith after the atrocities of the Holocaust. God, he says, speaks even from Auschwitz and gives Jews a new commandment to be added to the 613 he gave at Sinai.

Jews are forbidden to hand Hitler posthumous victories. They are commanded to survive as Jews, lest the Jewish people perish. They are commanded to remember the victims of Auschwitz lest their memory perish. They are forbidden to despair of man and his world, and to escape into either cynicism or otherworldliness, lest they cooperate in delivering the world over to the forces of Auschwitz. Finally, they are forbidden to despair of the God of Israel, lest Judaism perish. . . . A Jew may not respond to Hitler's attempt to destroy Judaism by himself cooperating in its destruction. In ancient times, the unthinkable Jewish sin was idolatry. Today, it is to respond to Hitler by doing his work.

Source: Emil L. Fackenheim, *God's Presence in History* (Northvale, NJ, and Jerusalem: Jason Aronson Inc., 1997), p. 84.

cannot be required to embrace the covenant, and yet they do so freely. Greenberg observes that this embrace takes on a wide variety of forms, from the extremely orthodox to the extremely secular. And after Auschwitz, he insists, all Jews, from the extremely orthodox to the extremely secular, are obligated to accept each other as Jews, accepting contemporary Jewish pluralism as an authentic covenantal pluralism. For Jews to turn their backs on other Jews, as some of the ultra-Orthodox in the state of Israel do when they refuse to acknowledge the Jewishness of non-Orthodox Jews, is another way of granting Hitler a posthumous victory. In a post-Holocaust and postcolonial world, Jews find themselves once more facing the question that arose in the first century of the common era: Which of all the ways of being Jewish is the right way? What has changed after Auschwitz, says Greenberg, is that Jews are free to observe or not to observe the covenant; they are not, however, free to reject Jews who exercise this freedom.

Post-Holocaust Judaism offers an alternative to the "one way" of ultra-Orthodoxy. This is a postmodern form of Judaism, in which there is not one single way to truth and to faithfulness but many. Covenantal pluralism is affirmed insofar as great diversity in thought *and* practice, both secular and religious, is allowed. Only one practice is not negotiable: the obligation of post-Holocaust Jews to accept one another in their diversity. Both ultra-Orthodoxy and the Judaism of Holocaust and Redemption seek a way out of what they see as the spiritual poverty of a modernism that made the Holocaust possible. The choice they offer to all Jews is either withdrawal from or involvement in the modern world, either back to what they view as premodern uniformity or forward to a new age of postmodern Jewish pluralism.

Finally, the post-Holocaust Jewish scholar Marc Ellis insists that Israeli Jews must never use the suffering of Jews in the Holocaust as an excuse for the oppression of their Palestinian neighbors. They must remember that the covenant relation of the Jews to the land includes the demands to ensure justice for all and to show compassion to the stranger. Not only must Jews accept other Jews in their diversity, they must accept their Christian and Muslim Palestinian neighbors in Israel in an environment of justice and peace for all. Such a task is not easy when extremists on all sides seek to undermine genuine efforts at compromise and cooperation, and yet many in the state of Israel continue the struggle to find that middle ground.

Challenges to Jewish Existence After the Holocaust

This new Judaism of Holocaust and Redemption, which has proven very attractive to American Judaism, Israeli Judaism, and Israeli nationalism, has a postmodern and postcolonial orientation. That is, instead of seeking to return to some premodern orthodoxy emphasizing one truth and one way, it attempts to find unity in the diversity of religious and secular Jews. Even its new "holy days" (or "holidays") display characteristics of both the holy and the secular. Indeed, two days that seem to be entering the Jewish calendar are recollections of seemingly secular events—*Yom Hashoah* (Day

TALES OF SPIRITUAL TRANSFORMATION

The Nobel Prize–winning author Elie Wiesel, a survivor of Auschwitz, remembers an event that took place while he was a prisoner there. His tale shows that not even consignment to the death camps of the Holocaust could destroy Jewish faith.

The Jewish festival of the giving of the Torah by God to Moses, *Simhath Torah*, arrived. However, there was no Torah in the camp that Jews could use to ritually carry in celebration. Indeed, during this celebration Hasidic Jews pick up the Torah and literally dance with it to express their joy. So an old man looks around for a substitute to use for the Torah celebration. He sees a young boy and asks him,

"Do you remember what you learned in heder (Torah school)?" "Yes I do," replied the boy. "Really," said the man, "you really remember Sh'ma Yisrael" (the confession of faith in the oneness of God). "I remember much more," said the boy. "Sh'ma Yisrael is enough," said the man. And he lifted the boy, clasped him in his arms and began dancing with him—as though *he* were the Torah. And all joined in. They all sang and danced and cried. They wept, but they sang with fervor—never before had Jews celebrated *Simhath Torah* with such fervor.

Source: Elie Wiesel, *A Jew Today* (New York: Random House, 1978), p. 146.

of Desolation), recalling the Holocaust, and *Yom Ha'atzmaut* (Independence Day), celebrating the founding of the modern state of Israel.

The impact of the Holocaust on Jewish consciousness cannot be overstated. During the Holocaust the Nazis nearly succeeded in their goal of eliminating Jews from the face of the earth. Nearly a third of all Jews died in the Holocaust; nearly two-thirds of the Jews of Europe died. The eastern European Jewish communities were hit the hardest. Ninety percent of these Jews and more than 80 percent of all the rabbis, Talmudic scholars, and Talmudic students then alive were murdered.

Jews might have despaired after the devastation of the Holocaust, but the founding of the state of Israel by the United Nations in 1948 gave them hope. The counterbalancing of the Holocaust and the founding of the state of Israel fits the great formative story of Jewish existence—exile and return. After 2,000 years without a homeland, many Jews experienced the ability to return to Israel as a Jewish state as a miraculous act of divine redemption akin to the return to the land of promise after slavery in Egypt or after exile in Babylon. That redemption makes it possible for Jews to remember the Holocaust without despairing.

It is in this context that we review the history of the establishment and development of the state of Israel, which marks an important turning point in the demise of colonialism and the emergence of a postcolonial, post-Holocaust Judaism. In 1922 the League of Nations gave Britain a mandate over Palestine, which had been under Muslim control. Meanwhile, the Balfour Declaration of 1917 had already set the stage for the establishment of a homeland for Jews in the area, alongside the existing Palestinian population. In supporting this policy, Britain legitimated the goal of the international Zionist movement while doing little to hasten its implementation. Thus at the conclusion of World War II, Palestine was still under the British mandate.

In 1947, as a member of the newly formed United Nations, Britain asked the General Assembly to establish a special committee on Palestine. The report of this committee, UNSCOP, led to a resolution to divide Palestine into two states—one Jewish and the other Arab (see Map 3.5). The state of Israel was established on May 14, 1948, the date on which Great Britain gave up official control of the area. Within a year Israel would be admitted to the United Nations.

The creation of a Jewish state was supported by two key UN member nations, the United States and the Soviet Union, and it represented the triumph of the Zionist movement. The Arab states, however, refused to accept the UN partition plan, and on May 15, 1948, the armies of seven Arab states invaded the newly formed nation and the war for independence was under way. The war was fought in two phases, with an intervening cease-fire, and ended in the defeat of the Arab forces and an armistice with the Egyptians in February 1949. Later agreements were signed with Jordan, Lebanon, and Syria; however, none was signed with Iraq. Relations with neighboring Arab states remained tense throughout the decades that followed, flaring again into the wars of 1967 and 1973.

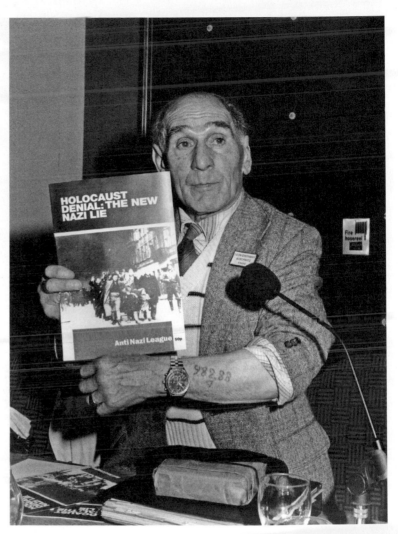

Leon Greenman, a Jewish survivor of Auschwitz, displays his Auschwitz serial number tattoo after addressing an Anti-Nazi League meeting in Brighton, England.

It is hard to overstate the impact of the 1967 war on Judaism. In June of that year, the state of Israel was seriously threatened by four predominantly Muslim nations: Egypt, Jordan, Syria, and Iraq. Israeli forces were overwhelmingly outnumbered, and the country was surrounded by 250,000 troops, having at their disposal some 2,000 tanks as well as 700 fighter planes and bombers. A UN Emergency Force had withdrawn in May, and Israeli diplomatic initiatives seeking intervention from European

Map 3.5 The creation of the state of Israel.

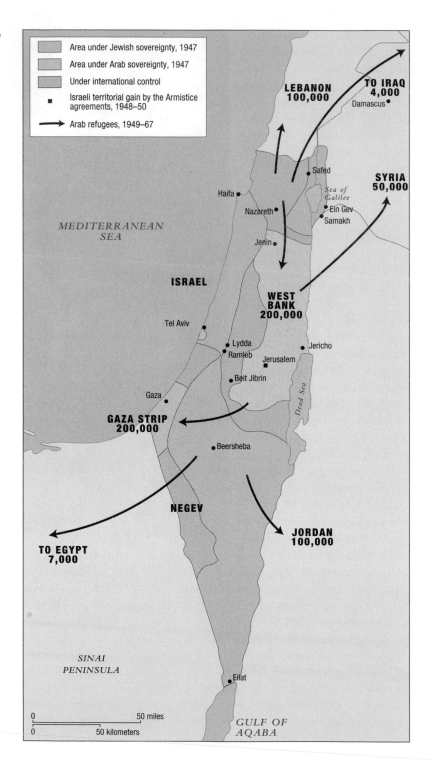

Area under Jewish sovereignty, 1947

Area under Arab sovereignty, 1947

Under international control

Israeli territorial gain by the Armistice agreements, 1948–50

Arab refugees, 1949–67

LEBANON
100,000

TO IRAQ
4,000

Damascus

Safed

Sea of
Galilee

SYRIA
50,000

Haifa

Nazareth

Ein Gev
Samakh

MEDITERRANEAN
SEA

Jenin

ISRAEL

WEST
BANK
200,000

Tel Aviv

Lydda
Ramleh

Jericho

Jerusalem

Beit Jibrin

Dead Sea

Gaza

GAZA STRIP
200,000

Beersheba

NEGEV

JORDAN
100,000

TO EGYPT
7,000

SINAI
PENINSULA

Eilat

0   50 miles
0   50 kilometers

GULF OF
AQABA

This Israeli Rosh Hashanah card celebrates Moshe Dayan and Yitzhak Rabin as heroes of the victory of Israel in the 1967 Six-Day War.

Youths celebrate the founding of the modern state of Israel at the Western Wall, waving an Israeli flag. The new state has deep religious significance for many Jews, who see it as a sign of God's saving activity after the near annihilation of European Jews in the Holocaust.

countries and America met with feeble responses. Israel perceived itself to be alone, without allies and doomed to what many feared would be a second holocaust. Israeli armed forces, under the leadership of General Yitzhak Rabin, staged a surprise air attack on the morning of June 5. In a brilliant series of military moves, Israel routed the combined Arab forces in a war that was over in six days.

At the end of the war, Israel occupied territory formerly under the control of the Egyptians and the Syrians—from the Suez Canal to the Golan Heights. In the process Israel had taken control of the entire area west of the Jordan River, including the Old City of Jerusalem (on June 7), recovering one of the holiest places for all Jews, the Western Wall of the Second Temple (destroyed by the Romans in 70 CE), which had been under Jordanian control (see Map 3.6). As the dust of the Six-Day War settled, Jews both in the land of Israel and in Diaspora were overwhelmed with a sense of awe at their seemingly miraculous deliverance. Even among the most secular or nonreligious Jews, many could not help but see the redemptive hand of God in these events.

In response to this unexpected defeat, at a conference held in Khartoum in August 1967, Arab nations adopted a policy of no recognition of or negotiations with Israel. Under new leadership, the three-year-old Palestinian Liberation Organization began a long and systematic policy of guerrilla warfare against Israel.

But the essential fact for Jews has been that Israel exists and has withstood all onslaughts against it. For many Jews the 1967 war was the turning point. From that time forward the meaningful connection between the

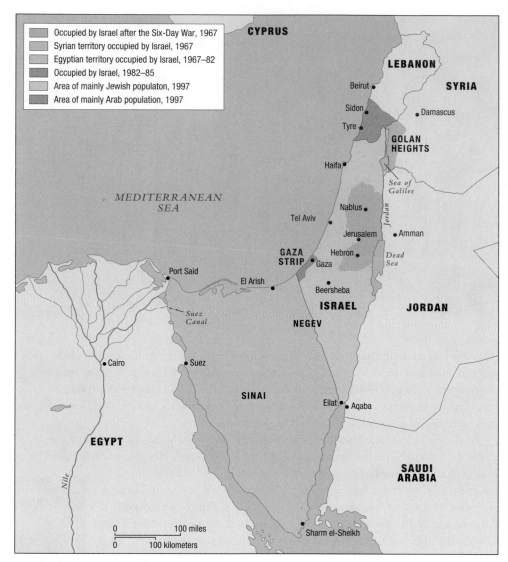

Map 3.6 Arab-Israeli conflict from 1967.

Holocaust and the founding of the state of Israel could not be ignored. The two events became indissolubly linked in Jewish minds, and the days of remembrance of these two events became ever more prominent in the Jewish calendar.

The Yom Kippur War of 1973 was less decisive than the 1967 war in military terms, but it sparked a resurgence of religious Zionism. On October 6, 1973, the Egyptian army penetrated the Israeli–occupied territory of the Sinai peninsula, while the Syrians invaded the Golan Heights. The surprise attack occurred on Yom Kippur, one of the holiest days in the Jewish calendar. Although caught off guard, Israel

The signing of the Camp David Peace Accord on March 26, 1979. U.S. President Jimmy Carter (center) is flanked by President Anwar Sadat of Egypt on his right and Israeli premier Menachem Begin on his left.

rallied and successfully rebuffed its attackers, but the event undermined confidence in the leadership of the Labor Party. Thus the ground was prepared for the rise of the conservative Likud Party, with the election of Menachem Begin as prime minister in 1977. Another result was increased political influence from religious Zionists like the Gush Emunim.

The Gush Emunim were committed to the notion that none of the occupied territories from the 1967 War was to be given back in any peace agreement after the 1973 war. Believing strongly that the Jews were chosen by God to inherit this land, they were no more inclined to share it with their Palestinian neighbors than many Christian and Muslim Palestinians were to share it with the Jews. Consequently, the Gush Emunim began an intensive program of establishing settlements in the occupied territory, an activity that was not authorized by the Israeli government. When Menachem Begin came to power, however, he supported the settlements. In this fashion, religious Zionism began to play an important role in Israeli public policy.

While the settlements were in their infancy, however, Begin signed a peace treaty with the president of Egypt, Anwar Sadat. This agreement, signed at Camp David in 1979 with the encouragement of U.S. President Jimmy Carter, called for Israel to return occupied territory in the Sinai. The Gush Emunim saw the territorial rollback as a betrayal of God's will. The movement splintered in 1982 with the death of its spiritual leader, Rabbi Zvi Yehuda Kook, and some adherents began to wage guerrilla warfare against Palestinian militants. Some even planned to blow up the mosque on the Temple Mount in Jerusalem, but they were discovered before the plan could be carried out. The leaders were arrested in 1984, and the movement lost a large measure of the public support it had enjoyed.

The Struggle over Jerusalem

The present struggle for sovereignty over Jerusalem is symbolic of the convergence of the spiritual and the physical, the religious and the political in the Middle East. This "holy" city is historically as well as scripturally claimed by Jews, Muslims, and Christians. For the Jews, Jerusalem is the "mountain of the Lord." The Mishnah (second-century compendium of Jewish laws) asserts that the Shekinah, or divine presence, has never left the Western Wall. Jerusalem is a predominant symbol and source of Jewish religious as well as nationalist identity.

In 70 CE the Romans destroyed the second temple in Jerusalem and expelled its Jewish population. Jews scattered throughout the world. Although many assimilated into the countries of their Diaspora, they retained their faith and Jewish identity. Each year, Jews across the world conclude the Passover ceremonies with the determined wish "Next Year in Jerusalem." The prophetic idea of an eventual gathering of all Jewish exiles into the land of their origin has influenced the attitudes of Westerners, Jewish as well as Christian, toward Jerusalem. The repeated assertion by Israeli leaders that a united Jerusalem is the eternal capital of Israel is an articulation of this biblical belief translated into a political vision. For 2,000 years, Jews have nursed the idea of returning to reclaim Jerusalem.

For Christians, Jerusalem is the site of their faith's origins and early history, where Jesus preached his message, was crucified, died, and was buried. It was there that in Christian belief Jesus was miraculously resurrected from the grave and ascended into heaven. The religious significance of Jerusalem was translated into the political when Pope Urban II summoned the First Crusade to recover Jerusalem and establish a Christian kingdom there.

Christian political interest in Jerusalem was manifest more recently in the British mandate over Palestine and in continuing U.S. support for Israel. Christian groups and institutions such as the World Council of Churches and the Vatican have also maintained keen interest in the status of Jerusalem.

At the same time, Jerusalem and Palestine continue to be the home of Arab Christians, who have lived there for centuries. It is also significant to the many Christians who make pilgrimages to the historical Christian churches and sites in Jerusalem.

Jerusalem is one of the three most sacred places of Islam. It was the first city to which Muslims turned in prayer (subsequently changed to Mecca), and in Muslim belief it is the place from which the Prophet Muhammad ascended to the heavens (miraj haqq) on a winged horse. According to Muslim eschatology (an aspect of theology that addresses the final events of human history), Jerusalem is the place where the end of time commences. Today, the loss of control of Jerusalem indicates to Muslims their ultimate defeat in what many regard as the unending Crusades launched by Christians against Islam. Failure to regain sovereignty over Jerusalem, they believe, is indicative of the decline of Islamic civilization and the failure of Palestinian aspirations to decolonize their land.

Jerusalem has also become a symbol of Western imperialism for many Muslims, who see the continued expansion of Israel as a Western plot to dominate their lands and destroy Islam. They fear that under Israeli rule, Islam's third most important mosque (al-Aqsa/Bait-ul-Maqdis) will eventually be destroyed. Indeed, some Jewish religious leaders and groups have expressed plans to rebuild the temple of King Solomon on that very site. The continued settlement of Jews in Arab East Jerusalem and the forced evacuation of Palestinians, both Christian and Muslim, have only reinforced Muslim fears.

Finally, the myth of supersession shared by Christians and Muslims further complicates things. Much as Christians have seen themselves as inheritors of Judaism who supersede or replace Judaism with a new and more complete revelation (Christianity), so Muslims see themselves as the inheritors of Judaism and Christianity. They believe that Islam is a continuation and completion of Abraham's faith and that the Quran is the final revelation sent by the same God who sent his revelations through Moses and Jesus. In that same vein, many believe that they are the true inheritors of the Holy Land, symbolized by the conquest of Jerusalem by Umar ibn al-Khattab, the second of the "Rightly Guided Caliphs," in 637 CE.

The situation became more complicated in contemporary times. In 1948, the status of Jerusalem became a global issue when, in the aftermath of the Holocaust, the United Nations partitioned Palestine to create the state of Israel as a homeland for the Jews.

The struggle for Jerusalem is indeed representative of the intersection of religion and politics in the Middle East, now with global ramifications. It is in Jerusalem that the temporal, spiritual, political, cultural, and territorial converge. Jerusalem is both modern and traditional. It is modern in its status as the aspiration of Jewish and Palestinian nationalism, and it is traditional in its sacred significance to three religions. For many there can be no political solution for Jerusalem without a religious solution. In Israel, where some forms of Zionism fuse religion and nationalism, the modern and the traditional are not distinguishable; neither are the religious and the political.

A particular reading of postcolonial history created the false expectation that the Middle East was well on the way toward secularization. History is not progressing according to the script that modernity had envisaged for the region. Religion has once again become a major theme in the study of world politics, particularly in the context of the Middle East. Rather than receding, religion has returned to the center stage. The region is developing both in political as well as economic terms, but not along the lines that Western social sciences had predicted. The long history of the nexus between power and religion and current conditions in the Middle East suggests that Western-style secularism will continue to be challenged by the contemporary religious resurgence.

In recent years, new Islamic republics have been declared in Iran, Sudan, and Afghanistan.

In Morocco, as in Saudi Arabia, the monarchy is strongly legitimized by its close association with Islam. In Jordan, King Hussein never forgot to mention his lineage, which he traced back to the Prophet Muhammad. Muslim rulers remain acutely sensitive to the power of religion, and opposition movements also appeal to Islam for legitimacy and popular support.

Similarly, Israel's very existence and identity remain tied to Judaism. Many believers base their political agenda on issues and sites that their faith holds sacred. Whether to defend the status quo or to condemn it, politicians in the Middle East, Jews as well as Muslims, invoke religious categories. The difference between the role of religion in contemporary politics, in politics in the precolonial past, and in politics in the postcolonial secular era has been one of degree, not of kind.

In the twenty-first century, religion will continue to be a major driving force in global politics. It performs many political functions, just as politics serves many religious functions in the traditional land of God, the Middle East. Religion is a source of identity as well as signification, providing symbols of authentication and meaning for social and political existence. It is the basis for states as well as a source of civil society. It is invoked to give legitimacy to systems and regimes and to provide revolutionary fodder to challenge the legitimacy of states, systems, and regimes. Jerusalem represents the locus where all three Abrahamic faiths have come together in the past and remains the subject of common and at times competing claims. The challenge for the religious politics of the Middle East in coming years, as with the issue of Jerusalem, will be to develop a pluralistic mode of existence based on the recognition of shared principles, values, and interests amid acknowledged religious and political differences.

Source: Adapted from "Religion in the Middle East" (by John Esposito with Muqtedar Khan). In Deborah J. Gerner, ed., *Understanding the Contemporary Middle East* (Boulder, CO: Lynne Rienner, 1999).

The existence of the state of Israel represents for many Jews a redemption from 2,000 years of powerlessness, persecution, and exile. The state of Israel represents, for Jews, a new age of politics, power, and a capacity for self-defense in a world that has often been bent on subjugating or destroying them. Today, Jews continue to struggle to find a way to live constructively with their own diversity in the Diaspora. And they struggle as well to maintain the autonomy of the state of Israel, while seeking a just and lasting peace in the Middle East.

Conclusion

What we learn from the study of the diverse ways of being Jewish is that religion can either reject the secular or accommodate it. What form shall the life of the people Israel take in the modern world? That is the issue being debated among Jews as they move into the future. Those like the ultra-Orthodox, who reject the secular, see religion as being about a sacred, eternal, and unchangeable way of life that must not be profaned by accommodation with the world. Consequently, they are segregationists. The ultra-Orthodox, like fundamentalists everywhere, see modern secular society as profane—a contradiction of the sacred order embodied in premodern religious forms. All modern and postmodern/post-Holocaust religious forms of Judaism, by contrast, see the holy and the secular less as opposites than as complementary, and they tend to see historical change as the medium through which God reveals himself in time.

For modernist and post-Holocaust Jews, knowledge of the historical development of Judaism (in varying degrees) became an inherent component in their self-understanding and has made it possible for each person to admit new levels of diversity and change into the tradition. The modernist forms of Judaism (Reform, Conservative, and Orthodox) tend to regard diversity as competition in which one is "more right" than the others although all are Jews. The postmodern Judaism of Holocaust and Redemption envisions the diverse forms of Judaism as equal and mutually supporting. To the ultra-Orthodox, by contrast, diversity is apostasy, and segregation from the non-Jewish modern world and from all forms of Judaism that compromise with that world is the only path to being the true Israel or covenant people.

For most ultra-Orthodox, to admit any change is to condone relativism, and with it unbelief. For modernist and post-Holocaust Jews, to admit change is a matter of intellectual integrity: Since time cannot be stopped, some change is inevitable. Jews at the two ends of the spectrum disagree over how much change is permissible, with the Orthodox demanding a return to the fundamental truths and practices of premodern Judaism and the secular Judaisms accepting at least some integration with the non-Jewish world. For Reform, Conservative, and Holocaust and Redemption Jews, God reveals himself in the continued unfolding of history. For ethnicists, socialists, and Zionists, meaning is to be found not in the God of history but in the history itself. Such "secular" Jews are not "religious" in the traditional sense of biblical theism, but they do display one type of religious behavior commonly found in the history of religions—reverence for the ways of the ancestors, ways that are held sacred.

All but the ultra-Orthodox are convinced that to be the true Israel not only does not require Jews to go back but allows them to go forward. The strength of the modern/postmodern forms of Judaism is in their ability to adapt Jewish life to new environments and situations. The strength of the Orthodox and ultra-Orthodox is in challenging those who would adapt not to sacrifice the heart of Jewish religious existence as a people—God, Torah, and Israel. They would argue that history and Jewish ethnicity are not an adequate substitute.

The adventure continues as Jews everywhere wrestle with each other and with the world around them over what it means to be a Jew—especially in the state of Israel, where there can be no peace unless accommodation both among Jews and with their Christian and Muslim neighbors is found. And yet the very struggle of Jews everywhere, whether secular or religious, among themselves and with the non-Jewish world around them, is very Jewish. We need only recall the story of how Jacob's name was changed to Israel (Genesis 32:23–32). Jacob wrestled with the stranger who would not tell Jacob his name but instead blessed Jacob and changed Jacob's name to Israel, meaning "he who has wrestled with God and human beings and prevails." Throughout history, the drama of Judaism has been to wrestle with God and the stranger. Today, whether secular or religious, Jews are still deeply shaped by the stories of Israel, they still wrestle with the stranger, and they still prevail.

> Jacob was left alone; and a man (a stranger) wrestled with him until daybreak. . . . Then he said, "Let me go, for the day is breaking." But Jacob said, "I will not let you go, unless you bless me." So he said to him, . . . "you shall no longer be called Jacob, but Israel, for you have striven with God and with humans, and have prevailed. . . . So Jacob called the place Peniel, saying, "For I have seen God face to face and yet my life is preserved."
>
> —NRSV, Genesis 32:24–30

Discussion Questions

1. What does it mean to say that Judaism is a form of the "myth of history"? Give examples from both the biblical and postbiblical periods.

2. At what point in biblical history did the fundamental pattern of Jewish experience emerge, and what shape did it take? Give two examples from the history of Judaism, one secular and one religious.

3. What is the Talmud, and what is its significance for the religion of Judaism?

4. Compare and contrast Enlightenment Judaism (Haskalah) and Hasidic Judaism.

5. Whom would you nominate as the three most important postbiblical figures in the history of Judaism, and why?

6. In what ways have secular forms of Judaism transformed the shape of contemporary religious forms of Judaism? Give examples and explain.

7. How does the history of anti-Judaism in Western Christianity and Western civilization relate to the Holocaust?

8. What was the impact of the Holocaust on the shape of modern and postmodern forms of Jewish life, religious and secular?

9. What is the Judaism of Holocaust and Redemption, and how does it relate to modern and premodern forms of Judaism? Also, why might it be seen as the alternative to ultra-Orthodoxy?

10. Is Zionism a secular form of Judaism or a religious form, or both? Explain, with historical examples.

Key Terms

Ashkenazi	Hasidism	synagogue
bar mitzvah	Holocaust	Talmud
bat mitzvah	Israel	Tanak
circumcision	Kabbalah	Tannaim
covenant	kosher	temple
Diaspora	Marranos	Tisha B'Av
dual Torah	Mishnah	Tzaddik
Gemara	*mitzvot*	Zionism
gentile	Rabbinic	*Zohar*
halakhah	Sephardic	
haredim	*Shema*	

Suggested Readings

Fasching, Darrell J. *Narrative Theology After Auschwitz: From Alienation to Ethics* (Minneapolis: Fortress Press, 1992).

Greenberg, Irving. *The Jewish Way* (New York: Summit Books, 1988).

———. *For the Sake of Heaven and Earth: The New Encounter Between Judaism and Christianity* (New York: Jewish Publication Society of America, 2004).

Isaacs, Ronald H., and Kerry M. Olitzky, eds. *Critical Documents of Jewish History: A Source Book* (London: Jason Aronson, 1995).

Johnson, Paul. *A History of the Jews* (New York: Harper & Row, 1987).

Keppel, Gilles. *The Revenge of God: The Resurgence of Islam, Christianity, and Judaism in the Modern World* (University Park: Pennsylvania State University Press, 1991, 1994).

Lawrence, Bruce B. *Defenders of God: The Fundamentalist Revolt Against the Modern Age* (Columbia: University of South Carolina Press, 1995).

Neusner, Jacob. *The Death and Birth of Judaism* (New York: Basic Books, 1987).

———. *Self-fulfilling Prophecy: Exile and Return in the History of Judaism* (Boston: Beacon Press, 1987).

Schwartz, Barry. *Judaism's Great Debates: Timeless Controversies from Abraham to Herzl* (Lincoln: University of Nebraska Press, 2012).

Notes

1. Jacob Neusner, *The Death and Birth of Judaism* (New York: Basic Books, 1987), p. 116.
2. Elie Wiesel, *A Jew Today* (New York: Random House, 1978), p. 146.

Additional Resources

The Chosen (1981, feature film). Set in 1940s Brooklyn and based on a novel by Chaim Potok (published in 1967 by Simon and Schuster), this film presents the story of two young men, one from an ultra-Orthodox Hasidic family and the other from a more "modern" Orthodox family at the time of the Zionist struggle of Israel for statehood. A dramatic examination of the conflict between different ways of Jewish life and thought responding to the "modern" world at a critical moment in Jewish history. Color, 107 minutes, dir. Jeremy Kagan.

Genocide (1981, documentary). Academy Award–winning documentary on the Holocaust narrated by Elizabeth Taylor and Orson Welles. An Arnold Schwartzman production available from the Simon Wiesenthal Center (http://www.kintera.org).

Heritage: Civilization and the Jews (1984, documentary). A nine-part PBS video series on the history of the Jews narrated by Abba Eban. Available on interactive DVD-Rom from PBS. There is also an accompanying PBS website, including timeline and lesson plans. Here you will also find links to a wealth of web resources on the history of the Jews (http://www.pbs .org/wnet/heritage/HeritageGuide.pdf).

CHRISTIAN DIVERSITY 4

and the Road to Modernity

Overview

Somewhere in rural India, a small group of Christians, virtually indistinguishable from their neighbors, who are Hindus, gather to pray and offer flower petals before a statue of Jesus. In yet another place, somewhere in Africa, villagers gather to dance and sing tribal chants in praise of the risen **Christ**, even as in a small unadorned room in England, a dozen Quakers sit in wordless prayer, waiting for the Holy Spirit to inspire one of them to speak a message to the rest. At the same time, if we turn to the United States, we find a woman priest consecrating bread and wine as the body and blood of Christ at an inner-city Episcopal church in the Northeast. Southward, in a small village in Latin America, a dozen peasants sit in a circle on a hillside under the morning sun, preparing to share the bread and wine as the body and blood of Christ and studying the Gospel of Luke. Remembering that the word *gospel* means "good news," they are encouraged by Jesus' words of hope to the poor and the downtrodden. At the same time, televangelist Joel Osteen tells an American television audience of millions that Christ's message is that God has good things in store for them.

Elsewhere, in a storefront church in the Midwest of the United States, Christians—male and female, black and white—stand and raise their arms above their heads, their hands extended toward heaven. The eyes of many are closed; soon some begin to speak in an unknown language. These worshippers are **Pentecostal**, or charismatic Christians who believe they have gifts or abilities to speak a special spiritual language, known as *speaking in tongues*. They believe that the Holy Spirit of God has descended

Christ: title Christians apply to Jesus of Nazareth; from the Greek translation of the Hebrew word meaning "anointed one" or "messiah"

Pentecostal: churches that emphasize possession by the Holy Spirit and speaking in tongues

147

For some Christians, worship is a powerful and physically involving emotional experience, as in this contemporary charismatic service in a stadium in Anaheim, California.

Catholic: churches that define their Christian authenticity through apostolic succession

on them and speaks through them, even as this Spirit guides their daily walk with Christ. Meanwhile in Rome, the pope, leader of the largest Christian denomination in the world, the Roman **Catholic** Church, processes into the great Cathedral of St. Peter escorted by a long line of men in flowing robes. The procession makes its way between the majestic rows of stone pillars led by one man carrying a processional cross. Incense bearers follow, swinging pots of richly aromatic incense whose smoke wafts through the air as if carrying the sounds of organ music and chanting up to heaven. Soon the pope will arrive at the altar to celebrate Mass.

Despite their incredible diversity, all these believers are Christians engaged in Christian prayer and worship. The challenge before us is to understand the unity and diversity among Christians, especially in the contemporary world. In addition, in this chapter we will need to get a more complete picture of the history of the process of modernization and globalization that began in Western culture in an ambivalent relationship with Christianity. This will also give us the background necessary to better understand the reaction of other religions to modernization.

Like Jews and Muslims, Christians believe that there is but one God, the God who made all things and rules over history. This God is the highest reality, and to act in harmony with the will of this God is the highest goal of life. Christians are unique, however, in believing that God is one God yet three persons (Father, Son, and Holy Spirit) and that the reality of this God is uniquely revealed in the life and person of Jesus of Nazareth. Christians believe that the eternal Word of God was united to humanity through the person of Jesus, who suffered and died on the cross for the sins of the world. They believe that Jesus was raised from the dead three days later and after forty days ascended to heaven, where he will reign until he comes again at the end of time to judge the living and the dead at the final resurrection.

Like Jews and Muslims, Christians believe that the gravest problem in human life is sin—the failure to live in harmony with the will of God. Sin has two dimensions: idolatry and injustice. Idolatry is more than worshipping the images of false deities; it is treating anything that is not God as if it were more important than God. Idolaters shift the focus from the God who seeks the good of all to their selfish desires, thus sowing the seeds of injustice, for if nothing is more important than achieving such selfish goals as wealth and power, treating other human beings unjustly can be seen as necessary to ensure that these ends are met.

However, Christians differ from Jews and Muslims in their view of sin and how it is to be overcome. Most Christians define *sin* in terms of the concept of **original sin**, which says that the will to do good in all human beings was corrupted by the first human beings—Adam and Eve, who, through their disobedience to God's will, brought sin and death into the world. Thus, most Christians believe that while human beings were created good, their good will (the desire to do what is good) was corrupted by the inherited consequences of the sin of Adam and Eve, so humans feel compelled to act selfishly. Humans are enslaved to the power of sin and not fully capable of obeying the will of God. Out of compassion for human beings, God chose to send a savior, Jesus Christ, to redeem them by dying in reparation for their past sins and restoring human nature (re-creating a good will in them) in order for obedience to the will of God to be possible and in order to restore human destiny to its true goal of eternal life with God.

God sent into the world his only son, to become incarnate—that is, fully embodied—in the person of Jesus of Nazareth. In doing so, God united his divine nature to human nature, healing its flaws. The primary means for Christians to overcome sin and live in harmony with the will of God is to die spiritually and be reborn through faith in Christ. The Christian who has undergone this conversion experience believes he or she has become a new person, one who is free to obey the word of God as revealed in the scriptures. Christians believe that during their earthly lives they are called to help bring about the **Kingdom of God**—the beginning of a new creation of love, compassion, and justice in which death will finally be overcome, even as Jesus overcame death on the cross.

In century after century, Christians have sought this Kingdom of God, also referred to as the *kingdom of heaven* in scriptures. Constantly they have struggled to establish it. This goal has forced Christians to try to understand the relationship between the church and the world and how their faith and way of life should be related to the non-Christian world around them. Both Catholic Christianity, which took definitive shape in the early and medieval church, and the sixteenth-century **Protestant** movement to reform Catholicism have struggled with this question in every age, including the present one.

Despite the explanation of Christianity just given, it would be misleading to think that all Christians in all times and places would agree with it. Like all religions, Christianity is more than one thing. It has taken many forms and been many things

original sin: sin of Adam and Eve, who disobeyed God when they ate the fruit of the tree of knowledge of good and evil. This sin was said to weaken the will to do good of all humans born after them

Kingdom of God: occurs whenever humans live in accord with the will of God

Protestant: churches that emphasize direct personal relationship with God in Christ (rather than through the mediation of the Church established by apostolic succession) as necessary for salvation to many people. In the remainder of this chapter we shall try to understand both the unity and the diversity of Christianity.

Today Christianity is the largest religion in the world. With over 2.2 billion adherents, of whom about 1.1 billion are Roman Catholic, all together Christians represent approximately one-third of the world's population. Approximately 37 percent of Christians are Protestant, and 12 percent are either Greek or Russian Orthodox. Other minority Christian communities make up 1 percent of the global Christian population. Our primary task in this chapter is twofold: (1) to understand Christianity in all its diversity and (2) to appreciate the unique role that this religion has played in the development of the modern society that presented such a formidable challenge to it and all other faiths. So, unlike in our other chapters, here we will focus not just on religion but also on the emergence of the modern world out of the ancient world. So this chapter will trace important aspects of the social, intellectual, and political history of modernization as it emerged in the West. Since modernity grew up within the womb of Western Christian civilization, we will

Christianity Timeline

31 CE	Crucifixion of Jesus of Nazareth
48–60	Letters of Paul of Tarsus
70	Fall of the Jewish temple in Jerusalem to the Romans; Gospel of Mark written
80–100	Gospels of Matthew and Luke and John written
313	Edict of Milan by Constantine permitting Christianity in Roman Empire
325	Council of Nicaea declares Word of God to be same as (homoousios) God
380	Christianity declared the official religion of the Roman Empire by Emperor Theodosius
451	Council of Chalcedon, doctrine of two natures in the one person of Christ
500s	Development of Benedictine monasticism in the West
590–604	Pontificate of Gregory the Great, first great pope of the Middle Ages
732	Muslim invasion of Europe stopped at Tours by Charles Martel
800	Coronation of Charlemagne
1095	First Crusade against Muslims and mass violence against Jews
1184	Inauguration of church inquisitions by Pope Lucius III
1198–1216	Pontificate of Innocent III, most powerful pope in history
1224–1274	St. Thomas Aquinas, greatest theologian of Middle Ages
1414	Council of Constance—papal decadence and the declaration of conciliar rule in the church
1517	Luther's Ninety-five Theses posted on church door at Wittenberg, beginning of Protestant Reformation
1545–1563	Council of Trent, Catholic Counter-Reformation
1555	Peace of Augsburg—first attempt to end religious wars of the Reformation

have to understand not only the history of Christianity as a religion but the way it has influenced and been influenced by social, political, and intellectual trends in Western history.

As with Judaism and the other religions found in the modern world, pluralism presents a challenge. Some Christians believe there should not be diversity among Christians and blame modernization for this development. So some Christians, who identify themselves as **fundamentalists**, have argued that the alliance of Christianity with modernization is a mistake. This mistake could be corrected by returning to the "fundamentals" of the faith as they believe these fundamentals were understood and practiced before the emergence of the modern scientific and secular view of the world. Others (*modernists*) have argued that the historical evidence shows there has always been diversity within Christianity. For them modernization is not a problem but is itself evidence of the power of the Christian **Gospel** to transform the world. In their view, Christians should embrace modernization as the path to human dignity and liberation.

fundamentalist: the most conservative wing of Evangelical Protestants, who believe modern interpretations threaten certain Gospel truths

Gospel: literally "good news"; refers to Jesus' message of salvation in the New Testament

1648	Peace of Westphalia—end of religious wars, quest for religious tolerance
1703–1791	John Wesley, founder of Methodism
1768–1834	Friedrich Schleiermacher, father of modern theology
1791	First Amendment to U.S. Constitution, guaranteeing religious freedom for all
1813–1855	Søren Kierkegaard, Christian existentialism
1851	Karl Marx publishes *Communist Manifesto*
1859	Charles Darwin publishes *On the Origin of Species*
1869–1870	First Vatican Council
1910–1915	Publication of *The Fundamentals* begins fundamentalist/modernist controversy
1939–1945	World War II and the Holocaust
August 6, 1945	Atomic bomb dropped on Hiroshima, Japan, leading to end of World War II
1947	India achieves independence; Church of South India is formed
1950s, 1960s	Emergence of civil rights movement under Martin Luther King Jr.; Pope John XXIII and the Second Vatican Council
1970s–1990s	Religious resurgence of evangelical fundamentalism and emergence of liberation theology movements
2005	Death of Pope John Paul II and election of Pope Benedict XVI
2013	Pope Benedict XVI resigns (the first resignation since the thirteenth century) to permit the election of a new Pope, which occurred on March 13, 2013, when Jorge Mario Bergoglio, an Argentinean Jesuit, became Pope Francis

The Christianity of yesterday helped give birth to the modern world in all its diversity; and to understand the latter we need also to understand the former. We shall begin with the Protestant encounter with modernity and then look at Catholicism's struggle with the modern world. Then, to see how things came to be the way they are today, we shall return to the beginning in the first century and journey forward.   ○ ● ○

Encounter with Modernity: The Fundamentalist–Modernist Controversy (1859–)

The Protestant Confrontation with Modernity

When the first followers of Jesus of Nazareth looked up into the night sky in the first century, they did not see what modernists did when they looked upward in the nineteenth century. For modernists saw a cosmos with stars and planets scattered in infinite space. They knew that the earth is not at the center of the universe but just one of the planets circumnavigating a star (the sun) in one of many galaxies. When individuals in the first century looked up they saw a world shaped not by the modern scientific imagination but by the imagination of the ancient Greeks. They accepted the Greek view that the earth was at the center of seven spheres. The higher spheres of the stars and the planets embodied spiritual beings (Paul of Tarsus called them the "principalities and powers") that governed the universe. Everything above the moon, they believed, belonged to the realm of the spiritual and eternal. Everything below the moon belonged to the realm of the physical and temporal. The Greeks thought that the souls of all humans had their origin in the spiritual realm and had descended into the material or bodily realm. But the spiritual goal, each individual's hope of salvation, was to return to the eternal realm above, beyond time, decay, and death.

In addition to the legacy of the Greeks, the worldview of the first Christians owed a debt to the Hebraic tradition of ancient Israel, namely, that creation is a story unfolding in time. In the beginning God spoke and the story began. The story has many dramatic ups and downs as it unfolds, but at last God will bring the present world to an end, judge it, and transform it into a new creation. Today "modern" believers wrestle with the question of whether being a Christian requires adherence to the ancient worldview or can accommodate changing worldviews, including the modern scientific one.

The nineteenth century marked a critical turning point in the history of Christianity as it sought to coexist with an increasingly "modern" secular and scientific world whose views challenged many of the fundamental truths and practices of Christians.

The central issue in modern Christianity has been the struggle between modernism and fundamentalism. Indeed, the term *fundamentalism* originated with the American Protestant encounter with *modernism*.

Modernization in nineteenth-century America was fueled by the growth of science, industrialization, and concomitant urbanization. In this period the United States was becoming increasingly secular, especially in the area of higher education. This was a major cultural shift, for in the mid-1800s most colleges were under **evangelical** Protestant leadership. This form of Christianity emphasized the centrality of the powerful "born-again" experience of spiritual transformation and the primacy of the Bible as a source of true knowledge. By the end of the century higher education was more and more in the hands of universities modeled on the German scientific ideal of scholarship, in which each discipline has its own rational and empirical standards that make no direct appeal to the Bible or Christian beliefs. In this context, Charles Darwin's theories on the biological evolution of humanity from lower primates had caught the popular imagination. Less generally known but very much on the minds of evangelical preachers was the new "biblical criticism" that had come out of Germany. Although by *criticism* proponents meant "analysis," not "finding fault," this new scholarship, which looked on the Bible as a historical, humanly created document, challenged many pious beliefs about its teachings.

evangelical: Christian movements that emphasize the emotional power of conversion as a spiritual transformation

The challenges stemming from Darwinism and biblical criticism were a double blow to Christian beliefs and elicited two opposing responses: the modernism of liberal Christian evangelicals on the one hand and the fundamentalism of conservative Christian evangelicals on the other. Liberal evangelicals developed a new theology to show how modernism and Christianity were compatible. They saw God at work in evolution and in history and embraced a "Social Gospel" oriented to making this world a better place for all. Christians, they argued, have an ethical calling to cooperate with God's will, operative in evolution and history, to transform this world into the Kingdom of God. By the end of World War I, liberal evangelical Christianity dominated the northern Protestant churches. However, in the eyes of many other evangelicals, the attempt to adapt Christianity to the modern world was doomed to failure. What one ended up with was a Christianity emptied of everything that made it Christian and filled with everything that was secular and modern.

It was modernization that split evangelical theology in two: opposing the liberal Social Gospel was Protestant fundamentalism. Whereas the theologians of the Social Gospel believed they represented the next logical stage in the historical development of Christianity, evangelicals who responded in a fundamentalist mode were convinced that there could be no historical development in this respect. If there was a conflict between the scriptures and modern science, then it must be modern science, not the Bible, that was in error.

In a series of twelve paperback books entitled *The Fundamentals,* published between 1910 and 1915, champions of the fundamentalist movement spoke in defense of Bible-based religion and against the apostasy, as they perceived it, of modernism. Convinced that liberal theology and Darwinism were undermining American

"If thou lovest God and all mankind, I ask no more: 'give me thine hand.'"

—John Wesley

civilization, they took their stand on the inerrancy of the Bible, pure and simple. If you did not share this belief, the fundamentalists did not consider you to be a true Christian.

The development of two American schools of evangelical Christianity was paradoxical. Evangelical Christianity had originated as a strategy for transcending the theological disputes and religious wars that occurred in the aftermath of the Protestant Reformation. The original evangelicals, in Europe, believed that a true Christian was identified not by acceptance of the right doctrines but by being "born again"—an emotional transformation undergone through a spiritual surrender to Christ that produced a life of love and compassion and enabled Christians to accept each other, despite disagreements over fundamental beliefs. One of the most influential proponents of evangelical Christianity, John Wesley (the founder of Methodism), was famous for insisting that doctrinal differences should not separate Christians who are truly united in their love of God and their neighbor.

Many later evangelicals, however, feared that the shock of modernism threatened Christian faith to the core, and by the 1920s the movement dubbed *fundamentalism* by the popular press was understood to refer to militantly antimodernist evangelical Protestants. The event that decisively formed the public image of Christian fundamentalism in America was the Scopes trial held in Dayton, Tennessee, in 1925. John Scopes, a high school teacher, had been accused of breaking a law that banned the teaching of evolution in the state's public schools. Three-time candidate for president of the United States William Jennings Bryan appeared for the prosecution. The defense was led by the legendary Clarence Darrow, a favorite of the international press corps that attended the trial. Although Bryan won the case in court, he lost the cause in the media, which portrayed fundamentalism as the philosophy of ignorant backwoods hicks. Fundamentalism then lost popular support, and Protestant liberalism, which sought to embrace modernity, held sway largely unchallenged until the surprising resurgence of fundamentalism in the last quarter of the twentieth century.

The Catholic Confrontation with Modernity

In 1864 Pope Pius IX issued a Syllabus of Errors listing eighty "modern" teachings that challenged the control of all knowledge and politics by the church. Pius IX thought that modern ideas could only lead to a godless society that would no longer heed the eternal and unchanging fundamental truths of the one true church, and he admonished Catholics to reject them. In 1869 Pius IX called the First Vatican Council of cardinals and bishops to shore up the teachings of the church against the threat of modernism. In 1870 the papacy was besieged not only by modern ideas but by modern secular politics. In that year the new secular kingdom of Italy seized the papal estates from Pius IX and the Vatican lost the political power it had enjoyed for centuries.

Thus Vatican I, as the council is now known, was in session precisely at the time when the intellectual and political authority of the papacy was at its weakest and most vulnerable. In 1870, at the insistence of Pius IX, Vatican I declared the pope to be infallible. This meant that a pope's official declarations on faith and morals could not be altered, even with the consent of the church, including any future councils.

There is a striking similarity between Protestant and Catholic antimodernist responses. Both attempted to prevent modernization and historical change from entering the church by an appeal to an infallible or inerrant authority that they believed was higher than scientific and secular authority. However each responded by appealing to a different form of authority. For Protestants it was the Bible; for Roman Catholics it was the pope, as the final authority on how the Bible was to be interpreted.

It is all the more remarkable, therefore, that almost a century later a new pope would seek to reverse many of the decisions of Vatican I and come to terms with the modern world. When Pope John XXIII called the Second Vatican Council in 1962, in one dramatic gesture he sought to reverse the more than four centuries of church attempts to reject the emerging modern world. And he sought to heal the bad feelings generated by religious divisions in Christianity going back to the Protestant Reformation and even earlier. Moreover, in its Declaration on the Relationship of the Church to Non-Christian Religions, the council expressed a new openness to the teachings of other world religions. Indeed, it declared: "The Catholic Church rejects nothing which is true and holy in these [non-Christian] religions."

The Second Vatican Council's meetings lasted from 1962 to 1965. John XXIII did not live to see them completed, but in his brief papacy (1958–1963) he unleashed a spirit that transformed the Catholic Church from a world-shunning institution into one that was open to the modern world. In the decades since Vatican II, Catholics have wrestled with their future, with some wanting to return to the fundamentals of the Catholicism of Vatican I, and others wanting to follow the road to modernization.

Pope John XXIII, who opened the doors of the Roman Catholic Church to modernity by calling the Second Vatican Council, in a portrait from 1963.

The Nineteenth-Century Historical and Social-Scientific Revolution

In the confrontation with modernity, both Catholics and Protestants responded to the scientific revolution in human thought that had marked the nineteenth century. This revolution was precipitated by the emergence of new academic disciplines, representing the final shock wave of modern consciousness.

The first wave had been created by the natural sciences. Copernicus had outraged the European world when he suggested in 1543 CE that the earth was not the center of the universe. Later, geologists had concluded that the earth was far older than had been calculated by anyone who used the Bible as a guide. Then in 1859 Charles Darwin published *On the*

Origin of Species, rendering completely implausible the biblical account according to which human beings appeared on earth on the sixth day of creation. Darwin claimed that evolution had been proceeding for many hundreds of thousands of years and was the result of a struggle between members of the various species culminating in the survival of the fittest.

The social sciences delivered the second shock wave, especially critical historiography, which showed that popular legends about the past often did not accurately describe the events they purported to chronicle. The other social sciences did little to ease the shock. Sociologists and anthropologists who studied societies comparatively suggested that humanity had invented gods to make the ways of life of various cultures seem sacred. This view was reinforced by Sigmund Freud's suggestion that God was a projection or instance of wish fulfillment—an illusion that human beings needed to create to give them a feeling of security in a dangerous world. Now human beings were asked to think of both society and human identity as created by human choices rather than by divine actions and decisions, as claimed by traditional teachings.

This new awareness created a profound problem. The question that came to divide modern Christianity was whether to reject the developments of modernity, as did Protestant evangelical fundamentalism and Vatican I Catholicism, or to accept them, seeing God at work in evolution and historical change, as did Protestant evangelical liberalism and Vatican II Catholicism—or strike some kind of compromise in between. Paradoxically, although modernity appeared to be a threat to Christianity, it had been nurtured, in significant part, by Christianity itself. Our task now is to return to the beginning of Christianity so that we can better understand the historical circumstances that led its adherents and its institutions, the churches, to contribute to the development of the modern world. In this we will focus entirely on tracing the role of Christianity in relation to the emergence of modernity in Europe and the role that Christianity has played in promoting European colonialism. Then we will further trace the new developments coming out of African and Asian Protestantism and Vatican II Catholicism. These trends seem to be leading to a post-European diaspora form of Christianity open to religious pluralism in an age of globalization.

Premodern Christianity: The Formative Era (31–451 CE)

The New Testament and the Life of Jesus

The journey of Christianity from the ancient to the modern world begins in the first century with the life and teachings of Jesus of Nazareth as communicated in the Gospels of the New Testament. Being a Jew, Jesus participated in a religious tradition that went back 2,000 years before his time. This is acknowledged in the Christian Bible, which is made up of two parts. What Christians call the Old Testament is basically an adoption of the Pharisaic and Hellenistic Jewish collections of sacred writings that have been the official scriptures of Judaism since the end of the first century of the common era (CE). The scriptural writings of Christians called the New Testament did not assume the form of the twenty-seven books we have now until the year 367 CE—more than 300 years after the death of Jesus. During those centuries there were in circulation many stories of the life and sayings of Jesus (other gospels such as the *Gospel of Thomas* and the *Acts of John*), most of which do not appear in the New Testament. Even after 367, extending into the sixth century, some of these "other gospels" appear in "new testament" Bibles.

What is striking is that the tradition did not settle on a single story of Jesus for its Bible but actually included four distinct yet overlapping stories—the Gospels of Matthew, Mark, Luke, and John. To these were appended letters by the apostle Paul and others, a short history of the early church (the Acts of the Apostles), and a vision of the end of time (the book of Revelation). Christians believe that these scriptures show that Jesus of Nazareth is the Christ—the anointed one, or messiah—whose coming was foretold by the Hebrew prophets.

According to tradition, the Gospels were written in the order of their appearance in the New Testament: Matthew, Mark, Luke, and John. After careful scrutiny of the literary structure and probable historical context of each Gospel, however, many modern scholars concluded that Mark's Gospel probably was written first (at the time of the fall of the temple in 70) and that both Matthew and Luke used Mark's material as a model in writing their versions (sometime between 80 and 90). The Gospel of John (written after 90) is so different in literary tone, content, and structure that it seems to have been a largely independent creation.

Also, according to tradition, the Gospels were written by disciples (or disciples of disciples) of Jesus. Taking advantage of historical and archaeological findings that shed additional light on the biblical period, modern scholars do not believe any Gospel had

Christians in every culture tend to imagine the birth of Christ in terms of their own culture, as in this Chinese painting.

a single author. Rather, each one began in shared oral traditions as told in different communities of believers after Jesus' death on the cross and attested resurrection. These traditions were eventually written down and edited to place the sayings of Jesus in the context of different remembered events from Jesus' life.

As we have noted, the sacred scriptures of Christianity were first examined critically in the nineteenth century. Within Christianity the validity of this modern approach is in dispute. Fundamentalists reject it, while other Christians see it as helpful for understanding the development of faith in the early church. And yet for all their differences, and quite apart from historical questions of "what really happened," all forms of Christianity share a common reverence for the stories of Jesus as they are found in the New Testament.

The Stories of Jesus

The power of the Christian message is revealed in the stories of Jesus. What the stories of Jesus tell is that God's true being manifested itself in the life of a human being, Jesus of Nazareth. Ancient philosophies often denigrated the human body as a prison to be escaped from and unworthy of association with God, who was pure spirit. The story of Jesus, in whom God's word was made flesh, affirmed that being human was not to be belittled, for God embraced it.

Jesus was born roughly at the beginning of the first century and grew up in Nazareth in ancient Palestine, then under Roman rule (see Map 4.1). Little is known of his youth, but according to the gospel stories he was raised by Joseph, a carpenter, and his wife, Mary, the child's mother. The birth of Jesus was said to have been miraculous, for Mary became pregnant through the power of God as announced by an angel rather than through marital relations with Joseph.

Around the age of thirty, Jesus had a traumatic experience. Someone he knew, admired, and was related to—John the Baptist—was arrested on orders from Herod and eventually beheaded. To everyone's surprise, soon after John's arrest Jesus began teaching the very message that had gotten John in trouble with Herod—"Repent, for the kingdom of heaven is at hand" (Matthew 4:17).

"Love your enemies and pray for those who persecute you, so you may be children of your Father in heaven; for he makes his sun rise on the evil and on the good, and sends rain on the righteous and on the unrighteous."

—NRSV, Matthew 5:44–45

While his family and childhood friends at first thought he had gone mad, Jesus soon attracted followers who thought otherwise and called him rabbi, which means "teacher." The power of the Christian story is especially revealed in the Sermon on the Mount (Matthew 5–7), with its message of loving all persons, even your enemies. It is that message of compassion and forgiveness that has moved millions.

In addition to preaching repentance and love, according to the scriptures, Jesus began working miracles—healing the sick (Mark 1:40–45; Matthew 9:18–22), walking on water (Mark 6:45–52; John 6:16–21), casting out evil spirits (Mark 1:23–28; Matthew 8:28–34), and miraculously multiplying a few loaves and fishes to feed a multitude, a story recounted in all four Gospels. As the fame of Jesus spread, some of the Sadducees and Pharisees (see Chapter 3), according to the stories, grew jealous of him and began to plot his demise. They had him handed over to the Romans who had heard some call him "messiah." While the Gospels typically make it appear

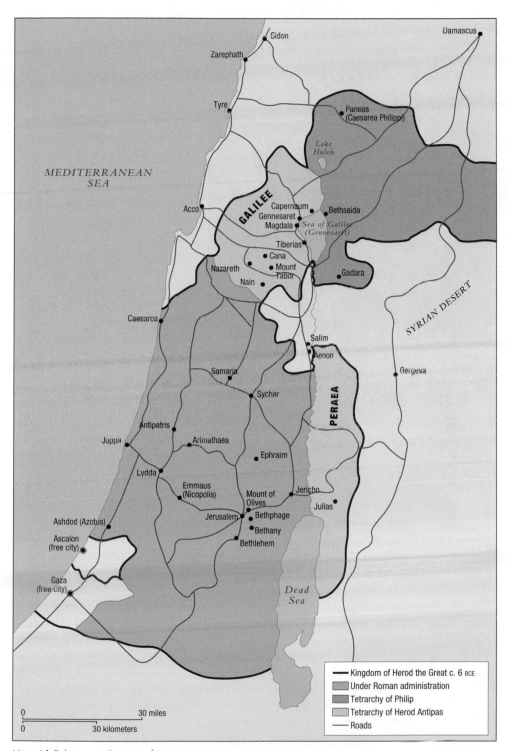

Map 4.1 Palestine at the time of Jesus.

Map labels:
MEDITERRANEAN SEA
SYRIAN DESERT
Dead Sea
Lake Huleh
Sea of Galilee (Gennesaret)
GALILEE
PERAEA

Sidon
Damascus
Zarephath
Tyre
Paneas (Caesarea Philippi)
Acco
Capernaum
Bethsaida
Gennesaret
Magdala
Tiberias
Cana
Mount Tabor
Nazareth
Gadara
Nain
Caesarea
Salim
Aenon
Gergesa
Samaria
Sychar
Antipatris
Arimathaea
Joppa
Ephraim
Lydda
Emmaus (Nicopolis)
Mount of Olives
Jericho
Julias
Ashdod (Azotus)
Jerusalem
Bethphage
Bethany
Ascalon (free city)
Bethlehem
Gaza (free city)

Legend:
Kingdom of Herod the Great c. 6 BCE
Under Roman administration
Tetrarchy of Philip
Tetrarchy of Herod Antipas
Roads

0   30 miles
0   30 kilometers

Illustration of Jesus healing a leper from a biblical manuscript found at Mount Athos Monastery in Greece.

Second Coming: belief that Jesus will return at the end of time to establish a new heaven and a new earth

as if the Jews, not the Romans, are the cause of Jesus' crucifixion, historians have pointed out that only the Romans had that power. Moreover, for the Romans the term *messiah* was associated with their enemies the Zealots. A militaristic sect of Judaism that engaged in guerrilla warfare against the Roman legions, the Zealots openly announced their expectation that God would send a messiah, a political revolutionary who would overthrow the Roman Empire. Historically, the reason the Romans condemned Jesus to die nailed to a wooden cross was that they thought of him as such an enemy of the state.

Whatever the political facts, the followers of Jesus came to find deep spiritual meaning in the Crucifixion. What is striking about Mark's account (15:34) of the event (found also in Matthew 27:46) is the bleakness of Jesus' final words: "My God, my God, why have you forsaken me?" This is very different from the final words of Jesus reported in other Gospels: "Father, into your hands I commend my spirit" (Luke 23:46) and "It is finished" (John 19:30). Mark presents a Jesus with whom even a hearer in the depths of despair can identify. And yet the Gospels do not allow despair to be the final word. For they offer the hope that just as Jesus was raised from the dead, so may be those who have faith in him.

As the story continues (John 20), some of the disciples came to Jesus' grave on Sunday morning, the first day of the week, only to find an empty tomb; later Jesus appeared among them, displaying his wounds to prove it truly was he, risen from the dead. Now the disciples, who had been afraid, began to be filled with a new spirit—the Holy Spirit of the God who had raised Jesus from the dead (Acts 2). Emboldened by this spirit they began to proclaim the message of the risen Lord who had conquered death and would return very soon. At this **Second Coming**, or Parousia, Jesus would raise the dead, judge the heavens and the earth, and inaugurate the Kingdom of God, in which all injustice would be overcome and suffering and death would be no more.

In a world filled with injustice, suffering, and death under the oppressive rule of the Romans, such a message inspired hope and joy. The world was not a cold and uncaring place, for the love of God nourished every creature. The life of Jesus presented people with a story of suffering and tragedy that was real yet not final, for suffering and death were overcome in the resurrection. In the life of Jesus, people could see their own lives reflected, leading to the hope that their own tragedies would not be final and that they too would be resurrected. To understand these things is to understand some of the reasons why Christianity is the religion of one-third of the world's population.

Apocalypse: The Book of Revelation

The New Testament not only describes the life, death, and resurrection of Jesus but also offers a vivid description of how Jesus will return as Messiah to judge the heaven and the earth and bring about a new creation. In the Book of Revelation he is described as leading a battle against Satan or the Devil, banishing him to a "lake of fire" along with all sin and death, so that all remaining can share in the eternal life of God.

The *Apocalypse* or *Book of Revelation* is the last book of the New Testament. It is perhaps the most controversial and confusing book of the Christian bible (*Apocalypsis*, a transliteration of the Greek word for "revelation," leads to the familiar English title, *Apocalypse*). According to the opening chapter of the Book, it is written by a man named John who had visions given to him on the island of Patmos. These visions showed how God would soon bring about the destruction and recreation of the world. This would entail a final judgment, the end of the world as it had existed, and the establishment of a new creation in which all sin and death would be conquered in a final resurrection and the survivors would share eternal happiness with God.

Scholars disagree on the date the book was written. Some scholars say shortly before the year 70 CE when the Jewish Temple in Jerusalem was destroyed by the Romans. This might be consistent with the Gospel of Mark, Chapter 13, where Jesus predicts the destruction of the Temple as coming soon, and the world coming to an end. Others, noting that the end of the world did not follow upon the destruction of the Temple, think that it was written some twenty years later during the persecutions in the reign of the emperor Domitian and predicting a destruction to come at some later time. This has some plausibility since the Roman Empire is painted as the instrument of Satan and the enemy of the Gospel in the book.

A helpful way of reading the book is to see it organized around five sections, each describing a series of seven events, preceded by an introduction and followed by a conclusion.

Introduction (1:1–20)
    Seven Letters to the Churches (2:1–4:11)
    The Opening of the Seven Seals (5:1–7:17)
    The Sounding of the Seven Trumpets (8:1–14:5)
    The Casting of the Seven Bowls (14:6–18:24)
    The Seven Visions of New Creation (19:1–22:5)
Conclusion (22:6–21)

God and Satan: Zoroastrianism and the Biblical Tradition

In the time of Moses (ca. 1280 BCE), the religion of Israel was technically not yet monotheistic but rather henotheistic, which means the worship of one God above all others. The first commandment given to Moses by this God is: "I am the Lord Your God, you shall have no other gods before me." It does not say there are not other Gods, but rather that the God of Israel is a jealous God who will not tolerate the tribes worshipping these other gods. It was only in the time of the Prophets, between 1000 and 400 BCE that tribal henotheism was transformed into a true monotheism, asserting that there is only one God and all others are false gods.

After the time of King David, Prophets like Amos and Hosea, Jeremiah, and Ezekiel and Isaiah proclaimed the God of Israel to be the one creator of the world and so of all peoples. This God, according to exilic prophets like Ezekiel and Isaiah, determined the destiny of all peoples and shaped the direction of history. As such, God was the source of all good and evil (Isaiah 45:7–8). When Solomon's temple was destroyed and the people of Israel were conquered and taken into slavery in Babylon (586 BCE), the Babylonians were said to be the instruments of God's will, punishing the Israelites for their sins. In the same way, Ezekiel promised that one day God would forgive and restore the people of Israel to their land. Indeed, Isaiah actually sees the King of Persia, Cyrus, who conquered the Babylonians, as a "messiah" or "anointed one" (Isaiah 45:1) sent by God to restore the people of Israel to the land of Israel (538 BCE) and even rebuild their temple. And both Ezekiel and Isaiah promised a resurrection of the dead—a new idea not part of the earlier biblical beliefs in the era from Moses to David. In Isaiah's view, there would be a coming Day of the Lord, when all nations would be gathered in Jerusalem (Isaiah 66:18ff), leading to a final judgment of all nations and a resurrection of the dead.

By the time Christianity emerged from Judaism in the first century, a new view of God and evil had emerged. Early Christianity adopted the Septuagint or Greek translation of the Bible used by Hellenistic Jews. This Septuagint included apocryphal books, meaning books containing "hidden meanings." The genuine biblical status of these books was often challenged, but they are of great historical value in assessing historical developments in Jewish and Christian beliefs. Many of these, such as the Book of Enoch, reflect a changing view of the Devil during the period in which Christianity was emerging from Judaism. In this new view it was not God who was the source of evil, but the Devil. An elaborate cosmology emerged in which there were minions of angels serving God in the heavens, and some of these, led by Satan, rebelled and sought to oppose God's plan for creation. The devil's minions or demons sought to enlist humans in this rebellion against God by seducing them into embracing selfishness and sin.

In the earlier biblical tradition, Satan, as we see in the Book of Job (chapters 1 and 2), is a member of God's court who acts as an *adversary* (the meaning of the word *satan*), who can do nothing without God's permission. God gives Satan permission to send misfortune into Job's life but forbids him from taking his life. God does this to test Job's faithfulness but in the end rewards Job for remaining faithful. By the time of the emergence of Christianity in the first century, the new popular mythology of evil asserted that Satan, acting in rebellion, seeks to defeat God and God's saving intentions for the history of the human race. In the Christian Gospels, we see Satan portrayed as the enemy of the Kingdom of God or Kingdom of Heaven. He tempts Jesus (Matthew 4:1–11) and incites his enemies. Jesus, himself, is portrayed as an exorcist who can cast out those demons who serve the Devil's purposes. Indeed, in the final book of the Christian bible, *The Book of Revelation*, the resurrected Jesus is portrayed as returning to earth as Messiah for a final battle with Satan in which he casts Satan and those who serve him into a lake of fire, and then a new earth comes down from heaven in which all evil and death are eliminated, bringing a final resurrection (Book of Revelation, chapter 20).

Where did this newer view of Satan as a powerful adversary and enemy of God come from? According to historians of the biblical literature, it seems likely that biblical thought was deeply influenced by the emergence of Zoroastrianism in Persia. For it was the Persians who conquered the Babylonians in 538 BCE and allowed all who had been enslaved by the Babylonians to return to their original homelands, including the people of Israel. Thereafter the imagery of Zoroastrianism seemed to inspire new more dramatic accounts of the nature of evil.

Zoroastrianism emerged as a religious phenomenon in Persia in the time approximately parallel to that between Moses in the thirteenth century and the Babylonian Exile in the sixth century BCE. Its teachings are attributed to a prophet/teacher known as Zoroaster or Zarathustra, depending on the transliteration. The revelations given to Zarathustra are contained in scriptures called Gathas, which also contain other later materials from the Zoroastrian tradition offered by the *magi*—its hereditary priestly caste (reference to the magi is found in the birth story of Jesus in the Gospel of Matthew 2:1–12). The complete book of Zoroastrianism is known as the Avesta and includes the Gathas, as well as the rituals and laws of the Zoroastrian tradition. The Gathas reveal the wisdom and benevolent power of Ahura Mazda, the "Wise Lord" and his attributes the "Amesha Spentas" or "bounteous immortals," which are aspects of God's power in the universe, later personified as angelic powers.

The beneficent power of Ahura Mazda is opposed by another power, that of Angra Mainyu. If the first represents the highest power of Good in the universe, the latter represents the opposing power of Evil. The view developed that the universe was caught in a cosmic struggle between these two powers of Good and Evil. Zoroastrians saw the universe as a struggle in time between Good and Evil—the holy spirit and the evil spirit—which will end with the final victory of Good over Evil at the end of time. As Zoroastrian cosmogony developed, human history was said to be predetermined to last 12,000 years. Zoroastrians developed a view of final judgment for each person leading to either a heavenly existence or punishment in a hell-like state until the end of time, when evil will be overcome and all will be redeemed. This struggle between good and evil culminates in the last 3,000 years in which a savior figure is born for each thousand-year period and ending finally in the resurrection of the dead, the exile of Evil, and the creation of a new world and eternal life.

Zoroastrianism was eventually challenged in Persia by the seventh century CE emergence and spread of Islam. Islamic persecution of Zoroastrians followed, and many Zoroastrians sought refuge in other lands. By the tenth century CE, the most significant diaspora community existed in India, where Zoroastrians are known to this day as Parsis (Persians), who continue to practice the rituals of their fire ceremony as a celebration of beneficent divine power in the universe. The obvious parallels between Christian beliefs and Zoroastrian beliefs about good and evil; divine and angelic powers; and heaven, hell, and final judgment suggests that much of the belief of New Testament-era Christianity was influenced by Zoroastrian cosmology. There are some similar parallels in Judaism and especially in Islam. The influence of Zoroastrianism on all three traditions is plausible because Zoroastrianism predates the biblical religions of Judaism, Christianity, and Islam. However, this influence is complicated by the fact that they all coexisted and seemed to have influenced each other over centuries. So the biblical religions influenced Zoroastrianism as well. Today, the total world population of Zoroastrians is very small, estimated at about 200,000.

Joyful Iranian Zoroastrians celebrate the ancient mid-winter Sadeh festival around a ritual fire near Tehran in January 2012.

The plot of the book reveals that God is bringing time to an end in a final resurrection of the dead and a final judgment, and the churches must remain faithful and be prepared. First there will be a reign of 1,000 years of peace. Then there will be a great battle between the forces of good (led by the Messiah) and the forces of evil (led by Satan). After a battle led by the Messiah against Satan and his minions, the forces of evil will be defeated and cast into a lake of fire. Then all suffering, death, and injustice will be destroyed; the dead will be raised; and the New Jerusalem will appear, where all will live with God in eternal happiness.

In the history of Christianity the book has been very controversial. Although some thought the author, John, must be the same as the author of the Gospel of John, modern biblical scholars find that unlikely. Its style and vocabulary are too different from that of the Gospel's author. Many communities in the early church did not accept the book as genuine revelation, especially among the Eastern Greek-speaking churches. Eventually the Latin churches of European Christianity accepted it, but even as late as the Protestant Reformation in the sixteenth century, Luther questioned whether it really belonged.

In the New Testament itself, Jesus is quoted as saying that no one knows the day or hour of the coming end of time, not even he, only his Father in heaven (Matthew 24:36). Despite this, the Book's vivid and often violent descriptions of signs of the coming end of the world have led many Christians in later centuries to believe its descriptions suggested the end was coming in their own time. All such expectations have been disappointed.

Famous passages in the Book of Revelation include the opening of the first four seals of a seven-seal scroll that reveal the four horses of the apocalypse, bringing war, famine, economic disaster, and death. The sounding of seven trumpets announces the coming judgment of the earth. The pouring of the seven bowls of judgment brings partial destruction to the earth, especially to the city of Babylon, which embodies the evil of all the cities of the world, and the battle between the Messiah and Satan, described as a defeated dragon who is, along with the two beasts who assist him, cast into the lake of fire. Finally, seven visions are presented of the coming of a new Jerusalem, a new heaven, and a new earth in a new city of God that has no temple but only the living presence of God. In this city all suffering and death are overcome and all the nations live by the light of God.

The Book of Revelation has struck both fear and hope in the hearts of its readers over the centuries as they have puzzled over the possible meanings of its mysterious symbolism and whether it is to be read literally or symbolically.

Christianity's Emergence from Judaism

Jesus was born a Jew; lived as a Jew, participating reverently in traditions that had originated as long as 2,000 years before his birth; and died as a Jew. His gentile followers, however, thought that Jews did not understand his message. As a consequence, what began as a way of understanding Judaism was embraced almost exclusively by gentiles (non-Jews), who thought of themselves as practicing a new and improved faith—Christianity. These gentile Christians came to teach what some scholars have called the myth or story of supersession—that God had rejected the Jews and chosen gentiles instead. It was a myth that would endure until the twentieth century.

Christianity, in fact, began as a Jewish sectarian movement. After 2,000 years of biblical history, especially after the Babylonian exile (586–538 BCE), a variety of movements (such as those of the Sadducees, Pharisees, Hellenists, Zealots, Samaritans, Essenes, and Nazarenes, discussed in Chapter 3) developed in Judaism. There was no agreement on a common set of sacred writings among them. Only at the end of the first century of the common era did the Hebrew Bible as we know it come into existence, largely owing to the influence of the Pharisees and the Hellenists. At the beginning of the century, however, these groups and others were engaged in an ongoing argument about the right way of life for the people of Israel.

Naturally, each movement saw itself as the model for the right way of life and all others as deviant. The result was a diverse set of sectarian movements, each proclaiming a message something like this: "We are the true Israel (i.e., the true Jews); you are not. The end of the world is at hand when God will come to judge the heaven and the earth. Jews who have strayed, who are thus no better than pagans, must repent and be ritually immersed. Then they will become true Israel again—true Jews who, by definition, live the way we do." The "we" here naturally was a different "we" depending on who was preaching the message. Of course any Jews who were not part of that "we" were likely to find the message an insult, for traditionally the baptismal rite of ritual immersion and purification was required only of non-Jewish converts to Judaism (along with circumcision for males).

Essential to the emergence of Christianity from Judaism is the preaching and teaching of Paul. Without Paul of Tarsus, a Pharisee and Hellenistic Jew, Christianity would not be the religion we are familiar with today. It is one of the paradoxes of Christianity that the one person, after Jesus himself, who has most deeply influenced the Christian tradition is a man who began as a persecutor of it. Paul of Tarsus at first treated the movement that began with the rabbi Jesus as a heretical form of Judaism. Yet he eventually came to argue that Christianity was not really a heresy but a way for gentiles to share in the promises made by God to the Jews. Paul, who came to be known as an apostle of Jesus, was not one of the original twelve apostles selected by Jesus and never met Jesus before his crucifixion. He came to know Jesus as the risen Lord after an extraordinary encounter on the road to Damascus, an experience that led to his conversion. Paul became the first great missionary of the Christian movement, and we know of Paul's thoughts and actions primarily from his letters to the churches that he founded in places like the ancient Greek cities of Corinth and Ephesus. The letters form approximately one-fourth of the New Testament. Other accounts of Paul's ministry appear in the Acts of the Apostles, in the New Testament, a book attributed to the author of the Gospel of Luke.

Throughout history the Crucifixion has captured the imagination of great artists such as Matthias Grünewald, creator of this sixteenth-century altarpiece now in Isenheim, Germany.

"God has imprisoned all (both Jews and gentiles) in disobedience so that he may be merciful to all."

—NRSV, Romans 11:32

Paul was born in what today is Turkey and educated in Jerusalem. Hellenistic Jews were very successful missionaries to the gentiles in first-century Judaism. They presented Judaism as open to Greek patterns of thought and behavior. When Paul became a convert to the Nazarene movement, as a Hellenistic Jew he continued this Hellenistic missionary activity but with a new twist: He argued that the task of the followers of Jesus was to bring the gentiles into Judaism as a "wild olive branch" grafted onto a cultivated olive tree of Judaism (Romans 11:16–18). Neither Jews nor gentiles were perfect but God did not hold their faults against them. Through Jesus, Paul taught, the gentiles were now called to share with the Jews in the promises made to Abraham (Ephesians 2:11–22). After the fall of the Jewish temple in Jerusalem (ca. 70), this teaching was ignored in favor of the view that Christians supersede or take the place of the Jews as God's chosen people. Tradition says that Paul was martyred in Rome, probably around the year 60 CE.

The Fall of the Temple

The whole picture of diversity in first century Judaism changed dramatically in the year 70 CE, when the Romans marched into Jerusalem with thousands of troops, burned down the temple, and drove the Jews out of their holy city. In the aftermath of the fall of the temple, two movements emerged to shape Western religious history: the Pharisaic movement, which became Rabbinic Judaism, and the Nazarene movement, which became gentile Christianity.

The Pharisees survived the destruction of the temple because they were able to provide flexible Jewish leadership under dramatically new conditions. Unlike Pharisaic Judaism, the Nazarene movement never had a large following among Jews. Its greatest success was a missionary movement for the conversion of gentiles. The Nazarenes were an apocalyptic movement, believing that the end of time was at hand and that their special mission was to convert the gentiles before the final judgment. In this they were inspired by the prophecies of Isaiah that in the last days all nations would be gathered into Jerusalem (Isaiah 66:18–20).

A critical issue for the Nazarenes was the status of new gentile converts. This was taken up around the year 48 at a meeting in Jerusalem. The Christian tradition refers to this meeting as the first church council or the "Council of Jerusalem." The conservatives from Jerusalem argued that gentile converts had to be circumcised and obey the whole Mosaic law, as required of other Jews. Paul of Tarsus came to this meeting from Antioch, where he and other Hellenistic Jews were converting large numbers of gentiles. Hellenistic Jewish missionaries believed in adopting Greek culture and language to make Judaism attractive to gentiles. Paul and others sympathetic to the Hellenistic mission argued that gentiles should be exempt from the requirement of circumcision and from most of the ritual obligations, focusing instead on obeying the moral commandments of the Mosaic covenant. The faction led by Paul won the argument, and a letter urging these changes went out to all the mission communities (Acts 15:19–21).

This ruling was decisive for the growth of the Nazarene movement among gentiles. Released from those Jewish practices that gentiles were most reluctant to embrace (circumcision, kosher food restrictions), they flooded into the movement. By the second century Jewish-born people made up a smaller and smaller proportion of the total membership. And as the leadership fell more and more into the hands of gentiles, the movement lost its sense of identity as a Jewish movement and began to take on a separate identity as a new religion—Christianity.

The Origins of Christian Anti-Jewish Sentiment

We are now in a position to discuss a problem that has plagued the relationship between Jews and Christians throughout the history of Western civilization. The New Testament reflects the context of the Jewish sectarian arguments that had been going on in the first century, in which groups like the Zealots, the Essenes, and the Nazarenes were saying to each other: "We, not you, are the true Israel, the true Jews. Therefore repent, be baptized, and become Jews the way we are, for the end of time and God's judgment are at hand."

TEACHINGS OF RELIGIOUS WISDOM: Paul on Faith, Hope, and Love

With the possible exception of Jesus' Sermon on the Mount, no teaching of Christianity is better known than the apostle Paul's teaching on faith, hope, and love from his letter to the Corinthians (1 Corinthians 13:1–13, New American Bible*). These three—faith, hope, and love—came to be known as the "three cardinal virtues" of Christianity.

If I speak in human and angelic tongues but do not have love, I am a resounding gong or a clashing cymbal. And if I have the gift of prophecy and comprehend all mysteries and all knowledge; if I have all faith so as to move mountains but do not have love, I am nothing. If I give away everything I own, and if I hand my body over so that I may boast but do not have love, I gain nothing.

Love is patient, love is kind. It is not jealous, (love) is not pompous, it is not inflated, it is not rude, it does not seek its own interests, it is not quick-tempered, it does not brood over injury, it does not rejoice over wrongdoing but rejoices with the truth. It bears all things, believes all things, hopes all things, endures all things.

Love never fails. If there are prophecies, they will be brought to nothing; if tongues, they will cease; if knowledge, it will be brought to nothing. For we know partially and we prophesy partially, but when the perfect comes, the partial will pass away. When I was a child, I used to talk as a child, think as a child, reason as a child; when I became a man, I put aside childish things. At present we see indistinctly, as in a mirror, but then face to face. At present I know partially; then I shall know fully, as I am fully known. So faith, hope, love remain, these three; but the greatest of these is love.

These first-century Jewish sectarian arguments were incorporated into the sacred writings of Christianity found in the New Testament. However, when these statements were read and repeated by the leaders of the "Christian" movement in the second and later centuries, they were no longer seen as exhortations from one Jewish group to another. Now gentiles who had come to identify themselves as Christians took up the refrain: "We are the true Israel; you are not." And thus was born the Christian myth of supersession, or divine rejection. Christians now argued: "We Christians have replaced you Jews as God's chosen people. Because you did not recognize Jesus as messiah and had him crucified, God has rejected you and chosen us to supersede you." In the next chapter we will see that in the seventh century CE, Islam emerged with Muhammad's similar teaching of supersession: namely, that Muslims replace both Jews and Christians as God's chosen people.

In Christianity the teaching of supersession took an especially violent turn. Soon this logic was disastrously extended to include the claim that since "the Jews" had brought about the death of the very son of God who was sent to save them, not only had God rejected the Jews for all time, but it was the Christians' duty to punish them. It was a view that played a tragic role in the persecution of Jews throughout much of Western history. It was not until the time of Vatican II (1962–1965) that a commission created by Pope John XXIII condemned the teachings of supersession and divine rejection of the Jews and affirmed Paul's view, that gentiles are like a wild olive branch grafted onto the tree of Judaism to share in God's promises to Abraham. By the end of the twentieth century, most Protestant churches had renounced the teachings of supersession as well.

Jesus as Son of God

In the first four centuries after the time of Jesus, as gentile Christianity separated itself from Judaism, Christians struggled to formulate an authoritative understanding (dogma) of who Jesus is and what his significance is. The essential problem that faced the early followers of Jesus, who, like the apostle Paul, believed that they had a special mission to convert the gentiles, was how to translate an essentially Jewish message about a coming "messiah" into terms non-Jews could understand. These missionaries did not want pagans to confuse Christian claims about Jesus being **Son of God** with pagan myths in which divine beings come down to earth in humanlike bodies. The challenge was to speak correctly and clearly about the being and meaning of Jesus of Nazareth without claiming either too little (that Jesus was just a good man) or too much (that Jesus was not really human but rather a supernatural being like the gods of pagan mythology). For about 300 years, Christians debated the various possible ways of thinking and speaking about Jesus and held several church councils. By the time the argument was settled, both extremes had been deemed **heresy**.

The most important councils were those of Nicaea in 325 and Chalcedon in 451. Some bishops and theologians argued that Jesus was a divine being with neither a mortal mind nor a body. Some argued that Jesus had a human body and a divine mind, others said that although his mind too was human and mortal he had a divine will, and so on. Such views made Jesus a kind of half-man and half-god, not unlike other characters in pagan mythology. The Council of Chalcedon rejected all such views, insisting that Jesus had a human body and a human mind. He was fully and completely human, with a birth and a death like every other person. Jesus' humanity differed from that of others in only one way—he was without sin. Moreover, in this man Jesus, God was wholly present. The formula arrived at to reconcile the apparent paradox was that in the "one person" of Jesus there were "two natures" (divine and human) united "without confusion" or mixture. That is, in the person of Jesus divinity and humanity were united yet completely distinct.

Two beliefs had to be held together in this formula, that of Nicaea—that the Word through which all things were created was the "same as" (**homoousios**) God (i.e., eternal)—and that of Chalcedon—that the man Jesus was a mortal human being to whom was united that eternal Word (which had existed before its incarnation in the man Jesus). If the Word was not eternal, it could not confer eternity; and if Jesus was not mortal, his resurrection offered no hope to other mortals. This formula was meant to combat Gnostic Christian views, eventually declared heretical, to the effect

"We all with one accord teach . . . the same Christ, Son, Lord, Only-begotten, recognized in two natures, without confusion, without change, without division, without separation; the distinction of natures being in no way annulled by the union . . . coming together to form one person."
—Church Council of Chalcedon

Son of God: title applied to Jesus of Nazareth

heresy: negative term in Christianity for choosing to believe in doctrines viewed as erroneous by more orthodox believers

homoousios: Greek term for the belief that the Word of God through which all things were created is "the same as" God that Jesus was a divine being (i.e., pure spirit)—a god who only appeared to be a "flesh and blood" human being and therefore could not really have died on the cross, nor would it have been necessary for him to arise from the dead.

The formula of two natures in one person developed at Chalcedon was complemented by another unique doctrine or belief of Christians—the belief in a triune God, which had been affirmed earlier at the Council of Constantinople in 381. The doctrine of the **Trinity** asserts that God is one essence but three persons. The formula "three persons in one God: Father, Son, and Holy Spirit" is not really about mathematics. Rather, it means that God, the creator of the universe, can at the same time be present in the life of Jesus and in all things in the world through God's Word and Spirit—without ceasing to be transcendent or beyond the universe. The doctrine of the Trinity states that God is *in* all things without accepting the pantheistic notion that God *is* all things.

Jews and Muslims, with their theology of a prophetic monotheism, according to which God is one and not three, have typically misunderstood the meaning of the doctrine of the Trinity. But then so have many Christians. Nevertheless, the intent of both the "**two natures, one person**" doctrine concerning Jesus and the doctrine of the Trinity concerning God is to affirm the uniqueness of a God who is both present in and transcendent to the cosmos. This is the true God who has no equals—the God of Abraham—the very same God affirmed by Jews and Muslims.

Constantinianism: The Marriage of Christianity and Empire

Perhaps the single most important political event in the history of Christianity was the conversion of the Roman emperor Constantine, the first monarch to champion the rights of Christians. Constantine, who issued the Edict of Milan in 313, was baptized on his deathbed. With his imperial declaration, Christianity went from being an often-persecuted religion to a permitted (and eventually the favored) religion in the empire.

Up until this point, many Christians had tended to look at Roman civilization, with its imperialism and colonial domination of foreign territories, as the work of the devil. That is how it is portrayed in the book of Revelation, for instance. After Constantine, Christians began to see Roman imperialism as a good thing, as a way of spreading the Gospel throughout the world. This was a decisive step in shaping the Western religious vision of a Christian civilization. The **Constantinian** vision achieved the status of official political policy in 380, when Christianity became the official religion of the Roman Empire under Emperor Theodosius. Within ten years, pagan worship was declared illegal and all pagan temples were closed. Only Judaism was permitted as an alternative to Christianity, and it existed under severe legal restrictions, with Jews losing many of the freedoms they had had under pagan Rome.

Trinity: God as Father, Son, and Holy Spirit; God is not many gods but one God in three persons

two natures, one person: doctrine that in the one person of Jesus are two natures (divine and human) coexisting in unity but without mixture

Constantinian: under first Christian Roman Emperor, Constantine, the view that the Emperor rules over both the church and the state, and protects the church as the official religion of the Roman Empire

The Greek-speaking churches of the East took Constantine's relationship to the church as a model of how things should be. There were four great centers of Orthodoxy: Constantinople, Alexandria (Egypt), Antioch (Syria), and Jerusalem, each ruled by a patriarch. In the Eastern Byzantine part of the Roman Empire, centered in Constantinople, church and state existed symbiotically. The Christian emperor called church councils and even appointed the bishops. The emperor ruled over both church and state in the name of Christ.

However, the pattern of Western civilization that shaped the road to modernity was not that of Orthodox Christianity from the East but an important modification of it that put church and empire in a precarious relationship combining cooperation and antagonism. The Constantinian model thrived in Byzantium until the fifteenth century; but in the West, Roman political rule collapsed after the time of Theodosius. The political vacuum created by the absence of an emperor in the West allowed the bishops of the Latin-speaking churches to assume much greater independence with respect to the state. This was especially true of the bishop of Rome, whose power and authority grew as secular Roman political power and authority collapsed, leading to the idea of the primacy of this bishop of Rome as *pope* (father) over all other bishops. In the Latin church the idea of separation between church and state developed. The chief architect of this alternative vision was Augustine of Hippo.

The Constantinian unification of church and state is illustrated in this Roman mosaic showing the Roman emperor at the center as the unifying ruler of both the state (on his right) and the church (on his left).

Augustine, Architect of Western Christianity

From the fifth century on through the Protestant Reformation and the emergence of modernity, the West has been deeply influenced by the theological thought of Augustine of Hippo, whom Christians typically refer to as *St. Augustine*. After Jesus and the apostle Paul, probably no other individual in history is more responsible for the shape of Western Christianity. Augustine's vision deeply shaped the development of Roman Catholicism from the fifth through the twelfth centuries. Then he was eclipsed by Thomas Aquinas, only to be recovered by the Protestant reformers Luther and Calvin in the sixteenth century, who drew heavily on the writings of Augustine.

Constantine died in 337. Augustine, who was born in 354 and died in 430, lived through the time of Theodosius and witnessed firsthand the transformation of the Roman Empire from a pagan empire into a Christian one. This stunning transformation could not fail to impress contemporary observers. They could not believe that the pagan Roman Empire had become Christian through chance or good luck. They concluded instead that God intended to use the Roman Empire to provide the political unity and stability needed to spread the Gospel to the ends of the earth.

In century after century, Christians turned to Augustine's spiritual autobiography, *The Confessions* (400), as a model of conversion and piety. And in century after century, rulers of church and state turned to his book *The City of God* (423) as a model for the political order. Indeed, the first great medieval pope, Gregory I, used Augustine's vision to justify his exercise of power over the political order, and Charlemagne, who on December 25, 800, became the first Holy Roman Emperor, is said to have slept with a copy of *The City of God* under his pillow. The influence of *The Confessions* and *The City of God* on the history of European Christianity and European society is so vast and profound that it is almost impossible to calculate.

The Confessions: *Faith, Reason, and the Quest for Wisdom*

"I was not encouraged by this work of Cicero's to join this or that sect; instead I was urged on and inflamed with a passionate zeal to love and seek and obtain and embrace and hold fast wisdom itself, whatever it might be."

—Augustine, *Confessions,* Book III

A key turning point in Augustine's life, as he relates it, was the awakening of his mind and heart to a passion for wisdom when he was nineteen years old. Before that event, the young man had devoted himself to fulfilling selfish desires (*cupiditas*) for wealth, fame, power, and sexual pleasure. About the time Augustine was completing his studies in Carthage in Africa, he came across a book entitled *Hortensius*, by the pagan author Cicero. This book, says Augustine, set him on fire with a new kind of desire (*caritas*)—the selfless desire for wisdom.

And so Augustine resolved to follow his doubts and questions wherever they might lead him. Augustine doesn't say that *Hortensius* changed his thinking but, rather, that it "altered my way of feeling . . . and gave me different ambitions and desires" (III, 4). Augustine's wording here is very important. His experience changed his feelings and desires, which in turn changed his thinking and eventually led to his full conversion. Christianity is a religion of the transformation of the heart as the symbolic location of the emotions. In the first century of the common era, Jesus had called his hearers to undergo a change of heart, and virtually every great reform and renewal movement in Christian history has returned to this theme.

Augustine's story of his conversion became a model for understanding the relationship between faith and reason. Theology, he said, is "faith seeking understanding." Some interpretations to the contrary, this does not mean "you first have to believe to be able to understand." Rather, you will be led to deeper understanding if you have faith and trust that God is working through your very doubts to lead you to deeper understanding. In his *Confessions* Augustine says that only after his full conversion did he come to realize that when he had the faith to doubt, he already had an implicit faith in Christ, who was leading him to doubt and so to find true wisdom.

The City of God: *Augustine's Tale of Two Cities*

In the same way that *The Confessions* provided a model for faith and reason, *The City of God* provided a model for church and state. The meaning of history is unraveled for Augustine by a symbolic reading of the biblical stories as a history of two cities that exist side by side in history—the human city and the city of God. These two cities are guided by two different loves, *cupiditas* (selfish love) and *caritas* (selfless love), respectively. These, of course, are the same two loves Augustine saw at war in his own life in his *Confessions*. Augustine's formulation of the appropriate relationship of these cities provided the decisive model of relations between church and state, religion and politics, and sacred and secular for most of Western history.

For Augustine the story of the human city was the story of the history of civilizations going through endless cycles of progress and decline—a story without any clear purpose or meaning. But hidden within that history was another story—that of the city of God. This story, which is revealed in the Bible, has a clear purpose and direction. It is the story of a journey with God through time toward a final resurrection and eternal life for all who belong to the city of God. The city of God, however, was not identical with the church. In his view, some within the institution were not faithful believers and some outside of it were. Only at the final judgment will human beings come to know who truly belongs to the city of God.

In defining the relationship between the two cities Augustine argues that both state and church exist through God's will to serve God's purposes. God uses the state to establish the peace necessary for the spread of the Gospel by the church. In the journey through history each entity should serve the other. The state should be subject to the church in spiritual matters, and the church should be subject to the state in earthly matters. Neither should seek to dominate the other. However, in actual history the sides could never fully agree on where to draw the line between earthly matters and spiritual matters. And too often each side forgot the part about not dominating the other. Indeed, throughout most of Western history both popes and emperors maneuvered to upset the balance between the two by trying to dictate to the other.

This fifteenth-century miniature painting by Nicola Polani depicts Augustine writing *The City of God.*

Augustinian: views of St. Augustine emphasizing the separation of church and state, pope and emperor, rather than a Constantinian unity of both in the emperor

While our main emphasis is on Latin (Western) Christianity, because that is the form of Christianity that fostered the emergence of modernity, the Eastern churches have great historical and cultural significance. The earliest churches of Christianity were in communities that spoke Greek, not Latin. By the fourth and fifth centuries the Latin-speaking churches grew in number and influence to rival the Orthodox churches and declared the bishop of Rome to have unique authority among all bishops and came to treat him as "the holy father" or "pope." While the Greek churches followed the Constantinian model and gave ultimate religious authority to the emperor, the Roman churches came to reject that model. The Greek churches, by contrast, did not accept the central authority of one bishop that the Roman churches affirmed. All the bishops answered to the emperor, but internally these churches were conciliar, placing ultimate authority not in a single bishop (a pope) but in church councils as meetings of all the bishops.

Eastern Orthodox Christianity was distinctive for its mystical emphasis: Christ became human, it is said, so that humans could become divinized and share mystically in the eternal life of God—a process known as *theosis.* Orthodoxy is also distinctive for its understanding of sin as ignorance rather than as corruption of the will through original sin as put forward in Latin-Augustinian Christianity. For the Orthodox churches, Christ is the great teacher who comes to dispel human ignorance of oneness with God and to restore humans to mystical unity with the creator. The emphasis is not on Christ as the lord of History but on the cosmic Christ through whom all things are created, held together, and brought to fulfillment. From the beginning there was tension between the Eastern and Western churches, but a formal split did not occur until 1054.

The pure Constantinian vision of the Eastern churches sees the church as a branch of the state and the emperor as both the religious and political leader of the state. The **Augustinian** vision separates church and state by expecting there to be two ultimate authorities, both a pope and an emperor, each with their separate spheres of authority. Yet Augustine's vision is not yet the modern one that insists on a secular, or nonreligious, state that promotes religious pluralism and "freedom of religion." On the contrary, he assumes that the two powers will work together to achieve a worldwide Christian civilization. Since the time of Augustine, most Christians have assumed that the task of Christianity is to transform every society into a "Christian society" comprising two branches: church and state. This pattern continued even after the Holy Roman Empire collapsed and the Protestant Reformation helped usher in the modern era. In more recent times, modern European culture replaced Roman civilization as the political order thought to be willed by God for the purpose of spreading Christianity around the world. Only gradually, after the religious wars the Protestant Reformation provoked, did Christians begin to explore an alternative— the modern idea of a secular, or nonreligious, state as the guarantor of freedom to worship in a religiously pluralistic world. We will return to this observation when we discuss modernization.

Premodern Christianity:
The Classical Era (451–1517 CE)

In 476 Romulus Augustulus, the last Roman emperor in the West, was deposed. Less than a century after the time of Augustine of Hippo, the Roman Empire and its civilization collapsed in the West. Most commerce ceased, for example, and the Roman money economy was replaced by a barter system. Over several centuries Europe was invaded by tribes from the north; and as tribal leaders upgraded themselves into lords of their domains, feudalism began to take shape. The feudal system was a network of loyalties established between a landholder (a king or a nobleman) and those who served him and his estates. It was a hierarchical arrangement, with the nobility on the top, subordinates called vassals in the middle, and serfs and slaves at the bottom. The nobles were members of either a secular warrior aristocracy or the religious aristocracy consisting of bishops and abbots (the heads of monasteries), for the church was a major landholder and church officials too could be feudal lords.

The Middle Ages roughly span the sixth through the fourteenth centuries. It was a world without printing presses, and so the few existing books were handwritten. Only the elite among the clergy and the nobility could read, in any event. The average Christian got his or her religious view of life from sermons delivered by priests and from images depicted in the stained glass windows and on the walls of the churches and cathedrals.

In this new world, the church carried civilization forward into Europe, accomplishing this primarily through the spread of Christian monasteries. It was monasticism that provided the bridge of civilization between the ancient world and the modern world, bringing technological development and the light of learning to a European period that has been otherwise described as the Dark Ages.

Monasticism was the first serious reform movement in the church. Once Christianity became the official religion of the Roman Empire, many who became Christians did so for reasons of expediency rather than piety. The practice of Christianity came to be more about social acceptability and worldly success for them. By the late third century, members of the Eastern (Greek) churches who wanted to lead an exemplary

Before the printing press was invented, all books were written by hand. Depicted is a medieval monk transcribing a text at his desk.

> "Idleness is the enemy of the soul; and therefore the brethren ought to be employed in manual labor at certain times, at others, in devout reading."
>
> —*The Holy Rule of St. Benedict*, chapter 48.
>
> SOURCE: Rev. Boniface Verheyen, OSB, trans. *The Holy Rule of St. Benedict*, 1949 edition.

Christian life often felt they had to separate themselves from the corrupt world around them, moving into the desert to live simply, with much time for prayer. The first monks tended to be hermits, but gradually many of these solitary men began to form monastic communities. The most outstanding of these monks, called the *desert fathers*, had a powerful influence on the church throughout the Middle Ages. For example, Gregory I, the first medieval pope, was born to aristocracy but abandoned his privileges to become a monk in the desert. It was the beginning of a pattern. Whenever Christianity tended to grow corrupt with worldly power and success, it was monasticism that provided reform movements to call the church back to its spiritual mission.

By the late fourth century, monasticism had spread to the Western (Latin) churches. Whereas Greek Orthodox monasticism was supported by church and state, the Latin communities, set up according to the model of Benedict of Nursia (480–543), were self-supporting communities of work and prayer under the leadership of an abbot. In the ancient world work was viewed as a task for slaves, but Benedict taught that "to work is to pray" and integrated physical labor into the daily schedule of group prayer and private devotions. Consequently, the Benedictine monasteries preserved and developed not only spiritual knowledge but also ancient learning and technology. The Benedictines were the great engineers of the Middle Ages, who developed impressive waterwheel and windmill technologies to improve the monks' productivity. The goal was to make work more efficient so that there would be more time for prayer. Thus, the monasteries brought to the West not only spiritual renewal but also intellectual and technological advances, making profound contributions to the full flowering of technological civilization in the modern period.

The Medieval Worldview: Sacraments and Festivals

In the medieval world, life on earth was seen as a test and a place of waiting to enter one's true home in heaven, if one passed the test. Christians believed that when they died their souls would be separated from their bodies and would come before God for individual judgment. In the future (at an unknown time) the world would come to an end and Jesus would return to raise the bodies of the dead and unite them with their souls. Those who had been faithful and good would be rewarded for all eternity in heaven, enjoying the "beatific vision" or presence of God; the rest would be consigned to eternal punishment in hell.

The church was God's gift to this world to help Christians prepare for their final judgment. The church was founded by Jesus Christ, the Son of God, who had passed on leadership of the church to his chief apostle, Peter (Matthew 16:18). This apostolic succession was continued by the popes, who were seen as the direct successors of Peter, guaranteeing that the church would be divinely guided because the pope speaks with the authority of Christ on earth. The Catholic Church claimed that apostolic succession proved that it alone was the one true church and that its task was to confer God's guiding and protecting grace upon all believers through the sacraments.

Sacraments

Through the descending hierarchy of the pope, the bishops, and the lower clergy, as Christ's priesthood, the **grace** of God was conferred on humankind, mediated to every Christian through seven **sacraments** that guided and assisted them from birth to death and beyond. These sacraments were baptism, confirmation, Holy Eucharist (communion), marriage, ordination (holy orders), confession, and extreme unction. These sacraments were taken to be the outward and visible signs of God's inward, invisible grace (forgiveness and assistance), helping Christians grow spiritually and morally toward holiness or saintliness. Grace, considered an undeserved gift from God, was also seen as an invitation to a renewed spiritual life that required human cooperation, accepting the aid offered by God and consciously trying to use that aid for spiritual and moral improvement. Because the sacraments could be administered only by ordained clergy, every Christian was dependent on the priests and bishops of the church, under the rule of the pope, to be in a right relationship to God. Outside the institutional church, it came to be thought, there was no salvation.

grace: the idea of unmerited divine love and assistance given to humans

sacraments: ritual materials and actions (such as pouring water over infant at baptism), usually through mediation of ordained clergy, said to impart the grace of God to Christians

Festivals

If the sacraments carried Christians from cradle to grave, the annual cycle of religious festivals carried them through the seasons of the year and created for them a world of stories in which to dwell. The early church saw itself as living in the time between Easter and the *advent*, or "Second Coming" (Parousia) of Jesus Christ to raise the dead and judge the heavens and the earth. By the Middle Ages a church calendar had developed to immerse the faithful in a cycle of festivals and stories that reminded Christians of their origin and destiny. The church year began with Advent, whose stories evoke hope for the Second Coming. Gradually a concurrent theme of Advent as preparation for Christmas developed, overshadowing the earlier theme. Christmas and Epiphany were festival seasons designed to celebrate the stories of the birth of Jesus, the visit of the wise men from the East, and the baptism of Jesus. No one knew the date on which Jesus was born; December 25 was chosen to compete with a popular pagan festival honoring the sun god.

Children reenacting the nativity story.

The season of Christmas/Epiphany is followed by Lent, a time of penitence, fasting, and prayer in preparation for Easter. Its stories recall the temptations, healings, and teachings of Jesus. Lent culminates in Holy Week, in which the stories of Jesus' trial and death are recalled. In the Easter season, the church retells the stories of the resurrection and the subsequent appearances of Jesus to his disciples. The final season of the church year, Pentecost, recalls the descent of the Holy Spirit upon the apostles and the birth and growth of the church. After Pentecost, of course, comes Advent again and a new year of hope and expectation. Thus, for many centuries the cycle of festivals has allowed Christians to dwell in a world of stories that tie and bind them into the great cosmic drama in which God is bringing salvation to the whole world.

Medieval Christians were grounded in the sacraments and oriented by the festivals, and their stories also sought divine aid through prayers to the saints and angels in heaven. That is, they prayed that exemplary Christians (*saints*) who had died and other spiritual beings, known as *angels*, would present their petitions to God in heaven. This was, after all, how things got done in medieval feudal society. If you wanted a favor from a member of the nobility or the king, it was best to ask someone at court to intercede for you. Hierarchies of saints and angels were believed to exist in heaven and to work in a similar fashion. On the other hand, it was believed that some angels who rebelled against God, the devil and his minions, exercised an evil influence over human beings that must be resisted through the power of prayer and the sacraments.

In this medieval worldview, we have the full integration of the biblical worldview of life, death, and resurrection of the body with the Greek metaphysical worldview rone des hauitce œuuxee du noble Charlemaine ror de franc

De plusieurs batailles que Charlemaine eut alencontre

of the cosmos as a hierarchical order. It forms the essence of the Catholic world-view. Lacking the historical consciousness that came after the Renaissance, medieval Christians thought this amalgamated worldview was exactly what Jesus had pro-claimed in the Gospels.

A depiction of the coronation of Charlemagne as the first Holy Roman Emperor by Pope Leo III on Christmas Day in the year 800 CE.

The Two Cities Revisited

Throughout the Middle Ages there was a struggle between the two cities that Augustine had described. From the time of the Holy Roman Emperor Charlemagne (800–814), the emperors sought to dominate the church and the popes sought to dominate the state. A turning point in the development of the power of the papacy was its emulation of a monastic model of church discipline that originated in France. Because Benedictine monasticism had a strong work ethic, many monasteries became great centers of wealth, which in turn led to abuses. In 910 a new reform movement swept through monasticism, and a new monastery was founded at Cluny, in east central France. The Cluny reforms aimed at spiritual renewal and reorganization.

In addition to their emphasis on spirituality, the Cluniac monasteries provided an important organizational model for the development of colonialism, first adopted

RITUALS AND RITES: The Seven Sacraments and the Life Cycle

The seven sacraments, which Catholicism (both Orthodox and Roman) developed by the late Middle Ages, provided ritual assistance to the Christian at every stage of life, from birth to death. The word *sacrament* comes from a Latin translation of the Greek word for "mystery," a term borrowed from first-century pagan cults known as *mystery religions*, whose rituals were performed in the hope of achieving immortality.

The sacraments of Christianity, by uniting humans to God and eternal life, were said to guarantee salvation from sin and death. With the coming of the Protestant Reformation in the sixteenth century, only baptism and communion retained the status of sacraments. The other five rituals were rejected by Protestants on the ground that they could not be found as such in the New Testament. However, many of these "rejected" practices are observed in some Protestant denominations as rituals but not as sacraments in the full sense.

Baptism

The early Christians followed the Jewish practice of ritual immersion for new gentile converts in which the person's whole body was submerged in a river, lake, or special pool. For Christians, however, full submersion was seen as participation in Christ's death in the tomb; the emergence of the body from the water was equated with Christ's resurrection and departure from the tomb. The submersion was accompanied by the words "I baptize you in the name of the Father, the Son, and the Holy Spirit." As the practice of infant baptism developed in later generations, pouring of water over the baby's forehead was adopted as an alternative. Both types of baptism are still performed today.

This ritual is believed to flood the soul with divine grace (divine love, forgiveness, and assistance), erasing all stain of original sin, the sin of Adam and Eve that is said to mark every newborn child. Baptism changed one's destiny from death to eternal life.

Communion

Equal in sacramental importance was the Eucharist, or Holy Communion. This practice seems to have been an adaptation of the Jewish blessing of the bread and wine at meals, especially as it was practiced at Passover, the Jewish remembrance of the people's deliverance by God from slavery in Egypt. In the Gospels, at Jesus' last Passover, he broke the bread, blessed it, and said, "This is my body." He blessed the wine, too, and told his disciples, "This is the cup of my blood, shed for you and for many for the forgiveness of sins." By eating the bread and drinking the wine consecrated by a priest or minister who represents Jesus, Christians believe they are partaking of the body and blood of Jesus (for some literally, for others spiritually), who died for their sins on the cross and brought them to eternal life. Both baptism and communion were established well before the Middle Ages. However, to these, five other sacraments were added in the Catholic traditions.

Confirmation

The first converts to Christianity were adults who made a conscious decision to be baptized and to follow

Anglican Bishop Desmond Tutu, a Nobel Peace Prize winner, gives children communion during mass in Saint-Barnabas Church in South Africa.

Christ. As the practice of infant baptism developed, so did a controversy over whether this was appropriate, since the infant was too young to make such a choice. Infant baptism, it was decided, signifies that God is choosing the child rather than that the child is choosing God. At some point, however, a young Christian was expected to make a conscious choice to live for Christ. In the ritual of confirmation, young people at about the age of thirteen demonstrated their knowledge of the faith, were anointed on the forehead with oil, and made a public declaration of commitment to Christ. Thus, young adults were *confirmed* in the faith, accepting responsibility for the commitment made for them at baptism.

Marriage

During the Middle Ages, marriage was transformed from a civil proceeding into a sacrament. The union between a man and a woman came to be compared to the union between Christ and the church. As such it became more than a union between the couple for the purpose of raising a family. It became a ritual for uniting the spouses to each other in Christ. The husband and wife promised to love and care for each other as Christ loved and cared for his church.

Holy Orders

In the Middle Ages, a ritual also developed for inducting men into the priesthood. Bishops, Christ's representatives in the community of the faithful, ordained others, priests, to assist them in their pastoral work. In the ritual of ordination, bishops anointed the new priests' hands with oil to symbolize their sacred role in conferring the grace of God upon their parishioners through the administration of the sacraments. Bishops themselves were consecrated to their new office by the laying on of hands by other bishops.

Until the late Middle Ages, ordained priests could also be married. In the Western church, later reforms established the requirement that priests remain unmarried, or celibate. From this point on a man had to choose between the sacrament of marriage and that of ordination. In the Eastern church priests have always been allowed to marry, but bishops must be celibate.

Confession and Extreme Unction/ Anointing of the Sick

Two additional sacraments were developed during the Middle Ages: confession, to mediate God's forgiveness for sin, and extreme unction anointing of the sick, to confer God's power of healing in times of illness. In the early church it was common for people to put off baptism until death was near, for fear that sins committed after baptism could not then be washed away. To encourage baptism in infancy, the church developed a sacrament for the forgiveness of sins: The penitent would confess his or her sins and express true sorrow for them to a priest, who would then absolve the person, that is, forgive the sins of each in the name of Christ, thereby reconciling the sinner with God. The priest would also assign an appropriate penance for the absolved sinner to complete in reparation for his or her sins. Penance varied depending on the seriousness of the sin but most frequently required the penitent to repeat certain prayers or make a pilgrimage to a sacred place and resolve not to fall into sin again.

Closely associated with the practice of confession was the anointing of the sick with oil. In cases of serious illness, a priest would be called to anoint the Christian with oil in hopes of mediating God's grace to heal the person. Since this ritual of healing was administered to a person who was near death, it was called *extreme unction* and came to be thought of as the sacrament of the dying.

by the church and later emulated by such secular institutions of modernity as the multinational corporation. Whereas each Benedictine monastery was a world unto itself, under its own abbot, all the Cluniac monasteries, regardless of location, were answerable to a central command—the monastic headquarters in Cluny. Under Pope Gregory VII (1073–1085), Rome adopted this form of organization, thus imposing papal authority centered in Rome over all the bishops in the church.

The height of papal power occurred under Pope Innocent III (1198–1216), who forced the kings of England and France into submission, authorized the Fourth Crusade, and carried forward an immensely punitive inquisition against all heretics without interference from civil authorities. Innocent actually had both absolute spiritual power over the church and temporal political power over the state, to which the papacy had long aspired. The weakest moment of papal power, by contrast, occurred, as we have noted in connection with the First Vatican Council, under Pius IX in the late nineteenth century, when the church lost most of its temporal power.

The Promise and Threat of Christian Mysticism

Like every great religion, Christianity has a long tradition of mysticism—referring, in this context, to beliefs and practices thought to lead to a direct and immediate experience of God in Christ. The meaning of this experience is communicated through the biblical claim that human beings are created in the image and likeness of a God who is without image. The closer one comes to being like God, the more one is emptied of ego-identity.

Christian mysticism expresses itself in two dramatically different forms—the mysticism of love and union (the divine–human marriage) and the mysticism of identity. The former is exemplified by Spanish mystics of the sixteenth century, Teresa of Avila and her student, John of the Cross; the latter by the German mystic Meister Eckhart. Unlike early Christian theology, Christian mysticism has for centuries been enriched by the contributions of women: Teresa of Avila, Catherine of Siena, Thérèse of Lisieux, and Julian of Norwich, to name a few. In part this is because mystical experience is viewed as a gift from God that cannot be institutionally controlled. Consequently, it unleashes a powerful impulse toward equality. The mystical experience is accessible to male and female without distinction—all are equally in the image of the God without image.

As with the Jewish tradition, so too in Christianity, mysticism has been viewed ambivalently. This is because some mystics seem to speak as if they are not just in union with God but, in some sense, *are* God. This sometimes seems to be the case for the mysticism of identity. Yet despite this strain of what some consider to be blasphemy, Christianity has continued to affirm the validity and importance of mysticism.

"Christ has no body now but yours. . . . Yours are the feet with which he walks to do good. Yours are the hands through which he blesses all the world."

—St. Teresa of Avila

Christianity, Judaism, Islam: Crusades and Inquisition

Islam, which seemed to appear abruptly in the Arabian desert in the early 600s, grew within the span of a century into a civilization larger than the Roman Empire had been. For a time the Muslims seemed poised to proceed east of Spain to conquer most of Europe. But Charles Martel, whose initiative led to the formation of the Carolingian dynasty and the Holy Roman Empire, turned the Muslims back at Tours in 732. Europe remained Christian, but its holy sites, in Palestine, were in the hands of Muslims.

The Crusades were meant to change that. There were four main Crusades, in 1095, 1147, 1189, and 1202. Armies were organized to march to the Holy Land (Jerusalem and surrounding territories) and free it from the Muslims. But as the crusading armies marched through Europe they unleashed devastating violence on the Jewish communities they encountered along the way, fed by ancient Christian stereotypes of Jews as a "rejected people," killing an estimated 10,000 Jews in Germany alone during the first expedition.

This fourteenth-century manuscript painting depicts the Crusaders at the gates of Jerusalem.

As the Crusaders advanced toward Jerusalem, considerable violence was done even against Orthodox Christians, who were considered semi-heretics by the papal troops. The Muslims were the Crusaders' primary targets, however, for the Muslims held the Holy Land in their possession and threatened the Eastern church, whose main center was Constantinople. Thus the Crusades were ostensibly for the purpose of driving back the Muslims, reclaiming Jerusalem, and reuniting the Eastern and Western branches of the church. Pope Urban II, who preached the First Crusade, promised that all soldiers who participated would have their sins forgiven and would enter heaven. In addition, Crusaders were promised that they could keep the lands they conquered. The Crusaders laid siege to Jerusalem in June 1099, and the city fell on July 15. Muslim men, women, and children lost their lives in a bloody massacre.

The Crusades brought dramatic changes to Christendom, opening up new trade routes and fostering interactions between cultures, all of which stimulated economies. As a result of their exposure to new ideas and attitudes and new religious beliefs and practices, some Europeans embraced new forms of ancient "heretical" beliefs. For example, a religious movement known as the *Cathari* or Albigensians took root in southern France and began to spread. The Cathari believed in reincarnation, and their goal was to liberate the spirit from the evil of a fleshly body. This led Pope Lucius III (1184) to initiate the Inquisition, an effort to stamp out heresy. The Fourth Lateran Council in 1215 authorized the punishment of all heretics by the state and also prescribed distinctive dress for Jews and Muslims (e.g., pointed hats or yellow badges) and restricted Jews to living in ghettos. Soon, inquisitions under church auspices would become infamous for their cruelty.

There were positive consequences of the Crusades as well. Most of Aristotle's work, lost to the West, had been preserved by Islamic scholars. The rediscovery of Aristotle led to new and controversial ways of thinking in the new universities of Europe in the twelfth and thirteenth centuries. And for a brief time Jewish, Muslim, and Christian philosophers, such as Maimonides (1135–1204), Averroes (Ibn Rushd, 1126–1198), and Thomas Aquinas (1224–1274), all used a common philosophical language to learn from each other's traditions, even if only, in the end, so that each could argue for the superiority of his own.

Christianity and Modernity (1517–1962)

The Emergence of Modernity

By the year 1500, Europe had been transformed from a primitive land of farms and undeveloped regions into a network of significant urban centers. In these cities, incorporation, a form of legal agreement that gave citizens the right of self-governance in exchange for taxes paid to the nobility, facilitated the emergence of individualism, an independent economy, and democratic self-governance. With increased craftsmanship and trade, corporate charters were also granted to the new craft guilds or "universities." These corporations mark the beginnings of the secularization of social institutions. Indeed, one of the defining characteristics of modernization is the existence of self-governing institutions that operate independent of direct religious authority (pope and bishops) and also of traditional medieval political authority (kings and lords). Education, too, declared its independence from the monasteries and cathedral schools, as scholars banded together to form their own universities. It was in these institutions of learning that intellectual secularization first appeared, as scholars began to think about their subject matters with a sense of independence from direct church authority. These changes facilitated the development of the institutional and intellectual diversity characteristic of modern secular societies. And in this environment three trends converged to shape the modern West: the millennialism of historical progress, the *via moderna* of autonomous reason, and the *devotio moderna* of emotional transformation.

Millennialism: History as Progress

One strand of modernity had its roots in the apocalyptic visions of Joachim of Fiore (1132–1202), a monk and abbot from southern Italy whose vision of history deeply influenced the modern age. Joachim's *"everlasting Gospel"* suggested that history can be divided into three ages corresponding to the three persons of the Trinity: the age of the Father (beginning with Abraham), which was superseded by the age of the Son (beginning with Christ), which would in turn be replaced by a third and final age, that of the Holy Spirit. Joachim thought of himself as living at the beginning of the *millennium*, the final age of the Spirit, in which there would no longer be any need for the institutional church and its clergy—nor for any other institution, including the state. Joachim, a mystic, expected the Holy Spirit to inspire a natural spontaneous harmony between all individuals, rendering existing institutions superfluous. This third age, which Joachim believed was predicted in the book of Revelation, would be the beginning of the Kingdom of God on earth, an age of perfect freedom and harmony that was destined to last a millennium, that is, a thousand years.

Joachim's version of the myth of history as proceeding through three ages profoundly shaped the modern view of history as a story of progress—history was seen as moving forward from the ancient period through the medieval, culminating in the modern age. For Joachim the third age was identified with the triumph of mysticism over the institutional church. But his three ages became increasingly secularized in the eighteenth century, during the Enlightenment in western Europe. As a result, while the three-age model persisted, the Holy Spirit was no longer identified as the force behind the millennium. For instance, Gotthold Lessing, the great Enlightenment scholar, held that the education of the human race passed through three phases: childhood, adolescence, and adulthood. The last, or third, age he identified with the Age of Enlightenment, in which the autonomy of reason (instead of the Holy Spirit) would lead to a natural and rational harmony among human beings. This vision of three ages was carried forward into the nineteenth century. Auguste Comte, the founding father of sociology, divided history into the ages of myth, philosophy, and science. One can find further parallels in the visions of other nineteenth-century philosophers, such as Hegel and Marx.

The Via Moderna and Devotio Moderna

According to Thomas Aquinas, the greatest of the medieval theologians and also generally regarded as the most influential Roman Catholic theologian, faith complements and completes reason. For Aquinas the Prime Mover known through Greek philosophy (especially Aristotle) is the same as the God of the Bible. One can have some knowledge of God through reason, independent of faith, but scripture enriches this knowledge immeasurably. Faith and reason, rightly used, can never contradict each other. However, the generation of theologians that followed Aquinas, known as *nominalists*, radically disagreed with him. William of Ockham (1287–1347) and other nominalists rejected this view as "ancient" (they called it the *via antiqua*) and outmoded. Espousing instead a *via moderna,* or modern way, these later theologians argued that reason was of little help in discerning the will of God. The split between faith and reason had made its appearance.

The "modern way" secularized the world by separating faith and reason. The only way to know what God wills is through faith as a deep emotional trust in God and a fervent reading of scriptures as the revealed word of God (the *devotio moderna*). The only way to know the world God has created is through rational empirical investigation of the world God has actually created. Thus, when it comes to knowledge of the world, faith requires the secular *via moderna* of rational scientific or empirical inquiry. And when it comes to knowledge of God, only revelation understood through "faith alone" will do. Protestantism and modernity are like two sides of the same coin, arising out of the *via moderna* and *devotio moderna* of the late medieval theology to flourish in the Renaissance and the Reformation. Therefore, unlike all other religious traditions, Protestantism did not, at first, experience modernization as the intrusion of an outside force but rather as a form of experience nurtured from within. It was only as modernization and secularization took on lives of their own, independent of the Protestant Reformation, that they began to appear threatening.

The Renaissance and the Reformation are siblings that grew up together. The intent of the first Renaissance thinkers was to recover the pre-Christian wisdom of the ancient world of Greece and Rome. The Reformation, in a parallel fashion, sought to reach back into antiquity and recover the original New Testament Christian vision as it existed before medieval theologians integrated it with Greek metaphysics. The new ideas of modernity were greatly facilitated by new technology, the printing press. With the introduction of movable type in 1454, a growing popular literacy made possible the rapid and wide dissemination of new ideas. The printing press also greatly accelerated the development of national identities by promoting a common language and shared ideas within a geographic area.

The initiator of the Protestant Reformation was Martin Luther (1483–1546), an Augustinian monk who embraced the new, modern way of thinking. While Luther thought that reason could be useful in secular matters, when it came to matters of faith, Luther called reason a "whore" that could not be trusted to lead one to God. Knowledge of God, rather, can be obtained only through faith and scripture undistorted by reason. "By faith alone," in fact, became the central doctrine of the Protestant Reformation, also embraced by the second major figure of the Protestant Reformation, John Calvin (1509–1564).

The Renaissance and the Reformation fostered a new individualism in the new, free cities by encouraging people to affirm their individuality and to have a sense of personal dignity and equality with others. This way of thinking could not be sustained without a shift from the medieval hierarchical view of authority to a democratic view. Knowledge through empirical inquiry and political authority based on the consent of the governed lie at the heart of the revolution called *modernization*. It is the encounter with these modern notions of knowledge and power, throughout the nineteenth and twentieth centuries, that has placed anxiety in the hearts of traditional or premodern societies around the globe. Such societies, like those of premodern Europe, typically are imbued with a sense of sacred, cosmic hierarchical order in which those in power ruled with sacred authority from above. As suggested earlier, Protestantism was unique in that from the beginning it was part of the revolutionary shift away from divinely decreed hierarchies toward individuality, equality, and dignity.

Devotio Moderna and the Protestant Reformation

The *devotio moderna* is exemplified in Martin Luther's emotional experience of be-

In this portrait of Martin Luther, by the sixteenth-century painter and eyewitness Lucas Cranach the Elder, the fiery reformer, once an Augustinian monk, appears peaceful and contemplative.

IN SILENCIO ET SPE ERIT   FORTITVDO VESTRA

ing "born again." Luther grew up in a medieval Catholic world in transition toward the modern world of the Renaissance. At the insistence of his father he began to train in law as a young man, but after nearly getting hit by lightning in a rainstorm, he abandoned that path, became an Augustinian monk, and was ordained as a priest as well. His quest for moral and spiritual perfection drove him into feelings of great anxiety and hopelessness, for he felt that he could never live up to what was expected of him by God. Then, somewhere between 1511 and 1516, he had a powerful spiritual experience. While studying Paul's letter to the Romans, he suddenly came to see the meaning of the phrase often translated as "The just shall live by faith" (Romans 1:17).

What Luther came to realize, he said, was that he was acceptable before God with all his imperfections, as long as he had faith in Christ, who had died for his sins. There is nothing one can do to be saved. God has done everything. Salvation is a gift of grace. All sinners must do is have faith; and because of that faith, God will treat sinners as if they were saints, as if they were without sin. As this realization came over him, Luther said he was overcome by a liberating and exhilarating experience of having been in the immediate presence of a forgiving and compassionate God.

And Luther now knew that *justification* (i.e., being considered to be just and good) before this God was not by a person's works but by God's grace. One cannot will faith; it is received as a gift from God or pure grace. So salvation is by faith through grace—faith alone understood through scripture alone—not, as the Catholic Church had insisted, through grace *and* works, faith *and* reason, scripture *and* (hierarchical) tradition. This understanding of **justification by faith** is the cornerstone of the Protestant Reformation.

In 1516, Pope Leo X authorized the selling of indulgences to raise funds to rebuild the Cathedral of St. Peter in Rome. That is, the pope promised that the sins of generous donors would be wiped away so that after death, they would avoid all punishment due them for their sins. For Luther, this was the last straw. Salvation was not to be purchased, since it comes by grace and faith alone. On October 31, 1517, Luther posted *Ninety-five Theses Against the Sale of Indulgences* on the church door of Wittenberg Castle, calling for public debate. That event marks the beginning of the Reformation.

Luther's problem was how to reform a church tradition gone corrupt. His solution was to criticize the tradition by raising faith and scriptures to a higher level of authority than church tradition, using scripture to judge and reform the tradition. This was an option open to him that was not available to Christians before the *canon*, or list of books in the New Testament, had been agreed on (after 387). It was the Catholic tradition that picked the scriptures and created the Christian Bible, as Catholics would say, "under the guidance of the Holy Spirit." Without the success of Catholicism, Protestantism's "faith alone, scriptures alone" would not have been possible, and without the failures of Catholicism, Protestant reform would not have been necessary.

Luther started out protesting abuses in the church, but he quickly moved on to challenge the entire mediating role of the church, the sacraments, and the papacy. Luther did not start out to create a new form of Christianity, only to reform the existing tradition. But events took on a life of their own that very quickly turned a reformation into a revolution, and Protestant Christianity was born in a radical break with the ancient, medieval way. In addition to the ancient Catholic way of faith *and* reason, scripture *and* tradition, guided by papal authority, there would be the new, modern Protestant way of faith alone, through scripture alone, and the individual alone before his or her God.

Calvin and the Protestant Ethic

Protestantism was unique in that from the beginning it was part of the revolutionary shift away from sacred hierarchy toward not only secular rationality but also individuality and equality. In this, Protestantism, in conjunction with Renaissance humanism, laid the groundwork for the emergence in the West of the idea of human dignity and human rights. And yet, in the relation of Christianity to the state and to society, the

---

justification by faith: doctrine that humans are saved by faith as a gift from God rather than through works of obedience

---

"Thereupon I felt myself to be reborn and to have gone through open doors into paradise. The whole of scripture took on a new meaning."

—Martin Luther

basic assumptions of the Constantinian/Augustinian visions of the unity of church and state remained operative, at least for the major strands of the Protestant Reformation. The state should be a Christian state, only now that meant Protestant.

Next to Luther, John Calvin was the greatest of the reformers. Calvin spent his life transforming the city of Geneva in Switzerland into a model for Protestant civilization. Arguing that human sinfulness requires that all power be limited, he created a Christian democratic republic with a division of powers among its representative bodies. This institutional strategy served as a model for later secular democracies.

The Protestant work ethic associated with Calvinism really represents the secularization of the Benedictine motto "to work is to pray." Indeed, a major teaching of Luther and Calvin is the idea that work in the world (whether as a shoemaker or doctor, etc.) is as holy a task as praying in a monastery—indeed, a holier task. What makes work holy is not where it is done but doing it as a result of God's call. The **Protestant ethic** demanded that one live simply and work hard: "earn all you can, save all you can" to be able to "give all you can" for the greater glory of God. The early twentieth-century sociologist Max Weber suggested that this ethic helped to fuel the emergence of capitalism in Europe by encouraging both hard work, which allowed individuals to prosper, and savings, which were needed for investment.

Calvinistic concepts are important to note here because in Europe and North America, it was Calvin's rather than Luther's vision of Protestant civilization that most influenced the future, not only of democracy but also of Western capitalism and colonialism.

Protestant ethic: sociologist Max Weber's observation that Calvinist beliefs about holiness and work contributed to accumulation of wealth and facilitated the growth of capitalism

Other Reform Movements

If the *via moderna* split faith and reason apart and confined reason largely to the secular parts of life, the *devotio moderna* of mystical piety played a parallel role, restricting faith to the domain of spiritual emotions. By the fourteenth and fifteenth centuries, a new kind of "this-worldly" mysticism—the *devotio moderna*—was creating popular pietistic movements for spiritual renewal that grew up spontaneously and without official church approval. These "grassroots" movements focused on personal piety founded on intense, emotionally transforming religious experiences. The experiences fostered a new, democratic spirit by emphasizing the equality of all before God and the spiritual benefits to be obtained from living simply. They were typically critical of the medieval Catholic Church, its wealth and its hierarchical order.

The Anabaptist Rebellion Against Both Church and State

We have described the Lutheran and Calvinist center of the Protestant Reformation. However, there were wings to the left and right of this center as well. On the left were the radical reformers and on the right the Anglicans. The radical reformers have deep roots in the mystical and millennial "grassroots" movements of the late Middle Ages.

The Anabaptists were Christians who denied baptism to infants because the practice is not mentioned in the New Testament and because they believed that only those who freely choose to join the church should be baptized. The views of the Anabaptists alienated them from Protestantism and Catholicism and led to their severe persecution by both traditions. By 1535 over 50,000 Anabaptists had been martyred.

Interestingly, the pacifist strands of this movement stand out in the history of Christianity because the Anabaptists do attempt to break with the Constantinian vision of a Christian civilization, rejecting both the authority of the hierarchical church and the authority of the state. This meant that pacifist Anabaptists refused any role in public service on the grounds that the state condones killing and that taking an oath of office goes against one of Jesus' statements in the Sermon on the Mount: "No one can serve two masters" (Matthew 6:24). The Hutterites, the Mennonites, and the Amish are all products of the Anabaptist wing of the Reformation. The most pious of their twentieth-century descendants among the Amish are distinctive for refusing to compromise their principles by taking advantage of modern conveniences such as electricity and motor vehicle transportation.

The Anglican Reformation and the Puritan Revolt

At the other extreme, the English Reformation was initiated by the state rather than by Christians in the churches. Initially the English monarch championed Catholicism against Luther's views as "heretical." Indeed, Pope Leo X conferred the title "Defender

The struggle to keep the premodern traditions pure is difficult. But note that this Amish woman is using in-line skates while pushing a baby stroller to reach her destination faster without utilizing gas or electricity.

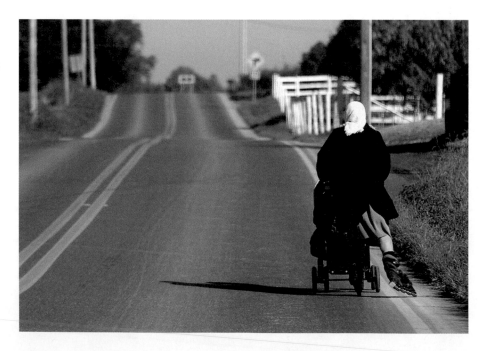

of the Faith" on King Henry VIII. Problems arose, however, when Henry, who had no male heir to the throne, wanted to divorce his first wife, Catherine of Aragon, and remarry in hopes of fathering a son. Pope Clement VII refused to give his permission. So in 1534, Henry VIII nationalized the church, making himself the head of what was now the Church of England. Then the archbishop of Canterbury declared the marriage to Catherine invalid. Nevertheless, apart from breaking with the papacy, the English church remained essentially Catholic, and Henry continued to oppose and often punish those he considered to be heretics. Only after Henry's death were Protestant reformers safe in England.

As Protestants made inroads in Britain, the Church of England's doctrine did not seem pure enough for the Puritans, Calvinist radicals who were intent on returning to a New Testament Christianity shorn of all "popery." After a short period of dominance under their military leader, Oliver Cromwell, Puritans became the object of persecution. Puritanism was a diverse and fragmented movement that had splintered into Congregationalists, Presbyterians (who prevailed in Scotland), Separatists, and Nonconformists, including Baptists—all rejecting the thirty-nine Articles of Religion, the official statement of doctrine of the Church of England. In 1620, 101 Pilgrims sailed for North America. Over 40,000 Pilgrims fled England in the next two decades, bringing to the new colonies their propensity for sectarian diversity.

The Catholic Counter-Reformation

The Council of Trent was a series of meetings held between 1545 and 1563 for the purpose of responding to the reformers. The positions hammered out in these meetings reinforced the absolute power of the pope and made the medieval theology of Thomas Aquinas normative for the Catholic Church. Trent, for the most part, froze Catholicism in its late medieval form. It affirmed that the Catholic "tradition" was equal in authority to scripture and that Latin should remain the language of the Bible and of worship. It also retained the seven sacraments (which Protestantism had reduced to two, baptism and communion) and the importance of the saints, relics, and indulgences. Indeed, the buying and selling of indulgences was not even discussed. At the conclusion of the meetings of the Council of Trent, Pope Pius IV declared that there was "no salvation outside the Catholic faith."

Religious Diversity: Church and State in War and Peace

The Reformation led to political divisions and open warfare between Catholics and Protestants throughout Europe. Like Catholics, all Protestants except the Anabaptists assumed that the goal of Christianity was a Christian civilization. For the most part, however, neither side considered the other side Christian. Each tended to think the other was doing the work of the devil. Consequently, Christians resorted to warfare to settle whose religion would shape the public order. In Germany, a series of wars between Protestants and Catholics ended in the Peace of Augsburg in 1555, with its compromise statement *"cuius regio, eius religio"* (the religion of the ruler shall be the religion of the land). As a consequence, the splintering of the church seemed to match the splintering of Europe into nation-states. Another series of battles, known as the Thirty Years War, erupted but was brought to a conclusion with the Peace of Westphalia in 1648. This was a general settlement that reestablished the conditions of the Peace of Augsburg, with additional protections for minorities and encouragement of religious toleration (see Map 4.2).

Clearly the Protestant Reformation created not a new and purer unity but a new and chaotic diversity. The more people learned to read the Bible for themselves, the more a diversity of interpretations emerged, leading in turn to more and more diverse forms of Christianity. The Protestant Reformation and the religious wars that followed had relativized and privatized religion, making the very act of interpreting the Bible seem more and more private and subjective. Thus, the Reformation helped to create a key element of modern consciousness, the awareness of the relativity of one's understanding of the world and the need to choose one's identity. The result, after much bloodshed, was the gradual transformation of both Protestantism and Catholicism into denominational religions. Whereas in medieval Catholicism and the early sectarian movements of Protestantism, each group had seen itself as the sole repository of truth to which all in society should conform, denominational religions accept the establishment of religiously diverse communities, each expressing the private views of their adherents.

With the emergence of denominationalism, Christianity was on a path leading to a new relationship to the public and political order of society. In North America first and then in Europe, a new understanding of the state emerged—the state as a secular and neutral political institution that favored no one religion. Hence, after the French and American revolutions, the secular, democratic nation-state that functioned by privatizing religion (restricting it to peoples' personal/denominational lives) increasingly became the normative model for the modern Western world. Paradoxically, this development coexisted with the continued assumption by many Christians that the task of Christianity was to Christianize the world. Consequently, as Europe's public order was becoming more and more secular in the nineteenth and twentieth centuries, European Christians were setting out to Christianize the world in concert with Western colonialism's political and economic attempts at global conquest.

Enlightenment Rationalism and Christian Pietism

Pietism and rationalism, two responses to the doctrinal, social, and political divisions created by the Reformation, were rooted in the split between faith and reason that we have already described. And both contributed to the development of Western notions of universal human rights.

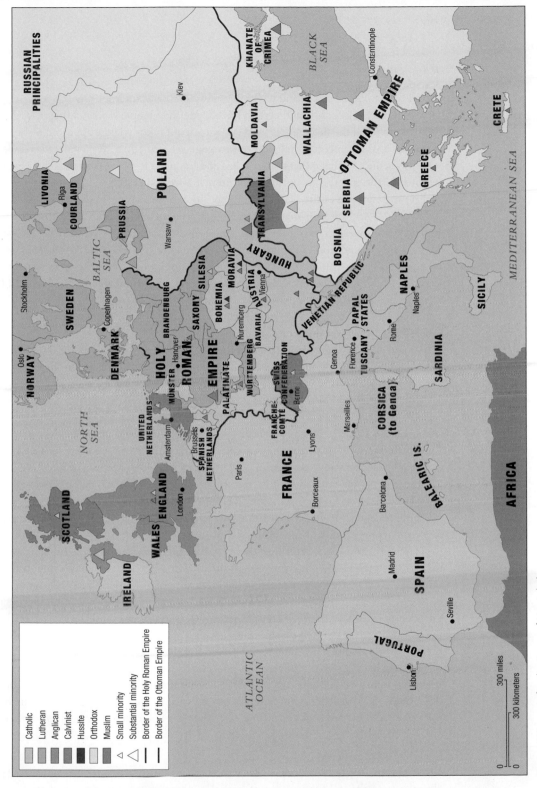

Map 4.2 Europe after the Peace of Westphalia.

Legend:

Catholic
Lutheran
Anglican
Calvinist
Hussite
Orthodox
Muslim

△ Small minority
△ Substantial minority
Border of the Holy Roman Empire
Border of the Ottoman Empire

0   300 miles
0   300 kilometers

**Map labels:**

RUSSIAN PRINCIPALITIES
Kiev
KHANATE OF CRIMEA
BLACK SEA
Constantinople
OTTOMAN EMPIRE
MEDITERRANEAN SEA
CRETE
GREECE
SERBIA
WALLACHIA
MOLDAVIA
BOSNIA
TRANSYLVANIA
HUNGARY
VENETIAN REPUBLIC
LIVONIA
Riga
COURLAND
PRUSSIA
POLAND
Warsaw
BALTIC SEA
Stockholm
SWEDEN
Copenhagen
DENMARK
BRANDENBURG
Hanover
MÜNSTER
SILESIA
SAXONY
MORAVIA
BOHEMIA
Nuremberg
AUSTRIA
Vienna
HOLY ROMAN EMPIRE
BAVARIA
WÜRTTEMBERG
PALATINATE
SWISS CONFEDERATION
Berne
FRANCHE-COMTÉ
NAPLES
Naples
PAPAL STATES
Rome
TUSCANY
Florence
Genoa
SARDINIA
SICILY
CORSICA (to Genoa)
BALEARIC IS.
AFRICA
Marseilles
Lyons
Bordeaux
FRANCE
Paris
Brussels
SPANISH NETHERLANDS
UNITED NETHERLANDS
Amsterdam
NORTH SEA
NORWAY
Oslo
SCOTLAND
IRELAND
WALES
ENGLAND
London
ATLANTIC OCEAN
SPAIN
Madrid
Seville
Barcelona
PORTUGAL
Lisbon

Rationalism

The rise of modern science and technology was dramatic and impressive. Science came to express the most public and certain knowledge that people believed they had about their world. And the more public and certain scientific knowledge appeared to be, the more private and uncertain religious knowledge seemed to be. As science developed, scientists came to believe that they had less and less need to bring God into their explanations. In the nineteenth century, the French astronomer Pierre Laplace announced that he had no need of the "God hypothesis" to explain the world scientifically.

We have seen that in the view of Enlightenment philosopher Gotthold Lessing human beings were entering the third age of history. Lessing called this era the *age of reason*, or the adulthood of the human race. People no longer needed to be told what to believe. To be "enlightened" was to "think for oneself, using one's capacity to reason." Enlightenment rationalism became the foundation of all scientific and public knowledge. The Enlightenment was built on four key concepts:

1. use of one's own reason,
2. freedom from tradition through the rational critique of the past,
3. a view of nature as a finely tuned machine whose mechanisms can be rationally understood, and
4. the belief that history is guided by hidden laws of progress.

deism: enlightenment view that God created the world as a watchmaker does a watch, leaving it to run without interference

The power of reason was assumed to be capable of freeing human beings from the irrationality of the past (including the irrationality of much of religion), of discovering how the universe really works, and of introducing a golden age of progress.

Enlightenment rationalism fostered the emergence of **deism**, which likened the world to a clock and God to a divine clockmaker. Just as a clockmaker makes a perfect machine that runs on its own without assistance from its maker, so God, as creator, does not actively guide or influence events in the world.

The Enlightenment promised to overcome the divisions among human beings that had generated the religious wars of the Reformation by reducing religion to its rational elements. By thus eliminating the emotion-laden "superstitions" of traditional religions, rationalists believed they would create a more tolerant world. Enlightenment rationalists, who identified reason as the one universal that all humanity shared, expected the exercise of universal reason to lead people of every religion and culture into greater harmony. Such an enlightened deism was characteristic of denominations such as the Unitarians and the Universalists and played an important role in championing universal rights. Enlightenment morality contributed to the emergence of a modern ethic of human dignity and human rights by stressing the fundamental unity of the human race. And indeed, in England and elsewhere laws of toleration began to be passed.

Pietism

What was missing in the clockwork universe of deism was warmth or emotion. The alternative to the cold rationality of both Enlightenment rationalism and Protestant rationalism was supplied by Pietism, a new movement that gave rise to evangelical Christianity. In their search for a way of uniting people of faith, who had been divided since the Protestant Reformation, the Pietists explored the nonrational aspects of religion, those in the realm of emotion. Indeed, Pietism was a movement to recover the *devotio moderna* of the late medieval and Reformation periods.

Pietists sought to transcend religious differences by minimizing the role of sectarian dogma, which seemed to divide Christians, and maximizing the role of religious emotion, which they hoped would be a unifying factor. The true test of Christian faith, Pietists argued, is found not so much in right belief or dogmas as in a changed heart. Thus the goal of evangelical piety was in the beginning antisectarian and antidogmatic. One of its greatest representatives, John Wesley (1703–1791), believed passionately that doctrinal differences should not separate Christians. He saw the deep emotion of faith as the way to Christian unity.

The first wave of Pietism came in the seventeenth century. It included such groups as the Moravians and the Quakers. The greatest and most far-reaching expression of Pietism in the eighteenth century was the Methodist movement begun by John Wesley, who was deeply influenced by the Moravians as well as by Catholic and Anglican mystics. Wesley, whose conversion had "strangely warmed" his heart, rejected some of Calvin's ideas and questioned the doctrine of original sin by emphasizing freedom of choice, suggesting that humans were capable of achieving spiritual and moral perfection.

Wesley's message was aimed primarily at the new working class created by the Industrial Revolution. Factory owners did not always pay just wages, and working conditions and hours were often inhumane. The Methodist movement was one of the first constructive responses of Christianity to these changing conditions. Methodist communities were committed to a morality of perfecting both self and society. Mystical piety is a great equalizer in social experience because it is contagious and can overtake anyone, without regard to social status, race, gender, or creed.

Methodism's most striking accomplishments include leading roles in the abolition of slavery in England (1833) and in introducing women into the ministry. Both exemplify the importance of evangelical piety in the development of the modern commitment to human dignity, equality, and rights.

The tremendous power of the Methodist and other evangelical movements tapped a long tradition in the history of Christianity. This is the tradition of combining a simple regimen of prayer and devotion with life in small communities of discipline and mutual encouragement oriented toward improving the world. This formula fueled the monastic movement that missionized the tribes of Europe and brought learning and the heritage of Greek civilization to Europe. This same spirit was carried forward in Calvinism and was transferred to evangelical Christianity, primarily (but not exclusively) through Methodism. In these Protestant formulations, it would be

John Wesley, the founder of Methodism, often preached to the men, women, and children of the new working class during the Industrial Revolution.

carried around the world in the global missions of the nineteenth century. Thus, paradoxically, the Augustinian vision of a mission to Christianize the world that had had such consequences as the Inquisitions and the excesses of the Crusades also afforded a model for promoting human dignity and equality. The arrogant side of Western colonialism brought with it the seeds of its own demise as it spread around the world. Today, the base communities of liberation theology and the communities of indigenous (non-European) spiritual renewal among African and Asian Christians are touched by a postcolonial form of the evangelical missionary message.

Nineteenth-Century Romanticism and Existentialism

The rationalism and pietism of the Enlightenment shared a faith in the progress of the human race. Drawing on the myth of the three ages as formulated by Joachim of Fiore in the thirteenth century, members of these groups shared a millennial faith that they lived in the final age of history, when people would throw off the authoritarianism of past tradition and institutions and instead be guided by a direct inner light that would bring with it progress and harmony. For this to come about, the rationalists relied on the *via moderna* of the light of reason. For the Pietists it was the *devotio moderna*—the warm emotional light of spiritual illumination that comes from being born again. Thus both share the millennial mysticism (of Joachim of Fiore) that has driven the modern spirit of progress. But the progress and harmony they expected from piety and from reason did not come.

The French Revolution in the Wake of the Failure of Reason

At the end of the eighteenth century economic conditions grew very bad in France, and they were not helped by the extravagance of the court of King Louis XVI. This led to a massive revolt, the French Revolution, which began in 1789. In addition to replacing the government, the new leaders created a revolutionary religion featuring a "Cult of Reason" and later a "Cult of the Supreme Being" (deism). The churches were transformed into "Temples of Reason," and statues of the Virgin Mary were replaced by icons of "nature goddesses" and "the goddess of reason." King Louis and his wife, Marie Antoinette, were executed in 1793, and in the Reign of Terror that followed, thousands of clergy and nobility were arrested and beheaded.

The bloody events of the 1790s brought about considerable disillusionment with reason. Reason had been embraced at the beginning of the Enlightenment as the way of avoiding fanaticism, dogmatism, violence, and intolerance. And yet in the French Revolution reason had shown itself to be fanatical, dogmatic, violent, and intolerant. People grew weary of the violence and complexity of urban life and longed for the simplicity of nature uncorrupted by civilization. With the failure of reason, many people turned to emotion as the foundation for renewal of life. If the Enlightenment was rationalistic and mechanistic, the Romantic period that followed was emotional and organic. If the Enlightenment had sought to escape the suffocation of past tradition

GENDER FOCUS: Women in Christianity

Christianity (like Judaism, Islam, and the religions of Asia) arose in *patriarchal* (male-dominated) societies. Historically, women have played the greatest roles in forms of Christianity that valued direct and immediate religious experience (mystical piety) as more authoritative than the institutional authority of the bishops. Thus in the early church women played a greater role in Gnostic (mystical and otherworldly) and Montanist (apocalyptic and ecstatic) Christian movements than in Catholicism, which was institutionally hierarchical. And yet there were always some women who were exceptions to the rule. According to the letters of Paul, women had leadership roles in some of the early Christian communities. As the early church became institutionalized, however, prevailing customs of male dominance seemed to reassert themselves, and the pattern of excluding women from roles as priests and bishops took hold.

During the Middle Ages women found ways to exercise autonomy and independence by founding female monastic orders. With the Protestant Reformation, however, even that option was taken from them, and women were largely confined to the home and child rearing. This began to change in the nineteenth century, when the evangelical missionary movements with deep roots in the mystical traditions of piety (*devotio moderna*) offered new opportunities for women in leadership roles. The role of women in these missions played an important part in the political development of the woman's movement for independence and the right to vote. Also, among the more unusual forms of Christianity, with mystical or Gnostic roots, women founded new traditions. For example, the Shakers, the Unity School of Christianity, and Christian Science were begun by Ann Lee, Emma Curtis Hopkins, and Mary Baker Eddy, respectively.

Another major source of women's autonomy was the *via moderna* as expressed in the denominations influenced by Enlightenment secularization

A civil rights activist who marched with Martin Luther King Jr. in Selma, Barbara Harris was ordained a bishop in the Episcopal Church in 1980.

and rationalism. Consequently, in the nineteenth century women began to be ordained in some Protestant denominations. The Congregationalists led the way in 1853. They were followed by the Universalists, the Unitarians, and other denominations. The mainline Protestant churches (e.g., Methodist, Presbyterian, Episcopal, and Lutheran) did not follow suit until the twentieth century. The Roman Catholic and the Orthodox churches still do not ordain women, arguing that the maleness of Jesus and the apostles reveals the divine intent for an all-male priesthood.

The last four decades of the twentieth century saw the rise of a theologically based feminism. The issue that divides feminists and fundamentalists is whether God created a sacred natural order in which men's and women's roles are eternally defined. Fundamentalists say yes, feminists say no. Feminists say that fundamentalists confuse the cultural attitudes and common practices of premodern societies with the will of God. Fundamentalists turn this argument around, saying that feminists and other liberation advocates confuse the cultural attitudes and common practices of modern societies with the will of God.

and enter a bright new future of scientific advances, Romanticism sought to return to the organic, familial, and deeply emotional connections of traditional agricultural or village society. An ambivalent struggle between these alternative visions is still very much a part of our contemporary culture.

From Reason to Emotion: The Romantic Alternative to Enlightenment Rationalism

"The sum total of religion is to feel that, in the highest unity, all that moves us in feeling is one; . . . that is to say, that our being and living is a being and living in and through God."

—Schleiermacher

The German philosopher Immanuel Kant (1724–1804), the greatest of the Enlightenment philosophers, argued for religion within the limits of reason that focused on ethics, on the grounds that there is no rational way at arriving at belief in God. Friedrich Schleiermacher (1768–1834), considered to be the father of modern Christian theology, offered the Romantic solution to Kant's rationalist challenge, suggesting that knowledge of God comes to people not through reason (the *via moderna*) but rather through emotion (the *devotio moderna*). Consequently, knowledge of God can coexist with scientific knowledge of the world: There is no conflict because the outer, secular, public sphere of reason is separate from the inner, private sphere of faith.

Moreover, Schleiermacher disputed the opinion of some Christians that the affirmation of faith in the resurrection of Jesus Christ depends on historical proof. When a person does not believe in the resurrection one day and then confesses such faith the next day, the theologian argued, the altered conviction was not the result of that person's having learned a new historical fact but of that person's having had a powerful transformative emotional experience. This emphasis on transformative emotion places Schleiermacher directly in the tradition of the *devotio moderna* and evangelical Pietism.

Kierkegaard and the Existentialist Response to Cultural Relativism

"To have a self, to be a self, is the greatest concession made to man, but at the same time it is eternity's demand upon him."

—Kierkegaard

Another important development in modern Christianity was existentialism, marking the start of the postmodern exploration of the implications of cultural relativism. Existentialism was responding to the new thinking that accompanied advances in historical and social scientific consciousness. The results of both historical and ethnographic studies made people aware that various cultures interpreted "human nature" differently. Cultural relativism entails the acknowledgment and examination of these differences.

According to the existentialists, one is not born with an essential human nature. Rather, "existence precedes essence"—that is the core insight of existentialism. When you plant an acorn, you know you will get an oak tree. The essence of the tree is there from its beginnings. But when a human child is conceived, biology is not definitive because human freedom enters into the equation. No one can predict who or what that child will become. The life task of a human being is to create a self through his or her choices.

Søren Kierkegaard (1813–1855) invented what came to be called *Christian existentialism*. Kierkegaard argued that if we have no innate human nature, each person must make a "leap of faith" inspired by faith in Christ to trust God to help him or her construct an identity as a loving and compassionate human being. Like Schleiermacher, Kierkegaard wrote that such faith depends neither on logical reasoning nor on historical proof but on a personal choice driven by powerful emotions that lead one to make the leap of faith.

From the Holocaust to Hiroshima: The Global Collapse of the Modern Myth of History as Progress

The existentialist response to the social sciences and cultural relativism led some philosophers, such as Friedrich Nietzsche (1844–1900), to conclusions quite the opposite of Kierkegaard's—namely, that history and ethnography show "God" to have been a human invention, who is now dead, a circumstance that obliges us to invent our identities without God.

Christian faith is proved not by scientific and/or historical facts, nor by metaphysical arguments, but by the emotional, moral, and spiritual transformation of the individual. In making this argument, Friedrich Schleiermacher became the founder of modern Protestant theology.

For Nietzsche, the modern world was incompatible with belief in the biblical God: History had demythologized the sacred stories of the Bible and shown them to be false even as science had demythologized the biblical view of creation and replaced it with Darwin's theories of evolution. As Nietzsche saw it, European Christians who acted as if Christianity and modernity were compatible would one day realize that in embracing modernity they had killed God. Recalling the argument between fundamentalists and modernists at the beginning of this chapter, we can now see that Nietzsche and fundamentalists shared at least one conviction—that belief in God is incompatible with modernity. But for fundamentalists this meant that Darwin's theories had to be rejected, whereas for Nietzsche it meant belief in God had to be rejected.

Nietzsche, having rejected the God of the Bible, believed that history is guided by a struggle for existence that takes the form of a "will to power." Like Kierkegaard, he argued human beings must choose who they will become, but he believed their choices should be preceded by a rejection of Christian values and beliefs. The problem with Christianity, said Nietzsche, is that biblical morality teaches "weak values" such as forgiveness and pity that ultimately lead to resentment against persons who are strong and courageous. They lead, the philosopher believed, to an ideal of "equality" that rewards mediocrity. Nietzsche therefore called biblical values bad for civilization. The future, he believed, should belong to the strong—those superior and creative individuals who had the courage to "transvalue all values" and to make their own morality.

Little more than half a century after Nietzsche announced the death of God, the Nazis came along to embrace Nietzsche's vision of a will to power. Nietzsche's model for a world ruled by superior persons was not that of the Nazis, who distorted the philosopher's ideas when they cast themselves as those superior human beings destined to re-create the world. What Nietzsche's vision did have in common with that of the Nazis was contempt for the ideals of equality and democratic rule that Nietzsche associated with Christianity.

Nietzsche, who had characterized Christians as weak because their religion taught them to show compassion and pity, might have been surprised by the number of churchgoers who showed themselves quite willing to abandon their weak values of compassion in exchange for the Nazi ideals of elitism and the will to power. Between 1933 and 1945, Hitler and the Nazi Party ruled Germany and drew Europe and America into World War II (1939–1945).

One of the key factors in Hitler's rise to power was his successful appeal to anti-Semitism in German and Austrian culture. Hitler was able to achieve power, in large part, by appealing to long-standing prejudice against the Jews created by the churches over the centuries. By the time of the Middle Ages, Christians viewed Jews as deserving to suffer for rejecting and crucifying the messiah, the Son of God. Consequently, the Nazis were able to strip the Jews of their citizenship, confiscate their property, and send them off in boxcars to concentration camps without serious resistance from the churches and often with their assistance. Over 6 million European Jews are estimated to have been killed, mostly in the gas chambers of the Nazi concentration camps.

> "Being a Christian is less about cautiously avoiding sin than about courageously and actively doing God's will."
>
> —Dietrich Bonhoeffer

The Christian churches might have been a powerful force against the Nazi attempt to exterminate the Jews, but they were not. In Germany, by some estimates, only 20 percent of the Protestant churches resisted Hitler and the Nazi message, as the famous Protestant theologian and martyr Dietrich Bonhoeffer did. Even fewer took issue with the treatment of the Jews. Pope Pius XI signed a concordat with Hitler in hopes of protecting the autonomy of the German Catholic churches. Most Christians passively acquiesced in the Nazi program of genocide, and many actively cooperated.

A minority of Christians held fast to what Nietzsche called the "weak values" of Christianity (love and compassion) and rescued Jews, but with a few important exceptions they were lone individuals of conscience. Christians in Denmark were one notable exception, and most of Denmark's Jews survived because of collective resistance by church and state. Le Chambon sur Lignon in France is another such exception: This small village of mostly French Protestants saved over 5,000 Jewish lives. Wherever the churches led resistance to the Nazis, Jewish lives were saved. Unfortunately, that did not happen often. As the church historian Franklin Littell has noted, the irony is that more priests and ministers died in Hitler's armies than died resisting Hitler.

Reflection on the lessons of the Holocaust brought unprecedented change to Christianity in the last decades of the twentieth century. Since Vatican II and in response to the Holocaust, not only the Catholic Church but also the main Protestant denominations have sought to correct past teachings about the Jews as a rejected people (the myth of supersession) and have replaced these teachings with an affirmation that the Jewish covenant is an authentic covenant with God—one that exists both prior to and apart from the Christian covenant. This public acknowledgment of the Jewish people as chosen by God and of the religion of Judaism as a valid expression of monotheism is unprecedented in the history of Christianity.

The horrors of World War II made Nietzsche's claim that God was dead seem more plausible. The killing of millions on the battlefields and in the camps, achieved by means of the latest science and technology, represented the death of what "God" had become for many in Western civilization, namely, the "God of progress." The millions upon millions of dead and the shameless reality of the Nazi death camps gave modern persons good reasons to question whether modernity and "progress" were truly worthy human ideals. Science and technology had become essential instruments in the propagation of mass death.

Finally, with the dropping of the atomic bomb on Hiroshima, Japan, at the end of World War II and the accumulation of nuclear weapons by the USSR and the United States in the second half of the twentieth century, a turning point may have emerged. The possibility of a nuclear war that would destroy the planet made belief in the progress of history and a better future through science and technology seem far from inevitable. As the world moves beyond its modernist phase, many Christians are beginning to explore the possibility of separating the church's message from the myth of history as progress and from the assumptions of the cultural superiority of the West that reinforced colonialism.

> "The madman jumped into their midst and pierced them with his eyes. 'Whither is God?' he cried; 'I will tell you. *We have killed him*—you and I. All of us are his murderers.'"
>
> —Friedrich Nietzsche, "The Parable of the Madman"
>
> SOURCE: Friedrich Nietzsche, *The Gay Science* (1882, 1887) para. 125; Walter Kaufmann, ed. (New York: Vintage, 1974), pp. 181–82.

Christianity and Postmodern Trends in a Postcolonial World (1962–)

From Colonial to Postcolonial Christianity

For most of its history Christianity has been predominantly a European religion. The Christianity that fostered the rise of modernization and the myth of progress was not that of the Eastern Orthodox churches, which saw Christian civilization as a sacred unity of church and state. It was Western Augustinian Christianity, with its model of two cities, one sacred and the other secular.

Europe gave birth to Roman Catholicism during the Middle Ages and to modern Christianity with the Protestant Reformation. In 1600 the overwhelming majority of Christians in the world lived in Europe. However, the invention of the modern three-masted sailing ship (ca. 1500) unleashed massive changes that began when the countries of Europe acquired their first colonies and seems to be culminating in the birth of a global civilization. Colonial expansion was accompanied by worldwide missionary activity, led first by Catholic countries such as Portugal and Spain and later by countries with new Protestant centers of power, especially England. By 1900 only half of all the Christians in the world lived in Europe, and by the end of the twentieth century the majority of the world's Christians resided elsewhere, in Latin America, Africa, and Asia. Thus, postcolonial Christianity is decisively non-European.

Even as church membership was waning in Europe, it was planting the seeds of its possible transformation and renewal in postcolonial forms elsewhere in the world. On the one hand, while birthrates among Christians declined in Europe, the number of children born to Christians elsewhere increased dramatically. On the other hand, the secularization of Europe led to a large decline in the practice of Christianity there. Paradoxically, at the same time, through European colonial expansion, Protestant evangelical Christians engaged in a massive missionary enterprise whose aim was the Christianization of every part of the world touched by colonization (see Map 1.3 in Chapter 1). This plan was justified by the assumption that the political and economic colonization of the world by Europe was part of God's plan to make possible the spread of the Gospel to the very ends of the earth.

The feeling of the superiority and global destiny of European civilization that accompanied colonialism communicated itself through an attitude of paternalism. At first many in the premodern cultures were impressed with the wonders of Western science and technology. Before long, however, indigenous peoples came to feel demeaned and diminished by the Westerners' attitude toward them.

In former colonial areas, whether in Africa, Asia, or the Americas, resentment against western Europeans inevitably led to a political backlash that typically coalesced around liberation movements. Activists called for rejection of some Western values, such as capitalism and individualism, in favor of political and economic independence and restoration of traditional values and customs. Paradoxically, at the same time, other values espoused by the West, such as dignity and equality, lent support to these indigenous liberation movements. We see this paradox, for example, in Gandhi's campaign to liberate India from English colonial domination, which appealed both to Hindu values and to modern Western values in just this way.

If colonialism brought modernity to the non-European world, the rejection of Western colonialism can be said to mark the beginnings of postcolonial and postmodern trends in Christianity. It is among postcolonial Christians that we might find the beginnings of a new postcolonial and non-Eurocentric form of Christianity, more open to coexistence with other religions and cultures.

Latin America

liberation theology: liberation theology emerged in Latin America in the twentieth century; the goal was to show that the Gospel was more radical than Marxism in its promotion of justice for the poor

Latin America was colonized in the sixteenth century by Spain and Portugal, two Roman Catholic countries untouched by the Protestant Reformation. Thus the Spanish and the Portuguese brought to the New World medieval patterns of social order that were hierarchical and antidemocratic. By the mid-twentieth century, however, the forces of secularization and Marxism had taken their toll, and while 90 percent of Latin Americans were baptized, only about 15 percent were estimated to be practicing their faith. This situation set the context of the emergence of postcolonial movements of **liberation theology** and evangelical–charismatic Christianity.

In the last decades of the twentieth century, Latin American Christians (mostly Catholics) exposed to the Marxist analysis of European colonial exploitation criticized the traditional hierarchical order of society that reinforced privileges for the few and ensured poverty and oppression for the many. Their response was called liberation theology. These ideas, in turn, produced a backlash among some branches of Evangelical and Pentecostalist Protestant Christianity, the movements that had inspired the missionary zeal of the nineteenth century. These evangelical and Pentecostal Christians saw liberation theologies as a new form of the social gospel and its ultimate sellout of Christianity to modern culture. In an effort to return to the premodern spiritual foundations of their faith, Pentecostalists and others downplayed issues of cultural and economic oppression. Rather, they focused on issues of personal conversion (being born again) and/or ecstatic experience (e.g., speaking in tongues). Their idea was to transform society through personal virtue that could be cultivated by spiritual means within the parameters of any social system in which individual Christians happened to live.

For Christians in the liberation movements, the heart of the Gospel is love for the poor and the struggle for social justice. For evangelical Christians it is personal conversion, personal regeneration in the Spirit, and the shaping of a public order that will give priority to these goals. Despite their differences, however, both parties regard Christianity as the only appropriate means of shaping the public order of political and economic life.

For some Christians, worship inspires hope for a world of justice and compassion. A liberation theology base community meets in Panajachel, Guatemala, to hear the good news from scripture that Jesus Christ has come to liberate the poor and the oppressed.

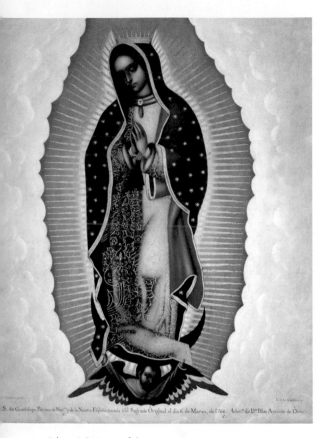

S. de Guadalupe, Patrona de Mex.ᵒ y de la Nueva España, tocada à su Sagrado Original, el dia 6. de Marzo, de 1760.   Adevᵒ de Dᵗ Blas Antonio de Oviñ

Africa

For models of Christianity that break with both the premodern and modern visions of a "Christian civilization" one must look primarily to the African and Asian churches, where we see the emergence of a "diaspora" model of Christianity. A diaspora religion is one whose adherents are "dispersed" as minority communities among many nations and cultures.

Except for the ancient Coptic Church in Egypt and the Church of Ethiopia, Christianity in Africa is the result of missionary efforts primarily from the colonial period. At the beginning of the twentieth century there were scarcely any Christians in Africa. At the end of the century it was the fastest-growing geographic area for Christianity, and more than a fifth of the world's Christians can be found there today. Almost half of the population of Africa is now Christian, with Islam a close second.

As the number of converts to Christianity grew, the people overcame the tight control missionaries had sought to maintain over African Christianity by developing indigenous forms. One of the most interesting of the African independent church movements is Isaiah

(above) Painting of the Virgin of Guadalupe, who is said to have appeared to a peasant in Mexico in 1531. The Virgin Mary, mother of Jesus, conveys God's love and compassion to Catholic believers around the world.

(right) In Africa and everywhere around the world, entry into the Christian faith is through the ritual of baptism, as shown here in Mozambique.

Shembe's Nazareth movement, whose members openly long for a black Christ. Shembe is described as having a miraculous birth and being born of the Spirit—as one who came from heaven so that native Africans might know that God is with them. In general in the twentieth century, even among the more traditional denominational native African congregations, Christianity became more and more African and less and less European. Such African churches involve strong **syncretistic** elements; that is, some of their beliefs and practices are Christianized versions of indigenous pre-Christian religious elements.

syncretistic: identification of the gods of one religion with the gods of another

There is a liberation theology in Africa, but, as the leadership of retired Anglican bishop Desmond Tutu in South Africa illustrates, it is less on the model of Latin American Marxist theory and more on the model of the nonviolent civil rights movement in the United States. Indeed, the movement led by Martin Luther King Jr. is an interesting blend of the liberation passion for justice with an evangelical ecstatic piety that is revealed in his moving and passionate public speaking style that moves both heart and mind. This type of evangelical/Pentecostalist piety has also left its stamp on African Christianity, commingling with the experiential/ecstatic elements of traditional African tribal religions. In the twenty-first century, African Christianity is likely to be a major contributor to the development of a postcolonial Christianity. However, in Africa, Christianity's success tempts believers to envision a "Christian Africa."

Archbishop Desmond Tutu and Nelson Mandela triumphantly greet the crowds at the City Hall in Cape Town, South Africa, after Mandela's election as State President (May 11, 1994).

Asia

European colonialism moved into Africa and Asia simultaneously. The British went into Ceylon (Sri Lanka), India, Burma (Myanmar), Malaysia, Singapore, Hong Kong, and various Pacific islands (also Australia and New Zealand). The French expanded into the Indochina peninsula, including Laos and Cambodia. As in Latin America and Africa, the spread of Christianity that accompanied this colonial expansion was driven by the same Augustinian sense of the providential link between the expansion of European civilization and the spread of the Gospel.

Asia presented Christianity with interesting new challenges. The expansion of a great world religion, it seems, can be stopped only by another great world religion, such as Hinduism or Confucianism. In Asia, Christianity is a distinct minority presence and seems unlikely ever to become the religion of civilizational order. Asia's contribution to the development of a postcolonial Christianity may well be the development of a diaspora model of Christianity,

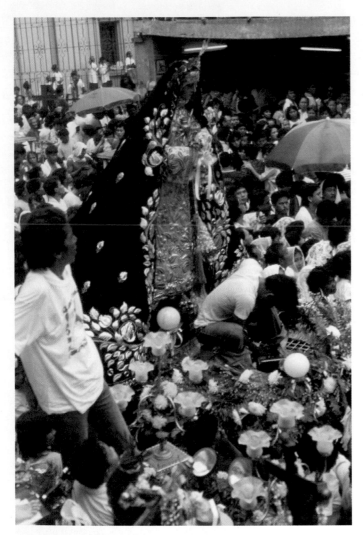

The Black Nazarene festival in the Philippines is illustrative of the indigenization of Christianity in local cultures.

one that will transcend traditional Western civilizational and denominational boundaries and be open to creative coexistence with other religions and cultures. We shall briefly survey this movement as it is unfolding in South and East Asia.

India

According to ancient Christian traditions, Thomas, one of the twelve apostles of Jesus, brought Christianity to India. In the sixteenth and later centuries Jesuits, Dominicans, and representatives of other Catholic orders spread their faith in India and elsewhere in Asia. As in Africa and Latin America, the major Protestant incursion was the wave of mission activity that accompanied nineteenth-century colonialism. Once India had won its independence from British colonial rule in 1947, there was increasing pressure on the churches in India to become less European and more Indian. In response, Indian Christians began to move beyond European denominational Christianity.

In 1947 Anglicans merged with Methodists and other Protestant bodies to form the Church of South India. Much later, the Protestant Church of North India was founded and also a Protestant Church of Pakistan (1970). With these changes there was also a shift of emphasis from conversion to dialogue, with the goal of showing the compatibility of Hinduism and Christianity. Christians have had to learn how to live as a diaspora religion in a largely Hindu culture, renewing efforts to indigenize Christianity with the appearance of Christian ashrams (both Protestant and Catholic) and syncretistic trends resulting in Hinduized forms of Christian worship.

China

Similar patterns of missionary activity by Catholics followed by Protestants occurred in China and Japan. Although Christian missionary activity goes back to the seventh century, it was aggressive colonial missionizing that led to backlash and persecution

Everywhere the story of Jesus has been told, believing artists have tried to present the events in terms of their own cultures. In this way the universal appeal of the story of Jesus is demonstrated, as in this depiction by the Indian artist Jamini Roy of the Holy Family's flight to Egypt.

in the nineteenth and twentieth centuries. Nineteenth-century colonialism brought the first large-scale attempts to convert the Chinese. China did not welcome the missionary movements and permitted them only under the military and economic duress that accompanied colonialism. After the Communists came to power in 1949, many missionaries were either imprisoned or expelled. Chinese Christians were persecuted and often forced to undergo "reeducation."

With the coming of Mao Zedong's Cultural Revolution in 1966, churches were closed, Bibles burnt, and Chinese priests and ministers sent to work camps. All public worship was banned. Nevertheless, Chinese Christians persisted by secretly worshipping in private homes (*house churches*). When Western relations with China improved in the 1980s, it was discovered that indigenous forms of Christianity had survived and were still being practiced in that country.

Today, Christianity, an estimated 5.1 percent of the population of China, is thriving and growing, with government tolerance—including house churches—so long as it appears indigenous and not the result of "foreign" missionaries. Government persecution seems to be focused on those Christian movements that advocate unpatriotic political issues, such as human rights, that threaten the Confucian ethos of Chinese society.

Japan

Until the nineteenth century Japan was largely closed to all Western enterprises, including missionary activity. While as early as the 1500s, the Jesuit Francis Xavier (1506–1552) had established a Catholic community in Japan, the Jesuits were driven out by severe persecution in the next century. Nevertheless, when missionaries returned in the mid-nineteenth century they found a thriving community of "hidden Christians" at Nagasaki. These believers were considered by Japanese rulers to be unpatriotic and subversive. Very quickly, Japanese Christians moved to assert their independence from Western forms of Christianity and to develop indigenous forms.

The Japanese Protestant leader Uchimura Kanzo is famous for having started the "nonchurch" movement. He saw Western church structures as culturally inappropriate to Japanese culture and sought to restructure Christianity on the Asian teacher–disciple model. He tried to demonstrate in his life that it was possible to be both a patriotic Japanese citizen and a Christian. Ironically, the atomic bomb dropped on Nagasaki destroyed the oldest center of Christianity in Japan. After the war, Japanese Christians turned strongly pacifist and sought to break with the Japanese state by resisting any move toward government involvement with Shintoism.

Korea

Korea is the great success story of Christian missionary activity in Asia. A Catholic presence in Korea goes back to the eighteenth century. Protestant missionaries came in the 1870s, but significant growth did not occur until Korea began signing trade agreements with the West in the 1880s. Korean interest in Christianity mounted after the Japanese victory over China in 1895, which Koreans rightly felt was threatening to their own autonomy. Christianity became identified not only with modernization and Westernization but also with anti-Japanese sentiments, which increased in 1910, when Japan annexed Korea.

After World War II, the victorious Allies divided the country into North and South Korea, and civil war followed (1950–1953). Communists in North Korea have driven out Christians there, although house churches may survive. South Korea has the highest percentage of Christians of any nation in Asia except for the Philippines. Nowhere in Asia (except for the Catholic Philippines) has Christianity played as strong a role in public life as it has in South Korea, whose first two presidents were Christians. Since the 1970s a highly political liberation theology similar to that developed in Latin America, known as *minjung* theology, has emerged. And as in Latin America, Africa, India, China, and Japan, Korea too developed its own indigenous forms of Christianity, the most famous of which is the Unification Church of Sun Myung Moon, who is heralded by his followers as a new messiah—in this case an Asian messiah.

Given that the majority of Christians in the world are now non-European, it is likely that much of postcolonial Christianity will draw on the experiences of the various Asian "mission churches." The question remains whether the dominant model will be an African model, aspiring against the odds to Christianize the continent, or an Asian model of diaspora churches, creatively relating to the consequences of globalization and a world that is religiously diverse.

North America—the United States

Although the first explorers and settlers in North America were the Vikings and then later and more successfully the Spanish, and although France extended its reach to the continent as well, the United States came to be primarily as a result of colonization by the British. Indeed, it was a revolt against British colonialism by the citizens of its colonies that led to the Declaration of Independence in 1776 and later to the Constitution of the United States of America as the foundation for a new nation as formulated in 1787.

The citizens of the thirteen colonies that became the United States of America were largely but not exclusively refugees from the political intolerance toward sectarian religious minorities experienced in Europe. At first the European pattern of sectarian rivalry continued in the New World, but it soon became clear to the colonists that the uniqueness of America as an alternative to Europe had to lie in toleration of diversity. Consequently, the very first amendment to the U.S. Constitution declares: "Congress shall make no law respecting an establishment of religion, or prohibiting the free exercise thereof." These words guarantee religious freedom to all Americans by forbidding the government to name any religion as the state religion. This amendment, which became effective in 1791, created a major break with the Constantinian and Augustinian models of Christian civilization and opened the door to diaspora models of Christianity. It was, however, a legal transformation that took on cultural embodiment only as non-Christian populations in America began to grow.

In the nineteenth and twentieth centuries Protestant denominationalism emerged as a new pattern for a culture characterized by religious diversity, and new denominations proliferated out of all proportion to Protestant divisions in Europe. Gradually, diverse religious communities in North America came to think of the church as an invisible reality embracing all Protestants and denominations as voluntary associations that one joined according to one's preferred style of being Protestant.

Enlightenment rationalism and evangelical Pietism, both of which de-emphasized dogmatic divisions, deeply influenced the emergence of denominationalism. But this new perspective was, at first, developed around the notion of America as a Protestant nation. Therefore, it was very traumatic when, beginning in the latter half of the nineteenth century, Catholic and Jewish immigrants poured into the United States and tipped the balance away from a Protestant majority. This led to a strong reaction of anti-Catholicism and anti-Judaism, which did not disintegrate until the last half of the twentieth century, when Protestant, Catholic, and Jew came to be seen as acceptable alternatives within the denominational pattern. In the twenty-first century, the modern equilibrium is being further challenged by influxes of immigrants from Asia and the Middle East. In an emerging global civilization, U.S. citizens who are Muslim, Hindu, or Buddhist are increasing in numbers and in prominence.

TALES OF SPIRITUAL TRANSFORMATION: Martin Luther King Jr.'s Kitchen Experience

Martin Luther King Jr. transformed the social and political landscape of America in the 1950s and 1960s by leading a movement of nonviolent protest against the practices of racial segregation in American life. The "civil rights movement," as it came to be known, led to equal rights under the law for people of all races and opened the way for the election of the first black president of the United States in 2008.

During the civil rights movement, King's life was threatened on a regular basis. There was a defining religious experience that lay behind his courage to continue despite these threats. King came home late from a bus boycott meeting when the movement was just beginning in Montgomery, Alabama. He was sitting in his kitchen when the phone rang. A voice said: "Nigger . . . we are tired of you and your mess now, and if you are not out of this town in three days, we're going to blow your brains out and blow up your house." Although he had received dozens of such calls before, this one got to him. Fear gripped him and he could not sleep, so he went to the kitchen for a cup of coffee. James Cone records King's telling of what happened.

Something said to me, you can't call on daddy now; he's in Atlanta, a hundred seventy-five miles away. . . . You've got to call on that something, on that person that your daddy used to tell you about, that power that can make a way out of no way. And I discovered then that religion had to become real to me and I had to know God for myself. And I bowed down over that cup of coffee. I never will forget it. Oh yes, I prayed a prayer. And I prayed out loud that night. I said, "Lord, I'm down here trying to do what's right. I think I'm right. I think the cause that we represent is right. But Lord, I must confess that I'm faltering, I'm losing my courage and I can't let the people see me like this because if they see me weak and losing my courage they will begin to get weak." . . . Almost out of nowhere I heard a voice . . . "Martin Luther, stand up for righteousness. Stand up for justice. Stand up for truth. And lo, I will be with you, even until the end of the world." After that experience . . . I was ready to face anything. (James Cone, *Martin and Malcolm and America: A Dream or a Nightmare* [Maryknoll, NY: Orbis Books, 1991], 124–125).

Three days later King's home was bombed. Fortunately no one was hurt. While some gathered with guns seeking to protect him, he urged them to remain nonviolent, and he reminded them that no matter what happened, God would be with them in their struggle.

Consequently, the decision of whether to be a Christian civilization or adopt a diaspora model of Christian life is playing itself out not only in the developing world but in North America as well. Fundamentalism wants to create a public order focused on creating a "Christian America," yet a North American form of liberation theology seems to be embracing a diaspora model of Christianity. The liberation movement sees itself as one force among many, seeking social justice for all in a pluralist society. The roots of North American liberation theology lie not so much in Marxist liberation theology as is the case in South America. Rather, North American liberation theology is shaped primarily by the civil rights movement, initiated by the Reverend Martin

Not all Christian houses of worship in America have that New England look. This adobe mission church is in Taos, New Mexico.

Luther King Jr., perhaps the most important figure for understanding postmodern Christianity in an age of globalization.

On December 1, 1955, Rosa Parks, a black woman in Montgomery, Alabama, refused to move to the segregated section at the back of a public bus. Her subsequent arrest aroused the churches in the black neighborhoods of Montgomery to organize a boycott of the buses and to demand repeal of the state's bus segregation laws. The Reverend Martin Luther King Jr., pastor of the Dexter Avenue Baptist Church, himself the son of a Baptist minister, was elected to lead the boycott. The boycott marked the beginning of the struggle to end segregation (ca. 1954–1966). The boycott came to a successful conclusion when the Supreme Court declared Alabama laws requiring segregated buses unconstitutional. The ruling, on November 13, 1956, took practical effect on December 21, 1956.

King introduced a diaspora model of Christianity into American social and political life. He was open to the wisdom of other religions, for he believed that God spoke to humanity in every time and in every culture. Indeed, he drew on the principles of nonviolence and civil disobedience first perfected by the great Hindu leader Mohandas K. Gandhi to bring about a nonviolent racial revolution

CONTRASTING RELIGIOUS VISIONS

As the following contrasting visions indicate, every religious tradition is capable of generating both visions that encourage peace and understanding and visions that encourage conflict and violence.

Martin Luther King Jr.— the Gospel of Divine Mercy

The single most important Christian example of postmodern Christianity, open to other religions and global diversity, is Martin Luther King Jr. It is he that others, such as Bishop Desmond Tutu of South Africa, took as their model. King lived and died by Jesus' teachings from the Sermon on the Mount, found in the Gospel of Matthew (chapters 5–7). Here Jesus tells his hearers to love their enemies, do good to those who persecute them, and, when struck, turn the other cheek. God's love, like the rain, says Jesus, falls on the just and the unjust alike. In addition, the apostle Paul explains that God's love of his enemies is expressed in the fact that Christ died for "the ungodly," all who were "still sinners" so that "while we were enemies we were reconciled through the death of his Son" (Romans 5:6–11, NRSV). For Martin Luther King Jr., these teachings of Jesus are the heart of the Gospel and therefore the heart of Christianity. Christians must follow these teachings and love their enemies.

For centuries Christians were inspired by these teachings yet sought ways to avoid having to put them into practice. It was typically argued that "in the real world" to love your enemies while "turning the other cheek" was the equivalent of turning the world over to the rule of those who were most violent and unjust, which would be disastrous. So early Christian theologians like Augustine of Hippo developed the idea of "just war" or the just use of violence to protect the weak and the innocent. It was Martin Luther King Jr.'s study of Gandhi's philosophy of nonviolence that enabled him to see that there was another alternative—nonviolent resistance to evil.

Martin Luther King Jr. transformed the social landscape of American society by integrating the Sermon on the Mount with Gandhi's techniques of nonviolence to further racial and social justice in the United States.

King argued that the way of violent retribution, "an eye for an eye," only escalates the violence (even in a "just war") and leaves everyone blind. With the strategy of nonviolent resistance, however, you do not simply hand the world over to those who are most violent. On the contrary, you create a mass movement of nonviolent noncooperation that brings the normal business of society to a standstill until your enemy consents to compromise and begins to act more justly. This was the strategy King used to organize the bus boycott in Montgomery, Alabama, in 1955–1956. A major portion of the users of the bus system were black, and when they stopped riding the buses the city could not bring in enough income to run the bus system, which many whites also needed to use. This in turn affected the amount of shopping that was being done in the city, which hurt the economy. Within a year the city was forced to rescind the law requiring racial segregation of the buses, and justice for all its citizens was increased without resort to violence by King's movement.

Tim LaHaye and Jerry B. Jenkins: *Left Behind*—the Gospel of Divine Judgment

Reportedly, more than 65 million books in the *Left Behind* series have been sold, and a children's series has sold more than 10 million copies. In addition there are a variety of related materials—movies, clothes, games, music, and so on. The series of novels on the coming end of the world is the core of a religious media sensation in contemporary American life and culture. In an interview for the television news program *60 Minutes* (broadcast April 14, 2004), the books' authors, Tim LaHaye and Jerry B. Jenkins, insisted that according to the Bible, when Jesus comes to judge the earth at the end of time he will not be forgiving his enemies. On the contrary, he will be God's warrior who comes to slay God's enemies in a final battle between believers and unbelievers, in which all believers will be "raptured" (lifted up into heaven) and all nonbelievers will be "left behind."

Martin Luther King Jr. put the emphasis on the Jesus of the Sermon on the Mount, who emphasizes that God who loves the "just and the unjust" alike, while the authors of the *Left Behind* series emphasize the Jesus who comes to judge the world at the end of time. In the *60 Minutes* interview with Morley Safer, *Left Behind* coauthor LaHaye explains: "Unfortunately, we have gone through a time when liberalism has so twisted the real meaning of scripture, that they have manufactured a loving, wimpy Jesus that would never

Not all Christians have embraced Martin Luther King Jr.'s nonviolent Christian message. In their best-selling "Left Behind" book series, Tim LaHaye and Jerry B. Jenkins portray the violence and terror of the God who comes to destroy his enemies at the end of time

do anything in judgment, and that is not the God of the Bible." To this, coauthor Jenkins adds that they stay as close to the Bible as you can get. Jesus' "slaying the enemy . . . and the fact that the enemies' eyes melt in their head, their tongues disintegrate, their flesh drops off—I didn't make that up, that is out of the prophecy." For these authors, the Gospel's final message is not God's love for his enemies as found in Jesus' Sermon on the Mount but the violence and terror of the God who comes to destroy his enemies, which they believe can be found in the book of Revelation.

in the United States. Moreover, he worked to bring an end to the war in Vietnam that was raging in the 1960s by participating in a cooperative nonviolent protest movement with Jewish and Buddhist leaders such as Abraham Joshua Heschel and Thich Nhat Hanh.

Dr. King and the Southern Christian Leadership Conference, which he founded in 1957, were at the forefront of these efforts. In 1963, *Time* magazine named Martin Luther King Jr. "Man of the Year"—the first black American ever so designated. In June 1964 the Civil Rights Act was passed, and in December King became the youngest person ever to win the Nobel Peace Prize. Then in the spring of 1965, King, accompanied by Rabbi Heschel and others, led a successful march from Selma to Montgomery, Alabama, to emphasize the need for laws to protect the right to vote for all blacks. He compared it to Gandhi's march to the sea to protest the Salt Act. It was, indeed, a turning point, for on August 6, 1965, the Voter Rights Act was signed by President Lyndon Johnson. On April 4, 1968, at the age of thirty-nine, King was assassinated by a sniper in Memphis, Tennessee, but the civil rights movement went on to transform America to the extent that in 2008 the United States elected its first black President, Barack Obama.

Conclusion: The Challenge of Religious Pluralism

A significant gulf divides the fundamentalist and postmodern ways of affirming Christian faith. Modern Christians tended to privatize religion and segregate personal piety from public life. Religion is a personal and family matter: public life should be secular and therefore free of religion. Neither fundamentalist nor postmodern Christians are willing to accept that model. Both insist that their faith should affect public life. The question is how to do this in an age of global pluralism, for the form that public faith takes in each is very different. Fundamentalism champions either a Constantinian or an Augustinian vision of a global Christian civilization. Postmodern, postcolonial Christianity affirms a pluralistic world and a diaspora model of Christianity, in which those who believe in Jesus seek, as King did, to cooperate with others, religious and nonreligious, in achieving a compassionate social order with justice for all. We should not expect that Christians will eventually favor one view at the expense of the other. More likely, as in the past, there will be diverse expressions of Christianity in diverse social, historical, and political circumstances.

Discussion Questions

1. What were the issues that were resolved by the development of the doctrine of "two natures in one person" (Council of Chalcedon) and of the Trinitarian nature of God (Council of Constantinople)? Do these doctrines put Christianity into fundamental disagreement with the prophetic monotheism of Judaism and Islam? Explain.

2. What is original sin, and why does it lead to the need to expect a savior? Is original sin a universal belief among Christians? Explain.

3. Why are Jesus, Paul, and Augustine often thought to be the three most important figures in the history of Western Christianity?

4. It can be argued that Eastern Christianity, Western Christianity, and postcolonial Christianity offer three different models for understanding the relationship between church and state and the relation of Christianity to the non-Christian world: a Constantinian model, an Augustinian model, and a diaspora model. Explain these models, and identify their strengths and weaknesses.

5. The idea of "modernity" is deeply rooted in the Christian version of the myth of history as it was interpreted by Joachim of Fiore. Explain how this is so. Give examples.

6. What is secularization, and how is it related to the history of Christianity?

7. How did Luther's understanding of Christianity differ from that of the medieval church? What was the political and religious significance of this difference?

8. How did the emergence of Protestantism contribute to the development of the secular nation-state?

9. How did Western colonialism contribute to the emergence of a post-European or postcolonial Christianity? Define and explain.

10. What are the issues that separate premodern from modern and postmodern Christianity, and how do they exemplify the fundamentalist–modernist debate?

Key Terms

Augustinian	heresy	sacraments
Catholic	homoousios	Second Coming
Christ	justification by faith	Son of God
Constantinian	Kingdom of God	syncretistic
deism	liberation theology	Trinity
evangelical	original sin	two natures, one
fundamentalist	Pentecostal	person
Gospel	Protestant	
grace	Protestant ethic	

Suggested Readings

Bettenson, Henry, and Chris Maunder, eds. *Documents of the Christian Church*, 4th ed. (New York: Oxford University Press, 2011).

Fasching, Darrell J. *The Coming of the Millennium* (New York: Authors Choice Press, 1996, 2000).

Johnson, Paul. *A History of Christianity* (New York: Atheneum, 1976, 1979).

Keppel, Gilles. *The Revenge of God: The Resurgence of Islam, Christianity and Judaism in the Modern World* (University Park: Pennsylvania State University Press, 1991, 1994).

Lawrence, Bruce B. *Defenders of God: The Fundamentalist Revolt Against the Modern Age* (Columbia: University of South Carolina Press, 1995).

Littell, Franklin. *The Crucifixion of the Jews* (New York: Harper & Row, 1975).

Marsden, George M. *Understanding Fundamentalism and Evangelicalism* (Grand Rapids, MI: William B. Eerdmans, 1991).

McManners, John, ed. *The Oxford Illustrated History of Christianity* (New York: Oxford University Press, 2001).

Roof, Wade Clark, and William McKinney. *American Mainline Religion* (New Brunswick, NJ: Rutgers University Press, 1987).

Ruether, Rosemary. *Faith and Fratricide* (New York: Seabury Press, 1974).

———. *Liberation Theology* (New York: Paulist Press, 1972).

Stendahl, Krister. *Paul Among Jews and Gentiles* (Philadelphia: Fortress Press, 1976).

Tillich, Paul. *A History of Christian Thought*, Vols. 1 and 2 (New York: Harper & Row, 1967, 1968).

Von Campenhausen, Hans. *The Formation of the Christian Bible* (Mifflintown, PA: Sigler Press, 1997).

Additional Resources

Ad Hoc: Resources for Teaching and Research Relating to the History of Christianity. Yale University Library. (www.yale.edu/adhoc/research_resources/links.htm) This source provides links to a variety of scholarly online resources.

From Jesus to Christ: The First Christians. This four-hour PBS video series traces Christianity from Jesus to Constantine. The entire series can be watched online at http://www.pbs.org/wgbh/pages/frontline/shows/religion/watch/. Includes timelines, study guides, etc.

A History of Christianity: The First Three Thousand Years, by Oxford historian Diarmaid MacCulloch. DVD available from PBS. Episode 1: The First Christianity; Episode 2: Catholicism: The Unpredictable Rise of Rome; Episode 3: Orthodoxy: From Empire to Empire; Episode 4: Reformation: The Individual Before God; Episode 5: Protestantism: The Evangelical Explosion; Episode 6: GOD in the Dock.

The Longest Hatred. A documentary on anti-Semitism in Christianity and Islam. Two videos, total of 150 minutes (Copyright Thames Television 1993 and WGBH Boston 1993).

ISLAM

The Many Faces of the Muslim Experience

5

Overview

Allahu Akbar. . . . There is no God but God. Come to prayer." Five times each day, Muslims throughout the world, in Algiers and Mindanao, London and Paris, Bosnia and New York, are called to prayer.

The images and realities of Islam and of Muslims across the world are multiple and diverse. Poor villagers and wealthy urban professionals from Nigeria, Egypt, and Saudi Arabia to Afghanistan, Pakistan, and Indonesia make their way to the Friday congregational (*juma*) prayer. At the same time, attacks by suicide bombers in Iraq, Afghanistan, or Pakistan kill other Muslims at prayer. On the streets of Cairo, Geneva, Kuala Lumpur, and Jakarta, Muslim women walk, some in stylish Islamic dress, some in dresses and veils that cover their faces and bodies. They join others adorned in Western fashions.

While in many Muslim societies women's status and rights are undermined by patriarchal cultures and reflect serious inequality in education and literacy, at the same time there are significant indications of change. On the one hand, in Yemen, women's literacy is anywhere from 26 percent to 47 percent (vs. 81 percent for men); in Pakistan, the rate is anywhere from 12 percent to 40 percent (vs. 69 percent for men). On the other hand, women's literacy rate in Iran is 70 percent and the rate in Saudi Arabia is 81 percent, and they are as high as 89 percent in Jordan and 85 percent in Malaysia. In the United Arab Emirates, as in Iran, the majority of university students are women. Educated Muslim women in some sex-segregated countries are not visible in the workplace, but in other countries they work as engineers,

Islam Timeline

ca. 570	Birth of Muhammad
610	Muhammad receives first revelation, commemorated as "Night of Power and Excellence"
620	Muhammad's Night Journey to Jerusalem
622	Emigration (*hijra*) of the Muslim community from Mecca to Medina; first year of the Muslim lunar calendar
632	Muhammad's final pilgrimage to Mecca, farewell sermon, and death
632–661	Rule of the Four Rightly Guided Caliphs, formative period for Sunnis
638	Muslim conquest of Jerusalem
661–750	Umayyad Empire
680	Martyrdom of Husayn and his followers at Karbala, Iraq
750–1258	Abbasid Empire: height of Islamic civilization, patronage of art and culture, development of Islamic law, and rising trade, agriculture, industry, and commerce
756–1492	Andalusia (Muslim Spain): period of interfaith coexistence of Muslims, Christians, and Jews
765	Death of sixth Shii imam, Jafar al-Sadiq; succession disputed, causing split between Sevener and Twelver Shiis
8th–9th c.	Formation of major Sunni law schools
1000–1492	Christian reconquest of Muslim-ruled territories in Spain, Sicily, and Italy
1095–1453	Crusades
12th c.	Rise of Sufi orders
1187	Saladin and Muslim forces reconquer Jerusalem
1281–1924	Ottoman Empire (Middle East, North Africa, and portions of Eastern Europe)
1453	Fall of Constantinople/Istanbul, capital of former Byzantine Empire, to Ottomans
1483–1857	Mughal Empire (South Asia)
1501–1722	Safavid Empire (Iran)
1876–1938	Muhammad Iqbal, Islamic modernist and ideologue for foundation of Pakistan
1897–1975	Elijah Muhammad, leader of the Nation of Islam in the United States
1903–1979	Mawlana Abu Ala Mawdudi, founder of the *Jamaat-i-Islami* in India/Pakistan
1906–1949	Hassan al-Banna, founder of the Muslim Brotherhood in Egypt
1906–1966	Sayyid Qutb, radical, militant ideologue of the Muslim Brotherhood in 1950s and 1960s
1975	Wallace D. Muhammad (name later changed to Warith Deen Muhammad) succeeds his father, Elijah Muhammad, and progressively brings his followers into conformity with mainstream Sunni Islam
1979	Iranian Revolution and foundation of Iranian Islamic Republic under leadership of Ayatollah Khomeini; seizure of the Grand Mosque in Mecca by Muslim militants; Soviet Union invades Afghanistan
1990	FIS (Islamic Salvation Front) wins Algerian municipal and regional elections
1993	Bombing of World Trade Center in New York City by Muslim militants
1995	Welfare (Refah) party wins parliamentary elections; Dr. Necmettin Erbakan becomes Turkey's first Islamist prime minister

1998	U.S. embassies in Tanzania and Kenya bombed by Muslim militants
September 11, 2001	Terrorist attacks against the World Trade Center in New York City and the Pentagon in Washington, D.C.; sparks U.S.-led war against global terrorism and the hunt for Osama bin Laden and al-Qaeda
2003	U.S.-led invasion of Iraq and overthrow of Saddam Hussein; Iran's Shirin Ebadi becomes first Muslim woman to win Nobel Prize for Peace; first female judge appointed to Egyptian Supreme Constitutional Court
2004	French Parliament bans Muslim headscarf in schools and public places; terrorist train attack by Muslim militants in Madrid, Spain
2005	Series of bombings on London subways and a bus kill fifty-one people; London bombings (also called the 7/7 bombings) were a series of coordinated terrorist attacks on London's public transport system during the morning rush hour.
2006	Hamas landslide victory in Palestinian elections; Bangladeshi economist Muhammad Yunus and his Grameen Bank win the Nobel Peace Prize. Yunus pioneered the concept of microcredit—giving unsecured loans to poor people
2007	Turkey reelects Prime Minister Erdogan and Justice and Development Party in parliamentary elections; Declaration on Muslim-Christian relations signed by some 138 Muslim religious leaders and authorities
2009	Popular protests in Iran following controversial presidential elections marred by corruption. Nicknamed the "Twitter Revolution" because of its use of social networking tools to organize nonviolent protests.
2011	Reelection of Erdogan in Turkey; beginning of the "Arab Spring," sparked in Tunisia and Egypt, largely through social networking tools, as series of nonviolent protests calling for greater levels of democracy, freedom, and an end to government corruption.
2011	Osama bin Laden, the founder and head of the Islamist militant group al-Qaeda, killed in Pakistan by American military
2011	Ennahda (the Renaissance Party), in Tunisia's first democratic election, wins a plurality of votes in the Constituent Assembly
2012	In first open democratic elections in Egypt, the Muslim Brotherhood wins a majority of the vote in the parliamentary election to the People's Assembly, and the Brotherhood's Mohammed Morsi is elected president
2013	Egypt's first democratically elected president, Mohammed Morsi, after widespread antigovernment demonstrations on July 30, overthrown in a military backed coup
August 14, 2013	Egyptian security forces use lethal force against Morsi supporter sit-in, killing more than 625 and injuring thousands. The interim government moved quickly to declare the Muslim Brotherhood a terrorist organization and attempted to totally suppress it, using mass arrests and military trials that drew sharp criticism from major international human rights organizations. The government cracked down and arrested foreign journalists and Egyptian critics and democracy activists.
January 27, 2014	Tunisian Assembly passes new constitution
March 24, 2014	An Egyptian court sentences 529 members of the outlawed Muslim Brotherhood to death, the largest mass death sentence in modern Egyptian history

doctors, scientists, teachers, and lawyers alongside their male colleagues. In contrast to those in many Muslim countries, Muslim women in America are as educated and earn as much as American Muslim men.

Islamic associations in the slums and lower-middle-class neighborhoods of Cairo and Algiers, Beirut and Mindanao provide families who cannot afford state services or who live under governments that do not provide adequate social services (such as the West Bank and Gaza) with inexpensive and efficient educational, legal, and medical social services. At the same time, the terrorist attacks of 9/11 signaled a decade of global terror from Morocco, Spain, Scotland, and Britain to Iraq, Saudi Arabia, Yemen, Pakistan, Afghanistan, Indonesia, and the Philippines.

If a militant minority has turned to bullets, many mainstream Muslims have turned to the ballot box when given the opportunity by their governments, many of which are authoritarian. Members of Islamic organizations have been elected to parliaments in Turkey, Algeria, Jordan, Egypt, Kuwait, Yemen, Pakistan, Thailand, and Malaysia. They have been elected prime minister of Turkey and served as president of Indonesia and Turkey and in cabinet-level positions in many countries. Others have been elected officials in professional associations of doctors, lawyers, engineers, journalists, and teachers.

This chapter will look at the history and heritage of **Islam** and impact on **Muslim** societies and world events today. It will explore the challenges and struggles within the global Muslim community in defining the meaning of Islam for modern and postmodern life.

Islam: submission or surrender to God

Muslim: one who follows Islam

Mecca is the holiest city of Islam: the birthplace of the Prophet Muhammad, where the earliest revelations occurred and toward which Muslims turn in prayer five times each day. Muslims on pilgrimage gather near Mecca's Grand Mosque following Friday dawn prayers.

The study of Islam and Muslim societies, yesterday and today, is a fascinating trip across time and space. It requires a bridging of the gap between religion, history, politics, and culture. Let us begin by briefly discussing what Islam is and where the Islamic world is.

The word *islam* means "submission" or "surrender." A Muslim is one who submits, who seeks to follow and actualize God's will in history. The Muslim community (**ummah**) is a transnational community of believers, God ordained and guided, whose mission is to spread and institutionalize an Islamic Order, to create a socially just society: "You are the best community ever brought forth for mankind, enjoining what is good and forbidding evil" (Q. 3:110).

Islam belongs to the Abrahamic family of great monotheistic faiths. Muslims like Jews and Christians view themselves as the children of Abraham, as proclaimed in each of their sacred scriptures: the Old and New Testaments and the Quran. Despite specific and significant differences, Judaism, Christianity, and Islam share a belief in one God, the creator, sustainer, and ruler of the universe who is beyond ordinary experience. And all believe in angels, Satan, prophets, revelation, moral responsibility and accountability, divine judgment, and reward or punishment. Yet while Jews and Christians claim descent from Abraham and his wife, Sarah, through their son Isaac, Muslims trace their religious roots back to Abraham (Ibrahim) through Ismail, his firstborn son by Hagar, Sarah's Egyptian servant.

Today, Islam is the world's second-largest religion. Its 1.5 billion followers can be found in some fifty-seven predominantly Muslim countries, extending from North Africa to Southeast Asia (see Map 5.1). Because Islam has often been equated simply with the Arabs, only about 20 percent of the worldwide Muslim community, few realize that the vast majority of Muslims live in Asia and Africa: Indonesia, Bangladesh, Pakistan, India, and Nigeria. Islam's presence and impact extend beyond countries in which the majority of the population is Muslim. In recent years, Islam has become a significant presence in the West as the second- or third-largest religion in Europe (in particular, France, Germany, and England) and in North America. Today the capitols or major cities of Islam are not only exotic-sounding places like Cairo, Damascus, Baghdad, Mecca, Islamabad, and Kuala Lumpur, but also London, Paris, Marseilles, Brussels, New York, Detroit, and Los Angeles.

A dynamic religion that interfaces and at times competes with other faiths, Islam has had a significant impact on world affairs. In contrast to the modern secular belief in the separation of church and state, Islam for many Muslims represents a more comprehensive worldview in which religion and society, faith and power, have been and are more closely bound. Throughout much of history, to be a Muslim was not simply to belong to a faith community or to worship in a given place but to live in an Islamic community or state, governed (in theory if not always in practice) by Islamic law. Historically, Islam has significantly informed politics and civilization, giving rise to vast Islamic empires and states as well as Islamic civilization.

From Islam's origins to the present, Muslims have been engaged in a continuous process of understanding and interpreting the word of God (**Quran**): defining,

ummah: Muslim community of believers

"Say: He is Allah, the One and only; Allah, the Eternal. He did not beget, nor is He begotten; And there is none like Him."
—Quran, 112

Quran: Muslim scripture

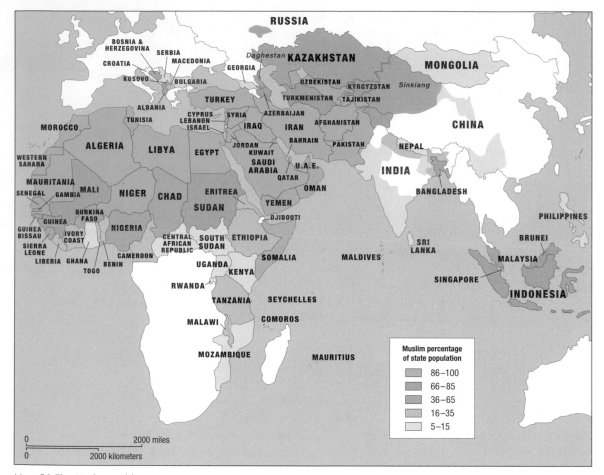

Map 5.1 The Muslim world.

redefining, and applying Islamic practices to the realities of life. Thus, while it is correct to say that there is one Islam, revealed in the Quran and the traditions of the Prophet, as we shall now see, there have been many interpretations of Islam, some complementing each other, others in conflict.

Muslims today, like other people of faith, struggle with the relationship of their religious tradition to modernity and postmodernity. How does a faith revealing a God-centered universe speak to a modern, post-Enlightenment, human-centered secular world that emphasizes reason and science? Like Judaism and Christianity, Islam contends with questions about a range of issues, from evolution, birth control, abortion, artificial insemination, and organ transplants to ecology, nuclear energy, chemical warfare, religious extremism, and terrorism. The questions are many: What is the relationship of Islam to secularization? Should Islam today be restricted to personal life,

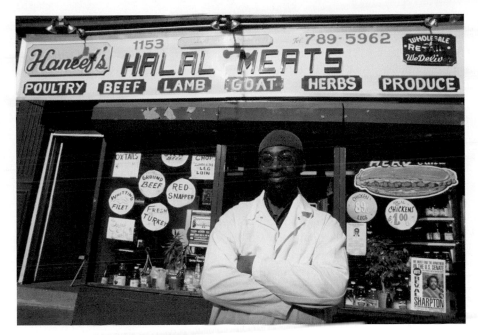

Muslim dietary law, like Judaism's kosher law, requires the ritual slaughter of animals permitted to be eaten. Today across America, *halal* butcher shops may be found, providing these religiously prepared meats for their Muslim customers.

or should it be integral to the state, law, and society? Is Islam compatible with modern forms of political participation, such as democracy? In the twenty-first century, what should be the Islamic positions on treatment of religious minorities, non-Muslims, and women?

Encounter with Modernity: The Challenge of Western Colonialism

When Muslims were asked in the Gallup World Poll (2007) what they feared most, majorities cited intervention, invasion, or occupation by foreign powers. This concern can be seen in widespread opposition to the invasion of Iraq and Afghanistan by America, Britain, and other Western powers and the charge that this is but another form of Western colonialism. The Islamic world has witnessed upheaval and renewal since the nineteenth century as Muslims absorbed the impact of European colonialism. European colonialism challenged Muslim historical self-understanding and pride. A common belief throughout history had been that the early and rapid expansion of Islam and Islamic empires, extending from Africa to Asia and their continued success and power until the nineteenth century, were signs of God's guidance and pleasure with the Islamic community.

Yet by the nineteenth century, Europeans had colonized many Muslim areas: the French in North, West, and Equatorial Africa and the Levant (Lebanon and Syria); the British in Palestine, Transjordan, Iraq, the Arabian Gulf, and the Indian subcontinent; and in Southeast Asia, the British in Malaya (Malaysia, Singapore, and Brunei) and the Dutch in Indonesia.

Muslims found themselves on the defensive against a European imperialism that threatened their political, religious, and cultural identity and challenged time-honored beliefs and practices. Muslim responses to colonialism and Western culture and ideas varied from rejection and confrontation to admiration and imitation.

While many conservative religious leaders dug in their heels and resisted any significant change and new Western-oriented elites opted for a Western secular approach, Islamic modernist reformers staked out a middle path. They sought to restore the pride, identity, and strength of their debilitated community by bridging the gap between their heritage and modernity. They emphasized the compatibility of Islam with reason, modern science, and technology, reminding Muslims of the development of Islamic civilization and its contributions to philosophy, science, medicine, mathematics, and architecture. Reformers championed the need for ***ijtihad***, the reinterpretation of Islamic law to meet the needs of the modern world. However, they failed (1) to produce a systematic reinterpretation of Islam; and (2) to develop effective organizations and institutions to preserve and propagate their reformist message. These two failures led to the emergence of modern Islamic activist organizations (sometimes referred to as fundamentalist movements), such as the Muslim Brotherhood in the Middle East and *Jamaat-i-Islami* (the Islamic Society) in South Asia. Both these organizations criticized Islamic reformers for tending to Westernize Islam. In particular, they condemned the tendency of most Muslim countries to adopt Western models of development uncritically. Islam, they insisted, is a total, comprehensive way of life that offers an alternative path to Western capitalism and communism/socialism. These movements and their many offshoots, from mainstream social and political organizations to radical revolutionary groups, continue to be major forces today.

During the post–World War II era, most of the Muslim world regained its independence. However, the boundaries of modern nation-states such as Lebanon, Syria, Sudan, Jordan, Iraq, Kuwait, Malaysia, and Pakistan were arbitrarily drawn by the European states that had colonized the areas. Indeed, many Muslim rulers were appointed by colonial governments; others, often military officers or former officers, simply seized power. As a result, instead of elected governments, much of the Muslim world received a legacy of autocratic rulers (kings, military and ex-military) not of their choosing.

The political legitimacy of rulers and issues of national identity and unity have plagued many of these nations to this day; governments have relied heavily for control and stability on internal security forces rather than elections. Because the West provided the models for development, it was widely supposed that modernization and progress would depend on Westernization and secularization. Iran's Islamic revolution of 1979–80 shattered this assumption.

ijtihad: interpretation or independent reasoning in Islamic law

The Islamic Resurgence

The Iranian revolution signaled the resurgence of Islam in Muslim politics. Although Iran drew attention to the reassertion and power of Islam in politics and society, Islam had already become a major factor in Muslim politics for more than a decade before 1979 in Egypt, Libya, and Pakistan. The crushing military defeat of combined Arab forces in the Six-Day War of 1967 and the consequent loss to Israel of major territories (the Sinai, the West Bank and Gaza, the Golan Heights, and especially Jerusalem, the third-holiest city of Islam) became "*the* disaster" in Muslim literature and consciousness. This key event triggered a period of doubt and self-examination.

Despite national independence, most Muslim countries had remained politically and economically weak, underdeveloped, and dependent on the West. What went wrong? To regain their past power and glory, many Muslims believed that they must return to the straight path of Islam. The 1973 Arab oil embargo and the later Islamic revolution in Iran reinforced the belief that Muslim economic and political power could be attributed to the resurgence of Islam in contemporary Muslim politics and society.

During the late 1960s and 1970s, Islam enjoyed a higher profile in personal and public life, demonstrated by greater religious observance and Islamic dress as well as the growth of Islamic political and social organizations and institutions: banks, publishing houses, schools. In addition, governments in Egypt, Libya, Sudan, and Pakistan as well as their opposition political parties turned to Islam in politics during the 1970s and 1980s to enhance their legitimacy and mobilize popular support. At the same time, Islamic activist organizations mushroomed in number and size throughout the Muslim world. Alongside Islamic organizations such as the Muslim Brotherhoods of Egypt, Syria, Jordan, and Sudan, there were violent revolutionary organizations with names like Jund Allah (Army of God), Hezbollah (the party of God), and Islamic Jihad.

Yet, by the late 1980s and 1990s, a quiet (nonviolent) revolution had also occurred. From North Africa to Southeast Asia, Islam was playing an increasingly more visible and important role in the socioeconomic and political life of society. In the twenty-first century, Islamic activists and parties are a significant factor in electoral politics in Egypt, Algeria, Morocco, Sudan, Lebanon, Jordan, Turkey, Palestine, Pakistan, Malaysia, and Indonesia. Many authoritarian rulers have experienced the power of religion in Muslim politics through ballots of Islamic supporters as well as bullets of the more radical groups.

Islam in the West

To speak of Islam in the twenty-first century is not only to speak of Islam and the West but also of Islam in the West. Islam is the fastest-growing religion in North America and in Europe, the second-largest religion in France, Holland, Belgium, and Germany, and the third-largest in Britain and the United States. Even without increases in Muslim immigration and conversions to Islam, in several decades Muslim projected birthrates will result in Islam's replacing Judaism as the second-largest religion in the United States.

Muslims in the United States, like other religious or ethnic minorities before them, face many questions about their faith and identity: Are they Muslims in America or American Muslims? Can Muslims become part and parcel of a pluralistic American society without sacrificing or losing their identity? Can people be Muslims in a non-Muslim state that is not governed by Islamic law? Is the U.S. legal system capable of allowing for particular Muslim religious and cultural differences?

In the West, it has sometimes been fashionable to speak of a post-Christian society; but for many Muslims, talking about a post-Islamic society is not relevant. For many Muslims, the debate is not over whether religion has a place and role in society, but rather what kind of Islam or Islamic presence should exist. Understanding Islam today requires an appreciation of the full spectrum of Muslim responses to the modern world, ranging from those who view Islam as a personal faith to others who wish to see it implemented more formally in state and society.

Throughout the ages, when Muslims have sought to define or redefine their lives, the starting point has always been an understanding of the past. Thus, we need to go back in order to go forward. To understand Islam's present and future, we must learn about the history and development of Islam and the Muslim community.

Premodern Islam: The Formative Era

Like all the world's religions, Islam places great emphasis on its early history. For Muslims, the formative period is the time of the Prophet Muhammad, a period that included the revelation of the Quran and Muhammad's founding of the first community. It is often seen as the "best of times," the time of the purest and most authentic Islamic community, a society that was to be emulated by future generations, a model to return to for inspiration and guidance.

At the core of Muslim belief and faith are the messenger and the message. As Christians look to Jesus and the New Testament and Jews look to Moses and the Torah, Muslims regard Muhammad and the Quran as the final, perfect, and complete revelation of God's will for humankind. Also, because of the remarkable success of Muhammad and the early Muslim community in spreading the faith of Islam and the rule of Muslims, an idealized memory of Islamic history and of Muslim rule became the model for success, serving as a common reference point for later generations of reformers.

Allah: God

The foundations of Islam are belief in God (**Allah**, Arabic for "The God") and in God's messenger, Muhammad. Though God is beyond our ordinary experience, or transcendent, Islam teaches that he can be known directly through his messengers and revelations. Thus, Muhammad and the Quran, the final messenger and the message/revelation, are key in the formation and development of the Islamic tradition, its beliefs, laws, rituals, and social practices. Learning more about the messenger and the message will increase our understanding of Islam today and our insights about the sources Muslims use to guide their lives in the twenty-first century.

Muhammad's Early Life

Few observers in the sixth century would have predicted that Muhammad ibn Abdullah and central Arabia would come to play pivotal roles in world history and world religions. Most would have seen as limited at best the future impact of an orphan raised in a vast desert region marked by tribal warfare and divisions and bounded by two great imperial powers, the Eastern Roman, or Byzantine, Empire and the Persian (Sassanid) Empire. And yet the message Muhammad brought from God and the force of his personality would quite literally transform Arabia and have a significant impact on much of the world, past and present.

Because Muhammad regarded himself as a religious reformer and not the founder of a new religion, it is important to understand pre-Islamic Arabian society and religion, which were tribal in structure and organization. Individuals lived in extended families; several related families constituted a clan; a cluster of several clans comprised a tribe. Al Ilah (Allah) was seen as the high god over a pantheon of tribal gods and goddesses who were believed to be more directly active in everyday life. Each city or town had its divine patron/protectors and shrine. Tribal gods and goddesses were respected and feared rather than loved, the focal points of the rituals of sacrifice,

Muhammad: The Final Messenger

No prophet has played a greater role in a world religion and in world politics than Muhammad. Both in his lifetime and throughout Muslim history, Muhammad ibn Abdullah has served as the ideal model for Muslim life. Some Muslims have called him the "living Quran," that is, the embodiment in his behavior and words of God's will. He is viewed as the last or final prophet, who brought the final revelation of God. He is so revered that the name Muhammad (or names derived from it—Ahmad, Mahmud) is the most common Muslim name. In some Muslim countries, every male child has the Prophet's name as one of his forenames. Thus, the Prophet and his example, or *Sunnah*, are central to Islam and Muslim belief and practice. Muhammad is not only the ideal political leader, statesman, merchant, judge, soldier, and diplomat but also the ideal husband, father, and friend. Muslims look to his example for guidance in all aspects of life: eating; fasting; praying; the treatment of a spouse, parents, and children; the creation of contracts; the waging of war; and the conduct of diplomacy.

prayer, and pilgrimage. The tribal polytheism of Arabia was embodied in a cube-shaped building that housed the idols of 360 tribal gods and was a center of pilgrimage. Located in the ancient city of Mecca, this cube, *Kaaba*, would be rededicated to Allah in the seventh century.

Tribal polytheism was a very "worldly" religion, with little concern about or belief in an afterlife, divine judgment, or reward or punishment after death. Individual identity and rights were subordinated to tribal and family identity, authority, and law. The key virtue, "manliness," included loyalty to family and protection of its members, bravery in battle, hospitality, and honor. There was little sense of moral responsibility and accountability beyond tribal and family honor. This era, in which justice was guaranteed and administered not by God but by the threat of retaliation by family or tribe, is referred to as the period of ignorance (*jahiliyya*) before Islam.

jahiliyya: unbelief; ignorance; used to describe pre-Islamic era

Forms of monotheism did exist in Arabia; both Arab Christian and Jewish communities had long resided in the region. The Quran also speaks of Arab monotheists, *hanifs*, descendants of Ibrahim (Abraham). In addition, Arab traders would have encountered Judaism and Christianity, since Jewish and Christian merchants regularly came to Mecca, a major center for trade as well as pilgrimage. However, monotheism's most powerful appeal to the Arabs came only when the Prophet Muhammad received his revelation from Allah, a message that would change the lives of hundreds of millions of people throughout Arabia and beyond.

There is little information about Muhammad's life before his "call" to be God's messenger; the portrait of his early years is drawn from early Muslim writers, legend, and Muslim belief. Muhammad ibn Abdullah (the son of Abdullah) was born in 570 into the ruling tribe of Mecca, the Quraysh. Orphaned at an early age, Muhammad was among the tribe's "poorer cousins," raised by an uncle and later employed in Mecca's thriving caravan business. Muhammad had one wife, Khadija, for twenty-eight years, until her death. Much is recorded about Muhammad's relationship with Khadija, who was his closest confidante and strongest supporter. The couple had six children, two sons who died in infancy and four daughters. After Khadija's death, Muhammad married other women, all but one of them widows.

By the age of thirty, Muhammad had become a prominent, respected member of Meccan society, known for his business skill and trustworthiness (he was nicknamed al-Amin, the trustworthy). Reflective by temperament, Muhammad would often retreat to the quiet and solitude of Mount Hira to contemplate his life and society. Here during the month of Ramadan in 610, on a night Muslims commemorate as the Night of Power and Excellence, Muhammad the caravan leader became Muhammad the messenger of God. Muhammad at the age of forty received the first message, or divine revelation, from a heavenly intermediary identified by later tradition as the angel Gabriel: "Recite in the name of your Lord who has created, / Created man out of a germ cell. / Recite, for your Lord is the most generous One, / Who has taught by the pen, / Taught man what he did not know."

Muhammad became a link in a long series of biblical prophets, messengers from God who served as a conscience to the community and as God's messenger. Like

Moses, who had received the Torah on Mount Sinai, Muhammad received the first of God's revelations on Mount Hira: "It is He who sent down to you the Book with the truth, confirming what went before it: and He sent down the Torah and the Injil ["Evangel," "Gospel"] before as a guidance to the people" (Q. 3:3). Also, like Amos and Jeremiah before him, Muhammad served as a "warner" from God who admonished his hearers to repent and obey God, for the final judgment was near:

> Say: "O Men I am only a warner." Those who believe, and do deeds of righteousness—theirs shall be forgiveness and generous provision. And those who strive against our signs to avoid them—they shall be inhabitants of Hell. (Q. 22:49–50)

Muhammad continued to receive revelations for more than two decades (610–32); together these revelations constitute the text of the Quran (literally, "the recitation or reading").

The first ten years of Muhammad's preaching were difficult. At first he revealed his religious experience to his wife and close friends only. When he finally began to preach God's message, critiquing the status quo, he encountered the anger of Mecca's prosperous, powerful political and commercial leaders. In the name of Allah, the one true God, Muhammad increasingly denounced polytheism and thus threatened the livelihood of those who profited enormously from the annual pilgrimage, which was the equivalent of a giant tribal convention. Equally problematic, Muhammad preached a message strong on issues of social justice, condemning the socioeconomic inequities of his time. The Prophet denounced the exploitation of the poor, orphans, and widows as well as prevailing business practices such as false contracts and usury. Muhammad claimed an authority and legitimacy, as God's prophet, that undermined the primacy of Mecca's rich and powerful masters. He called all true believers to join the community of God, a universal community that transcended tribal bonds and authority, a community led by Muhammad, not by the Quraysh.

As Muhammad continued to preach his message, the situation in Mecca became more difficult. After ten years of rejection and persecution in Mecca, Muhammad and his followers migrated to Yathrib, renamed Medina, "city" of the prophet, in 622. Invited to serve as arbiter or judge, for Muslim and non-Muslim alike, Muhammad became the political and religious leader of the community. Medina proved a new beginning, as the Muslim community prospered and grew.

After the *Hijra*

The emigration (*hijra*) from Mecca to Medina in 622 was a turning point in Muhammad's life and in Islamic history. The central significance of *hijra* and the birth of the Islamic community (the *ummah*) led to Muslims dating their calendar not from the birth of the Prophet or from the first revelation but from the creation of the Islamic

hijra: migration of Muhammad from Mecca to Medina; marks first year in Muslim lunar calendar community at Medina. Thus, 622 CE became 1 AH, "after the *hijra*." Muslims, then and now, believe Islam is a world religion, a global community of the faithful, with a universal message and mission.

Muhammad did not intend to create a new religion; rather, he was a prophet and reformer. His message proclaimed an absolute monotheism, the unity (***tawhid***), or oneness, of God and God's final revelation. Polytheism and idolatry—putting anything in place of the one, true God—were to be condemned and suppressed. Islam was to be a corrective to Arabian polytheism, and, Muslims believe, the distortions of God's original revelation to Moses and Jesus by the authors/editors of the Bible that had occurred over time. Muhammad called all to repentance, to turn away from the path of unbelief and false practice and toward the straight path (***sharia***) of God. Thus, Muhammad (the last, or "seal," of the prophets; Q. 33:40) and the Quran (the complete, uncorrupted revelation) were a corrective, a restoration of the true faith and message of God.

Muhammad taught that submission (*islam*) to God was both an individual and a community obligation. Tribal identity must be replaced by identification with Islam, now the primary source of community solidarity. This belief was reinforced by the Quran's emphasis on social justice, social welfare, in particular protection of women, orphans, and the poor. Muhammad rejected or reformed some rituals and introduced

tawhid: oneness of God; monotheism

sharia: Islamic law

The courtyard of the Mosque of the Prophet in Medina, the first mosque in Islam, is among the most sacred sites in Islam. The original structure has been rebuilt and expanded several times.

others. He reinterpreted the pre-Islamic Arabian pilgrimage to the Kaaba at Mecca. The Kaaba was cleansed of its 360 tribal idols and rededicated to Allah. Pilgrimage to the Kaaba in Mecca, like prayer five times each day, became one of the Five Pillars, or required practices, of Islam.

During the short decade that Muhammad led the community at Medina, he, in light of continuing revelations, defined its mandate and mission. He forged its identity, consolidated its political base, and established its basic religious law and practice.

Muhammad skillfully employed both force and diplomacy to defeat the Meccans and then to unite the tribes of Arabia under the banner of Islam. In 624 Muhammad and his followers successfully engaged and defeated the far greater Meccan forces at the Battle of Badr. For Muslims, then and now, this battle has special significance, a "miraculous" victory in which the forces of Allah and monotheism were pitted against those of Meccan polytheism. Yet despite overwhelming odds, the army of God vanquished the unbelievers. The Quran itself tells of God's assistance (Q. 8:42ff, 3:123) in securing the victory. The Battle of Badr became a symbol of divine favor and intervention remembered and invoked throughout history, as witnessed in the 1973 Egyptian-Israeli war, when President Anwar Sadat used the code name Operation Badr to inspire and motivate his forces.

After a three-year series of battles, a truce was struck at Hudaybiyah. However, in 630, Muhammad, charging that the Meccans had broken the truce, led an army 10,000 strong on a march to Mecca; the Meccans surrendered without a fight. Muhammad proved magnanimous in victory, rejecting vengeance and plunder and instead granted amnesty to his former enemies. The majority of the Meccans converted to Islam, accepted Muhammad's leadership, and became part of the Islamic community.

In his early preaching, Muhammad had looked to Jews and Christians as natural allies. As "**People of the Book**" (*ahl al-kitab*) who had received prophets and revelation, they had much in common with Muslims, and so he anticipated the approval and acceptance of Islam by the Jews of Medina. Muhammad initially presented himself to the Jews of Arabia as a prophetic reformer reestablishing the religion of Abraham. However, the Jewish tribes of Medina, who had lived there a long time and had political ties with the Quraysh of Mecca, did not accept the reformer's message. While the majority of tribes converted to Islam, Medina's three Jewish tribes, half the population of Medina, did not. Until that time, Muslims had faced Jerusalem to pray and, like the Jews, fasted on the tenth day of the lunar month. However, when the Jews rejected Muhammad's claims and proved resistant to conversion, Muhammad received a revelation and changed the direction of prayer from Jerusalem to Mecca. Thereafter, Islam was presented as a distinct religious alternative to Judaism.

Because of the multireligious and multitribal nature of Medina, Muhammad promulgated the Charter or Constitution of Medina, which set out the rights and duties of all citizens and the relationship of the Muslim community to other communities. Jews were recognized as a separate community, politically allied to the Muslims but retaining internal religious and cultural autonomy. However, political loyalty and

People of the Book: those possessing a revelation or scripture from God; refers particularly to Jews and Christians allegiance were expected. The Jews' denial of Muhammad's prophethood and message and their political ties with the Meccans became a source of conflict. The Quran accuses some Jewish tribes of regularly breaking treaties: "Why is it that whenever they make pacts, a group among them casts it aside unilaterally?" (Q. 2:100). Muslim perception of intrigue, rejection, and betrayal by the Jewish tribes led first to exile and later to warfare. After the Battle of the Ditch in 627, the Jews of the Banu Qurayza, a Jewish tribe who lived in Yathrib at the time, were denounced as traitors who had consorted with the Meccans. In the end, Muhammad moved to crush the remaining Jews in Medina, whom he regarded as a political threat to Muslim consolidation and rule in Arabia.

Muhammad's use of warfare was not alien to Arab custom or to the Hebrew prophets' belief (Exodus 14:14, Deuteronomy 20:4, and 2 Kings 10:25–31) in God-sanctioned battle—the conquest and the punishment of "enemies of God" in which the men were often killed and the women and children were spared but enslaved. Both believed that God had sanctioned battle with the enemies of the Lord. However, it is important to note that the motivation for Muhammad's actions was political rather than racial or theological, a fact often overlooked by critics of Islam as well as militant Muslims.

In 632, Muhammad led the pilgrimage to Mecca. There the sixty-two-year-old leader delivered a farewell sermon in which he emphasized:

> Know ye that every Muslim is a brother unto every other Muslim, and that ye are now one brotherhood. It is not legitimate for any one of you, therefore, to appropriate unto himself anything that belongs to his brother unless it is willingly given him by that brother.[1]

This event continues to be remembered and commemorated each year by millions of Muslims who make the annual pilgrimage to Mecca, in modern Saudi Arabia.

The Message of the Quran

The Quran is the foundation and heart of Islam. Muslims believe that the Quran is the eternal, uncreated, literal, and final word of God revealed to Muhammad as guidance for humankind (Q. 2:185). Thus, for Muslims, Islam is not a new religion but rather the oldest, for it represents the "original" as well as the final revelation of God to Abraham, Moses, Jesus, and Muhammad. In fact, it has become common for many who convert to Islam to be referred to as "reverts" rather than converts.

The Prophet Muhammad is seen as a conduit, an intermediary, who received God's message and then communicated it over a period of twenty-two years. The text of the Quran is about four-fifths the length of the New Testament. The Muslim scripture consists of 114 chapters (**surahs**) of 6,000 verses, arranged by length, not chronology.

surahs: chapters of the Quran

The God (Allah) of the Quran is seen as the creator, sustainer, ruler, and judge of humankind. He is merciful and just, the all-knowing and all-powerful, the lord and ruler of the universe. The Quran teaches that God's revelation has occurred in several forms: in nature, in history, and in scripture. God's existence can be known through nature, which points to or contains the "signs" of its creator and sustainer (Q. 3:26–27). The record of humankind also contains clear examples and lessons of God's sovereignty and intervention in history (Q. 30:2–9). And finally, God's will for humankind has been revealed through a long line of prophets and messengers: "Indeed We sent forth among every nation a Messenger saying: 'Serve your God and shun false gods' " (Q. 16:36). As a result, throughout history, people could know not only that God exists but also his will, what God desires and commands, for humankind.

Muslims believe that the Quran, like the Torah and the Evangel (Gospel), is taken from an Arabic tablet, the source, or mother, of all scriptures, preexisting with God in heaven. From it, the teachings of the three Abrahamic faiths (Judaism, Christianity, and Islam) were taken and revealed at different stages in history. Indeed, many Muslims take their names from the biblical prophets Ibrahim (Abraham), Musa (Moses), Sulayman (Solomon), Dawud (David), Yahya (John), Maryam (Mary), and Issa (Jesus). Equally striking to many is the fact that the name of Mary, the mother of Jesus, is cited more often in the Quran than in the entire New Testament.

God's word, as revealed in the Quran, is the final and complete revelation. It provides the primary and ultimate source of guidance, the basis for belief and practice in Islam. Study, memorization, recitation, and copying of the Quran have been central acts of piety. The noble art of copying the Quran has produced a rich tradition of calligraphy. This manuscript page provides a beautiful example.

Throughout history, Jesus and Mary (Maryam), his mother, have been held in high esteem. Jesus enjoys a special place among the prophets in Islam. The Quran affirms the virgin birth of Jesus, the promised Messiah, who declared from his cradle: "I am God's servant; God has given me the Book, and made me a prophet" (Q. 19:30).

Because Arabic is the language of the Quran, all Muslims memorize, recite, and pray the Quran in Arabic, whether they understand it fully or not. Much as the Roman Catholic Mass until the middle of the twentieth century was always said in Latin, Arabic is viewed as the sacred language of Islam; in a very real sense it is regarded as the language of God. Whatever their local language, Muslims pray in Arabic five times each day. Whereas Christianity, at an early stage translated its scriptures into Latin and Greek and after the Reformation into local languages, Muslims maintain Arabic as the language of the Quran, the primary source for religious learning and of formal worship.

Because the Quran is regarded as God's sacred Word, it is handled with reverence. A devout Muslim will not write in a Quran that is used for spiritual reading or prayer. Memorization of the entire text of the Quran is a time-honored act of piety. For many Muslims the clearest evidence of the Quran's power and uniqueness is its impact on its hearers; indeed, many have been moved to conversion after hearing the beauty of a Quranic recitation. Recitation or chanting of the Quran is a major art form as well as an act of worship. Muslims gather in stadiums and auditoriums around the world to attend international Quran recitation competitions as many in the West might attend an opera. To win an international competition can be a source of great national pride.

A Golden Age of Expansion, Conquest, and Creativity

caliph: successor of Muhammad as political and military leader of the Muslim community

Sunnah: example set by Muhammad of living the principles of the Quran

Because Muslims believe that the Quran is God's Word or revelation, from an early age children are taught to recite the Quran.

The rule of Muhammad and his first four successors, or **caliphs**, is seen as the formative, normative, exemplary period of Muslim faith and history. After God sent down his final and complete revelation for humankind through his last prophet, the Islamic community/state was created, and the sources of Islamic law, the Quran and **Sunnah** of the Prophet, originated. Both reformers and Islamic revivalists today look to this period as the reference point for divine guidance and historical validation. Muslims believe that the revealed message of the Quran and the example of the Prophet and his successors were corroborated in the full light of history after "miraculous" victories at Badr and elsewhere, by the spread of Islam as a faith as well as its phenomenal geographic and political expansion, which produced *Islamic Empires*.

Through force and diplomacy, Muhammad united the tribes of Arabia under the banner of Islam. During the century after his death, the period of the four Rightly Guided Caliphs, Muslim armies were inspired by their new faith, material (bounty from richer societies) and spiritual rewards, especially paradise for those who died and were remembered as martyrs. These highly motivated armies overran the Byzantine and Persian empires, which had already been greatly weakened by internal strife and constant warfare between them.

Christendom experienced the early expansion of Islam as a threat to its religious and political hegemony. Muslim rule, and with it the message of Islam, quickly spread from the Byzantine and Persian empires to Syria, Iraq, and Egypt and then swept across North Africa and into Europe, where Muslims ruled Spain and the Mediterranean from Sicily to Anatolia (see Map 5.2).

For non-Muslim populations in Byzantium and Persia, who had been subjugated by foreign rulers, Islamic rule meant an exchange of rulers rather than a loss of independence. Many in Byzantium willingly exchanged Greco-Roman rule for that of new Arab masters, fellow Semites, with whom they had closer linguistic and cultural affinities and to whom they paid lower taxes. Upon declaration of their allegiance to the Islamic state and payment of a poll (head) tax, these "protected" (***dhimmi***) peoples could practice their faith and be governed by their religious leaders and law in matters of faith and private life.

Islam proved more tolerant than imperial Christianity, providing greater religious freedom for Jews and indigenous Christians. Under Muslim rule, most local or indigenous Christian churches, persecuted as schismatics and heretics by the "foreign" Christian orthodoxy of their rulers, could practice their faith.

The rapid spread and development of imperial Islam produced a rich Islamic civilization that flourished from the ninth to the twelfth centuries. Urban cultural centers emerged in Cairo, Baghdad, Cordova, Palermo, and Nishapur. With significant assistance from Christian and Jewish subjects, Muslims collected the great books of science, medicine, and philosophy from the West and the East and translated them into Arabic from Greek, Latin, Persian, Coptic, Syriac, and Sanskrit. The age of translation was followed by a period of great creativity as a new generation of educated Muslim thinkers and scientists made their own contributions to learning in philosophy, medicine, chemistry, astronomy, algebra, optics, art, and architecture. Towering intellectual giants dominated this period: al-Farabi (d. 950), Ibn Sina (known as Avicenna, 980–1037), Ibn Rushd (known as Averroes, d. 1198), al-Biruni (973–1048), and al-Ghazali (d. 1111). Avicenna (Ibn Sina) exemplified these multitalented men of genius:

I busied myself with the study of Fusus al-Hikam (a treatise by al-Farabi) and other commentaries on physics and mathematics, and the doors of knowledge opened before me. Then I took up medicine. . . . Medicine is not one of the difficult sciences, and in a short time I undoubtedly excelled at it, so that

dhimmi: "protected"; refers to non-Muslim peoples who were granted religious freedom under Muslim rule in exchange for payment of a tax

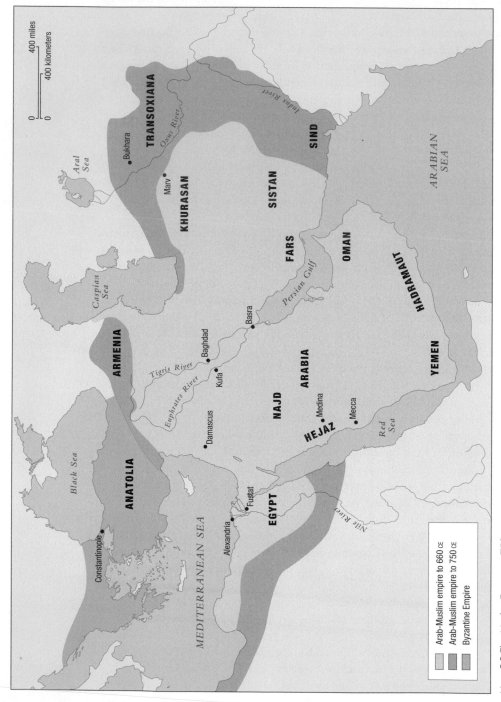

Map 5.2 The Muslim Empire to 750 CE.

Arab-Muslim empire to 660 CE
Arab-Muslim empire to 750 CE
Byzantine Empire

TRANSOXIANA

Bukhara

Aral Sea

Oxus River

Indus River

SIND

ARABIAN SEA

KHURASAN

Marv

SISTAN

FARS

OMAN

HADRAMAUT

Caspian Sea

Persian Gulf

ARMENIA

Basra

Baghdad

Tigris River

YEMEN

ARABIA

Euphrates River

Kufa

NAJD

Medina

Mecca

Damascus

HEJAZ

Red Sea

Black Sea

ANATOLIA

Constantinople

MEDITERRANEAN SEA

Fustat

Alexandria

EGYPT

Nile River

physicians of merit studied under me. . . . At the same time I carried on debates and controversies in jurisprudence. At this point I was 16 years old. Then, for a year and a half, I devoted myself to study. I resumed the study of logic and all parts of philosophy. During this time I never slept the whole night through and did nothing but study all day long. . . . Thus I mastered logic, physics, and mathematics. . . . When I reached the age of 18, I had completed the study of all these sciences. At that point my memory was better, whereas today my learning is riper.[2]

The cultural traffic pattern was again reversed when Europeans, emerging from the Dark Ages, turned to Muslim centers of learning to regain their lost heritage and to learn from Muslim advances. They retranslated the Greek philosophers and the writings of their great Muslim disciples: men like al-Farabi, who had come to be known as "the second teacher or master" (the first being Aristotle) and Ibn Rushd (Averroes), remembered as "the great commentator on Aristotle." Many of the great medieval Christian philosophers and theologians (Albert the Great, Thomas Aquinas, Abelard, Roger Bacon, Duns Scotus) acknowledged their intellectual debt to their Muslim predecessors.

The failures and reforms of Muslim societies today, as in the recent past, are often measured against this history, at times romanticized, of an earlier period of brilliant success.

Diversity, Division, and Dissent

The victories and accomplishments during the early history and spread of Islam were also accompanied by deep division and dissent. During the lifetime of the Prophet, the community had been united by Muhammad's prophetic claims, his remarkable leadership skills, and the divine revelations he continued to receive. However, Muhammad's death precipitated crises, dissent, and civil wars.

Given the pivotal role of Muhammad in the life of the community, his death in 632 was a traumatic event. What was the community to do? Who was to lead? Issues of political succession and secession or civil war were to plague and threaten its survival.

Muhammad's senior followers, known as the *Companions* of the Prophet, moved quickly to reassure the community. In proclaiming Muhammad's death to the faithful, the Companion Abu Bakr declared: "Muslims! If any of you has worshipped Muhammad, let me tell you that Muhammad is dead. But if you worship God, then know that God is living and will never die." The Companions selected Abu Bakr as caliph (*khalifah*, "successor or deputy"). As caliph, he was not a prophet but rather Muhammad's successor as political and military head of the community.

This next stage in the history of the Muslim community, the Caliphate (632–1258), has traditionally been divided into three periods: the time of the Rightly Guided Caliphs (632–661), followed by the Umayyad (661–750) and Abbasid (750–1258)

This enameled glass mosque lamp, made in the early 1300s, was dedicated to a Muslim ruler. Quotations from the Quran decorate the lamp.

dynasties. During these centuries a vast empire was created, with successive capitols at Medina, Kufa, Damascus, and Baghdad. Stunning political and military success was complemented by a cultural florescence, resulting in powerful Islamic empires and a brilliant Islamic civilization. However, it was the earliest period, that of the Rightly Guided Caliphs and the Companions of the Prophet, that was to become the example for later generations of believers.

Abu Bakr (632–34), the first successor of Muhammad, was tested almost immediately when some Arab tribes attempted to bolt from the community, declaring their independence. Abu Bakr crushed the tribal revolt, consolidated Muslim rule over the Arabian Peninsula, and preserved the religiously based unity and solidarity of the Islamic-community state.

Abu Bakr's successor, Umar ibn al-Khattab (634–44), initiated a period of expansion and conquest. During the reign of the third caliph, Uthman ibn Affan (644–56), from the Umayyad clan, tribal factionalism resurfaced with a series of rebellions that would plague the Islamic community's development.

A second crisis of leadership, with repercussions down through the centuries, occurred when civil war broke out during the reign of the fourth caliph, Ali. Although in 632 the majority of the community had supported the selection of Abu Bakr as caliph, a minority dissented, believing that leadership should stay in the family of the Prophet and thus pass to its senior male member, Ali. In addition to being Muhammad's cousin, Ali was the Prophet's son-in-law, having married Fatima, a daughter of Muhammad and Khadija. Shortly after Ali's accession to power, his authority was challenged by a triumvirate that included Muhammad's widow, Aisha, who was the daughter of Abu Bakr. This was followed by the rebellion of Muawiya, the governor of Syria. Arbitration proved inconclusive but did lead to two results that have had a profound impact on the history of Islam.

First, a group of Ali's followers, the Kharajites (those who "go out," or secede), broke away. They maintained an uncompromising faith, believing that Ali's failure to subdue his opponents rendered him no better than Muawiya. The Kharajites held both Ali and Muawiya to be unbelievers whose revolt against God was punishable by death. Second, Muawiya remained recalcitrant in Syria, biding his time until Ali was assassinated by a group of Kharajites. Muawiya then seized power and established a monarchy, the Umayyad dynasty (661–750).

The Umayyad dynasty was responsible for the rapid spread of Islam and the emergence of imperial Islam, with its capital in Damascus. However, opposition to what later Muslim historians would characterize as impious Umayyad caliphs also resulted in important movements for renewal and reform. Some movements, such as the Kharajites and the Shiah, were revolutionary, while others led to the development of Islamic law and mysticism (Sufism).

The Kharajites, who had broken with Ali, emerged as revolutionaries who, although unsuccessful in their own times, continue to inspire contemporary radical groups. Like some religious extremists today, the Kharajites interpreted the Quran and the Sunnah literally and sought to follow their beliefs absolutely and to impose them on others. They viewed the world as divided into belief or unbelief, into Muslims, defined as those who agreed with the Kharajites, and infidels, the enemies of God: those who differed with the Kharajites and therefore should be excommunicated, or cut off from the community.

Like extremist groups today, who have taken such names as Jihad, the Soldiers of God, and al-Qaeda, the Kharajites, claiming to follow the letter of the Quran and the example of the Prophet, adopted their own interpretation of Muhammad and the experiences of the early community. Seeing themselves as the instruments of God's justice, God's righteous army, they believed that violence, guerrilla warfare, and revolution were not only legitimate but obligatory in their battle against the usurpers of God's rule. Other Muslims, however pious, who committed an action contrary to the letter of the law, as interpreted or understood by the Kharajites, were guilty of grave (quite literally mortal) sin. According to the Kharajites, they were apostates and thus had committed treason against the Islamic community-state. If they did not repent, they were to be fought against and killed. Many of the components of this early Islamic worldview may be found in twentieth- and twenty-first-century Muslim extremist writings, including those of the Muslim Brotherhood's Sayyid Qutb, who will be discussed below, and in the ideology of groups such as Islamic Jihad, the Army of God, the Armed Islamic Group, Muhammad's Youth, Takfir wal Hijra (Excommunication and Flight), and al-Qaeda.

The Origins of the Sunni and Shiah Split

A second major revolutionary movement spawned by opposition to Umayyad rule was the rebellion by the followers of the fourth caliph, Ali. The results of this violent disagreement would lead to the two major branches of Islam, the communities of the **Sunni** majority and the **Shiah**, or Shii, minority.

The followers (*shiah*, "partisans") of Ali had been thwarted twice: when Muhammad's cousin was not appointed as the first caliph, and later when Muawiya seized the caliphate from Ali, who had been the Prophet's fourth successor. In 680, when the Umayyad ruler Yazid, the son of Muawiya, came to power, Husayn, the son of Ali, was persuaded by a group of Ali's followers in Kufa (a city in modern Iraq) to lead a rebellion. However, the support promised to Husayn did not materialize, and Husayn and his army were slaughtered by the Umayyad army at the city of Karbala (also in modern Iraq).

The memory of Karbala and the "martyrdom" of Husayn resulted in a Shii worldview, a paradigm of suffering, oppression, and protest against injustice. The mentality encouraged by this paradigm was reinforced by the Shiis' minority status and discrimination against them through the centuries. It sustained the community throughout history and became a major source of inspiration and mobilization during Iran's "Islamic" revolution of 1978–79.

Sunni Muslims constitute 85 percent and Shiah approximately 15 percent of the global Islamic community. Although united in their common confession of faith in

Sunni: Muslims who accept the *sunna* and the historic succession of the Caliphs

Shiah: followers of Ali, the cousin and son-in-law of Muhammad

The Blue Mosque, Shrine of Ali bin Thabit, cousin and son-in-law of Prophet Muhammad. Ali was the fourth caliph of Sunni Islam and the first imam of Shiah Islam. Built in the fifteenth century, the mosque has survived countless wars in near perfect condition. While some believe that it houses the tomb of Ali, most believe that he is buried in the Imam Ali Mosque in Najaf, Iraq.

imam: in Sunni Islam, the prayer leader and one who delivers the Friday sermon; in Shia Islam, refers to Ali's descendants, who are believed to be the legitimate leaders (not the Sunni caliphs) of the global Muslim community or *ummah*

God, the Quran, and the Prophet Muhammad, their notions of leadership and history differ. The reality of the dynastic Umayyad and Abbasid caliphates notwithstanding, in Sunni Islam, the caliph ideally is the selected or elected successor of the Prophet. He serves only, however, as political, military leader of the community, not as prophet. In Shiah Islam, the **imam**, or leader, is not selected from among the members of the community but must be a direct descendant of the Prophet's family. Moreover, he is the religiopolitical leader of the community. Though not a prophet, he is the divinely inspired, sinless, infallible, and final authoritative interpreter of God's will as formulated in Islamic law.

Sunnis and Shiah also developed differing interpretations of history. For Sunni, the early success of Islam and the power of its rulers were signs of God's guidance, rewards to a faithful community that were seen as historical validation of Muslim belief and claims. In contrast, the Shiah saw the same events as the illegitimate usurpation of power by Sunni rulers. For the Shiah, therefore, history is the theater for the struggle of a minority community, righteous but historically disinherited and oppressed, that must restore God's rule on earth under his imam. The early centuries of Islamic history would witness ongoing struggles between Sunnis and Shiah but also the remarkable development of religious thought (Islamic law, theology, and mysticism), institutions, traditions, and civilization.

Premodern Islam: The Classical Era

A critical issue faced by all religious believers today is the connection or continuity of current religious belief and practice with centuries-old sacred traditions. So, too, Islamic tradition and heritage become important reference points to justify contemporary beliefs and practices and as the basis for Islamic reform.

Law and Mysticism: The Outer and Inner Paths to God

Dissatisfaction with Umayyad rule, in which wealth led to abuse of power and corruption, resulted in the development of two nonrevolutionary reform movements or institutions: the **ulama** (religious scholars, or learned ones), with their Islamic law, and the Sufis, whose Islamic mysticism we shall discuss later.

In contrast to Christianity's emphasis on doctrine or theology, Islam, like Judaism, places primary emphasis on what believers should do, on religious observance of and obedience to God's law. Muslims are commanded by the Quran to strive or struggle (the literal word for struggle is **jihad**) in the path (*sharia*) of God, to realize, spread, and defend God's message and community. The faithful are to function as God's vicegerents (representatives or stewards) on earth, promoting the good and prohibiting evil (Q. 3.104, 3:110). All Muslims are responsible as individuals and as a community for the creation of the good society. Despite vast cultural differences, Islamic law has provided an idealized blueprint, a moral compass, that has provided a source of identity and guidance, a code of behavior, among Muslims throughout the ages.

Islamic law developed during the Umayyad dynasty in the eighth and ninth centuries as a response to real religious and political concerns and issues. Law was standardized by legal experts, with a view to limiting the power of the caliph or his appointed judges. Law continued to flourish during the tenth century under the Abbasid caliphs, who overthrew the Umayyads and legitimated their revolution by becoming the patrons of Islam and Islamic law. It is important to note that law did not develop primarily from the practice of courts or from government decrees but through the interpretation of scholars. In Sunni Islam, the *ulama* set out a religious ideal or blueprint based on four official sources of Islamic law: the Quran, the Sunnah, *qiyas*, and *ijma*.

The primary material source of Islamic law is the Quran, God's will for humankind: "Here is a plain statement to men, a guidance and instruction to those who fear God" (Q. 3:138). The Quran contains only eighty prescriptions that would qualify as law in the strict sense of the term; the majority of Quranic texts provide general principles and values, reflecting what the aims and aspirations of Muslims should be.

The Sunnah (example) of the Prophet comes from the Quran, early biographies, and especially prophetic traditions, the richest sources of information about Muhammad and his times. The Sunnah consists of volumes of hundreds of thousands

ulama: religious scholars

jihad: armed struggle in defense of Islam or the Muslim community; often, terrorists have also used this term to legitimate their actions

"Goodness is not turning your faces towards the East or West; goodness is to believe in Allah, the Last Day, angels, and the Book, and the prophets; to spend money, out of love for Him, for your kin, for orphans, for the needy, for the wayfarer, for those who ask, and for the freeing of slaves; to be steadfast in prayer, and pay the alms tax regularly; to fulfill contracts you have made; and to be firm and patient, in pain (or suffering) and adversity, and throughout all periods of panic. Those are truthful and God-fearing people."

—Quran 2:177

hadith: narrative report of Muhammad's sayings and action

qiyas: legal term for analogical reasoning

ijma: in Islamic law, consensus

ibadat: worship, ritual obligations

muamalat: social interactions

fatwa: legal opinion or interpretation from a Muslim legal expert (*mufti*)

mufti: legal expert who issues *fatwas* to judges and litigants

of narrative stories or reports (***hadith***) about what the Prophet said and did. The material seemingly covers every situation. The centrality of the Prophetic traditions, yesterday and today, cannot be overestimated: "They are associated with the person who is 'alive' here and now and who is as revered and loved by all Muslims now as he was fourteen centuries ago."[3]

The third source of law is analogical reasoning (***qiyas***). When confronted by a question or issue not addressed specifically and clearly, in the Quran or Sunnah, jurists looked for similar or analogous portions of scripture to identify principles that could be applied to a new case. For example, there is no specific text dealing with the use of mind-altering drugs, but from *qiyas*, jurists can justify the condemnation of such substances on the basis of sacred texts that plainly forbid the consumption of alcohol.

Finally, consensus (***ijma***) is based on a statement traditionally attributed to the Prophet: "My community will never agree on an error." In reality, consensus has generally amounted to acceptance or consensus about an issue from the majority of religious scholars who represented religious authority.

The two main divisions of Islamic law concern a Muslim's duties to God (***ibadat***), which consist of obligatory practices such as the Five Pillars of Islam, and duties to others (***muamalat***), which include regulations governing public life, from contract and international law to laws on marriage, divorce, and inheritance.

Islamic law is a source of unity and guidance, but individual jurists and legal scholars from diverse social backgrounds and cultural contexts have ever differed in their interpretation of texts, in their personal opinions, and in their notions of equity and public welfare. Diversity and disagreement in Islamic law are reflected in the acceptance of different law schools and the validity of their different (*ikhtilaf*) opinions.

We see these differences in official legal opinions or interpretations (***fatwas***) of Muslim jurists (***muftis***) who advised judges and litigants in recent times. In the Gulf War of 1991, some muftis supported Iraq, and others supported a U.S.-led armada that included troops from Egypt, Kuwait, and Saudi Arabia. Similarly, sharp differences have existed among religious leaders over the religious legitimacy or illegitimacy of suicide bombing in Israel-Palestine. But however different and contentious interpretations of Islamic law have been throughout Islamic history, the Five Pillars of Islam unite all Muslims in their worship and following of God.

The Five Pillars of Islam

If God, the Quran, and the Prophet Muhammad unite all Muslims in their common belief, the Five Pillars of Islam provide a unity of practice in the midst of the community's rich diversity. These are the Five Pillars:

shahadah: Muslim declaration of faith

1. *The Declaration of Faith.* A Muslim is one who bears witness that "There is no God but the God and Muhammad is the messenger of God." One need only make this simple statement, known as the ***shahadah***, to become a Muslim.

The first part of the *shahadah* affirms Islam's absolute monotheism, an unshakable and uncompromising faith in the oneness or unity (*tawhid*) of God. The second part is the affirmation that Muhammad is the messenger of God, the last and final prophet, who serves as a model for the Muslim community.

The action, or doing, orientation of Islam is illustrated by the remaining four pillars or duties.

2. *Prayer.* Five times a day (dawn, noon, midafternoon, sunset, and evening), Muslims throughout the world are called to worship God. In many cities of the world, the quiet of the night or daily noise of busy city streets is pierced by the call of the **muezzin** from atop the tower (*minaret*) of the mosque: God is Most Great (Allahu Akbar)!, God is Most Great!

> I witness that there is no god but God (Allah) . . .
> I witness that Muhammad is the Messenger of God . . .
> Come to prayer . . . come to salvation . . .
> God is Most Great! God is Most Great! There is no god
> but God!

Prayer (**salat**) is preceded by a series of ablutions to cleanse the body and to symbolize the purity of mind and body required for worshipping God. Facing the holy city of Mecca, Islam's spiritual homeland where the Prophet was born and received God's revelation, Muslims recall the revelation of the Quran and reinforce a sense of belonging to a single, worldwide community of believers. Muslims may pray in any appropriate place wherever they happen to be: at home, in an airport, on the road. They may do so as individuals or in a group. For Muslims, *salat* is an act of worship and adoration of God and remembrance of his word, not one of request or petition.

"Recite what has been revealed to you of the Book and perform prayer regularly: for prayer restrains from shameful and unjust deeds. Allah's remembrance is the greatest (thing in life) and Allah knows what you do."
—Quran 29:45

muezzin: one who issues the call to prayer from the minaret of a mosque

salat: prayer performed five times each day

These Uzbek Muslims, like fellow believers across the world, perform their prayers five times each day.

mosque: a building used for public and community worship

khutba: sermon delivered in a mosque on Fridays

minbar: mosque pulpit from which khutba is preached

zakat: almsgiving

Ramadan: ninth month of Muslim calendar, during which Muslims fast

A muezzin calling the faithful to prayer in the city of Kashgar in western China.

On Friday, the noon prayer is a congregational prayer that usually takes place in a **mosque** (*masjid*, "place of prostration"). A special feature of the Friday prayer is a sermon (*khutba*), preached from a pulpit (*minbar*). Since there is no priesthood in Islam, any Muslim may lead the prayer. In many communities, larger mosques do have an imam who leads the prayer and is paid to look after the mosque.

3. *Almsgiving.* The third pillar of Islam is the *zakat*, almsgiving. As all Muslims share equally in their obligation to worship God, so too they all are duty bound to attend to the social welfare of their community by redressing economic inequalities. This is accomplished through an annual contribution of 2.5 percent of one's accumulated wealth and assets, not just on income. Strictly speaking, *zakat* is not charity, since almsgiving is seen not as voluntary but as a duty imposed by God, an act of spiritual purification and solidarity. Just as the Quran condemns economic exploitation, it warns against those who accumulate wealth and fail to assist others (Q. 3:180). Those who have benefited from God's bounty, who have received their wealth as a trust from God, are required to look after the needs of the less fortunate members of the Muslim community.

In most countries, Muslims determine to whom they will pay the *zakat*. However, in recent years, some governments, such as those of Pakistan, Sudan, and Iran, in the name of creating a more Islamic state, have collected and distributed the *zakat*. This has proved to be a point of contention, for some charge that the central government misappropriates funds, and others prefer to have the freedom to distribute it themselves to needy relatives, friends, or neighbors.

4. *The Fast of Ramadan.* Muslims are required to fast (*sawm*) during **Ramadan**, the ninth month of Islam's lunar calendar. From dawn to dusk, all healthy Muslims must abstain from food, drink, and sex. The primary emphasis is less on abstinence and self-mortification as such than on spiritual self-discipline, reflection, and the performance of good works.

The fast is broken at the end of the day by a light meal, called breakfast. In the evening, families exchange visits and share foods and sweets that are served only at this time of the year. The month of Ramadan comes to an end with a great celebration, the Feast of the Breaking of the Fast, Id al-Fitr, one of the great religious holy days and holidays of the Muslim calendar. Family members come from near and far to feast and exchange gifts in a celebration that lasts for three days.

5. *Pilgrimage to Mecca*. The pilgrimage season follows Ramadan. Every adult Muslim who is physically and financially able is expected to perform the pilgrimage (**hajj**) to Mecca in Saudi Arabia at least once in his or her lifetime. Those who are able may go more often. Just as Muslims are united five times each day as they face Mecca in worship, each year believers make the physical journey to this spiritual center of Islam, where they again experience the unity, breadth, and diversity of the Islamic community. In the twenty-first century almost 2 million Muslims gather annually from every part of the globe in Saudi Arabia for the *hajj*.

The focus of the pilgrimage is the Kaaba, the cube-shaped House of God that Muslim tradition teaches was originally built by the prophet Ibrahim (Abraham) and his son Ismail to honor God. The black stone is believed to have been given to Abraham by the angel Gabriel. Thus the stone is a symbol of God's covenant with Ismail and, by extension, with the Muslim community. Like *salat*, the pilgrimage requires ritual purification; no jewelry, perfume, or sexual activity is permitted. Pilgrims wear white garments, symbolizing for everyone, rich and poor alike, the unity and equality of all believers before God. Men and women worship together. There is no segregation of the sexes.

As the pilgrims near Mecca, they shout: "I am here, O Lord, I am here!" When they reach Mecca, they proceed to the Grand Mosque that houses the Kaaba. There they pray at the spot where Abraham, the patriarch and

hajj: annual pilgrimage to Mecca, in which all adult Muslims are expected to participate at least once if physically and financially able to do so

"Alms are for the poor, the needy, and those employed to administer the (funds); for those whose hearts are bound together; as well as for freeing slaves and [repaying] debts; spending in the cause of Allah and for the wayfarer: thus Allah commands, and Allah is All-Knowing and Wise."

—Quran 9:60

Muslims are required to abstain from food and drink from dawn to dusk during the month of Ramadan. At dusk each day during Ramadan, families gather to break the fast and share a meal. This practice is called "breakfast."

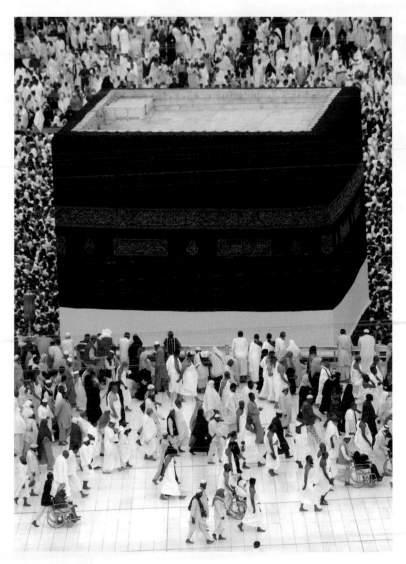

The Kaaba. The pilgrimage (*hajj*) to Mecca, one of the Five Pillars of Islam, takes place during the first ten days of the twelfth month of the lunar calendar. The focus of the pilgrimage is the Kaaba, "the cube," also known as the House of God, which tradition says was built by Abraham and his son Ismail. Pilgrims circumambulate the Kaaba, located within the Great Mosque of Mecca. This is a ritual act that many believe symbolizes the angels' circling of God's throne in heaven.

father of monotheism, stood, and they circumambulate the Kaaba seven times. Another part of the *hajj* is a visit to the Plain of Arafat, the site of Muhammad's last sermon, where pilgrims seek God's forgiveness for their sins and for those of all Muslims throughout the world.

The pilgrimage ends with the celebration of the Feast of Sacrifice (Id al-Adha). The "great feast" commemorates God's testing of Abraham by commanding him to sacrifice his son Ismail (in the Jewish and Christian traditions it is Isaac who is put at risk). Commemorating God's final permission to Abraham to substitute a ram for his son, Muslims sacrifice animals (sheep,

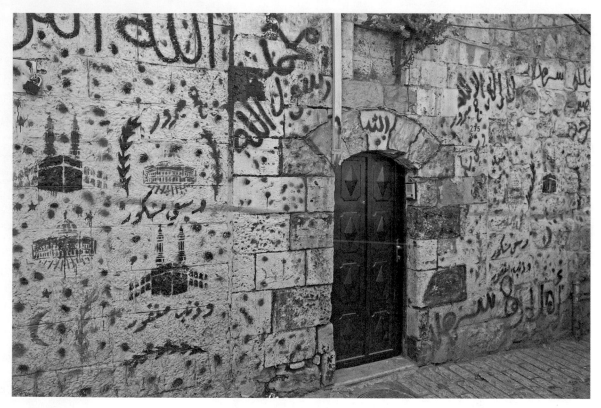

Those who have made the *hajj* often use the honorific title *hajji*. Many, as demonstrated by this house in Jerusalem, decorate the facade with illustrations to show that the owner has been to Mecca.

goats, cattle) not only in Mecca but across the Muslim world. While some of the meat is consumed, most is distributed to the poor. The three-day Feast of Sacrifice is a time for rejoicing, prayer, and visiting with family and friends.

Women and Muslim Family Law

Few topics have received more popular attention than women and the family. If many Muslims speak of Islam as liberating women, others in the West as well as in Muslim countries decry the continuing oppression of women. The position of Muslim women must be viewed within the dual context of their status in Islamic law and the politics and culture of their societies. Islamic law itself reflects both the Quranic concern for the rights and protection of women and the family (the greater part of its legislation is devoted to these issues) and the traditions of the male-dominated society within which Islamic law was developed.

The Quran introduced reforms affecting the status of women both through new regulations and by teachings that led to the modification of prevailing customs. The Quran recognized a woman's rights to contract marriage, to receive and keep her

Jihad: The Struggle for God

Jihad, "to strive or struggle," is sometimes referred to as the sixth pillar of Islam, although it has no such official status. In its most general meaning, *jihad* refers to the obligation incumbent on all Muslims, as individuals and as a community, to exert (*jihad*) themselves to realize God's will, to lead a virtuous life, to fulfill the universal mission of Islam, and to spread the Islamic community through preaching Islam to convert others or writing religious tracts ("jihad of the tongue" and "jihad of the pen"). Thus, today it can be used to describe the personal struggle to keep the fast of Ramadan, to lead a good life, to fulfill family responsibilities. Popularly it is used to describe the struggle for educational or social reform—to establish good schools, to clean up a neighborhood, to fight drugs, or to work for social justice. However, it also includes the struggle for or defense of Islam, holy war. Although *jihad* is not supposed to include aggressive warfare, this tactic has been invoked by early extremists such as the Kharajites, by rulers to justify their wars of conquest and expansion, and by contemporary extremists such as Osama bin Laden and his *jihad* against America as well as *jihadi* organizations in Lebanon, the Persian Gulf, and Indonesia.

dowry, and to own and inherit property. No equivalent rights existed in Christianity or in Judaism during or long after the lifetime of the Prophet. In fact, women in the West did not gain inheritance rights until the nineteenth century. These Quranic reforms and others would become the basis for Muslim family law.

As the Five Pillars are the core of a Muslim's duty to worship God (*ibadat*), family law is central to Islam's social laws (*muamalat*). Indeed, Muslim family law has often been described as the heart of the *sharia*, reflecting the importance of the family in Islam. Because of the centrality of the community in Islam and the role of the family as the basic unit of society, family law has enjoyed pride of place in the development of Islamic law and in its implementation throughout history. Similarly, though the emergence of modern Muslim states has often seen the adoption of Western-oriented civil and commercial laws or legal systems, in most countries Muslim family law has remained in force. While in some countries family law has been reformed rather than replaced, often this reform has generated considerable conflict and debate. In the 1980s, the resurgence of Islam was often accompanied by attempts to return to the use of classical or medieval family law and to reverse modern reforms. Thus today, as in the past, the subject of women and the family remains an important and extremely sensitive subject in Muslim societies.

The status of women and the family in Muslim family law is the product of many factors: Arab culture, Quranic reforms, foreign ideas and values assimilated from conquered peoples, and the interpretation of male jurists in a patriarchal society. Regulations developed in the early centuries of Islamic history regarding marriage, divorce, inheritance, and bequests have guided Muslim societies, determining attitudes toward women and the family.

"For Muslim men and women—for believing men and women, for devout men and women, for true men and women, for men and women who are patient and constant, for men and women who humble themselves, for men and women who give in Charity, for men and women who fast (and deny themselves), for men and women who guard their chastity, and for men and women who engage much in Allah's praise—for them has Allah prepared forgiveness and great reward."

—Quran 33:35

The Quran teaches that men and women are equal before God in terms of their religious and moral obligations and rewards (Q. 33:35). However, husbands and wives are seen as fulfilling complementary roles, based on differing characteristics, capacities, and dispositions and their traditional roles in the patriarchal family. Men function in the public sphere, the "outside" world; they are responsible for the financial support and protection of the family.

A woman's primary role is that of wife and mother; she is responsible for the management of the household, raising her children and supervising their religious/moral training. In light of women's more sheltered and protected status and men's greater experience in public life and broader responsibilities, the Quran (and Islamic law) teaches that wives are subordinate to husbands (Q. 2:228), and in Islamic law the testimony of one man is worth that of two women. Similarly, because men in a patriarchal system were responsible for the economic well-being of all women and other dependents in the extended family, the male portion of inheritance was twice that of a female.

Marriage is a primary institution in Islam, regarded as incumbent upon all Muslims. It is a civil contract or covenant, not a sacrament. It safeguards chastity and the growth and stability of the family, legalizing intercourse and the procreation of children. Reflecting the centrality of the family and the identity and role of individual family members, marriage is not simply an agreement between two people but between two families. Thus, marriages arranged by the two families or by a guardian are traditional, although the majority of jurists agreed that a woman should not be forced to marry a man against her will.

Many non-Muslims are ignorant or unaware of Quranic reforms affecting women; indeed, most equate Islam with polygamy or, more accurately, polygyny. The Quran explicitly permits a man to marry four wives while in the same verse (Q. 43) noting that if all cannot be supported and treated equally, then only one is permitted. The purpose of this provision is not to discourage all men from practicing monogamy but to afford protection to unmarried women as well as to limit and regulate the unfettered rights of men. Islamic modernists in recent years have used this same spirit and another verse ("You are never able to be fair and just between women if that is your ardent desire," Q. 4:129) to argue that the Quranic ideal is monogamy and that plural marriages should be restricted or eliminated. In particular, they note that the original revelation was given to a premodern community in which losses in battle left many widows who needed protection. More important, many maintain that the demands of modern life make it extraordinarily difficult for any man to provide equally for more than one wife, especially in terms of time and affection.

Islamic law, reflecting the spirit of the Quran (Q. 4:35) and a saying of the Prophet ("of all the permitted things divorce is the most abominable"), regards divorce as permissible but reprehensible. One authoritative legal manual calls divorce "a dangerous and disapproved procedure . . . nor is its propriety at all admitted, but on the ground of urgency of relief from an unsuitable wife."[4] Islamic law itself, as if to underscore the seriousness of divorce, prescribes that a man must pronounce the words or formula of divorce three separate times to make it irrevocable.

The strong influence of custom can be seen in the more limited rights of divorce accorded women. The Quran had declared: "Women have rights similar to those (of men) over them; while men stand above them" (Q. 2:228). For example, while the *ulama* extended more limited divorce rights to women, in contrast to men, women had to go to court and present grounds for divorce far more specific than unsuitability; they were limited to charges like physical abuse, abandonment, and failure to provide adequate maintenance. Beginning in the 1920s, some Muslim governments relaxed these and other legal restrictions on women.

Historically, divorce rather than polygamy has proved to be the more serious social problem, especially since women have often been ignorant of their legal rights or unable to exercise them in male-dominated social environments. Historically, a woman's Quranic and legal rights to contract and dissolve her own marriage, to receive and control her dowry, or to inherit often disappeared under the pressures and mores of strong patriarchal societies. Thus custom tended to prevail over Islamic law as well as the letter and spirit of the Quran.

A major example of the interaction of custom and scripture is the veiling (or covering) and seclusion (**purdah**) of women. These customs, assimilated by Islamic practice from the conquered Persian and Byzantine empires, have been viewed by many, though certainly not all, as appropriate expressions of Quranic principles and values. The Quran does not stipulate the veiling and seclusion of women, although it does say that the wives of the Prophet should speak to men from behind a partition. It tells women to dress and behave modestly (Q. 24:30–31), but the admonition applies to men, as well.

> **purdah:** seclusion of women from men who are not relatives

Veiling and seclusion have varied considerably across Muslim societies and in different historical periods. Originally veiling had been meant to protect women in upper-class urban surroundings, where they enjoyed mobility and opportunities to socialize. Village and rural women were slower to adopt the measure, which interfered with their ability to work in the fields.

Over the centuries, as the practices of veiling and seclusion spread, there were deleterious effects on the status of women religiously and socially. The institution of *purdah* served to cut off many women's access to the mosque, the social and educational center of the community, an isolation that further lowered their status. Poorer women were often restricted to small houses with limited social contacts. The serious negative impact of *purdah* in modern times was attested to in the 1940s by an Egyptian scholar and religious leader who bore the name of a distinguished predecessor. The twentieth-century Muhammad al-Ghazali (d. 1996) said: "Ninety percent of our women do not pray at all; nor do they know of the other duties of Islam other than their names."[5]

Although debate rages today in many Muslim societies about the status and character of "the Muslim woman," with greater opportunities for women's education and employment have come reforms to address the inequities of some Muslim laws that affect women only. Modernizing governments from the 1920s to the 1960s reformed Muslim family laws in marriage, divorce, and inheritance.

Reforms included measures that restricted a male's right unilaterally to divorce his wife as well as to practice polygyny. In fact, a wife was permitted to specify in her

The Sufi Path

At the heart of Sufism's worldview and spirituality is the belief that one must die to self to become aware of and live in the presence of God. For guidance in the way Sufis relied on a teacher or master (*shaykh* or *pir*), one whose authority was based on direct personal religious experience. The master leads his or her disciples through the successive stages of renunciation of the transient phenomenal world, purification, and insight. Along the way, God is believed to reward and encourage the disciple through special blessings and certain religious experiences or psychological states.

marriage contract that a husband must obtain her permission before taking another wife. A wife's grounds for divorce were increased, as well. These reforms were partial and were imposed from above through legislation. They were often resisted or reluctantly accepted by the *ulama*. Moreover, with the resurgence of Islam, more conservative religious forces and many Islamic activists have rejected family law reforms as Western inspired, calling instead for a return to classical Islamic laws and seeking again to limit and control women's role in society.

The Interior Path of Love: Islamic Mysticism

Alongside the path of law (*sharia*) is the interior path or way (*tariqa*) of Sufi mysticism, a major popular religious movement within Sunni and Shii Islam. Whereas the *sharia* provided the way of duties and rights to order the life of the individual and community, Sufism offered an esoteric path or spiritual discipline, a method by which the Sufi sought not only to follow God but also to know or to experience God's presence.

Islamic mysticism, like Islamic law, began as a reform movement. With the phenomenal success of Islam uniting the tribes of Arabia and conquering the Byzantine and Persian empires, the *ummah* entered another phase in its development. In a new capital, Damascus, the Umayyad caliphs set up a court characterized by an imperial lifestyle and material luxuries. Increasingly, pious Muslims in many locations saw these changes as evidence that God and submission to his will were being replaced in the royal courts of dynastic rulers by concerns for power and wealth. To counter this trend, the critics began to study the Quran, the traditions of the Prophet, and the performance of religious duties, with an emphasis on asceticism and love of God, re-emphasizing the centrality of God over worship of the material world and its rewards.

Sufism: Islamic mysticism

The term **Sufism** comes from the coarse woolen garment (*suf*, "wool") worn by many of these early ascetics. The reformers did not reject the world so much as dependence on the things of this world; they did not wish to allow creation to obscure the Creator or to forget the Absolute Reality in the course of being swept along and away from God by material realities. Desiring a more faithful return to the purity and simplicity of the Prophet's time, men and women pursued a path of

Turkish Sufi order (Mawlawi *tariqah*), founded by Jalal al-Din Rumi (d. 1273), one of the most famous Sufi mystics. These men are popularly known as *whirling dervishes* because of one of their meditation rituals, a dance in which they revolve to the music of Sufi songs.

self-denial and good works. The **Sufis** were known for detachment from the material world, which they viewed as ephemeral, a transient distraction from the divine; repentance for sins; fear of God and the Last Judgment; and selfless devotion to the fulfillment of God's will.

Sufis: Muslim mystics

Early emphasis on ascetic detachment (worldly renunciation) and meditation was complemented by the fusion of asceticism with an undying devotional love of God exemplified by Rabia al-Adawiyya (d. 801). The joining of the ascetic with the ecstatic permanently influenced the nature and future development of Sufism. An attractive and desirable woman, Rabia declined offers of marriage, not willing to permit anyone or anything to distract her from dedication and total commitment to God. Nothing captures better the selfless devotion she espoused than the following words attributed to her:

> O my Lord, if I worship Thee from fear of Hell, burn me in hell, and if I worship Thee in hope of Paradise, exclude me thence, but if I worship Thee for Thine own sake, then withhold not from me Thine Eternal Beauty.[6]

Over the years, a variety of ascetic and ritual practices were adopted as part of the mystic way, including fasting, poverty, silence, and celibacy. Among the Sufi techniques to "remember" God, who is always present in the world, are rhythmic repetition of God's name and breathing exercises that focus consciousness on God and place the devotee in the presence of God. Music and song as well as dance are also used to express deep feelings of love of God, to feel or experience his nearness, and to show devotion to God and Muhammad. The best-known use of dance is that of Turkey's whirling dervishes, who circle their master to imitate the divinely ordained motions of the universe.

One popular practice of Sufism is the veneration of Muhammad and Sufi saints as intermediaries between God and humanity. Despite the official Islamic belief that Muhammad was only a human being and not a miracle worker, his central role as the ideal model of Muslim life had generated stories of the Prophet's extraordinary powers. In Sufism these stories mushroomed and were extended to Sufi saints, the friends (**wali**) or protégés of God, who are said to have had the power to bilocate, cure the sick, multiply food, and read minds. The burial sites or mausoleums of Sufi masters became religious sanctuaries. Pilgrims visited them, offering petitions for success in this life and the next, and miracles were reported.

wali: Sufi term referring to a saint

The many faces of contemporary Islam include not only the more visible reassertion of Islam in Muslim politics but also the revitalization of Muslim piety and spirituality. These adherents of the Sufi Naqshbandi order at the Islamic Institute in Cairo represent one of the major mystical orders in Islam. Not only did they play an important role in reformist and anticolonialist movements throughout the Islamic world in the past, they also do so today.

Though Sufi spirituality complemented the more ritual and legalistic orientation of the *ulama* and the *sharia*, the relationship between the two was often tense. The *ulama* tended to regard Sufi masters and the mystic way as a challenge to their authority and their interpretation of Islam. Sufis tended to regard the *ulama's* legalistic approach to Islam as lesser, incomplete, and subordinate to the Sufi way.

The majority of the *ulama* reacted to these challenges to their authority and worldview by condemning Islamic mysticism in the name of Islamic orthodoxy. At this critical juncture a prominent Islamic scholar, Muhammad al-Ghazali (1058–1111), emerged to save the day.

Al-Ghazali spent many years traveling to major Sufi centers in Arabia and Palestine, practicing and studying Sufism. During this time, he wrote *The Revivification of the Religious Sciences*, in which he showed that law, theology, and mysticism were neither incompatible nor inconsistent with one another. This brilliant *tour de force* reassured the *ulama* about the orthodoxy of Sufism and countered the rationalism of the philosophers. In al-Ghazali's great synthesis, law and theology were presented in terms that the *ulama* could accept, but they were grounded in religious experience and interior devotion (Sufism). Rationalism was tempered by the Sufi emphasis on religious experience and love of God. Al-Ghazali reconciled the *ulama* and the Sufis, producing a religious synthesis that earned him the title "Renewer (**mujaddid**) of Islam." While the tension between many of the *ulama* and Sufism continued and, as we shall see, in later centuries led to attempts to reform or suppress Sufism, al-Ghazali had secured an important place for Sufism within Islam. Indeed, Sufism in the twelfth century and later swept across much of the Islamic world. Sufi orders became the great missionaries of Islam, and Sufism became integral to everyday popular religious practice and spirituality.

However, the strength of Sufism as a popular religious force also proved to be its weakness. Its flexibility, tolerance, and eclecticism, which enabled it to incorporate local religious practices and values as Islam spread to new regions, also led at times to the indiscriminate incorporation of superstitious and otherwise non-Islamic activities, ranging from magic and fetishism to drunkenness and sensuality. Sufism's concern about the dangers in the *ulama's* religious legalism and ritual formalism gave way to rejection, by some, of the official practices of Islam in favor of a highly individualistic and idiosyncratic brand of devotion. Emphasis on the limits of reason and the importance of religious practice and experience devolved into an anti-intellectualism that rejected all Islamic learning and authority and promoted superstition, passivism, and fatalism. Premodern reformers and modernists, both secular and Islamic, have blamed Sufism for the ills of the Muslim world, yet throughout much of the history of the *ummah*, Sufism has remained a vital spiritual presence and force.

Islam and the State

As we have seen, the early success and power of Islamic empires greatly influenced the development of Islamic law and mysticism. From Muhammad's establishment of the first Muslim community at Medina in 622 CE and down through the centuries, the faith of Islam became a central force in the development of state and society. The soldiers, traders, and Sufis of Islam spread God's word and rule, creating a vast land or region of

> **mujaddid:** "renewer"; one who comes to restore and revitalize Islamic community and practice

Sheikh Lotf Allah Mosque in Isfahan, Iran, completed in 1618, is one of the architectural masterpieces of Safavid Iranian architecture.

dar al-Islam: territory controlled and ruled by Muslims

Islam (**dar al-Islam**). The caliphate, with its centralized Islamic empires, the Umayyad (661–750) and Abbasid (750–1250) dynasties, was followed by an extensive series of Muslim sultanates extending from Timbuktu in Africa to Mindanao in Southeast Asia. During this period great medieval Muslim empires emerged: the Ottoman in the Middle East (1281–1924), the Safavid (1501–1722) in Iran, and the Mughal (1483–1857) in South Asia.

However different these empires and sultanate states, Islam constituted the basic framework for their political and social life. Islam provided legitimation, a religio-political ideology, and law, informing the state's political, legal, educational, and social institutions. The *caliph* or *sultan*, as head of state, was seen as the political successor of Muhammad. Though not a prophet, he was the protector of the faith who was to implement Islamic law and to spread Islamic rule. The *ulama* were the guardians of religion, its interpreters, and as such often served as advisers to *caliphs* and *sultans*. They were not an ordained clergy, nor were they associated with organized "congregations." Rather, they were a major intellectual and social force or class in society. They played a primary role in the state's religious, legal, educational, and social service institutions. The *ulama* were by this time theologians and legal experts, responsible for the application of the law and the administration of *sharia* courts. They ran the schools and universities that trained those who aspired to public as well as religious office. They administered funds that were applied to a broad range of services, from the

The Taj Mahal, the mausoleum built (1631–47) by the grief-stricken emperor Shah Jahan for his beloved wife Mumtaz Mahal, who died in childbirth. Situated in a forty-two-acre garden, it is flanked by two perfectly proportioned mosque complexes. This crowning achievement, a landmark of world architecture, symbolizes the wealth and splendor of the Mughal Empire. The project brought together craftsmen and calligraphers from the Islamic world who worked with Muslim and Hindu craftsmen from the empire.

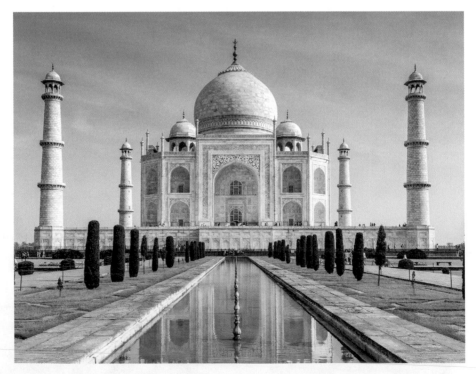

construction and maintenance of mosques, schools, student hostels, and hospitals to roads and bridges. In time, they came to constitute a religious establishment alongside and often dependent on the political establishment. Indeed, in many empires the ruler appointed a senior religious leader, *Shaykh-al-Islam*, as head of religious affairs, a post that still exists in many Muslim countries today.

In an Islamic state, citizenship, or perhaps more accurately degree of citizenship, was also based on religious affiliation. Muslims were full citizens, enjoying all the rights and duties of this position. As discussed earlier, Jews and Christians as People of the Book, were also citizens, but they had the status of protected people (*dhimmi*). Islam also informed the international relations of the state. The spread of Islam as a faith and a religiopolitical system was legitimated by the Quran and by the teaching and example of Muhammad. Muslims sought to create a "Pax Islamica," much like the "Pax Romana" and what U.S. policy makers would later speak of as a "Pax Americana." Conquest and diplomacy, force, persuasion, preaching, and alliances were its means.

The obligation to strive (*jihad*) to follow and realize God's will entailed opposition to evil and injustice and included *jihad* as an armed struggle to defend Islam or the community and to spread Muslim rule and empire. As such, *jihad* became part and parcel of Islam's doctrine of war and peace. As Islamic empires spread, non-Muslims could pick one of three options: to convert to Islam, to become "protected people" and pay a poll tax, or to become enemies to be fought.

For the believer, the role of Islam in state and society was mirrored in the continuum of Muslim rule, power, and success from the time of the Prophet Muhammad to the dawn of European colonialism. Despite the contradictions of life, civil wars, impious rulers, and dynastic usurpers, the presence and continuity of an Islamic ideology and system, however different the reality might at times be from the ideal, validated and reinforced a sense of a divinely mandated and guided community with a purpose and mission. Thus for many Muslims the history of Islam is that of a vibrant, dynamic, and expansive faith. Islam and Muslim rule were extended over major areas of Africa; the Middle East; South, Southeast, and Central Asia; Spain; and southern Italy. As a result, Sunni Muslim history contains the belief that following the Islamic community's divine mandate to spread God's guidance and governance will lead to prosperity and power in this life as well as the promise of eternal life in heaven.

The rapid spread and expansion of Islam as a dynamic faith and imperial power challenged and was regarded as a theological and political threat to Christendom, epitomized by the launching of the Crusades.

Islam and the West (Christendom): The Crusades

Despite common religious roots and instances of cooperation, the history of Islam and Western Christendom has been marked more by confrontation than by peaceful coexistence and dialog. For the Christian West, Islam is seen as the religion of the sword; for many Muslims, the spirit of the Christian West was epitomized first by the Crusades and centuries later by a movement seen as largely equivalent, European colonialism.

Unlike Judaism or any other world religion, Islam constituted an effective theological and political challenge to Christendom and its hegemonic ambitions. Muslim armies overran the Byzantine Empire, Spain, and the Mediterranean, from Sicily to Anatolia. At the same time, Islam challenged Christian religious claims and authority. Appropriating Christianity's insistence that the New Testament describes a new covenant and revelation superseding that of the Jews, Muslims now claimed to represent a third major stage in God's revelation, a third covenant. Therefore, Christians and Jews should acknowledge that they had corrupted their original revelations from God and that the one, true God, in his mercy, had sent his revelation one final and complete time to Muhammad. Islam now claimed to have a divinely mandated universal mission to call all to worship God and to join the Islamic community and live under Islamic rule. From the seventh to the eleventh centuries, Islam spread rapidly, extending Muslim rule over Christian territories and winning Christian hearts, in time creating large numbers of converts. Christianity and Islam were on a collision course.

By the eleventh century, Christendom's response to Islam was twofold: the struggle to reconquer Andalusian Spain (1000–1492), where the coexistence of Muslims, Christians, and Jews had produced a cultural florescence, and the undertaking of the Crusades (1095–1453).

Jerusalem had been taken by Arab armies in 638. Thereafter, for five centuries, Muslims lived in peaceful coexistence with Christians and with Jews. Although banned by Christian rulers, Jews were permitted by Muslims to return to live and worship in

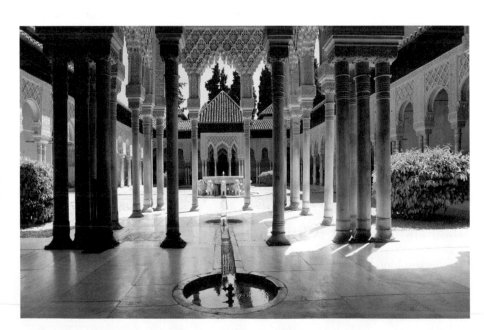

Courtyard of the Lions, Alhambra Palace, the fourteenth-century residence of the Nasrid dynasty in Granada, Spain, one of the remarkable monuments remaining from the several centuries of Muslim rule in Andalusia, when Muslims, Jews, and Christians coexisted and produced a high culture.

the city of Solomon and David. However, in the eleventh century political events and an imperial-papal power play that pitted Christendom against Islam began a period of misunderstanding and distrust that has spanned nearly a millennium.

In 1071, the Byzantine emperor Alexius I, whose army had been decisively defeated by a Seljuq (Abbasid) army, feared that all Asia Minor would be overrun. He called on other Christian rulers and the pope to come to the aid of his capital, Constantinople, by undertaking a "pilgrimage," or crusade, to free Jerusalem and its environs from Muslim rule. For the leader of the Western church, Pope Urban II, Jerusalem provided an opportunity to gain recognition of papal authority and the pontiff's role in legitimating the actions of temporal rulers. In addition, Christian rulers, knights, and merchants were driven by the promise of booty as well as trade and banking opportunities coming from the creation of a Latin kingdom in the Middle East. This enthusiastic response to the call for help by Alexius served to unite a divided Christendom in a holy war against the "infidel," ostensibly to liberate the holy city. The appeal to religion captured the popular mind and gained its support. This was ironic because, as one scholar has observed, "God may have indeed wished it, but there is certainly no evidence that the Christians of Jerusalem did, or that anything extraordinary was occurring to pilgrims there to prompt such a response at that time in history."[7]

Few events have had a more shattering and long-lasting effect on Muslim-Christian relations than the Crusades. Three myths pervade Western perceptions of the Crusades:

- that Muslims were the protagonists
- that Christendom triumphed
- the sole purpose of the Crusades was to liberate Jerusalem.

In fact, the Crusades were launched by Urban II and secular Christian rulers for causes as much political and economic as religious, and on balance Muslims prevailed.

For Muslims, the collective memory of the Crusades lives on as the clearest example of militant Christianity, an early harbinger of the aggression and imperialism of the Christian West, a vivid reminder of Christianity's early hostility toward Islam. If many regard Islam as a religion of the sword, Muslims down through the ages remember July 15, 1099, when the crusaders from Western Europe conquered Jerusalem, slaughtering all its Jewish and Muslim inhabitants in a massacre of unbridled violence. Western chroniclers spoke of Crusaders wading in blood up to their ankles. In Europe Christian monks hailed it as the greatest event in world history since the crucifixion of Christ. Muslims contrast this behavior with that of Salah al-Din (Saladin), the great Muslim general, who, in reconquering the holy city in 1187, spared noncombatants.

By the fifteenth century the Crusades had spent their force. Although ostensibly launched to unite Christendom and turn back Muslim armies, the opposite had occurred. One unintended result of the Crusades was the deterioration of the position of indigenous Arab Christian minorities in the Holy Land. These minorities had had rights and privileges under Muslim rule, but, after the establishment of the Latin Kingdom, they found themselves treated as "loathsome schismatics." In an effort to obtain relief from persecution by their fellow Christians, many Arabs abandoned their beliefs, and adopted either Roman Catholicism, or—the supreme irony—Islam.[8] Amid a bitterly divided Christendom, the Byzantine capital, Constantinople, fell in 1453 to Muslim armies, was renamed Istanbul, and became the seat of the Ottoman Empire. For Muslim-Christian relations, what actually happened in the Crusades is less important than how the period has been remembered. Each community (Islam and Christianity) sees the other as militant holy warriors, somewhat barbaric and fanatic in their religious zeal, determined to conquer, convert, or eradicate the other, and thus an enemy of God—an obstacle and threat to the realization of God's will. As we shall see, the history of their contention continued through the next wave of European colonialism and finally in the superpower rivalry that began in the twentieth century.

How do we get from a centuries-long history of Muslim vitality, creativity, power, and success vis-à-vis the West to a time in which much of the Muslim world is part of the developing rather than the developed world? How do we get from the confrontations of the past, on the one hand, and the coexistence and tolerance of Andalusia, on the other, to contemporary concerns about a clash of civilizations? Why is Islam equated by many with violence, religious extremism, and terrorism: from hostage taking and hijackings to holy wars, assassinations, and bombings?

Understanding Islam today requires an appreciation of key historical events from the eighteenth to the twentieth centuries as well as of the causes and nature of premodern and modern reform movements. Sacred texts and long-held religious beliefs, combined with the specific sociopolitical contexts of Muslim communities, have been critical factors in producing a diversity of Muslim experiences and interpretations of Islam.

Premodern Revivalist Movements

From the eighteenth to the twentieth centuries, the Islamic world witnessed a protracted period of upheaval and renewal. In many countries Muslim societies, already threatened by European colonialism, failed and declined for internal reasons, as well. Such crises sparked responses from religious social/political revivalist movements that quite literally spanned the breadth of the Islamic world: from the Mahdi in the Sudan, the Sanusi in Libya, the Fulani in Nigeria, the Wahhabi in Saudi Arabia, to the Padri in Indonesia. Though their political and socioeconomic conditions varied, all were concerned about religious, political, and social disintegration, and all were convinced that the cure for the societies was a renewal of the Islamic way of life.

Islamic revivalist movements draw on a long and rich history and tradition of revival (*tajdid*) and reform (*islah*). Throughout Islamic history, the failures of and threats to Muslim societies have given rise to individual reformers and to reformist movements led by scholars or mystics. Islamic revival and reform involve a call for a return to the fundamentals, the Quran and Sunnah, and the right to interpret (*ijtihad*, or use of independent judgment) these primary sources of Islam.

In the eighteenth and nineteenth centuries, this belief took on popular religious forms. While such Islamic renewers or revivalists claimed simply to return to the original teachings of the Quran and the Prophet Muhammad, in fact each one produced new religious interpretations and cultural syntheses needed to guide his age. We shall discuss the Wahhabi movement in Arabia and the Mahdiyya in Africa, perhaps the best known of the postmedieval revivalists. Each exerted a formative influence on modern Muslim states: the Wahhabi in what is now Saudi Arabia and Qatar and the Mahdist in Sudan.

Geometric design plays a major role in Islamic art. Artists use circles, triangles, hexagons, and squares to create ornate patterns to express and reinforce the unity of the Islamic world vision. This striking illustration comes from a Moroccan Quran tablet.

A religious leader, Muhammad ibn Abd al-Wahhab (1703–92), and a local tribal chief, Muhammad ibn Saud (d. 1765), joined forces to produce a united, militant religiopolitical movement. Ibn Abd al-Wahhab was dismayed by the condition of his society, which he saw as having degenerated to that of pre-Islamic Arabia, the *jahiliyya*, or period of ignorance of Islam. He was appalled by such popular religious practices as the veneration of Sufi saints, which he believed compromised the unity or oneness of God, and he was very critical of the Islamic community in Arabia, which had fallen back into tribalism and tribal warfare. He condemned some devotional rituals as idolatry, the worst sin in Islam, and dismissed others as pagan superstitions. Abd al-Wahhab wished to purify Islam from all foreign un-Islamic practices.

The Wahhabi movement waged a rigorous holy war to subdue and unite once again the tribes of Arabia. Muslims who did not go along were declared enemies of God who must be fought. Unlike other revivalist movements, the Wahhabi chose to completely suppress rather than merely reform Sufism.

The Mahdi of the Sudan, on the other hand, was a charismatic Sufi leader who initiated a militant reformist religiopolitical movement. The founder of the Mahdiyya order, whose name was Muhammad Ahmad, proclaimed himself **Mahdi** ("divinely guided one") in 1881. Thus, he went beyond most other revivalist reformers who claimed the right to interpret Islam and instead said that he was a divinely appointed and inspired representative of God.

Mahdi: "divinely guided one" who is expected to appear at the end of time to usher in a perfect Islamic society of peace and social justice

The *Mahdi* established an Islamic community, uniting his followers, who like the Prophet's Companions were called *Ansar* ("helpers"). He also justified waging holy war against other Muslims, declaring Sudan's Ottoman Muslim rulers infidels who "disobeyed the command of His messenger and His Prophet, . . . ruled in a manner not in accord with what God had sent, . . . altered the sharia of our master, Muhammad the messenger of God, and blasphemed against the faith of God."[9] During this period, Sufism was reformed, and alcohol, prostitution, gambling, and music were outlawed as foreign un-Islamic practices that had corrupted society. After a four-year struggle, Mahdist forces overcame Egyptian forces of the Ottoman Empire, and an Islamic state was established in Khartoum in 1885.

Islam and Modernity

By the nineteenth century, the decline of Muslim societies made them vulnerable to external powers. Sharing the fate of many, they fell victim to European imperialism, which ultimately did much to shape the modern Muslim world politically, economically, religiously, and culturally. When Europe overpowered North Africa, the Middle East, South Asia, and Southeast Asia in the nineteenth century, reducing most Muslim societies to colonies, many experienced these defeats as a religious crisis as well as political and cultural setbacks.

Colonialism brought European armies and Christian missionaries, who attributed their conquests not only to their military and economic power, but also to the superiority of Western civilization and the truth inherent in Christianity. The French spoke of a "mission to civilize" and the British of "the white man's burden." Thus the missionaries who accompanied the armies of bureaucrats, soldiers, traders, and teachers were quick to spread the message of the superiority of their religion and civilization.

Muslim responses to Europe's political/religious penetration and dominance varied significantly, ranging from resistance or warfare in "defense of Islam" to accommodation to Western values, if not outright assimilation. Some advocated following the example of the Prophet Muhammad, who in the face of rejection and persecution in Mecca chose initially to emigrate from Mecca to Medina and later to fight. However, the military defense of Islam and Muslim territory generally proved fruitless in the face of the large, modernized weapons of superior European forces; and emigration to a "safe, independent" Muslim territory was logistically and physically impossible for most.

The response of many Muslim rulers, from Egypt to Iran, was an attempt to emulate or adopt that which had made the West triumphant, its knowledge, science, and technology as well as its culture. From Muhammad Ali, an early nineteenth-century ruler of Egypt, to the shahs of Iran in the twentieth century, the goal was development of modernized societies with modern militaries. Even Muslim rulers who sought an end to Western hegemony seemed convinced of the superiority of the culture and were drawn by its accomplishments and power. Students were sent to the West to study, to learn the sources of its success. "Modern" schools and institutions, based on European models and curricula, were created in many parts of the Muslim world to provide a "modern" education for a new generation. As a result, a modern elite quickly emerged.

Modern Muslim elites, intellectually and culturally influenced by, if not dependent on, the West, regarded the traditional Muslim religious establishment, the *ulama* or scholars who interpreted Islam, as relics of the past, incapable of inspiring and responding to the demands of the day. Most advocated a Western, secular model of development, and to this end they favored appropriating Western political, economic, and social institutions. In addition, however, they wanted to introduce a process of secularization, entailing separation of church and state and the restriction of religion to private, rather than public, life.

Islamic Modernism

In the late nineteenth and early twentieth centuries, Islamic reformers sought to bridge the gap between conservative religious leaders and modernizing secular elites, to demonstrate that Islam was compatible with modernization. Islamic modernists advocated a bold reinterpretation (*ijtihad*) of religious doctrine and practice in light of the needs of modernizing societies through programs of religious, educational, and social reform. They rejected the tendency of many *ulama* to cling blindly to past traditions and religious interpretations no less than the indiscriminate Westernization promoted by many secular modernists.

Islamic modernism asserted the compatibility of faith and reason, of Islam and modernity. It provided an Islamic rationale for the reinterpretation of Islamic doctrine and law, for the adoption or adaptation of modern ideas, science, technology, and institutions. Declaring Islam to be a religion of reason, science, and progress, reformers called on Muslims to reclaim the beliefs, attitudes, and values that had made the Islamic community so successful in the past, contributing to the creation of Islamic empires and a world-class civilization.

Maintaining that the decline of the Muslim community was not due to Islam but to Muslims' departure from the dynamic faith of Muhammad, Islamic reformers advocated a process of purification and reconstruction, of renewal and reform, to overcome what they viewed as the prevailing static medieval religious worldview. Centers of Islamic modernist thought sprang up across the Muslim world from Cairo to Jakarta.

Islamic modernism challenged both the doctrines and the leadership of the conservative religious establishments, rejecting blind acceptance of the authority of the past. Many of these reformers were not traditionally trained religious scholars but modern educated "laymen" who claimed the right to interpret and reinterpret Islam. They repudiated the authority of the *ulama* as the sole "keepers of Islam" as well as the tradition that the *ulama's* legal doctrines/interpretations were binding.

The rationale of Islamic modernism was simple: The corpus of Islamic law consisted, on the one hand, of divinely revealed and thus immutable laws and, on the other, of laws that were human interpretations that met the needs of past historical and social contexts and were therefore subject to change to accommodate modern circumstances and conditions. Thus, they distinguished between the unchanging laws of God (observances governing prayer, fasting, pilgrimage) and social legislation or regulations that were capable of reformulation and change.

Islamic modernism inspired movements for religious reform and for national independence but remained primarily attractive to the intellectual elite. Its major contribution was to provide much of the vocabulary for Islamic reformism and to legitimate a modernist agenda. In particular, it stressed the compatibility of religion and reason, the need for reinterpretation of traditional sources, and thus the need for religious, political, and social reforms. Islamic modernism provided the precedent for accepting or Islamizing "modern" ideas and institutions (from the nation-state and parliamentary government to women's education) as well as the notion that those qualified to interpret Islam should be extended beyond the monopoly exercised historically by the *ulama*. However, it failed to produce a systematic reinterpretation of Islam or to develop effective organizations to preserve, propagate, and implement its message. These failures contributed to the emergence of revivalist activist organizations like the Muslim Brotherhood in Egypt and the Islamic Society in South Asia.

Modern Revivalist (Fundamentalist) Movements

The presence and power of Europe in the Muslim world and the seeming failure of reformers to block Western political and cultural penetration effectively spawned two major Islamic revivalist movements in the Middle East and South Asia in the 1930s, the Muslim Brotherhood (*Ikhwan al-Muslimin*) and the Islamic Society (*Jamaat-i-Islami*). Islamic activist organizations have been the driving force behind the dynamic spread of the contemporary Islamic resurgence. Their trailblazers, Hassan al-Banna (1906–49) and Sayyid Qutb (1906–66) of the Brotherhood and Mawlana Abul Ala Mawdudi (1903–79) of the *Jamaat*, have had an incalculable impact on the development of Islamic movements throughout the Muslim world. Both movements constructed an ideological worldview based on an interpretation of Islam that informed social and political activism. Their founders are the architects of contemporary Islamic revivalism, men whose ideas and methods have been studied and emulated by scholars and activists from the Sudan to Indonesia.

Hassan al-Banna, a schoolteacher, established the Muslim Brotherhood in Egypt in 1928, and Mawlana Abul Ala Mawdudi, a journalist, organized the *Jamaat-i-Islami* in India in 1941. Both leaders combined traditional Islamic educational backgrounds with knowledge of modern Western thought. Believing that their societies were dominated by and dependent on the West, politically and culturally, both al-Banna and Mawdudi posited an "Islamic alternative" to conservative religious leaders and modern elites, whose orientation was Western and secular. The *ulama* were generally regarded as passé, a religious class whose fossilized Islam and co-optation by governments was a major reason for the backwardness of the Islamic community. Modernists were seen as having traded away the very soul of Muslim society out of blind admiration for the West.

The Brotherhood and the *Jamaat* proclaimed Islam to be a self-sufficient, all-encompassing way of life, an ideological alternative to Western capitalism and Marxism. These movements did not simply retreat to the past. Joining thought to action, they provided Islamic responses, ideological and organizational, to their twentieth-century Muslim societies to address such issues as how best to respond to European colonialism and to revitalize the Muslim community. In contrast to Islamic modernists who justified adopting Western ideas and institutions because they were compatible with Islam, al-Banna and Mawdudi sought to produce new interpretations, using Islamic sources. For Hassan al-Banna and Mawlana Mawdudi, the cultural penetration of the West in education, law, customs, and values, which threatened the very identity and survival of the Muslim community, was far more dangerous in the long run than political intervention.

Though they opposed Westernization, the Brotherhood and the *Jamaat* were not against modernization per se. They engaged in modern organization and institution building, provided modern educational and social welfare services, and used modern technology and mass communications to spread their message and to mobilize popular support. Their message itself, though rooted in Islamic revelation and sources, was clearly written for a twentieth-century audience. It addressed the problems of modernity as seen through Muslim eyes: government accountability, the relationship of Islam to nationalism, democracy, capitalism, Marxism, modern banking, educational and legal reform, women and work, Zionism, and international relations.

Organizationally, the Brotherhood and the *Jamaat* believed that, like Muhammad and the early Muslim community in Mecca, they were a vanguard, righteous communities within the broader *ummah* of Islam. Both organizations recruited followers from mosques, schools, and universities: students, workers, merchants, and young professionals, primarily city dwellers from the lower middle and middle classes. The goal was to produce a new generation of modern, educated, but Islamically oriented leaders prepared to take their place in every sector of society.

RITUALS AND RITES: Ideological Origins of Contemporary Revivalism

Despite differences, Hassan al-Banna and Mawlana Mawdudi shared the following ideological worldview based on a historical tradition that has inspired and guided many contemporary reform movements.

1. Islam is a comprehensive way of life, a total, all-embracing ideology for personal and public life, for state and society.
2. The Quran, God's revelation, and the example (Sunnah) of the Prophet Muhammad are its foundations.
3. Islamic law (the sharia, the "path" of God), based on the Quran and Sunnah, is the sacred blueprint for Muslim life.
4. Faithfulness to the Muslim's vocation to reestablish God's sovereignty or rule through implementation of God's law results in success, power, and wealth of

the Islamic community (ummah) in this life as well as eternal reward in the next.

5. Muslim societies fail and become subservient to others because they have strayed from God's divinely revealed path, following the secular, materialistic ideologies and values of the West or of the East—capitalism or Marxism.
6. Restoration of Muslim pride, identity, power, and rule (the past glory of Islamic empires and civilization) requires a return to Islam, the reimplementation of God's law, and the acceptance of God's guidance for state and society.
7. Science and technology must be harnessed and used within an Islamically oriented and guided context to avoid the Westernization and secularization of Muslim society.

While al-Banna and Mawdudi viewed an Islamic revolution as necessary to introduce an Islamic state and society, they advocated a process of reform rather than violent political revolution. To establish an Islamic state required first the Islamization of society through a gradual process of social change. Both the Brotherhood and the *Jamaat* maintained that Muslims should not look to Western capitalism or communism and that faith in the West was misplaced. Western democracy had not only failed to check but also had contributed to authoritarianism, economic exploitation, corruption, and social injustice. These early Islamic activists believed that the inherent fallacy of Western secularism, separation of religion and the state, would be responsible for the moral decline and ultimate downfall of the West. Finally, the Brotherhood maintained that years of Arab subservience to the West had not prevented the West from betraying Arabs by supporting Israeli occupation of Palestine.

Radical Islam

The worldviews and interpretations of Hassan al-Banna and Mawlana Mawdudi were shaped by their historical and social contexts as much as by faith. The Muslim Brotherhood had a confrontation with the Egyptian state in the late 1950s and 1960s that caused a group within the movement to become more militant and radicalized. The chief architect of this transformation, Sayyid Qutb, recast the ideological beliefs of Hassan al-Banna and Mawlana Mawdudi into a rejectionist revolutionary call to arms.

Like Hassan al-Banna, Sayyid Qutb had studied at a modern college established to train teachers. A devout Muslim, he had memorized the Quran as a child. Like many young intellectuals of the time, he studied Western literature and grew up an admirer of the West. Qutb was a prolific writer and an active participant in contemporary literary and social debates.

In 1949, a turning point in his life, Qutb traveled to the United States to study educational organization. Although he had come to the United States out of admiration, Qutb's experiences convinced him that the sexual permissiveness, moral decadence, and anti-Arab bias, which he perceived in U.S. government and media support for Israel, had corrupted all of Western civilization. Shortly after his return to Egypt in 1951, Sayyid Qutb joined the Muslim Brotherhood.

During the 1950s, Qutb emerged as a major voice of the Muslim Brotherhood, especially influential among the younger, more militant members. Government harassment of the Brotherhood and Qutb's imprisonment and torture in 1954, for alleged involvement in an attempt to assassinate Egyptian strongman Gamal Abdel Nasser, increased his radicalization and made his worldview even more confrontational. During ten years of imprisonment, he wrote prolifically. In his most influential Islamic ideological tract, *Signposts*, or *Milestones*, he took the ideas of Hassan al-Banna and especially Mawlana Mawdudi to a militant radical revolutionary conclusion.

Qutb regarded Egypt and other Muslim governments as repressive and anti-Islamic. Society was divided into two camps, the party of God and the party of Satan, those committed to the rule of God and those opposed to it. There was no middle ground between the forces of good and of evil. Qutb advocated a vanguard, a group of true Muslims within the broader, corrupted society. The Islamic movement was a righteous minority adrift in a sea of ignorance and unbelief. Muslim governments and societies alike were seen as un-Islamic, atheist, or pagan entities.

Qutb maintained that the creation of an Islamic system of government was a divine commandment and therefore an imperative, not an alternative. Given the authoritarianism of many regimes, Qutb concluded that *jihad* as armed struggle was the only way to implement a new Islamic order. Islam, he declared, stood on the brink of disaster, threatened by repressive anti-Islamic governments and the neocolonialism of the West and the East. Qutb went beyond his predecessors when he declared Muslim elites and governments atheists as enemies of God, against whom all true believers should wage holy war. Many later radical groups have used Qutb's formulation of the two options to bring about change: evolution—a process that emphasizes change from below, or revolution—violent overthrow of established (un-Islamic) systems of government.

In 1966, Qutb and several other Muslim Brotherhood leaders were executed. Thousands of Brothers were arrested and tortured, while others went underground or fled the country. Many concluded that the Brotherhood had been crushed, a prediction that was to prove false a decade later.

It is difficult to overstate the impact of Hassan al-Banna, Mawlana Mawdudi, and Sayyid Qutb. Their worldviews and organizations became formative influences for contemporary Islamic movements. Combining religiopolitical activism with social protest or reform, contemporary Islamic movements represent a spectrum of positions from moderation and gradualism to radicalism and revolutionary violence, from selective criticism of the West to rejection and attacks on all that the West stands for. Indeed, these movements reflect the multiple issues facing Muslims in their struggle to determine the relationship of Islam to modern state and society:

- countering Western political and cultural hegemony
- dealing with the seeming challenge of modernity to Islamic belief
- redefining Islam and its relevance to modern life and society
- addressing the clash of cultures not only between the West and the Muslim world but within Muslim societies over religious and national identity and development

Islam and Postmodern Trends in a Postcolonial World

The Impact of the Islamic Resurgence

Since the last decades of the twentieth century, the Muslim world has experienced the impact of the contemporary resurgence of Islam. New Islamic governments or republics were established in Iran, Sudan, and Afghanistan. Rulers, political parties, and opposition movements used Islam in attempting to attract supporters. Islamic activists have led governments, served in cabinets and in the elected parliaments, and served as senior officials in professional associations. At the same time, a minority of radical Islamic organizations in Egypt, Algeria, Lebanon, the West Bank, and Gaza have engaged in violence and terrorism to topple governments or to achieve related goals. Extremists have left a legacy of kidnapping, hijacking, bombing, and murder from the Middle East to Southeast Asia, from Paris to New York and Washington. Understanding this complex and multifaceted phenomenon is often difficult and requires an awareness of its roots and sources. What were the causes and conditions that led to the contemporary resurgence of Islam?

Islam in Modern State and Society

A map of the modern Muslim world reveals both old and new realities and begins to explain visually the upheaval in Muslim societies. During the twentieth century, former Islamic empires and sultanates were replaced by modern nation-states, carved out by European colonial powers after World War I. By World War II, most of these newly designated states had won their independence, but it was an independence of artificial creations, and the new rulers, in Jordan, Syria, and Iraq had been placed on their thrones by Britain or France. Moreover, European education, culture, and values strongly influenced the elites in most states and societies. As a result, issues of government legitimacy as well as of national and cultural identity remained unresolved. After World War II, the stability of many rulers was due more to Western or Soviet support and strong military-security apparatus than to supportive indigenous culture or widespread political participation.

Once these modern nation-states had been created in the Muslim world, it was expected that they would generally follow a "modern," that is, Western, secular path of development. Outwardly, this seemed to be the general case. While Saudi Arabia proclaimed itself an Islamic state, based on the Quran and *sharia* law, most new nations adopted or adapted Western political, legal, social, economic, and educational institutions and values. In contrast to Saudi Arabia, Turkey positioned itself at the opposite end of the religion-versus-secularism spectrum. Under the leadership of Mustafa Kemal Ataturk, it suppressed Islamic institutions, banned Islamic dress and Islamic law, and transplanted Western secular laws and institutions to create its own version of a secular state.

However, Egypt, Syria, Iraq, Pakistan, Malaysia, and Indonesia created what may be called "Muslim states." In these and most other countries in the Islamic world, the majority populations are Muslim, but, despite some religious prescriptions, Western-inspired institutions have been adopted: parliaments, political party systems, legal codes, educational systems and curricula, banks, and insurance companies. Western dress, movies, and culture became prominent and pervasive among the wealthy and powerful in urban centers.

Throughout much of the twentieth century, progress and prosperity in Muslim societies were regarded by most governments and by those with key positions in government and society as dependent on the degree to which Muslims and their societies were "modern." The degree of progress and success for individuals, cities, and governments was measured in terms of conformity to Western standards and values. Based on these criteria, Turkey, Tunisia, Egypt, Lebanon, and Iran were often seen as among the more modern, advanced, and "enlightened," that is, Westernized and secular, countries. Saudi Arabia, the states of the Persian Gulf, Afghanistan, Bangladesh, and Pakistan were generally regarded as more traditional, religious, and thus "backward."

The Failure of Modernity and the Islamic Revival

The 1960s and 1970s shattered the hopes and dreams of many who believed that national independence and Western-oriented development would usher in strong states and prosperous societies. These were decades that proved a powerful catalyst for a religious resurgence and revival. The crises of many Muslim societies underscored the failure of many governments and societies to become strong and prosperous, even after national independence. The realities of many Muslim societies raised profound questions of national identity and the political legitimacy of rulers as well as of religious faith and meaning. Such pervasive conditions as poverty, illiteracy, failed economies, high unemployment, and unequal distribution of wealth could not be blamed entirely on Western influences.

The signs of these profound problems would not become fully appreciated in the West until the Iranian revolution of 1978–79. There were previews, however, during the preceding decade: the 1967 Arab-Israeli war, Malay-Chinese riots in Kuala Lumpur in 1969, the Pakistan-Bangladesh civil war of 1971, and Lebanon's civil war of the mid-1970s. Such catalytic events triggered a soul-searching reassessment among many Muslims. Their disillusionment and dissatisfaction were accompanied by an Islamic revival, a quest for self-identity and greater authenticity, as many reaffirmed the importance of Islam and Islamic values in their personal and social lives. Along with a reemphasis on religious identity and practice (prayer, fasting, dress, and values) came an equally visible appeal to Islam in politics and society made by governments as well as Islamic political and social movements. Islamic ideology, discourse, and politics reemerged as major forces in the development of the Muslim world, forces that both Muslim and Western governments have had to accommodate or contend with for several decades.

The return of Islam as an international political force was seen by many as signaling a return of God's guidance and favor. However, the fall of the shah and an *ulama*-led revolution were as threatening for many Sunni Muslim governments and elites, especially those in Gulf states like Iraq, Saudi Arabia, Bahrain, and Kuwait, which have significant Shiah populations, as these events were to the West, America and Europe.

Perhaps the most significant symbolic event, which sparked Muslim disillusionment and dissatisfaction, was the 1967 Arab-Israeli war, now often called the Six-Day War. Israel defeated the combined forces of Egypt, Syria, Iraq, and Jordan in a "preemptive" strike, which the Israeli government justified as necessary to counter a planned Arab attack. The Arabs experienced a massive loss of territory: Sinai, Gaza, the West Bank, and in particular Jerusalem, the third-holiest city (after Mecca and Medina) of Islam.

Muslims, like Jews and Christians, for centuries have looked to Jerusalem, a city central to Muslim faith and identity, a place of religious shrines and pilgrimage. Muslims hold Jerusalem to be sacred because of its association with prophets (from David and Solomon to Jesus) and because of its central role in the Prophet Muhammad's Night Journey and ascension.

When Muslim armies took Jerusalem without resistance in 635, they built a large mosque (al-Aqsa) and then a magnificent shrine, the Dome of the Rock, on the site associated with the Night Journey and the biblical site of Abraham's sacrifice and Solomon's temple. Muslim loss of Jerusalem in the 1967 war was a traumatic experience, which made Palestine and the Arab-Israeli conflict not just an Arab Muslim and Arab Christian issue but a worldwide Islamic issue. Many who asked what had gone wrong also wanted to know why Israel had been able to defeat the combined Arab forces. Were the weakness and failure of Muslim societies due to their faith? Was Islam incompatible with modernity and thus the cause of Arab backwardness and impotence? Had God abandoned the Muslims? These were questions that had been raised before.

The Dome of the Rock in Jerusalem, a major holy site and place of pilgrimage erected by the Umayyad caliph Abd al-Malik, was completed in 692. The famous shrine is built on the spot from which Muslims believe Muhammad ascended to God and then returned to the world. In this story, one of the grand themes of Islamic scholarship and popular piety, the Prophet, in the company of the angel Gabriel, was transported at night from the Kaaba in Mecca to Jerusalem. From there, he ascended to the heavens and the presence of God.

As we have seen, from the seventeenth to the nineteenth centuries, internal threats to Muslim societies were followed by the external threat of European colonialism. The mid-twentieth century, however, was a period of independence and Muslim self-rule. The failures of the "modern experiment" led many to turn, or perhaps more accurately to return, to a more authentic, indigenous alternative to modern nationalism and socialism. Despite significant differences from one country to the next, many Muslims worldwide sought an Islamic alternative to Western capitalism and Soviet Marxism. In this context, Islam became a rallying cry and symbol for political organization and mass mobilization.

The Religious Worldview of Contemporary Islamic Activism

Islamic activists shared the following beliefs or points of ideology:

1. Islam, a comprehensive way of life, is and must be integral to politics and society.
2. The failures of Muslim societies were caused by departing from the path of Islam and depending on Western secularism, which separates religion and politics.
3. Muslims must return to the Quran and the example of the Prophet Muhammad and reintroduce Islamic laws.
4. Modern development must be guided by Islamic values rather than those that would lead to Westernization and secularization of society.

As Islamic symbols, slogans, ideology, leaders, and organizations became prominent fixtures in Muslim politics, religion was increasingly used both by governments and by reform and opposition movements to enhance their legitimacy and to mobilize popular support. Islamic movements and organizations sprang up across the Muslim world. A variety of opposition movements appealed to Islam: In Iran Ayatollah Khomeini led the "Islamic revolution" of 1979–80; militants seized the Grand Mosque in Mecca in 1979, calling for the overthrow of the government; religious extremists assassinated Egyptian President Anwar Sadat in 1981. At the same time, Afghan freedom fighters (*mujahideen*, "holy warriors") in the late 1970s and early 1980s led a resistance movement against the Soviet Union's invasion and occupation. Islamic movements and organizations throughout the 1980s created or extended their influence over religious, educational, social, cultural, and financial institutions as well as professional organizations of physicians, lawyers, and journalists.

The leadership of most Islamic organizations (particularly Sunni groups) was and remains outside the control of the *ulama*. Many have degrees in modern science, medicine, law, engineering, computer science, and education. Most Islamic organizations have attracted individuals from every stratum of society. While the majority of Islamic organizations work within the system, a minority of radical extremists insist that Muslim rulers are anti-Islamic and that violence and revolution are the only way to liberate society and impose an Islamic way of life.

From the Periphery to Mainstream Politics and Society

The 1980s were dominated by fear of "radical Islamic fundamentalism," embodied in Iran's announced desire to export its "Islamic fundamentalist revolution" and the activities of clandestine extremist groups. Feeding these fears were disturbances by Shiah in Saudi Arabia, Kuwait, and Bahrain; Iran's strong backing of a Lebanese Shiah group, Hezbollah, which emerged in response to the Israeli invasion and occupation of Lebanon; and a series of hijackings, kidnappings, and bombings of Western embassies. Although Muslim rulers and Western leaders alike were on edge, no other "Irans" occurred.

By the late 1980s and early 1990s, it was increasingly clear that a quiet, or nonviolent, revolution had taken place in many parts of the Muslim world. Islamic revivalism and activism had in many contexts become institutionalized in mainstream society. From Egypt to Malaysia, Islam played a more visible and important role in socioeconomic and political life. Islamically inspired social and political activism produced schools, clinics and hospitals, and social service agencies, such as day care, legal aid, and youth centers. Private mosques were established alongside those controlled by governments, and financial institutions such as Islamic banks and insurance companies appeared. In addition, an alternative elite emerged consisting of modern educated but Islamically (rather than secularly) oriented doctors, engineers, lawyers, businesspeople, university professors, military officers, and laborers. Perhaps nowhere was the impact of the Islamic revival experienced more visibly than in political elections.

The majority of Muslim countries are under authoritarian rule, a legacy of premodern Muslim history, European colonial rule, and post-independence. During the late 1980s, in response to "food riots," protests, and mass demonstrations over the economic failures of governments, elections were held in authoritarian countries like Jordan, Tunisia, Algeria, and Egypt. Participating Islamic organizations such as the Muslim Brotherhoods of Jordan and Egypt, Tunisia's Nahda (Renaissance) party, and Algeria's Islamic Salvation Front (FIS) emerged as the major political opposition.

In Algeria, the FIS swept municipal and, later, parliamentary elections and thus was poised to come to power peacefully, through the electoral process. The Algerian military intervened, however, installing a new government, canceling the election results, and imprisoning and outlawing the FIS. This set in motion a spiral of violence and counterviolence that polarized Algerian society and produced a civil war costing more than 100,000 lives.

By the mid-1990s, Islamic activists could be found in the cabinets and parliaments of many countries and in the leadership of professional organizations. In Turkey, the most secular of Muslim states, the Welfare (Refah) party swept mayoral elections, and in 1995 Turkey elected its first Islamist prime minister and also the leader of the

Welfare Party, Dr. Necmettin Erbakan. The Turkish military, claiming the need to save Turkish secularism, brought about the resignation of Erbakan and was influential in having the party outlawed and some of its leaders imprisoned.

The Road to 9/11

At the same time, radical extremist groups such as Egypt's *Gamaa Islamiyya* (Islamic Group) and Islamic Jihad attacked Christian churches, businesses, foreign tourists, and security forces. Extremists were convicted in the United States and Europe for terrorist acts, such as the 1993 bombing of the World Trade Center in New York. Terrorist attacks increased throughout the decade. Osama bin Laden was increasingly regarded as the "godfather" of global terrorism and a major funder of extremist groups. His involvement was suspected in the bombing of the World Trade Center in 1993, the killing of eighteen American soldiers in Somalia in 1993, and bombings in Riyadh in 1995 and in Dhahran in 1996. In February 1998, bin Laden and other militant leaders announced the creation of a transnational coalition of extremist groups, the World Islamic Front for Jihad Against Jews and Crusaders. His own organization, al-Qaeda, was linked to a series of acts of terrorism: the truck bombing of American embassies in Kenya and Tanzania in August 1998 that killed 263 people and injured more than 5,000, followed in October 2000 by a suicide bombing attack against the USS *Cole*, which killed seventeen American sailors.

September 11, 2001, would prove to be a watershed, signaling the extent to which Muslim extremists had become a global threat, in particular emphasizing the role of Osama bin Laden and al-Qaeda in global terrorism.[10]

Bin Laden's message appealed to the feelings of many in the Arab and Muslim world. A sharp critic of American foreign policy toward the Muslim world, he denounced U.S. support for Israel and sanctions against Iraq, which he said had resulted in the deaths of hundreds of thousands of civilians. He dismissed as the "new crusades" the substantial American military presence and economic involvement in his native Saudi Arabia. To these messages were added other populist reminders of Muslim suffering in Bosnia, Kosovo, Chechnya, and Kashmir.[11]

Al-Qaeda represented a new global terrorism, associated at first with the Muslims

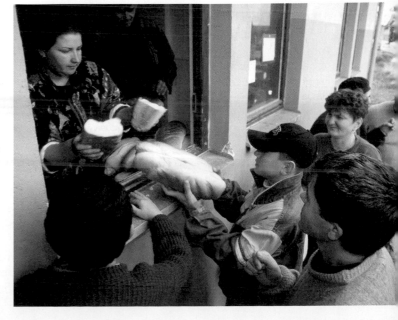

The ethnic warfare that accompanied the breakup of Yugoslavia had tragic effects in Bosnia, one of the oldest Muslim communities in Europe. Refugees of all ages, at Mihatovici, near Tuzla, line up to receive food.

CONTRASTING RELIGIOUS VISIONS

As the following contrasting visions indicate, every religious tradition is capable of generating both visions that encourage peace and understanding and visions that encourage conflict and violence.

Muhammad Iqbal (1876–1938)

Educated at Government College in Lahore, Pakistan, he studied in England and Germany, where he earned a law degree and a doctorate in philosophy. Iqbal's modern synthesis and reinterpretation of Islam combined the best of the East and the West, his Islamic heritage with Western philosophy. Both admirer and critic of the West, Iqbal acknowledged the West's dynamic spirit, intellectual tradition, and technology but was sharply critical of European colonialism as well as of the materialism and exploitation of capitalism, the atheism of Marxism, and the moral bankruptcy of secularism.

The Reconstruction of Religious Thought in Islam succinctly summarizes Iqbal's reformist vision, which can also be accessed in his extensive writings and poetry. Like other Islamic modernists, Iqbal rejected much of medieval Islam as static and stagnant. He saw Islam as emerging from 500 years of "dogmatic slumber" and compared the need for Islamic reform now to that confronting Christianity at the time of the Reformation. Iqbal emphasized the need to reclaim the vitality and dynamism of early Islamic thought and practice, calling for a bold reinterpretation (*ijtihad*) of Islam. He attempted to develop alternative Islamic models for modern Muslim societies. Thus, for example, drawing on Islamic traditions, he sought to "rediscover" Islamic principles and values that would provide the basis for Islamic versions of Western concepts and institutions such as democracy and parliamentary government.

Osama bin Laden (1957–2011)

Born in Riyadh, Saudi Arabia, bin Laden received a degree in public administration in 1981 from King Abdul-Aziz University. A major turning point in bin Laden's adult life occurred in 1979, when the Soviets occupied Afghanistan. From 1979 to 1982, he used his financial resources to support vigorously the *jihadi* resistance against the Soviets, providing construction materials, building roads and airfields, and then moving to Afghanistan to set up his own camps and command Arab *mujahideen* forces, who became known as "Arab Afghans." He later created al-Qaeda, "the base," to organize and track the fighters and funds being channeled into the Afghan resistance.

Bin Laden's opposition to the American-led coalition in the Gulf War of 1991 placed him on a collision course with the Saudi government and the West. In 1994 the kingdom revoked bin Laden's citizenship and moved to freeze his assets because of his support for militant fundamentalist movements. Bin Laden joined other dissident activists and religious scholars, moving to Sudan and then back to Afghanistan. Assuming a vocal leadership role in international terrorism, in 1996 he issued a Declaration of Jihad, created to drive the United States out of Arabia, overthrow the Saudi government, liberate Islam's holy sites of Mecca and Medina, and support revolutionary groups around the world. In 2000 he was among the founders of the World Islamic Front for the Jihad Against Jews and Crusaders, an umbrella group of radical movements across the Muslim world, and issued a *fatwa* emphasizing the duty of all Muslims to kill U.S. citizens and their allies.

who had gone to Afghanistan to fight the occupying Soviets in the 1980s, and reflected in acts of terrorism in Central, South, and Southeast Asia, often attributed to the influence of Saudi Arabia and Wahhabi Islam. Bin Laden and other terrorists transformed Islam's norms about the defense of Islam and Muslims under siege to legitimate the use of violence, warfare, and terrorism. Their theology of hate espouses a bipolar view of a cosmic struggle between the armies of God and of Satan, the forces of good and evil, right and wrong, belief and unbelief: those who are not with them, Muslim or non-Muslim, are judged to be against them. These extremists "hijacked" the Islamic concept and institution of *jihad* in an attempt to lend legitimacy to their acts of violence and terror.

Globalization and Hijacking of *Jihad*

Since the late twentieth century the word *jihad* has gained remarkable currency. On the one hand, the term's primary Quranic religious and spiritual meanings became more widespread: *Jihad* was the "struggle" or effort to follow God's path, to lead a moral life, and to promote social justice. On the other hand, the idea of *jihad* as armed struggle has been widely used by resistance, liberation, and terrorist movements alike to legitimate their cause and recruit followers. Thus the Afghan *mujahideen* waged *jihad* in Afghanistan against the Soviet Union and subsequently among themselves; Muslims in Kashmir, Chechnya, the southern Philippines, Bosnia, and Kosovo have fashioned their struggles as *jihads*; Hezbollah, Hamas, and Islamic Jihad Palestine have characterized war with Israel as a *jihad*; and Osama bin Laden, speaking as head of al-Qaeda, declared global *jihad*, targeting Muslim governments as well as the West. Understanding the multiple meanings of *jihad* is critical to understanding Islam and Muslim politics today.

Jihad is a term with multiple meanings and usages, both past and present. The central importance of *jihad* is rooted in the Quran's command to "struggle or exert" (the literal meaning of the word *jihad*) oneself in the path of God. *Jihad* has several major meanings. First and foremost it refers to the moral struggle to be virtuous, to do good works. Depending on circumstances, it also can mean fighting injustice and oppression, spreading and defending Islam, and creating a just society through preaching, teaching, and, if necessary, armed struggle. These two broad meanings of *jihad*, nonviolent and violent, are contrasted in a well-known tradition that reports that when Muhammad returned from battle, he told his followers, "We return from the lesser jihad to the greater jihad." The greater *jihad* is the more difficult and more important struggle against one's ego, selfishness, greed, and evil.

Jihad as Armed Struggle

The earliest Quranic verses dealing with the right to engage in a "defensive," armed *jihad* were revealed shortly after the *hijra* (emigration) of Muhammad and his followers to Medina. At a time when they were fleeing from persecution in Mecca and forced to fight for their lives, Muhammad is told in the Quran: "Leave is given to those who fight because they were wronged—surely God is able to help them—who were expelled from their homes wrongfully for saying, 'Our Lord is God'" (Q. 22:39–40). The defensive nature of *jihad* is emphasized in 2:190, "And fight in the way of God with those who fight you, but aggress not: God loves not the aggressors."

The Quran and Islamic law provide detailed guidelines and regulations regarding the conduct of war: who is to fight and who is exempted (48:17, 9:91); when hostilities must cease (2:192); and how prisoners should be treated (47:4). Verses such as 2:294 emphasize that warfare and the response to violence and aggression must be proportional: "Whoever transgresses against you, respond in kind." From the earliest times, it was forbidden in Islam to kill noncombatants as well as women and children and monks and rabbis, who were promised immunity unless they took part in the fighting.

But what of those Quranic verses, sometimes referred to as the *sword verses*, that call for killing unbelievers, such as "When the sacred months have passed, slay the idolaters wherever you find them, and take them, and confine them, and lie in wait for them at every place of ambush" (9:5)? This is one of a number of Quranic verses that are cited by critics to demonstrate the inherently violent nature of Islam and selectively used (or abused) by some Muslim religious extremists to develop a theology of hate and intolerance and to legitimate unconditional warfare against unbelievers. The privileging of the sword verses dates back to the early centuries of Islam.

During the period of expansion and conquest, many of the *ulama* (religious scholars) enjoyed royal patronage and provided a rationale for caliphs to pursue their imperial dreams and, in the name of spreading Islam, to extend the boundaries of their empires. Classical jurists argued that the sword verses (9:5 and 9:123) abrogated, or canceled, the earlier verses that limited *jihad* to defensive war, thus permitting unprovoked military action in the cause of God. However, the full intent of the sword verse "When the sacred months have passed, slay the idolaters wherever you find them" is missed or distorted. First, the verse refers to the specific context: The early Muslims were being persecuted and attacked by their Meccan enemy. The term *idolaters* here refers to the Meccan polytheists, not to "unbelievers" in general or, as extremists would hold, to Jews and Christians. Second, the tendency to quote the first part of the verse in isolation distorts the full intent of the passage, which is followed and qualified by: "But if they repent and fulfill their devotional obligations and pay the zakat [the charitable tax on Muslims], then let them go their way, for God is forgiving and kind" (9:5).

Bin Laden and other terrorists choose the selective militant interpretation of the so-called sword verses, ignore the criteria of Islamic law for a just *jihad*, and recognize no limits but their own. They reject the tenets of Islamic law regarding the goals and means of a valid *jihad*: that the use of violence must be proportional; that innocent civilians, noncombatants, should not be targeted; and that *jihad* can be declared only by a ruler or head of state. Today, extremists from Madrid to Mindanao legitimate unholy wars in the name of Islam itself, bypassing the Quranic requirement that authorization for *jihad* be given by a nation's ruler.

While bin Laden and al-Qaeda have enjoyed support from a significant minority of Muslims and religious leaders, the majority of Muslims and major Islamic scholars and religious leaders across the Muslim world condemned such attacks as unjustified. For example, the Gallup Organization in 2005–8 surveyed some thirty-five predominantly Muslim countries (from Morocco and Pakistan to Indonesia) as part of its World Poll. The vast majority (93 percent) of all those polled said the 9/11 attacks were unjustified; 7 percent said the attacks were completely justified. The Islamic Research Council at al-Azhar University, regarded by many as the highest moral authority in Islam, and other prominent religious leaders issued authoritative declarations (*fatwas*) against bin Laden's and other terrorists' initiatives:

> Islam provides clear rules and ethical norms that forbid the killing of non-combatants, as well as women, children, and the elderly, and also forbids the pursuit of the enemy in defeat, the execution of those who surrender, the infliction of harm on prisoners of war, and the destruction of property that is not being used in the hostilities.[12]

Timothy Winter (Abdul Hakim Murad), a British Muslim, Cambridge University professor, and prominent Muslim religious leader, represents many Muslims in his clear and straightforward rejection of Al-Qaeda as religiously illegitimate and inauthentic. Winter dismisses bin Laden and his right-hand man, Ayman al-Zawahiri, as unqualified, un-Islamic vigilantes who violate basic Islamic teachings:

> Their proclamations ignore fourteen centuries of Muslim scholarship, . . . [and they use] lists of anti-American grievances and of Koranic quotations referring to early Muslim wars against Arab idolators. . . . All this amounts to an odd and extreme violation of the normal methods of Islamic scholarship. . . . An insurrectionist who kills noncombatants is guilty of *baghy*, "armed transgression," a capital offence in Islamic law. A jihad can be proclaimed only by a properly constituted state; anything else is pure vigilantism.[13]

Suicide Bombing: War of the Fatwas

Few issues have been more contentious among religious authorities than suicide bombing, demonstrating the extent to which both sacred texts and human interpretation of sociopolitical contexts influence the formulation of *fatwas*. The issue of suicide bombing and the question of its legitimacy or illegitimacy crystallized in the Israeli-Palestinian conflict during the second intifada. Amid escalating Israeli and Palestinian violence, many Palestinians and other Arabs argued that suicide bombers were committing not an act of suicide but one of self-sacrifice, the only option for resistance and retaliation against an enemy with overwhelming military power and foreign support. As student posters at universities in the West Bank and Gaza declared: "Israel has nuclear bombs, we have human bombs."

Suicide attacks, especially those that target innocent civilians or noncombatants, have precipitated a sharp debate among prominent religious authorities in the Muslim world. Their advice and *fatwas* illustrate the debate today. Sheikh Ahmad Yasin, the late religious leader and founder of Hamas, as well as many other Arab and Palestinian religious leaders have argued that suicide bombing is necessary and justified when faced with Israel's illegal occupation and overwhelming military power.

Although Yusuf Qaradawi, a prominent religious scholar and public figure, condemns acts of terrorism and suicide bombings, he has made a clear exception when it comes to the Palestinian-Israeli conflict. His strong opposition to Israeli occupation and policies led to early support for suicide bombing in Israel. Qaradawi was one of the first religious scholars to issue a *fatwa* that justified suicide bombings in Israel, based on the premise that Israelis were not civilians but combatants in a war of occupation waged against the Palestinians.

In sharp contrast, Abdul-Aziz Al Al-Shaykh, the former Grand Mufti of Saudi Arabia, condemned all suicide bombing as un-Islamic and forbidden by Islam. Similarly, Timothy Winter rejects any use of suicide bombing and targeting of civilians as an aberration:

> This kind of targeting of civilians, for instance, the aberrant use of terrorist violence, is something that really is very new. . . . It hasn't gained much inroad into the leadership of the religion, but in the masses on the streets, as it were, particularly in very tense, unnatural places like Gaza, the slums of Baghdad, and other places, it does have a certain standing unfortunately. And this is the great challenge of the leadership of the religion—how to reassert orthodoxy in the face of a growing groundswell of fundamentalist revolt.[14]

Post 9/11: Impact and Response

The 9/11 bombings in the United States and subsequent acts of terrorism globally were accompanied in the United States and some European countries by an exponential growth of far right politicians, political commentators, media personalities, and some religious leaders who conflated mainstream Islam with terrorism. They fed an increase in discrimination against Islam and Muslims ("Islamophobia"), resulting in widespread suspicion of mainstream Muslims, hate crimes, and the belief that Islam, not just Muslim extremism, is a threat.

At a 2004 UN conference, "Confronting Islamophobia: Education for Tolerance and Understanding," Kofi Annan addressed the international scope of this problem, warning: "When the world is compelled to coin a new term to take account of increasingly widespread bigotry—that is a sad and troubling development. Such is the case with 'Islamophobia.' "

A *Washington Post*/ABC News poll in 2006 "found that nearly half of Americans—46%—have a negative view of Islam, seven percentage points higher than a few months after Sept. 11, 2001."

In Europe, Islam was overwhelmingly singled out as the religion most prone to violence, with percentages of those who agreed with this ranging from 63 percent in Britain to 87 percent in France and 88 percent in the Netherlands.

In the Gallup World Poll, when U.S. respondents were asked what they admire about the Muslim world, the most common response was "nothing" (33 percent); the second most common was "I don't know" (22 percent). Despite major polling by Gallup and PEW showing that American Muslims are well integrated economically and politically, a January 2010 Gallup Center for Muslim Studies report found that more than 4 in 10 Americans (43 percent) admit to feeling at least "a little" prejudice toward Muslims—more than twice the number who say the same about Christians (18 percent), Jews (15 percent), and Buddhists (14 percent). Nine percent of Americans admitted feeling "a great deal" of prejudice toward Muslims, while 20 percent admitted feeling "some" prejudice. Surprisingly, Gallup data revealed a link between anti-Semitism and Islamophobia, that contempt for Jews makes a person "about 32 times as likely to report the same level of prejudice toward Muslims."

Time Magazine and *The New York Times* in August 2010 reported that 33 percent of those interviewed believed that Muslim Americans were more sympathetic to terrorists and 60 percent had negative feelings about Muslims. Other studies from Gallup, the *Washington Post*, and the Pew Forum indicate similar findings.

Over the years, a common charge has been that Muslims do not condemn terrorism despite the fact that post 9/11 many statements have been issued by Muslim leaders and organizations from all over the world, including a major joint statement by global religious and intellectual leaders (the Amman Message). Unfortunately, major media outlets do not seem to find them "newsworthy," and thus they are relegated to the Internet. See, for example, http://www.ammanmessage.com/; http://www.cair-net.org/html/911statements.html; http://www.beliefnet.com/story/111/story_11121_1.html.

Over the past few decades, the vast majority of American Muslims have become economically and increasingly politically integrated into mainstream American society. Students account for 31 percent of the American Muslim population as compared to 10 percent in the general population; 40 percent have a college degree or more, compared to 29 percent of Americans overall. Muslim women are equal to men in holding college or postgraduate degrees and report incomes nearly equal to men.

Muslims span the socioeconomic spectrum: professionals (doctors, lawyers, engineers, and educators), corporate executives, and small business owners, as well as blue-collar workers. Only 2 percent of Muslims represent low-income families. Seventy percent have a job (paid or unpaid) compared to 64 percent of Americans overall.

Despite this integration, however, many American Muslims believe that they are singled out by the government for extra surveillance. This experience, however, has not soured the attitudes of the majority of Muslims, 71 percent of whom agree that most people who want to get ahead in America can succeed if they are willing to work hard. This is a higher proportion than the American public as a whole.

If some blamed the religion of Islam for the growth of radicalism and the appeal of bin Laden and other terrorist leaders, others identified U.S. and European policies in the Muslim world: uncritical support for authoritarian regimes, Palestinian-Israeli

In China, followers of traditional Islam (Gedimu, from the Arabic for "old," *qadim*) build communities around small central mosques. Muslim men meet here in Beijing for communal prayers in the central congregational mosque.

policies, and the West's double standard in promoting democratization as major catalysts.

That Osama bin Laden and many of the 9/11 hijackers were from Saudi Arabia and Saudi support for some Islamic groups and *madrasas* in countries like Afghanistan and Pakistan have raised questions about the role of Wahhabism in global terrorism. Wahhabi Islam, the official form of Islam in Saudi Arabia, is among the most ultraconservative interpretations of Islam.

As we have seen, the Wahhabi movement takes its name from Muhammad Ibn Abd al-Wahhab and the eighteenth-century revivalist movement. Over time, the ideas of many uncompromising interpreters of Wahhabi Islam have resulted in an ultraconservative or "fundamentalist" brand of Islam: literalist, rigid, puritanical, exclusivist, and intolerant. Wahhabis believe that they are right and all others (other Muslims as well as people of other faiths) are wrong. Presenting their version of Islam as the pristine, pure, unadulterated message of the Prophet, Wahhabis have sought to propagate and sometimes impose throughout the world their strict beliefs and interpretations, which are not shared by the majority of Muslims.

Since the last half of the twentieth century, domestic and foreign conditions have led to the emergence of militant, violent interpretations of Islam. In 1979, when militants seized the Grand Mosque in Mecca, they called for the overthrow of the Saudi monarchy. At the same time, Islamic activists from Egypt and other countries, often fleeing their home governments, had found refuge in Saudi Arabia, teaching in universities and religious schools or working in government ministries and organizations. As a result, alongside the puritanical Wahhabi Islam of the establishment, a radical brand of Wahhabi Islam, having both internal and external sources, infiltrated Saudi society. Its theology and worldview was one of militant *jihad*, domestic and global.

Both government-sponsored organizations and wealthy Saudi individuals have funded the export of Wahhabi Islam, in its mainstream and extremist forms, to other countries and communities in the Muslim world and in the West. Wahhabi theology, funding, and influence were exported to Afghanistan, Pakistan, the Central Asian Republics, China, Africa, Southeast Asia, the United States, and Europe. They offered financial aid for the building of mosques, libraries, and other institutions; funded and distributed religious tracts; and commissioned imams and religious scholars. At the same time, some wealthy businessmen and organizations in Saudi Arabia and the Gulf have provided financial support to extremist groups that actively promote a holy war ("jihadi") culture. The challenge is to distinguish between those who preach and propagate an ultraconservative Wahhabi theology and militant extremists and terrorist organizations. Similar divisions between mainstream Muslims and violent extremists exist in other religions, with Jewish, Christian, and Hindu fundamentalists sometimes acting in ways not condoned by the majority of their coreligionists.

In sharp contrast, in a world in which some in the Muslim world and in the West speak of or even promote a clash of civilizations between the Muslim world and the West, a historic event occurred on October 11, 2007. In a dramatic and groundbreaking display of interreligious solidarity, 138 of the world's most senior Muslim leaders wrote a letter, "A Common Word Between Us and You," to the heads of all Christian churches. The letter's authors—Muslims from around the world and from both the Sunni and Shiah, Salafi and Sufi traditions—declared their belief that with over half of the world's population consisting of Muslims and Christians, meaningful world peace can only come from peace and justice between the two largest global faiths despite their differences. The letter, based on a close study of both the Bible and the Holy Quran, was an open invitation to Christians to unite with Muslims to cooperate in creating peace and understanding and diffusing tensions, based on what is most essential to their respective faiths—the commandments of love: the shared belief of both Muslims and Christians in the principles of love of one God and love of neighbor.

Islam and the Arab Awakening: Between Authoritarianism and Pluralism

The "Arab Spring" or "Arab Awakening" marked a historic transition in the political makeup of countries like Tunisia, Egypt, Libya, and Syria. A broad sector of society, eager for change and democratic reforms, made their voices heard, reclaiming their dignity and national pride and insisting that they would decide the direction and the future of their countries. Though initially not among the leadership, in postuprising elections Islamist candidates and parties swept into power in Egypt (the Muslim Brotherhood's Freedom and Justice Party and Salafi, especially the Noor Party) and Tunisia (Ennahda, the Renaissance, Party), although not in Libya. If many voted for Islamists, many others were dismayed and feared Islamist rule would lead to increased religiosity in politics. Some asked: "Can the Islamists lead?"

Indeed, many in countries like Egypt and Tunisia agreed that election results, while polarizing, were the product of a free and fair process. Far from monolithic, Muslim Brotherhood and Ennahda and Salafis incorporate diverse currents, ideologically, politically, and socioeconomically. Many in leadership positions were challenged to move beyond the elder-dominated hierarchical structure and authority of the past and to engage in greater power sharing by bringing in support from younger representatives and opposition members. American and European policymakers were equally challenged to work with Islamically oriented government leaders. The question of "how" Islam and democracy will be compatible became even more real and relevant. New governments in both Egypt and Tunisia spoke of a civil state with an Islamic reference and equality of citizenship for all, and what that will mean regarding implementation of shariah and the rights and freedoms of religious minorities, secularists, and women. However, the ability of new governments to satisfy the expectations of diverse sectors of society, in particular to jump-start failed economies and address issues of high unemployment and now high expectations, was formidable. At the same time, the Egyptian and Tunisian governments were challenged by secular parties, including illiberal secularists, and especially the entrenched remnants of the Mubarak and Ben Ali regimes (military, police, judiciary, and a vast bureaucracy), often referred to as "the deep state," who remained in power.

By 2013, the Arab Spring began to look like an Arab winter. In Syria, the death toll in the struggle to oust the regime of Bashir Al-Assad and his opposition saw the death toll rise to 100,000, with vast destruction of the country. Both the governments of Egypt and Tunisia struggled to govern and to deal with opposition critics and movements. The hardest hit was Egypt, where a nationwide anti-Morsi and anti-Brotherhood protest movement galvanized on June 30, around the anniversary of Morsi's troubled first year in power.

The Morsi government made many mistakes and mishandled opportunities. The anti-Morsi opposition included many (liberals, marginalized revolutionary Arab youth, secularists and leftists, and Copts) with genuine concerns and grievances regarding the failure to reach out more effectively and build a more representative coalition government and to improve Egypt's failed economy, unemployment, poverty, and cost of living. However, the backbone of the movement consisted of individuals and institutions that represented the deep state legacy of the Mubarak regime (the military, the judges of the state constitutional court, the interior ministry, police, and state media as well as a strong contingent of illiberal secularists, including intellectuals, businessmen, and TV and media personalities). While some called for a second revolution, others warned of a civil war, and still others feared an end to the promises of Tahrir Square and democracy in Egypt. Politics became polarized into a growing "culture war" between the opposition and the Morsi government and its supporters. An opposition of millions in large-scale demonstrations across Egypt moved from demands for major reforms to violent clashes and a demand that Morsi resign or be driven from office, providing an excuse for a military-backed coup and a return to authoritarianism.

Three weeks after the military coup that removed President Mohamed Morsi and the Muslim Brotherhood from power, the interim government appointed nineteen generals as the governors of Egypt's provinces, and the military launched an operation against unarmed Muslim Brotherhood demonstrators, using lethal force that left more than 1,000 dead (other estimates ranged in the thousands), and thousands injured, the worst violence in Egyptian modern history.

On August 14, Egyptian security forces used lethal force against the Morsi supporter sit-in, killing more than 625 and injuring thousands. The interim government moved quickly to declare the Muslim Brotherhood a terrorist organization and attempted to totally suppress it, using mass arrests and military trials that drew sharp criticism from major international human rights organizations. The government cracked down and arrested foreign journalists and Egyptian critics and democracy activists. On March 24, 2014, an Egyptian court sentenced 529 members of the Muslim Brotherhood to death, the largest mass death sentence in modern Egyptian history.

Questions for Postmodern Times: Issues of Authority and Interpretation

The primary question for Muslims is not change, for most accept its necessity. Rather, it is how much change is possible or permissible in Islam and what kinds of change are necessary. This issue is central to virtually all the questions that Muslims face with respect to their faith in contemporary life: the relationship of Islam to the state, political participation or democratization, reform of Islamic law, promotion of religious and political pluralism, and the rights of women.

Although the sources and sacred texts of Islam, the Quran and the Sunnah of the Prophet, remain the same, the political, social, and economic contexts have changed. While all Muslims continue to affirm belief in God, Muhammad, and the Quran, Muslim interpretations of Islam today vary significantly. Some believe that Islam, like most faiths in the modern age, should be primarily a private matter; many others have struggled to implement Islam in public life as well. Although categories are not clear-cut and at times overlap, four general Muslim orientations or attitudes toward change may be identified: secularist, conservative traditionalists, Islamist or neofundamentalist, and Islamic reformist or neomodernist.

Like their counterparts in the West, secularists believe religion is a personal matter that should be excluded from politics and public life. Calling for the separation of religion and the state, they believe that Islam belongs in the mosque, not in politics, and that the mosque should solely be a place of prayer, not of political activism.

Conservatives emphasize following past tradition and are wary of any change or innovation that they regard as deviation, or *bida*, the equivalent of Christian heresy. Conservatives are represented by the majority (though certainly not all) of the *ulama* and their followers, who continue to assert the primacy and adequacy of centuries-old Islamic law. Advocating the reimplementation of Islamic law through the adoption of past legal doctrine, they resist substantive change.

Traditionalists or neotraditionalists, too, believe in the centrality of tradition and classical Islamic law, but they also believe that Islamic traditions based primarily on human interpretation rather than a sacred text can be reinterpreted, changed, or expanded in light of new social, economic, and political realities. Thus, for example, some prominent religious authorities, such as Sheikh Ali Gomaa, Grand Mufti of Egypt, have given *fatwas* that women may run for parliament or president and serve as judges.

Islamic activists or Islamists (often commonly referred to as fundamentalists) are in some respects similar to conservatives, though more flexible. They represent a broad spectrum, from ultra-orthodox, literalist, and puritanical movements to more flexible and reform-minded believers, from militant extremists to those who hold mainstream political and social positions. In contrast to conservatives, they are not wedded to the classical formulations of law. In the name of a return to the Quran and Sunnah, fundamentalists speak of purifying Muslim belief and practice by a rigorous and literalist embrace of the past, whereas more mainstream Islamists are prepared to interpret and reformulate Islamic belief and institutions.

Islamic activists emphasize the self-sufficiency of Islam over compatibility with the West. Few of their leaders are religious scholars or imams. Like the Muslim Brotherhood and other Islamic revivalist organizations from the twentieth century, their comprehensive understanding of Islam fosters social and political activism, often challenging the political and religious status quo.

In contrast to modernizers, neomodernists, despite some overlap with mainstream Islamists, are more open to substantive change and to borrowing from other cultures. Like Islamists, they root their reforms in the Quran and Sunnah and are not wedded to classical Islamic law. However, their approach to change is different: They distinguish more sharply between the principles and values of Islam's immutable revelation and certain historically and socially conditioned practices and institutions, which they believe can and should be subject to widespread change to meet contemporary circumstances.

fiqh: "understanding"; human interpretation of divine law (*sharia*)

At the heart of reformist approaches to Islam is the core issue, the relationship of the divine to the human in Islamic law. Thus reformers focus on the need to distinguish between the *sharia*, God's divinely revealed law, and *fiqh* ("understanding"), including the areas of human interpretation and application that are historically conditioned. Reformers go further than conservatives or traditionalists in their acceptance of the degree and extent to which classical Islamic law may be reinterpreted or changed. They place more emphasis on the finite nature of early doctrines. They argue that just as early Muslim jurists applied the principles and values of Islam to the societies of the past, again today a reinterpretation or reconstruction of Islam is needed. But who has the authority to do this work?

As in the past, both the *ulama*, the religious scholars of Islam, and Muslim rulers continue to assert their right to protect, defend, and interpret Islam. The *ulama* persist in regarding themselves as the guardians of Islam, the conscience of the community, its only qualified interpreters. Many rulers, through cooptation and coercion of religion, combine their obligation to protect and promote Islam with the state's power to influence, control, and impose a certain "brand" of Islam. Governments control and distribute funds used to build mosques and to pay the salaries of religious officials and functionaries. Even topics or outlines for Friday mosque sermons are subject to government approval.

Today, many argue that it is not rulers or the religious scholars but the laity and parliaments that should be major actors in the process of change. While the *ulama* base their authority on their training in traditional Islamic disciplines, lay Muslims

Islam and Democracy

A primary example of Islamic reformism and its method today is the debate over the relationship of Islam to democracy. Some Muslims reject any discussion of the question, maintaining that Islam has its own system of government. Others believe that Islam and democracy are incompatible, claiming that democracy is based on un-Islamic Western principles and values. Still others reinterpret traditional Islamic concepts like consultation (*shura*) and consensus (*ijma*) of the community to support the adoption of modern forms of political participation or democratization, such as parliamentary elections. Thus, just as it was appropriate in the past for Muhammad's senior Companions to constitute a consultative assembly (*majlis al-shura*) and to select or elect his successor through a process of consultation, Muslims now reinterpret and extend this notion to the creation of modern forms of political participation and government, parliamentary governments, and the direct or indirect election of heads of state. This process is sometimes called "Islamization." Similarly, in legal reform some Muslims believe that Islam is totally self-sufficient; they demand the imposition of Islamic law and reject any outside influences. Others argue that Islamic law can be reinterpreted today to incorporate new interpretations or formulations of law as well as laws from elsewhere that do not contradict the Quran and Sunnah.

counter that they possess the legal, economic, and medical qualifications necessary to address contemporary issues and should be counted among the "experts" along with the *ulama*.

Islam in the West[15]

As we discussed at the beginning of the chapter, Muslims have in modern times become part of the American and European landscapes.

Muslims were long an invisible presence in the West. Most came as immigrants. Many wanted to fit into their new societies, to be accepted, gain employment, raise families, and live quietly in their adopted countries. Others wished to live apart, to avoid any prospect of loss of identity or assimilation into a Western, non–Muslim society. Political events in the Muslim world reinforced a desire for a low profile in any country to which Muslims had relocated; in some cases Muslims found themselves on the defensive. Images and stereotypes from the past, of camels and harems, were replaced by modern impressions of violence and terrorism associated with the threat of militant "Islamic fundamentalism." The result has often been Muslim bashing and what some have called *Islamophobia*: harassment, discrimination, and violence toward Muslims on the basis of their faith or race.

Today, Muslims in Europe and America no longer live primarily in clusters of immigrants; rather they are members of second- and third-generation communities, participating in professional and civic life. Yet many continue to face issues of faith and identity as a religious minority.

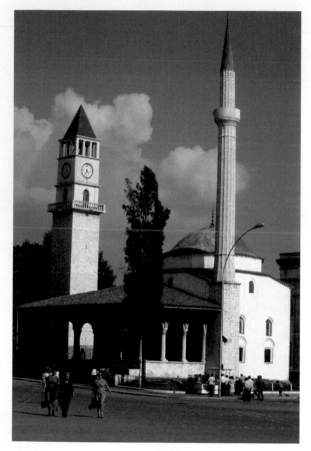

For many years, Islam and other religions were suppressed and persecuted in Albania by a communist regime that declared the state officially atheist in 1967. Many mosques in this Muslim majority country were closed or destroyed, and religious symbols were banned. In 1990 the ban was lifted, and this and other mosques were rededicated and opened.

The Muslims of Western Europe

More than 44 million Muslims may be found in Europe. Because many, though certainly not all, wish to retain their religion, culture, and values, the presence and citizenship of Muslims in western Europe, as in America, have made assimilation, acculturation, integration, and multiculturalism major religious, social, and political issues.

In contrast to America, in Western Europe the Muslim presence is due in large part to immigration based on a vestigial colonial connection. After independence, many professionals and skilled laborers from former European colonies in Africa, South Asia, and the Arab world immigrated to Europe, seeking a better life. In the 1960s and 1970s, unskilled workers flooded into European countries whose growing economies welcomed cheap labor. In addition, from the 1970s onward, increasing numbers of Muslim students came to Europe, as they did to America, to study. While many returned home, others chose to stay for political or economic reasons.

The largest Muslim population in Western Europe is in France, with 4.7 million Muslims (70 percent of whom come from North Africa), followed by Germany (4.3 million) and the United Kingdom (2.9 million). The Muslims of France, comprising almost 7.5 percent of the population, now exceed Protestants and Jews in number and are second only to France's Catholic community. There are grand mosques in Paris and Lyon and more than a thousand mosques and prayer rooms throughout the country. The majority of Germany's 4.3 million Muslims are of Turkish origin (63 percent); Britain's 2.9 million Muslims come primarily from the Indian subcontinent.

The issue of Muslim identity has been particularly acute in France, where the government has taken a firm stand in favor of total assimilation or integration. The issue was symbolized in a celebrated case in which the wearing of a headscarf by Muslim female students was outlawed. In February 2004, France's National Assembly ignored protests and criticism from around the world and voted 494–36 to approve the controversial ban in public schools. Although the new law was aimed primarily at Muslims wearing the *hijab*, other religious apparel (large Christian crucifixes and Jewish skullcaps, or *yarmulkes*) was included; violators face suspension or expulsion. The government argued that this law is needed not only to protect France's secular traditions but also to ward off rising Islamic fundamentalism. Controversy over Islamic

In all Islamic communities, mosques are the social and community centers. Here, at the end of the Ramadan fast, women prepare to pray in the mosque in Regent's Park, London.

dress continued in 2010, when France, along with Belgium, moved to ban the *niqab*, wearing of a full face veil, in public places. The growth of far-right anti-immigrant political parties has created similar pressures in the Netherlands and elsewhere.

Islam in America

Islam is the fastest-growing religion in the United States. Many believe that in the first half of the twenty-first century, Islam will become the second-largest religion in America, after Christianity. The estimates of the number of American Muslims vary significantly, from 3 million to 7 million. Muslim Americans are racially diverse communities in the United States; two-thirds are foreign-born.[16] The majority of American Muslims, 60 percent, are South Asians (from the Indian subcontinent), and 35 percent are indigenous African Americans. The majority of American Muslims are Sunni, but there is a strong Shiah minority. Racial, ethnic, and sectarian differences are reflected in the demographic composition and politics of some mosques, as well: Many houses of worship incorporate the diversity of Muslims in America, but the membership of others is drawn along ethnic or racial lines.

Muslims were present in America prior to the nineteenth century. Perhaps 20 percent of the African slaves brought to America from the sixteenth to the nineteenth centuries were Muslim. However, most were forced to convert to Christianity. It was not until the late nineteenth century, with the arrival of waves of immigrant laborers from the Arab world, that significant numbers of Muslims became a visible presence in America. In recent decades many more have come from the Middle East and South

The Muslim community in America is a rich racial, ethnic, and cultural mosaic of indigenous believers, the majority of whom are African American, and immigrant Muslims. Thousands of Muslims from New York's varied ethnic communities pray next to Coney Island's landmark Parachute Jump to celebrate the Feast of Sacrifice (Id al-Adha). This major religious holiday commemorates God's command to Abraham to sacrifice his son Ismail.

Asia. In contrast to Europe, which attracted large numbers of Muslims as immigrant laborers in the 1960s and 1970s, many who have come to America in recent decades have been well-educated professionals, intellectuals, and students. Many have come for political and economic reasons, leaving behind the constraints of life under authoritarian regimes and failed economies.

The Transformation of "The Nation of Islam"

African American Islam emerged in the early twentieth century when a number of black Americans converted to Islam and established movements or communities. Islam's egalitarian ideal, in which all Muslims belong to a brotherhood of believers, transcending race and ethnic ties, proved attractive. Whereas Islam was seen as part of an original (African) identity, Christianity was associated with the legitimation of slavery and thus a legacy of white supremacy and oppression of black Americans that extended into the twentieth century. The early twentieth century saw the appearance of quasi-Islamic groups, combining a selective use of Islamic symbols with black nationalism. The most prominent and lasting movement, the Nation of Islam, was associated with Elijah Muhammad (formerly Elijah Poole, 1897–1975).

Elijah Muhammad had been a follower of Wallace D. Fard Muhammad, who preached a message of black liberation in the ghettos of Detroit in the early 1930s. After Fard mysteriously disappeared in 1934, Elijah Muhammad became the leader of the Nation of Islam. Adopting the title of the Honorable Elijah Muhammad, he claimed to be the messenger of God. Under his leadership, the Nation of Islam, popularly known as the Black Muslims, was redefined and transformed into an effective national movement. Elijah Muhammad preached black liberation and nationalism, black pride and identity, strength and self-sufficiency, black racial supremacy, and strong family values. The spirit and ethic of the Nation of Islam was embodied in the phrase "Do for self," a doctrine of economic independence that emphasized self-improvement and responsibility through hard work, discipline, thrift, and abstention from gambling, alcohol, drugs, and eating pork.

Malcolm X (d. 1965), also known as El-Hajj Malik El Shabazz, African American Muslim leader, civil and human rights advocate. An early disciple of Elijah Muhammad, chief minister of the Nation of Islam, he became one of its most prominent leaders and spokespersons. He withdrew from the Nation in 1964, becoming a follower of Sunni Islam. He was assassinated in 1965 by members of the Nation of Islam.

The Nation of Islam differed significantly from mainstream Islam in a number of basic beliefs. It claimed that Allah (God) was human—the black man named Wallace D. Fard—and that Elijah Muhammad (not the Prophet Muhammad) was the last messenger of God. The Nation taught black supremacy and black separatism, whereas Islam teaches the brotherhood of all believers in a community that transcends racial, tribal, and ethnic boundaries. The Nation did not subscribe to major tenets of the faith, such as the Five Pillars of Islam.

Three individuals epitomize the development and transformation of Elijah Muhammad's Black Muslim movement: Malcolm X, Wallace D. Muhammad (Warith Deen Muhammad), and Louis Farrakhan.

Malcolm X (1925–65), born Malcolm Little, exemplified the personal and religious transformation for which the Nation of Islam was noted. His experience of racism and prejudice led to his alienation from and rejection of American society. A prison sentence was the result of an early life of drugs and crime in the ghettos of Roxbury, Massachusetts, and later in New York's Harlem. It was during his incarceration (1946–52) that he became self-educated, reading widely in history, politics, and religion. Malcolm became convinced that Christianity was the "white man's religion" and that the Bible "[in the] white man's hands and his interpretation of it, have been the greatest single ideological weapon for enslaving millions of nonwhite human beings."[1] In 1948 he formally turned to Elijah Muhammad and accepted the teachings of the Nation of Islam. Malcolm Little became Malcolm X.

A gifted speaker, dynamic and articulate, and a charismatic personality, Malcolm X rose quickly through the ranks of the Nation of Islam to national prominence in the 1950s and early 1960s. He organized many of the Nation's temples; started its newspaper, *Muhammad Speaks*; and recruited new members, including the boxer Cassius Clay, renamed Muhammad Ali.

However, Malcolm's increased involvement in domestic and international politics as well as his contacts with Sunni Muslims in America and in the Muslim world led to a gradual shift in his religious/ideological worldview. This development put him increasingly at odds with some of Elijah Muhammad's teachings. While Elijah Muhammad advocated separation and self-sufficiency that excluded involvement in "white man's politics," Malcolm came to believe that "the Nation of Islam could be even a greater force in the American Black man's overall struggle if we engaged in more action."[2] He spoke out forcefully on a variety of issues: the civil rights movement, the Vietnam War, solidarity with liberation struggles in colonial Africa. Such statements made him an easy target for those within the Nation who were jealous of his prominence, and as a result he found himself increasingly marginalized.

In March 1964 Malcolm X left the Nation of Islam to start his own organization and a month later went on pilgrimage to Mecca. Here Malcolm underwent a second conversion—to mainstream Sunni Islam. The pilgrimage brought Malcolm and the religious/separatist teachings of the Nation face to face with those of the global Islamic community, vividly exposing their conflicts and contradictions. Malcolm was profoundly affected by the Muslim emphasis, which he experienced firsthand during the hajj, on the equality of all believers.

The 1960s were a transitional period for the Nation of Islam. Not only Malcolm X but also Elijah Muhammad's son, Wallace D. Muhammad, each in his own way, questioned the teachings and strategy of the senior Muhammad. At one point, Wallace was excommunicated by his father. Despite their disagreements, however, Elijah Muhammad had designated his son as his successor, and in February 1975 Wallace D. Muhammad succeeded his recently deceased father as supreme minister. With the support of his family and the Nation's leadership, Wallace set about reforming the doctrines of the Nation and its organizational structure. He simultaneously integrated the Nation within the American Muslim community, the broader American society, and the global Islamic community.

The Nation and its teachings were brought into conformity with orthodox Sunni Islam, and the organization was renamed the World Community of al-Islam in the West (WCIW). Wallace Muhammad made the pilgrimage to Mecca and encouraged his followers to study Arabic to better understand Islam. The community now observed Islam's Five Pillars. Black separatist doctrines were dropped as the community proceeded to participate in the American political process. The equality of men and women believers was reaffirmed; women were given more responsible positions in the ministry of the community. In 1980, as if to signal his and the community's new religious identity and mission, Wallace changed his name to Warith Deen Muhammad and renamed the WCIW the American Muslim Mission.

Muhammad Ali, renowned heavyweight boxing champion of the world. Born Cassius Clay in 1942, he revealed in midcareer that he had become a member of the Nation of Islam and changed his name to Muhammad Ali. He became the most prominent and popular Muslim public figure in America and globally.

TALES OF SPIRITUAL TRANSFORMATION: Malcolm X

After leaving the Nation of Islam in March 1964, Malcolm X made the hajj, pilgrimage to Mecca. The experience transformed his life and changed his perspective on racism:

> There were tens of thousands of pilgrims, from all over the world. They were of all colors, from blue-eyed blondes to black-skinned Africans. But we were all participating in the same ritual, displaying a spirit of unity and brotherhood that my experiences in America had led me to believe never could exist between the white and the nonwhite.
>
> You may be shocked by these words coming from me. But on this pilgrimage, what I have seen, and experienced, has forced me to rearrange much of my thought patterns previously held, and to toss aside some of my previous conclusions. . . . During the past eleven days here in the Muslim world, I have eaten from the same plate, drunk from the same glass, and slept in the same bed (or on the same rug)—while praying to the same God with fellow Muslims, whose eyes were the bluest of the blue, whose hair was the blondest of blond, and whose skin was the whitest of white. And in the words and in the actions and in the deeds of the "white" Muslims, I felt the same sincerity that I felt among the black African Muslims of Nigeria, Sudan, and Ghana.
>
> We are truly all the same—brothers. All praise is due to Allah, the Lord of the worlds.

He returned a Muslim rather than a Black Muslim, changing his name to El Hajj Malik El-Shabazz. On February 21, 1965, Malcolm Shabazz was assassinated as he spoke to an audience in New York.

The transformation of the Nation of Islam under Warith Deen Muhammad did not occur without dissent. Louis Farrakhan (born Louis Eugene Walcott, in 1933), a bitter foe of both Malcolm and Wallace, broke with Wallace in March 1978. Farrakhan retained the name and organizational structure of the Nation of Islam as well as its black nationalist and separatist doctrines. However, from 1986 onward, while using many of the political and economic teachings and programs of Elijah Muhammad, he moved the Nation closer to more orthodox Islamic practices.

While Farrakhan's militancy and anti-Semitic statements brought condemnation and criticism, the effectiveness of the Nation in fighting crime and drugs in ghettos and in rehabilitating prisoners earned the Nation praise. Farrakhan's leadership of the Million Man March on Washington in 1995 received widespread media coverage and support among Christian as well as Muslim leaders and organizations. Though the Nation of Islam has far fewer members than Warith Deen Muhammad's American Muslim Mission, Farrakhan's persona and actions gave him a disproportionate amount of visibility and recognition as the twentieth century drew to a close.

Issues of Adaptation and Change

Islam and Muslim identity in North America reflect the diverse backgrounds of the community: from immigrants who came to America in pursuit of political, religious, or economic freedom to native-born African Americans seeking equality and justice. Muslims, like Hindus and Buddhists, have been challenged by an America that, despite separation of church and state, retains a Judeo-Christian ethos in which Judeo-Christian values are regarded as integral to American identity and Jewish and Christian holidays are officially recognized holidays. The tendency of some in America, as in Europe, to contrast American "national culture" with Islamic values further complicates the process of Muslim assimilation. Finally, the American media's disproportionate coverage of violence and terrorism (as reflected in the maxim "If it bleeds, it leads") has brushstroked mainstream Muslims and projected the image of Islam as a particularly militant religion, reinforcing those who talk of a clash of civilizations.

Islam in America provides many examples of significant change and reform. Both mosques and their leaders, or imams, have been transformed by the American experience. Because Friday is a workday and a school day in America, many Muslims are not able to attend the Friday congregational prayer. Therefore, for many, Sunday at mosques and Islamic centers is the day of congregational prayer, religious education ("Sunday school"), and socializing. Teaching materials and syllabi on Islam and Muslim life are available for the instruction of children and adults at mosques and in schools. Imams in America not only are responsible for the upkeep of mosques and leading of prayers, but often take on the duties of the clergy of other faiths, serving as counselors to military and as hospital and prison chaplains.

In the twenty-first century, Muslim-minority communities have become a global and permanent phenomenon. Today, American Muslims increasingly seek to empower themselves, participating in rather than simply reacting to life in America. Like American Jews and other minorities before them, Muslims are developing grassroots institutions that are responsive to their realities. The contemporary American Muslim community is increasingly more integrated both politically and economically. Muslim advocacy and public affairs organizations promote and lobby for Muslim rights and community interests.

Moreover, Muslim educational associations monitor textbooks and the teaching of Islam to ensure accuracy and objectivity. Public affairs organizations monitor publications and respond to misinformation in the media and to objectionable policies and actions by legislators and corporations. Islamic information services develop and distribute films, videos, and publications on Islam and Muslims in America to further better understanding. Some communities have primary and secondary Islamic schools.

Islam: Postmodern Challenges

Islam and Muslims today are again at an important crossroads. The struggle today, the world over, is one of faith, identity, and reform. What does it mean to be a Muslim in an increasingly globalized and pluralistic world and society? How should Islam's sacred sources and heritage be interpreted to respond to issues of religious authority, secularism, the role of *sharia*, the rights of women and minorities, religious extremism, and terrorism?

Like the other Children of Abraham, their Jewish and Christian cousins, Muslims face questions of faith and identity in a rapidly changing world. The process of reform bears witness to the fact that monotheistic does not mean monolithic. As in the past and as in all faiths, the unity of Islam embraces a diversity of interpretations and expressions, a source of dynamism and growth as well as contention and conflict among believers and, at times, with other faith communities. The challenge for all believers remains the rigorous pursuit in a world of diversity and difference of "the straight path, the way of God, to whom belongs all that is in the heavens and all that is on the earth" (Q. 42:52–53).

Like Catholic and Jewish communities before them, which created their own schools to safeguard and preserve the faith and identity of the younger generation, some Muslim communities have created Islamic schools that combine a standard academic curriculum with training in Arabic and Islamic studies.

While the Quran and Sunnah of the Prophet Muhammad remain normative for all Muslims, vigorously debated questions have been raised in the areas of interpretation, authenticity, and application. If some Muslims see little need to redefine past approaches and practices, others strike out into new territory. Some Muslim scholars distinguish between the Meccan and Medinan *surahs* (chapters). The former are regarded as the earlier and more religiously binding; the latter are seen as primarily political, concerned with Muhammad's creation of the Medinan state and therefore not universally binding. Still other Muslim scholars say that whereas the eternal principles and values of the Quran are to be applied and reapplied to changing sociopolitical contexts, many articles of past legislation addressed conditions in specific historical periods and are not necessarily binding today.

Although the example (Sunnah) of the Prophet Muhammad has always been normative in Islam, from earliest times Muslim scholars saw the need to examine critically and authenticate the enormous number of prophetic traditions (*hadith*). A sector of modern Western scholarship questioned the historicity and authenticity of the hadith, maintaining that the bulk of the Prophetic traditions are pious fabrications, written long after the death of the Prophet. Most Muslim scholars and some from outside the Islamic world have taken exception to this sweeping position. If many of the *ulama* continue to accept the authoritative collections of the past unquestioningly, other Muslim scholars have in fact become more critical in their approach and use of tradition (*hadith*) literature.

Contemporary Muslim discussion and debate over the role of Islam in state and society reflect a broad array of questions: Is there one classical model or many possible models for the relationship of religion to political, social, and economic development? If a new Islamic synthesis is to be achieved that provides continuity with past tradition, how will this be accomplished? Will it be imposed from above by rulers and/or

As in other world religions, in Islam marriage is solemnized in a religious ceremony. This Baghdad wedding is an occasion for great joy and celebration among the couple's family and friends.

the *ulama* or legislated in populist fashion through a representative electoral process? These questions are reflected in the debate over the nature and role of Islamic law in Muslim societies.

Islamization of the Law

What should the role of *sharia* be today? Does Islamization of law mean the wholesale reintroduction of classical law as formulated in the early Islamic centuries or the development of new laws derived from the Quran and Sunnah of the Prophet? Or can it include the acceptance of any laws, whatever their source (European, American, etc.), that are not contrary to Islam? Who is to define, determine, and oversee this process: rulers, the *ulama*, or parliaments?

The implementation of *sharia*, where it has occurred, has not followed a fixed pattern or set interpretation even among those countries dubbed conservative or fundamentalist, such as Iran, Sudan, Afghanistan under the Taliban, Pakistan, and Saudi Arabia. Women in Saudi Arabia cannot vote or hold public office. In Pakistan and Iran, despite other strictures and problems, women vote, hold political office in parliaments and cabinets, teach in universities, and hold responsible professional positions. However, Islamization of law has underscored several areas that have proved particularly problematic: the *hudud* (Quranically prescribed crimes and punishments for alcohol consumption, theft, fornication, adultery, and false witness), the status of non-Muslims and minorities, and the status of women. All potentially involve changes in Islamic law.

While some call for the reimplementation of the *hudud* punishments, other Muslims argue that harsh measures such as amputation for theft and stoning for adultery (not mentioned in the Quran) are, like stoning in the Old Testament or many

hudud: Quranically prescribed crimes and punishments adopted by some countries and advocated by some groups as evidence of the "Islamic" nature of their political rule and law corporal punishments practiced by governments in centuries past, no longer suitable. Among those who advocate imposition of the *hudud*, some want it introduced immediately and others say that it should be contingent on the creation of a just society in which people will not be driven to steal to survive. Some critics charge that while appropriate relative to the time they were introduced, *hudud* punishments are unnecessary in a modern context.

Women and Minorities

As we have seen, one result of contemporary Islamic revivalism has been a reexamination of the role of women in Islam and, at times, a bitter debate over their function in society. More conservative religious voices among the *ulama* and many Islamists have advocated a return to veiling and sexual segregation as well as restrictions on women's education and employment. Muslim women are regarded as culture bearers, teachers of family faith and values, whose primary role as wives and mothers limits or prevents participation in public life. The imposition of reputed Islamic laws by some governments and the policies of some Islamist movements reinforced fears of a retreat to the past. Among the prime examples have been the enforcement of veiling, closure of women's schools, restriction of women in the workplace, and extremist attacks and killings. In fact, the picture is far more complex and diverse, revealing both old and new patterns.

Modern forms of Islamic dress have the practical advantage of enabling some women to assert their modesty and dignity while functioning in public life in societies where Western dress often symbolizes a more permissive lifestyle. It creates a protected, private space of respectability in crowded urban environments. For some

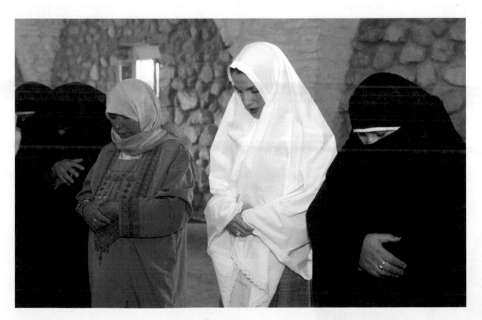

Queen Rania of Jordan (center) at prayer with other Muslim women.

GENDER FOCUS: Women and Empowerment

Muslim women in the twentieth century had two clear choices or models before them: the modern Westernized lifestyle common among an elite minority of women and the more restrictive traditional "Islamic" lifestyle of the majority of women, who lived much as their grandmothers and great-grandmothers had lived. The social impact of the Islamic revival produced a third alternative that is both modern and firmly rooted in Islamic faith, identity, and values. Muslim women, modernists, and Islamists have argued on Islamic grounds for an expanded role for women in Muslim societies. Rejecting the idea that Islam itself is patriarchal and distinguishing between revelation and its interpretation by all-male *ulama* in patriarchal

settings, Muslim women have reasserted the right to be primary participants in redefining their identity and role in society. In many instances, this change has been symbolized by a return to the wearing of Islamic dress or the donning of a headscarf, or *hijab*. Initially prominent primarily among urban middle-class women, this new mode of dress has become more common among a broader sector of society. For many it is an attempt to combine religious belief and Islamic values of modesty with contemporary freedoms in education and employment, to pair a much-desired process of social change with indigenous Islamic values and ideals. The goal is a more authentic rather than simply Westernized modernization.

Benazir Bhutto, former prime minister of Pakistan, was one of several Muslim women to have served as president or prime minister in an Islamic nation. She served two terms in the 1990s as prime minister (1988–October 1990), and again from 1993 until her final dismissal in November 1996. She was assassinated in 2007.

it is a sign of a real Islamic feminism that rejects what is regarded as the tendency of women in the West and elite Westernized Muslim women in many Muslim societies to go from being defined as restricted sexual objects in a male-dominated tradition to so-called free yet exploited sexual objects. Western feminism is often seen as pseudo-liberation, a new form of bondage to dress, youthfulness, and physical beauty, a false freedom in which women's bodies are used to sell everything from clothing to automobiles to cell phones. Covering the body, it is argued, defines a woman and gender relations in society in terms of personality and talents rather than physical appearance.

New experiments by educated Muslim women to orient their lives more Islamically have also resulted in more women "returning to the mosque." In the past, when women were restricted to the home and allowed only limited education, they did not participate in public prayer in mosques. While some attended the Friday congregational prayer, sitting separately from the men, it was more common for women to pray at home and to leave religious learning to men. Today in many Muslim countries and communities, particularly those that have been regarded as among the more modernized, such as Egypt, Jordan, Malaysia, and the United States, women are forming prayer and Quran study groups, which are led by women. To justify these public activities, women cite the examples of Muslim women in early Islam who fought and prayed alongside their men and of women who were held in high repute for their knowledge and sanctity. Women from the United States to Malaysia, as individuals and in organizations, are writing and speaking out for themselves on women's issues. They draw on the writings and thought not only of male scholars but also, and

The Quran and Islamic tradition enjoin modesty, and thus everyone is required to wear modest dress. The diversity of attire found across the Muslim world is reflected in this group of young Muslim women in the United States. Though all are dressed modestly, some wear a headscarf (*hijab*) while others do not.

most importantly, on a growing number of women scholars who utilize an Islamic discourse to address issues ranging from dress to education, employment, and political participation.

Contemporary Muslim societies reflect both the old and the new realities. Old patterns remain strong and are indeed reasserted and defended by those who call for a more widespread return to traditional forms of Islamic dress and segregation or seclusion of women (*purdah*). However, at the same time, Muslim women have become catalysts for change. While the women's literacy rate in Pakistan is anywhere from 12 percent to 40 percent (vs. 69 percent for men), women's literacy rates are much higher in Egypt (63.5 percent), Iran (70 percent), Saudi Arabia (81 percent), and as high as 89 percent in Jordan and 85 percent in Malaysia. In the United Arab Emirates, as in Iran, the majority of university students are women. Women have increasingly empowered themselves by entering the professions, running for elective office, and serving in parliament, becoming students and scholars of Islam, and establishing women's professional organizations, journals, and magazines. Women's organizations such as Women Living Under Muslim Laws, based in Pakistan but international in membership; Musawah: Global Movement for Equality and Justice in the Muslim Family; and Malaysia's Sisters in Islam are active internationally in protecting and promoting the rights of Muslim women.

Islamic Reform

Islamic reformers face formidable challenges and obstacles, including the discrediting of militant ideas and ideologies and the reform of *madrasas* and universities that perpetuate

Indonesia has the largest Muslim population in the world. These women from the province of Aceh, contestants seeking to become Miss Indonesia, learn how to perfect the application of makeup.

a "theology of hate" and train so-called jihad-ists. Another obstacle to reform, however, is the ultraconservatism of many (though not all) *ulama*, which hinders reform in the curriculum and training of religious scholars, leaders, and students.

The struggle of Islam is between the competing voices and visions of over a billion mainstream Muslims and a dangerous and deadly minority of terrorists. While the extremists dominate the headlines and threaten Muslim and Western societies, the vast majority of Muslims, like other religious believers, wish to pursue normal, everyday activities. For decades, quietly, persistently, and effectively, a group of reform-minded Muslims have articulated a variety of progressive, constructive Islamic frameworks for reform. These intellectual activists represent voices of reform from North Africa to Southeast Asia and from Europe to North America. They respond to the realities of many Muslim societies, the challenges of authoritarian regimes and secular elites, the dangers of religious extremism, and the dead weight of well-meaning but often-intransigent conservative religious scholars and leaders.

Islamic reform is a process not only of intellectual ferment and religious debate but also of religious and political unrest and violence. The lessons of the Protestant Reformation, the Catholic Counter-Reformation, and more recently Vatican II demonstrate that religious reformations take time and are often fraught with conflict

TEACHINGS OF RELIGIOUS WISDOM: A Bosnian Prayer

Our Lord
Do not let success deceive us
Nor failure take us to despair!.
Always remind us that failure is a temptation
That precedes success!
Our Lord
Teach us that tolerance is the highest degree of
    power
And the desire for revenge
The first sign of weakness! . . .
Our Lord

If we sin against people,
Give us the strength of apology
And if people sin against us,
Give us the strength of forgiveness!
Our Lord
If we forget Thee,
Do not forget us!

Source: A Bosnian Prayer cited by Mustafa Ceric, Grand Mufti of Bosnia-Herzegovina, in his "Judaism, Christianity, Islam: Hope or Fear of Our Times," in James L. Heft, ed., *Beyond Violence* (New York: Fordham University Press, 2004), pp. 54–55.

and even danger. Generations of reformers, often a minority within their communities, struggle today against many powerful forces, including conservative religious establishments, with their medieval paradigms; authoritarian regimes able to control or manipulate religion, education, and the media; and political and religious establishments that often see reformers as a threat to their power and privilege.

Conclusion

With 1.8 billion members, one-fourth of the world's population, the global Muslim community is second only to Christianity's 2.3 billion. Despite setbacks, for fifteen centuries Islam has proven vibrant and dynamic, growing spectacularly as a faith and empire, from the time of the Prophet Muhammad. Islam's message and way of life has attracted followers of every race and culture, adapting to diverse cultures from Africa to Asia and Europe to America. Unity of faith has been accompanied by a diversity of expressions. In the twenty-first century, Islam is at a crossroads. Muslims face yet another watershed as they struggle to implement their faith and practice within the realities and challenges of contemporary life.

The struggle for reform is religious, intellectual, spiritual, and moral. But it must be a more rapid and widespread program of Islamic renewal that not only builds on past reformers but also more forcefully follows the lead of today's enlightened religious leaders and intellectuals and more effectively engages in a wide-ranging process of reinterpretation (*ijtihad*) and reform.

The pace of reform has been slow in many countries and societies that are dominated by authoritarian regimes, entrenched elites, and a global politics in which Western governments, despite their democratic principles and values, are often willing to support autocrats to protect their own national interests. The process has been compounded by the threat and attacks of Muslim extremists within Muslim countries and in the West.

In contrast to Christianity's centuries-long Protestant Reformation and Vatican II in Roman Catholicism, the forces of globalization and development today necessitate a more rapid process of change. At the same time, religious, like political, reform often brings heat as well as light. Religious reformations often include not only bitter and divisive theological debates, but also, as in Christianity, the religious wars (1516–1750) between Protestants and Catholics. The result of theological and legal differences can be seen in the results—the many Christian denominations and the various branches of Judaism: ultra-orthodox, orthodox, conservative, reform, reconstructionist, and humanistic.

While the trajectory of Islamic reform and its outcome remain uncertain, Muslims are challenged to exemplify the Quranic prescription that the Islamic community (*ummah*) pursue a just and middle (*wasat*) path: "Thus We have made you a just community, that you may witness to humanity" (2:143) as, like those before them, it seeks to follow "the straight path, the way of God, to whom belongs all that is in the heavens and all that is in the earth" (42:52–53).

Discussion Questions

1. Identify and describe the Five Pillars of Islam.

2. What are the differences between Sunnis, Shiah, and Sufis?

3. What is the difference between the *sharia* and *fiqh*? What impact have these aspects of Islam had on modern revivalism and reformism?

4. What are the origins of the Crusades? Explain their long-term effects on Muslim-Christian/Western relations.

5. Discuss the impact of European colonialism on the Muslim world. What are some of the ways in which Muslims responded to it?

6. What is *ijtihad*? Why is this concept at the heart of the question of the relationship between Islam and modernity?

7. Describe the different themes and techniques used for the revival and reform of Islam in the eighteenth century.

8. Discuss the basic tenets and significance of the Muslim Brotherhood and the *Jamaat-i-Islami*.

9. What are the causes and conditions that led to the contemporary resurgence of Islam?

10. How is Islam used both to support and to oppose the state? Give examples.

11. Describe the diverse meanings of *jihad*. How has the concept been used by different Islamic movements to justify their activities?

12. Discuss the origin and development of the Nation of Islam. Do African American Muslims differ from mainstream Muslims?

13. How has Islam affected or changed the status of women? How are women influenced by Islamic movements today? How are they influencing these movements?

14. What are some of the major issues facing Muslims living in non-Muslim-majority countries today, particularly in Europe and America?

15. Identify and discuss several key areas of Islamic reform.

Key Terms

Allah	*dhimmi*	*hadith*
caliph	*fatwa*	*hajj*
dar al-Islam	*fiqh*	*hijra*

hudud	*muamalat*	*sharia*
ibadat	*muezzin*	Shiah
ijma	*mufti*	Sufi
ijtihad	*mujaddid*	Sufism
imam	Muslim	Sunnah
Islam	People of the Book	Sunni
jahiliyya	*purdah*	*surah*
jihad	*qiyas*	*tawhid*
khutba	Quran	*ulama*
Mahdi	Ramadan	*ummah*
minbar	*salat*	*wali*
mosque	*shahadah*	*zakat*

Suggested Readings

Armstrong, Karen. *Islam: A Short History* (New York: Modern Library, 2002).

Brown, Jonathan. *Hadith: Muhammad's Legacy in the Medieval and Modern World* (Oxford: Oneworld Publications, 2009).

———. *Very Short Introduction: Muhammad* (Oxford: Oxford University Press, 2010).

Donohue, John, and John L. Esposito, eds. *Islam in Transition: Muslim Perspectives*, 2nd ed. (New York: Oxford University Press, 2006).

Esposito, John L. *The Future of Islam* (New York: Oxford University Press, 2010).

———, ed. *Islam: The Straight Path*, 4th rev. ed. (New York: Oxford University Press, 2010).

———. *The Islamic World: Past and Present*. 3 vols. (New York: Oxford University Press, 2004).

———, ed. *The Oxford History of Islam* (New York: Oxford University Press, 2000).

———. *Unholy War: Terror in the Name of Islam* (New York: Oxford University Press, 2000).

———. *What Everyone Needs to Know About Islam*, 2nd ed (New York: Oxford University Press, 2011).

——— with Dalia Mogahed. *Who Speaks for Islam? What a Billion Muslims Really Think* (New York: Gallup Press, 2008).

Lings, Martin. *What Is Sufism?* (London: I. B. Tauris, 1999).

Nasr, Seyyed Hossein. *The Heart of Islam: Enduring Values for Humanity* (San Francisco: Harper, 2002).

The Quran: A Modern English Version, trans. Majid Fakhry (Berkshire, UK: Garnet, 1996).

The Qur'an, trans. Haleem, M. A. S. Abdul (Oxford: Oxford University Press, 2008).

Ramadan, Tariq. *Western Muslims and the Future of Islam* (New York: Oxford University Press, 2005).

Sonn, Tamara. *A Brief History of Islam* (Malden, MA: Wiley-Blackwell, 2010).

Notes

1. Ibn Hisham, quoted in Philip K. Hitti, *History of the Arabs*, 9th ed. (New York: St. Martin's Press, 1966), p. 120. For the text within the context of a major biography of the Prophet

Muhammad, see Ibn Ishaq, *The Life of Muhammad*, trans. A. Guillaume (London: Oxford University Press, 1955), p. 651.

2. Bernard Lewis, ed. and trans., *Islam: From the Prophet Muhammad to the Capture of Constantinople* (New York: Harper & Row, 1974), pp. 179–81.

3. Seyyed Hossein Nasr, *Muhammad: Man of God* (Chicago: Kazi Publications, 1995), p. 90.

4. *The Hedaya*, trans. Charles Hamilton, 2nd ed. (Lahore, Pakistan: Premier Books, 1957), p. 73.

5. As quoted in Reuben Levy, *The Social Structure of Islam* (Cambridge: Cambridge University Press, 1955), p. 126.

6. Margaret Smith, *Rabia the Mystic and Her Fellow-Saints in Islam* (Cambridge: Cambridge University Press, 1928), p. 30.

7. Francis E. Peters, "Early Muslim Empires: Umayyads, Abbasids, Fatimids," in Marjorie Kelly, ed., *Islam: The Religious and Political Life of a World Community* (New York: Praeger, 1984), p. 85.

8. Roger Savory. "Christendom vs. Islam: Interaction and Coexistence," in Roger Savory, ed., *Introduction to Islamic Civilization* (Cambridge: Cambridge University Press, 1976), p. 133.

9. John O. Voll. "The Sudanese Mahdi: Frontier Fundamentalist," *International Journal of Middle East Studies* 10 (1979), p. 159.

10. For perceptive discussions of Osama bin Laden, see A. Rashid, *Taliban: Militant Islam, Oil, and Fundamentalism in Central Asia* (New Haven, CT: Yale University Press, 2000), and J. K. Cooley, *Unholy Wars: Afghanistan, America and International Terrorism* (London: Pluto Press, 2000).

11. Osama bin Laden, "From Somalia to Afghanistan, March 1997," in *Messages to the World: The Statements of Osama Bin Laden*, ed. Bruce Lawrence (New York: Verso, 2005), 44–57.

12. *Al-Hayat*, November 5, 2001.

13. http://groups.colgate.edu/aarislam/abdulhak.htm.

14. Timothy Winter, "The Poverty of Fanaticism," available at http://www.islamfortoday.com/murad02.htm (accessed 19 May 2011).

15. This section is adapted from John L. Esposito, *Islam: The Straight Path*, 3rd ed. (New York: Oxford University Press, 1998), and *Muslims on the Americanization Path* (New York: Oxford University Press, 1999).

16. http://en.wikipedia.org/wiki/Islam_in_the_United_States#cite_note-PewForum-60#cite_note-PewForum-60 (accessed May 14, 2011).

Additional Resources

Oxford Islamic Studies Online (http://www.oxfordislamicstudies.com). A comprehensive scholarly resource for the study of Islam.

Oxford Bibliographies Online (http://oxfordbibliographies.com). Developed cooperatively with scholars and librarians worldwide, the "Islamic Studies" portal at this site is an excellent starting point for research and further understanding.

Islamicity (http://www.islamicity.com). This extensive site provides a nonsectarian, comprehensive, and holistic view of Islam and Muslims to a global audience.

CDs

Michael Sells, *Approaching the Qur'an* (contains CD of Qur'an recitation)
Sami Yusuf, *Without You* (http://www.youtube.com/watch?v=7-ROGqpdRf8)
Zain Bhika, *Allah Knows* (http://www.youtube.com/watch?v=RpjIsSdsT6A)

Films/DVDs

Cities of Light: The Rise and Fall of Islamic Spain (http://www.pbs.org/programs/citiesoflight/)
Great World Religions: Islam
    (http://www.thegreatcourses.com/tgc/courses/course_detail.aspx?cid=6102)
Inside Islam: What a Billion Muslims Really Think
    (http://www.youtube.com/watch?v=FFDyDHSlTfc)
Islam: Empire of Faith (www.pbs.org/empires/islam)
Muhammad: Legacy of a Prophet
    (http://upf.tv/about-upf/our-work/shop/shop-muhammad-dvd.html)
National Geographic, *Inside Mecca,*
    (http://video.google.com/videoplay?docid=-6916375781663065887)

HINDUISM, JAINISM, AND SIKHISM

6

South Asian Religions

Overview

"*Namaskar.*" Millions of Hindus every day extend this ancient Sanskrit greeting to holy seekers and other respected individuals as well as to their gods. Whether they are in the ancient city of Varanasi (Benares) or a newly consecrated sanctuary in Minneapolis, Minnesota, this greeting gives clear indication that we are entering the religious domain of South Asian religions. As impressive new temples are built by a rising number of immigrants throughout the Western world, devotees such as those who attend the Minneapolis temple field standard questions from friends and neighbors: Are all Hindus vegetarians? Do you really believe that cows are sacred? Is that blue figure on the poster a male or a female? Why does everyone leaving come out with that dot on their forehead? Where do the Jains and Sikhs fit into this complicated mosaic?

Yet what immigrants from all over modern South Asia practice as Hinduism is much less varied than what their relatives back in their homeland observe. For example, in a suburb of Calcutta, devotees lead a goat toward the small temple, where a priest sprinkles pure water on its head; after seeing it "consent" to its fate by shivering, the priest skillfully wields a sharp knife to slit the animal's throat, severs the head, and pours the spurting blood from it on the icon of goddess Kali, saying, "*Om namaskar Kali-Ma*" ("*Om* homage to Mother Kali"). Elsewhere, in the Himalayan foothills town of Haridwar, a sadhu who has renounced all family ties in quest of liberation walks slowly down a narrow byway, wearing only a humble robe and carrying an alms bowl, where a housewife, as she does each day, offers some fruit, bows, and says, "*Namaskar baba-ji*" ("Homage to respected father"). Even with the contradictions easily witnessed in modern India, no one would dispute that animal sacrifices to Kali and absolutely nonviolent ascetics are following ancient and legitimate Hindu traditions.

What this means is that ancient beliefs and practices continue to thrive today despite all the revisions and reforms introduced by colonial rule, independence, and the advent

Hinduism Timeline

ca. 3500–1600 BCE	Indus Valley civilization in northwestern South Asia
1500 BCE	Decline of major Indus cities; populations migrate east to Gangetic plain
1500–500 BCE	Formative period of Vedic civilization
900–400 BCE	Shramana period of wandering ascetics and composition of the Upanishads
300–100 BCE	Texts of brahmanical orthodoxy formulated (e.g., *Laws of Manu*)
100–400 BCE	Composition of devotional texts and epics *Ramayana* and *Mahabharata*
50–300 BCE	Composition of the *Bhagavad Gita* and Patanjali's *Yoga Sutras*
100 CE–700 CE	Hindu traditions established along rim of Indian Ocean in Southeast Asia
320–647	Classical temple Hinduism established
500–ff	Development of Advaita Vedanta school; textual expressions of Hindu tantrism as counterculture
788–820	Life of Shankara, exponent of Advaita Vedanta and creator of Hindu monasticism
800–1200	Six brahmanical schools established as divisions in elite philosophical Hinduism
1025–1137	Life of Ramanuja, philosophical defender of *bhakti* faith
1200–1757	Muslim rule of North India; Buddhism virtually extinguished in South Asia
1420–1550	Era of great devotional saints (e.g., Mirabai, Ravidas, Kabir, Chaitanya, Surdas)
1469–1539	Life of Nanak, the founder of the Sikh faith
1526–1707	Mughal dynasty; Muslim rulers move from ecumenical views to anti-Hindu, anti-Sikh policies
1708	Death of tenth guru, Gobind Singh; Sikh text *Adi Granth* declared guru of the community
1757–1857	British East India Company dominates Indian political life
1815	Christian missionaries present in most cities and towns of British India
1828	Founding of the Brahmo Sabha (later Brahmo Samaj) by Rammohan Roy
1830–1890	First Hindu texts reach North America, influence the Transcendentalists Emerson and Thoreau, and the Theosophy movement
1834–1886	Life of Ramakrishna, charismatic guru with ecumenical teaching
1858–1947	After uprising, British crown assumes direct rule over India; South Asian ethnic groups recruited for government service across British Empire spread Hinduism globally

of science. In India and across the Hindu diaspora, there are newly built monasteries for study (**mathas**) in the traditional way, at the feet of recognized masters, or **gurus**. And there are also yoga centers in the major urban centers like Mumbai that cater to India's new middle class, which resemble those found in London or Chicago. Add to these the Jain and Sikh temples, as well as the new sects that have arisen around charismatic teachers, gurus who combine classic doctrines with ideas from other Asian traditions or the West. Many by now use video and Internet media to extend their outreach. Today there are also communities in which very conservative priests memorize, recite,

matha: Hindu monastery

guru: a spiritual and cultural teacher, regarded by students as semidivine

1863–1902	Life of Swami Vivekananda, Ramakrishna's disciple, who led global Ramakrishna Mission
1875	Foundation of the Arya Samaj by Swami Dayananda Saraswati
1893	Speeches by Swami Vivekananda inspire interest at Parliament of World Religions in Chicago
1920–1948	M. K. Gandhi (1869–1948) leads civil disobedience campaigns, articulating ecumenical Hindu reformism influenced by Western culture
1923	Founding of the Rashtriya Svayamsevak Sangh (RSS), Hindu nationalist group
1940	Ashram established by Sathya Sai Baba, beginning of large global movement
1947	Independence of India from Britain; prime minister, J. Nehru, declares India a secular state
1948	Gandhi assassinated by Hindu extremist
1964	Vishva Hindu Parishad (VHP) founded to unite Hindu leaders and devotees worldwide
1964	International Society for Krishna Consciousness (ISKON) established by Bhaktivedanta (1896–1977)
1984	Sikh extremists occupy Golden Temple in Amritsar; armed removal by Indian army; assassination of the prime minister, Indira Gandhi
1987	Weekly Indian television series *Ramayana* inspires rising sentiments of Hindu nationalism
1992	Hindu agitation in Ayodhya culminates in destruction of Babri Mosque; Hindu-Muslim riots across South Asia
1995	The Swaminarayan Mandir opens in London, the largest traditionally built Hindu temple outside India
1998	The Bharatiya Janata Party (BJP), a Hindu nationalist political party, wins parliamentary majority for the first time; rules until 2004
2002	Hindu hooligans riot in BJP-led Gujarat state, killing 2,500 Muslims, looting Muslim businesses, and displacing 200,000
2004	BJP loses national parliamentary elections but retains control of ten states across India
2007	During Kumbha Mela, Hindu holy men stage demonstration against Ganges pollution
2011	Death of global Hindu teacher Sathya Sai Baba
2014	BJP wins national parliamentary elections, returns to power

and pass down the earliest hymns and rituals orally, some dating back 3,000 years. And in the great centers such as Varanasi, pilgrims come by the hundred thousands each year to make offerings and see the deities enshrined in their magnificent temples, while musicians and dancers in traditional training studios nearby continue to perfect their dramatic renditions of religious themes. In many villages across the Indian subcontinent, where 60 percent of the population still lives, ritual practices within families and in local temples remain vigorous.

In this chapter we will explore such examples from near and far to understand how Hinduism and the other South Asian religious traditions are unlike the monotheistic world religions surveyed already. All except Sikhism lack a canonical text accepted by all followers and have no single elite or institution that ever exerted control over the development of their fundamental beliefs and practices. Our goal is to provide a "map" of this diverse territory by using the thread of South Asia's unfolding history to follow its many additions and innovations and by highlighting just how and where there is unity in diversity in what we call "Hinduism." To start with, we need to understand what this term does and does not mean.

Defining Hinduism: Unity, Diversity, Localities

What we label "Hinduism" ranges from monotheism to polytheism to atheism; from nonviolent ethics to moral systems that see as imperative blood sacrifices to sustain the world; from critical, scholastic philosophical discussion to the cultivation of sublime, mystical, wordless inner experiences. "Hinduism" as we use the term indicates the amalgam of spiritual traditions originating in South Asia that comprises the third-largest world religion today. The term owes its origins to *Sindhu*, the Persian word for the great Indus River. Conquering Muslims used *Hindu* to designate people who lived east of the Indus, and later the British applied the term to the non–Muslim natives of the region.

A singular term for "Hinduism" was never in vogue in premodern South Asia, and it never stood for a single way of being religious. Some South Asian intellectuals and politicians in the last two centuries did adopt it to stand amid the apparent singularities of the Muslim and Christian. What is meant, or what should be meant, by "true Hinduism" has remained contested throughout history, especially in the modern and postcolonial eras.

Religion in South Asia has been the most pluralistic and least centrally organized in the world, a characteristic dating back at least a millennium, when the Arab geographer Alberuni identified forty-two discrete "religions" in South Asia. While conservative religious ideology still is used by some to justify the caste system and social inequality, other ancient traditions argue forcefully—in ways similar to those in the Western prophetic faiths—for the reform of society and for "God-given" egalitarianism. Hinduism itself thus incorporates differences at least as fundamental as those between Judaism, Islam, and Christianity. Therefore, it is only by distinguishing the various "Hindu" traditions from the more general and monolithic term *Hinduism* that we can compare this tradition with other world religions.

Though the great majority of Hindus live on the South Asian subcontinent, an important postcolonial development has been their global diaspora. Their migration to other parts of the world has made Hinduism a global faith today. The estimated number of Hindus had surpassed 800 million by the turn of the millennium; after Islam, it is the second-fastest-growing world religion.

Among the contemporary nation-states, India remains the heartland of Hinduism (see Map 6.1). The modern state of India has been a secular democracy since its inception in 1947. It has over eighteen major culture regions, whose ethnic groups speak over a thousand languages. Every region in South Asia has its distinctive religious history as well. The most profound differences are seen between the traditions of North and South India.

Among the other South Asian states, Nepal was until 2006 the world's only Hindu nation, with a large majority of its 30 million people identifying themselves as Hindu. Two Muslim nations, Pakistan and Bangladesh, contain Hindu minorities (3 percent and 16 percent, respectively), most of whom remained despite the chaos and bloodshed occasioned by partition of British India in 1947. Fifteen percent of Buddhist Sri Lanka's population of 25 million is Hindu. Five to 10 percent of Malaysia's large population is Hindu. Small communities of Hindus are also found in Myanmar (Burma), Indonesia, Fiji, and the Caribbean.

In North America there are over 2.25 million Hindus, with immigrants far outnumbering converts, making Hinduism the fifth largest group. In the United States, as across Europe, Hindu temples serve as centers of religious teaching and ritual practice. The yoga traditions that involve training the body for flexibility and mental peace have been the most influential vehicle for spreading Hinduism among non-Indian peoples. The best-known Hindu tradition that has attracted Euro-American converts since the 1960s has been the so-called **Hare Krishna** movement (ISKON) and **Transcendental Meditation (TM)**.

This chapter surveys this multicentric spiritual tradition of Hinduism and provides an overview of its two great independent traditions, Jainism and Sikhism. Buddhism, the third great heterodox religion of South Asia, is the subject of the next chapter. Beginning with the first records of urban civilization in South Asia, the chapter describes the earliest form of religious life shaped by the Vedas, texts that are among the oldest (3,500 years old) in human history. Building on them and citing later revelations, we move through a succession of religious beliefs and practices that have found expression since then, without a priestly hierarchy or any institutional authority stifling the religious imagination. We finally focus on how these loosely connected traditions were affected by Islamic rule (1200–1780), and the founding of the separate world religion called Sikhism. It then traces how British colonial rule (1800–1947) in reordered religious life in South Asia. A final goal of this chapter is to convey a sense of modern and postcolonial change amid what still are extraordinary continuities in

Hare Krishna/ ISKON: global devotional movement focused on Krishna founded by Swami Prabhupada (1896– 1977)

Transcendental Meditation (TM): movement founded by Maharishi Mahesh Yogi that brought yoga meditation teachings to the West

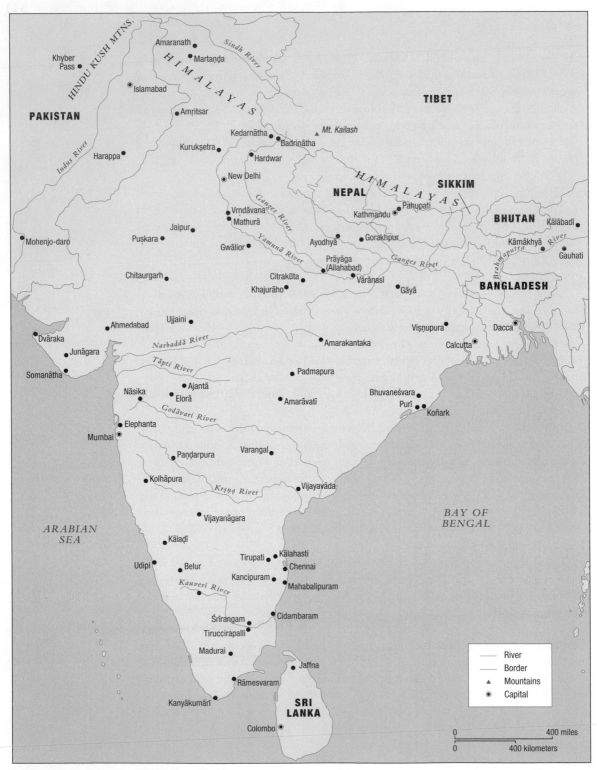

Map 6.1 India, with major cities and holy places.

religious life today, some of which date back three millennia. In addition to an array of traditions that can be described as falling within the circle of "orthodox Hinduism," so vibrant has religious life in South Asia been that it also spawned three major heterodox religions that have themselves become global in scope today: Buddhism and Jainism, which began 2,500 years ago (see Chapter 7); and the Sikh tradition, which began about 500 years ago (and is covered in the latter portions of this chapter).[1]

Encounter with Modernity: Hindu Challenges to India as a Secular State

Religion in South Asia has undergone a continuous development process throughout its history, one that has tended to preserve the past, even amid striking innovations that thrived and multiplied; this was possible, in part, because no single priestly group, theologian, or institution ever imposed a universal or reductive definition of the core beliefs. Hindus have since antiquity respected the remote past as a more refined era of spiritual awareness, and no one forced adherents to believe in any one way. Regional diversities made this religious freedom even more pronounced, and in South Asia the religious imagination, and questing after spiritual experience, was extraordinary. There have been no heresy trials or inquisitions in South Asia's long history; in fact, debating spiritual truths, often with great subtlety, was a regular feature of premodern court life and in society at large. Hinduism contains within it every conceivable religious belief and practice that has ever been recorded in human history. This pattern of exuberant pluralism continues to the present, with the result that Hinduism's multiplicities are continuously extended: Very ancient traditions are preserved alongside those originating in the medieval era, and these threads weave together with the traditions introduced by nineteenth- and twentieth-century reformers.

Because of this diversity, leaders such as M. K. Gandhi and Jawaharlal Nehru, who led South Asia to independence, firmly believed in the prevailing Western political norm of the secular state, insisting that for India to be modern it should be a secular democracy, formally favoring no religion. In the last decades of the twentieth century, however, this stance was questioned by many Hindu citizens.

In reacting to perceived threats from modern secularism and non-Hindus, Hindu revivalist groups have created new organizations styled on Western prototypes. Among the many responses to British colonial rule and the changes it brought to South Asia, one of the most enduring has come from institutions calling for thoroughgoing reform of "Hindu-ness" (**Hindutva**) in national life and the reconstitution of India as a Hindu state. With roots among nineteenth-century reformers, this ideology began to be forcefully articulated in 1923 across the nation by the **Rashtriya Svayamsevak Sangh** ("National Union of [Hindu] Volunteers"). This group, known as the **RSS**, proposed a nativist definition of "Hinduism" as devotion to "Mother India." Members

Hindutva: "Hindu ness"; Hindu identity

Rashtriya Svayamsevak Sangh (RSS): "National Union of [Hindu] Volunteers"; group advocating "Hinduism" as devotion to "Mother India"

have worked in the political arena to promote candidates wishing to repeal the secular rule of law India instituted in 1947, when the country gained independence from Great Britain. By 2014, RSS membership had grown to over 5 million.

Bharatiya Janata Party: Hindu nationalist political party

It was only with the most recent incarnation of an RSS-allied political party, the **Bharatiya Janata Party (BJP)**, that Hindu nationalists finally found success in electoral politics across the nation. In the elections of 1995, the BJP won more seats than any other party in the national parliament, defeating the Congress Party, which had dominated Indian politics since independence. In the 1998 elections, the BJP became India's ruling party, a position it held until 2004. Campaigning on economic themes, the BJP won back control over the Indian Parliament again in the spring of 2014.

The BJP is led mostly by high-caste politicians and appeals primarily to middle-class urbanites. It rose in prominence as its leaders sought to symbolize the unity of a militant and revived Hindu India through a series of motorized "chariot festivals" across the nation, culminating in reworked traditional rituals in which the waters from all the country's sacred rivers were brought together and merged. The BJP and its allies also stoked popular resentment over government-sponsored affirmative action initiatives that set quotas for civil service hiring and admission to state colleges for the most disadvantaged, or "scheduled caste," members, a move aimed to break disproportionate high-caste control over the nation's governmental and educational institutions.

The most strident and hard-line RSS policy is to foment confrontations with South Asian Muslims by accusing the secular government of favoring them in its civil laws and of protecting medieval-era mosques that were purportedly built on North Indian sites sacred to Hindus. The BJP today seeks to have the Hindu majority undo acts of centuries past and repress Islamic activism. The first and most violent focus was on Ayodhya, where in 1528 the Mughal ruler Babar built a Muslim house of worship known as the Babri Mosque. Modern BJP partisans claim that the site was the birthplace of Rama, a human incarnation of the god Vishnu. Responding to the call made by many Hindu nationalist groups, one that was dramatized in a widely distributed video production suggesting that the activists had been miraculously given Rama's blessing for this "service," thousands of volunteers converged on the site in December 1992. They attacked and subdued government troops protecting the site and then broke up the Babri Mosque with hammers, steel rods, and crowbars. In the aftermath, rioting broke out between Muslims and Hindus in other Indian towns and in Pakistan. Over 2,000 people perished.

The RSS- and BJP-led movements advocate paths to religious modernization found elsewhere in the world: They adopt the latest media yet reject the Enlightenment-inspired critiques of religious belief; they insist that the secular political systems established in the colonial and postcolonial eras give way to a religious state. They have used the ancient idea of Mother India to express symbolically their sense of her being "raped" during Muslim, colonial, and postcolonial secular rule. Guru Golwalkara, the RSS chief between 1940 and 1973, put it this way:

> When we say this is a Hindu nation, there are some who immediately come up with the question "What about the Muslims and Christians?" But the

crucial question is whether or not they remember that they are children of this soil. . . . Together with the change in their faith, gone is the spirit of love and devotion for the nation. They look to some distant holy land as their holy place. It is not merely a change of faith, but a change even in national identity.[2]

Beyond declaring loyalty to the land and the Hindu state, however, nationalist literature remains elusive and necessarily vague on what exactly "Hindu-ness" means, and for good reason: Hindus have remained divided on this question since antiquity and remained so throughout the era of colonial rule and up to the present.

More recently in 2007, the BJP leaders who still rule in the state of Madhya Pradesh passed laws requiring the public school curriculum to include the elementary yoga practice of sun worship (*surya asana*), a series of movements that are accompanied by devotional chanting. A state court soon after struck down the legislation, concluding that yoga is a religious practice and that the law contradicted India's secular constitution. The outcome is not surprising, but controversy that India is a secular state again served to roil the Hindu majority across the country.

Despite these setbacks, the appeal of the Hindu-India movement has shown persistent strength. Hindu nationalists have provided a focal point for political action by those involved in guru-oriented sects, with their emphasis on personal devotional enthusiasm (discussed later in this chapter), and for those middle-class Hindus now drawn to yoga centers of today (also discussed later), both of which offer different versions of "Hinduism." Nationalist politicians thus appeal to the simplest level of religious identity and arouse anti-Muslim sentiments to attract a large number of middle-class Hindus across the nation.[3] To understand better the significance of Hindu nationalism's challenge to modern secular India, we must go back to the beginning and trace the historical development of this tradition.

Premodern Hinduism: The Formative Era

The Aryans and Religion in the Vedic Era

The recounting of ancient South Asian history was once a tale of the subcontinent being invaded from the northwest by an aggressive, light-skinned people who called themselves *Aryans*; their warriors, in their horse-drawn chariots, were imagined as destroyers of the cities of the Indus Valley, a civilization as ancient as those of Egypt and Mesopotamia. After forcing their dark-skinned inhabitants to flee southward and inhabit south India, the Aryan hordes moved east and subdued the tribes they encountered across the Gangetic plain. This rendition of history was used to explain the modern distribution of "north" and "south" India as separate linguistic and racial zones. The Aryans, supposed to be militarily if not also culturally superior by these

Bull seal, Harappa, ca. 1800 BCE. Although the meaning of the zebu bull symbol here is uncertain, this animal was later regarded as the vehicle of the great god Shiva.

theorists, allegedly forced the invaded people to migrate southward over the Vindhya Mountains to settle in the lower peninsula.

Built on very forced readings of the evidence, this view of history contained a racial assumption welcomed by early European scholars and by high-caste Hindus in the modern and postcolonial era. Then, when Sanskrit, the language of Hinduism's Vedic hymns, was discovered to be an Indo-European language and so related to most languages of Europe, it was also concluded that the ancestors of the modern Hindu elite were distantly kin to the British. Western archaeologists and the British colonial government supported such research and found this imagined history attractive. British imperial apologists, in particular, welcomed support for their view of modern Indians as superstitious and modern Hindu priests as corrupt, thereby justifying their presence.

Although migration in prehistory is accepted by objective historians as a factor explaining the linguistic geography of Eurasia, scholars now find no justification for understanding *Aryan* as a racial term, and they reject utterly any suggestion that the ancient Aryans or their descendants were or are culturally superior to those living in south Asia before them. The Indus Valley cities likewise are now thought to have declined not through conquest but owing to regional climatic changes. There are also signs that the Indus Valley culture in fact contributed significantly to subsequent "Aryan" culture. Indeed, "Aryan" in social terms really had no meaning beyond designating participants in early Vedic sacrifices and festivals. By 700 BCE, "Aryan culture" had been adopted by most politically dominant groups across the Indo-Gangetic plains, but most of the religious beliefs and ritual practices of Hindus today are those recorded in texts that were composed *after* the original four Vedas, which we'll discuss more in this next section.

Vedic Religion

Vedas: collection of earliest Hindu hymns

Knowledge of early Indic religion comes from the four **Vedas**, a collection of over a thousand hymns of praise and supplication addressed to the gods, the oldest of which is the *Rig Veda*. Composed in archaic language and set in poetical form, these hymns show no systematic development, ordering, or single mythological framework. It is likely that the Vedic hymns were collected and appreciated by only the most elite social groups of that earlier millennium (1500–500 BCE).

Brahmin: highest caste, many serving as priests

Early Vedic religion was centered on the fire sacrifices (*yajna* or *homa*). The sacrifice depended on the knowledge of a special, hereditary group of priests called **brahmins**, who chanted the Vedic hymns and orchestrated highly intricate and time-consuming rituals intended to gratify the numerous Aryan deities. Accompanied by carefully cadenced chants, the brahmins placed grain, animal flesh, and clarified butter in a blazing fire, thereby transforming the offerings into fragrant smoke to nourish and please the gods. The entire universe was thought to be maintained by this sacrifice: If kept happy, well fed, and strengthened through the offerings, the deities would sustain creation and ensure the prosperity of the sacrificers.

A brahmin priest in Nepal prepares a sacrificial fire pit for his patrons.

The language of the Vedic hymns, called *Sanskrit*, was thought to be divine in origin. The hymns were memorized by brahmin priests and taught to men in succeeding generations. The Vedas existed for over two millennia in oral form; the earliest extant written manuscripts, which date back only to the eleventh century of the common era, include annotations showing proper accents and supplying ritual contexts. This very archaic tradition still is followed in scattered communities across India today.

The major deities of the Vedic world, all male, were those connected to sacrifice, martial conquest, mystical experience, and maintenance of moral order. Agni, the fire god whose flaming tongue licks the offerings, was essential for the successful ritual. The warrior deity par excellence was Indra, and he has the greatest number of hymns dedicated to him. It was Indra who subdued alien deities, and it was Indra who was called on to lead the Aryan men into battle. Soma was conceived to be a divine presence dwelling within a psychoactive substance of the same name, which was drunk by humans and deities before battle and at the end of major rituals. Another strong deity, Varuna, was thought to enforce the moral order of the universe and to mete out punishment or reward. The hymns indicate that humans approached Varuna with personal petitions for forgiveness.

Death and afterlife in the early Vedic era were envisioned as alternative destinies. There was the possibility of becoming an ancestor (*pitri*) and reaching a heavenly afterlife if one lived morally, but only if one's family, in the first after-death year, performed special memorial rituals (*shraddha*). These were designed to embody the initially disembodied spirit in its arduous journey to become, as several hymns poetically describe it, one of the twinkling evening stars. Some Vedic texts imply that the essence of a father is also born in his sons, resulting in the continuation of his life. Alternatively,

"In your offspring you are born again; That, O Mortal, is your immortality."

—Taittiriya Brahmana

SOURCE: Quoted in Patrick Olivelle, *Samnyasa Upanishads* (New York: Oxford University Press, 1992), p. v.

those whose deeds were immoral or whose families failed to do the proper shraddha rituals lost their individual identity and merely dissolved back into the earth.

Vedic religion was marked by faith in the power of the gods, ritual acts to influence them, and the spiritual resonance of Sanskrit words. The Aryans believed with absolute certainty in the primacy of their deities. But by 100 CE however, the dominant devotional tradition placed all the central deities of the earliest pantheon into minor roles: Indra is the king of the minor heavenly hosts, Agni is confined to be a guardian of ritual, Soma is seen as the deity residing in the moon, and Varuna becomes the lord of the ocean. Similarly, the Vedic concept of *rita*, the natural human order that the gods enforced, is replaced by three dominant themes in subsequent Hinduism: reincarnation, the law of karma, and the concept of **dharma** (duty).

dharma: "duty" determined by caste and gender

Karma, Yoga, and the Quest for Liberation

Scattered references in later Vedic hymns indicate that a very different spiritual orientation had entered the Aryan world. The practice of asceticism—involving retreat into the forest, silent introspection, and the cultivation of trance states—was likely the first indigenous pre-Vedic spiritual tradition absorbed into the dominant religion. Such practices found a receptive community in certain circles, and their synthesis of this spirituality emerges clearly in the **Upanishads**, the remarkable tracts that began to be appended to the Vedic hymns after 1000 BCE. The dialogues themselves and the name they are given—*upanishad* means "sitting near devotedly"—convey a context of disciples learning at the feet of masters who have gone beyond the Vedic sacrificial framework to adopt ascetic practices. These gurus developed new teachings and practices aimed at realizing the more fundamental realities underlying all existence.

Upanishads: appendices to the Vedas that record early Hindu mystical teachings

The central idea they introduced is that of **samsara**, "the world," in which all phenomena are really only secondary appearances. But blinded by illusion (*maya*), humans act foolishly and thereby suffer from samsara's pains and privations. These last until the realization dawns that the underlying reality is everywhere the same, and it is the unchanging spirit (**Brahman**). The individual soul (**atman**) wanders from birth to death again and again until it finds release from the cycle by realizing that it is nothing other than Brahman, the ultimate reality of the world, the universal spirit.[4]

samsara: "the world" of rebirth subject to the law of karma

Brahman: unchanging world spirit that arises at creation

atman: the soul, which transmigrates after death

An individual's destiny in samsara is determined by actions (deeds and thoughts) the person performs. Good deeds eventually bear good consequences, while bad deeds ripen into evil consequences. This natural law, which operates throughout samsara and affects the destiny of the atman, is called **karma**, a complex term whose meaning is often oversimplified. It is important to note that all the world religions that emerged in India accept the samsara paradigm: the "orthodox" traditions that accept the authority of the Vedas as well as the "heterodox" religions—Buddhism, Jainism, and Sikhism—that do not. Although all three hold different doctrines about the precise nature of the soul and the mechanisms of karma, each advocates specific yoga practices designed to realize the highest truth and achieve **moksha**, release from further reincarnation.

karma: "action"; effects of actions that condition a being's future

moksha: "release" from future rebirths and deaths; salvation

TEACHINGS OF RELIGIOUS WISDOM: A Maid Teaches a Holy Man How to Discern Rebirth Destiny

A certain holy man, well skilled in Brahmanical lore and who had spent his whole life in the study of the *Vedas* and other religious works, went on a journey. At the first town he entered he, . . . while resting himself [near a domicile], saw a funeral pass, . . . when, to his astonishment, he heard the mistress from within the house inquire from the maidservant as to whether the deceased had gone to heaven. Commanded to do so, the girl went out, and in a short time returned, giving an answer in the affirmative. A similar occurrence took place, but in this instance the maidservant's reply was in the negative. Lost in amazement, the sage demanded how she was able to make known the workings of karma which were to him, notwithstanding all his learning, inscrutable. The maid replied that it was an extremely easy task to ascertain the destination of departed souls . . . as it was only necessary to attend at the . . . place of cremation and listen to the opinion expressed regarding them by their neighbors. If ten of them concurred in speaking in praise of the deceased, it was almost certain that he had gone to a heavenly rebirth; if, on the contrary, they agreed in asserting that he was an evildoer, it was equally sure that he went to a worse rebirth.

Source: A. K. Ramanujan, *Folktales from India* (New Delhi: Penguin Books India, 1993), p. 55.

The teachers in the Upanishads argue that through a cosmic process that is inexplicable, this unitary ultimate reality in the world's creation became subdivided into myriad atmans. Flesh-and-blood individual human beings are ultimately transitory physical beings, and thus illusory. Atmans are the truly real entities in the world, however subtle and difficult to perceive they may be. All beings, then, have a spiritual center, sharing with one another and the forces that move the universe a common essence. This truth is stated concisely in the Chandogya Upanishad when the teacher simply states literally, "That [i.e., Brahman] thou art," or more directly, "You are divine." As we will see, it is not enough simply to know intellectually that Brahman equals atman: One must realize this truth in one's own life through the discipline called yoga.

Yoga

Yoga refers to the various sets of disciplined practices by which human beings can unify and focus their bodily powers for the purpose of realizing their true spiritual essence, the atman within. First surfacing clearly in the late Upanishads, these practices were codified in a text, the **Yoga Sutras**, attributed to a sage named Patanjali (ca. 150 BCE). The yoga meditation tradition is for the highly advanced spiritual elite, for those attempting to escape *samsara* by ending, or "burning up," all past karma.

The *Yoga Sutras* assume that yoga can be performed properly only by individuals of high moral character, who have renounced most material possessions, live

"By austerily a man achieves goodness, and through goodness he takes hold of the mind. Through the mind he reaches the self, and reaching the self he comes to rest."

—Maitreya Upanishad

SOURCE: Patrick Olivelle, *Samnyasa Upanishads* (New York: Oxford University Press, 1992), p. 160.

yoga: "union"; practices that lead to union with the divine

Yoga Sutras: ancient text codifying yoga practices, attributed to Patanjali

Seeking to discern Brahman within themselves, ancient Hindu holy men practiced many forms of austerity, as shown in this Punjabi painting of yoga positions.

in simplicity (including vegetarianism), and study the teachings regarding the "inner reality." Practice begins first with postures (*asana*) designed to make the body flexible and to awaken its energies, then develops breath control (*pranayama*) to harness and enhance the body's primal energy. After focusing the mind on a single object for long periods, the *yogin*, or adept practitioner, experiences a series of increasingly refined states of consciousness as the mind is withdrawn from external sensation. These experiences culminate in a trance state (*samadhi*). It is in samadhi that the yogin develops a direct and eventually unbroken awareness of the luminous origin of consciousness itself: the life-giving, pure, and blissful atman.

The progressive practice of yoga opens up an inner vision of the commanding reality of the soul within, thereby weakening the power of ignorance and egotistic desire that naturally distort human consciousness. The ultimate goal in yoga meditation is to dwell for extended periods in trance, reaching the highest state, *kaivalya*, an awareness that is perfectly at one with and centered in the atman. The yoga practitioner who reaches this state is said to put an end to all past karma and to experience moksha, liberation from future rebirth. This adept, freed from desire and ignorance, is thought to be omniscient and capable

OM ॐ

First appearing in the Upanishads, where it is described as the "seed sound" of all other sounds, OM (also written in full phonetic rendition as AUM) is one of the most prominent symbols of Hinduism. Repeated as part of almost every mantra for offerings and meditation as well as written calligraphically on icons and other symbols, OM has become an ever-present and multivalent symbol, often reflecting sectarian differences. Upandishadic interpretations were carried on and developed in, for example, yoga, where OM is seen as a symbol of cosmic origination and dissolution, and past-present-future-dissolution (A/U/M/ silence) in its one resonating sound. OM's components

also include all four states of consciousness in yoga theory, with A as waking, U as dreaming, M as dreamless sleep, and the syllable as a whole "the fourth." OM is the sound-form of *atman-Brahman*. Repeating OM is thus the key to meditation that leads to *moksha*. The theological schools discussed in the text have suggested yet further meanings: The three letters AUM represent Brahma, Vishnu, and Shiva; Vaishnavites identify OM with Vishnu; Shaivites see Shiva as Lord of the Dance creating from OM all the sounds for musical notes from his drum. The written OM, shown in the title bar to this box, adorns all the major deities as represented in the popular art forms.

Sadhus have been a part of the Hindu tradition for three thousand years. Wandering Hindu ascetics today adhere to a variety of paths, from the bhakti devotional devotees to yogins seeking the divine without form.

of supernormal feats, such as telepathy, clairvoyance, and extraordinary travel. This *enlightenment* experience and the capacity to know others' tendencies and thoughts makes the yogic sage an ideal spiritual guide for other religious seekers.

The great majority of Hindus from the formative period onward have oriented their religious lives around the reality of karma. Although subject to various interpretations, Hindu karma doctrine asserts that all actions performed by an individual set into motion a cause that will lead to a moral effect in the present and/or future lifetimes. This belief holds that a natural mechanism functions to make the cosmos orderly and just. One Sanskrit name for the Indian subcontinent—*karmabhumi*, "realm of karma"—reflects the doctrine's centrality in Hindu life. This has meant that inclinations to do good and avoid evil were backed up by the belief in karmic retribution for one's actions. Since old karma is coming to fruition constantly and new karma is being made continuously, it is—in most explications—incorrect to see karma doctrine as instilling an irresistible fatalism. Further, not all events in life are due to karmic accounting; Indic religious philosophies and medical theory have also recognized natural causalities as part of the human condition.

"This is the entire aim of yoga: rendering in personal experience of the Truth which universal nature had hidden in herself. . . . It is the conversion of the human soul into the divine soul and of natural life into divine living."

—Aurobindo Ghose

SOURCE: Stephen Hay, ed., *Sources of Indian Tradition*, 2nd ed., vol. 2 (New York: Columbia University Press, 1988), p. 155.

What is implicit in karma theory for typical human beings is that one's karma in daily life is in fact unknown. In practice, this uncertainty principle (similar to the belief of some Protestant Christians that no one can be certain about his or her salvation) has sustained a strong tendency for Hindus to resort to astrology for guidance at times of important decisions, such as when first to plant the fields, the choice of marriage partner, or when to set off on a journey. As Indian society developed, other ideas were tied to karma, weaving tighter the socioreligious fabric of classical Hinduism.

Premodern Hinduism: The Classical Era (180 BCE–900 CE)

There were very few periods in South Asian history when transcontinental empires unified the subcontinent. The first great empire was that of the Mauryas (300–180 BCE), whose emperors helped to spread Buddhism and its ideal of compassion as a principle of just rule. As Buddhism expanded and thrived, it competed with early brahmin-led traditions.

Classical Hinduism, the product of response to Buddhism by the orthodox brahmin priests and spiritual teachers, absorbed and synthesized aspects of this missionary faith while also embracing pre-Aryan deities and other indigenous Indic traditions. As a result, nonviolence and vegetarianism became ideals of high-caste religiosity, Hindu monasteries for training and meditation were begun, and a distinctive theistic dimension of Hinduism (not part of early Buddhism) found vast elaboration and increasingly popular acceptance. Classical Hinduism in North India reaches a mature synthesis in the Gupta dynasty (320–647 CE), when wealth and the cultural expressions of devotional Hinduism flowered in all the fine arts. This tradition was so compelling that by 1200 CE, Hinduism had slowly absorbed the Buddha within its panoply of gods and Buddhism had virtually disappeared from South Asia except for the Himalayan (Nepal) and Sri Lankan peripheries. Brahmin literati in the classical age composed Sanskrit literature that codified and disseminated expressions of this new synthesis in the realms of philosophy, theology, and law. These texts and leaders gave the subcontinent a source of unity through one fundamental paradigm: An individual's place in society is defined in terms of karma.

"Early Heterodox" Indic Religions: Jainism and Buddhism

By 700 BCE, the religious movements that had emerged in South Asia were especially diverse. Most were organized around brahmin teachers, who set themselves to the task of reinterpreting the Vedic sacrifice or finding new ascetic methods to experience the ultimate reality, what many called Brahman. Most of these teachers taught that the Veda was sacred and formed the bedrock of all revelation; from this time onward, the traditions that adopt this view, and that accept the legitimacy of caste and brahmin priesthood, have been regarded by traditional scholars as "orthodox" Hindu schools.

But there were other charismatic teachers who formed organized Indic religions who did not accept the Veda, adopt orthodox caste ideology, or revere brahmins as innately superior beings. They regarded brahmin ascetics that were still concerned with cosmic order and social hierarchy as deluded. These great, separate, heterodox religions—first Jainism and Buddhism in ancient times, and then Sikhism by 1520—become world religions in their own right. Significantly, each was founded by members of the warrior caste; and each consciously shaped a community of elite disciples who carried forward the movement, insuring its long-term survival; and each developed its own distinctive spiritual practices that won the loyalty of communities of warriors and merchants. Buddhism is covered in the next chapter, and Sikhism later in this chapter. We now turn our attention to Jainism.

Jainism: The Tradition of Spiritual Conquerors

Among the many seekers who retreated to the forests of ancient north India, were some totally committed to liberation from death and rebirth. Texts recount certain groups of wanderers who experimented with every variety of practice to reach that goal, discarding what did not serve their purpose. Little is known about most of these seekers; aside from the names scattered in the Upanishads, the only accounts that survive are those of the few successful religions that emerged in this era, Buddhism and Jainism. The former, the most successful, is the subject of the next chapter; the latter, Jainism, is one that has survived until the present day. Found now in parts of India, as well as in small communities in East Africa, England, and North America, Jainism is a minor world religion, with between 5–8 million followers today.

Jain tradition records the existence of twenty-four sages who have realized the true nature of the world and discovered the only path to overcome human bondage in it. These sages are called Tirthankaras "ford finders," whose name refers to those places called "fords" where crossing to the other shore of the river is shallow and easiest. The last two Tirthankaras are key, Parsavanath (ca. 850 BCE) and Mahavira (599–527 BCE). The latter was influenced by the former, and both are revered for attaining release (moksha) from samsara by adopting a rigorous ascetic life that included naked wandering and fasting.

Like all the sages in this era, the Jain saints believed in samsara and in release from it, moksha. Their precise understanding of these is distinctive, however, compared to the other great Indic religions. This world, they agree, is suffering, harsh, and ultimately meaningless; unlike Hindu and Buddhist philosophy, however, samsara is real in a material sense, and not an illusion. The Jains regard the only solution is to escape it and their sages taught that only through non-action can individuals find true happiness.

This non-action is particularly grounded in stopping any practice in life that involves killing in any form, intentional or not. Hence, Jains describe their path as *ahimsa paramo dharma*, "non-killing is the supreme path."

Like the Upanishadic teachers, Jains regard the soul (jiva) as the repository of all deeds. Although in itself a pure, crystalline entity, the soul is caught in a karmic trap, blackened due to killing done in this and previous lives, intentional or not. It is this killing karma residue that corrupts spiritual awareness. Total non-violence in thought, word, deed dissolves this precipitate; non-interference in all worldly connections is the only way to end even subtle violence. The religious life of Jain householders seeks to limit new karma; the religious occupation of monks and nuns is more intensive, seeking to stop making any new karma and rapidly burn up the residue of the old.

Purification of this past underlies all Jain practices, whether for the householder majority, who undertake periodic fasts or periods of renunciation, or those who dedicate themselves to attain the highest goal of *samyak darshan*, "complete intuition" into the world's workings, a momentous awakening. All Jains seek to develop "detachment and forgiveness," a mind that cultivates self-control and renunciation, as stated in verses called the *micchami dukkadam* that are commonly recited in community rituals:

> We forgive all living beings
> We seek pardon from all living beings
> We are friendly toward all living beings
> And we seek enmity from no one.

Jains believe that to achieve moksha requires taking monastic vows, and so with community support the elite undertake more austere fasting, meditation, and scripture study. These three cause past karma to ripen prematurely and end karma quickly. In the ancient past, and as is still seen today, a Jain monk occasionally undertakes *Sallekhana*, a fast unto death leading to final complete detachment from the body, the end of all karma, and moksha.

After Mahavira's death, the Jain community of monks and householders developed and spread, attracting the patronage of ancient Indic kings. But around 310 BCE, the community split due to differences in interpretations of the rules of asceticism and the role of women, and what were the authoritative texts. Some moved south, to Gujarat and Rajasthan; they called themselves the Digambara ("Sky-clad") who require male monastic nakedness. This group believes the true texts were lost and so rely on treatises called the Prakaranas. Those who remained in the north called themselves the Svetambara ("White clad monks"). They held that their texts were valid, most notably the Kalpa Sutra. Women are given a full spiritual place, and up until the present day, nuns far outnumber Svetambara monks. From antiquity until the modern era, these two groups developed in isolation. Despite some points of difference, their commonalities are large, especially in holding the view that only monastics can reach moksha.

By the fifth century CE, Jains began building temples housing images of the Tirthankaras; these included shrines to some Indic gods as well. Jains (like the Buddhists, as we'll see) viewed gods not as world creators or sustainers, but merely as powerful beings still bound by karma who are destined to return for future rebirth. From this time, Jains cautiously integrated their religious tradition in the wider Hindu society: gods affecting worldly life could be worshipped by Jain householders, even in Hindu temples; caste hierarchy was accepted, but Jains rejected the doctrine that brahmins were born as spiritually superior human beings. Jinasena, the ninth century CE Jain philosopher, justified these accommodations, and even adapted for the Jains a system of life cycle rites based on Brahmanical precedents.

Jainism thus found a niche in the religious pluralism of South Asia over the last millennium. Jain businessmen—who worked hard, consumed modestly, emphasized education, and were masters of accommodation—have been extremely successful in many enterprises and served as lavish patrons of their faith, securing its future.

The Reality of Karma and Caste

As we have seen, the idea of karma provided a way of explaining the destiny of a being according to its moral past. Evil deeds lead to evil destiny, and vice versa; people get what they deserve, although not necessarily in a single lifetime. This idea of karmic retribution had become widely accepted by the classical era, and brahmin social thinkers built on it to formulate the basis of the ideal Hindu society in a series of texts called the *Dharmashastras* (*Treatises on Dharma*). These texts, the most famous of which is known by the English title *The Laws of Manu*, make a series of arguments about karma while also charting practices and social policies designed to keep the world in order.

The *Dharmashastras* assume that one's birth location is the most telling indication of one's karma. They also argue that high-status birth gives one a higher spiritual nature, reflecting one's good karma past. Rebirth, then, is assumed to fall into regular patterns, and this natural process justifies seeing society, like the animal kingdom, as broken down into groups with very separate natures and capacities. These groups have come to be called *castes* in English; the Sanskrit word for them is *jati*.

Hindu law codes became the basis of Indian law in the early classical period. They prescribed that those born into a caste should marry within that group. Such individuals were believed to have closely matching karma so that if they segregated themselves to bear and raise children, reincarnation patterns should be maintained consistently and clearly. Those born into a caste were also expected to perform the traditional tasks of that group. The four main groups were called *varnas*, or classes: *brahmins*, who were to master the Vedic and ritual practice; *kshatriyas*, who were to rule justly and protect society, especially the brahmins; *vaishyas*, who were to specialize in artisanship and trade, multiplying the wealth of the society; and *shudras*, the workers needed to perform laborious and menial tasks for those in the upper jatis.

The *Dharmashastras* also identify the top three classes as *dvija*, or twice born, meaning "born again" through a Vedic initiation. Groups despised by the higher castes, such as *chandalas*, were assigned to perform polluting tasks, such as street sweeping and carrying dead bodies. Under each varna, hundreds of caste subgroups were arrayed, and to this day these vary regionally in their surnames and specific social functions. It is also important to note that in antiquity (as in real life today), intercaste marriages, political events, and local history resulted in much more social flexibility than is prescribed in the brahmanical texts.

Each caste was thought to have a singular proper duty to perform in life; the term for this, *dharma*, is central throughout the subsequent history of Hinduism. The *Dharmashastra* texts argue that one must live in accordance with one's place in the world, which has been assigned from all earlier lives. Only by doing so does one make the good karma needed to move "upward" in samsara. As one passage in *The Laws of Manu* [10:97] warns, "Better to do one's own dharma badly than another caste's dharma well." This also implied that women should always be subordinate to men.

Hindu religious law, therefore, does not see all human beings as having the same social and religious status or as being subject to the same legal standards. While religious views underlie this system of social inequality, Hindu social theorists argued that in the fullness of time—beyond a single-lifetime framework—samsara and its law of karmic retribution allow for certain, inescapable cosmic justice, matching karmic past to social function. In the end, every soul will move upward through samsara to be reborn as a brahmin male and reach liberation. Individual freedom is sacrificed for harmony and for society's ultimate and eventual collective liberation.

Thus, in theory, the religious underpinning of the caste system has served to legitimate the social hierarchy beyond Vedic times. It preserves the purity and privileges of the highest castes and argues that society depends on brahmins: If they live in purity and use their ritual mastery to worship the gods properly, they ensure that divine grace will sustain a fruitful society and a nonthreatening environment.

Consistent with this belief system, high-caste Hindus view their superior status as based upon exemplary actions in previous lives. As we shall see, this sanctioning of high-caste privilege had early critics among Buddhists and Jains and, later, among Sikhs as well. Modern reformers from the lowest social groups point out that these Hindu doctrines were (and are) a metaphysical justification for the high-caste minority to rule over the low-caste majority. As Bhimrao Ambedkar, one of the legal reformers of the early twentieth century, stated,

> To the Untouchables, Hinduism is a veritable chamber of horrors. The sanctity and infallibility of the *Vedas* . . . the iron law of caste, the heartless law of *karma*, and the senseless law of status by birth are to the Untouchables veritable instruments of torture which Hinduism has forged against the Untouchables.[5]

The classical Hindu writers also prescribed other endeavors to realize the ideal Hindu life. To explain the extraordinarily precise attention shown to detail and to the ideal human lifetime, we must consider the individual's quest to fulfill his or her dharma fully.

The Four Stages of Life

The male becomes a full person only after he has passed through the first of four stages, known as the student; the prescribed life then proceeds to that of the householder, the forest dweller, and the homeless wanderer (*sadhu*). A student studies in the house of his teacher, learning to the extent appropriate to his caste and individual aptitude a curriculum that formerly included memorizing major portions of Vedas as well as acquiring proficiency in archery, medicine, astrology, and music. Upon completing the student phase, a man returns to be married; as a householder, his duty is to perform the traditional rites and raise children in the proper manner to continue the father's lineage. The *Dharmashastras* require women to subordinate themselves to men, although husbands are supposed to respect their wives and maintain happiness within the household. Marriage is treated as a sacrament, and divorce is not allowed.

Once a couple notices their hair turning white, "sees their son's sons," and finds the household well handled by their male descendants, they are directed to become forest dwellers. In this stage, they focus on spiritual matters by retreating to the forest, living only on wild foods and with bare necessities; they renounce sensuality and sex, with rituals and meditation becoming their chief concern. The fourth portion of life, the homeless wanderer, builds on the third, on the supposition that knowledge and discipline have led the forest dweller to the gateway of moksha realization. Persons now wander alone; no rituals need be done, and they renounce all but what can be carried, as the remaining days are devoted to pilgrimages to holy sites and to yoga practice. From the classical era onward, the widespread dissemination of teachings about caste and stages in life, called *varnashrama Dharma*, has given "Hindu doctrine" its area of strongest consensus.

A sadhu Hindu ascetic, coated in ash, consults a ritual text.

The Four Aims of Life

Since individuals differ in their karma-determined capabilities according to caste and stage of life, the classical Hindu theorists in the *Dharmashastras* also identified four legitimate aims or ends that could be the focus of legitimate, divinely prescribed human striving.

The first, *artha*, can be translated as material gain or worldly success. South Asian folk literature of animal stories and human parables imparts instructions toward this goal in life, an indication that belief in karma has never stifled pious Hindus' interest in "getting ahead."

The second aim, *kama* ("sensory pleasure"), was seen as an acceptable goal for embodied beings, especially householders seeking to fulfill the duty of propagating the family line. Many in the West have seen the *Kama Sutra*, a text that treats the cultivation of sexual pleasure explicitly, but many chapters are devoted to achieving "the good life" in many other spheres as well.

The third aim, *dharma*, fulfilling the duty prescribed by one's caste, we have already discussed; the other ends of life are justly pursued only if they remain consistent with one's caste and gender-appropriate duties.

The last of the four goals, *moksha*—release from the cycle of future rebirth and redeath—is adopted by few, but the texts counsel that true ascetics pursuing this goal should receive everyone's respect and support through almsgiving. Hindus still venerate the sadhu saints, who follow this path of spiritual wandering.

Epics and the Development of Classical Hinduism

For the majority of Hindus, the ideals of the law books, the theologies of classical Hinduism, and the models for religious life are conveyed in the sacred stories and by characters of the great epics. By the classical era, the two great Hindu epics had been composed from oral sources that doubtless originated in heroic accounts of early battles fought by warriors in the Aryan clans. The longer of the two, the *Mahabharata*, records an escalating and ultimately devastating feud between rival sides of a family as they vied for control of the northern plains, each one aided by supernatural allies. The moral element of this story—one side has usurped power from the other, but the rightful heir has no desire to shed the blood of his kin to take it back—is explored with great subtlety. The *Mahabharata* conveys the existential dilemmas of Hindu life, its characters encountering moral issues in family relations, gender conflicts, caste duty versus individual wishes, and so on. Through textual recitations, dance dramas, art, and now comic books, Hindus have "dwelled in these stories" and subplots. This rivalry ended in a war of immense carnage that in theological interpretation marks the onset of the current age, the **Kali Yuga**. The *Mahabharata* and its most famous portion, called the **Bhagavad Gita**, allowed for diverse and nuanced evaluations of dharma, especially that pertaining to warriors, kin, and women and regarding the role of divinity in human affairs. The epic reveals the many difficulties, paradoxes, and ambiguities that face those who wish to apply the lofty religious ideals of the *Dharmashastra* to often-gritty and ambiguous real-life circumstances.

The same quality of "speaking with many voices" is true of the second great epic, the *Ramayana*. Here, the underlying historical circumstance is the rivalry between one Aryan clan—symbolized by the hero Rama—and the non-Aryans of the south, portrayed as powerful demons subject to unbridled lust, immorality, and disrespect for Vedic sacrifices. Invoking the forces of nature and his animal allies, Rama does succeed in defeating the demon Ravana and establishing a unified Hindu kingdom. The tale has proven very malleable in giving groups across South (and Southeast) Asia a narrative to express their own views on ethnic relations, the good king, gender relations, and the relationship between northerners and southerners. In fact, there is

Kali Yuga: the dark age in which the world is currently

Bhagavad Gita: Hindu scripture extolling the divinity of Krishna; part of the epic *Mahabharata*

no one *Ramayana* today, for through its telling and retellings hundreds of groups have claimed their particular version as sacred and central to their own Hindu ideal.

Mainstream Hinduism and the Rise of Devotion to the Great Deities

Most of the deities who became the focus of Hindu devotional life by the classical age differed in name and conception from those of the earliest Vedic hymns. An entirely new collection of Sanskrit texts, called **puranas**, was composed to extol the glories of these great gods, specify their forms of worship, and celebrate the early saints who cultivated divine love for them. The purana stories recount examples of human incarnation, instances of divine omniscience, and episodes of grace. Heroes in these stories become models of exemplary devotional faith, or **bhakti**. Just as Hanuman the monkey king serves Rama and Radha the consort loves Krishna without limit, so should one devote the full commitment of heart and mind to one's own bhakti practice.

puranas: texts extolling glories of Hindu deities

bhakti: devotionalism to a Hindu divinity

All the puranas—which many Hindus revere today as the "fifth Veda"—share an important assumption about humanity living in the Kali Yuga, the post-Vedic age: This era, said to have begun in 3102 BCE, is defined as the period of degeneration, in which human spiritual potential is declining. The puranas declare that the deities have extended their grace to humanity in ever-increasing measure in return for their devotees' unselfish devotion to them: While the ascetic practices of yoga do not end (and not all Hindus accepted Kali Yuga theory), this ideal of bhakti became the predominant one for Hinduism from the classical era until the present day.

Hinduism's shift toward bhakti follows its characteristic "add-on pattern" in merging a new theology with the fundamental ideas of the formative era: samsara, karma, and moksha. The devotional tradition accepts the early cosmic model but builds on it by asserting that the great deities, such as Shiva, Vishnu, and Durga, have the power to reward devotion by altering the karma of the *bhakta* (devotee). Though these deities are omnipotent and omniscient, they are usually seen as augmenting the earlier tradition, not challenging it. By absorbing human karma, they can bring their grace to persons seeking liberation from worldly suffering and ultimately from samsara. This view is most dramatically expressed in the *Bhagavad Gita,* where the deity Krishna argues that desireless action is possible only through egoless bhakti faith and that the true suspension of all action (which produces additional karma) is impossible.

By the classical era, purana texts asserted the existence of 330 million deities. How could the theologians account for such mind-numbing diversity? The bhakti saints and theologians argued that the existence of countless gods reflects the grace of the divine, since the diverse needs of a humanity comprising innumerable individual karmas could only be met be a diverse set of gods. The crucial goal facing each Hindu is to find and focus on the one deity whose form is most appropriate to his or her level of spiritual maturity.

The common principle of simplification in later Hinduism was that each devotee should choose a personal deity (*ista deva*) to be at the center of his or her religious life, a focus for personal communion through an emotional relationship. Although most teachers (and families) believed that "good Hindus" should respect all the great deities as well as the lesser spirits thought to dwell in each locality, it was nonetheless essential for each person to establish a single divinity to meditate on and to venerate as a channel for grace. Among theologians, the terms and mechanisms of liberation vary; in many of the puranas, rebirth in one's chosen deity's heaven—not exit from samsara—is proclaimed as the highest human goal.

The concept of "chosen deity" entailed commitment to knowing extensively and loving selflessly that particular god. This meant making offerings (*puja*, to be discussed later in this chapter), meditating, and studying the purana stories to be able to discern as completely as possible the divine personality. One formula for the stages of bhakti progress described the stages of devotion, moving from listening, singing, and worshipping to achieve an existential self-surrender that leads to liberation from samsara.

A linga, the image commonly used to worship Shiva.

Each of the great deities of Hinduism has come to be known through the purana texts, and theologians provide different explanations for how and why the divine beings have manifested themselves to save humanity from mundane dangers and to bestow ultimate liberation. It is noteworthy that for many on the bhakti path, rebirth in the heaven of their respective divinity became their highest goal, not the vague, difficult-to-comprehend moksha of the yogins or philosophers. In the following sections we'll examine the great deities in more detail, starting with Ganesh.

Ganesh

Judged by the number of shrines and the universality of his image, the elephant-headed Ganesh is the tradition's most popular divinity. Most Hindus worship Ganesh not as a divinity who will help them achieve liberation but more to secure his aid in worldly life. With a potbelly and love of sweets signaling his sensual orientation, Ganesh, who is commonly honored with offerings at the start of most rituals and journeys, is regarded as the kind, "fix-it" god in the pantheon.

Shiva

Shaivite: devotee of Shiva

The **Shaivite**, or one whose chosen deity is Shiva, focuses on two beliefs: that Shiva's essence is found in all creative energies that saturate this world, and that one can find one's own divine nature by dedicating bhakti practice to this lord. Shiva's identity in the puranas merges opposing sides of Hindu life: He is the ideal ascetic revered by yogins, the god who in the Himalayas underwent long penances while dwelling with cobras, clad in deer skin, and covered in ash. Also conceived as a divine householder, Shiva marries the goddess of the snow mountains (Parvati) and fathers the divine sons Ganesh and Kumar.

In Hindu legend, Shiva saves the world repeatedly and requites devotion with his grace. However, Shiva also has a wrathful side and will punish humans as well. The puranas attribute to Shiva the periodic cosmic upheavals that return the universe to a formless, empty resting state. The sectarian Shaivite theologians see the linking of world creation, fertility, and destruction as signifying Shiva's omnipresence, making him the supreme "Great God."

Vishnu and His Avataras

Although they may respect Shiva, Vishnu devotees (**Vaishnavites**) believe that their chosen deity is the one who truly underlies all reality. Vishnu alone is mentioned in the Vedas. He alone sleeps atop the cosmic ocean in the universe's eras of dissolution, and he alone begets the god Brahma, who then begins another cycle of creation.

Vaishnavite: devotee of Vishnu

The great theme of Vishnu theology is that of incarnation. The puranas dedicated to him recount many episodes in the earth's history when demons or evil threatened creation. At these times, Vishnu assumed the form of whatever was needed to smash the threat. Some of these incarnations, or **avataras**, were animals and most were local heroes.

avatara: incarnation of a god that descends to earth to assist creation and fight evil

Vishnu remains alive and connected to the human community of devotees through temple icons and rituals and through the singing of songs recounting his greatness. The texts also sense his being poised for humanity's future liberation, and one avatara, Kalki, is expected to come riding on a white horse to guide humanity as the Kali Yuga turns darker.

Avatara theory thus provides the most systematic example of Hinduism's theological pattern that spawned a profusion of sects, moving readily from the acceptance of multiple particular deities to arrange them in ordered hierarchies. But most Hindus, whether intellectuals or commoners, will assent to the same theological understanding, namely, that "ultimately all the gods are one." There is also a long history of Hindus (and Buddhists) refraining from staking out one final dogmatic position, since many traditions hold that Ultimate Reality is beyond all human naming or philosophical comprehension. Accepting this limitation has given Hinduism its flexible strength and its adherents an openness to ongoing revelation.

Bearing a mace, a discus, and a conch, Vishnu is represented as Lord of the Universe.

Rama

We have already encountered Rama, hero of the *Ramayana*, who slays the demon Ravana and reveals the ideal of proper filial obedience to parents, loyalty to brothers, and the exemplary conduct of Hindu kings. His alliance with

shakti: innate, creative
force of this universe,
understood as feminine

shaktas: devotees of
Devi

the monkey leader Hanuman also signals the ideal of harmonizing the divine with the natural world. A second form of Rama is one dedicated to destroying any evil kings who would molest brahmins or their rituals.

Krishna

The most complex and multifaceted of the Vishnu avataras, Krishna is revered in many forms: the infant trickster god, whose every prank and every gesture reveal his underlying divinity; the child who as "the butter thief" also steals the hearts of the world's mothers and fathers; the brave youth who rescues villagers from the poison of evil serpent deities (*nagas*) and from the cruel rains sent by the Vedic god Indra; and the divine paramour and consort of the female cowherds (*gopis*). Finally, Krishna is the mature guru who offers counsel about the necessity of serving the world according to one's dharma, clarifying choices among the many spiritual practices. Many of his sectarian devotees believe that Krishna is in fact the reality from which all the gods originate.

The Devis

The consolidating pattern in Hindu theology is readily apparent in the development of the myths of the goddess. Hindu goddesses are born of the earth and can bestow its wealth. Rivers are all goddesses. Early Indian art depicts the fertile, creative power of the universe in scenes where a young woman touches a tree, her innate energy (**shakti**) causing it to burst into bloom. Those who predominantly worship goddesses are thereby called **shaktas**, and theirs is the third general group among Hindu deity worshippers, alongside Vaishnavites and Shaivites.

The earth goddess may be addressed as Ambika ("Mother"), Sita ("[born of the] tilled furrow"), or Sati ("the Virtuous"). All these forms draw on the creative, mothering female force. Another widespread and primordial sense of female divinity is that associated with destruction; this has been primarily in the form of the smallpox goddess, called in the north Shitala or Ajima (so vibrant is this devi theology today that with the disappearance of this disease, Shitala has become the deity to appeal to against the rising scourge of HIV/AIDS).

Yet other related female forms are the goddesses who destroy demons, Durga and Kali. Those needing to confront death to arrive at mature spirituality can make Kali their "chosen deity": To visualize the dance

Durga, riding her vehicle, the tiger, carries the weapons of the male gods.

The Dance of Shiva

One of the most lyrical and evocative symbols of Hinduism, especially in the sweeping design of South Indian artisans, is that of Nataraja, Shiva as Lord of the Dance. The upper right hand holds the twin-sided drum, from which sacred sound emerges, counting time and originating sound's creative resonance. The opposite hand holds a flame; Shiva's holding a fire points to his being a refuge to followers in the fires of *samsara*. Fire also alludes to this deity's role as destroyer at the end of a great world era. Both hands move together in Shiva's great dance, ceaselessly integrating cosmic creation and destruction, including all the gods. Another hand shows the "fear-not" gesture, and the fourth points to his upraised foot, the place Hindu devotees touch most often in ritual. Shiva dances while treading on a demon who symbolizes delusion. Thus, to enter into the Dance of Shiva means to brave the circle of rebirth, transcend the limitations of time and apparent opposites, and join with the divine powers of the great deity whose grace and eternal energy can remove spiritual obstacles. Because the cosmos has become a manifestation of Shiva's power, a dance done simply for the purpose of his own entertainment, wherever individuals can cultivate artistic pleasure, they can find union with Shiva.

Shiva Nataraja, Lord of the Dance: twelfth-century bronze image from southern India.

of Kali means seeing that life inevitably becomes encircled by death and so always keeping in mind that the gift of human life should not be frittered away. Devotional communion with Durga and Kali requires bhaktas to offer them life blood through animal sacrifice to secure their blessings.

Hindu theology also views the pantheon as balancing the distinct powers that are uniquely those of male and female. The cosmos, like the human species, is seen as created and sustained by the same combination of gender energies: the male shakta and the female shakti. Each is incomplete and even dangerous without the balancing influence of the other. Thus, most of the Hindu deities are married. Shiva is married to Parvati, or Uma, Vishnu to Lakshmi (important as the wealth goddess), Brahma to Saraswati (goddess of learning), Krishna to Radha, Rama to Sita, and so on. We shall see later how tantric Hinduism carries the implications of this theology into individual yoga practice.

Premodern Hinduism: The Postclassical Era (900 CE–1500 CE)

The Formation of Major Hindu Schools of Thought

During the late classical era, the brahmin elite concerned with philosophical views (called *darshana*) consolidated their positions in systematic expositions, which became and have remained authoritative for the tradition. Every school's texts sought to explain the nature of the physical world, the boundaries of individuality, the basis for establishing human knowledge, and the means to liberation. All told, these texts and the epics comprise an extraordinarily large sacred literary tradition.

The orthodox schools formed in response to the heterodox, or nonstandard, schools of Buddhism and Jainism. Some of them were confined to small circles of high-caste scholastics, but the others, discussed here, came to dominate the Hindu intellectual tradition.

Sankhya

One of the oldest systematic philosophy schools to appear, and closely aligned to the yoga classical school, the Sankhya school's ideas were especially important in subsequent Hindu thought. The Sankhya school (literally, "analysis") posits a dualistic universe of matter (*prakriti*) bonded in various combinations with spirit (*purusha*). Both matter and spirit are eternal, with an infinite number of purushas eternally distinct from one another.

Sankhya admits the reality of gods but denies the existence of a transcendent, personal God. The purpose of spiritual life is isolating purusha from prakriti. Although its goal is to go beyond the material world, the Sankhya nonetheless developed a powerful analysis of material formations, specifying twenty-five *gunas*, the qualities by which matter can be clearly understood. Sankhya's differentiation of spirit-matter combinations, which has informed Hindu culture to the present, is applied to the analysis of human personality, gender, species, the seasons, aesthetics, medicine, and even foods.

One typical use of Sankhya theory is to assess the spiritual status of human beings. All beings are combinations of three primary material qualities or "strands" that bind spirit to the material world: *sattva* (associated with purity, goodness, subtlety), *rajas* (passion, raw energy), and *tamas* (darkness, inertia, grossness). In the Sankhya view, too, even the gods are qualitatively similar to humans, different only by having more sattva. This school thereby sees the incarnation of divinities in human form as part of the universe's natural processes.

Advaita Vedanta

The Advaita Vedanta school is monistic; that is, it regards the singular reality of the universe as impersonal spirit, a view that draws on the Upanishads' formula Brahman = atman. This school of thought began at the time of the Buddha and became the prevailing scholastic philosophy of South Asia after 500 CE, and it is most often emphasized by modern Hindu reformers. Advaita Vedanta's enduring central place among Hindu philosophies was due to the brilliance of the great religious virtuoso **Shankara** (ca. 788–820). His succinct commentaries and original treatises received additional exposure through public debates with proponents of other schools (including Buddhists).

Shankara argued that the apparent difference between the material and physical worlds is pure illusion (*maya*). Only study and yoga practice can enable a seeker to gain true knowledge, reversing the "superimposition" on pure spirit of deluded perceptions of two worlds. This path the Vedantins called *jnana yoga*, "union through discriminating knowledge."

Shankara admitted that one could in elementary and intermediate stages of spiritual development relate to Brahman as a personal divinity with characteristics (*sa-guna*) such as power and grace (**saguna Brahman**). But ultimately, moksha can be achieved only by going beyond this projection of a deity in terms of human characteristics to experience Brahman by merging one's own soul with **nirguna Brahman**, that reality "without characteristics."

Shankara also organized the first great network of Hindu monasteries (*mathas*) that supported male ascetics whose rule of conduct specified vegetarianism, dress in an ochre robe, use of a walking staff, and horizontal forehead markings. At monasteries established originally at Dvaraka in the west, Puri in the east, Badrinath in the north, and Shringeri in the south, this order grew, expanded, and survives to this day.

The Theology of Qualified Monism: Vishishta Advaita

While Shankara's monistic thought and practice appealed to intellectuals and ascetics, it was quite distant from the religious experience of most devotees who revered the gods. It remained for later theologians, particularly **Ramanuja** (ca. 1025–1137), to link scholastic theology with popular theistic practice. Ramanuja argued that human beings could not really recognize the divine, except in the perceivable world. Why? Since Brahman pervades all reality, the religious path to moksha cannot and need not proceed beyond saguna Brahman. Like Shankara, Ramanuja wrote his own commentary on the Upanishads, but he reached a very different theistic conclusion about their ultimate spiritual truth. He emphasized Vishnu as the form of Brahman most effectively worshipped.

Ramanuja asserted that each individual is ultimately a fragment of Vishnu, wholly dependent on him, and that a perfect continuous intuition of this could be realized only through concentrated and intense devotion (*bhakti yoga*). This theology also holds that souls do not ultimately merge with Brahman, maintaining a "separate nondifference," even in moksha.

Tantric Hinduism

Post–classical era Hinduism produced two major innovations: sectarian monasticism and **tantra**. Like the bhakti theology already mentioned, the tantric tradition built on

Shankara: influential Hindu philosopher, advocating the impersonal ultimate reality

saguna Brahman: human form of the world spirit

nirguna Brahman: impersonal form of the world spirit

Ramanuja: Influential theologian who emphasized worship of Vishnu

Shri Yantra, symbol of the goddess used in meditation.

tantra: esoteric practices leading to moksha

earlier ideas and practices but advocated new forms of spiritual experience. The name *tantra* relates to weaving, signifying "warp and woof," in this case likely indicating the interweaving of teaching and texts. The emergence of tantra can be seen in both Hinduism and Buddhism, indicating how thoroughly these later traditions affected each other.

Tantric teachers accepted Kali Yuga theory, and their texts typically begin by underscoring how the tantric path to liberation in this lifetime is suited for the Kali Yuga age, when individuals and the world itself are in spiritual decline. The assumption is that what worked for the Vedic sages is too subtle for today. Similarly, what was then prohibited to the seeker is precisely what is needed today for spiritual breakthrough. Still, tantric teachings are not given openly or universally, but are bestowed by teachers only to those deemed capable of practicing methods that, as we shall see, contradict the dharma-based morality of the upper castes. The method of transmitting the teachings from guru to student, of course, goes back to the ancient period. However, the vows not to reveal to noninitiates the lessons of the teacher are more highly restrictive than in earlier practice.

There are many tantric traditions, each deriving from an enlightened saint called a **siddha**, who discovered in an intensive personal quest a method of meditation and understanding that culminates in moksha. This personal lineage was passed down in small circles following specific beliefs and practices derived from the original master.

siddha: tantric saint

The six centers of the tantric body, displayed in relation to a yogin.

All the tantric paths are rooted in the ancient yoga traditions we have discussed. *Tantric yoga*, too, regards the body as a microcosm of the universe; adepts believe that all bodily energies, if harnessed and focused, are capable of producing a transformative religious experience. What is distinctive in tantric yoga is that the primal energies of male and female become essential and focal. Thus, tantra incorporated the devotional worship of female deities in union with their consorts. Many tantric teachings prescribe the practice of ritualized sexual union during which both partners visualize themselves as divinities, cultivating in each other an enlightened awakening through the transformative energy that arises through their union. The goal is realization of the one blissful spirit that is beyond gender and is universal.

Most tantric traditions invite practitioners to experience this ultimate reality, one that can be found only by suspending the norms imposed by Hindu social law and caste-determined individual conduct. Tantric yoga entails mastering complex rituals and practices that invert status and gender hierarchy norms, breaking down a person's construction of his or her identity on such conventional lines. Thus, one can select a tantric partner from a lower caste, and practitioners perform rituals designed to transform their inner being, ingesting foods such as meat, fish, and alcohol that are otherwise unacceptable for high-caste groups. Places of tantric practice include cremation grounds, the most polluted ritual sites; ritual implements include human bones and skulls. The sexual yoga and the use of gruesome items shocked orthodoxy, but they were deployed for the highly traditional goal of freeing the individual's mind to realize moksha.

Ritualized sexual union in Hindu tantra seeks to arouse an otherwise-dissipated primal power conceived of as a serpent coiled at the base of the spine; this force, called the *kundalini*, is made to rise up the spine through a series of centers (*cakras*), visualized as wheels or lotuses. These centers are found proximate to the genitals, navel, heart, throat, eyes, forehead, and top of the skull. If the energy can be raised to this topmost center, the "thousand-petaled lotus," one's spirit is perfected and a host of supernormal powers unfold. The unorthodox practices and extraordinary experiences were thought to be dangerous for those unready for them; this made the siddha teachers wary of instructing unproven individuals and led them to prescribe dire penalties for any initiate who revealed anything about tantric practice to outsiders.

While early on tantra grew to become a "counterculture" juxtaposed against orthodox Hinduism, its influence slowly grew, even among the high castes. Later, tantric ideas shaped Hindu life-cycle rites and temple ritualism, as priests over the centuries who had delved into tantric practice revised ancient rituals to be multidimensional, keeping the older outward practices and adding meaning for the general public as well as communicating inner truths for those attuned to esoteric tantric symbolisms.

The Early Islamic Era: Delhi Sultanate (1192–1525)

Soon after the conversion of central Asian and Turkic peoples to Islam in the first centuries after the death of the Prophet Muhammad (632 CE), Muslim converts came to South Asia, and the region began to absorb Islamic influences. Muslim traders enhanced transregional trade, settled in caravan and port towns. They built mosques, and eventually brought religious scholars and clerical authorities to guide the slowly growing Islamic communities. Missionaries preaching the tolerant and mystical tradition of Sufi Islam won an especially strong reception in some quarters. The conquest of northern India by Ghuride armies from central Asia (1192) defeated the Hindu kings. This conquest was the most devastating to Buddhists, whose already-declining monasteries on the Gangetic plain were leveled and whose monks fled to bordering lands.

Over 500 years of Muslim rule followed, an era of increasingly centralized government. In many areas, Muslims displaced kshatriyas as heads of regional states; in many other places, Hindu rulers continued as their vassals. The Delhi Sultanate included the northern sections of modern Pakistan and India, from the Indus to the Upper Ganges. In general, authorities of the sultanate did not attempt to regulate indigenous traditions in their own regions or in kshatriya-ruled states, and Hindu traditions continued. Indeed, the great bhakti saints who rose to prominence in this era have dominated the popular Hindu devotional imagination ever since. Some, called *bhaktas* (including

"In men of animal nature, Shakti sleeps, but for tantrics she is wide awake. He who serves shakti is the 'true worshipper.' Whoever knows the rapture of the soul's union with the ultimate is the true adept at lovemaking. All others are merely enjoyers of women."
—Kularnava Tantra V. 107–13

SOURCE: India Sinha, *Tantra: The Cult of Ecstasy* (London: Hamlyn, 1993), p. 144.

Basavanna [1106–68], Chaitanya [1486–1533], and Mirabai [1540–?]), taught that the highest human goal in devotion was to experience the divine in human manifestation; others, called *sants* (including Ravidas [1450], Kabir [1440–1518], and Nanak [1469–1539]), insisted that true liberation was found when seeing the divine beyond any particular form, that is, nirguna brahman. The devotional songs of these revered teachers are still sung across the Hindu world today.

Religion in the Mughal Era (1526–1707)

The great Mughal Empire that controlled northern and central India from 1526 until 1707 represented the second era of Muslim rule across much of South Asia. In its first century, Mughal rule was prosperous and peaceful, ushering in an efflorescence of Indo-Islamic culture in architecture and the fine arts. The Taj Mahal in Agra is the most famous among hundreds of magnificent buildings erected in this period. There was a significant rise in converts to Islam across North India during the Mughal dynasty.

The Rise of Sikhism

One of the principal bhakti saints, Guru Nanak (1469–1539), achieved unparalleled success as founder of the last great heterodox religion to originate in India, Sikhism. His disciples now number over 30 million, eclipsing the number of Jews in global population.

Guru Nanak was born in 1469, before the beginning of Mughal rule. His home region was the Punjab, a fertile west-central region on the trade routes leading to the northwest. Born into the warrior caste, he was well-educated in the religious literatures of Sanskrit, Persian, and Arabic; he showed a strong interest in the sant bhakti teachers, especially Kabir. By the age of twenty-nine, Nanak was married, father of two children, and employed as a civil servant. Around then, in 1498, he underwent a three-day mystical religious experience that changed his life. His first pronouncement after a long silence indicated the vision that he would pursue: "There is neither Hindu nor Muslim, so whose path shall I follow? I shall follow God's path. God is neither Hindu nor Muslim and the path that I follow is God's."[6]

For the next twenty years, Nanak wandered far and wide as a pilgrim. He was drawn to answer the paradoxical question of why, if God is one and indivisible, humanity should be divided into competing and very different faiths. Conveyed in poetry and song, his spiritual experiences and moral teachings were collected and recorded in the **Janam Sakhis**, the traditional stories about his life that include encounters with animals, rulers, commoners, and holy men—Hindu sadhus and Muslim Sufis alike. Legends concerning Nanak's life describe his travels throughout South Asia, his visits to Tibet and then Mecca. Everywhere his spiritual understanding and supernormal powers are said to surpass those of all others. Sikh tradition avers that Nanak respected both Hindu and Islamic traditions, but that his mission was to correct the mistaken practices and beliefs of both, thereby revealing the full spiritual truth and the proper path to realize it.

Janam Sakhis: traditional stories about the life and teachings of Guru Nanak

When he returned home from his wandering at age fifty, Nanak set out to do just this. Back in the Punjab, he taught all who were interested and soon attracted many disciples—"*Sikhs*"—who were drawn by the charismatic guru as well as by the community whose rules and rituals he established. He continued to compose religious verse, with 974 hymns in total forming the core of the Sikh scriptures when they were compiled by his successor a half century later. Nanak acted on his belief that the caste system was wrong by having all his disciples eat as one family from a common kitchen; he also was insistent that women deserved respect and religious equality. As one of his hymns states;

Of women we are born, of women conceived,
To a woman engaged, to woman married
Woman we befriend, by women is civilization
   continued. . . .
It is by woman that order is maintained
Then why call her evil from whom great men are
   born?[7]

Many disparate Hindu groups were drawn to this new community, which offered an indigenous monotheistic alternative to Islam. After designating a successor, Nanak died in 1539.

Traditional image of Guru Nanak.

The Ten Gurus and the Development of the Sikh Community

After Nanak there were nine other gurus (spiritual teachers who guide disciples) who managed the burgeoning Sikh communities being established across the region. The second and third gurus gathered the songs and sermons composed by Nanak, adding hymns of their own and those composed by Hindu sants and Muslim Sufis, to form the holy scripture called the **Adi Granth**. This text, containing over 7,000 hymns filling 1,948 pages in its final form, remains the unique focus of Sikh worship to this day. The Adi Granth is organized in chronological order beginning with hymns composed by Nanak, then hymns composed by the other Gurus, followed by the hymns of other saints. Each hymn came to have its own traditional tune for singing.

    The gurus also refined the community liturgies, making the group a compelling alternative to and socially separate from similar Hindu groups. The town of Amritsar ("Pool of Ambrosia") was built and became the center of the faith up to the present day. Its Golden Temple, set in a lake, is the crown jewel of Sikh architecture. Tradition holds that the site on which the Golden Temple stands was sanctified by

Adi Granth: scripture worshipped by Sikhs

In the Gurmukhī script, *Ek Onkar* is a combination of three letters: *Ek, Aum,* and *Kar,* which is a line drawn over the Om, signifying continuity, timelessness, and eternity.

Khalsa: "The Pure"; Sikh organization for defense of the faith

Om-kara: "Divine One"; Sikh term for the formless ultimate reality
Sat Guru: "True Teacher"; Sikh term indicating the active mode of Om-kara

the visit to it by Guru Nanak, who instructed succeeding gurus to develop the area into a great spiritual center that would radiate a message of love and peace to mankind. The tenth guru, Gobind Singh (1666–1708), declared that in the future, the guru of the Sikhs in spiritual matters would be the holy text itself, when the second name for it became the Guru Granth Sahib. From the time this temple was opened in 1604 until the present day, this has been taken out and its hymns chanted from dawn until dusk.

In the early years of Mughal rule, the Sikhs gained popularity and were welcomed at court. The emperor Akbar (1561–1605) found in the faith a tolerant monotheistic theology and regarded the followers as a disciplined moral community. Akbar's successors, however, felt distrustful about the Sikhs' growth and political influences. The fifth guru, Arjan (1581–1606), was tortured and martyred on the order of one emperor, and in 1669, when another Mughal ruler ordered all Hindu temples and schools demolished, Sikhs resisted, and many died defending their faith. It was in response to this growing persecution that the Sikh tradition came to emphasize training in martial skills and bravery in defending the community. At this time, too, a group called the **Khalsa** ("The Pure") was formed, a dedicated elite order of men and women ready to struggle and die if necessary in defense of the faith. Training camps in archery, swordsmanship, and cavalry fighting were established to empower men to perform this religious duty. The Khalsa, who adopted a strict and determined lifestyle as guardians of the faith, marked themselves by their appearance: uncut hair (covered with a turban), short trousers, steel wristlet, comb, and sword. Sikhs in the Khalsa also adopted the names Singh ("lion") for men and Kaur ("princess") for women, to eliminate caste distinctions within the community. A ceremonial baptism marks an individual's entrance into the Khalsa: The man or woman joining it kneels and is given a taste of *amrita,* a mixture of sugar in water that is stirred with a ceremonial sword; some is then sprinkled on the head.

Sikh Theology, Morality, and Spiritual Practices

Nanak's spiritual path contained elements found in both Hindu and Muslim traditions. As in Islam, Nanak taught that there is only one "God," who never walked the earth as a man (i.e., had not had an incarnation). Nanak also set his teaching firmly in the Hindu nirguna tradition, mystically affirming that this God is entirely beyond form and human categories. To specify this god, Nanak introduced the terms **Om-kara** ("Divine One") and **Sat Guru** ("True Teacher").

Anticipating reformers of colonial and postcolonial Hinduism, Sikhs deny that asceticism is necessary or of value, holding that householders are perfectly capable of realizing the highest goal of liberation. Similarly, they say that ritual acts and pilgrimages have no spiritual effect. In addition, they reject the authority of the Vedas and the innate sanctity of the brahmin caste. As we have seen, the Sikhs' non-Vedic orientation has caused high-caste Hindus to regard them as heterodox.

Residing in the human heart and communicating with those who live rightly and develop their spiritual faculties, Sat Guru freely bestows grace that ends individual karma and rebirth. In Sikh spiritual understanding, the human struggle involves rejecting ego-centered living and embracing the inner life of opening to the divine Sat Guru within. Revelation occurs through the effect of divine sound on one's consciousness. The Adi Granth is the center of their rituals and ceremonies. Therefore, Sikh religiosity is centered on listening to, and congregationally singing, the hymns composed by Nanak and other saints and sitting in the presence of the holy book, whose very words both reflect and impart this grace.

Consciously rejecting the norms of caste society while living among a Hindu majority, Sikhs affirm the social equality of all humanity, regardless of caste, race, creed, or gender. Women can join the Khalsa and, following the views of Nanak, Sikh women were emancipated from conformity to the gender practices of both Islam and Hinduism. They were not required to wear veils, widows could remarry, and women could be religious preachers and the political heads of administrative districts in the fledgling Sikh states in Punjab. Sikhs are expected to refrain from drugs including tobacco and alcohol, and many do not eat meat. Community service is an important and expected expression of faith; hard work and attaining wealth is encouraged; onerous work undertaken for others is highly respected. Being fit and active in defense of the weak and oppressed is an important part of the Sikh ethos on life.

There is no priesthood or ordained ministry in Sikhism; men and women pray together. Sikhs have had to make accommodations yet establish separate boundaries through their rituals. To become a Sikh requires making a profession of belief, affirming the essentials of nirguna theology and the need for each individual to earn liberation:

> There is one God, his name is truth eternal
> He is the creator of all things, the all-pervading spirit
> Fearless and without hatred, timeless and formless.
> Beyond birth and death, he is self-enlightened.
> He is known by the Guru's grace.[8]

Sikhs find their liberation in combining public and private worship with social action, earning an honest living, giving alms, and doing community service. The great sixth guru, Harogobind (1595–1644), established the Sikhs' main religious institution, the **gurudwara**, based on the teachings and examples of Nanak. This architectural and institutional form came to be the norm for Sikh communities everywhere, providing a common focal point for Sikh devotion and a place for communal gathering. The gurudwara hall is typically plain and undecorated, completely lacking in images or other religious decorations. At one end is a raised platform with a fine silk covering on which a copy of the Adi Granth is central. From dawn until dusk a learned member of the community reads from the text, singing in places; those Sikhs in attendance can join in to sing as they sit below the text on the floor that is covered with white cloth. Any time the text is opened in the gurudwara, a member of the community must sit by it, just as a human guru must have a disciple in attendance. There is no priesthood in Sikhism; anyone can give teachings or read the scripture. This sanctuary can also accommodate individuals coming for prayer or meditation at any time.

"Omkar
True name
Being who creates
Beyond fear and
    opposition
A form beyond time
Unborn, self-born
The guru's grace."
—Nanak

SOURCE: *Songs of the Saints of India*, p. 78.

gurudwara: Sikh temple

The Golden Temple in Amritsar, Punjab. This great landmark for Sikhs worldwide, and the faith's chief pilgrimage center, was occupied in the early 1980s by militants seeking Punjab's secession from India.

The gurudwaras also contain a common kitchen (*langar*) where community vegetarian meals are prepared for all who come and where all eat together. Thus, kitchen service reflects the moral teachings of Sikhism: the centrality of community, its egalitarian nature, and social action. Within India's Hindu caste society, the Sikh religious lifestyle and social norms were revolutionary, bringing all members together regardless of caste and station in life. Today, the serving of community meals for all needing to eat is a central practice. It is a form of service to the poor seen every day at the Golden Temple in Amritsar and in Sikh communities globally. Its spirit is reflected in the aphorism "Where there are Sikhs, there is no hunger."

Hinduism and Modernity

In the modern period, the innovative openness and additive practice of Hindu tradition continues, with global influences entering the South Asian experience. Although some South Asians preserve elements of premodern religious culture with a vigor matched in few places, others have adopted new beliefs and practices as the circumstances of their lives and societies have changed: Scientific ideas associated with the Enlightenment affected nearly everyone through education, technology, and medicine; the views and practices of Christian missionaries as well as the political practices of the modern state impacted almost everyone as well. Most important, the pattern of reform and synthesis that has kept this religion so flexible and fluid has continued, launching neo-Hindu teachers not only in South Asia, but in the global religious arena. Classical and reformed forms of Hinduism as well as political movements emphasizing religious identity have proven extremely successful, from highly educated intellectuals to illiterate villagers. We turn to this time of immense change and innovation now.

Hinduism Under British Colonialism

The first Europeans known to have settled in South Asia in Mughal times were Roman Catholic missionaries, initially the Dominicans in the Portuguese colony of Goa by 1510 and, after 1540, the Jesuits, led by Francis Xavier. Early merchants also arrived by sea to trade for spices, silks, indigo, and cotton goods. Although they had competitors among early Dutch, Portuguese, and French traders, the British under the East India Company eventually were the most successful at establishing themselves permanently. As the Mughal Empire over its last fifty years slowly disintegrated and the region's "Hindu states" asserted their independence, civil disorder increased, causing trade and tax revenues to decline. In this unstable atmosphere, the British augmented their trade missions with garrisoned fortresses, and by 1730 military detachments were integral to the British mercantile presence. From these centers, the British leaders were drawn into conflicts; when they defeated local rulers in battle, they made alliances and extended their command and control inward. South Asia soon became a patchwork of British territory and "princely states" that submitted to the British but were still ruled in their internal affairs by Hindu or Sikh royalty, or by Muslim sultans.

Modern scholarship on India and Hinduism originated in this context of Europeans seeking to learn about native peoples in order to tighten imperial control. British officials believed that it was their duty as white Europeans to spread enlightened

British Viceroy Lord Curzon (1859–1925) with a ruler of a princely state. British rule produced both crises and new opportunities for Hindu elites.

civilization to the "backward peoples" of South Asia. This message was, in turn, repeated back in Europe to justify the expanding colonial enterprise that had begun with merchants.

British schools were established in South Asia to train young Indians to serve in the lower echelons of the colonial bureaucracy. In large part, it was this new class of Indians that made first in-depth contact with modern ideas from Europe, especially in political thought, the natural sciences, and Christianity. This process unfolded in the colonial urban centers, the first of which was Calcutta. English quickly became the lingua franca of the subcontinent; knowing the English language and culture became the necessary path for any ambitious Indian subject living under British rule.

By 1813 missionaries had arrived from every major Christian denomination. Many challenged Hinduism on every front, from theology and ritual practices to morality and caste norms. Some ministers suggested that the British triumph in India represented God's judging Hinduism to be an idolatrous and demoniac heresy. Many South Asians came to regard the missionaries as in league with the colonialists. Crude depictions of Hindus and Indian culture fomented resentments.

In 1857 widespread civil disturbances swept across British-held territories. During this period, called "the mutiny" by the British and regarded by many Indians as "the first war of independence," Indian troops and peasants gave vent to resentments over colonial law and administrative insensitivities, executing some British officers and murdering their families. Colonial troops and loyal mercenaries eventually put down the rebellion and there were brutal reprisals taken against Indian citizens. When order

Considered the "first war of independence" by Indian nationalists, the uprising in 1857 was fomented by alleged disrespect of Muslim and Hindu troops under British command.

had been restored, in 1858, the British parliament dissolved the company that had held the royal charter for trade with Asia and declared the Queen's direct rule. India became "the jewel in the crown" of the British Empire for the next ninety years.

Challenges and Responses to Colonialism

The early modern era thus presented individual Hindus and Hindu institutions with a series of challenges that they shared with other colonized peoples across the globe. Powerful outsiders were arriving in significant numbers, proclaiming new truths and boldly denouncing Hindu beliefs. This ideological challenge appeared simultaneously in several forms: the scientific worldview of the European Enlightenment, humanistic critiques of religion, racial theories of European superiority, and the triumphalist Gospel teachings of outspoken Christian missionaries.

The early Christian missionaries from Britain were largely Protestant. As a result, the ideas of nineteenth-century Protestantism had a distinct impact on Hindus, who sought to reform their own traditions. Protestant emphases that were significant among Hindu reformers included the use of historical and scientific methods in the search for core scriptures and doctrines, and criticism of ritual that was not consistent with these doctrines. Other Protestant perspectives were distrust of traditional priests as purveyors of "blind superstition" and the promotion of spiritual individualism, whereby each person is responsible for his or her own spiritual destiny. Hindu reformers were further influenced by the Protestant reliance on new lay-run institutions to organize new religious movements, the linking of social uplift initiatives with religious reforms, and the prestige of monotheism. (With the exception of monotheism, the same ideas had an impact in the colonial Buddhist territories of Asia, as we will see in the next chapter.) In colonial India, too, new forms of "Protestant Hinduism" mobilized the colonized to protest against British imperialism.

Although most South Asians did not convert to Islam or Christianity, many regions in which Hindus lived were ruled by non-Hindus (Muslims and the European successors). This state of affairs was distressing because conquest by outsiders suggested that the power and grace of the Hindu deities had been eclipsed. Further, the economic dislocations due to imperialism in many instances undermined the traditional channels of financial support for Hindu scholars, activists, and temples.

The colonial government's political practice was to use religious identity as the basis for official dealings with "native constituencies." Thus, "Muslim," "Hindu," and "Sikh" became politically defined identities. This created serious problems in the post-colonial period, although it gave the British a convenient manner in which they could divide and exert control over groups that opposed their policies or (eventually) their very presence as overlords of South Asia. As a result, too, Hindus, Muslims, and Sikhs competed against one another for favorable treatment at the hands of the colonial government. Communal divides opened where none had existed. Since 1947, tensions between these groups defined by religion have resurfaced, sometimes tragically.

Christian missionaries possessed overwhelming confidence in their work, but converted relatively few. Muslim and Hindu leaders of South Asia often criticized missionary hypocrisy, but some adopted reforms due to their influence. This cartoon captures local resentment to missionary practices and their calls to "destroy your gods, burn your books, be converted . . ."

The nineteenth century saw a variety of Hindu responses to colonialism, making it an era of tremendous cultural vitality and synthesis. The early influential leaders were mainly brahmins, the traditional priestly caste that had long emphasized literacy and education. Most supported old-fashioned, change-resistant orthodoxy. Yet among this elite group, especially those in areas of most intense contact (Bombay and Calcutta), the initial reaction to the British shifted from indifference to more engaged positions: either hostility or curiosity. Scattered terrorist groups, some led by militant sadhus, formed to attack British officers and institutions. These were mostly thwarted and went underground. Other Indians developed a genuine interest in European civilization, and increasing numbers traveled to Europe for education. We turn now to examine prominent examples among these Hindu responses.

The First Reformist Generation: Rammohan Roy, Brahmo Samaj, and the Tattvabodhini Sabha

The widespread issue that Hindus were forced to confront, one shared elsewhere by Muslims and Buddhists, centered on a question: How could it be that the world-preserving great deities have allowed non-Hindus to overshadow Hindus so utterly and to defame Hindu society? Some Hindus gave an answer similar to that heard from time to time in Islam and in other faiths struggling under colonialism: Revelation has not failed, but the community has lost true belief and practice. Therefore, the community needs to be reformed. The first to articulate this position for Hinduism was **Rammohan Roy** (1772–1833), who is regarded by many as "the father of modern India." Roy called for the reform of certain Hindu beliefs and practices prevalent across India, including superstition, caste discrimination, and the practice of widow immolation (*sati*). He argued for universal education in English so that Indians could study modern math, science, and medicine. Roy was equally outspoken in defending Hinduism against missionary attacks, drawing on his study of the Bible and rational analysis to critique Christian dogmas.

In 1828 Roy founded Brahmo Sabha, an organization to further his reformist views. In 1841 the name was changed to the Brahmo Samaj, whose official English title—"Fellowship of Believers in the One True God"—expresses its goal of uniting Hindus of all castes to proclaim a reformist, monotheistic ideology. The Brahmo Samaj's importance lies in its strong influence on subsequent generations of Hindu reformers and revivalists; their writings also reached America and Europe, among the first to describe Hinduism to the West.

The **Tattvabodhini Sabha** ("Truth-Propagating Society") was an especially influential group in Calcutta associated with Roy's teachings. Aimed at exploring and propagating the teachings of Vedantic Hinduism in light of enlightenment rationality, the group was funded by leading members of the rising middle class that was prospering under British rule. Its meetings attracted leading Hindu teachers and philosophers; their addresses were published in vernacular languages and circulated widely among the colonial-era native class called the *bhadralok*: entrepreneurs, landed gentry, school teachers, journalists, a mixture of high castes and newly rich businessmen. Most in this influential class were schooled in England, and some were themselves involved in the colonial education system.

The Tattvabodhini Sabha's revivalism was colored by their commitment to promote the "modern Hindu's" adaptation to India's new economic and political realities. The Sabha publications merged these values—working hard, living honestly, saving rationally, and promoting altruism—with their view of Vedanta's message of the individual controlling personal desires. Along with Roy, they saw reformed Hinduism now being led by the "godly householder," not the premodern elite of world-renouncing ascetics. Instead of seeking to extirpate all human desire, Hindus should accept desire's power but guide it "according to *dharma*" (here, "justice") and for society's overall betterment: "respect for your father and mother, love your neighbors, work for the welfare of the government, rescue people from the torment of suffering, provide religious instruction to your sons and students, and give knowledge to the ignorant."[9]

Like the ethos underlying the successful Protestant businessmen then leading the global spread of capitalism, this influential Hindu elite articulated a congruent view of human mission, though they built this on a very different metaphysical foundation. For the principled, hard-working, frugal, philanthropic, middle-class householder to become a "saint" (*mahatma*, a term applied later to Gandhi), their journal set forth the path thus:

Rammohan Roy: pioneering religious figure who called for the reform of Hindu beliefs and practices

Tattvabodhini Sabha: colonial Hindu sect in Calcutta that promoted adaptation to India's new economic and political realities

They always exert themselves with care, whether by keeping good company, providing counsel, quelling sorrow, treating illness, or bestowing knowledge. Such great-souled men are indeed wealthy and they alone are the true votaries of the Supreme Lord. . . . They alone are able to set aside their own interests and work for the welfare of all.[10]

Arya Samaj: religious organization that redefined and defended reformed Hindu traditions

Jaina pratīka: symbol of the Jaina faith, officially adopted during the 2,500th anniversary of Mahavira's nirvana (1975). The palm of the hand bears the word *ahimsa;* the svastika topped by three dots and the crescent represent the four destinies, the threefold path, and the abode of the liberated souls, respectively; the slogan below the figure of loka-akasa calls for the mutual assistance of all beings.

परस्परोपग्रहो जीवानाम्

PARASPAROPAGRAHO JĪVĀNĀM

More Strident and Sectarian: Dayananda and the Arya Samaj

Similar in many respects to the Brahmo Samaj but centered in Bombay and Lahore, the **Arya Samaj** was founded in 1875 by the brahmin teacher Swami Dayananda (1824–83). Dayananda held the fundamentalist view that only the four Vedas were valid sources for true Hinduism and that they were in fact "infallible," containing all knowledge, even the root ideas of modern science. India, he famously proclaimed, "needed nothing from the West." For him, as for Roy, the essential Hindu theological idea was monotheism. Accordingly, he rejected post-Vedic scripture and saw later polytheism as the reason for Hinduism's decline. Dayananda tirelessly denounced practices such as child marriage, untouchability, and the subjugation of women. He composed his own simplified list of ethical norms and a description of properly reformed Vedic rituals. He also denounced Sikhism.

Dayananda's successors made the Arya Samaj especially influential once the organization developed village institutions and schools. Numerous Dayananda Anglo-Vedic colleges and high schools continue the Arya Samaj revivalist tradition to the present day. Many of the current Bharatiya Janata party members and leaders have been influenced by the Arya Samaj. Its work was spread globally by émigrés from South Asia.

Jain Reformism

Like other communities, Jains in the last century have revitalized their traditions and spread them globally through their communities and businesses. Biographers of Gandhi have speculated that Jain principles of nonviolence and detached social action exerted a formative influence on him. Jains today have emphasized how their doctrines are compatible with science; they have also focused on the virtues of vegetarianism and animal protection. Movements focusing on environmental health have been led by Jains; and in recent decades, some teachers have accepted Westerners into the Jain monastic community, especially in England and the United States. To celebrate the 2,500th anniversary of the saint Mahavira, a new symbol was devised to represent the tradition. In 2010, the first Jain center in the United States was opened in Boston.

Sikh Reform and Resurgence

Through their resistance to the Mughals, the Sikhs eventually carved out their own kingdom in western India that lasted from 1799 until 1849, when it was absorbed into British India after the Anglo-Sikh Wars of 1845–46 and 1848–49. After this, Sikh men were recruited into the colonial army from 1870 to 1947, becoming renowned for their disciplined character and martial abilities. Sikhs also entered into many of the new colonial educational institutions, finding success as civil servants, educators, and businessmen. Soon, Sikhs were serving across the British Empire, and on retirement many settled outside India, from Singapore and Hong Kong to England. These migrants brought their faith with them, making Sikhism a large global faith today.

Sikhs also responded to the religious challenges posed by South Asia's colonial situation and the aggressive Christian missionaries who appeared in the Punjab. One reformist group, known as the Nirakaris, emphasized ascetic values and fervent devotion to the Formless One (*nirankar*). Its founder, Baba Dayal (1783–1855), like some Hindu reformers, wanted to purify the faith of superstitions and any Hindu practices. Another Sikh reformist organization, the Singh Sabha (Lion Society), was formed in 1879 to advocate traditional values and implement socioeducational uplift programs to defend the faith. Centered in Amritsar, the Singh Sabha sought to vitalize Sikhism through educational initiatives such as the founding of Khalsa College in Amritsar, and it sponsored magazines and newspapers that encouraged religious pride among the Sikh communities that were spreading across India and abroad.

By 1920, calls for independence were rising across South Asia. Sikhs joined the movement due to the abuses of the British government in two areas: the imposed national policy, called the mahant system, that placed appointed Hindu caretakers in control of Sikh gurudwaras; and the administrative decision to place control of the Golden Temple in the hands of a British Deputy Commissioner. A new Sikh political action group, the Akali Dal, was formed to address these problems. The Gurudwara Act of 1925 was successful in returning to a Sikh committee the sole authority to manage the historic gurudwaras in the united Punjab, including the Golden Temple. The Akali Dal then joined Muslim and Hindu groups seeking the end of British rule and they continue to pursue Sikh interests in postcolonial India.

> "Calling God Mother is a higher idea than calling Him Father, to call him Friend is still higher, but the highest is to regard Him as the Beloved. The highest point of all is to see no difference between lover and beloved."
>
> —Vivekananda
>
> SOURCE: Stephen Hay, ed., *Sources of Indian Tradition*, 2nd ed., vol. 2 (New York: Columbia University Press, 1988), p. 73.

Ramakrishna and Vivekananda: The First Global Hindu Mission

A brahmin like Roy and Dayananda but with a much more humble educational background, Ramakrishna (1834–86) was a charismatic guru who attracted reform-minded Hindus. In Ramakrishna's revivalism, however, the teacher emphasized mystical experience and ecumenical monistic or nirguna theology. His spiritual experiences included long periods of trance in which he reported being possessed in turn by Kali, Sita, Rama, Krishna, Muhammad, and Jesus. Ramakrishna's teaching emphasized that the entire universe is permeated by the paramount divine spirit, a reality that is called different names by the world's different people, but whose essence is one. In articulating this view, Ramakrishna was updating to a global scale the interfaith ecumenical teaching of the classical Hindu school we have already discussed, that of Vedantic Hinduism.

It was Swami Vivekananda (1863–1902), Ramakrishna's foremost disciple, who became a guru in his own right and presented this theology in a forceful and systematic

TEACHINGS OF RELIGIOUS WISDOM: Same Water, Different Names

The following parable by Ramakrishna was found in a pamphlet from the Ramakrishna Mission in Calcutta, dated 1976.

God is one only, and not two. Different people call on Him by different names: some as Allah, some as God, others as Krishna, Shiva, and Brahman. It is like the water in a lake. Some drink it at one place and call it "*jal*," others at another place and call it "*pani*," and still others at a third place and call it "water." The Hindus call it "jal," the Christians "water," and the Muslims "pani." But it is one and the same thing. Opinions are but paths. Each religion is only a path leading to God, as rivers come from different directions and ultimately become one in the ocean.

Ramakrishna Mission: influential Hindu missionary and reform organization founded by Swami Vivekananda

manner. Vivekananda was the first great missionary representative of Hinduism on the global stage. His popularity grew through lectures on Hinduism across America and Europe. Most Westerners' first acquaintance with Hinduism is largely a product of the teachings of Vivekananda and his later followers.

Vivekananda organized the **Ramakrishna Mission**, whose institutions spread across India. The mission advocated reformist traditions and embraced a global ecumenical awareness. Its highly organized order of monks cultivated inner spiritual development through yoga, taught "the Gospel of Ramakrishna," and established educational institutions, hospitals, and hospices open to all. Some monks trained as doctors. In 2009 there were 23 mission hospitals, 120 dispensaries, and 6,500 educational centers in India.

The Ramakrishna Mission became the first great global Hindu organization with a vision of ecumenical Hinduism as the savior of the world, not merely of India. The mission's disciples in the West now support its global reach. By 2014 it had published many books and built retreat centers, libraries, and sanctuaries in major cities in seventeen countries.

The Work of Gandhi: Hindu Elements in Indian Nationalism

By the turn of the twentieth century, Britain's command over the subcontinent had grown, with its building of a vast modern infrastructure (roads, railroads, telegraph) that supported increasing trade. The presence of Christian missions and the colonial government's bureaucracy had also expanded as Europeans visited the region by the thousands yearly. Indian leaders and organizations seeking to strengthen and reform Hinduism were also multiplying through this period, however, and religious reformism and political activism frequently converged.

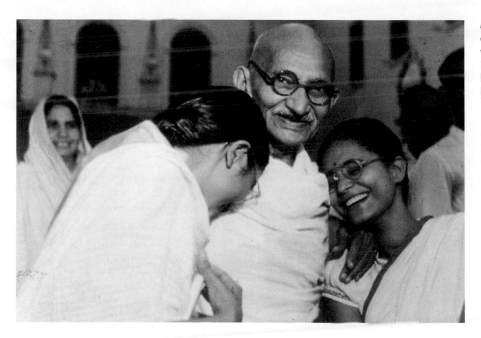

Mohandas K. Gandhi, a great political leader who merged European ideas with reformist Hindu teachings to lead India to independence.

The growing independence movement often drew on religious identity and pride. An important player in the independence movement was the Indian National Congress, founded in 1880 in Bombay. Although dominated by brahmins and a few Muslims, who were mostly urban, English-educated lawyers, the Congress sought to speak for all Indians. While it proclaimed loyalty to the Raj, as the British colonial government was called, the Congress increasingly agitated nonviolently for greater economic development and the incremental growth of self-rule. Thus, it gained acceptance as the party to articulate an Indian voice vis-à-vis the colonial government.

The spiritual background motivating many of the Congress leaders was that of the reformists who sought to regenerate Indian culture (both Hindu and Islamic). Indeed, many were convinced that India had a spiritual message for the future of humanity. Such a sentiment was heightened, of course, by the great world wars, whose devastation suggested that neither science, European political systems, nor Christianity was to be triumphant in global history.

It was **Mohandas K. Gandhi** (1869–1948) who became the most significant leader to guide South Asia to independence. Gandhi himself embodies the changes and syntheses affecting South Asia as the era of globalism under colonialism was brought to an end. As a paradigmatic reformist Hindu who merged European and Indian cultures, Gandhi became one of the greatest world figures of the twentieth century.

On the national stage, Gandhi linked the Congress elite with the masses. Although some disagreed with his stands, he was a nationally venerated guru, an activist who wrote and acted creatively to reinterpret Hinduism in an ethical, this-worldly manner. Gandhi went on hunger strikes to move British officials (or, at times, other Indian leaders) to

Mohandas K. Gandhi: iconic leader who inspired mass support and led India to independence by combining religious and political reforms *ahimsa:* nonviolence

satyagraha: "grasping the truth"; Gandhi's central principle of disciplined nonviolence that reflects ethical truth

reconsider their positions. The honorific *Mahatma* applied to his name, meaning "great-souled [one]," expresses the profound spiritual respect he garnered in his lifetime.

Carrying on the work of earlier reformers, Gandhi decried high-caste discrimination toward others, and he especially highlighted untouchability as a blight on Hinduism. He also extended the Hindu and Jain notion of **ahimsa** (nonviolence) to articulate an entire way of life, what he called **satyagraha**, guided by this ideal. Through following ahimsa in all spheres, Gandhi argued, the modern Hindu could find the truth in humble daily work. It was a principle that could transform the individual and society, imbuing each with a spiritual center.

Gandhi's life work was crowned in 1947, when India finally gained its independence. However, celebration of this long-anticipated moment was shattered by the violence that accompanied it. The British allowed no time for the orderly implementation of their partition, which divided India, a new secular nation, from the new Muslim state of Pakistan. A civil war broke out in which an estimated 4 million people perished. Nearing the age of eighty, Gandhi traveled to many of these areas in an

Gandhi

M. K. Gandhi was born in a merchant family in the western region of Gujarat. As a young man he was interested in secular subjects, and he traveled to London to study law. While there he encountered for the first time the classical Hindu texts, all in English translations. He was introduced to them not by an Indian *guru* but through meetings at the Theosophical Society, a group of European mystics interested in the secret doctrines they felt were at the root of all world religions. While in England, Gandhi also read the Bible avidly as well as books by European intellectuals like Tolstoy and Ruskin and the American Thoreau.

After becoming a lawyer, Gandhi settled in South Africa, then a British colony with a large Indian minority. He was soon drawn into political activism in opposition to the racist and discriminatory imperial practices directed toward South Asians as "coloreds." From experiences with protests and community organization, Gandhi developed his central principle, one that guided his future life. He called it *satyagraha* ("grasping the truth"). This concept has roots in the Hindu and Jain doctrine of nonviolence

(*ahimsa*) and in Christianity's injunctions to love one's enemy and turn the other cheek (as a reaction to being struck in the face). Gandhi required those opposing the government to confine their protests to nonviolent acts, accept suffering for the cause, to love the opponent, and to be disciplined in personal life. Gandhi's work in South Africa among Indian immigrants transformed him and drew attention to his teachings back in India, where Congress leaders urged him to return. He did so in 1915.

Although Gandhi always retained respect for British law and the moral ideals articulated in Western religions, back in India he abandoned the dress of the Western barrister for the humble *dhoti* (loincloth) of the Indian peasant. Gandhi's greatness as a political leader was likewise built on his connection with the Indian masses, a relationship that developed through his wide-ranging tours of the countryside, his involvement with a series of peasant protests, his self-imposed poverty, and an effective organization (including a daily newspaper) that he developed with those who lived in his *ashram*.

attempt to quell the chaos, but largely in vain. He was murdered in 1948 by a member of a fundamentalist Hindu group that had opposed partition and accused Gandhi of "concessions" to Muslims and the lowest castes.

India in many respects abandoned Gandhi's concept of spiritually centered, small-scale development. Only in civil law has India continued to embrace Gandhi's vision, albeit haltingly, in its attempts to eradicate caste discrimination. Though challenged by Hindu nationalists, the modern state of India holds fast to its fundamental identity as a secular—not Hindu—nation.

Hinduism and Postmodern Trends in a Postcolonial World

It is commonplace that many college students today want to go to India after graduation. Those who return report that it is "like nowhere else," and this is so for many reasons. One is that many pasts and ancient spiritual paths are alive among Hindus today and spiritual creativity is still very much alive. One can witness practices from the most ancient period, and study yoga with a guru quoting third-century BCE texts; one can also go to an urban park where newly formed modern groups practice "laughing yoga" before going to work; and one can witness a demonstration organized by a Hindu fundamentalist group that wants to make their version of "Hinduism" the state religion. But since we do not, in fact, have a single version of "Hinduism" on which to center our treatment of contemporary change, and there is no single institution or person in authority who can speak for all Hindus, we must be content to comprehend the nature of pluralism today. This is best done by focusing on a series of representative case studies that illustrate patterns of unity in the diversity evident in the postmodern period that continues until today.

The Persistence of Traditional Religious Understandings

Despite the modernization of India that daily reaches ever farther into the rural regions, there has been a remarkable persistence of traditional beliefs and practices in postcolonial India. While no single school or theology is representative of "Hinduism" in all its many forms, it is possible to trace broadly shared understandings and central ideas among the traditions that have remained influential to the present.

The Presence of the Divine

Whatever specific doctrines or practices an individual Hindu follows, what gives the tradition a measure of unity is the widely held conviction that there is something underlying the material world seen by our ordinary consciousness. For humans, therefore, life entails more than satisfying the needs dictated by survival. A divine reality enfolds human reality, interpenetrating the material world and human experience; this occurs primarily through the soul (atman), which animates an embryo in the womb and energizes human life.

If we were traveling to a typical village in South Asia today, we would readily notice that Hindu society is unique in its extraordinary veneration of the sacred in the daily rhythms of life. We might observe rituals honoring the rising and setting sun, see offerings being made at humble temples erected at unusual or aged natural features (stones and trees), and see the inhabitants showing reverent respect at rivers and local mountains as well as to animals such as elephants, snakes, monkeys, and, of course, cows. Devotees might invite us into shrines for the divine protectors of houses, families, artisans, and castes; farmers could take us to the guardian deities of the settlement and of their fields. The local brahmin priest could explain how everyone visits the temple to the goddesses when there are outbreaks of disease. He might direct us to speak with the local spirit medium, who could describe recent episodes of persons in the village possessed by ghosts or demons and how he intervened to cure them through offerings and trance. And then we might drop in to consult with the astrologer, who sits before a long line of patrons wishing to know how the distant deities who appear in the night sky can best be propitiated. Our brahmin host could also point out how at every key moment in a person's life—birth, coming of age, marriage, and death—he is called on to perform rituals to strengthen a family's collective spirit by seeking divine blessings.

In urban areas where some of the older traditions are less prominent, brahmins can be still found performing such rites and also adapting Hindu practices to changing times. For example, since 2004, a regular service offered to all customers of Maruti Udyog cars, the most popular automotive brand in modern India, is to have a brahmin priest perform a puja for the vehicle's good fortune; Maruti Udyog showrooms also feature a line of automotive accessories that include dashboard statues of the Hindu gods.

This excursion into Hinduism as lived tradition makes clear that there is no Hindu view that matches the Western deist notion, made popular in post-Enlightenment Western theology, that God set up creation as a mechanism and then, like a detached watchmaker, retreated to let it tick away. Across Hindu South Asia, the immanence of spirit is respected and the gods live next door. It is the human task to find harmony with them and eventually to seek liberation from rebirth by finding the spirit in whatever guise one is most suited to discover. Even in modern cities and among individuals who are highly educated, the wish to connect with and worship the divine remains strong today.

Hindu Inclusivity Accommodates Wide-Ranging Sectarianism

Another distinctive and enduring characteristic of Hinduism today is the broad range of ideas about the sacred and the widespread tendency for individuals to accept alternative, opposing views. The coexistence of so many competing theologies and religious practices and even the toleration of nonbelievers have been based on two notions. First is the belief that a human understanding of the highest truth, whatever that is held to be, is never complete or perfect. Second is the expectation that as individuals learn and practice more deeply, they will see reality more clearly. From these twin perspectives, persons thought to hold false views are simply located on a lower rank in a hierarchy, not rejected. A wrongheaded person may be ignorant, immature, or incomplete but not evil. Beginning with Islam and extending into the modern era with other "Western" religions, Hinduism's acceptance of pluralism has certainly endured.

Muslim–Hindu relations continue to be important and contentious in modern India. Communal enmity on religious lines was rare after Islam won acceptance in South Asia (1000 CE), mainly because group identity developed predominantly according to caste, region, and political loyalties. It was an acceptance of coexistence, as historian Ainslie Embree has pointed out, that characterized this relationship:

> Two great cultures and religious systems, the Hindu and the Islamic, while borrowing much from each other along the margins of their existence, retained their separate, core identities for 1,000 years. Coexistence, not assimilation, was the characteristic behavior of both communities, and it was made possible by the nature of Hindu society as well as the political policies of the Muslim rulers.[11]

A Hindu priest in Nepal offers *tika* powder, an essential part of the daily worship service for every god. The powder will later be used by the Brahmin priests to mark the foreheads of devotees.

Religious enmity is not an eternal, inevitable standpoint in South Asia or elsewhere; in the past, as today, it is the product of a specific historical context, shaped by human actions and political policies.

Though Hindu nationalists have rejected an accommodationalist stance, even questioning the loyalty to India of Muslims and Christians, the inclusivist religious attitude is still shared by many. It has encouraged ever new spiritual searches and the appearance of new religious sects that combine beliefs and practices from various traditions, including astrology, Buddhism, and "secular" traditions such as psychology.

The fact that Hindu groups accept others, Hindu and non-Hindu, and acknowledge their value should not cloud the recognition that many Hindus are indeed sectarian in their religious orientation. While the view "all the gods are one" is widely expressed, it is not a view shared by everyone. Adherence to the ecumenical strategy of inclusivity, of accepting the legitimacy of competing religious standpoints, does not oblige one to abandon one's own sect's truth claims. Inclusivity is ultimately a means of subordinating other truth claims, be they Vaishnava theism, Vedanta monism, or Christian trinitarianism. Thus Hindu worldviews have held their primacy throughout modern times and into the postcolonial era; it has mainly been in reforming and modernizing their social institutions that Hindus have adopted non-Hindu ideas.

Contemporary Hindu Practices

In many respects, what provides Hinduism with a measure of unity is not a single belief system, but a set of ritual actions that most individuals will observe. There is a common set of ritual actions that individuals can choose to connect with the divine, however they conceive it. There are also individuals whom most Hindus can consult with (ritualists, astrologers, gurus) to act on, and deepen, their beliefs. Beginning several thousand years ago, and continuing today, these have defined the Hindu life.

The Guru-Disciple Relationship

Dating from the time of the Upanishads, one central Hindu tradition has been the relationship connecting gurus and disciples. Just as Hindus perceive the divine in their natural and settled environments, they find spirit alive in its realization by those who reach moksha, achieve spiritual powers, and share their experiences for the benefit of humanity. Charismatic saintly gurus still hold a central place in both traditional and reformist Hinduism. There is even a festival day each year for honoring one's spiritual guide. *Guru Purnima*, or teacher's full moon, is a day for disciples to make the year's largest material donation to the guru and, ideally, to pay a visit to the teacher.

We have noted the lasting forms of organized Hinduism that emerged in the postclassical era. Then, as now, numerous spiritual teachers emerged in the traditional manner of undergoing long periods of training with independent gurus and then attracting their own disciples. Guru residences called **ashrams** sustain the community that performs rituals, meditates, and learns together under the guru's direction.

ashram: center of religious practice following a guru

Cyclic Time in Hindu Thought: Cosmic Eras

The Hindu view of time defines the universe as binding beings together in an eternal dance of life, death, and rebirth. The Vedic texts contain a multitude of creation accounts, and later texts combine them in a more circular vision of successive eras of cosmic dissolution followed by equally long eras when the created world undergoes a regular series of transformations. Once primal creation has begun, our world evolves through four eras called *yugas*.

The first and longest era, the *Krita Yuga*, is a golden age without suffering or wants: Meditation and virtue come naturally to all beings. In the second and third *yugas*, people are strongly inclined to proper duty (*dharma*); yet the inclination to virtue slowly wanes, and eventually there is the need for castes to be formed to keep order and the *Vedas* to be composed to aid those striving for truth and

goodness. But in the *Kali Yuga*, which in the current cycle began in 3102 BCE, human life moves from bad to much worse: Brahmins become unworthy, the Vedas are forgotten, castes mix unlawfully, and life spans decrease as a result of war and famine. The Kali Yuga ends with the destruction of the earth after a series of natural disasters culminating in a great flood, when Vishnu will again sleep on the waters. Some texts recount that after 1,000 of these four-era cycles, a greater destruction will take place, one in which all matter will be consumed in fire, reducing all reality to pure spirit. As an instance of Hinduism's diversity, we must also note that later sectarian groups proclaimed a dissenting, triumphal alternative to this pessimistic scenario, avowing that the grip of evil on the Kali Yuga has been (or will be) ended through the devotional practices of true believers.

Many Hindu guru-centered institutions tend to be short-lived, and the "school" that emerges lasts only as long as the charismatic teacher lives or only through his first generation of designated successors. Others continue, and in these cases we see the central Hindu notion of *parampara*, meaning "lineage, tradition, pedigree," that is, the belief that today's teachers are connected to earlier gurus, back to the first enlightened sage in the line.

The circle of intimate disciples must master the guru's instructions on the key spiritual practices (meditation, worship, etc.), most often memorizing them through intensive repetition. They may also collect their guru's teachings, sometimes only in memory, sometimes through writing, or, today, on video! Eventually, the tested and trusted disciples are also designated as gurus by the teacher, usually once they have reached an advanced age, and so the *parampara*, the succession, continues.

Accepting a guru entails assuming a new identity, which is symbolized in the widespread practice of receiving a new name. The true guru is the one who can open access to spiritual awakening, but the disciple can expect the guru's full grace and loving guidance only through the complete abandonment of ego.

Given the many material and psychological rewards bestowed on gurus, the possibility of clever charlatans, too, has long been recognized by the Hindu community. Yet even up to the present, most will show respect for all who conform to the role, acknowledging that, as one proverb goes, "Only Lord Shiva can say who is the true ascetic."

TALES OF SPIRITUAL TRANSFORMATION: Meeting the Guru

In the postcolonial era, Americans and Europeans who have sought Hindu teachers have left rich accounts of their first encounters. In this excerpt, Richard Alpert, the former Harvard researcher who became a popular Western interpreter of Hinduism as Ram Dass, describes his initial meeting with his guru, Maharaj-ji.

Some time later we were back with the Maharaj-ji and he said to me, "Come here. Sit." So I sat down

Ram Dass with his guru, Maharaj-ji.

and he looked at me and said, "You were out under the stars last night."

"Um-hum."

"You were thinking about your mother."

"Yes." ("Wow," I thought, "that's pretty good. I never mentioned that to anybody.")

"She died last year."

"Um-hum." . . .

"Spleen. She died of spleen."

Well, what happened to me at that moment, I can't really put into words. He looked at me in a certain way at that moment, and two things happened—it seemed simultaneous. The first thing that happened was that my mind raced faster and faster to try and get leverage—to get a hold on what he had just done. . . . And at the same moment, I felt this extremely violent pain in my chest and a tremendous wrenching feeling and I started to cry. I cried and cried and cried. And I wasn't happy and I wasn't sad. . . . The only thing I could say was it felt like I was home.

Source: *Be Here Now* (Kingsport, TN: Hanuman Foundation, 1978), p. 55.

New gurus continue to emerge and gather followers, a source of vitality and innovation that gives Hinduism today the impression of being "a sea of ever-shifting eddies and vortices that catch up individual believers in various aspects of their devotional lives."[12]

Living with Karma: Rituals, Astrology, and Rebirth

The classical doctrines associated with karma, reincarnation, and liberation are the center of Hindu (and Buddhist) belief, regardless of the school one follows or one's focus on a particular chosen deity. Karma is thus the most important spiritual force in the universe, determining one's place in the cosmos (as an animal, member of a human caste, etc.). What one does in a particular incarnation, however, then influences future destiny, so, properly speaking, Hindu belief does not posit a closed, fatalistic world-view. Nonkarmic causalities (natural forces, biological reactions, chance) also shape human life, so Hindus can say, like many Americans, "It was meant to be" as well as "Things just happen." Only enlightened saints are thought to be capable of knowing their karmic past and future; everyone else remains uncertain. For this reason, a steady menu of meritorious ritual is a sensible approach to living with karma, as is consultation with astrologers (again, a practice some Americans also incline to).

Karma doctrine assumes that a natural causal mechanism conditions individual destiny; but a person's destiny can be shaped by group actions, too. Husbands and wives worship together and act together in many ways. Marriage ritual ties couples for life and can include a vow to be reborn together in future incarnations (a popular motif in South Asian folklore). Entire families are thought to be shaped by the actions of elders.

Hindus today may explain their individual and collective destiny in terms of karma causality, but as the Maid's story on page 319 indicates, understandings about the workings of next-life destiny are anything but certain. For example, stretches in life may seem to be inexplicable except in terms of karma accumulated in the past, and some individuals do indeed see everything in life as fated from earlier lifetimes. But most Hindus believe that their destiny today and in future lifetimes is also determined in significant part by their future moral actions and ritual acts. The puranas and guru parables often state that being human and being Hindu are rare incarnations in samsara and should not be wasted. People may be reborn as other beings inhabiting this world, into purgatories (*naraka*) that receive evil human beings, or into heavenly realms (*svarga*) created by each great deity as dwelling places reserved for good and devout devotees. Indeed, many Hindus today regard rebirth in heaven, not union with Brahman, as the highest destiny.

A Hindu astrologer. Astrology provides suggestions about when to act in the world, in harmony with the planetary gods and one's own karma.

Gestures of Respect for the Divine

Despite the attraction of many middle-class Hindus today to the neotraditionalist movement, which we shall discuss later, respectful gestures and puja are the means by which Hindus relate to the divine wherever and in whatever form they find it. Stylized, formal greetings, prostrations, and a circumambulation are among the best-known ritual gestures.

Hindus greet each other by raising the joined palms to shoulder level and repeating "*Namaskara*"/"*Namaste*" ("salutation"/"greetings"), sometimes bowing. Some gurus teach that saluting other humans in this way is a theological statement: "I center my physical self in the atman located in my heart and salute your same holy center."

The core gesture of namaskara can be multiplied into any number of prostrations (*pranam*), principally either with the knees touching the ground or fully prone. This gesture, too, is one humans may do to other humans by, for example, grasping the feet of the one honored, such as a guru, a priest, an elder in the family, a mother-in-law (for a daughter-in-law), a husband (for a wife), or parents (for children).

Another Hindu perception of the body involves the differentiation between its two sides: The right side is the pure side and one eats with the right hand; the left hand is used to wash after calls of nature and is regarded as impure. As an extension of this, *pradakshina*, the circumambulation of an icon or temple, should be performed in a clockwise manner, keeping one's right side closest to the sacred object.

Namaskara or namaste, the gesture of respectful greeting directed to the gods and humans.

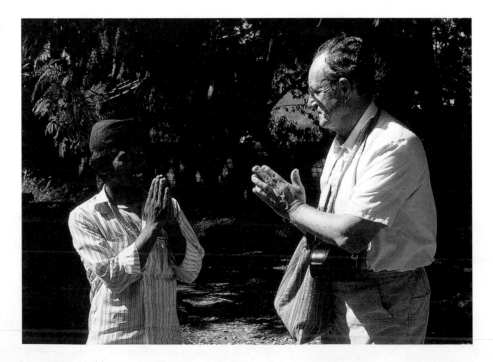

Puja

The concept of **puja**, or homage, is also built on the assumption that humanity and the divine must maintain an intimate connection, one marked by respectful hierarchy. For humans, the great deities (such as Shiva, Durga, and Vishnu) are superiors. Puja involves all the expressions by which an inferior can welcome, show respect for, and entertain a distinguished guest. Ideally, all ritual acts express a faithful bhakta's submissive, adoring, and self-negating service to the divine.

One doing puja seeks to please the deity as if the divine personage were human, that is, possessed five senses. All that Hindus offer as puja can be classified accordingly: Incense pleases the sense of smell; flowers please the senses of sight and smell; foods gratify the taste; mantras and music please the hearing; cloth and pastes please the deity's tactile sense.

The inseparability of otherworldly and mundane blessings is seen in the full process involved in making a puja offering and then receiving back the remains, *prasad*. These substances, having been proximate to the image, carry a subtle infusion of divine blessing, turning all prasad into "medicine." Food can be eaten, flowers worn in the hair, incense smoke wafted around the body, and holy water (*jal*) sipped. Colored powders that decorate an icon are carefully collected, mixed with water, and used to mark the forehead with a *tilak*, a spot in the center of the forehead above the eyes.

While the norms of different dharmas and of following one's own chosen deity have led Hindus to accept differences in religious orientation even among close family members, this "spiritual individualism" is balanced in most instances by the widespread and daily custom of families sharing from the same plate the prasad returned from the common family puja.

A good Hindu today, like a good Muslim, need never worship in public and may make all puja offerings to icons in a home shrine. In temples with priestly attendants, devotees usually place on the puja tray coins or uncooked rice to be taken by the priests, a meritorious service donation. It is through the medium of puja therefore that Hindu householders contribute to the subsistence of their priests and temples.

It is literally true that all the fine arts of South Asia developed as offerings made to the gods: instrumental and vocal music, dance, sculpture, and painting are all connected to temple rituals. Hindu temples are simply homes for ritually empowered icons that have been given "life" by brahmins chanting their heart mantras and by ritual painters who carefully paint in their eyes. They can be humble thatched buildings sheltering crude stones with no resident priests or magnificent palaces built to house jeweled images attended by hosts of priests and other temple servants. Great temples may be surrounded by monasteries, music pavilions, pilgrim hostels, and sacred ponds; these are the preeminent

puja: ritual offering to a deity

prasad: remains of any substance used in a puja, believed to have healing properties

Hindu puja. Ritual is the means of expressing individual devotion and soliciting divine grace.

centers of Hindu culture, and to visit them is to see all these cultural forms directed toward serving the gods with beauty, grace, and dedication.

Sacred Cows

One of the striking first impressions of South Asia is the free-ranging cows in villages and on city streets. Up through the 1960s, when India suffered its last major famine, many in the West said, "If only Hindus would eat beef, all their food needs could be met." What is certainly true is that cows are integral to Hinduism in many respects: One middle-period text suggests that all the divinities exist in the cow, and another sees the cow as an incarnation of the goddess Devi. Killing a cow is thus unthinkable. The cow's centrality is further seen in ritual practice: To mark and purify any space and make it suitable for puja, cow dung is a necessary ground coating; in addition, ingestion of any of the five products of the cow (milk, curds, butter, urine, dung) is the most potent source of ritual purification. Modern Hindu nationalists have chosen the cow to symbolize "Mother India."

Hindu Samskaras: Life-Cycle Rites

Being Hindu means following the proper path in life, determined by the dharma codes set forth by the ancient sages. An individual's life—like society's groups—should be properly organized. The *Dharmashastras* list over forty life-cycle rituals, *samskaras*; they are most observed today by families at the top of the caste hierarchy. We summarize the most popular contemporary practices briefly here, using terms and culture of northern India as representative.

Birth Rituals. Pregnant women are given empowered charms to protect the fetus and are made to stay within the family, isolated from demons and from sources of pollution. Despite the spilling of the mother's blood and bodily fluids, birth is a time of "happy pollution"; and for the period of the mother's recovery (up to ten days), the family abstains from puja and does not eat with outsiders.

Early Childhood Rituals. The ritual called *namkaran* serves to give an infant its formal name. Naming children after the deities is a common practice, and this can be done according to a parent's chosen deity, for the day on which the child is born, or simply for auspiciousness. The carefully noted birth time must be used to construct a horoscope, which will be kept for lifelong consultation. Before the first birthday, the final early childhood rite of first rice feeding introduces the baby to solid food.

Coming of Age. Boys and girls are led on different ritual paths emphasizing male dominance and female fertility. The rites marking adulthood for both sexes establish expectations and responsibilities of full Hindu personhood. Since the *Dharmashastra* forbids teaching Vedic verses to women, adult females are not assigned brahmanical rites but participate in their husbands' rituals. Women's ritual customs have nonetheless developed.

Hindus associated with large temples take out the images of the great gods yearly. The most dramatic of these outings is a large chariot, like this one in Puri, that is pulled by devotees (here in Madurai, Tamil Nadu, India) to earn merit.

Girls are initiated as women when they have their first menstruation, usually by going through a week of strict isolation, in which they are prohibited from seeing the sun or males. During this time, elder females in the family tell stories of the deities and instruct the girls on aspects of adult religious practice and the duties of Hindu women.

Boys of the top three castes are ceremonially given a sacred thread, after which they receive the first teachings from the family guru, including the rituals associated with the wearing of a multistranded thread (*janai*) over the left shoulder and right hip, a burden taken on from this day until death. (In modern times, this "wearing the thread" is maintained most consistently among brahmin families only.) Boys are also given their first mantra to memorize, the Rig Vedic Gayatri (3.62.10), to be repeated daily at the rising and setting of the sun:

We meditate on that excellent light of the divine sun
May he illumine our minds.

In adult initiation, boys become "twice-born" through this second birth into the knowledge of the Veda and Vedic ritual.

Householder. Marriage is usually arranged by the couple's families, although many young people today can veto a choice proposed for them. The relatives setting up the match must be satisfied that the individuals' horoscopes match harmoniously, to ensure that their characters and karmas are compatible. This is a judgment usually requested of an astrologer.

Upon marriage, a Hindu woman leaves her home, often with a dowry, to live with her mother-in-law, shifting forever her ritual center to the husband's family line. (This pattern is breaking down today in the urban middle classes, where employment patterns require transfers; also, among the rural population that is drawn to migrate to cities in search of jobs and education, nuclear families are common.)

Death. Death produces a crisis in the family and a state of corporate pollution that for immediate kin endures for an entire year. When someone dies, the family, out of love, wishes to perform all the rites carefully to ensure that the soul will go to its best possible rebirth. However, the death of a loved one also produces worry that the soul might be reincarnated as a dangerous or wandering ghost. This concern has given rise to the custom of cremating a corpse as soon as possible after death and before sundown. Carrying the body to the cremation site, the *ghat*, is men's work, with the eldest son lighting the pyre for the father and the youngest doing so for the mother. Some believe that when the heat of the cremation fire causes the skull to burst, the soul has been released to go to its next birth. The women, who stay at home during the cremation, must remove their ornaments and sweep the house, beginning to repurify the house polluted by death. The men who cremate must collect the burned remains so that the family can immerse them in a holy river.

After-Death Rites. Before the family may reestablish purity in their homes and resume social life, they must perform the first rites of feeding the departed soul, who is thought to wander as a ghost (*preta*) from twelve days up to one year. Here, Hindu tradition is preserved in the performance of the ancient Vedic rites: The mourners offer *pinda* puja, ritual rice ball offerings, to feed the soul and build up its intermediate-state body to be a preta and continue on its afterlife journey. Shraddha rites for parents and especially fathers are done yearly on the death anniversary.

Through this adherence to orthopraxy, we can see how ritual traditions define the individual Hindu's passage through the circle of life, from birth to death. The rituals generate good karma for the person, petition the gods for protection, and maintain the family in a state of ritual purity necessary for future pujas to be done. Similarly, we now survey the cycle of major festivals that mark the passage of the typical Hindu's day, month, and year. Here again, the unity of Hinduism is seen in the rituals that unite individuals, families, and communities to revere and petition the succession of deities in this ongoing cycle of festivals.

Hindu and Sikh Festival Practice

Many Hindus today carry a small pocket almanac that organizes the Western, lunar, and solar succession of days. Why are these so popular? Since the year is punctuated by a succession of great and small festivals, or *utsavas*, some lasting only a day, others stretching over ten days, Hindus must harmonize personal, family, and business affairs with the religious celebrations. Being a Hindu today entails celebrating this yearly cycle of festival observance: doing special rituals, recalling acts of divine grace, and feasting with family.

Part of the reason for this elaborate festival agenda is that across South Asia, it is customary for each important deity to have a special day and procession (*jatra*) that is the occasion for extraordinary acts of devotion. At these times, the god or goddess is felt to be more accessible to devotees and more inclined to extend grace to those who demonstrate their faith. The Hindu utsavas offer the chance to live in a profoundly different and sacred time, when the great salvific deeds known from legend and myth are retold by religious scholars (*pandits*) or enacted through live cultural performances. In many of the utsavas, special foods, drinks, and decorations are made that appear at no other time. Some festivals are reserved for fasting, ascetic acts, or other penances.

The greatest festivals celebrated in the notable religious cities of India are immense spectacles, and arranging for the myriad cultural performances and sideshows requires the participation of thousands. Arrays of electric lights, clouds of incense, and blaring loudspeakers (what one Hindu writer has called "the most important instrument of contemporary spirituality") overload the devotees' senses. The gatherings can create a marvelous sense of community among *bhaktas*, drawing pilgrims from afar to witness and to seek blessings.

Diwali

In India, the new year begins around the vernal equinox, a date also marking for Hindus the moment when creation in each world era begins anew. But across the north, the year begins with *Diwali*, the festival around the autumnal equinox that focuses on Lakshmi, goddess of wealth. On the main day families wear new clothes, sweep their houses clean, arrange a special altar with puja laid out for the goddess, and set up lamps (now, most are "Christmas lights") to guide her. On a subsequent day, brothers and sisters honor their kin ties, and individuals may do other special pujas to strengthen their health for the year ahead. Middle-class families now send "Diwali cards," akin to Christmas cards.

Sri Panchami

The festival of Sri Panchami is dedicated to Saraswati, the goddess of learning and the fine arts. Students, scholars, and artists all will flock to her temples. Some temples set up a whitewashed wall on which young children are to write their first letters, for traditional Hindu parents wait until this day to begin to teach their offspring to read and write.

Children enjoying Holi, the festival when humans join Krishna in living life as a divine sport.

Shiva Ratri

Shiva's Night, Shiva Ratri, is the end-of-winter festival, one of two festivals each year dedicated to Shiva. This festival emphasizes fasting and grand offerings to Shiva's phallic icon, the *linga*. Shiva Ratri also in some localities connects with the god's identity that imagines him controlling the myriad ghosts and goblins that occupy the lower portions of the Hindu pantheon. It is also the time for ascetics to make offerings at Shiva's great temples, which accordingly fill with thousands of sadhus and yogins who meditate, instruct devotees, receive donations, and demonstrate their powers.

Holi

lila: term reflecting theology of this world as a sphere of divine play

Hinduism's "feast of love," or Holi, is the year's primary festival honoring Krishna in his guise as the playful trickster god. In harmony with the theology called **lila** (divine play), devotees establish a set period for honoring the youthful Krishna. For the primary three or so days, all of society is at play, and normal caste and gender rules are suspended. In imitation of Krishna and to find harmony with his spirit, which transcends the mundane, all society should join in the lila, inverting established hierarchies and expectations. Women may sing lewdly in public or douse male passersby with buckets of water, and public officials such as policemen suffer usually playful pranks; in villages, an untouchable may be declared "headman" for the duration of the festival. On the last day, bonfires are lit to consume evil, commemorating Krishna's defeat of a female demon who sought his demise.

Tij

Tij is the festival for women, who can act in imitation of Parvati, one incarnation of Devi, who fasted, meditated, and underwent purification in the hopes of winning the husband she deserved. In her case, this was Shiva; for unmarried women, the hope is for a good human husband; for those already married, it is for the long life of one's spouse. For Tij, some women spend the night at a temple, where they sing devotional songs while fasting and listen to stories associated with Parvati and other exemplary women.

Dashara

In many places the largest yearly Hindu celebration, Dashara usually falls just before the first rice harvest. It has become the occasion for marking two separate divine events. For Rama bhaktas, this festival is *Rama Navami* (Rama's Ninth) the time for celebrating both Rama's birth and his victory over the demon Ravana, when he rescued his consort Sita and instituted an era of proper Hindu rule. *Durga Puja* similarly enfolds

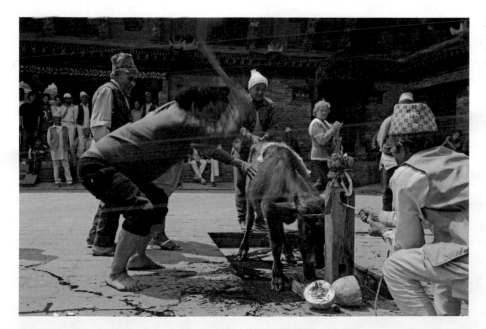

A male water buffalo is sacrificed to the goddess Durga in Kathmandu, Nepal.

the community in Durga's "Nine Nights" of struggle against Mahisha, the demon who could not be killed by a man and so threatened all creation. The "Victory Tenth Day" commemorates Durga's slaying of Mahisha, who had taken the form of a buffalo demon. To imitate the goddess in her moment of triumph and to bathe her images in the blood offerings that she most loves, devotees perform animal sacrifices at her temples, beheading primarily goats, fowl, and water buffalo.

Pilgrimage Festivals

From earliest times, Hindus believed the land bounded by the Himalaya mountains and the oceans to be holy. Thus the mountains and rivers of this region were imagined to be abodes of the deities and the places where enlightened sages have realized the highest truths. From then until now, devotees have gone on pilgrimage to see these sacred persons and places (for **darshan**, viewing the divine) and to dwell in the precincts blessed with spiritual powers. On their journeys today, Hindus do the rituals described for temples, make elaborate offerings and countless expressions of respect, and bring home treasured prasad. Modern transport has facilitated the expansion of pilgrimage in recent times.

darshan: seeing the divine; making eye contact with a god, holy site, or guru

Himalayas

The most dramatic and famous among the myriad Hindu sacred sites are located in the Himalayas, the world's highest mountain chain, where the very names of the snow-clad peaks reflect the perception of divine residence. According to one passage in the *Skanda Purana*, seeing any of the Himalayan peaks will

Pilgrims at the Amarnath Cave. Devotees worship the ice lingam of the great god Shiva found within this Himalayan hillside.

Temples like this in the Himalayas attract pilgrims and local devotees.

transform one's karma: "As the dew is dried up by the morning sun, so is the bad karma of mankind by the sight of Himalayas."

Ganges

Rivers are also focal areas for pilgrimage. The Ganges and its tributaries that flow down from the Himalayan glaciers all are associated with divinity: The Ganges itself, conceived as a goddess, was sent by the gods to succor humanity in the midst of a horrific drought. The Ganges is thus a divine entity; and as such, many bathing rites are done along its banks, where devotees hope to draw on her capacity to "wash away" bad karma. Ganges water is seen as the best source for purifying a ritual space, so pilgrims collect it and store it for future ritual use.

All rivers in South Asia are identified with the Ganges. A common legend known across the continent states that each river shares a subterranean connection with it. The points on the river best suited for human pilgrimage and ritualism are tributary confluences called **tirthas**. The literal translation of the word (ford, or river crossing) also indicates metaphorically that it is easier to cross the great river of samsara to reach heaven or moksha at a tirtha. Many of the great religious cities of South Asia are located along rivers.

tirtha: a holy space defined by a river confluence

The Kumbha Mela

The largest single religious gathering on earth in the early twenty-first century is not Muslims assembling in Mecca for the hajj but Hindus congregating at a holy tirtha for the Kumbha Mela. In 2013, at least 110 million Hindus gathered to bathe at Prayag

Ritual bathers in Varanasi, also known as Kashi or Benares. Located on the western bank of the Ganges and with its riverside *ghats* dominating the urban settlement, Kashi is the sacred city where pilgrims congregate.

("place of sacrifice"), on a riverside near modern Allahabad, where the Ganges, Yamuna, and invisible Saraswati rivers meet. The pilgrims entered the water at the exact auspicious moment connected with a story in the puranas in which the gods battled the demons over possession of a pitcher (*kumbha*) containing an immortality-giving elixir. After a long struggle, the gods won and became immortal; during the course of the battle, however, four drops of the elixir fell to earth at four places, and the site of the Kumbha Mela, which occurs every twelve years, rotates among them in a prescribed order. The Kumbha Mela draws hundreds of thousands of sadhus from their retreats to immerse themselves in the hyperdivinized river waters, where they are joined by millions of householders on pilgrimage, who bathe, offer puja, and sip the ambrosial river water, seeking an infusion of grace.

Ganges water purifies the Hindu devotee before puja.

Pilgrimage in Hinduism is not a requirement of the faith as in Islam, but the benefits are elaborately outlined in the later Hindu texts: healing, good karma, personal transformation. Pilgrims can go alone on foot or, with increasing popularity, in highly organized groups traveling on airplanes and buses. The goal may be to perform a ritual, such as a mortuary rite for a kin member. The more typical goal, however, is to seek general benefit through darshan and puja.

Sikh Festivals

The commonalities and divergences between Hindus and Sikhs are visible in the Sikh Festivals. These are known as *guru purb,* "guru remembrance" days for

The millions of Hindus who gather along the Ganges for a moment of grace at the Kumbha Mela form the largest religious gathering on earth today.

remembering the teachers. The birthdays of all ten gurus beginning with Nanak are spread over the year, as are commemorations of the martyrdoms of great leaders. All of these holy days involve chanting of the Adi Granth; during most of them the entire text is read in a day over the forty-eight hours prior to the festival day. At the end, the sweet food *karah parshad* (made of flour, semolina, sugar, and butter) is given to all in attendance after it is prayed over. There are three main festivals that coincide with the great Hindu celebrations but also mark key dates in early Sikh history. First in importance is the spring Baisakhi. It is during this festival, which celebrates the creation of the Khalsa in 1699, that new members of this group are initiated. On this day, the Sikh flag flown at homes and gurudwaras is replaced. The fall festival of lights, Divali, for Sikhs is the festival celebrating the release of the sixth Guru, Hargobind, and fifty-two followers from imprisonment by the Mughals; the lamps that Sikhs light celebrate their heroic return home. Hola Mohalla, a festival of mischief and play for Hindus, is the yearly occasion when Sikhs compete in martial arts and remember the Tenth Guru, Gobind Singh, and the Sikh teaching of protecting the weak and standing up for justice.

The Religious Institutions of Contemporary Hinduism

Although there is no single formal institution that unifies all Hindus, there are standard relationships that support the regular practice of ritual and the transmission of religious ideas. Most families have a relationship with a brahmin family priest whom they call on when there is the need for a life-cycle rite or when someone wishes to perform a special puja.

A Typical Smarta Shaiva Temple

One place of worship that can be found widely in upper-caste communities across the subcontinent is a Smarta temple, attended by a brahmin priest. In it, the major gods of the pantheon we have mentioned are enshrined, with the addition of the sun god, who presides over the astrological deities. Shiva usually is the central god, most often worshipped in his linga icon. The typical Smarta temple has the following standard layout:

The predominant religious institution of Hinduism, however, is the temple, and it is thought highly meritorious to build one that houses an empowered icon. Hindus from all classes, alone or collectively, have done so, but the temples built by the great kings enable the most complete expressions of Hindu religious culture. Yet the major temples are more than shrines: They include lands given to the deity and are supported by endowment funds that are continually augmented by the cash offered with puja.

Temple lands are usually rented out to tenant farmers, with part of the harvest going to the temple; other properties adjacent to the temple are often rented to merchants or artisans. Both rentals provide income for the upkeep of the temple buildings and payment for the priests. Through these relationships, Hindu temples have been integral to the local economies of South Asia, sometimes as the major landowners. Modern land reform has cut back on many of these holdings, forcing temples to find other means of support. In the summer of 2011, the hidden treasury of the Padmanabhaswamy Temple in southern India was found to hold $22 billion in gold, jewels, and statues.

The more organized sects and sadhu orders rely on the *matha*, or monastery, to serve as a venue for schooling and training for ritual service under an abbot (*mahant*). Some modern groups, such as the Ramakrishna Mission, have built their pan-regional reform movement through a network of mathas. Another familiar institution is the *ashram*, a retreat dedicated to supporting gurus and their disciples, thereby maintaining the relationship that is one of the central lifelines of Hindu culture.

Changes and Continuities: Examples of Postcolonial Hinduism

Across the Hindu world each day, brahmins memorize, recite, and pass on to their sons the millennia-old Vedic rituals and hymns as well as devotional songs composed centuries ago. Ancient rituals are vigorously practiced in millions of households.

Certain gurus are regarded by thousands as divine incarnations. Increasing numbers of pilgrims flock to the great temples, consulting the institutions' websites for guidance. Ascetic communities in ashrams train in yoga and engage in silent meditative retreats. Religious innovations among Hindus multiplied further through the colonial period and after independence, with recent teachers and globalization adding yet newer strands to the fabric of Hinduism. A 1986 gathering of nearly a thousand abbots of Hindu monasteries, one of the first ever held, assembled teachers representing 165 different organized spiritual traditions.

Yet modern medicine, mass media, and expanding transportation technology have changed how millions of Hindus understand and encounter Hindu doctrines and myths and even how they perform the puja rituals. Within major Indian cities today, a middle class is emerging whose lifestyle and experience have been highly influenced by Euro-American media culture, education, and connections. Institutions and "yoga centers" among this middle-class elite are developing newly synthesized approaches to Hindu spiritual practices, in forms similar to those found in European and American cities. The global spread of Hinduism now impacts the faith in South Asia. Digital CDs and videos posted online with sermons by gurus reach the global Hindu middle class, affording traditional doctrinal teachings far wider exposure than was ever possible by word of mouth.

Temple in Madras. Large temples are complex institutions with landholdings, charities, and resident priests.

Thus, Hinduism has assumed more forms today than ever in its history, and the linkage of religion to politics is growing. Since there is no one version or center of Hinduism that can stand alone, we will draw on a series of representative case studies to suggest the broad sweep of Hinduism in the postcolonial era: modernizers, guru-based movements *not* influenced by science, and finally proponents of Hindu nationalism who object to India's postindependence character as a secular state.

Modernizers abound in reformist Hinduism today. Some teachers and movements begun in the modern era (such as the Ramakrishna Mission) make strong assertions about the compatibility between scientific thought and venerable Hindu doctrines. The "big bang" hypothesis of creation, relativity theory, and the cosmological theories of multiple universes are referred to by these modernizers as compatible with—even anticipated in—the ancient scriptures. Hindu exponents have also proposed scientific explanations for rebirth and karma doctrines. Even the Vedas have been interpreted to credit the seers with awareness of contemporary technological possibilities (e.g., airplanes, genetics, brain waves). Hindu confidence that the traditional teachings will stand up to whatever science discovers is striking among modernists. Just as many scientists around the world (including many in India) refrain from suggesting that their discoveries are ever likely to disprove the existence of God or the reality of spirit, many highly educated Hindus have found no reason to abandon the essentials of their faith. Those with technological savvy have energetically expressed their faith on websites, and by 2014 an estimated 33,000 were dedicated to the many sides of Hinduism. Recent events and developments indicate how Hinduism has endured so strongly among such modernists.

Ganesh's Milk Miracle

A deity who attracts the devotion of nearly all Hindus is elephant-headed Ganesh, divine son of Shiva and Parvati. Ganesh is beloved for his earthy character, his potbellied silhouette, and his reputation as a remover of life's obstacles. Ganesh temples are found in nearly every locale where Hindus live. On September 21, 1995, at temples across North India, priests and devotees reported that icons of Ganesh had begun to drink the cows' milk that was being offered to them as part of the daily puja. The stories soon

Elephant-headed Ganesh, god of success, is found in every Hindu community. He is always worshipped first and before any major undertaking.

spread across the subcontinent by telephone and in press accounts, so thousands of Hindus from all walks of life rushed off to visit their local temples to offer milk, hoping to witness the phenomenon. Telephone and the Internet just as quickly spread the news across the globe, and Hindus in London, Jersey City, Los Angeles, and Toronto began to report similar experiences.

For believers, this was merely the latest in a long-running series of demonstrations that the divine is alive, connected to humanity and capable of conferring grace on those who serve the gods. From uneducated peasants to brahmin priests, people were citing the reports of disappearing milk as ample proof of the existence of a Supreme Being who accepts the offerings of his disciples. Whatever else this incident reveals about the role of the media and the Hindu diaspora, it also demonstrates that modern believers hold the conviction that the divine is immanent, a traditional view that has shifted little amid all the changes of the modern era.

The reaction was interesting, too: The "miracle" gave rise to widespread public debate and rallies organized by Hindu societies (such as New Delhi's "Guru Busters") whose purpose is to expose charlatans and promote rational faith. Predecessors for these modern skeptics and atheists can be traced as far back as the time of the Buddha (fifth century BCE). Although the popular Western imagination about India and Hinduism has been informed by romantic accounts highlighting mysticism and exotic theistic spirituality, it is important to note that there is an equally long-established South Asian tradition of hard-nosed skepticism.

Comic Books and Televised Epics

The modern printing press gave early Hindu reformers a means to reach a mass audience across the subcontinent more quickly than ever before. Ritual manuals, vernacular translations of texts, tracts on saints, interreligious debates, or even reformers' reductive definitions of "true Hinduism" (such as that proposed by the Arya Samaj or modern fundamentalists) reach the literate masses through such publications. South Asia's religious environment during the modern era has also been unified by the lithography of religious poster art, which has spread common inexpensive images of the deities.

An important mass media format appearing well after the end of colonialism is the religious comic book. Adopting reformist doctrines and linking far-flung Hindu communities is the Amar Citra Katha series of over 270 titles, in which newly standardized versions of the great stories of Hindu scripture are offered in colorful illustrated formats; the text is written in English and in various vernaculars. Under the editorship of Anant Pai (1929–2007), more than 90 million copies of 400 Amar Citra Katha texts have been sold, and in recent years they have been transposed into cartoons and animated programs. This series has emphasized for middle-class readers that "true Hinduism" is rational, opposed to violence and superstition, upheld by heroic devotees, and based on the respectful accommodation of other spiritualities (Hindu and non-Hindu) in the interest of national integration.

In India, there are countless comic books devoted to describing the stories of the Hindu gods and human saints. Most are printed in the vernacular languages of the subcontinent, as well as in English. Here, a pivotal scene from the great epic, the *Ramayana*.

Television broadcasts of religious epics have also been pivotal cultural events. In 1987 India's national broadcasting system, Doordarshan, began showing in weekly installments its Hindi version of the *Ramayana*, one of the two great religious epics that date back to the early classical era. Although most Indians do not own television sets, groups crowded into tea stalls or banded together to rent TVs and view the series. Many treated the experience of viewing the transmitted image like a visit to a temple. Bathing beforehand, they arrived carrying incense and garlanded the television sets. Some watched with their hands joined together, using the namaste gesture directed to the divinities on screen, and some muttered prayers as the sacred scenes unfolded, weekly for over a year.

An estimated audience of 80 million watched the one-hour Sunday morning program, and the pace of life on India's streets visibly slowed. The media's *Ramayana* gave the nation its first "national version" of the epic, one that celebrates the glories of the legendary Hindu king Rama and his struggle to establish a just and prosperous Hindu nation. Doordarshan had to extend the series to meet popular demand. It has subsequently produced and broadcast an even longer series on Hinduism's second great epic, the *Mahabharata*, as well as dramatizations of other devotional stories centered on the great deities, such as Krishna and Shiva.

The accessibility of lavishly produced TV productions of religious epics, complete with special effects, has in places undercut the relation between priest, teacher, and laity. Many argue, however, that Hindu nationalism has been strengthened by the common experience of viewing these sacred scenes.

The Dilemmas of Reform: A Young Bride Commits Sati

Following the norms of her caste and the Hindu law books, Roop Kanwar, an eighteen-year-old bride, went to live with her husband's family in Deorala, in the western Indian state of Rajasthan. But seven months later, on September 4, 1987, her husband, Mal Singh, died suddenly. Following ancient custom, the young man's kin prepared to cremate him on a pyre outside the town boundaries immediately before sunset. What happened next shocked India: Roop Kanwar was also burnt alive atop her husband's funeral pyre, becoming a *sati* ("virtuous [one]"), one of forty-two known cases since 1947. Five hundred people reportedly witnessed the act. What remains unclear were the widow's motivations and how freely she went to this death.

Rajasthan state officials were called to act on the basis of India's National Penal Code that holds widow immolation under any circumstances to be illegal. Reformers argued that those connected with Roop Kanwar's death should be prosecuted as murderers. Eventually, under pressure from national politicians and women's groups, members of Mal Singh's immediate family were arrested and an investigation ensued. Several months later the family members were released on bail, but no charges were ever filed. Few witnesses could be found who were willing to testify.

Sati is one Hindu practice that the British actively sought to end through explicit legal prohibition. The immolation of widows was held up for ridicule by many Hindu modernizers as evidence of how Indian society needed to break with blindly followed traditions and to reform its ways. Yet in 1987, over 50,000 devotees gathered for a commemorative ceremony for Roop Kanwar held thirteen days after her death. Some formed the Sati Dharma Raksha Samti (the "Committee for the Defense of the Religion of Sati"). The site of the burning pyre has been transformed into a shrine, outside of which artisans sell ritual photos of the site and other mementos. Since 1987, the Singh family has received many tens of thousands of rupees from donations. Throughout the town, the young widow is now celebrated by drummers and chanting youth as a brave *Sati-ma*, a divine figure who was blessed by and merged with the mother goddess, Devi.

The debate about this issue was renewed in 2008 when a seventy-one-year-old wife committed sati in eastern India; recent studies suggest that this practice is still far more common than officially reported. Again, controversy surrounded the question of whether the death was truly voluntary and whether the secular state should regulate this religious practice. Is the legal code that prohibits the custom and defines sati as barbaric binding? Or, as Hindu traditionalists insist—and many in this camp are again

GENDER FOCUS: The Divine Feminine and Hindu Women

Considering the role of women in Hinduism is a very confusing task, and the multivocalic nature of great religious traditions is especially clear here.

One impression can be found in viewing a performance of classical Indian dance, *Bharata natyam*, a tradition that has spread from southern India and is now found across India and is common in global performance. The woman dancer with subtle gestures and bold rhythmically timed steps portrays the great stories of the Hindu classics.

Another reality about Hindu women is that prescribed in the ancient texts. The *Laws of Manu* instruct men to control their women and for women to accept it as their sacred duty to obey first their fathers, then their husbands, and finally their sons. Lesser good karma is said to be the reason for birth as a female, and the troubles of menstruation and childbirth are accordingly their burden. In public life, the submission of women to men is clear, a norm underwritten by religious sanction. Among the many global Hindu gurus, there are a few women among a large male majority. Only in the esoteric tradition of tantra are women reckoned as equals.

Yet another powerful source of understanding the divine feminine in this tradition is the prominence of goddesses in the Hindu pantheon. There is the peaceful Lakshmi, nurturing goddess of wealth; Saraswati, the sustainer of arts and learning; Durga, slayer of demons; and Kali, the scary embodiment of death's inevitability. No religious tradition in the world has a richer diversity of goddesses who are worshipped, meditated on, and taken as embodiments of the ultimate reality.

local citizens and state politicians—should the state respect freedom of religion and allow Hindu women to follow this path to seek liberation?

The Spiritual Marketplace for Neotraditionalism: Popular Guru-Based Movements

Most conspicuous over the last decades has been the rise of cults and sects catering to the urban middle class. What is it like to live in the urban middle class today in South Asia? It involves confronting conflicting claims on one's identity and loyalty, as loyalty to one's "primordial" allegiances (caste, kin, home, region) clashes with the cosmopolitan and socially fluid urban culture that aspires to "be modern" and join the global culture of CNN, the Internet, and designer clothing. Traditional ties are to be honored at some level, but they no longer can fully contain the individual's deepest feelings of belonging.

Focused on sadhus and drawing inspiration from the reformists and revivalists of the nineteenth century, most of the new sects that have attracted the support of this new middle-class elite have proclaimed their own view of "essential Hinduism" as more belief oriented and less ritualistic. Just as modern technology has undercut to some extent the roles of priest and guru, the new sects have diminished the relevance of caste and regional social identity to spiritual seeking. Mass media and websites promote the teacher's message and link distant adherents. A number of the new sects have quickly built an international membership. In some cases they have benefited from praise and support for Hindu gurus active abroad, which has whetted an appetite for their teachings back home in South Asia. Most also emphasize women's participation. All engage their society and include community development, medical service, and educational initiatives, combining various traditional Hindu doctrines and practices with others adopted from Protestant missionaries.

Sathya Sai Baba. No modern Hindu saint has drawn devotees from as far and wide across India's urban middle classes as Sathya Sai Baba (1926–2011), a teacher known as much for the miraculous feats credited to him as for his instruction. A vigorous opponent of Western cultural influences on Hindu civilization and individual Hindus, Sai Baba advocated an active life informed by scriptural study and charitable giving; he taught a form of classical silent meditation that involves fixing one's gaze on a flame.

Sai Baba's trusts have established a vast network of service organizations: There are junior and senior Service Corps whose members feed the poor, act when disaster strikes, visit the sick, and so on. There are at present four Sai Baba colleges (three for women, one for men) that include educational outreach programs aimed to help small children. The ashram he established in 1943 marked the beginning of a large global movement toward neotraditionalism.

Sai Baba's fame and stature were based on accounts of his supernormal feats of multiple presence, miracle cures, and materializing out of the air items, including sacred ash, food, books, and even Swiss watches. Devotees see these powers of the traditional yogin saint as evidence that Sai Baba was an avatara of a divinity. Indeed, he said that he was Shiva and his consort in a single body. Through Sai Baba, disciples can see one of the perennial themes nurtured in the myriad South Asian traditions: that the divine is alive and appears in human form and that this world is still enchanted with grace. His death in 2011 was reported widely in the global media.

Brahma Kumaris. In India today, the most ardent sectarian proselytizers (especially across the northern states) are from the group called Brahma Kumari. Their Raja Yoga centers, also called "spiritual museums," are the organizing points around which each local chapter draws interested individuals and publicity, primarily among urban dwellers. The museums display doctrine-oriented pictures, with a member providing commentary; visitors who show interest are invited to attend meditation sessions and classes. By 2014, these institutions were being maintained by 15,500 full-time religious teachers. This is another group that stems from a charismatic teacher. The visions and spiritual experiences of the founding guru, Lekhraj (1876–1969), a jeweler from Hyderabad, inspired an early following. In 1936 Lekhraj established the Brahma Kumari sect and turned his entire wealth over to the first community.

Lekhraj attributed his vibrant visions portending the end of the world cycle to the grace of Shiva, the deity who commands the group's ritual attention. He also insisted that individuals must engage in radical purifications to survive and to inherit paradise. Such cleansing could come only through celibacy, vegetarianism, abstinence from tobacco and alcohol, and specific yoga practices. These traditional disciplines became the core practices of the Brahma Kumaris. The vow of celibacy, long an ideal for Hindu ascetics, is here extended to all householders. As a result, married couples who become disciples have to transform their marital relations to be expressions of "pure, noncarnal spiritual love." This teaching created serious domestic strife in the early community, forcing Lekhraj and his initially small circle of devotees to move to Karachi and later, after partition (1947), to Mount Abu in western India. Once there, the movement was transformed from a reclusive sect to an aggressively outgoing one. Soon missionaries had established centers across the major North Indian cities. Here is their mission statement:

> We teach a practical method of meditation that helps individuals understand their inner strengths and values. A worldwide family of individuals from all walks of life, we are committed to spiritual growth and personal transformation, believing them essential in creating a peaceful and just world. Acknowledging the challenges of rapid global change, we nurture the well-being of the entire human family by promoting spiritual understanding, leadership with integrity, and elevated actions towards a better world.[13]

Although its bhakti doctrines and cosmology could be characterized as drawn from premodern Hinduism and its silent meditation practices are drawn from traditional yoga, Brahma Kumari social practices are reformist and focused on women. Brahma Kumaris challenge Hindu society's patriarchal doctrines and ethical norms; the sect

Indian schoolchildren in Bhopal performing yoga exercises sponsored by the state government of Madhya Pradesh.

invites women to awaken to their divinity through connecting devotionally with the powers of traditional Hindu goddesses. Women leaders in the group also include members who serve as mediums, going into trance states to bring back messages from the gods as well as deceased teachers such as the founder, Lekhraj.

In recent years, the Brahma Kumaris have won recognition from India's leading politicians for supporting the establishment of a "value-based society," as members work with UN agencies on educational projects across South Asia. In the last decade, the Brahma Kumaris have claimed status as an independent religion, rejecting the label of "Hindu." In 2014 the group counted membership at 1 million. Over 8,500 Brahma Kumari centers exist, most in India, but also now found in over 100 other countries.

The Connection of Religion with Philanthropy and Social Reform

The impact of Christianity on Hinduism, as we noted earlier, was not primarily doctrinal but more in the arena of modeling the role of modern religious institutions and the scope of religious service in society. Just as Christian missionaries had shown that churches could be linked with schools and hospitals, Hindu reformers (e.g., the Ramakrishna Mission and Sai Baba) who have begun spiritual movements almost without exception have included social welfare initiatives to address the nation's undeniable needs. Initially, perhaps, this was done in competition with the Western missionaries; but the idea also found support from many Hindu teachers promoting the spiritual power of selfless, compassionate service and extolling individuals to engage in humanitarian merit-making.

As a result, most Hindu mathas have started educational institutions, and many sponsor clinics, orphanages, and hospitals staffed by their own trained staff. Hindu gurus cite a variety of reasons for the motivation that mathas now display for social work. Some state that the Indian people required inspiration from leaders who do not merely retreat to caves and meditate; another sadhu leader of one of India's largest monasteries described his work in education as necessary to make democracy a success. Yet another prominent swami, while acknowledging a desire to serve the people and foster humanitarianism, admits that his monastic order engages in social work primarily to dispel the impression that only other religions do it. New Hindu organizations are heavily engaged in addressing the poverty and suffering still endemic in modern South Asia. A prominent example of this engagement with contemporary problems is the pollution in the Ganges River. As elsewhere in the industrial world, urban municipal governments have used this sacred river as a sewer, and private companies have dumped their untreated factory wastes in it; hence, in many places, the Ganges has dangerous water toxicity and pollutant levels. So pernicious has this problem become that at the end of the great Kumbha Mela in 2007, thousands of Hindu holy men staged two days of protest and filed a lawsuit, threatening to lead others to boycott the next festival unless the government immediately began corrective actions to clean up the river. It remains to be seen, however, whether the convictions of religious leaders can really counterbalance the power of industrialists.

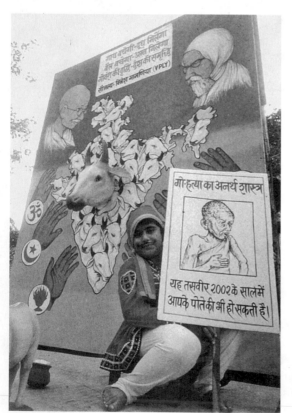

Poster at a political rally suggests that veneration of the cow provides the basis for unity among Indians of every religious group.

Religious Nationalism: Secular India and Its Discontents

As we noted earlier, many of India's anticolonial nationalist leaders were educated in England, and more than a few were unalterably committed to creating modern India as a secular democracy. They knew that religious strife in Europe had led to the formation of most modern Western nations, and they wanted to avoid the problems among the complex and competing religious communities in India that would inevitably result if any sectarian favoritism were shown. Indeed, most of the early political leaders, who were high-caste Hindus, feared what civil and partisan strife the Hindu majority might bring to the subcontinent. In the end, they succeeded, with British help, in marginalizing groups such as the RSS that wanted to establish India as a Hindu nation.

In practice, however, the democratic and secular Indian state has proved to be an ally of the high castes, particularly brahmins, in comparison with its British predecessor. This has led to the suggestion that in its actual workings, India's "secular state" really amounts to a form of "neo-Brahminism." Under British rule until 1947, brahmins held 3 percent of government jobs, a figure almost exactly equal to their proportion in the population. In 2000 (the latest year that statistics are available), however, their hold on civil service positions was as high as 70 percent, while their representation in the general population remained much the same as in 1947.

Yet in a curious and paradoxical development, and despite the state's administration's being heavily skewed toward their interests, high-caste politicians have convinced growing numbers of citizens that Hindus have been discriminated against by the laws and policies of secular India. Thus, throughout the 1990s, the BJP, the party controlled by members of the upper castes, campaigned on the basis of promises to establish a strong Hindu nation. Victories in state and national elections came in 1998.

The first national BJP government (1998–99) decided to explode India's first atomic bomb and several of its Hindu leaders periodically question the patriotism of Indian Christians. There have been incidents across the nation in which Hindu terrorists have burned down churches and murdered Christians.

The BJP and its high-caste supporters also want to reverse the secular state's efforts to uplift Muslims and others equally impoverished among the lowest castes. In regions where rich landholding, high-caste elites control local politics, lower castes have begun to mobilize to contest new elections in India's 700,000 villages; using their great demographic plurality, growing numbers among these humble groups, including many women, have been elected as village council leaders. As we have seen, this is an inversion of ancient Hindu caste law norms and traditional karma theory. During the first months of BJP rule, massacres in lower-caste settlements were reported across North India; in most cases investigated, the killings were found to represent efforts to intimidate groups that had voted against high-caste candidates or had sought state intervention to enforce lower-caste rights.

Then, in 2002, anti-Muslim riots in the state of Gujarat, allegedly abetted by its BJP government, left over 2,000 Muslim dead, with 35,000 homeless. A group of outside, independent judges collected testimony and summarized these horrific events:

> Hindutva hooligans came out into the streets . . . and in all flaming fury, targeted innocent and helpless Muslims. They were brutalized by miscreants uninhibited by police; their women were unblushingly molested; and Muslim men, women, and children, in a travesty of justice, were burnt alive. The

Violence between communities in India, especially along Hindu-Muslim and Hindu-Christian lines, has increased in recent decades. This photo depicts a Hindu mob advancing in Ahmedebad during the 2002 riots.

chief minister, oath-bound to defend law and order, variously connived at the inhuman violence and some of his ministers even commanded the macabre acts of horror.[14]

International human rights investigators joined in blaming this pogrom on the VHP (see below) and its youth wing, the Bajrang Dal, for planning these events. Yet few arrests were ever made in Gujarat. Not surprisingly, Muslim resentments, calls for revenge, and terrorist reprisals directed against the Hindu majority have increased across India. Did the BJP's subsequent national defeats in the national elections signal that the allure of strident Hindu nationalism has begun to wane? Secularists are concerned that Gujarat's chief minister during these riots, Narendra Modi, became Prime Minister of India in 2014.

The VHP: Hindu Leaders in Search of a Religious Nation

Vishva Hindu Parishad (VHP): organization of religious leaders that promotes the creation of a Hindu India

Linked to the RSS and the Bharatiya Janata party, the **Vishva Hindu Parishad (VHP)** (Council of All Hindus) was founded in 1964 as an organization of religious leaders who, while retaining their own disciples and spiritual agendas, wished to promote the interests of Hindus and a general kind of spiritual Hinduism. In agreement with earlier reformers and actually internalizing some of the criticisms made by European colonialists, the VHP views Hinduism as in decline, seeks the roots of the faith in the earliest texts, and considers the *Bhagavad Gita* to be Hinduism's preeminent scripture.

Although we have spoken of the lack of a central institution as a characteristic of Hinduism, one measure of the VHP's rise is its increasing success at securing unity among hitherto independent spiritual leaders. It has also spread to twenty-five countries, including the United States. Projects undertaken in common include religiopolitical festivals, missionary projects in tribal areas (including campaigns to "reconvert" some Indians from Christianity or Islam), and uplift initiatives among the "untouchable" castes. Critics have noted that such VHP efforts serve to add to the number the group can count as members of the "Hindu majority" in the state of India. But VHP supporters point out that uplift projects among the "untouchables" act on Gandhi's exhortation of Hindus to work to end the "evils of caste society."

The VHP argues that the era before Muslim rule (1200 CE) was a golden age for Hinduism, a time of social egalitarianism, prosperity, just rulers, and a wealth of enlightened seers. But with the Muslim conquest and such actions as the razing of temples to build mosques, Hindu culture declined; subsequent British domination of India made matters worse, causing further stagnation and division among all groups. The VHP views the secular state of India created in 1947 as a further means of dividing Hindus and thwarting the establishment of a great civilization centered on "Vedic spirituality." It further argues that if this secularism can be overthrown, and with it a mind-set of inferiority induced during the colonial period, another golden age can begin. Accordingly, the VHP has voiced support for dismantling any mosques that were (in the party's historical determination) built over Hindu temples in centuries past. The destruction of the mosque in Ayodhya in 1992 attracted attention to the group and support from ultranationalists, as did the VHP's marketing scheme to raise funds by selling bricks for the construction of the new Hindu temple planned for the site. The VHP leaders still express their wish to see other Muslim shrines removed from Benares and Mathura, and many defend the 2002 massacres against Muslims in Gujarat as being brought on by Muslims themselves.

Sikh Separatism and Globalization

Because the British invested heavily in irrigation and infrastructure in the Punjab, by the postcolonial era the Sikh home territory had become one of the most productive agricultural regions of India. But partition was a terrible blow to the Sikhs, as it divided their Punjab homeland and put Sikhs between fleeing Muslim and Hindu refugees, and the shocking massacres each inflicted on the other. Sikhs had to flee to India and abandon holy sites in the Pakistan Punjab; subsequently, Indian politicians divided up the Indian Punjab politically and in development initiatives in ways that were regarded as discriminatory against the Sikh majority. Anti-Brahmin sentiments grew. Although Sikhs became one of the wealthiest ethnic groups in postcolonial India, there were many who were left out and felt aggrieved by these events.

Despite Sikh prosperity, these grievances pulled more Sikhs toward the radical leaders who in the

With greater recognition of the religious pluralism of diverse global communities, differences in ritual beliefs and practices are becoming more widely known. In a parody of the cartoon *South Park*, Sikh cartoonist Dalbir points out difficulties of following religious law. Although many Sikhs are vegetarian, Sikh dietary rules allow the consumption of all meats if the animal was slaughtered compassionately. Some cartoons have also created inter- and intracommunity conflicts.

1980s revived a pre-independence demand for a Sikh homeland in Punjab, following the logic that had led to the creation of Pakistan as the homeland for South Asian Muslims. Guerrillas tried to transform this region into a de facto separate state they called Khalistan, extorting contributions they identified as "taxes" from Sikh farmers and merchants while randomly murdering Hindus living there. The movement had support in the Akali Takht and was funded as well by contributions from Sikhs abroad.

In 1984, after armed secessionist leaders occupied the Golden Temple in Amritsar, the Indian government sent troops to invade this shrine to arrest a separatist militant named Jarnail Singh Bhindranwale, who sought to establish an independent Sikh state in the Punjab province, killing many and declaring martial law in Punjab. In this operation, code-named Operation Blue Star, Bhindranwale was killed, along with casualties on both sides. The Golden Temple complex also suffered a great deal of damage due to the fighting. Many Sikhs regarded the attack as a desecration of their holiest shrine.

Later in the year, prime minister Indira Gandhi was assassinated by two Sikh bodyguards, who had been outraged by the sacrilege. The murder triggered waves of violence: In 1987 and 1988, over 2,700 Sikhs were murdered in anti-Sikh rioting, and antistate terrorist attacks in Delhi and other large cities resulted in the death of over 3,000 Hindus. By the turn of the millennium, the separatist agitation had largely dissipated as moderate Sikhs came back into power in national politics and international support for an independent state declined.

Through the last decades of the twentieth century, the Sikh global migration continued, and now almost 15 percent of Sikhs live outside India. With over 23 million followers worldwide, including a growing number of Western converts, Sikhism is slowly being recognized for its distinctive spiritual development and as the youngest of the three great heterodox faiths that originated in India, the other two being Buddhism and Jainism. Sikhs have for decades resisted Hindu nationalism; the first prime minister after the fall of the BJP in 2004 was the Sikh leader Manmohan Singh.

A Growing Global Tradition

Hinduism has entered into Western awareness strongly. As we will also see in the case of Buddhism, this interest is selective, centered on yoga and meditation, with much less focus on ritual or law. Many Westerners have been trained as yoga teachers by Indian masters, and nearly every major American city and college town has centers where one can go to practice. For many, of course, this interest is confined to the athletic or health benefits, with the religious beliefs underlying the practices often downplayed or tailored to fit into the customers' existing belief system. To see the panoply of traditions and applications of yoga in the West, one need only pick up a copy of *Yoga Journal*, a magazine that in 2013 reported over 604,000 subscribers and reached over 1.9 million readers monthly. It has been calculated that over 14 million Americans now practice yoga.

TALES OF SPIRITUAL TRANSFORMATION: Swami Satchidananda's Moksha

"My highest experience . . . of Advaita Oneness was in 1949, a few months after my *sannyas* initiation [as a celibate ascetic]. It was in midwinter, when I visited Vasishta Cave, where the sage Vasishta performed austerities. I went into the cave, . . . where I reached a large room with a seat. As I sat there and meditated, I had the experience of transcending my body and mind, realizing myself as the Omnipresent. I forgot my individuality. It is impossible to explain exactly what this is. I must have spent several hours in that state. Then I heard a humming sound, OM chanting, coming from a long distance away. Slowly, slowly, it became louder. As it neared I became aware of my mind and body . . . . For some time, I couldn't see anything in the normal way. All over I saw light, light, light. The whole world appeared as a mass of light. There was only peace and peace was everywhere. The state persisted the whole day. I have had this experience very often, mostly when I visit a holy place."

Swami Satchidananda went on to become a guru whose teaching was centered in North America, founding an ecumenical movement called *Integral Yoga* in 1966. Since 1986, Integral Yoga has been centered in Yogaville, a thousand-acre ashram in rural Virginia, and has spread to twenty-eight countries and nearly 400 centers across North America.

Source: From Sita Wiener, *Swami Satchidananda* (New York: Bantam, 1970), p. 88.

The bow asana, as demonstrated by the yoga master and guru Swami Satchidananda (1914–2002).

RITUALS AND RITES: Temple Ritual by Brahmin Priests

Then: A Traditional Visit to a Hindu Temple

No example of how, in the postmodern world, geography means less and less is better than the case of visiting a Hindu temple. In the past, if you wanted to "have darshan" of the great, holy icon in a major temple in India, this meant planning a trip, negotiating the journey, and timing the visit on a day and time when the inner shrine would be open for viewing. The auspicious days on the lunar calendar would be considered; and if you wanted special rituals to be performed on your behalf by a brahmin priest, you had to make the arrangements in person. Major donations to the temple, or special group rituals, including the recitation by a brahmin priest of texts telling sacred stories, meant going to the temple itself and negotiating the details. All of these factors made it difficult to visit the great temples and to make special ritual offerings, and personal contact with notable pandits and priests was rare.

Now: Online Temple Darshan and Puja

With the facilities on the Internet now having broad bandwidth and reaching extraordinary speed, it is now possible to "visit" the great temples of India from anywhere in the world. The website http://onlinedarshan.com serves as a clearinghouse for going to temple websites across Hinduism's global diaspora. At hundreds of listed temples, webcams offer live sacred viewing of the main images, including the live sound of devotees singing devotional songs and priests chanting mantras. At the click of the mouse, the devotee can order a lamp or food offering and see it being placed before the deity. There is also a welter of information and other services (including a site to make credit card contributions to a new building or shrine) and a library of information about divine stories of the chief gods (including testimonials of blessings received by others who made online offerings). Sources for teaching children about the faith are also popular choices of the online devotee.

The ubiquitous Indian diaspora is increasingly important in the process of Hindu globalization. First and second generations of Indians settled in the United States are the nation's richest ethnic group in terms of per capita income, and the majority, who are Hindu, has supported the internationalization of the faith. For example, the Hindus of the Greater Boston area have organized and collected several million dollars to build a large South Indian–style temple in Ashland, Massachusetts. Temple leaders hired artisans from Madras and had the chief icons made to order; they also created an endowment that pays for the lodging and full-time employment of two brahmin priests, who are recruited for long-term assignments to serve patrons of the temple. Dozens of similar institutions exist across North America and Europe.

Temples also are the natural centers for cultural awareness and revitalization movements among immigrant Hindus. For example, the Arya Samaj of North America regularly sponsors conferences in Hindu temples that seek to "empower the next generation with Vedic values" by having youth "practice those values in daily life, maintain a linguistic link to Sanskrit, inculcate a spirit of humility, give back to the community," and live by the founding motto, *Krivanto vishvam arya* ("Make this world noble").[15] Hindu nationalists have also spread their activism in America through temple institutions and summer camps for youth. The VHP has raised funds for causes back in India, and its members have sought to have public school textbooks in California rewritten to conform to their ideological interpretations of Indian history and Hinduism.

All immigrant Hindus today must submerge many of their regional traditions in joining with coreligionists from all over India to provide a homogenized working definition of "Hinduism." Indicative of this trend is the work of the Pancajanya Project founded by devout Hindus in the Asian-American Hotel Owner's Association: since 2008, they have placed over 150,000 copies of the *Bhagavad Gita* in hotel rooms in thirty states. As with other immigrant groups that assimilated in America, parents express some dismay and nostalgia for the traditions they followed back in Kerala or Bengal; their children are taught a simplified and essentialized version of "Hinduism": to chant "OM," do simple yoga, and interpret the *Bhagavad Gita* as a text lauding "caring and sharing."[16]

Converts and immigrant groups also have supported the global extensions of religious centers founded by modern gurus. In the West there are now hundreds of Hindu teachers who travel to the West to give teachings. Several dozen have shifted to ashrams and yoga centers outside India to dedicate their lives to their Western converts and South Asian immigrants. Perhaps the most successful of all the global Hindu gurus was the sadhu Maharishi Mahesh Yogi, who in the 1960s came to prominence by giving spiritual instruction to the Beatles. His movement, Transcendental Meditation

Across Europe and North America, increasingly affluent immigrant communities are building magnificent, traditional Hindu temples. This temple in Omaha, Nebraska, opened in 2004.

Global Hinduism: Transcendental Meditation (TM)

For fifty years until his death in 2008, Maharishi Mahesh Yogi brought mystical Hindu teachings to the West. Having introduced mantra-centered meditation to over 6 million seekers across the world, each of whom paid for the initiation (in 2006: $2,500), Maharishi's TM has established yoga centers around the world and founded a Vedic University in Fairfield, Iowa. TM now seeks to implement the guru's vision of rebuilding world spirituality and healing humanity, combining Vedic principles with those of quantum physics. With assets of $300 million in the United States, the group now focuses on (i) training advanced yogis in forty countries whose levitations can "produce quantum shifts to heal humanity's overstressed minds"; (ii) coordinating sessions across the globe in which meditators numbering the square root of the world's population (8,000, according to Maharishi's theory) will positively alter the planet's atmosphere and so the planet's humane consciousness; and (iii) building 3,000 "marble peace palaces" in major cities to offset the disharmonious locations. Having turned eighty-nine in 2006 and living in an ashram in the Netherlands, Maharishi expressed his aim: "My coherence-creating groups are going to put out all this mischief-mongering in the world. The world is going to come out to be a neat and clean world. All these countries will fade away." In recent years after the death of TM's founder, this organization has been vigorously promoted by the Maharishi's prominent disciple, the Hollywood director David Lynch. He launched the Foundation for Consciousness-Based Education and World Peace, which is dedicated to spreading TM globally, and in particular to troubled youth and underperforming schools. The foundation has drawn many celebrities to be initiated in TM spiritual practices and to promote its programs, including Oprah Winfrey, Russell Brand, Ellen DeGeneres, and Susan Sarandon.

Source: Lily Koppel, "Outer Peace," *New York Times Magazine*, October 8, 2006, p. 24.

Maharishi Mahesh Yogi (1918–2008)

(TM), has taken Hindu tradition across the globe and inspired a long agenda for utopian initiatives.

As India has become an important player in the global computer and software business, older Hindu institutions and new movements have adopted the Internet technology. For example, a famous Ganesh temple in Bombay has set up a website in which viewers can have live darshan of the main icons, hear hymns being sung, and, with a few additional mouse clicks, make credit card contributions to sponsor pujas. The website of a Vishnu shrine in the northern state of Jammu offers similar scenes and services, adding maps, regularly updated weather reports, and hostel bookings to aid the estimated 4 million pilgrims who visit the temple annually in person.

As Indian workers and entrepreneurs have become important in the global marketplace, especially in the computer and software industry, observers have discerned the rise of "karma capitalism." Here we can recognize Hindu teachings exerting a new and powerful influence in the global marketplace of ideas. Indian philosophies have been integrated in elite business schools in a variety of ways: "self mastery" courses that now help to train managers "to boost their leadership skills and find inner peace in lives dominated by work"; Hindu "business gurus" such as C. K. Prahalad now teach that executives should conceive of companies in more holistic ways, to redefine success as larger than monetary profit, including the well-being of employees, customers, and the environment. Human resources initiatives at companies such as General Mills, Google, Aetna Insurance, and Target now regularly include yoga and meditation to benefit their employees and improve corporate productivity. Classical Hindu beliefs and practices have now become a creative influence on the culture of modern multinational business, with many now explicitly managing their enterprises to generate "good karma."[17]

Like immigrant communities across the world today, Hindu parents create programs that instill traditional religious beliefs and practices.

(above) International organizations like the Boy Scouts have adjusted their programs to include other religious traditions.

(below) The blessings of the Hindu gods are sought in New Delhi by new car owners and, as shown here, by auto rickshaw owners. Hindu devotees today regularly perform pujas to avert accidents in cars, trains, and airplanes.

Conclusion

In the twenty-first century Hinduism assumes more forms than it ever has before, and the linkage of religion to politics is growing. Since it is impossible to take any religious tradition as standing for all of "Hinduism," we can only generalize about the broad patterns of change affecting the religion in South Asia. There is no doubt that India is changing, just as other parts of postcolonial Asia are. Newly built roads, transport systems, educational institutions, mass media, and industrialization are contributing to the rapid development of the economic system of the country, drawing migrants from rural settlements to burgeoning urban areas and transforming the life experiences of millions. In these settings, the Hindu traditions of the premodern world are in decline as new institutions and teachers arise to meet the needs of those living under these new circumstances.

But even with so much change, the belief in the spiritual presence of the gods, in yoga, and in the guru-centered spiritual life remains strikingly strong. It is easy to misinterpret surface changes as modifications to the religious tradition. Do cement buildings replacing cut stone temples or electric lights replacing the butter lamps for puja represent Westernization and the decline of traditional values? Or are they simply the transposition of new technologies in the service of the centuries-old wish to please the deities with artful decoration?

In the cities, among the rapidly expanding middle class as well as among slum dwellers, there are numerous new incarnations of "organized Hinduisms." Hitherto-independent groups such as sadhus from different regions are forming new organizations to work for common interests. Likewise, laity and priests associated with major temples have pressed for the establishment of management committees to orchestrate rituals and festivals as well as for supervising temple accounts. Thus, what in rural India was a largely preordained relationship with a family priest and local guru, in urban settings has become a matter of individual choice. Hindus in ever-increasing numbers, then, are faced with the "heretical imperative" (as discussed in Chapter 1) of making their own choices about their own religious paths. Media-savvy gurus appear on television, use video recordings and websites to link far-flung communities, and draw on a global network of disciples to build their movements. One of the most popular English-language magazines dedicated to promoting reformist Hinduism in India and abroad (*Hinduism Today*) is published not in Benares, but in . . . Hawaii.

As middle-class South Asians have raised their educational level, experienced rising prosperity, and encountered religions and societies elsewhere, they have been inevitably forced to consider "Hinduism" in comparison to these other belief systems and cultures. This process has been very

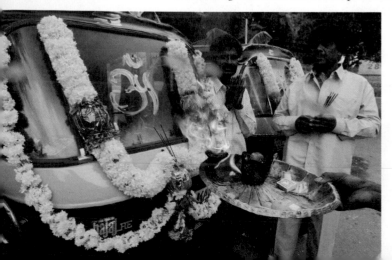

CONTRASTING RELIGIOUS VISIONS

As the following contrasting visions indicate, every religious tradition is capable of generating both visions that encourage peace and understanding and visions that encourage conflict and violence.

Peacemaker: Pandurang Shastri Athavale and the Swadhyaya ("Truth Seekers")

Pandurang Athavale (1920–2003) grew up in a family that was active in movements sponsored by M. K. Gandhi, the Mahatma. In 1956 he began organizing social uplift programs for the poorest low-caste groups, also drawing on a modernist reading of Hinduism's great spiritual classic, the *Bhagavad Gita*. Living modestly as a householder, Athavale prefers to be called Dadaji ("Elder Brother"), resisting the usual trappings of the title guru. His social programs have reached an estimated 20 million people living in 100,000 villages. The scope of this movement is due to the practice of *bhaktipheri*, or devotional visits, in which he or his followers spread the message of human service to new communities. His message is simple:

> It is my experience that awareness of the nearness of God and reverence for that power creates reverence for self, reverence for the other, reverence for nature, and reverence for the entire creation. And devotion as an expression of gratitude for God can turn into a social force to bring about transformative changes at all levels in the society.[a]

Acting on this conviction, members of Athavale's organization, called Swadhyaya, help build new temples that are ecumenical and open to all, and community centers for cooperative activities. Swadhyaya has become a worldwide movement, with 350 centers in the United States alone. The magnitude of the work and the authentic spirituality of the movement were the reason Athavale was awarded the 1997 Templeton Prize, the "Nobel for excellence in religious pursuits."

Confrontationalist: Voices from the Vishva Hindu Parishad

Arguing that Hindus have suffered from disunity, mindless pacifism, and Muslim predations over the last millennium, leaders associated with the "Council of All Hindus" have argued for revival by means of changing these old and decadent religious habits. An official inquiry on the Hindu-Muslim rioting in Bombay in 1993 reported that the responsibility lay in gangs of Hindus led by the Shiva Sena ("Shiva's Army"), a VHP ally. Members of this group went on a rampage, setting gasoline fires that burned Muslim businesses and homes. In the end, at least 1,200 Muslims died. A Shiva Sena leader commented several years afterward, "Who are these Muslims? If the Shiva Sena comes to power, everybody will take an initiation of the Hindu religion [to become Hindu]."[b] Similar uncompromising sentiments were expressed by the woman ascetic Uma Bharati, who proclaimed in 1991:

> Declare without hesitation that this is a Hindu country, a nation of Hindus. We have come to strengthen the immense Hindu shakti [force] into a fist. Do not display any love for your enemies. . . . The Qur'an teaches them to lie in wait for idol worshipers. . . . But we cannot teach them with words, now let us teach them with kicks. . . . Tie up your religiosity and kindness in a bundle and throw it in the Jamuna. . . . Any non-Hindu who lives here does so at our mercy.[c]

[a] *Hinduism Today*, June 1997, p. 35.
[b] *India Today*, January 15, 1996, p. 25.
[c] Thomas Hansen, *The Saffron Wave: Democracy and Hindu Nationalism in Modern India* (Princeton, NJ: Princeton University Press, 1999), p. 180.

Where in the world has the power of religious views on the environment successfully resisted the force of economic interests? Not, as yet, in India, where the Ganges is one of the world's largest sacred rivers.

poignant since the summer of 2007, as the Indian elite reflected about where their nation had traveled since independence in 1947 and how the country now measured up against earlier expectations and in comparison to the other great nation founded at roughly the same time, China. The widespread opinion expressed in the popular press was that while democracy was treasured and never to be surrendered and India's meteoric rise since 1990 in the global marketplace grows promisingly, there was also the hard truth pointed out that Hindu culture and religion have failed to transform Indian society in many of the positive ways evident in contemporary China. How could blatant caste discrimination endure? How could India's extreme poverty be tolerated with 43 percent of its children malnourished, while the rich get richer? How could the nation's leaders, drawn largely from the high castes, not have done more to change these realities? While no uniform answer emerged, and while not only religion was blamed, the frequent and often intense debates that swirled throughout that year signaled support for the view that Hinduism is part of the problem and needs reform.

Among the many voices of Hinduism today, nationalists seeking a religious state now contend with secularists for political power. The voices, aspirations, and wealth of Hindus now living outside of South Asia are also part of global Hinduism when new possibilities and reforms are being envisioned. The daunting task is for Hindus to demonstrate how their values, beliefs, and conscience can be mobilized to serve the needs of all its citizens, who now number over 1.3 billion.

Discussion Questions

1. Why is a brahmin essential to Vedic Ritual?

2. What reasons might be suggested for the transformation of the polytheism of the early Vedic peoples into the monism and theism of later Hinduism?

3. Compare and contrast the spiritual practice of the shaman (Chapter 2) with that of the yoga practitioner. Is it possible to know exactly how different their experiences are?

4. Why would the lowest castes regard the doctrines of karma, caste, and duty as a system designed to subjugate them?

5. What reasons would a woman have for abiding by her dharma?

6. To what extent can karma theory be considered to be a doctrine of fatalism? Do humans still have freedom of action?

7. If you were an Islamic judge in Mughal India, how would you advise the local sultan who asks if his subjects who follow Krishna (as depicted in the *Bhagavad Gita*) are in fact monotheists?

8. How does ritualism express the ideals of bhakti Hinduism?

9. Why was the influence of colonialism on the religions of India powerfully conveyed by the term *Protestant Hinduism*?

10. What reasons are Hindu nationalists giving to support their view that the creation of India as a secular country is a perpetuation of colonialism and a betrayal of Hindu ideals?

11. Explain why M. K. Gandhi's biography reveals many of the factors shaping modern Hindu reform.

12. Critique the following statement, from an ecumenical Hindu organization: "We can follow Jesus without contradiction, for he is none other than another *avatara* of Lord Vishnu."

13. What does it say about the power of ideas regarding the sacred versus the power of profane modern economic interests that the Ganges is now in danger of becoming a toxic waterway?

14. How do Sikh traditions differ from and find agreement with the teachings of the Hindu philosophy and also those of Islam?

15. If you visited a Sikh gurudwara, how would the activities there reflect Sikh beliefs?

16. What is lost, and what is gained, by the addition of virtual temple visits to the Hinduism of today?

17. A California state court in 2013 had to rule on a program called "Yoga for Kids" in the Encinitas public schools designed to "promote the children's physical and mental well-being." Local evangelical Christians had sued, arguing that the program is unconstitutional since it really represented "religious indoctrination" and so violated the U.S. Constitution's provisions for separation of church and state. How would you testify in informing the court?

Key Terms

Adi Granth	dharma	nirguna Brahman
ahimsa	Gandhi, Mohandas K.	Om-kara
Arya Samaj	guru	*prasad*
ashram	*gurudwara*	puja
atman	Hare Krishna/(ISKON)	*puranas*
avatara	*Hindutva*	Ramakrishna Mission
Bhagavad Gita	Janam Sakhis	Ramanuja
bhakti	Kali Yuga	Rammohan Roy
Bharatiya Janata Party	karma	Rashtriya Svayamsevak
(BJP)	Khalsa	Sangh (RSS)
Brahman	*lila*	saguna Brahman
brahmin	matha	samsara
darshan	moksha	Sat Guru *(continued)*

Key Terms (continued)

satyagraha	tantra	Vaishnavite
Shaivite	Tattvabodhini Sabha	Vedas
shakta	*tirtha*	Vishva Hindu Parishad
shakti	Transcendental	(VHP)
Shankara	Meditation (TM)	yoga
siddha	Upanishads	Yoga Sutras

Suggested Readings

Babb, Lawrence. *The Divine Hierarchy* (New York: Columbia University Press, 1975).

———. *Redemptive Encounters: Three Modern Styles in the Hindu Tradition* (Berkeley: University of California Press, 1986).

Dalrymple, William. *Nine Lives: In Search of the Sacred in Modern India* (New York: Knopf, 2010).

Dimmitt, Cornelia, and J. A. B. van Buitenen. *Classical Hindu Anthology: A Reader in the Sanskrit Puranas* (Philadelphia: Temple University Press, 1978).

Doniger, Wendy. *The Hindus: An Alternative History* (New York: Penguin, 2009).

Dundas, Paul. *The Jains* (New York: Routledge, 2002).

Embree, Ainslee, ed. *Sources of Indian Tradition*, 2nd ed., 2 vols. (New York: Columbia University Press, 1988).

Hawley, John, and Mark Juergensmeyer. *Songs of the Saints of India* (New York: Oxford University Press, 1988).

Hopkins, Thomas. *The Hindu Religious Tradition* (Belmont, CA: Wadsworth, 1982).

Jaffrelot, Christophe. *The Hindu Nationalist Movement in India* (New York: Columbia University Press, 1996).

Jaina, Padmanabh. *The Jain Path to Purification* (Berkeley: University of California, 1988).

Jones, Kenneth W. *Socio-Religious Reform Movements in British India* (Cambridge: Cambridge University Press, 1994).

Larson, Gerald James. *India's Agony over Religion* (Albany: State University of New York Press, 1995).

Mann, Gurinder Singh. *Sikhism* (New York: Prentice Hall, 2004).

Mittal, Sushil, ed. *The Hindu World* (New York: Routledge, 2004).

Narayan, Kirin. *Storytellers, Saints, and Scoundrels: Folk Narrative in Hindu Religious Teaching* (Philadelphia: University of Pennsylvania Press, 1989).

Smith, David. *Hinduism and Modernity* (London: Wiley–Blackwell, 2003).

Notes

1. Most Sikhs regard their faith as constituting a separate faith that rejects the authority of the Veda, the legitimacy of brahmin priesthood, and the associated ideology of caste. While we will point out how these and other contrasts came to define a very successful and distinctive tradition, we cover this tradition within this chapter for thematic consistency with other chapters treating similar patterns of diversity (Christianity and Islam).

2. *India Today*, January 15, 1996, p. 22.

3. Daniel Gold, "Organized Hinduisms: From Vedic Truth to Hindu Nation," in M. E. Marty and R. Scott Appleby, eds., *Fundamentalisms Observed* (Chicago: University of Chicago Press, 1991), p. 581.

4. For the sake of simplicity, in this text we use *brahmin* to indicate the priestly caste and Brahman to indicate the "world spirit," although in fact they are similar Sanskrit words: *brahman* and *brahmana*, respectively.

5. Bhimrao Ambedkar, *What Congress and Gandhi Have Done to the Untouchables* (Bombay: Thacker and Company, 1934), pp. 307–8.

6. W. Owen Cole, "Sikhism," in John R. Hinnells, ed., *A Handbook of Living Religions* (New York: Penguin, 1984), p. 240.

7. Patwant Singh, *The Sikhs* (New York: Doubleday, 1999), p. 27.

8. Ibid., p. 23.

9. Brian Hatcher, "Bourgeois Vedanta: The Colonial Roots of Middle-Class Hinduism," *Journal of the American Academy of Religion* 75 (2007), p. 313.

10. Ibid., p. 315.

11. "Hinduism," in Sumit Ganguly and Neil DeVotta, eds., *Understanding Contemporary India* (Boulder, CO: Lynne Reiner, 2003), p. 204.

12. John Stratton Hawley and Mark Juergensmeyer, *Songs of the Saints of India* (New York: Oxford University Press, 1988), pp. 44–45.

13. http://www.bkwsu.com/index_html.

14. Quoted in the *Financial Times* (London), March 31, 2007, Section FT, p. 1.

15. *India Abroad Weekly*, August 4, 2006.

16. "Camp Joins Summer Fun with Teaching the Hindu Faith," *New York Times*, February 11, 2007.

17. "Business Filter," *Boston Globe*, October 30, 2006, E-2.

Additional Resources

The Hindu Universe (www.hindunet.org). A gateway to many websites for case studies in belief and practice.

Hinduism Today (www.hinduismtoday.com). Online site of a leading magazine covering contemporary events and traditions.

BBC Religions: Hinduism (www.bbc.co.uk/religion/religions/hinduism). Excellent information and useful links, regularly updated.

Jain Dharma Online (www.jaindharmaonline.com). Website on Jain texts, traditions, and teachings in a modern perspective.

Sikhs.org (www.sikhs.org). A source for texts in translation and many other topics.

BUDDHISM

Paths Toward Nirvana

7

Overview

Today the West is being infused with images, stereotypes, and impressions of Buddhism. Hollywood movies such as *Seven Years in Tibet*, *Kundun*, and *The Little Buddha* attracted millions of viewers; a long list of celebrities from rock, sports, and show business have identified themselves as followers of the Buddha; the Dalai Lama is by now one of the most recognized religious leaders in the world. The adjective "Zen" is an overused but omnipresent cliché in advertising, while stress reduction techniques based on Buddhist meditation are now being used by millions. In popular culture, when people think of a "Buddha" they first picture a jolly fat man seen in Chinese restaurants. Many American converts now insist that Buddhism is "a philosophy, not a religion," and that it is "atheistic." Educated literary critics routinely write about the typical Buddhist as someone who should be oriented toward immediate nirvana realization; renowned newspaper reporters write stories based on the assumption that the "good Buddhist should be a poor Buddhist." The globalization of Buddhist tradition may be extraordinary in scope and accelerating in pace, but every assertion about Buddhism mentioned above is largely *wrong*. The goal of this chapter is to convey what has made Buddhism a vibrant living tradition, lay the above misconceptions to rest, and even to shed light on why these superficial impressions have proven so attractive in the West.

Indeed, when Asian Buddhists meet Western Buddhist converts, they often find their beliefs hard to comprehend. Take, for example, the simple recitation of "going for refuge." This practice is rarely done outside Asia and is largely ignored in America.

Buddhism Timeline

563 BCE	Birth of Siddhartha [some scholars determine as 463 BCE]
528	Enlightenment of Shakyamuni, the Buddha; creation of the *sangha*, the monastic order
ca. 510	Establishment of nuns' order
483	Death of the Buddha [some scholars, 383 BCE]
482	First Council collects and organizes oral accounts
383	Council of Vaishali leads to the first split in the sangha
273–232	Reign of Ashoka, convert to Buddhism, who spread Buddhism throughout India and beyond (Afghanistan, Burma, Sri Lanka)
250	Council of Pataliputra leads to division into "18 schools"
240	Sanchi stupa and other stupas built across India; relic cult at stupas central to community
ca. 100	Origins of the Mahayana school, beginning with *Prajnaparamita* literature
80	First collections of written canon begun, beginning with the Vinaya, the monastic code; Pali Canon collection begun in Sri Lanka
50 CE–180 CE	Spread of Buddhism into central Asia via the Silk Road
ca. 85 CE	Composition of the *Lotus Sutra*
124	Buddhist monks in western China
ca. 200	Writings of Nagarjuna, the most influential Mahayana philosopher; Madhyamaka school formed
220–589	Buddhist missions reach Southeast Asia, Java, Sumatra, Korea, Japan, Vietnam; Buddhist monasteries established throughout China in era of weak central state
ca. 300	Rituals and visualization meditations dedicated to bodhisattvas developed by Mahayana monks
ca. 300	Origins of Pure Land school in India
320ff	Development of Yogacara school, led by monastic brothers Asanga and Vasubandhu
ca. 425	Writings of a monk who shaped the Theravada school, Buddhaghosa, in Sri Lanka
ca. 500	Rise of the Vajrayana Thunderbolt school in India, which eventually dominates Buddhist communities in northeastern India, Nepal, and Tibet
ca. 600	Formation of the Ch'an school in China inspired by teachings of the legendary Indian monk Bodhidharma
700–1270	Buddhism dominates Sri Vijaya kingdom on Sumatra-Java; rulers build Borobodur stupa
749	First Buddhist monastery in Tibet
760–1142	Pala Dynasty rules North India, patronizes Buddhist monasteries, and promotes Mahayana traditions; tradition in decline elsewhere in India
841–845	Extensive destruction of monasteries in China and defrocking of Buddhist monks and nuns
850ff	Restoration of Chinese Buddhism, principally the Pure Land and Ch'an schools
ca. 1000	Second introduction of monastic Mahayana Buddhism into Tibet from India
1000–1400	Era of Pagan Kingdom in Burma, establishing one of the great centers of Buddhism
1192	Muslim rule established across northern India; final destruction of Indian monasteries and decline of Bodh Gaya as center of Buddhist pilgrimage

1193–1227	In Japan, formation of new schools: Zen brought from China by Eisei (1141–1215) and Dogen (1200–1253); Pure Land by Honen (1133–1212) and Shinran (1173–1262), and school founded by Nichiren (1222–1282)
1642–1959	Tibet dominated by Gelugpa monastic school under the Dalai and Panchen lamas
1686–1769	Life of Hakuin Ekaku, monk who revitalizes Zen in Tokagawa Japan
1815–1948	Era of British colonial rule; conflicts in Sri Lanka lead to reformist movement styled "Protestant Buddhism" that influences Buddhists across Asia
1851–1868	Rule of King Monghut in Siam, who revived the sangha and placed it under state control
1864–1933	Anagarika Dharmapala, Sri Lankan reformist, founder of the Mahabodhi Society, who spread reformism across Asia
1871–1876	Heavy Meiji persecution of Buddhism; 70 percent of monasteries lost as 75 percent of monks defrocked
1871	Fifth Buddhist Council held in Burma
1877–1945	Buddhist establishment in Japan supports nationalism, militarism, and territory seizures of Korea, Taiwan, and northern China
1893	Parliament of World Religions in Chicago; speeches by Zen monk and Dharmapala stir interest
1944	Buddhist Churches of America, a Pure Land organization, founded in California
1945	Soka Gakkai established in Japan, a branch of Nichiren school until 1991
1949–1976	Chinese Communist government persecutes Buddhists and seizes 250,000 monasteries and temples, with the Cultural Revolution (1966–1969) a period of intense destruction
1954–1956	Sixth Buddhist Council in Rangoon, Burma, culminating in the marking of the 2,500-year anniversary of Shakyamuni's death
1956	Founding of the Mahasangha Sahayaka Gana in central India, a Buddhist organization
1959–present	Exile of the fourteenth Dalai Lama from Tibet and the era of the globalization of Tibetan Buddhism
1976–present	Slow restoration of Buddhist institutions in China
1982–present	Civil war against Tamil minority in Sri Lanka polarizes Buddhist community
1987	Founding of Shakyaditya, a worldwide organization of Buddhist women
1989	Founding of the International Network of Engaged Buddhists by Thai activist Sulak Sivaraksa
1990	Revival of Buddhism in Mongolia after 88 years of suppression
1991	Founding of *Tricycle*, a Buddhist mass-market magazine in America
1998–present	Full ordination taken by Theravada nuns in Chinese monasteries, reviving a lost tradition
2007	Monks lead democracy protests in Burma, resulting in fierce government repression of sangha
2008	Uprisings across Tibet lead to Chinese government crackdown
2009	Civil War in Sri Lanka ends
2012–2014	Monks in Burma lead violent mobs that drive Muslims to refugee camps

But for over 2,500 years now, this taking refuge has been a daily practice for Asian Buddhist householders. "Going for Refuge" reaffirms one's devotion at the start of any ritual: *Buddham Saranam Gacchami* (I go for refuge in the Buddha), *Dharmam Saranam Gacchami* (I go for refuge in the teachings), *Sangham Saranam Gacchami* (I go for refuge in the community.)

For the student trying to understand Buddhism, how different those who "go for refuge" will appear. High in the Himalayas, a Tibetan monk wearing a warm red woolen robe seals himself into a cave retreat for three years and three months of meditative solitude. In the heart of urban Seoul, Korea, a layman wearing a stylish three-piece suit declares the opening of a twenty-four-hour Buddhist cable TV channel at a press conference in the ultramodern headquarters of a major Buddhist reform organization. In tropical Singapore, as householders gather to view 2,500-year-old bone relics of the Buddha, monks in yellow robes chant and extol the blessings of worshipping these mortal remains. All take refuge, all are following their country's Buddhist tradition, yet the diversity is astounding.

For Mrs. Suzuki of Tokyo, being a Buddhist means chanting set phrases tens of thousands of times to seek rebirth in a paradise created by a Buddha. For Mr. Chou of Taiwan, being a Buddhist means bestowing charity and doing good in order to achieve a better life in his next rebirth. For Mr. Shakya of Nepal, being a Buddhist means performing intricate rituals to honor the gods and Buddhas who out of their boundless compassion can bless his community. For forest monks in Sri Lanka and American disciples of a Japanese Zen master practicing in his monastery in the Catskills, being a Buddhist means only seeking enlightenment by meditation.

It is true that each of these Buddhists reveres an image of the Buddha, who is seated in meditation, serene and exemplary, but one cannot help but wonder what the historical Buddha might say today if he heard how differently these disciples now construe his teachings. The oldest of the world's missionary religions and perhaps the most accommodating in adapting to its widely varying communities in its global diaspora, Buddhism is in modest revival in most areas of the world today after having suffered debilitating setbacks throughout the modern era. Understanding Buddhism thus entails knowing about most of the peoples and cultures of Eurasia: from the homeland on the Ganges in South Asia into the high Himalayas, across the tropical states of Southeast Asia and over the central Asian deserts, and throughout the imperial domains of China, Korea, and Japan.

This chapter will examine how Buddhism in its creative diversity has sought to direct devotees to follow the three refuges. We will sketch the life of the Buddha, another of humanity's great and most significant religious teachers. We will then explore his basic teachings and chart the various interpretations as the tradition spread by monks, nuns, and merchants reached from northern India to East Asia, Southeast Asia, and in the last two centuries to Europe and the West.

Rough estimates place the number of Buddhists at 380 million, making it the fourth-largest among world religions. Over 98 percent live in Asia. Globally, there are as many Buddhists as there are Protestant Christians. Buddhists today are divided into two factions, those following the **Mahayana**, or "Great Vehicle," and those following the **Theravada**, or "Teachings of the Elders." Roughly 62 percent of people today are adherents of the Mahayana and 38 percent are Theravada followers. With most Mahayanists located in the countries north of the tropics, the label *Northern Buddhism* is sometimes used for this grouping, as opposed to the *Southern Buddhism* of the Theravadins. In a half-dozen Asian states (Sri Lanka, Myanmar, Thailand, Laos, Cambodia, Japan), Buddhists comprise the overwhelming majority of the population. They are significant minorities in Nepal, China, South Korea, and Singapore, while their presence in Malaysia (10 percent), Indonesia (3 percent), and India is less marked. (It should be noted that specific percentages, figures taken from Western almanac sources, are at best rough estimates, with wide margins for error.)

Buddhists today are becoming ever more aware of the diversity of Buddhist paths. Although modern activists and intellectuals may contest exactly "what the Buddha taught," Buddhism's basic teachings about life, mortality, and spiritual development continue to inspire adherents amid the often-traumatic changes of recent centuries. In every land, venerable institutions and reformist groups alike are seeking to adapt the faith to the changing world and to revive the essential practices that lead to Buddhism's perennial threefold goals: establishing moral community, securing worldly blessings, and realizing nirvana.

> **Mahayana:** "Great Vehicle," the dominant school of Buddhism in Nepal, Tibet, and East Asia
>
> **Theravada:** traditionalists; school of Buddhism dominant in South and Southeast Asia

Encounter with Modernity: Socially "Engaged Buddhism"

In the aftermath of the devastating December tsunami that struck the Indian Ocean on December 26, 2004, killing over 250,000 people, images of lived Buddhism filled the media. Press accounts of the first humanitarian responses reported that small groups of Buddhist householders immediately gathered what medicines, bandages, clothes, and food they could and headed directly to the coastal area to render compassionate assistance to compatriots. Those interviewed in Sri Lanka and Thailand typically explained in a self-effacing way that they were strengthened and motivated by their Buddhist tradition's teachings—that suffering is sad but inevitable in life and that acting compassionately is a central duty. This unprecedented tragedy showed how strong the adherence to basic Buddhist doctrines still is today, "at the grassroots level," as those doctrines are applied to modern situations of human suffering.

Other images of Asian Buddhists are of monks confronting war. In 1991, the monk Ghosananda of Cambodia led monks and householders into the countryside to intervene to end hostilities between Khmer Rouge remnants and the new government. Saying "We must find the courage to leave our temples and enter the suffering-filled temples of human experience," he braved falling shells and lethal firefights. Another image is that of a Vietnamese monk sitting cross-legged, engulfed in flames. This and

A monk rescues texts from a temple ruined by the 2004 tsunami.

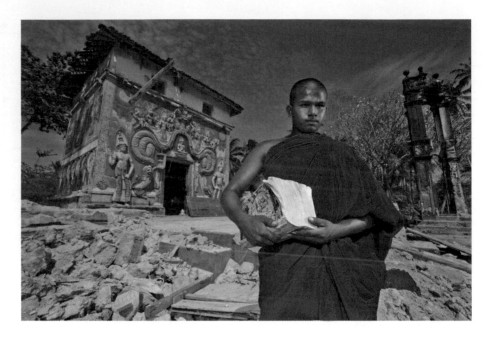

Protesting the Vietnam War, a Vietnamese monk commits suicide.

other monk suicides in 1963 protested the South Vietnamese government's failure to respect Buddhism and to adopt a policy of national reconciliation. Among the many Buddhist monks who challenged the corrupt South Vietnamese state was Thich Nhat Hanh, who argued that when faced with immense suffering, Buddhists must take action and engage their society. While Buddhism's ascetic traditions advocate renunciation of the household life and forest dwelling for nirvana-seeking meditation, Nhat Hanh drew on other sides of the tradition to urge Buddhist monks and nuns to defer solitary individualistic practice in favor of staging nonviolent confrontations with the governments and other agencies responsible for profound suffering.

Inspired by the monks of Vietnam, contemporary Buddhist activists in Asia and now in the West are responding to crises posed by environmental despoliation, political corruption, and global hunger. Accordingly, they are identified as "engaged Buddhists," and they refuse to turn away from suffering, counseling instead "mundane awakening." In this way, engaged Buddhists hope to elicit compassion on the part of individuals, villages, countries, and eventually all people, arguing that it is as ancient and as fundamental to Buddhism as the ascetic and solitary practices of the spiritual elite.

Buddhists engaging with society in political arenas now span the world, offering examples of revival from India to Japan: the Trailokya Bauddha Mahasangha Sahayaka Gana of India, which has worked since 1956 to convert from Hinduism low-ranked castes in India and help raise them out of poverty; the Sarvodaya Shramadana movement in Sri Lanka seeks to promote rural development through harnessing the service commitments of lay volunteers; various postwar Japanese Buddhist groups such as the Soka Gakkai work to transform society through political activism informed by Mahayana Buddhist ideals. On the ecumenical front, monk reformers such as Buddhadasa of Thailand and the Tibetan Dalai Lama have connected with those of other faiths to mobilize mutual seeking of the common good. In the late twentieth century, Sulak Sivaraksa, a Thai lay activist, formed the International Network of Engaged Buddhists to foster connections and develop this latest interpretation of the Buddha's teachings.

Zen Buddhist leader Thich Nhat Hanh in 2007, at the opening of a three day requiem for those killed on both sides of the Vietnam War.

Another major development in Buddhism since World War II has been the global diffusion of the tradition on a scale unprecedented in world history. Buddhist social activism has made the tradition more attractive to many in the West. In Asia, engaged Buddhists have no shortage of crises, given the region's rapid industrialization, the explosion of urban slum settlements, the alarming degradation of forests and watersheds, the predations of corrupt politicians, and the bloodshed from ethnic conflicts and civil wars. These profound changes have disrupted the regions' rural societies, including many of the communities that have long sustained Buddhist monastic institutions.

The engaged Buddhists, predominantly in the urban centers, now promote new understandings of Buddhism and organize Buddhist action, often confronting politicians and corporations. Can this movement revitalize the tradition from the capitals to the rural hinterlands and mitigate suffering without reducing or compromising its principal values?

Premodern Buddhism:
The Formative Era (600 BCE–100 CE)

To discover the rationale for such "social engagement" that this movement advocates, it is essential to go back to the very beginning of the tradition. Since it is the life of the Buddha that all followers look to for guidance, and from which all the later schools look for inspiration, we start our journey with the long life of the founder and examine his fundamental teachings. And because the historical destiny of Buddhism, the world's first missionary religion, is centered on the 2,500-year journey of the monastic community (sangha), understanding this institution's origins and development is essential to understanding the faith's expansion across Asia, and now in the West.

The Buddha: Context and Biography

We saw in Chapter 6 that North India during the Buddha's lifetime (563–483 BCE) was a place of spiritual questioning and ascetic searching unmatched in the history of religions. The dominant Aryan society was evolving from small pastoral settlements to city-states and a more diverse economy. In the context of this transformation, the old sacrifice-centered Vedic religion controlled by members of the brahmin caste was becoming for some much less plausible as an explanation of humanity's deepest connection to the universe. In remote retreats and near to the emerging urban centers, there were many seekers called **shramanas** who pursued ascetic practices (yoga) to realize the true essence of human consciousness, life, and reality. The society in which the Buddha was born was ordered by caste and brahmin ritualism. In addition, however, there were ardent, nonconformist shramana seekers who questioned almost everything the old Vedic tradition asserted about spirit, morality, and social hierarchy. Some lived naked, in silent retreat, or even sealed in clay pots; most explored various trance states, living as simply and with as little food as possible. Still other ascetics advocated materialism, nihilism, agnosticism, or fatalism.

shramana: wandering ascetic, a term applied to Buddhists, Jains, and others

Like the Upanishadic seers, most shramanas believed that life consists of a countless series of rebirths, that these are determined by an individual's karma, a natural and moral causal force that accrues from one's deeds, and that rebirths continue until through moral perfection and yoga practices one "burns off" one's karma to reach a state of liberation, which in Buddhism is termed **nirvana** or *sambodhi*. Shramanas differed widely on the exact means of reaching this goal, and they debated the details of personhood and universe. The most famous man ever to become an ascetic sought out these hermit teachers in midlife and learned from them, adopting many of their spiritual practices and doctrines. The one who would later call himself a Buddha started out life in very different circumstances, and we must now turn to his story.

nirvana: blissful state of liberation from rebirth, defined by the extinction of karma

As with other world religions, early accounts of the Buddha's life were passed down orally, and only centuries later were there any attempts to provide systemic biographies. What survives today are a variety of ancient accounts, each with its set of key events, many that are the same, but each with incidents and thematic emphases that are not. Among the many questions that face historians: Why are there so many similarities in the biography of the Jain religion founder Mahavira (see Chapter 6) and the Buddha? What follows here draws on the commonalities of ancient accounts, as well as more recent modern vernacular biographies.

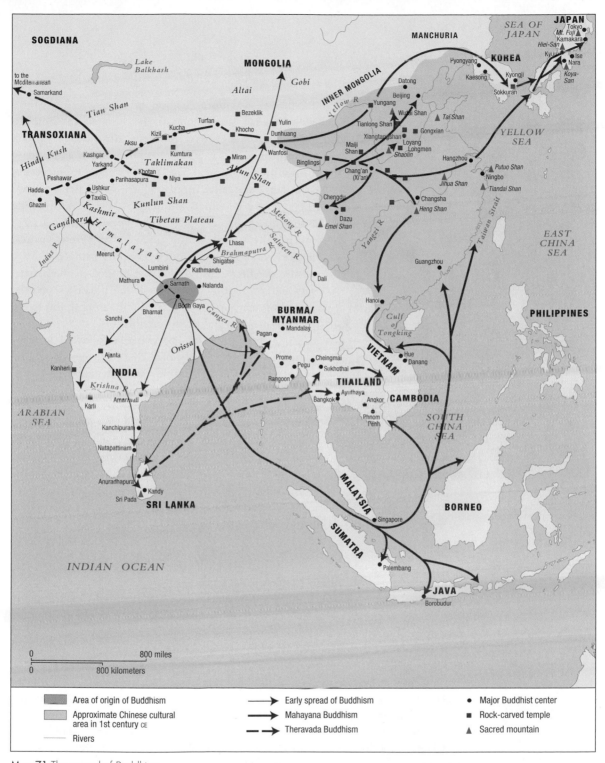

Map 7.1 The spread of Buddhism.

The Buddha's birth, depicted in a Chinese sculpture.

Siddhartha's Early Life

Siddhartha was born the son of warrior-caste parents who ruled a small state in the Himalayan foothills. According to legendary accounts, this boy's birth was accompanied by auspicious celestial signs and a wise man's prediction that the child would be successful as either a universal monarch or a great ascetic. Thus the infant was named Siddhartha, which means "the one who attains the goal." The young prince, whose mother died a week after giving birth, grew up in a palace where his father did everything in his power to ensure the first destiny. The son trained in the martial arts and was pampered with all the pleasures of rule, including marriage, a harem of concubines, and every form of pleasant artistic distraction.

Siddhartha's life changed when he followed an inclination to go with his faithful chariot driver to see the world beyond the palace walls. All the textual legends describe the profound impact of seeing a sick man, an old man, a dead man, and a shramana. These "four passing sights" overturned Siddhartha's rosy assumptions about life and also offered a vision of the ascetic path he could take to escape the spiritual emptiness he now felt in his sheltered existence. Within days, Siddhartha slipped away, abandoning his palace and family, including a newborn son. He began at that moment his search for a teacher among the forest-dwelling ascetics. The legends state that he was twenty-nine years old.

Siddhartha Begins His Quest

Siddhartha found a shramana guru, Arada Kalama, whose way of meditation allowed one to achieve a "state of nothingness." Siddhartha soon mastered this technique, but he also recognized that the accomplishment was limited in value. His quest led to a second teacher, Udraka Ramaputra, who taught a method of attaining trances that brought an experience of "neither perception nor nonperception." But again Siddhartha found that his fast-won mastery of this yoga still left him short of the highest goal.

He set forth alone again and soon joined five other men, who vowed to explore together a rigorous ascetic practice involving fanatical fasting (down to a few rice grains daily), breath control, and long periods seated in unmoving meditation. He adopted this lifestyle for about five years but finally rejected it, also, as too extreme, much to the dismay of his fellow seekers, who then ridiculed and abandoned him. Through this experiment, Siddhartha came to understand that the spiritual life is best undertaken as a middle path between the extremes of sense indulgence (the life in the palace) and asceticism so zealous that it weakens the body. One name for Buddhism, "the Middle Way," stems from this insight.

Although physically weakened and spiritually dismayed, Siddhartha did not quit. He was buoyed by a gift of rice and barley gruel from a village woman, and he came to sit beneath a great ficus tree by a river outside the town of Gaya. He vowed to find either success or death. The legends relate that his revitalized meditations were disturbed by Mara, a supernatural being regarded by Buddhists as the personification of death, delusion, and temptation. Mara summoned his demons, who appeared as armed soldiers to elicit fear and as alluring females to provoke lust, but Siddhartha touched his right hand to the earth, asking it to bear witness to his merit and eventual success. This earth-touching gesture, seen often in depictions of the Buddha in art, brought forth earthquakes and a cooling stream that washed away Mara and his hordes.

The Bodhi Tree and the Deer Park

Later that night, after resuming his meditations, Siddhartha reached more subtle and blissful perceptions and then the attainment of superfaculties, such as memory of former lives and psychic vision, that allowed him to survey the destinies of all beings according to their karma as well as the powers of levitation, telepathy, supervision, and superhearing. Finally he completely extinguished all desire and ignorance by fully realizing his capacity for insight (**prajna**). This "awakening" to the nature of reality under the *bo* (for *bodhi*, "enlightenment") tree, poetically recounted as occurring just as the dawn broke, provides the root meaning of the term *Buddha* that from this moment onward we can properly apply to Siddhartha. He is also referred to as *Gautama Buddha*, using his family surname, and *Shakyamuni*, "the sage," or *muni*, from Gautama's clan, the Shakyas.

For seven weeks the Buddha remained in the vicinity of the bodhi tree, enjoying the bliss of nirvana. The texts recount a story that his very first disciples were householders, merchants who made offerings and received his benediction for their continued worldly success. He also received the veneration of *nagas*, the snake deities, whose submission symbolized Buddhism's claim of "spiritual conquest" over all deities in every locality. Then Mara returned to tempt the Buddha to remain isolated, enjoying

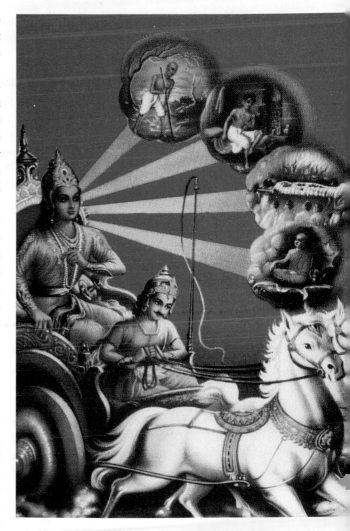

The Buddha encountering the "four passing sights" that inspired his religious quest and eventual awakening.

prajna: "insight"; quality of mind discerning reality clearly and calmly, its completeness necessary for enlightenment his solitary nirvana. In his attempt to prevent the Buddha from continuing to teach, the evil one cited humanity's hopeless stupidity. But the high gods also intervened to request that the Buddha live on to share his doctrine because, they assured him, there were people everywhere capable of realizing **enlightenment** by means of his teachings, or **Dharma**. This request inspired the Buddha's compassion, and he vowed to stay in the world, thus providing the ultimate model of the engaged Buddhist.

He then walked for days to reach distant Sarnath, a deer park outside the city of Varanasi, where he found his former ascetic colleagues. Their disdain turned to awe, however, after the now radiantly charismatic Buddha sat among them and taught for the first time the Four Noble Truths, which culminate in the Eightfold Path. The five ascetics became the first members of the **sangha**, and they were instructed to travel to different places in the four directions for the purpose of sharing the Dharma with all people of the world.

The Buddha's Life Work

For the next forty or so years, the Buddha empowered his enlightened disciples, called *arhats*, to act on his behalf, admit qualified seekers into the sangha, guide those who wished to meditate, and teach the Dharma to any who would hear it. Shakyamuni converted other ascetics, sometimes whole assemblies of them, as well as solitary shramanas, householders, and rulers. Buddha's faculty of psychic knowledge allowed him to preach according to the exact capacity of his audience.

As the Buddhist movement grew, new situations arose that required adaptation, so, in addition to his skill at teaching, the Buddha succeeded in creating an entirely new religious institution in ancient India: the sangha of monks (*bhikkhu*). It was established on the basis of formal ordination and vows to follow the extensive set of rules that he adapted to the many environments where Buddhist monks came to live.

After much urging (at least according to some legends), Shakyamuni also gave permission, around 510 BCE, for the creation of a sangha for female renunciants. He also bequeathed a mixed message by emphasizing, on the one hand, that women are capable of realizing enlightenment but also, on the other, specifying rules forcing the nuns, or *bhikkhunis*, to subordinate themselves to the monks in personal power and in matters of social etiquette. When admitting nuns, the Buddha also predicted that the tradition would decline. In subsequently allowing the sangha to receive lands, buildings, and other donated communal resources, the Buddha established a framework in which the sangha shifted its focus over time, from wandering to settled cooperative communal existence. This development, which also gave householder disciples a fixed focus for their patronage, in turn strengthened the sangha.

Late in life the Buddha began to suffer from various ailments, and he died in Kushinagar, a rural site, at the age of eighty. His body was cremated and the remains, divided into eight portions, were enshrined in relic mound shrines (**stupas**) that became the focus of Buddhist ritual and the visible architectural structure of the Buddha's presence across the world.

---

enlightenment: state of "nirvana" or liberation

Dharma: teachings of the Buddha

sangha: Buddhist monastic community

arhat: enlightened being; term applied to the Buddha and his disciples

bhikkhu/bhikkuni: Buddhist monk/nun

stupa: Buddhist shrine containing the relics of a Buddha or enlightened saint

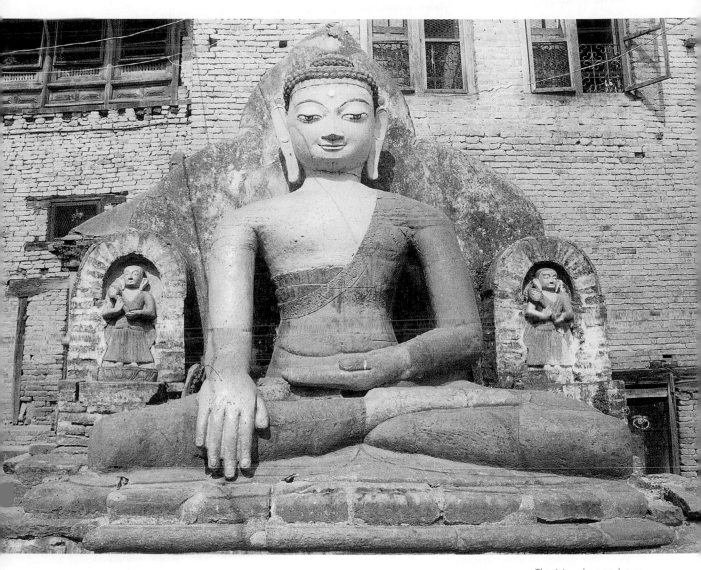

This Nepalese sculpture shows the Buddha in an earth-touching gesture, a frequently encountered icon that alludes to his calling upon the earth to bear witness to his fitness for enlightenment.

Shakyamuni's life story became for Buddhists a paradigmatic example of an individual's quest for enlightenment, and his exemplary role for subsequent generations was elaborated in hundreds of stories that describe incidents from this life as well as from his previous incarnations, in which he was reborn as a human, animal, or spirit. These narratives, called *jatakas*, along with stories of his path to Buddhahood, inspired arts and literatures across Asia that conveyed the essential doctrines in explicit, personified form. The Buddha, thus, embodies the Dharma, which, as in Hindu practice, is understood as comprising both the ultimate truth and the teachings that lead to that truth.

Buddhism as the Path to Nirvana

The spiritual tradition we refer to as *Buddhism* arose from the Buddha's wish to help others realize the transformative experience of nirvana. The Buddha emphasized the practical, goal-directed orientation of his way and urged his disciples not to engage in idle speculation or mere intellectualism. He taught that humanity comprises persons of very different kinds who bear different forms of karma. According to whether they are "ordinary persons," "learners," or "adepts," each is to be instructed differently. Regardless of an individual's level, to be born as a human at all, instead of as an animal or divinity, is a rare opportunity. A human life is not to be wasted; rather, people should live with purpose, with an awareness of the reality of karma, and make efforts to get closer to the highest goal, nirvana.

Unlike the other world religions, Buddhism has but a few universally accepted doctrines. Beyond the three refuges cited at the beginning of the chapter, Buddhists have adopted varying subsets of the Buddha's teachings and many rituals, always keeping the monastic community (the sangha) as its central institution. How could a world religion accommodate such pluralism in the course of establishing its essential doctrines?

The earliest Sanchi stupa with gateway and pathway for ritual circumambulation. This shrine, in Madhya Prodesh state, central India, was a major Buddhist pilgrimage site in ancient India.

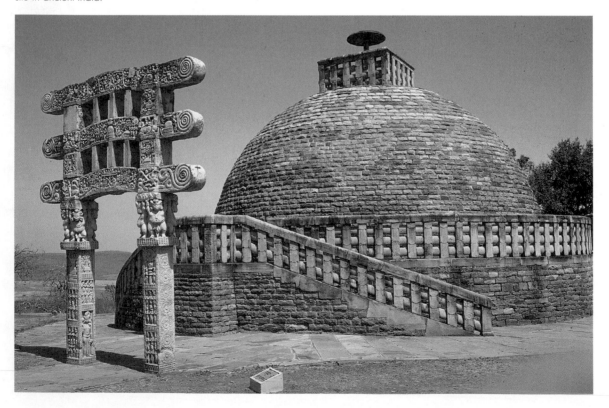

First, Buddhists (like Hindus) assume that since humanity contains persons of many sorts, many different spiritual avenues are needed to reach everyone. Teachers, therefore, formulated myriad practices, and philosophers offered multiple interpretations of the truth the Buddha had revealed.

The second reason for Buddhism's pluralism lies in an instruction from the Buddha himself: After his death, no one person or institution was to be allowed to fix a single canon or set a single norm of orthodoxy in doctrinal interpretations (the opposite extreme of premodern Christianity). As a result, by 600 years after the death of Shakyamuni Buddha, several different canons of collected teachings were made and the sangha aligned under two main divisions: the "elder traditionalists" and the Great Vehicle. The elders, or **Sthaviravadins**, were in South Asia more numerous, and their sole surviving school is called *Theravada*. Since about 100 CE, the Theravadins have taught that humanity should aspire to become enlightened arhats. *Mahayana* is the name given to the Great Vehicle division, and many schools survive today, including Pure Land and Zen, each with a great diversity of subgroups. Thus, in many respects it is quite artificial to posit a single "Buddhism" based on a common code or single text. Buddhism in popular practice among the laity, however, does show many continuities, as we will see. The first topic we will discuss is the highest ideal—nirvana.

Nirvana

The word *nirvana* is based on the Sanskrit verb meaning "to cool by blowing" and refers to one who has "cooled" the feverish *kleshas* ("hindrances," "poisons") of greed, hatred, and delusion. It is the kleshas that inflame desire, create karma, and bind the individual into *samsara*, the world of rebirth and suffering. Buddhists often present the concept of nirvana realization by likening it to the extinction of a fire, for as this phenomenon was understood in ancient India, the flames of an extinguished fire had been released to return to a diffuse, unagitated, and eternal state. The state of nirvana thus carries similar associations: freedom and existence in an eternal state beyond all material description. Both men and women, by moral living and mastering meditation, can realize nirvana through the cultivation of *prajna*, the direct "insight" into the nature of existence.

The Four Noble Truths

The earliest formulation of the Buddha's teaching, the **Four Noble Truths**, provides a central analysis of the human condition as well as a diagnosis: the path toward nirvana. The biographies recount that through the realization of these truths in his own experience, Shakyamuni reached final enlightenment.

The first Noble Truth, "All life entails suffering," instructs the Buddhist not to deny the inevitable experience of mortal existence: physical and mental disease, loss of loved ones, the bodily degeneration of old age, and the inescapability of death. The intention of this first truth is not to induce pessimism but to encourage clear, realistic observation. Even pleasure and good times, however enjoyable, have a fundamental

Sthaviravadins: traditionalists among early Buddhist monastic schools

"The Buddha declares the Law with a single voice,
While sentient beings, each in their own way, construe the meaning."
—*Vimalakirti Nirdesha Sutra*

Four Noble Truths: primary doctrinal formula describing human life as marked by suffering, distorted by desire, and a path to its extinction

"Compared with the man who conquers thousands in battle, the greatest warrior is the man who conquers himself. . . . If a man is strenuous, thoughtful, self-controlled, and morally disciplined, he grows immensely."

—*Dhammapada*

inadequacy because they are only temporary. The appropriate response to this truth is to make the most of the spiritual opportunities of human birth and to show compassion (**karuna**) and loving-kindness (**maitri**) to alleviate the suffering affecting all other beings.

The second Noble Truth states, "The cause of suffering is desire." The term for "desire" (*trishna*) literally means "thirst," a term that covers possessions, power, sex, and all that human beings "thirst after," far beyond mere food and drink. (At the advanced stages of Buddhist practice, desire for doctrinal learning and even the wish for one's own enlightenment must also be rejected to reach the final goal.) The emphasis on desire in the second truth makes plain the need for renunciation, detachment, and asceticism.

The third Noble Truth, "Removing desire removes suffering," is rooted in the central Buddhist idea of spiritual causation: The same pattern of cyclical cause and effect by which desire leads to further suffering can also be reversed and eventually extinguished in nirvana. The emphasis on renunciation also signals the importance of the sangha as a refuge for individuals who wish to remove themselves from the world of desire.

The fourth Noble Truth, "The way for removing desire is to follow the Eightfold Path," specifies the Buddha's treatment that will "cure" the human condition, with its continuous cycle of rebirth, suffering, and redeath. As the Buddhist progresses toward enlightenment, moving through moral practice, meditation, and the cultivation of the prajna, an understanding of the Four Noble Truths deepens. There are eight specific elements in the progressive path to nirvana.

The Eightfold Path

Among the many doctrinal lists compiled to describe Buddhist practices, The **Eightfold Path** has been the most widely disseminated. It outlines the necessary means for achieving the realization of nirvana. The usual order is as follows:

1. *Right Views*, especially of the Noble Truths, thoughts shaped by detachment from hatred and cruelty
2. *Right Intentions*, staying committed to final realization
3. *Right Speech*, which refrains from falsehood, gossip, and frivolity
4. *Right Action*, defined negatively as action free of killing, stealing, and harming
5. *Right Livelihood*, the refusal to earn a living through casting magic spells or careers that involve inflicting harm or killing
6. *Right Effort*, to clear and calm the mind
7. *Right Mindfulness*, the distinctive form of Buddhist meditation that observes clearly the mind and body and that cultivates detachment
8. *Right Concentration*, another form of advanced meditation that attains the mastery of trance states

Basic Buddhist Formula:
Buddhist Spiritual Progress and the Eightfold Path

MORALITY	→	MEDITATION	→	PRAJNA	→	NIRVANA
Right speech	→	Right mindfulness	→	Right views	→	
Right action	→	Right concentration	→	Right intentions		
Right livelihood	→	Right effort				

| Social context: | | | | | | |
| 95% of community | | 5% | | 1% | | exceedingly rare |

Another important arrangement of the Eightfold Path was organized according to three central categories of Buddhist practice:

Morality (Shila) entails Speech, Action, and Livelihood
Meditation (Dhyana) entails Effort, Mindfulness, and Concentration
Insight or Wisdom (Prajna) entails Views and Thought

The Sri Lankan Theravadin commentator **Buddhaghosa** (fifth century CE), who refers to the two legs of Buddhism as Morality and Meditation, on which the body of Insight stands, organized his entire summary of the faith on the basis of this division. The Eightfold Path emphasizes that moral progress is the essential foundation to successful meditation and that the measure of successful meditation is the awakening and deepening of prajna. The different elements of the path underscore Buddhism's practical emphasis on effectiveness, whether in the foundational goal of improving moral standards, good conduct, and the material welfare of society or in the service of the more advanced ideal of deconditioning desire-driven behavior, restructuring cognition, and focusing consciousness on enlightenment realization.

Buddhaghosa: great Theravadin monk-scholar

The First Community and Its Development

Life in the Buddhist sangha was a true refuge for "sons and daughters of the Buddha" (as monks and nuns were called) who wished to leave behind their homes and live for spiritual purpose. The ideal was simple: Material needs were met by householders, thus allowing the renunciants to meditate and study without encumbrances.

Texts regulating the early monks and nuns, called *Vinayas*, record how the rules and institutional life developed. For example, because the Buddha was sensitive to the state laws under which he lived, he declared criminals, runaway slaves, and army deserters ineligible to join the sangha. He also specified principles to govern the community (by seniority, as reckoned from the time since ordination) and insisted that the group meet every two weeks so that each monk or nun certified his or her personal compliance. This fortnightly ritual became a central feature of life in the sangha. The Buddha's organizational genius can be seen as well in his cultivation of a householder community that provided for the needs of the sangha. It was Buddhist householders who joined the sangha, and it was the patronage of other good Buddhist householders that established the faith's monasteries and shrines across India and, over time, throughout Asia.

After the Buddha's death, in accordance with his instruction that authority over his community was not to reside in a single person or institution, the monks and nuns settled in separate colonies, which became the monastic centers that perpetuated the faith. They repeated and memorized the sets of sermons they had heard and worked out a distinctive form of communal life. Within the first three centuries there were several gatherings of all monks, councils that met to focus on the exact rules of monastic practice.

Although the early sanghas also found considerable common ground, none of the recorded councils ever achieved exact consensus on matters of discipline or doctrinal formulation. Dissenters went off to practice as they felt proper in their own monasteries, but the monastic codes in the *Vinayas* are remarkably similar. Yet disagreements that led to schisms surprisingly involved relatively minor points. This early fact of sangha autonomy and divergent understandings of the Dharma became precedents that shaped the continuation of regional pluralism found across the Buddhist world right up to the present. As Chinese pilgrim Fa-Hsien noted in 400 CE, after traveling extensively in India, "Practices of the monks are so various and have increased so that they cannot be recorded."[1]

How Buddhism Became a World Religion

In the first two centuries after Shakyamuni's death, Buddhist monks and converts spread slowly across the Gangetic plain as simply another one of the many shramana groups that emphasized asceticism and rejected the brahmin caste's privileged status, its ritual system, and especially its claim to hold a monopoly on advanced spiritual practice. It was **Ashoka** (273–232 BCE), an emperor of the powerful Maurya dynasty, whose support propelled Buddhism's emergence as a broad-based religious tradition that reached beyond the ascetics. Now it was in a position to unify the social classes of Indic civilization and link the householder population with its monastic elite.

Ashoka: ruler whose patronage spread Buddhist institutions and teachings across his empire, and likely beyond

Just as the Mauryan Empire extended across most of the subcontinent, Ashoka, through his personal prestige and imperial edicts as well as the patronage of notable monks, helped spread Buddhism from Afghanistan to the Bay of Bengal, from the Himalayan foothills to the island of Sri Lanka. As a result, the first definite traces of Buddhist monuments (monasteries and stupa shrines) can be dated to this era, as can the first systematic oral collections of the teachings. Within a century after the end of the Mauryan period, Buddhist institutions dotted the major trade routes going north and south, east and west from the Buddhist holy land, with major shrines, monasteries, and pilgrimage traditions developing at sites associated with the founder's life.

Buddha from Gandhara, in the upper Indus River region, where icons were made by artisans skilled in the Hellenistic style.

The expansion northwest into the upper Indus River, in the region called **Gandhara**, and into the Kashmir Valley and then beyond them up the trade routes crossing the mountains north into central Asia made these areas a key Buddhist stronghold for the next millennium. It was here that the Indic world had already met the Hellenic, for hundreds of settlements across the upper Indus were populated by descendants of the troops of Alexander the Great (356–323 BCE). Indeed, the expansion of the Mauryan Empire was enabled in part because Alexander's campaign of world conquest had faltered on the Indus. Stranded far from home, some veterans of Alexander's army settled in the area, where their descendants established small states and became prominent regional traders. Many converted to Buddhism. To understand Buddhism's successful rise to popularity among kings and commoners, however, we must comprehend how the sangha became the center of Buddhism across Asia.

Gandhara: area of Indo-Greek interaction, influential in the creation of Buddhist art

Sangha and Monastery: The Institutional Vehicles of Buddhism's Expansion

Living in community, Buddhist monks, nuns, and devout lay followers established monasteries and shrines that rooted the faith in every locality. As Buddhist monasticism spread across Asia, it introduced independent, corporate institutions that transformed local societies and regional polities. In ancient India, the early sangha admitted new members without regard to caste as a limiting spiritual or social category. In Buddhism's subsequent missionary migrations, acceptance into the sangha offered ordinary citizens an opportunity for spiritual seeking and educational advancement that was otherwise unavailable.

Buddhism could not have existed in society at large without the support of the householders, for it was the laity that ensured the viability of the monastic institution. Throughout the Buddhist world, laypeople made donations to the sangha to "earn merit" as a means of improving their karma and garnering worldly blessings for themselves, their families, and their communities. It was this central exchange, maintained between sangha and society, that kept Buddhism vibrant.

Varieties of Buddhist Monasticism

The typical Buddhist community had its center in a monastery (*vihara*), where monks or nuns would take their communal vows, meditate, study. These institutions also supported monks who practiced medicine, performed rituals essential to the Buddhist lifestyle of the locality, or managed the institution as builders and groundskeepers. Over time, distinctions developed within Buddhist monasticism: There were forest monasteries, where meditation and optional ascetic practices (*dhutanga*) could be undertaken (often under the leadership of a charismatic monk teacher), and those monasteries in village and urban settlements, which offered the opportunity to blend compassionate service to the community with individual cultivation and study. A Buddhist monk or nun could move between village and urban monasteries.

In many areas, the focus and inspiration for followers was a monk whose spiritual charisma and exemplary teaching ability drew monastic disciples and donations from the laity. The common biography of such monks mirrors that of Shakyamuni (the Buddha): disillusionments, renunciation, retreat to the wilderness, nirvana realization, and then a return to society to teach.

Practical Mechanisms of Expansion

Many successful monasteries expanded. The pattern was to send out monks to establish satellite institutions following the teachings of the charismatic founder, thereby perpetuating the monastic lineage. This template of Buddhist expansion created "galactic systems" that extended Buddhism into unconverted frontier zones. The resulting network of "mother-daughter" monasteries shaped alliances of all sorts, religious and otherwise, providing the pattern of new Buddhist institution building found from Afghanistan to Bali and more recently from Bangkok to Los Angeles, Dharamsala to New York. This institutional system also resulted in the tendency for aristocratic/dominant caste families to control local monastic lineages. This pattern of certain ethnic groups dominating Buddhism in certain regions occurred in Buddhist Tibet and continues in the Kathmandu Valley, in Japan, and in Sri Lanka. In other contexts, Buddhist viharas were instrumental in breaking down ethnic and class boundaries, blurring divisions between peoples, and creating transregional spiritual communities.

Rulers across Asia were drawn to support Buddhism because of its emphasis on individual morality, its rituals designed to secure prosperity for the state as well as for its leaders, and the powerful legitimi-zation that respected monastics could bestow on a regime. History has also shown that states favoring Buddhism often placed controls on the sangha's de-velopment. For example, to orchestrate the early expansion of Buddhism in China and Japan, em-perors ordered each provincial governor to build a monastery. This command was eventually reissued to the subunits in each province as Buddhist insti-tutions came to mirror the state's own administra-tive networks. Buddhist exponents, in turn, held up Ashoka as a model for the ideal Buddhist ruler, who today would be called a benevolent dictator. A fair, generous king (governor, local official, etc.), the monastics might call "a future Buddha." The most praiseworthy title was *cakravartin*, a zealous protector and devotee. Thus leading monks in the sangha could offer those wielding political power the highest form of legitimation in the eyes of the faithful. In this manner, Buddhist doctrines, officials, and patrons permeated the secular and political lives of the societies Buddhism entered.

Buddhist monastery estate in China. By the end of the first Buddhist millennium, major monasteries had become complex institutions whose wealth helped popularize the tradition.

In places where Buddhism thrived, some mon-asteries in cities and villages evolved into complex institutions that were much more than refuges for ascetics. The monastery often housed the only local school, and members of the sangha served their societies by spreading literacy. Many urban mon-asteries also became lending institutions, appointing treasurers to see that when monies donated at shrines exceeded the sangha's requirements, the overage was reinvested (usually in trade loans) back into the local community. Interest earned through this practice was reinvested as well. On the trade routes especially, this practice, combined with profits from renting monastery-owned buildings to warehousing or retailing enterprises, garnered considerable income for the monastery treasuries. Such devel-opments, which are attested from 200 CE onward in India and China, explain how Buddhism traveled across the Asian landscape on the basis of trade, supported by traders, and in cities along the commercial routes.

Another component in the spread of vibrant Buddhist institutions across Asia was the accumulation of lands donated by individuals and the state as perpetual endowments. Since monks were forbidden to till the soil, the sangha (as typically organized by lay managers) would rent out the cultivated lands it was acquiring. Whether its laborers grew rice and wheat or cultivated orchards, the monastery derived the food or cash needed for the sangha's upkeep. Until the twentieth century, in fact, many of the large Buddhist institutions were given indentured workers or slaves (usually entire families). Finally, shrines located within the monasteries would also earn income for the sangha in the form of offerings and from levies imposed on artisans who sold icons and votive amulets. All these elements made running a major monastery a demanding job and ensured that both donors and managers wielded considerable influence in the community.

These practices of "monastic landlordism," banking, and shrine management were also central to Buddhism's successful missions across Asia, creating the means to endow the faith with reliable income and a strong material culture. Buddhists attracted a following not only with their spiritual teachings but also with well-constructed, often-remarkable buildings, shrines, and image halls that complemented the Dharma. Tied to the productive base of society, successful Buddhist monasteries were ornamented with masterpieces of art, their libraries grew with manuscript production, and their leaders could develop an effective presentation of the Dharma. Many viharas also organized endowed charities that fed the poor and dispensed free medical care.

But there was one problem. As a practical matter, monastery autonomy and the lack of an overarching authority to regulate the monks' and nuns' obedience to the Vinaya norms made political leaders the arbiters of the integrity of Buddhist institutions. These officials had to "purify the sangha" periodically—that is, remove those who were acting contrary to the Vinaya norms or perhaps had not entered the vihara through the proper ordination. Thus, Buddhism's strength through concentrating wealth and human resources was also its historical weakness: Viharas were vulnerable to the variability of state patronage and royal protection as well as to the devastating effects of internal corruption and civil disorder.

Premodern Buddhism: The Classical Era (100–800 CE)

The Pan-Asian Expansion of Buddhism

In his first sermon after receiving enlightenment, Shakyamuni Buddha told his former companions, the five ascetic monks, to spread the new teaching universally and to use the local dialects in these communications. Thus, from its inception Buddhism has been a missionary religion, teaching a message directed to and thought suitable for all peoples. As the first missionary religion in the world, Buddhism initially spread to places not unlike the urban and trading centers where it had begun. Within the first millennium of the common era, Buddhism was found throughout South Asia and well into central Asia on the overland routes. Monks also traveled on the maritime trade routes to Sri Lanka and across Southeast Asia. Monasteries welcomed all who would observe the rules of residence. By this time, small circles of philosopher monks had divided into more than eighteen schools of doctrinal interpretation. What gave the religion unity was a common reverence for the Three Refuges; however, Buddhism never was a unified tradition either doctrinally or institutionally.

By the year 100 CE, Buddhism had entered China through central Asia on the silk routes. As it grew more popular and spread across East Asia over the next six centuries, monks and pilgrims traveled on the land and then later on oceanic routes between the two great ancient civilizations of Asia. The taking root of Buddhism in this region constitutes one of the greatest instances of cross-cultural transmission and conversion in world history, parallel in scope only to the transformations wrought by the world's only other great missionary faiths, Christianity and Islam. Buddhism added original conceptions of space, time, psychology, and human destiny that challenged indigenous notions. It also introduced a new social institution that fostered its missionary success: the land-grant monastery, whose members could be drawn from diverse social classes and live free from taxation, forced labor, or military service.

The Core Doctrines

Scholars always emphasize the division between traditionalists (Theravada) and adherents of the Great Vehicle (Mahayana), which grew among intellectuals in Buddhism's first millennium. But to keep this in perspective, we must remember that for most householders, whose practice of Buddhism focused on moral living, merit making, and securing worldly blessings, there was little interest in such doctrinal complexities or philosophical differences. These householders were mainly concerned with the sangha's conformity to the Vinaya code because upright monks and nuns could be relied on for proper performance of rituals that benefited individuals and the community. In addition, householders would earn merit by making donations to the sangha itself.

We have suggested that an individual's beliefs and meditation practices were largely personal matters; indeed, from the earliest days, monks (or nuns) following very different interpretations of the Dharma coexisted under the same monastery roof. We first consider doctrines and ethical norms that all Buddhists shared and then move on to discuss teachings that differed from school to school.

"Enlightened beings are like lotus flowers,

With roots of kindness, stems of peace,

Petals of wisdom, Fragrance of conduct."

SOURCE: *The Flower Ornament Scripture*, translated by Thomas Cleary, from *Everyday Mind*, a Tricycle book edited by Jean Smith

Prajna and Realizing Nirvana

Necessary for the attainment of nirvana and often translated as "wisdom," *prajna* refers to the capacity for deep spiritual discernment. The term is better rendered as "insight," however. In Buddhism it means "seeing into" reality as it truly is, characterized by suffering, impermanence, and supporting the existence of those traits known as the **Three Marks of Existence**. Buddhist salvation is often referred to as *enlightenment* because this fullness of prajna eliminates ignorance and completely clears the mind to see reality.

The state a Buddha or an arhat, a fully enlightened follower, achieves at death is referred to as *parinirvana* ("final nirvana"), although the texts say that strictly speaking this after-death state is beyond conception. Nirvana has been described in both negative and positive terms: a deathless realm where there is neither sun nor moon, neither coming nor going, but also a state that is tranquil and pure. Most of the early scholastic treatises recognized nirvana as the only permanent reality in the cosmos. It

Three Marks of Existence: Buddhist terms for analyzing human reality as marked by impermanence, suffering, and no soul

RITUALS AND RITES: Buddhist Meditation

Then: Tradition of Monastery Meditation

Until about 150 years ago, Buddhist meditation was undertaken only by monastics and was a regular practice only by a minority of this small elite. In ancient India, there is much evidence for monks and nuns having quite variable aptitudes for this spiritual practice: Some were more inclined to textual memorization, rituals, teaching; some even specialized as managers and builders of the institution's properties. Those interested in meditation entered into a relationship with a spiritual mentor, from whom instructions in a specific practice were obtained, and with whom reports of progress and obstacles would be shared. The meditating monk or nun might practice in a monastery training hall, in his own cell, or in an isolated retreat such as a jungle hut or a Himalayan cave. Some teachers even instructed their disciples that all activities in daily life

could be times of meditation. The traditional Buddhist meditation master would try to discern the state of a disciple's spiritual aptitude (prajna), mainly by interpreting the individual's body, speech, and mind; this caring, personal interaction provided the basis for determining how best for the individual to move forward. Meditation, in short, relied on the communal support of the monastery, fellow monks securing living essentials and providing encouragement, and an abbot nurturing spiritual progress. In total, Buddhist tradition has dozens of different practices that can be prescribed by a meditation master; all are directed to the universal goals: calming the mind and discerning the real. Most famous, perhaps, are the traditions of Zen training monasteries. Monastery abbots (roshi) direct monks in two seasons each year called seshin when most in these monasteries meditate intensively; for each disciple, they assign either koans or silent meditation focused on the breath.

---

is not, as erroneously depicted by early Western interpreters, to be seen as "annihilation," which is an extreme position rejected by the Buddha.

anatman: "no-atman," the doctrine denying the reality of a permanent, immortal soul or ego at the center of a person

skandha: "aggregate"; term used to identify each of the five main components that define a human being

"Nonself" Doctrine

The concept of **anatman** ("no-atman" or "nonself") is used to reject any notion of an essential, unchanging interior entity at the center of a person. The "atman" the Buddha rejected is the indestructible soul posited in the Upanishads and subsequent Hinduism, as described in Chapter 6. Buddhist philosophers argued that the universal characteristic of impermanence, one of the Three Marks of Existence, most certainly applies to human beings. As a result they regarded the human "being" in terms of the continuously changing, interdependent relationship between the five aggregates called **skandhas**.

Buddhist analysts begin with the person as a collection of the skandhas: the physical body, which is made of combinations of the four elements (earth, water, fire, air); feelings that arise from sensory contact; perceptions that attach the categories good, evil, and neutral to these sensory inputs; habitual mental dispositions (samskaras) that

Now: Internet Meditation Guided by Cybermonks

The Buddhist tradition's openness to cultural adaptation continues into the present. Monks, who have always had the role of teachers and scholars, are becoming increasingly computer literate. So it is the cybermonk, skilled in the new medium of the Internet, who is experimenting today in freeing meditation from the monastery halls and monastics. Another profound innovation in Buddhist modernism across Asia has been the democratization of meditation, and its spread to householders. To meet the needs of householders in the West who may be too far from a monastery to practice meditation in a community, contemporary monasteries and institutions now utilize the Internet to foster practice. The magazine *Tricycle* has recently sponsored a "Commit to Sit" program using online signup; it posts video instructions and sends out e-mail encouragement to all who want to enhance their personal practice. Another example is the Zen Mountain Monastery, in Woodstock, New York. Since 2003,

this monastery has posted meditation instructions and a link where distant meditators can contact Cybermonk, "a senior monastic available through e-mail to answer your Dharma questions." While it is uncertain how well these initiatives can actually succeed without the face-to-face guidance of a living teacher, there is no doubt that Buddhist leaders today are embracing Internet media to pursue missionary outreach. As one cybermonk from Australia, Phra Pannyavaro, has recently written, "The new 'cyber temple' will become the meeting place for an online Buddhist community of *practitioners*, as is already happening in the newsgroups and chat channels worldwide. . . . There is a belief in some Buddhist traditions of a future Buddha, called Maitreya—who it is said will come to revitalise the Dhamma. I cannot honestly see how any future Buddha, or future followers of the historical Buddha, would not naturally use the available technology and be quite at ease surfing the Internet."[a]

[a] Web posting, August 11, 2010, at http://littlebang.org/2010/07/01/cyber-monks-ven-pannyavaro/.

connect karma-producing will to mental action; and the consciousness that arises when mind and body come in contact with the external world.

The spiritual purpose of breaking down any apparently unchanging locus of individuality is to demonstrate that there is nothing (or "no thing") to be attached to or to direct one's desire toward. The no-self concept, however, presented exponents of Buddhist doctrine with the perpetual problem of explaining moral causality: How can the doctrine of karma, with its emphasis on compensation for one's good and bad moral decisions, operate without the mechanism of the soul, as in Hinduism or Christianity? Early texts show that this question was clearly posed to Shakyamuni Buddha: If there is no soul, how can the karmic "fruits" of any good or evil act pass into the future of this life or into a later incarnation? The standard explanation given is that karma endures in samskaras that are impressed in the fifth skandha, consciousness. Although always evolving and so impermanent, one's consciousness escapes the body at death and passes over to be reincarnated in the next life form.

While the no–self or no–soul doctrine was at the center of Buddhist thought for the philosophical elite, householders across Asia still typically conceived of themselves in terms of a body and a soul. This contradiction may indicate how peripheral some philosophical doctrines were to the mainstream of popular Buddhist understanding.

Impermanence and Interdependence

dependent origination: twelve-part formula explaining how individuals are bound to future rebirth until they extirpate desire and ignorance

Another universally accepted doctrinal formula in Buddhism is one that specifies the causal pattern of psychic and bodily states conditioning a person's bondage to suffering and rebirth. Known as **dependent**, or *conditioned*, **origination** (*pratityasamutpada*), this doctrine views reality as an ongoing, impermanent, and interdependent flux in the form of a circle divided into twelve parts. (See diagram on the next page.) Whatever point of entry you take, the next clockwise element is the experience conditioned, and the adjacent element in the counterclockwise position is that condition directly affecting the present. Without spiritual exertion, we spin around, life after life, under these conditioning patterns. Used in this way, the twelve-fold formula reiterates the basic doctrines already cited: Craving and ignorance are the two chief causes of suffering (Noble Truths Two and Three); and the human being has no soul, only changing components of bodily life units (skandhas). This complicated formula can also be reduced to two key elements that Buddhism focuses on, the interaction of desire and ignorance that keeps humans being reborn in samsara.

Buddhist Moral Precepts

The early Buddhists specified that moral practice is the first and necessary foundation for moving farther on the path toward nirvana. Buddhist ethics entails an "ideology of merit," in which making good karma and avoiding bad is the only sensible approach to life. Popular Buddhist stories focus on the reality of rebirth, covering thousands of lifetimes, which leads to the realization that all contemporary beings have been one's parents and children throughout a vast number of rebirths. Thus, acting morally toward them should be natural and logical. Buddhist doctrine also emphasizes the wisdom of cultivating detachment, discernment, and compassion (karuna).

The earliest moral rules the Buddha established consisted of five precepts. In South and Southeast Asia, they are chanted regularly in modern Theravada rituals by both

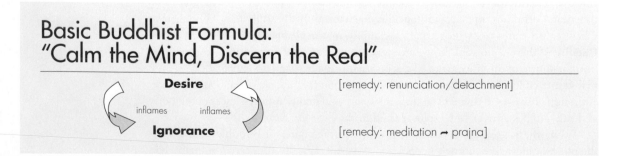

Basic Buddhist Formula:
"Calm the Mind, Discern the Real"

Desire   [remedy: renunciation/detachment]

inflames   inflames

Ignorance   [remedy: meditation → prajna]

Diagram representing the formula of dependent origination, including several interpretive schemes.

monks and laity. In these communities, the precepts are regarded as general ideals applicable to everyone. Mahayana schools tended to regard the precepts more as vows, to be chanted only if one intends to follow them completely. (One can omit reciting a precept if one does not expect to be able to observe it.) The five precepts listed here are paired with corresponding positive traits that can be developed to counteract the inclination to violate a precept.

1. Not to destroy life intentionally → kindness and compassion
2. Not to steal → generosity and renunciation
3. Not to have sexual misconduct → seeking "joyous satisfaction with one's spouse"

4. Not to lie → loving the truth, seeking it, pursuing discernment and insight
5. Not to become intoxicated → mindfulness, contentment, awareness via meditation

Later in the history of Buddhism, householders began to observe eight precepts on holy days, entailing a stricter observance of the original five along with three additional renunciations:

6. Not to eat (solid) food after noon
7. Not to view shows, dancing, or singing or to wear garlands, perfumes, jewelry
8. Not to sleep on high or wide beds.

In addition to the eight precepts, there is a set of ten precepts, observed by novice monks and undertaken as a long-term commitment. They comprise the eight but split one of these into two parts and add a final prohibition against handling money. This final rule was made to ensure that begging for food would be the norm for monks and nuns, an exchange between laity and sangha that bound together the Buddhist community.

Karma and Causality

punya: "merit"; good karma earned by moral practices, learning, and meditation

pap: "demerit"; bad karma earned by breaking the precepts

One can make the case from textual sources that karma doctrine is not fatalistic because one is continually making new **punya** ("merit") or **pap** ("demerit") to change the ongoing calculus of karmic destiny. Buddhist karma analysis holds that some good actions (e.g., building a monastery) and bad actions (e.g., harming one's parents) lead to powerful repercussions in the future, in either this life or the next. Nevertheless, the larger reality is that a person's karma, like all phenomena, changes every instant.

Further, the Buddhist understanding of causality is that not all contingencies in life are karma dependent. In fact, according to one Theravadin text, events are more likely than not to have had causes other than karma. Since only Buddhas can ascertain whether karma or other contingencies are at work in ongoing life, individuals are faced with uncertainty in evaluating events. Buddhists make a "general reading" of karma from birth station and biography. To be prepared for the future, however, the logic of the karma doctrine has motivated Buddhists everywhere to cultivate a lifelong practice of making punya and seeking guidance throughout life from astrology. Indeed, texts for householders emphasize that accumulation of wealth is the fruition of good past karma and that giving away wealth to earn merit is the best human expenditure. This giving, of benefit to all, is in a sense the social application of the Buddha's teaching about interdependence. These principles have been incorporated into Four Conditions and **Four Good Deeds**, doctrinal statements

Four Good Deeds: doctrinal formula guiding the laity on the uses of wealth that have been as influential for the laity as the Four Noble Truths were for monks and philosophers:

Four Conditions (to seek)

Wealth gotten by lawful means
Good renown in society
Long life
Birth in heaven

Four Good Deeds (to use wealth for)

Make family and friends happy
Ensure security against worldly dangers
Make offerings to family, friends, gods, and ghosts
Support worthy religious people

The core doctrines we have discussed—prajna and nirvana, anatman (nonself), impermanence and interdependence, and karma causality—comprise the most common foundation for Buddhist belief. For householders, these ideas translate into fostering family ties, striving for economic success, making offerings to hungry ghosts and local gods, pursuing worldly happiness and security, nurturing faith, and seeking heaven.

Now we consider how in specific places and times individual Buddhists and Buddhist communities have focused on these teachings that affect individual life.

The Classical Ideal: Buddhist Civilization

Buddhist civilization was sustained by ritual exchanges between householders and renunciants, the monks and nuns whose advanced ascetic practices entailed abandonment of worldly comforts. Many formulations of proper Buddhist practice were made in the course of early Buddhist history to guide the faithful among the spiritual alternatives specified by the Buddha. The triad of moral practice (*shila*), meditation (*dhyana*), and insight cultivation (*prajna*) was an early organizing schema, as we noted in our discussion of the Eightfold Path.

Buddhist monasticism arose to provide refuge and support for renunciants seeking enlightenment, but the tradition survived by building multifaceted relationships with lay followers who provided for the monks' and nuns' subsistence. Eliciting the loyalty of a cross section of all classes, Buddhists articulated the foundations for a society with spiritual and moral dimensions. Buddhism adapted to myriad local traditions, yet still—when vital—its community remained focused on the **Three Refuges**: the Buddha, the Dharma (the teachings), and the Sangha (the monastic community).

Three Refuges: the Buddha, the Dharma, and the Sangha

TEACHINGS OF RELIGIOUS WISDOM: Teachings on Compassionate Living

Given that the First Noble Truth holds that "all life is suffering," then it follows that all Buddhists should do whatever possible to alleviate it and should open their hearts to others. This underlies the universal Buddhist moral emphasis on compassion.

Thus as a mother with her life will guard her son, her only child, let him extend unboundedly his heart to every living being. And so with loving-kindness for all the world, let him extend unboundedly his heart, above, below, around, unchecked, with no ill will or hate.

—the Buddha[a]

In everything you do, simply work at developing love and compassion until they become a fundamental part of you. That will serve the purpose, even if you do not practice the more outward and conspicuous forms of Dharma, such as chanting, virtuous activities, and altruistic works. As a Sutra states, "Let those who desire Buddhahood not train in many Teachings but only one. Which one? Great Compassion. Those with great compassion possess all the Buddha's teaching as if it were in the palm of the hand."

—Tibetan monk and teacher
Patrul Rimpoche (1808–87)[b]

[a] *Samyutta Nikāyu* (1, 8).
[b] *Words of My Perfect Teacher*, trans. Padmakara Translation Group (1998), pp. 209–10.

The general ideals of Buddhist civilization were in place very early. Monks and nuns served the world through their example of renunciation and meditation, by performing rituals, and by providing medical services. As preservers, transmitters, and exemplars of the Dharma, the sangha's duty was to attract the lay community's merit-making donations by being spiritually worthy; complementing this, sangha members were to follow the *Vinaya* rules and seek out dedicated sympathizers and generous donors. Based on these guidelines, Buddhist societies came to exhibit an array of common traits: relic shrines as centers of community ritual and economy; monasteries as refuges for meditation, study, and access to material resources; and sangha members who assumed leadership of the community's spiritual instruction and ritual life.

Thus, Buddhism successfully developed a broad vision of the spiritual community and of proper practice. Texts speak of the devout layperson's duty to help others grow in faith, morality, knowledge, and charity, to live a life worthy of his or her family heritage, and to make offerings to the spirits of the dead. The Buddha also revealed several short texts (called *mantra* and *paritta*, later *dharani*) that, when chanted, help householders achieve the material blessings and protections needed for a good worldly life. All Buddhists are instructed to listen to the Dharma and try hard to resist its decline. Given the variety of possible practices, the only sound definition of a "good Buddhist" is simple: one who takes the Three Refuges and practices accordingly.

The Mahayana: Philosophies and East Asian Monastic Schools

Despite their prolific writings, Mahayana philosophers and followers were in fact a minority in ancient South Asia, for monks of this persuasion lived in monasteries alongside Sthaviravadins, the predecessors of today's Theravadins. Mahayana only became the "Great Vehicle," the dominant form of Buddhism and the center of a vibrant subculture, in the last era of Buddhism in India (700 CE until its extinction) as well as for a millennium until around 1300 CE in Burma, and the Khmer, Indonesian, and Funan regions of medieval Southeast Asia.

The contrast between traditionalists (Theravadins) and Mahayanists seems to reflect a universal human tendency to divide religious communities between those inclined to a literal approach (holding to the letter within a conservative tradition) and those inclined to a more open-ended and experimental approach to spiritual matters. The Mahayana in this light might be compared to the Sufis in Islam, opposed to the strict scholars of the law (ulama); the Christian analogy would be the mystics in opposition to the official medieval church.

On the philosophical level, there were fiercely contested disagreements between the Theravadins and Mahayanas that we know of chiefly from the Mahayana side. For the most part, the traditionalists ignored the Mahayanist polemics, dismissing proponents with the derogatory term Illusionists (*Vaitulika*). The pejorative label the Mahayanists applied to these opponents, the "Lesser Vehicle" (*Hinayana*), suggested diminished religious effectiveness, commitment, and vision.

We shall discuss the Madhyamaka and Consciousness Only schools of Mahayana thought as well as some minority schools that happen to be well known today and a tradition called the Thunderbolt Vehicle.

The Madhyamaka

Among the earliest texts expressing Mahayana ideas are those called the *Perfection of Wisdom* (*Prajnaparamita*). In these texts of varying length, comments attributed to the Buddha or notable monks poke fun at the Theravadin arhats and seek to poke holes in their scholasticism. More importantly, however, the *Prajnaparamita* texts represent a search for the ultimate truth behind the words of the oldest scriptures. Since Mahayana thought emphasizes interdependence, its exponents saw the Theravadins' focus on an individual's pursuit of nirvana as "selfish" and so reflecting ignorance of the Buddha's highest teaching. Most Mahayana exponents held that the laity as well as monks could potentially attain enlightenment.

Opposition to the Theravadins coalesced in the writings of the monk **Nagarjuna** (born c. 150 CE), one of India's greatest philosophers and founder of the **Madhyamaka** school. Nagarjuna developed a deconstructive method that reduces all assertions to arbitrary propositions and applied this analytical treatment to wide-ranging subject matter. In one of the most courageous explorations in the history of religions, he argued that all language is conventional and that all classifications set up by it are mere constructions, including all Buddhist constructs, even *nirvana* and *samsara*. It is through

Nagarjuna: influential analytical philosopher of the Mahayana school

Madhyamaka: Mahayana philosophical school whose goal is to clear away all attachments, making realization possible

shunyata: "zero-ness"; the term used to designate the emptiness of all constructs

understanding how humans construct reality arbitrarily, positing a "self" and then a "world of things" separate from it, that one reaches a bedrock existential realization that reality is empty or **shunya** of any "thing" the mind can construe. Seeing this analytically and existentially, one can be fully released from all illusions and desires and from the cycle of rebirths. Nagarjuna's deconstructive philosophical effort was religious. His aim was to clear away all false assumptions and even the subtle attachment to language and scholastic categories, thus opening the way to Buddhist meditation practices that transcend words, the only viable means of finding true refuge and final enlightenment.

"Consciousness Only" School

Cittamatra: Mahayana philosophical school that focuses on consciousness as the center of spiritual realization

The other major school of Mahayana thought continued to develop the Great Vehicle from Nagarjuna's standpoint. The "Consciousness Only" (**Cittamatra**) school largely agreed with the Madhyamaka critique of experience as empty but asserted that the real arena of spiritual transformation can therefore be further specified within human consciousness. This school's great thinkers were the brothers Asanga and Vasubandhu (active c. 380 CE), who developed intricate theories of consciousness and causality. They described how karma works within the stream of consciousness, where past actions may block pure, passionless seeing. Further, the spiritual life must be devoted to purifying mind or consciousness, since this is all that truly exists. Again, the practical effect of such theories was to promote the traditional Buddhist practice of meditation, as indicated by another name often applied to this faction: *Yogacara*, or "yoga practice," school.

Buddha-Nature School

Buddha-nature school: Mahayana belief that all beings possess the potential for enlightenment

Another Mahayana philosophy grew later from Madhyamaka roots in East Asia: the **Buddha-nature** (*tathagatagarbha*) **school**. Its proponents held that if it is true that nirvana and samsara cannot be separated in any meaningful way, then nirvana must interpenetrate all reality. And if this is so, one might say that all beings have a portion of nirvana and so possess the latent potential for its realization. Among the many metaphors developed to convey the interdependence of all reality with the Buddha nature, that of Indra's jeweled net had widespread appeal. Just as each jewel in the net reflects every other one, including the reflections of the reflections, even the tiniest thing contains the mystery of the universe. Although support for a school centered on this doctrine eventually declined in China, its ideas and metaphors influenced a Mahayana tradition in East Asia called *Ch'an* in China, *Sön* in Korea, and *Zen* in Japan. The Buddha-nature doctrine appeared to some as a

Manjushri, the bodhisattva of scholars, who cuts through ignorance and delusion with his sword of prajna.

reversion to belief in the soul; but it, too, reinforced the need for traditional meditation practices.

The Lotus Sutra and Celestial Bodhisattvas

One of the most popular Buddhist scriptures in East Asia was the **Lotus Sutra**. Originally written in Sanskrit by 100 CE, this work was later translated into every East Asian language spoken by Buddhists. Through parables, accounts of astounding magical display, and hammering polemics, the *Lotus* develops the Mahayana doctrine of cosmic Buddhahood. It recounts how amazed and confused the arhats became when Shakyamuni Buddha revealed that the human Buddha to whom they were so attached is in fact the embodiment of a more universal Buddha reality that can materialize in many forms simultaneously throughout the cosmos. The *Lotus* describes how the Buddha's preaching skillfully adapted the Dharma to suit the level of the audiences. Even his dying was a show, performed to encourage the active practice of devotees so that they would take seriously the shortness of mortal life. The *Lotus* asserts that the nirvana of arhats is incomplete, merely a preliminary stage in enlightenment seeking. Rather, all beings are destined for Buddhahood through eons of rebirth in samsara.

The religious ideal in the *Lotus Sutra* and in other Mahayana texts shifts from the arhat to the **bodhisattva**, or "future Buddha." Disciples following the Great Vehicle are encouraged not to be satisfied with the arhats' limited nirvana, when Buddhahood is the proper, final religious goal for all. Why? Mahayana teachers point out that given the reality of interdependence, no individual can be an enlightened "being" somehow independent of others. Bodhisattvas should therefore not imagine ending their careers until all beings are enlightened, a mind-boggling and very long-term commitment.

The *Lotus Sutra* is only one among a large class of texts that focus on bodhisattvas who have garnered the merit necessary to earn rebirth as divinities. These "celestial bodhisattvas" continue to serve humanity by offering compassionate intervention to secure worldly blessings and even the means to salvation. In the popular imagination, by the end of the faith's first millennium they had become the Buddhist parallels to Hindu or Chinese deities. The most popular and universal celestial bodhisattva was **Avalokiteshvara**, who came to be known as **Guanyin** in China, *Kannon* in Japan, *Chenrizi* in Tibet, and *Karunamaya* in Nepal. Wherever Mahayana Buddhism spread, texts recounting the compassionate deeds of this always kind divine being were

Lotus Sutra: early Mahayana text that reveals the universal cosmic character of Buddhas and the Dharma

Bodhisattva: a future Buddha," either in the present life or in a future life

Avalokiteshvara/ Guanyin: celestial Mahayana bodhisattva, popular across Asia

Tara, the popular female bodhisattva who is believed to have arisen from the tears of compassion from Avalokiteshvara.

commonly disseminated through storytellers, art, and popular texts. For the great majority of Buddhists in East Asia, being a Mahayana devotee meant performing rituals and asking for blessings from these and other compassionate bodhisattva divinities.

Pure Land Schools

Pure Land: a paradise for rebirth created by a bodhisattva, where humans can achieve enlightenment

Perhaps as an extension of the Buddha's injunction that the sangha should "show the householders the way to heaven," **Pure Land** Buddhism arose in India, around 300 CE, as yet another "cabin" within the Great Vehicle. This school's texts describe how certain bodhisattvas vowed to create celestial paradises on reaching Buddhahood. In these "Pure Lands," there existed all the conditions needed for the individual to be reborn and reach enlightenment. The popularity of this Buddhist orientation, which deferred enlightenment seeking from the human state until rebirth in a heaven, probably had its origins in Shakyamuni's predictions of Buddhism's decline after a thousand years. This expectation legitimated a new spirituality to match the changed times.

Amitabha/Amida: celestial Buddha whose Pure Land became the most popular in East Asia

The most important and highly developed of the Pure Land schools was that associated with the western paradise called *Sukhavati*, skillfully created by a Buddha named **Amitabha** in Sanskrit (*Amitofo* in Chinese, **Amida** in Japanese). An ordered system of Pure Land doctrine and practice developed in China and featured the chanting of Amitabha's name (*Namo A-mi-t'o Fo*) as a meditative act and communal ritual. Exponents assured Pure Land followers that by drawing on this Buddha's distinctive cosmic power through chanting and other devotional practices, even those with bad karma could be reborn in Sukhavati.

The Bodhisattva Vow:

"May I be a protector for the unprotected

A guide for wanderers

A boat, a bridge, a causeway for those who desire the other shore

A lamp for those who need light."

—Shantideva's *Bodhicaryavatara*

Avalokiteshvara, the most popular celestial bodhisattva in the Mahayana tradition.

In Japan, Pure Land Buddhism continued to evolve as devotees were taught that their own "self power" was insufficient to reach nirvana and only the "other power" of celestial Buddhas and bodhisattvas could be relied on. Rituals at death were dedicated to having an individual's lifetime accumulation of merit (punya) be directed to attaining rebirth in the Pure Land. Over the years these schools expanded, and hopes for Pure Land rebirth became extremely popular among the laity. Pure Land schools were also the first to deemphasize the requirement of monastic celibacy by its ordained sangha.

The Meditation School: Ch'an/Zen

By about 600 CE, a Mahayana school called **Ch'an** had formed in China. In contrast to the Pure Land emphasis on "other power," the Ch'an took a position on the "traditionalist" end of the Mahayana spectrum, insisting that individual effort to reach nirvana was the Buddha's true teaching. Ch'an masters stressed meditation, this-life realization, and "self power." This school still bases its authority on an unbroken line of enlightened teachers from Shakyamuni onward, with each subsequent enlightened master, in turn, transmitting a "mind of enlightenment" to his key disciple wordlessly, beyond all scriptures.

Less concerned with a single text and formed in close association with Daoist concepts and aesthetics (covered in Chapter 8), Ch'an lineages respected the Mahayana scriptures but also compiled their own texts recounting the teachings of their own patriarchs and masters, including their approaches to unlocking the gates of nirvana realization. This school also developed the use of paradoxical word problems called **koans** ("cases") that masters forced their disciples to ponder and answer. Resolution of the koans—with words, roars, bodily gestures, or composed silence—could lead to small awakenings of prajna or even to complete nirvana realization. Ch'an masters also insisted on the necessity of mindfulness meditation.

The paradigmatic figure of this school is Bodhidharma, the patriarch who reputedly brought the mind-to-mind transmission tradition from India to China, early in the seventh century of the common era. He is depicted as a fierce meditating monk dispensing terse spiritual admonitions. Later known as **Zen** in Japan, the Ch'an school also developed in monasteries upholding strict monastic rules. Its lineages eventually split along the line of those believing in gradual versus sudden enlightenment.

The Thunderbolt Vehicle: Vajrayana

One additional branch of elite doctrine and practice that emerged among Mahayana Buddhists was the **Vajrayana**, the **Thunderbolt Vehicle**, a tradition that some scholars would consider to be distinct from the Mahayana school. Also called *tantra* and similar to the Hindu tradition of that name, it developed after the faith's first millennium in South Asia. Initially the Vajrayana was the province of wandering mendicants whose spiritual seeking on the fringes of society began even before the Buddha's era. Perhaps in reaction to the complacency stemming from the mainstream view that final enlightenment would not be achieved until after many future lifetimes, the tantric traditions emphasized realizing salvation speedily and in this lifetime. It was also an esoteric tradition, meaning

Ch'an/Zen: Mahayana school emphasizing meditation, discipline, and individual effort to reach nirvana

koan: spiritual riddle used by Zen teachers to foster spiritual growth

"Unless you enter the great ocean of passions, you cannot get the treasure of full knowledge."
—*Vimalakirti Nirdesha Sutra*

Vajrayana/ Thunderbolt Vehicle: esoteric "vehicle" emphasizing practices that speed progress toward enlightenment

Milarepa, the great tantric saint of Tibet, whose songs are beloved for conveying the struggles of solitary meditation and the joy of enlightenment.

"That by which the world is bound, by that same energy its bonds are released; But the world is deluded and knows not this truth, and he who is deprived of this truth will not gain Enlightenment."

—*Hevajra Tantra*

that it was not public or openly shared but was passed on only to those the tantric teacher thought to be capable of understanding and practicing.

Tantric Buddhism used Indian yoga techniques and unconventional means under the guidance of an accomplished teacher, and it drew on the Mahayana philosophy that equated samsara with nirvana. It agreed that all beings partake of the Buddha nature, the *tathagatagarbha doctrine*, and identified the essence of the Buddha's teaching as the pursuit of unshakable, diamond-like insight by whatever means brought immediate success.

The central experience of tantric Buddhism is *sadhana*, communion with a celestial Buddha or bodhisattva through the experience of identification with his or her body, speech, and mind. Dozens of sadhanas emerged, based on existential identification with fierce beings such as Cakrasamvara or Hevajra. The sage who discovered each path is thought to have experienced this deity as the embodiment of enlightenment. Thus an initiate is taught to place the deity in his or her mind's eye, repeat mantras that resonate with that form, and build an existential connection with it, performing *mudras* (hand gestures) and other rituals that help to solidify the identification. When complete, one's identification ultimately leads to the attainment of enlightenment equal to that of the divine form.

Some tantric traditions consciously break the norms of orthodox caste society. Men and women assume identities as divine, enlightened consorts, and their sexual union is developed as a unifying experience of the dual energies of *prajna* (the feminine, as insight) and *upaya* (the masculine, as means of practice). Sexual consort yoga was doubtless once an element in some tantric traditions. (In modern Nepal and Tibet, "consorts" are often spouses.) But as these traditions were systematized in textual form by Buddhist monks after 900 CE in North India, the requirement of literal sexual yoga practice was reinterpreted to allow its replacement by symbolic visualization.

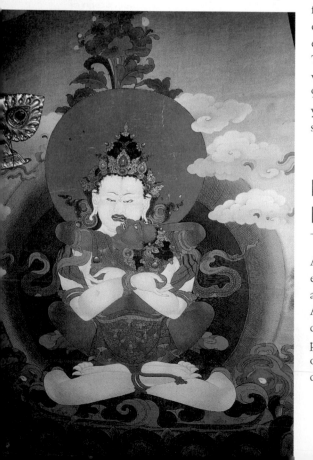

Tantric icon showing visualization of salvific insight and skillful practice as the union of female and male siddhas.

Premodern Buddhism: Buddhist Expansion (400–1500 CE)

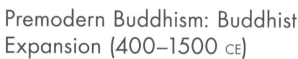

As Buddhism expanded across Asia up to the early modern era, in each cultural region monks, nuns, and disciples adapted the traditions to local cultural conditions. Across Asia, all the sanghas developed Buddhist rituals to help individuals through their lives, from birth to death. In applying the faith's resources to fulfilling the religious needs of the householders, monks and nuns from all Buddhist doctrinal schools served their lay communities in a similar manner. We will now survey the wide-ranging, trans-Asian pilgrimage of Buddhism; there is no other way to understand the history of this diverse tradition than to move across Asia by geographic region and then note the history of the faith's evolution and the distinctive beliefs and practices that characterize its regional adaptations.

South Asia

With the decline of the great Gupta dynasty in North India by 650 CE, small regional polities controlled the Hindu–Buddhist societies of South Asia. Buddhism survived mainly in the northeast under imperial patronage, its presence confined largely to monasteries that had also come to function as institutions of learning. The great centers Nalanda and Vikramashila, for example, fostered a vigorous articulation of Mahayana Buddhist philosophy, meditation, and popular piety. Ties to Tibet, Nepal, and centers in the Srivijaya kingdom of Sumatra-Java extended the influence of the Great Vehicle from these centers.

After Buddhism's successful transplantation in China, Sri Lanka, and Southeast Asia, monks and householders traveled to study in South Asia and to acquire texts. They also completed pilgrimage visits, venerating the "sacred traces" (cremation relics, begging bowls, etc.) of the Buddha and arhats that were entombed in the stupas. The Buddha's enlightenment tree in Gaya and the temple erected nearby were at the center of such visits. As Indic Buddhism declined, distant pious rulers from Sri Lanka and Burma sent funds and artisans to renovate the Gaya site, however. By 1296, when the last such donations were recorded, almost every Buddhist monastery in the Gangetic plain had been abandoned for centuries and many shrines had been left to decay. The decline of the faith in South Asia was due partly to the successful development of popular devotional Hinduism and by the Hindu monasticism organized by the saint-scholar Shankara, whose Advaita Vedanta school we discussed in Chapter 6.

Another factor in Buddhism's decline was the arrival in South Asia of Islam, another missionary faith that slowly spread throughout the region. By 750 CE, Muslim conquests and conversions to Islam in central Asia and in northwestern India were undermining the predominance of Buddhism. As we have seen, Buddhist monasticism was strongly tied to trade and mercantile patronage; and as the trade moving along the silk routes shifted to Muslim merchants with connections westward, the monasteries lost a major source of support. In addition, an era of raids into North India culminated in 1192 in the first period of Muslim rule from Delhi. Across the northern plains, most remaining Buddhist institutions were plundered, and the destruction dispersed Indian monks into the Himalayas, to coastal urban centers, and across the seas. In the southern peninsula of the Indian subcontinent, Buddhism also declined slowly, but scattered monasteries existed there as late as the seventeenth century.

Buddhism's dominant region shifted to East Asia after its major sacred centers in India lay in ruins. Because many early versions of the first Buddhist textual collections had been lost, each school settled on surviving texts and scholastic traditions to establish its own doctrinal authority. In East Asia, China became the strong center of Mahayana Buddhism. The cross-fertilization of Buddhism across Asia was further complicated after 1250, when Tibetan Buddhists exerted strong influences within China, south into the Himalayas, and north into Mongolia.

The island of Sri Lanka embraced Buddhism, and its early kings after 100 BCE supported the sangha and built monuments to express their devotion. Although both Mahayanists and Sthaviravadins practiced there throughout the first millennium, the Theravada school eventually prevailed. The "reforms" instituted by various Southeast Asian kings in the 1300s drew on respected Sri Lankan monks who came to reintroduce Theravada ordination and philosophical traditions. From this time onward, Theravada has remained the dominant tradition in Burma, Siam (now Thailand), and both Laos and Cambodia.

China

In East Asia, Buddhist schools formed around charismatic teachers whose interpretations favored one or another of the many texts as the Buddha's highest teaching. Mahayana Buddhism alone flourished, translated in terms compatible with Daoist mysticism, the indigenous gods, and aspects of Confucian morality and state governance (see Chapter 8).

Under the weak regional states of the pre-T'ang era (up until 645 CE), Buddhism found widespread support. Indian and Central Asian monks had begun a determined project of translating the hundreds of Buddhist texts into Chinese. In addition, monks, merchants, and rulers had obtained many precious relics and had them enshrined in monasteries across China. Finally, Chinese Buddhists came to recognize **Wu Tai Shan**, one of China's sacred mountains, as the home of Manjushri, one of Mahayana Buddhism's chief celestial bodhisattvas (a topic discussed earlier in the chapter). This belief grew as devotees by the thousands ventured to this extraordinary site and had powerful meditative visions of this future Buddha. So strong was belief in Wu Tai Shan's Buddhist holiness that its fame spread back to India; the Chinese annals note that hundreds of Indian pilgrims traveled to China in subsequent centuries to seek Manjushri's spiritual blessings at Wu Tai Shan. Through textual transmission, the location of relics in monastic shrines across the country, and the pilgrimages at this (and other) sacred mountains, Asia was unified by Buddhism.

Wu Tai Shan: sacred mountain in China revered as home of the bodhisattva Manjushri

With the consolidation of the T'ang state in Chang-an (modern Xian) and its revival of the traditional Confucian literati class, the destiny of Buddhism rose and fell according to the degree of support from the reigning emperor and his court. Despite the generosity of imperial patrons and wealthy donors who profited from trade along the legendary Silk Road, many Confucian officials who manned the permanent state bureaucracy criticized Buddhism. They argued that monks and nuns were disloyal to parents, country, and ancestors, asserting as well that the rising wealth of the monasteries weakened the overall economy.

Images of the corpulent and happy Maitreya, the next Buddha, called Mi-lo Fo in China, are popular in East Asia.

Anti-Buddhist sentiment culminated in the great persecution of 841–45. Nearly every Buddhist monastery was dismantled, metal images were melted down for the state treasury, and renunciants were ordered to return to lay life. Buddhism eventually rebuilt and rebounded, but the faith never permeated Chinese society so thoroughly again, nor did all the early Chinese doctrinal schools truly recover. From the Sung era onward, it was the Ch'an and Pure Land schools that survived, being less dependent on official recognition or aristocratic patronage. Leading monks repositioned the faith in Chinese society by emphasizing their disinterest in politics and their insistence that monastics must observe a disciplined lifestyle. In addition, they stressed the compatibility of Buddhism with Daoism and Confucianism.

During the short-lived Mongol conquest of China marking the Yuan dynasty (1271–1368), Tibetan Buddhism became the state religion and its distinctive Mahayana-Vajrayana traditions were granted strong support across the empire, primarily in imperial strongholds. The Mongols' conversion to Buddhism, soon after their thirteenth-century campaigns of violent conquest across Eurasia, marks another point at which Buddhism changed world history, in this case by undercutting Mongol martial values and expansionism.

With the return of native Chinese rule under the Ming (1392–1644), Mahayana traditions were embraced by a large sector of the population: worship of the celestial bodhisattva Guanyin; veneration of the sixteen saints designated as protectors of Buddhism until the coming of the next Buddha; and the practice of releasing animals (typically fish or birds) to earn merit. The corpulent form of the next Buddha **Maitreya** (Chi: **Mi-lo Fo**) appeared as a distinctive Chinese image. From the early Ming, too, the practice of householders keeping detailed merit account books gained

Maitreya/Mi-lo Fo: the next historical Buddha, uniquely depicted in China as corpulent and happy in popularity. In China as elsewhere, merit-making and ritual observances dominated the religious life of most Buddhists.

Southeast Asia

Southeast Asia after 1200 was ruled by regional states that sought their legitimacy in supporting the Theravada Buddhist monastic system introduced from Sri Lanka. Buddha relics were imported as well, and stupas in the Sri Lankan style were built across the region. The "reforms" already mentioned effectively reduced the presence of the Mahayana to a few isolated communities, and all of these eventually disappeared. The Khmer state for several periods was ruled by kings who favored Mahayana Buddhism, and they constructed magnificent temples and monasteries.

From the early eighth century, the large and prosperous Srivijaya Empire in Sumatra and Java also supported the efflorescence of both Hinduism and Mahayana Buddhism. These rulers created the colossal stupa at Borobodur, the crowning monument of this era. But with the empire's decline in the thirteenth century, the smaller states ruled by regional kings favored local religions or (later) the schools of Islam originating in India.

Yet in the majority of the Southeast Asian polities, it was Theravada Buddhism that thrived under rulers who claimed legitimacy under the cosmic law of karma, whereby they were reaping past merit to rule. Their states supported the sangha and sponsored rituals designed to have the powers of the Buddhist universe continually regenerated. In turn, they expected the people to emulate their example by following the Dharma, supporting a just Buddhist order in the territory, and accepting their

Archaeological remains of Pagan (Myanmar), one of the greatest Buddhist cities in the world between 1000 and 1400 CE.

place in the karma-determined social hierarchy. The many hundreds of grand stupas, image halls, and monasteries built in these prosperous states show the success of premodern Theravada Buddhism. The great Buddhist monuments legitimated the state, created spectacular sanctuaries, employed artisans and the masses, and lent prestige to the sangha. Across Theravadin Southeast Asia, this form of "state Buddhism" survived even after the kingdoms of the premodern era gave way to smaller regional states. However, this form of traditional, hierarchical Buddhism was to be challenged in the modern era as new ideas and political systems emerged.

Japan

Mahayana Buddhism was adopted across East Asia, originally reaching Japan in the seventh century. By 1230, Japanese monks again had traveled to China to undertake the last transplantations of Chinese schools: two forms of the Ch'an became the Soto Zen school (instituted by the monk **Dogen** [1200–1253]) and the Rinzai Zen school (under the monk **Eisai** [1141–1215]). Both vied for popularity among the aristocrats and warriors who controlled Japanese society in the post-Kamakura era (after 1350).

Dogen: Japanese monk; founder of Soto Zen school

Eisai: Japanese monk; founder of Rinzai Zen school

The Pure Land school also found widespread popular acceptance through the public preaching campaigns undertaken by charismatic monks. Since their simplification of Buddhist practice entailed only the *nembutsu*, the chant "*Namo A-mi-t'o Fo*," the honorific repetition of Amitabha Buddha's name imported from China, householders could hope for nirvana in Pure Land rebirth. A thirteenth-century Japanese monk named Shinran continued the basic rituals and textual interpretations imported from Chinese Pure Land teachers and added emphasis on *mappo*, the so-called decadent-age doctrine, reflecting acceptance of Shakyamuni's prediction of Buddhism's decline. Shinran argued that human beings were now completely dependent on the Buddha's grace to reach nirvana and had simply to acknowledge their grateful acceptance of it to enter the Pure Land. Shinran's school, the Jodo Shinshu, became a vital separate lineage, and its sangha was the first in Japan to drop the requirement of celibacy.

A third track in this era of new Japanese schools is represented by **Nichiren** (1222–82), a prophetic and charismatic monk who taught that the *Lotus Sutra* is the only true Buddhist text. Like Shinran, Nichiren subscribed to the doctrine of mappo and argued that the instability of the turbulent times confirmed it. He also accepted the ultimate reality of an omniscient cosmic Buddha immanent in the world and in persons. Practice in the Nichiren school was simplified to three devotional acts: a short honorific repetition of the *Lotus Sutra*'s title (*Nam-Myoho Reng-e Kyo*), meditation on an image of the cosmic Buddha designed by Nichiren, and pilgrimage to the school's national shrine. Later, the monk's followers taught that Nichiren himself was a bodhisattva. Their interpretation of Buddhism emphasized Japan's special significance in leading Buddhism through the declining stage of history, a

Nichiren: Japanese monk who taught that the *Lotus Sutra* is the only true Buddhist text

"Nichiren confuses his enemies," a woodcut print by Utagawa Kinuyoshi (1798–1861). Nichiren's disciples followed the teacher's example of practicing aggressive missionary exposition, a trend that has marked the school up to the present.

visionary view that endured to inspire several splinter movements in the modern and postwar eras.

The Himalayan Region

"In short, at all times and all occasions be not separated from these three, namely devotion to your teachers, an open heart to the world and all it contains, and compassion to sentient beings."

—Dolpo lama's advice

In Tibet, Mongolia, and Nepal, Mahayana schools also became supreme. Across the highland frontiers, Vajrayana traditions came to be regarded as the Buddha's highest teaching, and the monks who introduced Buddhism there taught that Buddhist belief and practice have both outer and inner levels of understanding, the highest of which was accessible only through tantric initiation and practice. In these regions, Vajrayana traditions developed in rich elaboration, and dedicated elites practiced exhaustive meditation regimens. Tibetan scholars translated a vast corpus of Sanskrit texts, commented on them, and composed their own interpretive tracts. Ritual masters also applied the texts and teachings to many aspects of life, designing rituals to promote health, prosperity, and the best possible rebirth. Even flags, watermills, and hand-turned wheels were adapted to broadcast the Buddha's teaching, continuously earning merit for individuals and communities.

In Tibet, too, the celestial bodhisattva doctrine was made more accessible to the laity: Extraordinary monks and nuns came to be identified as their incarnations (*tulku* in Tibetan) of these divinities. Indeed, after 1250 these "incarnate lineages" became institutions endowed with lands and households, and some tulkus assumed power as both religious and political leaders of their regions. Allied with the military might of the Mongols, leaders of the major Tibetan monasteries ascended to rule over central Tibet, a situation unprecedented in any other Buddhist society. The **Gelugpa** school,

Gelugpa: monastic school that came to politically dominate all others by 1640; its head, the Dalai Lama, ruled Tibet until 1959

under the Dalai and Panchen Lamas, came to rule Tibet in 1642, concentrating secular and religious power in its large, land-owning monasteries. Roughly 20 percent of the male population were monks.

Buddhism and Modernity

The current condition of Buddhism across Asia today is the result of its institutional development and how the tradition evolved in the very different social, political, and cultural contexts found there. The monastic institution that always has been at the center of Buddhist communities faced daunting challenges in the colonial era; the different crises, influences, and possibilities in each region led to different historical tracks, thereby increasing the diversity of Buddhism. The general pattern of Buddhism's adaptation in all societies, and especially the exchanges between monastics and householders that sustained it, are central to this story. Understanding these is the foundation for following how the various colonial influences and modern changes altered Buddhism in Asia.

The Potala in Lhasa, Tibet, was the palace of the Dalai Lamas from 1649 until 1959, when the fourteenth Dalai Lama went into exile.

Early Modern Buddhist Polities: Monastics, Householders, Kings

One decisive factor in Buddhist history has been the relation between the institutional religion and political power, a recurring source of controversy from the colonial period until the present, as we will see again shortly. Buddhists have always looked to the legend of Ashoka (273–232 BCE) to define their exemplary relationship with rulers as protectors and patrons. Only with such support can the sangha's integrity be ensured, the Buddha's monuments maintained, and the teachings passed down. In premodern Sri Lanka, the king appointed a senior monk as the *sangharaja* ("ruler of the sangha"); in every Theravada country today, leadership and jurisdiction over the sangha are found in the form of a single monk or monastic council appointed by the state.

A dramatic modern instance of this exemplary royal support was Burma's King Mindon, who convened the Fifth Buddhist Council (by Theravada reckoning) in 1871. The only complete textual canon among the early collections of the Buddha's teachings was recited and corrected at this conference. These writings, revered today as the **Pali Canon**, were then inscribed in their entirety on large marble slabs set up in the city of Mandalay. Postcolonial Buddhist governments across the world sponsored similar activities in 1956 on the occasion of the Theravadin school's determination of the 2,500-year anniversary of Shakyamuni's parinirvana.

Pali Canon: the only complete canon among the early collection of Buddha's teachings, split into three divisions: Vinaya (monastic code), Suttas (sermons), and Abhidhamma (advanced teaching formulas)

For most of its history, the Buddhist sangha has existed in polities ruled by kings or emperors. As a result, a mutually beneficial tradition developed: the sangha adopted rules in harmony with those of states and would applaud exemplary moral leadership on the part of the monarch. In premodern times, monastic Buddhism usually served to promote social stability, accommodating itself to local traditions. The monks also chanted mantras and performed merit-making rituals on behalf of rulers, a custom that continues in modern Japan, Thailand, and Nepal.

Buddhist Monasticism

A monastery (vihara) can be of humble construction or built to imperial, aristocratic standards. Each, however, must have a place for the monks to sleep and a building in which they gather for reception into the sangha, fortnightly recitations, and other proceedings. Monasteries may also have one or more stupas, a "bodhi tree," a meditation hall, and one or more image halls.

The subsistence of the monks and nuns has remained dependent on the donations of food and shelter by the lay community. Originally, all sangha members gathered their food in morning begging rounds, and the day's solid food had to be eaten by noon. By the modern period, however, Buddhists had developed other routines: In some places members of the laity would come to the monastery on a rotating schedule with food donations; in other places, monks cooked their own foods. Many Mahayana monasteries of East Asia interpreted the moral rules to require vegetarianism of the monks and nuns, but in recent centuries the restriction against alcohol was taken by most to mean "no intoxication," not complete abstinence.

Meditation Practices

As we have noted, meditation remained essential for all aspirants, lay and renunciant, seeking to move on the final path to nirvana. This practice by monks and nuns, even if only a few, certifies Buddhism's continuing spiritual vitality, inspiring layfolk to respect and take refuge in the sangha. Until the modern era, however, it was almost entirely the elite among monks and nuns who practiced meditation.

vipassana meditation: Buddhist meditation practice focusing on breath and body

Buddhism inherited and extended the spiritual experiments of ancient India. The practice of trance (*samadhi*) is accepted, even encouraged, but this state does not lead to nirvana realization, hence is not given highest priority. The key practice is called *mindfulness meditation* (**vipassana meditation**): a careful attending to, or being mindful of, the three characteristics of existential reality—suffering (*dukkha*), impermanence (*anitya*), and nonself (*anatman*).

The practice as taught today is simple: While remaining motionless, the practitioner seeks to focus all awareness on the breath, letting go of all intervening thoughts that arise. Attention to and comprehension of these realities opens up an awareness of the "inner life" we normally ignore. With such heightened awareness, mindfulness meditation has other critical effects: It shows how suffering and change are inevitable,

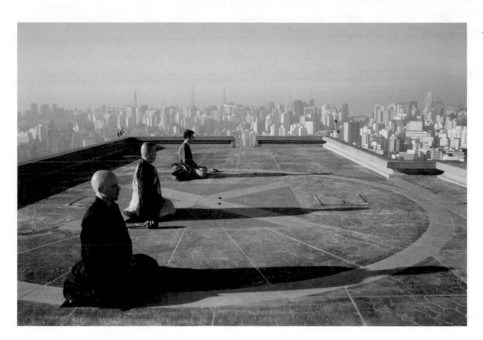

Japanese and Brazilian monks meditate and chant to bless the Copan Building in downtown São Paulo, Brazil, in 2010. Increasingly, converts and Asian monastics are members of the same sangha.

it nourishes personal detachment that stills desire, and it cultivates the spiritual insight (prajna) that dispels ignorance. The development of prajna and the removal of ignorance eliminate bad karma and create good karma. Perfection eventually leads to the fullness of prajna in a breakthrough, transformative experience of an enlightened mind (*bodhi*).

Mahayana meditations elaborated on these precedents. Ch'an or Zen mindfulness meditation, like Theravada vipashyana practice, focuses first on the breath. Given the Mahayana teaching that all beings possess the Buddha nature (*tathagatagarbha*), meditation can comprise any activity practiced with mindfulness, from walking to class to sipping espresso, or (more traditionally) from engaging in martial arts to arranging flowers.

In Pure Land meditation, the fervent wish to attain nirvana in an otherworldly western paradise (*Sukhavati*) encourages devotees to visualize that extraordinary paradise as described in the texts. These practices are especially important as death nears, for individuals who can visualize this realm are promised painless passage into heavenly rebirth through the boundless grace of the Buddha Amitabha.

Schools devoted to esoteric Vajrayana innovations developed yet other forms of meditation under the heading of *sadhana*. These tantric practices are based on mind's-eye visualizations of enlightened bodhisattvas and mantra recitations to jump-start spiritual development. By controlling the appearance of mental images, one sees all experience as mind-constructed and thus empty (*shunya*) of any ultimate reality.

Again, however, it is necessary to emphasize that most Buddhists—yesterday and today—concentrated their devotional activities on rituals and on accumulating merit rather than on meditation, and so we turn to gift giving as the foundation of Buddhist practice.

Punya and Dana: The Fundamental Buddhist Exchange

The Buddha set out a "graded teaching" to order the spiritual teachings to be given to disciples. This framework begins with the merit-making donations that enable a Buddhist community's diverse cultural activities. Still used as a guide for modern Buddhist teachers, the sequence counsels progression through the following stages of religious striving:

1. **Dana** ("self-less giving" to diminish desire)
2. *Shila* ("morality")
3. *Svarga* ("heaven")
4. *Dharma-deshana* ("instruction on doctrine") on the Four Noble Truths

This hierarchy of progressive practices defines a "syllabus" for advancing in spiritual attainment. Stages 1 and 2 lead to heaven birth (3), the fruit of merit; the doctrines in stage 4 are the instructions concerning reaching enlightenment, beyond good karma making.

Just as merit, or punya, has provided the chief orientation point and goal in the Buddhist layperson's worldview and ethos, dana has always been the starting practice

dana: "self-less giving" to diminish desire: the chief merit-making activity in Buddhist societies

A woman from a Buddhist merit-making society in Hong Kong releases shellfish into Victoria Harbor in 2010.

for accumulating it. Merit making for most Buddhists, including most monks and nuns, is the central measure of spiritual advancement. Merit making remains the universal, integrating transaction in Buddhist settings through the modern era, regardless of the respective intellectual elite's orientation toward competing Theravada, Mahayana, or Vajrayana doctrinal formulations or spiritual disciplines.

The wish for merit leading to rebirth in heaven has remained the most popular and pan–Buddhist aspiration; indeed, monks from the very beginning were instructed

Selections from a Chinese Buddhist Merit Account Sheet

In East Asia, followers interpreted Buddhist teachings in original ways, in some cases applying the basic ideas into new formulations. By the Ming era, Buddhist monks and householders thought it useful to assign mathematical values to articulate the hierarchy of moral actions, as in this example:

100 Merits: Save one life; save a woman's chastity; prevent a child from drowning; continue a family lineage

50 Merits: Prevent an abortion; provide for a homeless person; prevent someone from committing a serious crime; give a speech that benefits many

30 Merits: Convert another to Buddhism; facilitate a marriage; take in an orphan; help another do something virtuous

10 Merits: Recommend a virtuous person; cure a major illness; speak virtuously; save the life of a good animal; publish the Buddha's teachings; treat servants properly

5 Merits: Prevent a lawsuit; cure a minor illness; stop someone from slandering; make an offering to a saintly person; save any animal; pray for others

3 Merits: Endure ill treatment without complaint; bury an animal; urge those making a living by killing to stop

1 Merit: Give an article to help others; chant a Buddhist scripture; provide for one monk;

return a lost article; help repair a public road or bridge

100 Demerits: Cause a death; rape; end a family lineage

50 Demerits: Induce an abortion; break up a marriage; teach someone to do great evil; make a speech that harms many

30 Demerits: Create slander that dishonors another; disobey an elder; cause a family to separate; during famine, fail to share food grains

10 Demerits: Mistreat an orphan or widow; prepare a poison; kill an animal that serves humans; speak harshly to parent or teacher

5 Demerits: Slander spiritual teachings; turn away a sick person; speak harshly; kill any animal; write or speak lewdly; not clear an injustice when possible

3 Demerits: Get angry over words spoken; cheat an ignorant person; destroy another's success; be greedy

1 Demerit: Urge another to fight; help another do evil; waste food; kill insects; turn away a begging monk; take a bribe; keep a lost article

Source: Guide formulated by Liao-Fan Yuan (1550–1624), a Zen master of Jiang-su Province. Translated in *The Key to Creating One's Destiny* (Singapore: Lapis Lazuli Press, 1988), pp. 43–46. Passages edited and in places paraphrased.

to "show the laity the way to heaven" by acting as a "field of merit." Householders can "plant" donations in this field, and the "harvest" in good karma they earn will be great. Punya is needed for a good rebirth, and although Buddhist doctrine holds that heaven is a temporary state, the reward of heavenly rebirth has motivated many to be "good Buddhists."

Merit making can lead one closer to nirvana, but it also has practical, worldly consequences, impacting destiny both now and across future lifetimes. Therefore, Buddhists seek punya to change the karma "account" that affects them in this life as well as to modify future rebirth destiny.

To maximize punya and so enhance the course of spiritual advancement, popular texts urge all disciples, monastic and lay, to cultivate such practices as venerating images, fasting, taking extra precepts (as described at the very beginning of this chapter), organizing compassionate actions and charitable institutions, arranging public recitations of the texts, and undertaking meditation.

The most universal expression of lay Buddhist faith and punya seeking has been through dana. Making donations for spiritual purposes and setting aside time for moral observances, such as saving an animal and returning a lost object, remained the foundation for householder practice; these still comprise the most visible Buddhist activity today. Passages in the Mahayana texts also articulate the value of dana to the individual as an expression of compassion (*karuna*) and as a renunciatory practice that undercuts desire and attachment.

Rituals and Festivals

Buddhist monasteries developed ritual procedures and a yearly festival calendar. The monk's vocation came to include priestly duties, performing rituals that linked the Buddha's spoken words with simple gestures. In the simplest (and still most popular) universal Buddhist ritual, monks pour water into a vessel as they chant words revealed by the Buddha. Now imbued with healing powers, the liquid can be drunk or sprinkled over the bodies of those needing assistance. All Buddhist schools encourage meritorious offerings of lamps, incense, and flowers to Buddha images, bodhi trees, and stupas.

In the Mahayana schools, an important part of a bodhisattva's service to others is ritual; some monks specialized in chanting sound chains called *mantras*, known for their spiritual powers. Ritual chanting of the Buddha's own sayings is thought to further the foundations of spiritual practice and infuse towns and families with powerful blessings, including good karma. Ritual service thus came to dominate Mahayana Buddhism in its missionary program; mantra recitations were thought to activate the unseen cosmic Buddha powers promised in the Mahayana texts.

The bimonthly Buddhist holiday called *uposatha* occurs each fortnight on the new-moon and full-moon days. On uposatha, sangha members privately recite the details confirming that they are monastics in good standing according to the Vinaya rules. This recitation follows a private confession, to the renunciant's superior, of any

Theravada monk sprinkling a laywoman with water over which the sacred words of the Buddha have been chanted.

transgressions of the rules during the period. Uposatha continues in the modern era to serve as the regular occasion to review, correct, and certify the proper standards of monastery discipline in Theravada societies.

Emphasizing the fundamental interdependence between sangha and lay community, householders visit the local vihara on these days to make dana offerings. On these days, too, devout layfolk take the opportunity to don white robes, camp on the monastery grounds, and observe eight of the ten monastic rules. They join with many more layfolk who have come simply to release animals or to make offerings to Buddha images and remain to hear monks preach the Dharma. Thus, the lunar fortnight rhythm dominates the festival year. The regular succession of uposathas and the two half-moon days are when Buddhists typically undertake meritorious actions, perform rituals, and engage in meditation practices. In effect, each week has a special day for Buddhist observances. Like other great world religions, Buddhism also formed the basis of distinctive cultures that organized the year with regular monthly and yearly festivals. Some orchestrate reliving classical Buddhist events "in the beginning": Celebrations of the Buddha's birth, enlightenment, and nirvana are universal.

The Universal Buddhist Shrine

Caitya: Buddhist shrine

For all Buddhist schools, the stupa (or **caitya**, a term that can also signify any Buddha shrine) became a focal point and singular landmark denoting the tradition's spiritual presence. Buddhism eventually recognized "eight great relic caityas" for pilgrimage and veneration in South Asia. Stupa worship thus became the chief focus of Buddhist ritual activity, and this has continued through the modern era to the present. The Buddhist relic cult began early, inspiring monks, nuns, and householders to circumambulate the shrines (in the clockwise direction) and to have their own cremated remains deposited in the same great stupa or in smaller votive stupas located nearby.

Throughout Buddhist history, the stupa has served as a place to go to recall the Buddha's great acts, a "power place" tapping the Buddha's (or saint's) relic's healing potency, a site to earn merit through joyful, musical veneration, and a monument marking the conversion and control of local spirits. In the Mahayana schools, the stupa was also thought of as a symbol of Buddhahood's omnipresence, a center of Mahayana text revelation, and a perfect form showing the unity of the natural elements (earth, fire, air, ether) with the Buddha nature.

Later, Buddhists identified stupas as the physical representations of the eternal teachings. They also expanded the possible sacred objects deposited in them to include Buddha's words in textual form. Amid many understandings, Buddhists at every level of sophistication believe that ritually correct veneration of stupas will earn them merit. In practice, believers converge at stupas to mark events associated with the Buddhas or saints. Stupas thus remain the natural sites for Buddhist festivals of remembrance and veneration.

Buddhist stupa being whitewashed by a monk in Ladakh, in northern India near the Tibetan border. Monks, nuns, and laity have built these shrines since the Buddha's death.

Death Ritualism

In all Buddhist countries today, despite many regional differences, death rituals are the exclusive purview of the sangha and a key time for monks to expound core teachings and receive dana. Buddhist mourners carefully dispose of the corpse, relying on ritual performed by monks to ensure that the dead person does not become a hungry ghost (*preta*) or, worse, a demon (*yaksha*). They also seek to avert bad destiny for the deceased by making punya and then transferring it to the dead person. In adopting such practices, Buddhists straddle both alternatives to the ancient Indic question of whether destiny is based strictly on an individual's own karma over a lifetime or whether the proper performance of rituals during and immediately after death can override unfavorable karma and manipulate rebirth destiny. Since Buddhism is conceptually centered on the doctrine that the cosmos is governed by karmic law, ritual traditions naturally surround death, the critical time in the operation of such causal mechanisms. Both Theravada monks and—more expansively—Mahayana ritualists apply ritual expertise to this time. The tradition's dependence on after-death ritual service for sangha donations is evident in all modern Asian traditions; even when some people are otherwise hardly observant in modern urban areas of Japan, death rituals performed by Buddhist monks are universal.

Buddhism Under Colonialism (1500–1960)

The modern era was one of widespread decline for Buddhism across Asia. Medieval states either lost their autonomy or were destabilized by colonialism, first by European powers (the British in Burma, India, Sri Lanka, Tibet, and China; the French in Indochina; the Portuguese and Dutch in Sri Lanka; the Dutch in Indonesia) and

Typical gathering of devotees at the southern shrine of the Swedagon stupa, a Burmese temple in present-day Myanmar.

later, in the early twentieth century, by Japanese conquest and occupation. In East Asia, the imperial Chinese state was weakened by the colonial powers (primarily Britain), whose aggressive trade practices backed by military intervention disrupted the Chinese economy. The civil disorders that followed also undermined Buddhist institutions. (These events are discussed in Chapter 8.)

The impact of European colonialism on Buddhism can be summarized under two broad domains, institutional and doctrinal. Although Dutch, British, and French colonial governments had somewhat different ideologies guiding their rule in Asia, all administrations eventually declined to fulfill the traditional native king's role of patron and protector of the local religions, including Buddhism. As a result, the means of accommodation that had evolved over the centuries to perpetuate Buddhism ceased to exist, sometimes without warning, in every colonized polity. When the Portuguese and Dutch took power in Sri Lanka (1505–1658), for example, they seized the ports and lowlands, destroyed monasteries, persecuted Buddhists, forcibly converted many to Catholicism, and caused the Sinhalese king to flee to the central highlands. When all the island had become Britain's colony (1815), the British moved to end state support for the sangha and discontinued patronage dedicated to the upkeep of Buddhist buildings everywhere. Colonial administrations also typically ceased enforcement of indigenous land tenure relations and taxation, withdrew from supervision of monastic ordination, and halted ceremonies according respect to venerable monastic leaders, sacred symbols, and temples. The roots of modern crisis and Buddhism's decline across the region are easily traced to this abrupt deprivation of resources and political support.

Challenges from Colonialism, Communism, and Modern Critics (1800–Present)

In the realm of ideas, the colonial powers introduced two alien and often-contradictory systems of thought: on the one hand, the scientific notions derived from the Enlightenment, and on the other, theories of racial, cultural, and religious superiority that were used to legitimate the triumphant expansion of Euro-Christian peoples. Western medicine, often effective where folk remedies and rituals had unpredictable results, presented another challenge to every local society's worldview.

The fruits of the Enlightenment—democracy, modern science, and technology—were imported into Asia through schools built by the colonial governments. One motivation for establishing the schools was to provide trained native people who spoke the language of the colonizer. The reach of the colonial governments was broader, however, for in fact they were the official and secular extensions of the European home states. In addition, the colonial administrators were for the most part supportive of the expansion of the Christian missionary presence. (For example, in many places colonial law recognized as legitimate only marriages conducted by Christian ministers.) It was with such backing that the first modern global missions were created: Across Asia, lay and ordained Christians built churches and established educational institutions, hospitals, and charities; some proselytized aggressively through public preaching and pamphlets attacking Buddhist beliefs and practices.

After the fall of the Ching dynasty in 1912, socioeconomic conditions remained unstable under the Republic of China, only to worsen further with the rise of regional warlords and the Japanese invasion, first in Manchuria (1931) and then southward into the Chinese heartland. Throughout the twentieth century, the traditional Buddhist schools and Buddhist thought were subject to criticism by leaders of a modernizing faction called the May 4th Movement. To respond to those who claimed that Buddhism was parasitic and corrupt due to its landholdings, China's greatest modern reformer, Taixu (1889–1947), suggested that Chinese Buddhists should follow the ancient Ch'an school's policy of combining field labor with spiritual life, developing a "Buddhist work ethic" within the monasteries. Though critiqued fiercely by the elites, the Chinese sangha endured: In 1930, there were 730,000 monks and nuns who maintained 267,000 registered monastic temples. Later, the sustained Communist Party policy of thoroughgoing destruction, denigration, and disestablishment that began in 1949, however, had no precedent in Buddhist history.

Although at first disturbed and demoralized, Buddhists recovered from and responded to colonial-era challenges in various ways. Few converted to Christianity, however, despite such obvious inducements as access to charitable services and gaining an inside track to promotions into the British government service.

Although hampered by the disruption of their institutions, Buddhist intellectuals and preachers emerged to engage in the dialogue with science and Christianity. In Sri Lanka, for example, early Protestant missionaries, having assessed Buddhist monks as uniformly indolent and ignorant, felt themselves on the verge of mass conversion. Yet a series of public debates ended badly for those missionaries, a reversal that restored public faith in the ongoing relevance of Buddhist doctrine.

TALES OF SPIRITUAL TRANSFORMATION: The Enlightenment of Zen Master Sokei-an Sasaki

Although the canonical texts counsel monastics not to discuss their own spiritual attainments, the following account of his enlightenment is from a respected modern Zen master.

One day I wiped out all notions from my mind. I gave up all desire. I discarded all the words with which I thought and stayed in quietude. I felt a little queer—as if I were being carried into something, or as if I were touching some power unknown to me . . . and Ztt! I lost the boundary of my physical body. I had my skin, of course, but I felt I was standing in the center of the cosmos. I spoke, but my words had lost their meaning. I saw people coming toward me, but all were the same man. All were myself! I had never known this world. I had believed that I was created, but now I must change my opinion: I was never created. I was the cosmos; no Mr. Sasaki existed.

Source: *Zen Notes* 1, no. 5 (1954), pp. 17–18.

In Sri Lanka, the dialectic between the West and Buddhism was most intense, and decisive new directions for Buddhist modernization were identified in the island nation. Reformers involved the lay society more fully in Buddhist institutions and spiritual practices (primarily meditation), motivating some among the laity to take the place of former royal patrons. The lay reformers, in turn, insisted that monks respect the sangha rules and discipline, and they supported the revival of monastic meditation practice, usually in newly created reformist monastic schools. Finally, Buddhist intellectuals carried out historical investigations, offering modern demythologized reinterpretations of the Buddha and Buddhist doctrine analogous to the scholarly "search for the historical Jesus" that was emerging within Protestant Christianity at the same time. To publicize these reforms, Buddhists adopted one aspect of Christian missionary methodology: They began by investing in printing technology and undertaking publications that defined reformist doctrines and practices. They also rediscovered the practice of public sermonizing.

Reformers in Thailand, as in Sri Lanka, also articulated new interpretations of "true Buddhism." They taught that Buddhism in its pure form was not concerned with communal rituals or harnessing the cosmic powers of Buddhism to support the secular kingdom. Rejecting the adaptive local traditions that had developed in the process of the globalization of Buddhism, reformers insisted that the only genuine center of the faith was the individual's quest for mind cultivation and salvation. Doctrines describing the interdependent and impermanent nature of existence were emphasized, while the teachings about hungry ghosts and snake gods were rejected. Most reform leaders were critical of—even hostile to—"superstitions," rituals, and other local accommodations. Meditation was now the heart of "true Buddhism," and it was no longer restricted to monks and nuns: All Buddhists could and should feel capable of seeking nirvana.

The Buddhist Twentieth-Century Revival Gains Strength

By the early twentieth century, reformers had created new institutions to advance the revivalist goals directly. Also supporting the revival process in Asia was the first generation of Europeans sympathetic to Buddhism, who saw in the faith a nontheistic spirituality that was a compelling alternative to dogmatic monotheism. Many Western seekers interpreted Buddhism as encouraging spiritual experimentation through meditation rather than requiring blind faith. Its philosophy was seen as ancient wisdom marvelously preserved and still accessible.

The exigencies of imperialism had resulted in easier travel for Westerners, and this development enabled sympathetic Europeans and North Americans to assist native Buddhist modernists as they argued back against Christian ministers. Westerners both educated native intellectuals on Christianity and shared with them Enlightenment critiques of Christian dogma. Members of the Theosophical Society, a European group formed to pursue the secret, mystical teachings thought to underlie all the world religions, created new institutions, including English-medium Buddhist schools and lay organizations such as Buddhist teaching programs modeled after Christian Sunday schools. Buddhist nationalists also became involved in politics, seeking more favorable relations with—and eventually independence from—the European colonial governments. This experience in Sri Lanka was eagerly shared across Asia with modernists from Japan to Burma.

Early Western scholarship also added to the awareness of modern Asian Buddhists. Indeed, sites associated with Ashoka and many long-forgotten early monuments were discovered in the course of archaeological expeditions under the auspices of the British colonial government. European scholars used modern critical methods to translate and interpret the earliest canonical texts and then disseminated them globally. In fact, it was common for the newly educated indigenous intelligentsia in Buddhist countries to read their first passages from a canonical Buddhist text in English translation. (As in medieval Europe, only the elite among monk-scholars could read the original sacred texts.)

As Buddhist literature in English became available and was assimilated, voices from outside the sangha joined the contested discussion of "what the Buddha really taught." Thus, throughout the Buddhist world, the leaders of the old Buddhist establishments were often challenged to conform to the standards of discipline set forth in the monastic texts. In most Buddhist countries, colonial and postcolonial governments sought to eliminate sources of political dissent by imposing on the sangha regulations supposedly designed to "keep pure" the local Buddhist institutions.

Buddhism for Western Consumption: Meditation and Atheism

The efforts by the colonial powers to control Buddhism and Buddhists had a paradoxical effect. The global diaspora of Buddhism flowed "backward" on the networks of empire and through Western converts who became aware of Asian religions as a result of expanding communications and travel. For some Euro-Americans, the Enlightenment-based critiques of the Western monotheistic religions were persuasive and led to a search for religions that did not depend on belief in a personal God. By 1920, Buddhist centers in the West had been established by Euro-American converts and immigrants. As depicted in early popular and sympathetic accounts, the Buddha was a rationalist who rejected ritual and also a heroic social reformer. Buddhism was seen not as a religion but as an atheistic philosophy, compatible with science. Buddhist meditation, however, was regarded as an authentic, ancient spiritual practice, an aspect that attracted Westerners interested in the new field of psychology.

Euro-American contact with Mahayana Buddhism came strongest and earliest with Japanese Zen. Westerners were drawn to the spirit of iconoclasm and to meditation and to Zen's connection with the fine arts conveyed by early exponents, such as D. T. Suzuki (1870–1966). In the years immediately following the Second World War, Zen Buddhism particularly attracted segments of the bohemian and intellectual Western society, furthering an interest that still grows today. It was in the years leading up to World War II, however, that Japan embarked on an imperialistic course, one that showed the continuing strength of the tradition of Zen leaders supporting aristocratic warriors and rationalizing nationalistic violence.

Effects of Japanese Imperialism on Buddhism and on Asia

The role of Japan in twentieth-century Asia was undeniably pivotal. Once the country opened itself to the modern world with the restoration of the emperor in 1868, Japan's leaders sought to create a modern industrial state based on nationalism. Shinto was promoted as the shared national faith, and the emperor was revered as a living god. The nationalist movement also involved the deliberate diminishment of Buddhism. Despite its 1,400 years in Japan, Buddhism was criticized as "a foreign religion" inferior to Shinto. Many Buddhist monasteries and temples had their lands confiscated and state patronage withdrawn. Buddhist doctrines and practices were critiqued as "unnatural." In response to these changes, some Buddhist organizations instituted reforms that involved undertaking social work, educational initiatives, and the renewal of global missions. Some schools, such as Zen, even issued strong public pronouncements in favor of the government's nationalism and militarism, with prominent monasteries raising money for armaments. Many new Buddhist movements also began, but outside the older schools.

Japan's rapid and successful modernization effort encouraged not only nationalism but imperialism as well. Led by former samurai and others who had studied in Western countries, Japan annexed neighboring Korea (1910) and northern China (1934) and eventually invaded more distant Asian countries (Indochina, 1940; Burma, 1942). Soon after the Pacific phase of World War II began with the attack on the U.S. base at Pearl Harbor in 1941, the Japanese occupation extended from Manchuria, Korea, and China south to Micronesia and as far west as the borders of India through Southeast Asia.

Buddhism and Postmodern Trends in a Postcolonial World

With the end of World War II and, soon after, the demise of colonialism, most Asian nations faced the need to reinvent their societies politically and culturally. Those who sought the rebuilding and renewal of Buddhism in postwar China, Mongolia, Vietnam, and North Korea faced crippling hostility from communist rulers who regarded Buddhist doctrine as superstition and Buddhist institutions as parasitic on society. These nations engaged in "revolutionary campaigns" aimed at disbanding the communities of monks, nuns, and householders, destroying their buildings and images, and discrediting all forms of Buddhist belief and practice. There were other pressures as well, many of which have ultimately exerted more benign effects.

GENDER FOCUS: Buddhist Women

Yesterday and Today

According to many modern activists and historians, the central issue facing Buddhism today is the sangha's ability to adapt and lead in the rapidly changing postcolonial world. If this is true, how the tradition resolves its policies on the status of Buddhist women, especially renunciants, is a pivotal one in the twenty-first century.

We have seen how the Buddha reluctantly admitted women into the sangha, albeit with stricter rules and under the authority of monks. With this move the Buddha stated that women were the spiritual equals of men, capable of reaching enlightenment, yet that they still had to submit to the men in the sangha. The Buddhist sangha from its beginnings offered women a refuge from marriage, house-bound widowhood, and desperate poverty, and the work of women as nuns, devout householders, and patrons was an important factor contributing to its success throughout its history. In the distant past, as today, a visitor to a local Buddhist temple or a remote pilgrimage center would almost certainly find women in the majority of those present doing the rituals, walking the pilgrimage routes, and maintaining the shrines.

Through the vicissitudes of modernity, when monasteries declined and patronage suffered disruption under colonialism, the nun's order in many places disappeared, disrupting the traditional pattern. In the postcolonial era, women in many Buddhist societies have sought ways to restore their role and status in the Buddhist community. In 1987, at an international conference held in Bodh Gaya, 150 devout women formed a worldwide organization called Shakyaditya. The "Shakya Daughters" are dedicated to the restoration of the full ordination of *bhikkhunis* (nuns) among the Theravadins, a lineage most Buddhist monks of this school view as having died out almost a millennium ago. Throughout the

Buddhist world today, there are several hundred thousand highly committed women who have adopted an unofficial and unheralded ascetic lifestyle involving meditation, service, or study. In every country today, there is also a male-dominated sangha that controls the Buddhist institutions, and the great majority of monks strongly resist changes in the gender status quo and so oppose taking any action to restore the bhikkhuni order.

Yet some women who have adopted the lifestyle of the nun and donned white robes do not, in fact, even wish to take the full bhikkhuni ordination. Why? According to the Vinaya rules, fully ordained women admitted into the sangha must accept the formal supervision of the senior monks. Presently, in their unofficial status, these renunciants enjoy near-complete autonomy to manage their living arrangements and spiritual training. They argue that since their real loyalty is to the Dharma and their true concern is nirvana-seeking discipline, it is pointless to seek formal recognition. Yet remaining "unofficial" places severe limitations on the women's ability to build their institutions, since they are not recognized for state patronage, and householder donations to them do not yield the same prestige or merit-return that comes from donations to the fully ordained monks. As a result, most of the unofficial "nuns" today remain impoverished, without special honor in their societies at large, and marginal to the dominant Buddhist community.

Since 2000, over 400 women practicing in all the Theravada countries have gone to Chinese Mahayana monasteries (in mainland China or Taiwan) to receive full nun's official ordination, much to the consternation of the traditionalist monks. Can Buddhist traditions facing so many future challenges afford to relegate to the margins of their societies the energy, compassion, and merit of such women?

As Asia's rapid industrialization created new wealth, urbanization led to new forms of social dislocation, especially dramatic increases in the numbers of landless, wage-dependent workers and an unprecedented series of ecological crises. At the same time, Asia saw an expansion of higher education and the rise of educated classes alongside new commercial elites. As a result of these changes, Buddhism was transplanted into entirely new social contexts and drawn into political struggles and global dialogues.

By the mid-twentieth century, as East Asians had begun to recover from World War II, many conquered or colonized peoples were reclaiming their independence. The place of Buddhism in these new societies is as varied as ever. Buddhist movements today make use of the same approaches seen across the globe in other faiths. Some leaders reject modernity, seeking to return to practices that had been identified as "corrupted" by modernizers in the colonial era. Others strive to move Buddhism to an entirely new plateau, seeking to adapt it to the global realities of the postcolonial world. Still others blend traditionalism and reform, "rescuing" from the past what in their view is the essence of Buddhism while employing modern technologies to propagate the Dharma. New institutions have been created to champion strict adherence to monastic norms, scholastic learning, and meditation. Most commonly, organizations led by householders have been the most active and effective in adapting Buddhist teachings and practices to the world today.

South Asia

South Asia is the "holy land" where the Buddha was born, was enlightened, and died and where Buddhism has endured over 2,500 years. Among the contemporary countries of the region—India, Pakistan, Bangladesh, Sri Lanka, Bhutan, and Nepal—only in the Himalayan regions of the north and on the island of Sri Lanka to the south has Buddhism remained strong.

The Remnants of Buddhism in India: Reconstruction in the Places of Origin

Today, Buddhism is found in the modern nation of India only in very small, and recently established, communities. Most important for the faith's revival in the land of its origins are the sacred sites that were unearthed during the British-led archaeological digs of the nineteenth and early twentieth centuries. Among the hundreds of sites that were abandoned or had sunk into oblivion after the Muslim conquest of South Asia (since 1200 CE), the site where the Buddha was enlightened under the bodhi tree became the most significant and controversial. Identified by British officials in the mid-1800s and "restored" through colonial excavations and constructions (in the modern city of Gaya, Bihar), the "Great Enlightenment" temple, called the Mahabodhi, has again become a focal point for Buddhists. Its reformers in the colonial era focused on reestablishing the sanctity of this temple as their first step in reviving Buddhism. In recent decades, over twenty Buddhist monasteries have been erected there, as well as libraries, study centers, and pilgrim hostels. Reformist Buddhists are also attempting to reestablish the site as Buddhism's holiest center and pilgrimage destination, a shrine that unifies all Buddhists. Despite hard work by generations of reformers, this remains an unmet goal.

Even after decades of negotiations, control over the Bodh Gaya temple has eluded the Buddhist organizations, for Hindu priests and politicians have failed to turn over ownership of the shrine. By 1992, frustrations at unfulfilled promises peaked: Several resident monks threatened to immolate themselves, and several others began fasts unto death. The provocation for this confrontation was severe: Hindu priests had enthroned a *lingam*, the phallic icon of Shiva, on a temple altar and performed pujas to treat the five Buddha images in the temple as if they were deities in the Hindu epic, the *Mahabharata*. Hindu nationalists in the BJP, mentioned in Chapter 6, have increased their intervention in this fray by siding with the Hindu faction; in 2008, several attempting to make offerings were restrained by police. As of mid-2013, the stalemate continued.

"Protestant Buddhism": An Enduring Colonial-Era Reformation of the Faith

Anthropologist Gananath Obeyesekere has described the modern reformation of Buddhist tradition begun in colonial Sri Lanka as "**Protestant Buddhism**." He uses the term to convey two distinct but connected historic trends. The first is intuitively obvious: the adoption of aspects of missionary Protestant Christianity into the Buddhist framework to revitalize its institutions, practices, and doctrines. The second is a deeply ironic reference to a past marked by the arrogance of missionaries and British colonial discrimination against Buddhism.

The early influential mediator of such "Protestantism" in Sri Lanka was the American convert Henry Steele Olcott (1832–1907), who came to the country and helped activist Buddhist leaders organize their efforts. Olcott emphasized the importance of the laity in revitalization and the founding of Buddhist publications and schools. He also composed a *Buddhist Catechism* (1881) and invented a five-color Buddhist flag, both of which are widely used across the world today. Modern Protestant inclinations were evident in the reformist insistence that spiritual and scientific truth be compatible and that the only true practice was meditation, not the mindless observance of ritual. Furthermore, the reformers believed—in agreement with the Protestant missionaries—that the practice of Buddhism in Sri Lanka had been corrupted by idolatry, Hindu polytheism, and an undisciplined and corrupt monastic "priesthood." The laity, however, could reestablish "true Buddhism" through adhering to the pure philosophy and meditation practices taught by the human Buddha. Popular texts and village traditions were strongly critiqued, and two new sangha schools were created with ordination lineages from Burma, both requiring the strictest adherence to Vinaya rules.

A Sri Lankan protégé, who adopted the name Anagarika Dharmapala (1864–1933), continued Olcott's initiatives and went beyond them, preaching and publishing tracts

Protestant Buddhism: pattern of reform in which Buddhists adopted perspectives of Protestant Christianity to spread his vision of revitalized Buddhism. At the age of twenty-nine, Dharmapala addressed an ecumenical conference, the Parliament of World Religions, held in Chicago in 1893. He impressed hearers from all over the world with his definition of modernist Buddhism as compatible with science, free from dogma and superstition, tolerant of other faiths, and committed to social reform.

Dharmapala also found an enthusiastic reception among the Sri Lankan laity, especially among the newly educated professional elite and the merchant middle class, who owed their rising positions in the world to the changes wrought by the colonial modernization of the country. Dharmapala energized the Buddhist reformers in Sri Lanka; his speeches and writings also contributed to the linkage between the faith and the nationalist struggles.

Dharmapala celebrated Sri Lanka as a uniquely pure Buddhist country, elevated the Sinhalese ethnic group as a "chosen Buddhist people," and harshly demonized those opposing the country's Buddhist restoration. Scholars today see these influences as having set in motion the cultural forces that have made the postindependence state, Sri Lanka, a zone of extremes where bloody conflict has taken deep root alongside uncompromising reform.

Dharmapala's founding of the Mahabodhi Society in Calcutta extended "Protestant Buddhist" reform into other countries in Asia. In recent times, "Protestant Buddhism" has fostered an individualist ethos among those whose ties to a village or traditional sangha have been broken through urban migration. Those influenced by these reformist ideas see it as their own responsibility to practice meditation and study the Dharma (usually in English translations) in the quest for nirvana. Joining the sangha or seeking spiritual guidance from an ordained monk is also not necessarily the norm for those whose view of Buddhism has been affected by "Protestantism."

Buddhism in the Himalayas: No Shangri-La

Many Westerners first became aware of Buddhism through fictional works such as *Lost Horizon*, the film version of which was set in an idyllic, tropical valley amid the scenic, snow-blown Himalayan peaks. It is true that, in fact, Tibetan Buddhist communities have survived in the remote and picturesque settlements nestled among the world's highest mountains, but this region has hardly been a utopian zone for Buddhism in the post–World War II era. Along the southern Himalayan region, the isolation of the states on the Tibetan frontier (Ladakh, Sikkim, Bhutan) enabled them to retain their independence until the end of the Second World War. Since, however, religious conservatism also kept the monks and leaders of these states isolated and ignorant about the modern world, there was little impetus for reform or adaptation to the postwar international political order.

In 1949 most of the territories on the Tibetan plateau ruled by the Gelugpa school's Dalai Lama were declared part of the People's Republic of China, which sent its army to enforce this claim. The far peripheries of India and Nepal once oriented to Lhasa were isolated from the greater Buddhist centers, while central and western Tibet have been ruled by China as "the Tibetan Autonomous Region" until today. Up to the bitter end of China's Cultural Revolution (1976), all religious practices in the region were repressed and most Buddhist temples, monasteries, and shrines were destroyed. Thousands of Tibetans have died since 1949 in conflicts that set Chinese against Tibetan and Tibetan against Tibetan. The fourteenth Dalai Lama, Tenzin Gyatso, went into exile in 1959, and 15 percent of the population has left the country as well.

After 1980, official toleration of limited worship and monastic ordination returned, as did state-sponsored rebuilding of select monasteries. But increasing Tibetan protests since 1987 met with further restrictions and arrests, while increasing Chinese migration into the region, accelerated by the opening of a rail link in 2008, has reduced Tibetans to a minority in their homeland. Buddhist tradition is slowly being restored as the Chinese government allows but exerts close supervision of monastic training and ritual practices as long as they are not perceived as promoting Tibetan independence.

Three nations have remained free refuges of the Tibetan Buddhism. Nepal has several million Buddhists among the highland-dwelling Tibeto-Burman peoples, in its settlements of Tibetan refugees, and among the Newars of the Kathmandu Valley. Kathmandu is the modern capital of Nepal, and this valley is also Asia's largest center for international institutions connected with the major schools of Tibetan Buddhism.

Tibetan Buddhism also has survived in mountainous areas of northern India (in Ladakh, Himachal Pradesh, and Arunachal Pradesh). India has likewise accepted Tibetan refugees, for since 1959 the Dalai Lama's government in exile has been located in picturesque Dharamsala. Finally, there is Bhutan in the eastern Himalayas, a nation formed in 1907 as the royal kingdom ruled by the Wangchuck family. It is the world's only nation that has Tibetan Buddhism as its state religion.

Most regions where Tibetan Buddhism still flourishes have lost political autonomy. The central, northern, and eastern portions of Tibet were absorbed by China, while Ladakh and Sikkim were absorbed into modern India; Bhutan alone remained independent from India, but only in its internal affairs. In exile and in the isolated enclaves, Tibetan Buddhist institutions have sustained the faith, but these Buddhists struggle as refugees in poverty and as resident aliens within the larger states.

Yet amid the destruction, discrimination, and displacement that came to independent Tibet, there has also been the extensive migration of Tibetan Buddhist teachers into almost every country of the world. Now publishing houses, learned lamas, websites, and charismatic meditation teachers cross the globe to spread Buddhist teachings. While their predecessors were completely out of touch with the modern world and its spiritual challenges, contemporary monk-scholars and meditation teachers are now leaders in "bringing the Dharma to the West." The fourteenth Dalai Lama, Nobel Peace Prize winner in 1989, is well known as a world leader and is certainly the most recognized Buddhist in the world.

Theravada Buddhism Today in Southeast Asia

The first regions missionized in antiquity by Buddhist monks have remained the stronghold of Theravada Buddhism. In Sri Lanka and Burma, a new era began with the withdrawal of the British (1947). Buddhism became a pillar of the new nations' identity, and the Buddha was elevated to the status of cultural hero and ancestor.

While supportive of the respective struggles for independence, Buddhism in these states had also been enriched and enlarged by revival movements throughout the colonial period. Most of these involved the laity in the administration of its institutions and saw the establishment of new monastic schools emphasizing revival through strict discipline, meditation, and social service.

Buddhist leaders in the first decades after World War II were also at the forefront of addressing the relationship between socialism and communism, the political ideologies that had risen to popularity as alternatives to capitalism in guiding the newly independent states. Some monks were highly suspicious of communism and allied themselves with aggressive anticommunist campaigns, with one going so far as to say that "killing communists entails no demerit"! However, other, more leftist political activists and high civil servants used Buddhist rhetoric quite creatively to justify

Tobi Fudo: Protector of Airline Passengers

The sword-bearing Fudo has long been a protector of Buddhist teachings associated with the tantric school of Japanese Buddhism, Shingon. His dark body and fierce face symbolize his unshakeable devotion to the teachings of the Buddha; yet his nature is compassionate, as he has vowed to be of service to all beings who call upon him. A legend associated with a Fudo in Shoboin, a temple in old Tokyo, recounts the image flying back to the home temple after a monk had taken it on a pilgrimage. This temple's icon in the Edo period (1600–1868) thus came to be called Tobi (Flying) Fudo. Over the last thirty years, the sangha of this temple has sold *ema* boards like the one pictured here—Fudo with a Boeing 747—to Japanese air travelers, who write their flight numbers on the back and leave it at the temple, requesting protection. Carry-on talismans, called "Hiko-Omamori" 飛行守り, are also sold at the temple.

The adaptation of Fudo to be a protector of air travelers illustrates the social engagement, creativity, and adaptability of Buddhism in Japan today.

participation in communist regimes, as seen in this 1951 speech by a government minister of newly independent Burma:

> I declare that I have implicit faith in Marxism, but at the same time I assert that I am a true Buddhist. Both of these philosophies are correlated. . . . In the beginning, I was a Buddhist only by tradition. The more I study Marxism, however, the more I feel convinced in Buddhism. Thus I have become a true disciple of Lord Buddha by conviction and my faith in Buddhism has grown all the more. I now believe that for any man who has deeply studied Buddhism and correctly perceived its tenets there should be no obstacles to become a Marxist. Vexed by anxieties and fears in respect to food, clothing, and homes, human minds cannot dwell on old age, disease, and death. But with the satisfaction of men's material needs, humans can boldly face these three phenomena. Marxism cannot provide an answer to spiritual liberation. Neither can science. Only Buddhist philosophy can. It must, however, be conceded that material satisfaction in life can only be attained through Marxism.[2]

Tooth Relics and Anti-Muslim Riots in Myanmar

The Buddha's cremation relics have been the most sacred and precious objects for devotees from the faith's very beginnings. Not only are they the sole remnants of the enlightened one, a "sacred trace" of his earthly existence; they are also thought to

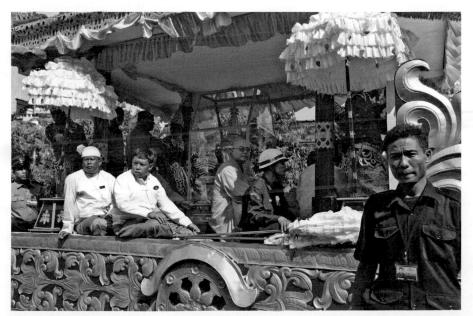

In 2011, the Buddha's sacred tooth relic was brought from China to Myanmar for the fourth time. Here, security officials and Chinese Buddhist monks accompany the relic as it Is transported to the Kabaaye pagoda in Yangon, Myanmar.

be infused with immense power, and mere proximity to them is believed to confer spiritual and worldly blessings.

In 1994 (and again in 2011) the Chinese government loaned a tooth relic to Myanmar. Placed in a jewel-embellished palanquin and conveyed from the Boeing 757 to a silk-draped float pulled by an elephant, the relic was taken to its shrine in the Maha Pasana cave in Rangoon, where over the next six weeks a half-million devotees came to venerate it and make offerings. The country's ruling junta, who had sponsored the visit, used the state-controlled media to emphasize that its members were exemplary Buddhists. In 1995 the junta underwrote the construction of a new temple in the capital where the relic has been displayed in 1996 and 2011. Displaying and respecting Buddha relics have been recognized as signs of just rulers in Buddhist states since antiquity, and the junta's generals no doubt intend their sponsorship of tooth relic veneration to win popular approval and counter dislike of their authoritarian rule. After regaining independence from the British Empire in 1948 and undergoing a short period of experimentation with "Buddhist socialism," Myanmar's government has often dealt harshly with persons suspected of fostering dissent. Nonviolent protests for democracy led by monks in 2007 were harshly put down by government troops, who arrested monastic leaders and shot demonstrators; however, a few years later, the government changed course, and since then has fostered the emergence of democracy and more public freedoms.

What happened in the last three years has surprised many observers, however. The relaxation of military control opened long-suppressed resentments felt by the Burmese Buddhist majority on two fronts: against the Christian tribal groups on their northern borders, whom the national army continues to attack; and toward Muslim citizens called Rohyingas whose ancestors had immigrated from Bangladesh into Myanmar's southwest border region. Claiming that "Myanmar is a Buddhist country" and challenging the Muslim Rohingyas' right to remain within the country's borders, Buddhist mobs have beaten and killed hundreds and driven 110,000 persons into refugee camps. Since then, the world press has shown unprecedented photos of Buddhist monks organizing rallies and even leading groups intent on expelling Rohyingas. Newly awakened Buddhist nationalism has released crowds intent on genocide; its protagonists have even threatened those calling for restraint and applying Buddhist ethics to all sentient beings.

Three Contemporary Faces of Thai Buddhism

A constitutional monarchy since 1932 and a country never ruled by a European nation, Thailand is another predominantly Theravada country. Thai Buddhism remains one of the most dynamic faiths in the world today. The society supports traditional and reformist scholarship, the ancient spiritual practices of forest monks, and pioneering reformist initiatives. Thai reformers have assumed active roles in working for the modernization of the country through government development programs

Monastics and house-holders of the modernist Dhammakaya school reside in individual tents of mosquito netting on a mass meditative retreat in Thailand.

in infrastructure building, agricultural innovation, education, and health care. Several notable independent monks have opposed the state's toleration of corruption, pollution, and environmental destruction. However, mainstream Thai Buddhist monastic institutions have benefited from royal patronage and the rising wealth that accompanied the economic boom of the late twentieth century. Certain charismatic monks and a host of new lay-oriented independent Buddhist institutions are also active in offering leadership to revitalize the faith. The burgeoning urban areas, where neither old community ties nor traditional monasteries effectively meet the needs of the new city dwellers, have been fertile ground for such reformists. Three examples illustrate the sorts of Buddhist innovators active in contemporary Thailand: the Dhammakaya, Santi Asoke, and the work of two monks, Phra Boonsong and Luang Pi Daeng.

The Dhammakaya. The Dhammakaya is the fastest-growing Buddhist reform group in Thailand, attracting the well-educated and newly affluent classes as well as the royal family. Founded by the charismatic monk Phra Monghon Thepmuni in 1978, Dhammakaya spreads its teachings and meditation practices through the sophisticated use of publications and mass media. The movement has established a presence in every major city and town across Thailand, where its very highly educated monks administer a program of rigorous training for the laity. Another binding force of Dhammakaya is Phra Thepmuni's meditation technique, one that has more in common with Mahayana practices of the Himalayas than with traditional Theravada methods. For its followers, the Dhammakaya has reduced the ritual complexity of the traditional monastery to a few simple practices. It has also emphasized that making money is compatible with Buddhism and has translated utopianism and interdependence teachings through the slogan "World Peace Through Inner Peace." As of 2014, the group numbered its supporters at over 1 million, with branches in twenty-four countries.

Santi Asoke. Santi Asoke differs in many respects from Dhammakaya: It has won a much smaller following (perhaps 100,000, as estimated in 2007) and has garnered much less wealth. Since its founding in 1976, however, movement activists have critiqued what they regard as the complacent establishment monastic schools' compromises with state and business power. Santi Asoke ("Peaceful Ashoka") are named after the first lay ruler in Buddhist history, the Indian emperor who (in Buddhist accounts) spread the faith across India and ruled according to the Buddha's ethical norms. Accordingly, this group seeks to reform Thai Buddhism through a return to austere ethical practices such as abstaining from meat, alcohol, and tobacco as well as avoiding gambling and hedonistic entertainment. Santi Asoke grew out of the work of forest monk reformers who in the 1920s and 1930s sought to revitalize the sangha by a return to an ascetic lifestyle for monks, complemented by rigorous meditation schedules. Santi Asoke's monks wear white robes instead of the traditional yellow because their founder, the charismatic but confrontational Phra Bodhiraksa, was defrocked by the Thai government's monk-monitoring body in the 1980s. The "Protestant" influence is evident in Bodhiraksa's criticisms of traditional rituals as "superstition and magic" and his outspoken rejection of the common Thai ritual of worshipping Buddha images. In recent years, Santi Ashoke has sought to promote ecological activism and sustainable environmental practices.

Phra Boonsong and Luang Pi Daeng. Not all reformers in Thailand have been new institution builders. Phra Boonsong (1941–), the abbot of Phranon Wat in central Thailand since 1972, is a dedicated environmentalist. When he arrived in the area, the ecosystem was sick. Runoff from the Chin River, which flows by the monastery, was polluting paddy fields, and declining agriculture and fishing yields were causing men and women to seek employment in the cities. So Phra Boonsong worked to improve the region's ecological balance by appealing to the traditional Thai prohibition against killing inside a monastery. He began by declaring the river adjacent to it a "pardon zone" for all water creatures. Next, from profits made by selling fish food to local Buddhists (who in turn gave it to the fish, earning merit), he was able to add fish stock to the river. The fish multiplied in that nearby stretch of the river, slowly adding to the breeding population available for harvest by many fishermen living along the river. This success enabled Phra Boonsong to convince the National Assembly to enact laws allowing monasteries nationwide to establish similar breeding zones, and over 200 have done so. He has also begun planting fruit trees on deforested hills, with organic orchards managed to reduce the use of expensive, watershed-polluting chemicals. The expertise of the Phranon Wat monks in species use, grafting, fertilizers, and marketing is now being shared across Thailand, allowing

TALES OF SPIRITUAL TRANSFORMATION: Maha Ghosananda, Witness to Buddhist Peacemaking in Cambodia

Ordained as a young boy in Cambodia, Somdet Phra Ghosananda (1928–2007) through middle age pursued a virtuoso monastic life, one that led to his spending years outside of his native land meditating in Thai forest monasteries and completing a doctoral degree in Pali textual studies. In 1976, when Maha Ghosananda heard of Cambodia's political upheaval and the atrocities of Khmer Rouge rule, he resolved to return to worldly action. So he left his forest monastery to work in refugee camps along Thailand's Cambodian border, where he built modest monasteries and trained new monks who helped meet the needs of the suffering population. He especially taught the *Metta-Sutta*, the classical expression of the Buddhist ideal of forgiveness and compassion.

After the fall of the Khmer Rouge, Maha Ghosananda returned to his native land, where he was named Supreme Monk Patriarch of Cambodia. Seeking to increase international support for Cambodia's people and to promote anti-landmine activism while drawn to invitations to preach Dharma and teach meditation among Cambodian immigrants in the United States, the great monk traveled there and founded over fifty international monasteries. But his first priority was to promote peace in Cambodia and foster national reconciliation through Buddhist morality.

Seeing the constant conflicts still common then in the countryside between Khmer Rouge remnants and the new government, he informed his fellow monks, "We must find the courage to leave our temples and enter the suffering-filled temples of human experience."[a] Even though he discovered that the Khmer Rouge had murdered his entire family and destroyed his native village, he never wavered from his conviction: "It is the law of the universe that retaliation,

hatred, and revenge only continue the cycle." So he began the practice of *Dhammayietra* ("Pilgrimages of Truth") in 1991.

Despite often finding his group close to the falling shells and lethal firefights, Maha Ghosananda led groups of monks and growing numbers of householders, who walked with heads down and hands folded, chanting the Buddha's words from the *Metta-Sutta*:

> Hate can never be appeased by hate;
> Hate can only be appeased by loving-kindness.

Recognized by the Japanese Niwano Peace Foundation and several times nominated for the Nobel Peace Prize, this beloved, self-effacing monk—called "Cambodia's Gandhi," gave up the satisfactions of scholarship and the bliss of meditation to take decisive action to heal a genocidal national conflict.

[a] *The Economist*, March 24, 2007.

other monks to spearhead similar efforts toward environmental awareness across the nation's rural hinterlands.

Abbot Luang Pi Daeng likewise could not ignore the world outside his monastery, Wat Hua Rin in Northern Thailand. His monastery buildings now include medical examination rooms, handicraft production outbuildings, and a meeting hall where people with HIV/AIDS come for health monitoring and support group meetings. Taking alms from households with an HIV-infected member to illustrate that the disease cannot be transmitted through casual contact, this monk has worked to end the abandonment of those who have contracted this disease and to find employment in new monastery-located handicraft industries for them. In addition to providing spiritual counseling, Luang Pi Daeng has applied the Buddhist teaching of suffering and interdependence to this crisis that has deeply affected Thai life: "I showed them that if we don't help those with AIDS, all of us suffer."[3] Luang Pi Daeng's work was instrumental in the establishment of the UNICEF-funded Sangha Metta Project, which has trained over 4,000 monks in seven countries about AIDS prevention and treatment.

Buddhist Revival in Postwar Indochina

By 1985, all the countries of the Indochinese peninsula had begun to liberalize their economies and relax restrictions on religious observances. As communist governments retreated from dogmatism to pragmatism and tolerated the enduring popular attachment to Buddhism and indigenous religions, civil authorities in Vietnam, Laos, and Cambodia began accepting the place of Buddhism in national culture and politics.

A French colony until 1953, Cambodia suffered through the Vietnam wars with the French and the United States and, in the aftermath (1975–79), the genocidal conflicts under the rule of the Khmer Rouge, led by Pol Pot. Under Pol Pot's communist regime, Buddhist monks and institutions were targeted for murder and destruction. While several Cambodian Buddhist centers were relocated among refugees over the border in Thailand, only after the withdrawal of the Vietnamese in 1989 did the restoration of Buddhism begin. Several prominent figures seeking national reconciliation have been Theravada monks.

Vietnam has increasingly tolerated the restoration of Buddhist monasteries and temples since north and south were reunited in 1975. Nevertheless, the government has imprisoned monks it regards as too involved in politics, and the officially sanctioned (and so-named) Vietnam Buddhist Church has won only minimum popular acceptance. Vietnam's population of 75 million resembles China in its religious orientation, with Buddhism the most widespread tradition existing alongside Chinese Daoism and Confucianism, indigenous cults, and Roman Catholic and Protestant Christianity. Vietnamese Buddhism today is predominantly Mahayana in the north, with Theravada monasteries found in the south.

The modern state of Indonesia contains the largest Muslim population in the world, though its western islands of Sumatra and Java were once at the center of an empire that supported both Hinduism and Buddhism. Under a constitution that officially protects all faiths, Indonesian Buddhists are a small minority (2 percent of 205 million), but the faith has undergone a vigorous revival since 1950. Small communities dedicated to predominantly Mahayana Buddhism likewise exist among minority ethnic Chinese communities in Malaysia and in Singapore, the city-state that separated from Malaysia in 1965.

East Asia

As devastated as Europe by the destruction of World War II, East Asia embarked on the long road to social, political, and economic recovery after 1945. Communist nations imposed new obstacles for Buddhist adherents and institutions for several decades afterward, but by 2013, only North Korea remained opposed to the tradition's reestablishment across East Asia. The examples that follow illustrate the remarkable rebound of Buddhist tradition, with followers once again drawing on the great ability of the Dharma to be adapted to changing circumstances and times.

Guanyin Rises Again in China

Mahayana Buddhists have for fifteen centuries shared a common faith in Avalokiteshvara, whose cult was found from central Asia to Japan in shrines located in almost every settlement and home. The celestial bodhisattva has come to be called Guanyin in China and Kannon in Japan. Originally depicted as a male, this divinity is now usually represented in female form. With Buddhism's missionary transplantation across East Asia, she became the refuge for all who desired rebirth in the western Buddhist paradise, for those who met dangerous life circumstances, and especially for women who wanted safe childbirth and sons. As Daoism organized and was systematized in response to Buddhism in China by the T'ang era (617–907), Guanyin was so popular (and Daoism so eclectic) that icons of Guanyin were accepted sights in Daoist temples or in clan temples otherwise dedicated to the veneration of ancestors.

The violently iconoclastic phase of Mao Zedong's Cultural Revolution (1966–69) nearly eliminated Guanyin from public places all across China and from private shrines as well, since Red Guards who found icons in their house-to-house searches claimed them as sure indicators of "reactionary elements." When icons were discovered, householders were in danger of being declared "enemies of the people," publicly humiliated, and even killed. Since the mid-1980s, however, Guanyin has returned to favor, and state-run factories have produced a large variety of images for sale, many at newly opened temple votive stores. Pilgrimage sites have been opened for Guanyin as well. Indeed, it is evident that even party members, especially among the younger and professional generations, tend to believe in the efficacy of worshipping this Buddhist divinity. Even so, the government's acceptance of the revival of Buddhist devotionalism stands in contrast to its harsh repression of other faiths that have taken root in China, from Christian sects to the syncretistic Falun Gong (see Chapter 8).

Since the death of Mao Zedong and the end of the Cultural Revolution in 1976, the Communist government of China has slowly allowed many Buddhist institutions to be reopened, including monasteries that train monks and nuns in traditional ritual and meditation practices. Augmented by meritorious gifts from Chinese living outside China, Buddhist institutions have been rehabilitated across the nation as the government has ended restrictions on lay devotees' setting up home shrines and undertaking pilgrimages.

Buddhist Revival in South Korea

The formerly unified Korean culture area, artificially split into North Korea and South Korea after World War II, was strongly influenced by Chinese cultural borrowings, including Buddhism, throughout its history. As South Korea experienced rising economic prosperity from the 1970s onward, it attracted patrons and activists who sought to build the spiritual programs of the monasteries, present the Buddha's teachings in modern media, and reverse the slide of Buddhism in the face of Christian proselytizing and government discrimination.

Despite many setbacks over the last century, the surviving Korean Buddhist institutions remain well endowed with landed income and have created an important niche in Korean society by establishing schools, universities, and lay meditation centers. As in other Buddhist countries undergoing successful economic modernization, Korean Buddhism is experiencing a renewal. Its modern institutions are upgrading monastic education, creating mass media publications, and developing an urban, middle-class Buddhist identity based on householder rituals, meditation, and youth organizations. The latest Korean innovation is the cable channel All-Buddhist Network Television, whose programs offer a mix of sermons, chants, rituals, and chefs teaching vegetarian cooking.

Buddhism in Japan Recovers After World War II

Japan, like the United States, is a country of ever-broadening religious expression. Buddhism has contributed to this through its classical monastic institutions and by its doctrines providing starting points for many of Japan's "new religions." In the mid-nineteenth century, the Meiji state's ultranationalist governments deliberately weakened Buddhism through ideological campaigns and institutionally. By the 1930s, many abbots of co-opted "establishment schools" were in fact actively fanning the flames of war. World War II left monasteries in ruins and prominent clergy in disgrace. But after the war, the sanghas of the oldest schools retained their nationwide presence under a system of head and branch monasteries developed in the late Tokagawa era (1600–1857), and some communities worked to restore their spiritual integrity. Today, most Japanese families are still registered as *danka* ("parishioners") of a monastery branch of one or the other Buddhist schools for, at the very least, the performance of family death rituals.

Boke Fuji ("Senility") Kannon: A New Incarnation of a Buddhist Deity

The late 1980s saw the appearance of icons that depicted the goddess Kannon holding a flower in one hand and opening the other in a gesture of mercy to two elderly people, one male and one female, who clutch at her robes in supplication. Consistent with her renown developed over one and a half millennia for compassionately "mothering" her devotees and bestowing this-worldly boons to those who call on her, this new form of the bodhisattva has arisen as senility or Alzheimer's disease has caused great emotional distress to many in Japan (as elsewhere). Both for the elderly and their families, who share a Confucian responsibility for parental

care at this stage of life, old-age suffering has surfaced as a weighty problem, suggesting a creative Buddhist response. Thus temples have established social and spiritual programs, developing amulets, shrines, and pilgrimage routes for devotees to visit in search of preventive blessings. Buddhist priests, aware of physicians' counsel that the best way to keep senility at bay is for the aged to keep active, are encouraging this approach. By organizing pilgrimages, for example, they make available to the elderly enjoyable, stimulating, and hopeful activity, in which the pilgrims can both articulate their worries and acquire peace of mind.

A contemporary Boke Fuji ("Senility") Kannon amulet from Japan.

But for many Japanese, Buddhism has remained in their lives. The great number of individuals undertaking pilgrimage circuits across the heartland of historical Japan to honor the Mahayana bodhisattva Avalokiteshvara, here called Kannon, attests to Buddhism's importance today. The Saikoku route, which is a sacred journey organized as far back as the thirteenth century, still attracts pilgrims to visit its many sites, including some of the greatest and most magnificent temples in Japan. This route has risen from postwar obscurity to host 30,000 participants in the late 1960s and over 90,000 by last count in the late 1990s. This "pilgrimage boom," as the popular religious revival has been labeled by journalists, was aided by the proliferation of modern pilgrim facilities. Moreover, the example of the Saikoku Kannon pilgrimage inspired the formation of other thirty-three-stage Kannon pilgrimage routes in at least seventy-two other regions of Japan. Scholars debate about how much this rapidly increasing pilgrimage is due to religious dedication to Kannon and how much is due to a less pious "cultural tourism, especially among the elderly."

Examples of recent revival show the continuing relevance of Kannon in Japanese life. One is lighthearted: The Zenshoji temple northwest of Tokyo has paired the bodhisattva with the Japanese craze for golf by erecting a six-foot Kannon who holds various golf clubs in her hands. Hundreds of golfers come daily to pray briefly for the mercy of lower scores. More serious is the recent creation of a thirty-three-stage pilgrimage route with a focus on worship of a completely new form of this bodhisattva: *Boke Fuji Kannon* ("Senility Kannon").

A final example of a new form of Kannon devotionalism in Japan is the cult organized to seek the forgiveness of the spirits of aborted fetuses (*mizuko*, "water children"). Buddhist temples throughout Japan have seen a revival in rituals on their memorial grounds as women have set up icons to which they offer food and other ritual gifts to spirits to whom they denied birth in human form. Kannon and another compassionate bodhisattva, named Jizo, are popular in this form of worship at many temples. Japanese women typically request that the compassionate deities guard and bless these wandering spirits until they fulfill their destiny and continue on to another human rebirth, as in classical Buddhist teachings. The **mizuko cult** has spread widely, promulgated by many temples that not coincidentally benefit from the income derived from the special ritual services they provide.

> **mizuko cult:** in Japan, form of Kannon devotionalism that seeks forgiveness from spirits of aborted fetuses

Buddhism Today in Diaspora and in Asia

Buddhism in the West

The economic boom that swept Asia in the 1990s and the global migration of Asians are the most recent developments affecting Buddhism today. To a large extent, newly affluent Buddhists have done what Buddhist householders have always done with a portion of their surplus wealth: make merit through pious donations. This infusion of new wealth has been used to rebuild venerable monasteries and temples, support new reform sects, and modernize Buddhist institutions by establishing schools, starting periodicals, and creating mass media outlets on television and the Internet. The most affluent and internationally minded, particularly those in East Asia, have shifted the traditional missionary ideal from national to global outreach, building on the migration of the home ethnic group (e.g., Taiwanese, Thai, or Japanese), but often seeking a wider audience beyond. One exception to the trend of new Asian affluence pushing the international expansion of Buddhism is the Tibetan diaspora, which has depended largely on donations by affluent Euro-American supporters, including Hollywood actors and rock stars.

The global migration of Buddhist monastic institutions and ideas has been so great that a representative of every major Asian school can now be found on every continent, and numerous non-Asians have by now been accepted for ordination as monks and nuns in every nation's sangha. In addition, awareness of the basic Buddhist doctrines of karma, nirvana, and Buddhahood, formerly confined to the educated classes

"Change Your Mind Day" in Central Park

Since 1993, the Buddhist magazine *Tricycle* has sponsored a gathering in New York's Central Park, on the first Saturday in June, that draws a variety of teachers who are active in America. Other attendees—"longtime practitioners, meditators-for-a-day, Dharma bums, and dog-walkers"—are led through a series of guided spiritual exercises in the half-day program. In 2007, following 108 gong strikes, American abbots from Zen monasteries and Westerners initiated as teachers in Tibetan lineages gave sermons, Japanese monks led chants, and an American meditation master directed the group in Theravadin-style vipassana meditation. A friend of the late Allen Ginsberg read poems by this famous convert to Buddhism. A perennial favorite followed: a spirited debate in Tibetan scholastic style punctuated by hand-slapping exclamations between a Tibetan lama and an American convert who argued about the nature of nirvana. In response to growing interest, *Tricycle* began providing international access to this event in 2007 by hosting a virtual Change Your Mind Day that features audio and video files of guided dharma talks on its website. By 2013, Buddhists in dozens of cities and across the globe had held "Change Your Mind" events.

Source: http://www.tricycle.com/p/1854.

of the world, is now accessible to all via the global mass media. In 2011 a search for "Buddhism" on the Web elicited over 3.1 million connections.

In the Zen and Tibetan schools in North America, especially, converts now speak of the emergence of new "American schools of Tibetan (or Zen) Buddhism." An explosion in publications, educational programs, and meditation sessions marks the unmistakable deeper adaptation of the faith within Western societies. Interestingly, these Euro-American Buddhist schools are selective in their adoption of Asian Buddhist traditions: They have eschewed celibate monasticism, featured meditation, and minimized ritualism, much like the "Protestant Buddhists" of Asia. This expectation of Westerners is especially noteworthy in the Pure Land schools established in America: These centers have found the need to offer programs in meditation for the laity, even though back in Asia their monastic life is more focused on chanting.

The modern diaspora of Buddhism in some respects can be seen as the global continuation of the faith's ancient missionary spirit. In North America, Buddhist missionaries have been led by teachers of Japanese and Korean Zen, all lineages of Tibetan Buddhism, Theravadins emphasizing vipassana meditation with ties to the countries of Southeast Asia, Japan's Soka Gakkai sect, and the various Pure Land schools (in rough order of importance).

In the 1950s the perceived iconoclasm of Zen—its nonconformist appeal—attracted Americans who participated in the Beat Generation culture of jazz, poetry, and experimental literature. The lure of Zen meditation practices has drawn Western practitioners from the 1960s onward. Zen's connection with Japanese fine arts and

Facts Regarding Buddhism in America

Self-identified Buddhists: 1.6 million
Those who report meeting a Buddhist teacher "at
   least a few times a year": 5 million
Those who practice Buddhist meditation:
   6 million

Those who say they read Buddhist literature:
   7 million
Those who report "Buddhism has had an important influence on their thinking about religion
   or spirituality": 28.3 million

Source: PEW Survey, 2011.

martial arts also helped Zen-oriented teachers and their institutions across the globe to reach a wider artistic and athletic audience.

The Japanese Soka Gakkai, a modern religiocultural offshoot of the Nichiren school, has an international following eager to reinterpret Buddhism and take political action to foster the development of a more enlightened world civilization. Pure Land Buddhism has been transplanted among East Asians who have migrated to urban areas worldwide, particularly the West Coast of North America and Hawaii. Indeed, migrants from every Buddhist country in the world have contributed to the globalization of their faith by establishing temples and monasteries in their adopted homelands. The latest groups of Asian Buddhists in America have emigrated from Southeast Asia.

Outside Asia, Buddhists still remain a small minority in the census figures and usually are found in urban areas. Among today's immigrants and Western converts, as in Asia, "being a Buddhist" does not necessarily imply an exclusive identity. Thus, the census figures, which show, for example, roughly a million Buddhists in North America as a whole, do not accurately reflect the penetration of Buddhist concepts and practices in contemporary national culture.

With intellectuals worldwide, however, awareness of Buddhist thought and practice is widespread. Advertising agents now deploy Buddhist ideas and practices routinely to promote materialistic attachments: Popular advertising since 1999 found the Dalai Lama's image being used to sell Apple computers, a Nike sneaker called "Nirvana," and a designer sandal called "Buddha." The word *Zen* has been reduced to a vapid cliché because it has by now been appended to hundreds of objects, certain to elicit consumer curiosity.

The Reshaping of Buddhism in Asia

In the postcolonial period, then, Buddhists have had to determine how to situate their tradition in the new secular polities. The effort has entailed reconstructing sangha–state relations after colonial neglect of the religious institutions, responding to scientific thought and modern medicine, reckoning with the religious pluralism introduced by Christianity and other faiths, and revising law codes in relation to national minorities. The results have been mixed. In Bhutan and Sri Lanka, the dominant ethnic groups

Buddhism as Commodity
and Buddhist Imagery as Sales Pitch

Although Zen is not mentioned in it, the ad on the left, for a truck, completely misunderstands the basic message of Buddhism, that is, that possessions and attachment undermine spiritual life. The image on the right makes the equally absurd suggestion that electronic distractions are somehow a kind of spiritual practice.

have promoted Buddhist nationalism at the expense of non-Buddhist minorities, while in Myanmar, members of the military have used Buddhist symbols in a manipulative way to prop up the legitimacy of their authoritarian regimes. Yet Buddhists in each of these countries have led democratic movements resisting repressive policies and violence.

Reformist monastic schools and lay movements begun in the modern era have continued to the present, with recent initiatives arising to address problems confronting the widely differing national contexts: Forest monks in Thailand respond to environmental crises, lay organizations in Japan campaign in elections to insert Buddhist values into the political culture, Mongolian leaders rebuild monuments and restore monastic education and ritual expertise, and Sri Lankan monks run for the national parliament vowing to keep their country's Buddhist identity strong.

As ethnic identity has held the loyalty of local communities, often against the demands of modern secular states, "being Buddhist" has drawn individuals to value, rediscover, and embrace Buddhism across Asia. In many cases, the postcolonial web of global interaction has shaped the process: The "Buddhism" that reformers discover has been filtered through and influenced by the thinking of Euro-American scholars and Westernized indigenous teachers.

An interesting and early example of this phenomenon occurred in Maharashtra, the modern state in central India. Since 1956, Mahar caste groups relegated to the bottom of the caste system have held mass ceremonies to convert to Buddhism, declaring their rejection of Hinduism and its institutionalization of social inequality. The Mahars' knowledge of Buddhism was informed in part by colonial scholarship; the presence in Maharashtra of ancient Buddhist sites revealed by British archaeology has obvious importance as well. The founder of this movement, Dr. Bhimrao Ambedkar (1891–1956), learned about Buddhism from his studies in the West, particularly at Columbia University, where Euro-American scholarship on Buddhism then held up the image of the Buddha as a social reformer. Statues of Ambedkar abound in Maharashtra villages today, monuments to the reinstatement of Buddhism tradition in the service of a twentieth-century social reform movement.

Buddhism's Elective Affinity for Modernization

At the beginning of the twentieth century, Western scholars such as Max Weber questioned whether Buddhism could prove compatible with economic modernization. Since the end of the Second World War, such skepticism has been laid to rest by the exceptional success of nations strongly influenced by Buddhism. We can now see that Weber erred in exaggerating the "otherworldliness" of mainstream Buddhism. He was not well acquainted with the unambiguous early doctrinal emphasis on "good Buddhists" attaining worldly success, an ethos that traveled well across the trade routes of Asia and, it seems, into the twenty-first century. Modern reformers have had many canonical texts to draw on to promote the compatibility between economic development and Buddhism. As an influential reformist monk of Thailand asserted several generations ago, "Education breeds knowledge, knowledge breeds work, work breeds wealth, and wealth promotes happiness."[4]

The economic boom in Asia since World War II has clearly benefited Buddhism as newly wealthy patrons have sponsored various renewal initiatives. Moreover, many do not involve the traditional sangha's leadership. For example, Thai and Korean projects are now under way that have transcribed the scriptures into digital form, a new mode of spreading the Dharma locally and globally to all with computer technology. Translation of the sacred texts into the global medium of English is another innovation. The Buddhist Publication Society, founded in Sri Lanka in 1956, has offered hundreds of vernacular (and English) translations and interpretive tracts on the Pali texts; its work overlaps with that of the Pali Text Society, founded in nineteenth-century England—a group that continues to extend its English translations of canonical work from the southern Buddhist tradition, including extracanonical commentaries.

Today each of the four Tibetan monastic schools has a modern publishing house in the West that yearly prints dozens of texts promulgating explanations of Buddhist doctrine by its own teaching monks. An even larger-scale project was initiated in

Socially Engaged Buddhism: Some Examples

Thai activist Sulak Sivaraksa puts the ancient Buddhist concept of suffering into the framework of today's world:

> In Buddhist terminology, the world is full of *dukkha* ["suffering"], i.e., the dangers of impending world destruction through nuclear weapons, atomic fallout, air, land, and sea pollution, population explosion, exploitation of fellow human beings, denial of basic human rights, and devastating famine. . . . World dukkha is too immense for any country, people, or religion to solve. We can only save ourselves when all humanity recognizes that every problem on earth is our own personal problem and our own personal responsibility. . . . The language of Buddhism must offer answers which fit our situation. Only then will Buddhism survive, today and tomorrow, as it has in the past, influencing humankind positively and generating love, peace, and nonviolence.[a]

An even more forceful exhortation is provided by the Vietnamese monk Thich Nhat Hanh:

> The word *Buddha* comes from the root *budh*, which means "awake." A Buddha is one who is awake. Are we really awake in our daily lives? That is a question. . . . Society makes it difficult to be awake. We know that 40,000 children in the Third World die every day of hunger, but we keep forgetting. The kind of society we live in makes us forgetful. That is why we need exercises in mindfulness. . . . Our earth is like a small boat. Compared with the rest of the cosmos, it is a very small boat, and it is in danger of sinking. We need a person to inspire us with calm confidence, to tell us what to do. Who is that person? The Mahayana texts tell us that you are that person.[b]

[a] Sulak Sivaraksa, "Buddhism in a World of Change," in Fred Eppsteiner, ed., *The Path of Compassion: Writings on Socially Engaged Buddhism* (Berkeley, CA: Parallax Press, 1988), pp. 16–17.
[b] Thich Nhat Hanh, "Call Me by My True Name," in Eppsteiner, *The Path of Compassion*, pp. 34–37.

1991 by the Japanese industrialist Yenan Numata. His foundation, the Bukkyo Denko Kyokai, is underwriting the scholarly translation into English of the entire Chinese canon. To do all 3,360 scriptures, the project is estimated to span the next 100 years!

The Sangha: Adaptive Reformism?

A recent survey of ordained Buddhist monks and nuns estimated that there are about 700,000 worldwide. Officially, monks outnumber nuns by six to one. Given the role of the sangha in maintaining the traditional goals in every society, the future of Buddhism is in the hands of the monks and nuns who will become the spiritual exemplars, scholars, teachers, and meditators.

Arguing that the sangha cannot keep Buddhism alive unless the monks keep pace with the educational level of the nation's population, countries such as Thailand have invested in making higher education available to them. This opportunity still attracts many young men from poor rural backgrounds to take ordination. Paradoxically, however, becoming a monk gives many the chance to live in better material circumstances

A Thai monk at an ATM in Bangkok. Monks across Asia face the challenge of adapting their lifestyle defined by monastic laws over 2,000 years old to the rapidly changing realities of the globalizing world.

than their parents are able to achieve and to gain skills that can be, and often are, taken back into lay life.

But at the same time, many Asian states have created national sangha bureaucracies, placing monastics under political supervision. These governments now scrutinize the preaching and personal lives of monks and crack down on any political activities that might arise in the monasteries. Seeing clearly the threat that the Buddhist Dharma represents to unjust or uncompassionate regimes, politicians have sought to weaken Buddhist institutions even while outwardly honoring them. In recent years, monks in Tibet and Vietnam have felt incidents of stern repression. It is hard to imagine Buddhist monks regaining the power they once enjoyed in the premodern era.

Since World War II, many developments have undermined the classical patterns and exchanges within Buddhist societies. Whereas formerly, monastic schools were an important part of the sanghas' service to local communities and a source of their recruitment, today public education has been removed from the monastery almost everywhere. If connection with and awareness of modern changes are essential to an institution meeting the needs of the lay majority, many question whether the Buddhist sangha today is capable of keeping Buddhist ideas and identity vibrant in the whirl of changes sweeping modern Asian societies.

Many progressive Buddhists think not. Noting that the modern sangha has a hierarchy of authority unknown in earlier times, they see little opportunity for young monks to fashion innovative applications of the Dharma in thought or action. Noting how powerful elder monks typically lack vision, purpose, or inspiration beyond the guardianship of ceremonies and tradition, many Asian householders now look to lay institutions for more promising avenues to keep Buddhism vital.

The number of men taking monastic vows across Asia has fallen far short of what population increases would predict. As a result, many village monasteries are understaffed, a trend reflecting the breakdown of rural communities that has contributed to the urbanization of Asia. While some Buddhists in Nepal, Korea, and Japan have countenanced sanghas of the "married ordained" to solve the problem of recruitment, these schools on the whole have actually shown even less inclination to revitalize or innovate. Again, it is easy to see why Buddhist reformers have almost always gone outside the boundary of the modern sangha to move ahead with their revitalization programs, at times even having to face opposition from the established monastic community.

State Buddhism and the Poison of Ethnic Passion

Few areas of Asian Buddhism have been removed from the crises and changes of the modern era: Scientific thought and technology derived from the European Enlightenment challenged traditional doctrines, cosmologies, and medical theories; the impact of European colonialism forced economic transformations that undermined traditional rulers and patronage; the ideologies of Christian missionary triumphalism and racism conflicted with indigenous beliefs about the superiority of Buddhism.

With colonialism now gone, shifts in the political, socioeconomic, and intellectual spheres have changed individuals and caused Buddhists to adapt their beliefs and practices to a transformed world. Countries with Buddhist majorities now must decide how to shape society—in economic and political spheres—to best realize the Buddha's ideal of a compassionate civilization. Exponents still debate whether Buddhism should endorse military authoritarianism (on the model of the benevolent dictator Ashoka) or representative democracy (on the model of the sangha's democratic norms). Is it more compassionate to establish a "pure Buddhist state" that privileges Buddhism and Buddhists or to opt for a secular state that guarantees evenhanded tolerance of a multireligious and multiethnic society? Can Buddhist ideals be more effectively implemented in a socialist or a free-market system?

In countries such as Myanmar and Sri Lanka, where adherence to Buddhism was a powerful force against colonialism, reform movements within the sangha weakened the older institutional lineages; but when "political monks" have gathered attention and public support, they have stoked an uncompromising Buddhist nationalism that targets minority ethnic groups of other faiths. In modern China and Vietnam, Buddhist monks are still called on to withdraw, study, and meditate. In India, Sri Lanka, and Thailand, on the other hand, monks have become leaders in political reform movements and in the implementation of economic development projects.

In revolutionary China and Mongolia, Buddhism was identified with the old feudal order and was fiercely disestablished. Across China's Tibetan and interior Mongol ethnic regions, the policy of the People's Republic of China, especially during the

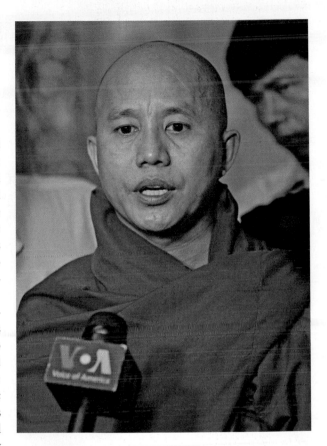

Buddhist monk U Wirathu has been accused of stoking anti-Muslim sentiments in Myanmar through his "969 Movement," which calls on Buddhists to boycott Muslim businesses.

CONTRASTING RELIGIOUS VISIONS

As the following contrasting visions indicate, every religious tradition is capable of generating both visions that encourage peace and understanding and visions that encourage conflict and violence.

Peacemaker: Thich Nhat Hanh

Since his early involvement in the peace movement in his native Vietnam, the Zen monk Thich Nhat Hanh (1926–) has projected a strong and ecumenical Buddhist voice. From exile in the West, he has been a firm advocate of toleration and the centrality of peacemaking when facing both personal challenges and international policy. A leading advocate of "engaged Buddhism" and author of several dozen books, Nhat Hahn has for decades argued that Buddhists must participate in social and cultural activities, with activism informed by the clarity arising from meditation. As he once affirmed, "In times like this, when people suffer so much, the bodhisattvas don't stay in the temple; they are out there."[a] His

Buddhist monks at a mass merit and blessings ceremony for Sri Lankan soldiers.

"12 Precepts of the Order of Inter-being" attempts to express universal principles of life beyond Buddhist sectarianism, rejecting absolutely killing, coercion, dogmatism, and untruthfulness while advocating a meditation-centered life.

Confrontationalist: Political Monks of Sri Lanka's Maha Sangha

Drawing on some of the nationalist pronouncements of reformists such as Anagarika Dharmapala, some monks have formed an entity called the Maha Sangha to engage in political action. These activist monks have urged their government to reply with relentless military action, not negotiated compromise, to resolve the Tamil revolt that has fueled Sri Lanka's tragic civil war since 1983. Arguing that "politics is the monks' heritage" and that Sri Lanka has special virtue as a Buddhist homeland, the Maha Sangha supports violence as the only solution. One poet has distilled their support for aggressive religious nationalism:

My brave, brilliant soldier son
Leaving [home] to defend the motherland
That act of merit is enough
To reach Nirvana in a future birth. . . .
Country, religion, race are my triple gems. . . .
The sangha is ever ready
At the front
If the race is threatened.[b]

[a]Sallie B. King, "Thich Nhat Hanh and the Unified Buddhist Church," in Christopher S. Queen and Sallie B. King, eds., *Engaged Buddhism: Buddhist Liberation Movements in Asia* (Albany: State University Press of New York, 1996), p. 351.
[b]H. L. Seneviratne, *The Work of Kings: The New Buddhism in Sri Lanka* (Chicago: University of Chicago Press, 1999), pp. 272–73.

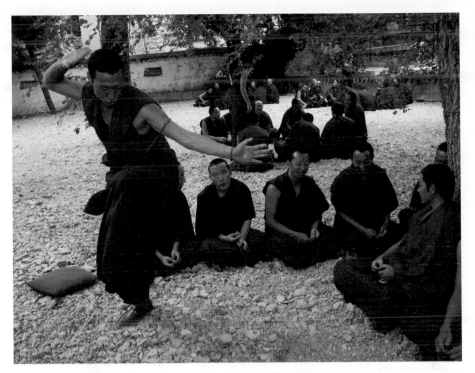

(left) Tibetan monks engaging in debate training, testing their ability to consistently expound the Buddha's teachings.

Cultural Revolution, was to destroy Buddhist monasticism, punish believers, and repress any public expressions of devotion. Just reestablishing stupas, ordination lineages, and traditional sangha life has been a challenge over the last decades in these nations. It was not until 1990 that Buddhism in Outer Mongolia experienced a revival after nearly a century of suppression.

In Sri Lanka, once the nationalistic Buddhist movements had ushered in independence, they turned their efforts inward. By seeking to legislate a "purer Buddhist state" and a restoration of past glories, they created an environment in which activist monks enflamed unprecedented ethnic conflict with non-Buddhist minorities long resident on the island. Paradoxically, Buddhist universalism and the ideology of compassion have not prevented modern attempts at "ethnic cleansing" there as well as in Burma and Bhutan. Some social historians see the further

(below) A monk from the Ravana Balaya, a Buddhist nationalist group that claims a sacred duty to safeguard Sri Lanka from "minority or outside influences," as he addresses the media during a 2013 protest in Colombo, Sri Lanka.

weakening of Buddhist ethics in the future: As populations rise and resources grow scarcer, politicians of Buddhist Asia, as elsewhere, will be increasingly tempted to use Buddhism to unify majorities to win votes and take power, inviting the temptation to discriminate against non-Buddhists. From 2007 until today, for example, Thai Buddhist monks have called for declaring Buddhism the official religion of the nation, in response to Muslim terrorist acts in its southern region that murdered monks and destroyed Buddhist sanctuaries.

Conclusion

As a refuge of intellectual freedom and spiritual imagination, Buddhist teachers nurtured and enriched the civilizations of Asia. Surveying the belief patterns of the world's Buddhist communities, one is challenged both by the sheer diversity of doctrinal

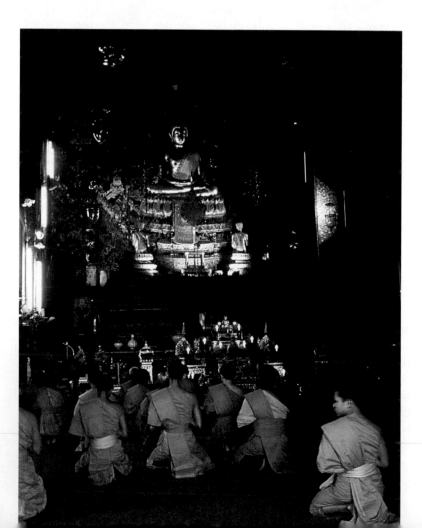

Members of the Thai sangha gather for chanting before a large Buddha in Bangkok.

expression and by the complexity of Buddhism's systematic thought. Such an outpouring of conceptualization from a tradition that held the ultimate reality to be beyond words! Buddhism's great migration across Asia and beyond has entailed the translation of texts, ideas, and rituals into non-Indic languages and cultures. In becoming a world religion, Buddhism in practice has promoted compassionate, medically advanced, disciplined, mercantile, and literate societies. Like other great religions today, Buddhism has shown that its definition of the human condition and its prescribed ways of addressing suffering and mortality have enduring value, even in new societies and in the midst of changes that have shaken the modern and postcolonial world.

The global migration of Asian Buddhists in the postcolonial era is an important source of global revival in the twenty-first century. As these groups grow and prosper in their new countries, they naturally channel a portion of their savings back to the home region. But these immigrants have also paid to sponsor monks and build storefront monasteries in the West and, in the process, internationalized the home country's institutions through a slow grassroots process of development. As Buddhist priests, monks, and expatriates move between their new and old countries, innovations and resources are being shifted as well. This immigrant-induced exchange also includes the cross-fertilization of ideas moving between Buddhist schools from distant areas of Asia and their Western exponents. It may well be that the future success—or perhaps even survival—of the modern national lineages and schools of Buddhism back in Asia will depend on an international membership, providing worldwide sources of funding and interpretive awareness. To date, only the Tibetan Buddhists in exile have been truly successful at linking the material support and ritual practice by Western converts to their traditional schools; otherwise, most Asian Buddhists and converts practice their religion completely separate from Westerners who have converted to Buddhism.

An especially promising development may be the growing presence of Buddhism in the emerging global culture. In the area of human rights, Asian Buddhist exponents have made impressive contributions. Buddhist doctrine offers many traditional ideals that have been rearticulated powerfully by reformists and activists who style themselves as "engaged Buddhists." These ideals include compassion, nonviolence, selflessness, interdependence, and detachment. There is no shortage of examples today of the existential "poisons" that Buddhists have always located at the center of their wheel of life—human greed, anger, and delusion. Yet the very compassion and selflessness that Buddhists have always embraced offer the means to lessen suffering of individuals, of communities, and of the earth itself.

An example of this determined insistence on applying Buddhist norms to modern crises is seen in the writings of the Thai activist Sulak Sivaraksa, founder (in 1989) of the International Network of Engaged Buddhists:

> When Prince Siddhartha saw an old man, a sick man, a dead man, and a wandering monk, he was moved to seek salvation, and eventually he became the Buddha, the Awakened One. The suffering of the present day, such as that brought about at Bhopal and Chernobyl, should move many of us to think

together and act together to overcome such death and destruction, to bring about the awakening of humankind.[5]

engaged Buddhism:
reformist movement among global Buddhists seeking to relate the teachings to contemporary suffering

Engaged Buddhism is uniting Asian Buddhists with Western converts, bringing together the energies of householders, monks, and nuns, and finding issues that connect Buddhist activists with similarly committed reformers from other faiths. It remains to be seen whether Buddhist revivalists can offer a compelling interpretation of the Dharma as Buddhists find themselves drawn into the marketplace of globalized capitalism, with its doctrines of individualism and competition and its vigorous encouragement of consumerism.

The late Gene Smith (at right), preserver of thousands of texts brought out of Tibet by refugees, presenting a gift of a hard drive containing thousands of sacred texts to a Tibetan Buddhist abbot. He made similar donations across the Tibetan world in 2008–9.

Discussion Questions

1. Pick three major episodes in the Buddha's life and discuss what lessons they impart to a typical Buddhist householder.

2. In what senses can the Buddha be called the Great Physician?

3. Many modern Buddhists regard the Buddha as a reformer. What teachings can be used to support this interpretation? What historical arguments can be made against this position?

4. Which of the Buddha's teachings are shared with post-Vedic Hinduism?

5. Explain how Buddhist doctrine can argue for reincarnation but against the existence of an "immortal soul."

6. Why is compassion a human ideal that is a logical extension of core Buddhist doctrines?

7. Why is Buddhism known as the *Middle Way*? Give at least three reasons.

8. Support or critique the statement "Vajrayana Buddhism is a school of Mahayana Buddhism."

9. Discuss the state of Buddhism across Asia in the year 750.

10. Why is the *Lotus Sutra* so important in China and Japan?

11. How does popular Mahayana Buddhism resemble and differ from devotional Hinduism?

12. How is the Mahar revival of Buddhism in India indicative of the effects of "Protestant Buddhism" and the backlash from the colonial era within the Buddhist world?

13. Name five aspects of Protestant Christianity that were adopted by Buddhist reformers, shaping the nineteenth- and twentieth-century revitalization movements called "Protestant Buddhism."

14. In your opinion, how would a modern Buddhist revivalist present the Dharma and argue that it remains a religion relevant to life in the twenty-first century?

Key Terms

Amitabha/Amida	bodhisattva	dependent origination
anatman	Buddhaghosa	Dharma
arhat	Buddha-nature school	Dogen
Ashoka	caitya	Eightfold Path
Avalokiteshvara/	Ch'an/Zen	Eisai
Guanyin	Cittamatra	engaged Buddhism
bhikku/bhikkhuni	dana	enlightenment

(continued)

Key Terms (continued)

Four Good Deeds	Nagarjuna	skandha
Four Noble Truths	Nichiren	Sthaviravadins
Gandhara	nirvana	stupa
Gelugpa	Pali Canon	Theravada
karuna	pap	Three Marks of
koan	prajna	Existence
Lotus Sutra	Protestant Buddhism	Three Refuges
Madhyamaka	punya	Vajrayana/Thunderbolt
Mahayana	Pure Land	Vehicle
Maitreya/Mi-lo Fo	sangha	vipassana meditation
maitri	shramana	Wu Tai Shan
mizuko cult	*shunyata*	

Suggested Readings

Gombrich, Richard. *Theravada Buddhism: A Social History from Ancient Benares to Modern Colombo* (New York: Routledge, 1988).

Heine, Steven, and Charles S. Prebish, eds. *Buddhism in the Modern World* (New York: Oxford University Press, 2003).

Lewis, Todd. *Buddhists: Understanding Buddhism Through the Lives of Practitioners.* (London: Wiley-Blackwell, 2014).

Lopez, Donald, ed. *Buddhism and Science: A Guide for the Perplexed* (Chicago: University of Chicago Press, 2008).

————. *Buddhism in Practice*, abridged ed. (Princeton, NJ: Princeton University Press, 2007).

Queen, Christopher, and S. King, eds. *Engaged Buddhism* (Albany: State of New York University Press, 1996).

Rahula, Walpola. *What the Buddha Taught* (New York: Publishers Resource, 1978).

Robinson, Richard, and Willard Johnson. *The Buddhist Religions: A Historical Introduction*, 5th ed. (Belmont, CA: Wadsworth, 2008).

Seager, Richard. *Buddhism in America* (New York: Columbia University Press, 1999).

Shaw, Sarah. *The Jatakas: Birth Stories of the Bodhisatta* (New York: Penguin, 2006).

Snellgrove, David. *Indo-Tibetan Buddhism* (Boulder, CO: Shambhala, 1987).

Strong, John S., ed. *The Experience of Buddhism*, 3rd ed. (Belmont, CA: Wadsworth, 2007).

Trainor, Kevin, ed. *Buddhism: An Illustrated Guide* (London: Duncan-Baird, 2001).

Wijayaratna, Mohan. *Buddhist Monastic Life* (Cambridge: Cambridge University Press, 1987).

Williams, Paul. *Mahayana Buddhism: The Doctrinal Foundations*, 2nd ed. (New York: Routledge, 2009).

Williams, Paul, and Anthony Tribe. *Buddhist Thought: A Complete Introduction to the Indian Tradition* (New York: Routledge, 2000).

Notes

1. Quoted in Samuel Beal, *Si-Yu-Ki: Buddhist Records of the Western World* (New Delhi: Munshiram Manoharlal, 1983), p. xxix.
2. U Ba Swe (Defense Minister of Burma) in *The Burmese Revolution* (Rangoon: Pyida Press, 1957), pp. 14–15.
3. *Tricycle*, Winter 2004, pp. 24–25.
4. Phra Kummsaen, quoted in Kenneth Landon, *Thailand in Transition* (Chicago: University of Chicago Press, 1939), pp. 67–68.
5. Sulak Sivaraksa, *Seeds of Peace* (Berkeley, CA: Parallax Press, 1988), p. 9.

Additional Resources

BBC Religion: Buddhism (www.bbc.co.uk/religion/religions/buddhism). Reliable information and updated links to sites with basic information.

BuddhaNet (www.buddhanet.net). Gateway to sources of scholarly information and current events in the Buddhist world.

Buddhist Studies WWW Virtual Library (www.ciolek.com/WWWVL-Buddhism.html). A directory of websites across the Buddhist world.

EAST ASIAN RELIGIONS

8

Confucianism, Daoism, Shinto, Buddhism

Overview

On public holidays and lunar days traditionally deemed favorable for approaching the gods, temples in China, Japan, and Korea are packed with morning visitors, the air thick with incense smoke. In Beijing, newly married couples flock to the White Clouds Daoist temple to light candles, requesting divine aid to ensure the birth of a son; at family shrines in Seoul, honor students approach ancestral altars to report their applications to study at universities abroad; in rural Japan, farmers gather at the village Shinto shrine for the annual harvest festival, clapping their hands to punctuate their prayers of thanks. Buddhist monasteries have also attracted new patronage as economic prosperity has enriched the region: Old women hoping for medicinal cures sip water that has been blessed, executive trainees sent by corporations for "toughening up" sit in meditation, and teenage girls requesting help for finding a boyfriend light incense sticks.

Today, public shrines for the sage Confucius are being built again, but there is no doubt that Confucian tradition has survived the wars, political tumult, and scathing denunciations of the twentieth century. In the colonial era, nearly every Chinese intellectual blamed Confucianism for retarding the region's development. Now its emphasis on education, strong families, individual discipline, and harmonious group relations is seen as holding the center of East Asia's stable societies and

East Asian Religions Timeline

1766–1122 BCE	Shang dynasty in China; cult of departed ancestors and oracle bone divination
1122–221	Zhou dynasty in China; yin-yang theory develops; era of intermittent civil disorder
ca. 551–479	Life of Master K'ung (Confucius)
ca. 520–286	Era of first Daoist sages, philosophers Lao Zi (d. 500 BCE?) and Zhuang Zi (365–290 BCE)
450–223	Era of Confucian sage scholars, Master Meng (Mencius, 371–289 BCE), Master Xun (298–238 BCE); origins of Confucian *Analects* and compilation of the *Five Classics*
221–206	Qin dynasty, the first to unify China; Great Wall completed
200 BCE–220 CE	Han dynasty in China; civil service based on Confucian teachings
220–588 CE	Period of weak central state and the growth of Daoism and Buddhism
ca. 450	"Three Caves" of Daoist scriptures collected
618–907	T'ang dynasty in China; period of Confucian revival; translations of Indian Buddhist texts
668–918	Silla dynasty in Korea, centered on Buddhism as state religion
710–784	Nara period in Japan; Shinto tradition organized; Buddhism made state religion
794–1185	Heian period in Japan, ends with emperor removed from rulership
918–1392	Koryo dynasty in Korea, with ecumenical development of Mahayana Buddhism
960–1279	Song dynasty in China; period of neo-Confucianism (the "Second Epoch")
1130–1200	Life of Zhu Xi, leading neo-Confucian exponent, who reestablished the tradition as preeminent among the Chinese literati
ca. 1150	Goddess Mazu becomes popular in China, recognized by the state
1185–1333	Kamakura era in Japan, era of civil disorder and the rise of new Buddhist schools
1279–1368	Yuan dynasty in China, era of Mongol rule
1336–1600	Ashikaga period in Japan; era of Shinto-Buddhist syncretism, popularity of Pure Land Buddhism; adoption of Zen among the literati and Samurai
1368–1644	Ming dynasty in China, the last era of Han Chinese rule; doctrine of harmonizing the "three faiths"
1380FF	In China, *The Canonization of the Gods* fixes folk pantheon in hierarchy mirroring state bureaucracy
1392–1910	Yi dynasty in Korea, an era marked by state-favored Confucianism
1472–1529	Life of Wang Yangming, a neo-Confucian who promoted mind cultivation and character development
1501–1570	Life of Yi T'oegye, important Korean neo-Confucian
1534–1582	Life of Nobunaga, Japanese shogun who persecuted Buddhism and gave support to Christianity
1592	Publication of *Journey to the West*, written by Wu Cheng-en
1600–1867	Tokugawa era in Japan, with capital in Tokyo; Buddhism under strong state support
1644–1911	Qing (Manchu) dynasty in China; era promoting Confucianism

1815–1888	Oldest new religions in Japan: Kurozumikyo (1814), Tenrikyo (1838)
1850–1864	Taiping Rebellion in China, led by Hong Xiuquan (1814–1864)
1860	Ch'ondogyo movement founded in Korea by Ch'oe Suun (1824–1864)
1868–1945	Return of emperor's rule in Japan and the rise of state Shinto; Japan adopts Western calendar, technology, imperialist political views
1871–1945	Japanese Buddhist establishment joins Shinto nationalists and Christians supporting militarism
1880–present	Best and brightest individuals across the East Asia region studying Western learning, technology to seek rapid modernization
1889–1890	New constitution and Japanese government initiatives draw heavily on Confucian doctrines
1900–1945	Founding of "new religions" in prewar Japan: P. L. Kyodan in 1924, Reiyukai Kyodan in 1925, Soka Gakkai in 1930, Rissho Koseikai in 1938
1912	Fall of Qing dynasty in China, ending state patronage of Confucianism
1946–present	Founding of "new 'new religions'" in postwar Japan: Sukyo Mahikari in 1963, Agonshu in 1971, Aum Shinrikyo in 1989
1949–1976	People's Republic of China established; Communist Party persecutes monks, priests, institutions
1966–1976	Cultural Revolution attacks the "Four Old Things": thought, culture, customs, habits. It reignites renewed persecution of religions and adherents in China
1984–present	Buddhist monasteries and Daoist temples reopen in China, many with new monks and nuns in residence; pilgrims increase rapidly and visit major sites to perform traditional rites
1994	Study of Confucianism in schools officially approved by Chinese state
1995	Aum Shinrikyo sect in Japan launches poison gas attack in Tokyo
1996–present	Images of Mao Zedong and other deceased Communist Party leaders found on popular religious amulets
1999	Falun Gong, a syncretistic Buddhist-Daoist group founded by Li Hongzhi claiming 100 million followers in thirty countries, protests in Beijing; within months, Chinese government bans the group and begins persecution of practitioners
2007	*Yu Dan's Reflections on "The Analects,"* a book on Confucius published in China, becomes a best-seller, with over 10.2 million copies sold; Chinese government begins funding of the first of 500 "Confucius Institutes" to be established in most countries across the world to promote the study of Chinese language and culture
2008	Chinese government declares Qing Ming, "Grave Sweeping Day," an official holiday; Confucian ancestor traditions return to graveyards across China
2010	Communist Party officially celebrates Confucius' birthday. It places image of Confucius in Tian'anmen Square, Beijing, then removes it a few months later
2012	Half a billion Chinese officially counted participating in Confucian grave visits and ritualism on Qing Ming
2013	Responding to many reports of neglected elders, Communist Party in China passes law requiring children to show filial piety to their parents through visits and calls

orchestrating this region's ascendancy in the global economy. One of the central goals of this chapter is to have the reader understand the Confucian world, in East Asia and beyond. Another is to understand how the Chinese emphasis on harmony was extended to "the unity of the three faiths" (*san-jiao heyi*, still a widely used phrase), meaning Confucianism, Daoism, and Buddhism.

Interreligious pluralism sets East Asia apart. Throughout the region's history, the great majority of East Asians regarded Confucianism, Daoism, deity cults, and Buddhism as complementary, dealing with different aspects of life. This applies to Japan as well, between Buddhism and its indigenous religion, Shinto. Most felt that these interrelated beliefs and practices enriched their spirituality, offering them the chance to meld the traditions harmoniously to solve personal problems and address life's questions. It was rare for individuals—elite or common folk—to feel that "being religious" meant choosing one religious tradition to the exclusion of the others. This openness stands in contrast to the common Western belief that religious conviction means adopting one creed and forsaking all others.

Studying religion in East Asia today entails grasping the existence of a popular common tradition that is rooted in the veneration of ancestors dating back to earliest antiquity. Over time these practices became blended with basic elements of Daoism, Buddhism, and Confucianism, comprising East Asia's **diffuse religion**. Given that roughly 30 percent of humanity is East Asian, no full reckoning of human religious life can be made without taking into account China, Korea, and Japan.

diffuse religion: spiritual tradition centered on family and locality, informed by common ideas from Confucianism, Daoism, and Buddhism

At a shrine atop the sacred mountain Tai Shan in southern China, devotees light incense and candles to honor the local gods. People hang heart-linking locks, hoping to secure the safety and happiness of their family members.

Geographical Orientation

Since this chapter is different from the others due to its treating together the religions of East Asia, the student must first become familiar with the geographical facts on the ground, and then understand the pattern of cultural diffusion that linked them for over two millennia in three separate but related religious timelines. Religion is closely tied to each nation's development, so it is imperative from this section onward that the history of China, Korea, and Japan be attended to carefully (see Map 8.1).

Countries: China, Koreas, Japan

What is today referred to as "China" is the People's Republic of China (PRC). With over 1.4 billion citizens, it is the country with the largest population in the world. Different dynasties up to the present have struggled to unify the dozens of minority peoples of the periphery regions with those of the core region who have called themselves Han and whose descendants speak the Chinese dialect Mandarin. Although spoken Chinese contains over twenty major dialects, the literate culture of China has used the same written language for more than 2,000 years. This has made the classical literary tradition (including all religious texts) accessible to the learned throughout the entire East Asian region. Mandarin language and Han culture effectively wielded by state officials did prove capable, at times, of unifying vast domains.

The formerly unified Korean culture area, artificially split into the separate countries of North Korea and South Korea since the end of the Second World War (1945), was most strongly influenced by Chinese cultural borrowings, including Buddhism. In the early modern period until the end of the Yi dynasty (1392–1910), Confucianism was the state religion, and ancestor worship was central. Among South Korea's 48 million people, shamanic traditions are today stronger in South Korea than elsewhere in East Asia, and they are practiced by most individuals regardless of any other religious affiliation. Little traditional religious activity is sanctioned or reported among the 24 million people of the modern isolationist and communist state of North Korea.

China also generated wave after wave of religious influence over the island nation of Japan, but beginning later than in Korea. Now a constitutional monarchy with all power vested in a parliament and prime minister, Japan had for fifteen centuries been ruled by an emperor and a single imperial line claiming mythological origins that are distinctively Japanese. Since the end of World War II, however, Japan's 125 million people have produced the world's third-largest national economy. As elsewhere, this rapid transition has worked in contradictory directions, enriching devotees of every persuasion who have rebuilt institutions and created new ones while changing the society profoundly and so causing individuals to see the world in ways previously unimagined. This explains why here and across East Asia, thousands of "new religions" have sprung up, offering creative spiritual responses to life in today's fast-moving societies.

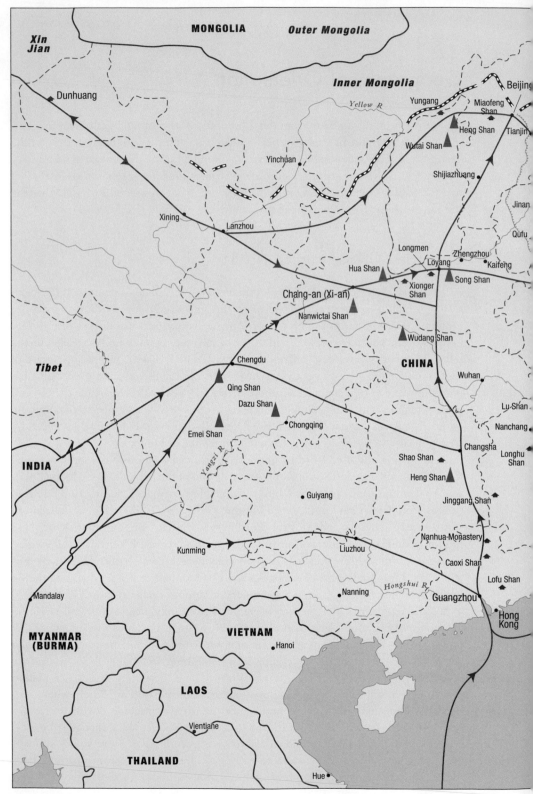

Map 8.1 Modern political map of China, Japan, and North and South Korea showing important religious sites.

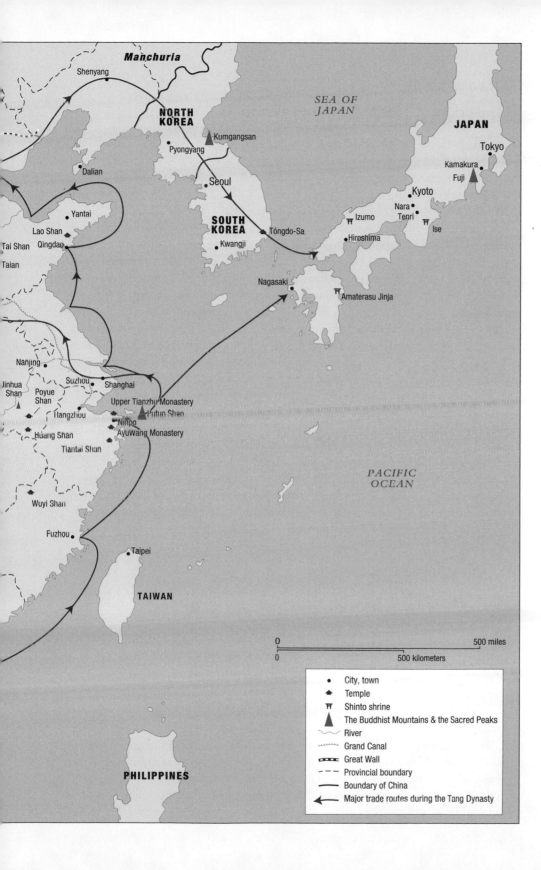

Manchuria

Shenyang

NORTH
KOREA

▲ Kumgangsan

Pyongyang

• Dalian

Seoul

• Yantai

SOUTH
KOREA

Lao Shan

Tai Shan

Qingdao

Taian

▲ Tóngdo-Sa

• Kwangji

Nanjing

Suzhou

Jinhua
Shan

Poyue
Shan

Shanghai

Upper Tianzhu Monastery

Hangzhou

▲ Putuo Shan

Ninpo

AyuWang Monastery

Huang Shan

Tiantai Shan

Wuyi Shan

Fuzhou

• Taipei

TAIWAN

PHILIPPINES

SEA OF
JAPAN

JAPAN

Tokyo

Kamakura
Fuji ▲

Kyoto

Nara
Tenri
Izumo
Ise

Hiroshima

Nagasaki

Amaterasu Jinja

PACIFIC
OCEAN

0   500 miles
0   500 kilometers

• City, town
▲ Temple
⛩ Shinto shrine
▲ The Buddhist Mountains & the Sacred Peaks
〰 River
···· Grand Canal
▭▭ Great Wall
--- Provincial boundary
— Boundary of China
← Major trade routes during the Tang Dynasty

493

Connections: Chinese Core and Periphery

China has been the formative center of the East Asian region from earliest antiquity. The emergence of a central state there predates the unification of Korea and Japan by at least twelve and fifteen centuries, respectively. Most modern national boundaries that demarcate the region date back to the premodern era. The two Koreas, the region of Tibet, and the republic of Taiwan are exceptions.

In very broad terms, all regions beyond China's early core can be seen as the periphery of Chinese civilization, where states and individuals selectively and creatively adapted the essential Chinese cultural forms. These forms encompass the full range of what "culture" entails: the fundamental material technologies needed for subsistence (intensive rice production, the making of iron, and porcelain pottery); the written Chinese characters used to record the spoken languages; and the beliefs and practices of its great religious traditions. As we have seen, even Buddhism, which the Chinese themselves adopted, was transmitted to the East Asian periphery in the same pattern, through China.

Yet despite the overwhelming magnitude of Chinese culture and the power of the Chinese states, Korean, Japanese, and, at times, Vietnamese peoples preserved their own separate identities. While importing and synthesizing much from China, each nonetheless developed a distinct spoken language, mythology, and spiritual connection to its territory. In all these periphery states, too, the national cultures inspired people to identify with being culturally and politically separate from China, however much their elites admired Chinese culture. (In some cases, especially given the destruction and changes that have swept modern China, Chinese cultural forms of earlier eras are now best preserved in Korea or Japan.) Further, as is all too evident in the modern era, the long-standing cultural ties connecting East Asian peoples did not prevent conflicts between nations that ranged from colonization and warfare to genocide.

Encounter with Modernity: The Fall and Return of Confucianism

The Postcolonial Challenge of Confucianism

By 1980 it was clear that modernity theorists who had predicted the decline of religion with the advent of science were incorrect in every instance. Nowhere have the flaws of this analysis been more striking than in East Asia, where indigenous intellectuals and reformers since the mid-nineteenth century blamed Confucianism for the region's decadence and failure to defend itself effectively against the imperialist West. The region's political despotism, social disintegration, economic retardation, scientific stagnation, poverty, and disease were all ascribed to its blind adherence to decadent Confucian ideals and practices.

The more quickly Confucianism could be abandoned in favor of Western cultural borrowings, reformers argued, the sooner East Asia would be on the road to prosperity. For this reason, many welcomed the fall of the Chinese (1910) and Korean (1912) imperial states and with them the domination of Confucian officials and intellectuals. Yet as events transpired, not only has religion in east Asia survived, it has revived and expanded, often in surprisingly strong forms.

For example, early modernity theorists once attributed Japan's postwar prosperity solely to its successful and rapid Westernization. Although the war fomented by European-style fascism destroyed many of Japan's material accomplishments through the country's first era of modernization (1868–1945), the Japanese after World War II were still able to rebound and build what is today one of the world's strongest economies.

Scholars now see the success of Japan as the result of much more than its early and rapid Westernization: The Meiji era (1868–1912) facilitated the region's first union of Western technology and reformed Confucian social policy, one that was accomplished, too, in postwar South Korea, Taiwan, and Singapore and is now under way in post-Mao mainland China.

Thus, the socioeconomic analysis has been completely reversed. We now find many scholars attributing the East Asians' success to the region's family-centered "bourgeois Confucianism" (as distinguished from the "high Confucianism" of the Mandarins, the former ruling elite).

The East Asian revival has also been realized in each instance by a strong post–World War II state that defines its duty in terms of providing leadership for the national economic agendas and takes responsibility for the nation's collective well-being. This recent reinvention of Confucianism has produced societies that today have low crime rates, social harmony, and efficient economic behavior. Given the disastrous state of the region right after World War II, the overall accomplishment has been called an "economic miracle."

Now what reformers had identified as Confucianism's intractable flaws have been reanalyzed in positive terms: Family-based businesses efficiently maximize scarce capital; tightly woven kin/family relations are excellent building blocks for supply and product distribution; an education system that fosters group cooperation, memorization, and imitation has proven adept at producing individuals able to work hard and master math, science, and technology. With strong states dedicated to achieving collective economic success, it was clear by 1990 that East Asian peoples with this reformed Confucian orientation had risen to top global positions in all the major manufacturing sectors of the postmodern world and created successful twenty-first-century societies. Thus, after East Asians had acquired Western know-how, they effectively drew on Confucian elements in their cultures to mobilize indigenous social resources and create political systems that ensured the social cohesiveness needed to promote national prosperity.

East Asia's success not only challenges the West's historical monopoly of wealth and economic power, especially after the global economic recession that began in

2008. In addition, the region's rise calls into question another former tenet of modernity theory: Is Westernization an inevitable consequence of modernization? Stated differently: Must all nations follow the Western model to succeed in the twenty-first century? Or is the Confucian route through strong authoritarian states an alternative for Asia, heralding what might be termed a "Third Confucian Epoch"? To understand better the ideas underlying this encounter with modernity, we must go back to premodern times and trace the historical development of religion in East Asia.

East Asian Religions in the Formative Era (1500 BCE–617 CE)

East Asia is extraordinary among the world's regions because many beliefs and practices documented from earliest antiquity (1500 BCE) survive there right up to the present. To convey just how strong this conservatism has been, consider the example of deities worshipped by China's imperial court: A list of the gods receiving sacrifices from the last Qing emperor in 1907 matches *exactly* the gods mentioned in a very early record (ca. 1100 BCE), with the sole exception of Confucius (who lived almost 600 years after the Shang court). Therefore, it is necessary to survey the emergence and early development of Chinese religions to discern religion's pivotal importance in Chinese civilization and to see how its religious beliefs and practices spread to other East Asian societies.

Earliest History: Shang (1766–1122 BCE)

In the fertile valleys of the Yellow River, urban societies formed by 2000 BCE, and their settlements reveal advanced metal technologies, a pictographic writing system, and religious practices. All three of these aspects of civilization are connected in the practice of oracle bone divination, which was discovered among the northern peoples who lived within walled cities and called their rulers the *Shang*. Questions were inscribed on dried large bones of animals. A ritualist then applied a hot metal bar to the bones and discerned answers from the cracking patterns produced. Among the over 150,000 Shang oracle bones found and deciphered to date, "this-worldly" concerns predominate—questions regarding whether to undertake military action, journeys, or ceremonies as well as the interpretation of omens believed to predict weather, illness, or the gender of unborn children.

Among the Shang were master metal casters who made finely decorated bronze vessels that were used in ceremonies to worship deities and ancestors. Elaborate offerings of drink and food, including animals dispatched on altars, were arrayed at early Chinese burial sites. Inscriptions on the vessels indicate that the Shang rulers boasted of the unrivaled supernatural power of their own ancestors to act on their and the society's behalf. This Shang notion of reciprocity between dead ancestors and living kin—food and honor bestowed by the living in return for blessings from the dead—remains a central aspect of East Asian religions up to the present day.

The cult of the dead assumed vast proportions in the case of the ruling elite, for whom large tombs were dug and around whom all the essentials for life in the "next world" were buried. Among the Shang, there was the practice of interring sacrificed human servants alongside the nobles; in the case of the later emperors, similar grand tombs were built, but terra-cotta replicas of servants and animals replaced living beings.

Humans' easy access to the gods is another important religious belief known from earliest antiquity. The Shang saw gods as immanent in rain, mountains, and rivers; early Chinese attributed significance to patterns and events in nature and made offerings to particular gods associated with them. Spirits were thought to affect all areas of life, from military battles and foreign relations to business fortunes, marriage, and illness. The presence of gods and ancestor spirits was most dramatically attested to by people who served as spirit mediums and were called *wu/xi* (women/men). Through their possession by the deities, the *wu/xi* shamans made ready contact with the supernatural: Some Chinese sought divine aid, and others hired them to exorcise the demons blamed for causing personal sicknesses or troubles.

There is also an interesting Shang concept of a high deity called **Shang-di**, "the Lord Above," regarded as so powerful that only the Shang rulers could petition him. The name signifies the elevation of one Shang ancestor to supreme status, though *Shang-di* endured subsequently in popular imagination as the superior deity who monitors human behavior. (Modern Chinese Protestants have used this term as a translation of *God*.)

Thus, the diffuse religion found later in East Asia stems from beliefs prevalent in early China: the organic view of an interconnected universe, one peopled by spirits including dead ancestors, and the belief that unseen forces in heaven and on earth could be influenced by the petitions of shamans, oracle readers, and divine kings.

Shang-di: heavenly Lord, thought to preside over early Chinese pantheon

Zhou, Chin, and Han Dynasties (1122 BCE–220 CE)

The millennium from the Zhou dynasty (1122–221 BCE) until the fall of the Han (206 BCE–220 CE) was "formative," in the sense that during this period most of the ideas and practices inherited from the past were developed in more systematic forms and recorded for the first time in textual compilations. It is also in this era that the great sages arose whose teachings would so strongly influence not only the Chinese elite but the entire region.

Ancestor veneration, deity worship, and the important role of spirit mediums all spread as the Mandarin-speaking population of China increased and dispersed south into the Yangtze River basin and then farther southward. Some extensions of early concepts can be noted. There was the development of **yin-yang theory** and the five

ancestor veneration: worship, feeding, and petitioning of the souls of dead ancestors

yin-yang theory: twin complementary forces by which the Dao is known

Tu-di Gong: "earth ruler" believed to control fertility worshipped by farmers in early China

substances theory (*wu-xing*: water, fire, wood, metal, earth) to make observations of nature and natural signs. The cult of **Tu-di Gong**, the "earth ruler" who controls fertility, became widespread among the largely agricultural populations. By Han times, Tu-di was addressed in legalistic petitions, reflecting the growing presence of law in Chinese society.

At court and among commoners, Chinese polytheistic theology regarded the deities as neither good nor evil but as potentially both: They can be agents of illness and disaster or the bearers of blessings. Most of the notable deities by the late Zhou were viewed with both hope and fear, as with the Lord of the Yellow River, whose waters usually bring lush harvests but who as bringer of floods can cause widespread death and destruction. The popular Chinese view was that well-disposed gods were pitted against chaos-disposed demons; this contrasted with the worldview of the elite that emphasized abstract reasoning or mysticism.

Ancestor veneration developed further in the formative era, with more elaborate concepts and practices surfacing regarding the afterlife. The family tomb became the key place connecting the living and the dead. Texts found in excavated tombs mention belief in a soul that survives into an afterlife, calling it a *chao-hun* ("cloud soul"). With the notable dead were buried objects that would be useful to a revived soul, including ritual vessels for eating and drinking.

Tian di: supreme overlord in Heaven believed in Han-era China to keep records on each individual soul

By the Han era, texts deposited in the tombs suggest the notion that a new supreme overlord, called **Tian di**, keeps records on each individual soul. Tomb scrolls detail personal acts that seem intended to verify the records kept by Tian di; there are written petitions asking that the deceased be released from blame for any evil deeds

Terra-cotta warriors, unearthed from an imperial tomb outside Xi'an, China, had been placed with the emperor to serve him in the afterlife.

performed in life. The belief that proper tombs can facilitate beneficial exchanges between living and dead grew stronger, for rulers had texts compiled to describe the proper rites, and these practices were then widely adopted across Chinese society.

The Zhou era was marked by considerable political instability and militarism. Regional states vied endlessly for control of territory and revenues, their rulers and officials showing little regard for moral order or respect for human life. Yet individuals arose who tried to formulate the principles on which a just society could be established and by which humane leaders should be guided. These ideas would become the central pillars of East Asian life. The emergence of these visionary thinkers at roughly the same time as the Greek philosophers and Indian sages makes them part of the world's *Axial Age*, so-called because future history changed course as a result of the teachings originating then. Those who advocated individualistic retreat, learning from the natural world, and noninterference by the state as the best way to ensure humanity's flourishing were called **Daoists**. Those who wished to cultivate their own humanity through disciplined learning, ritual practice, humility, and active social service were called **Confucians**.

Daoist: East Asian visionaries who advocated individualistic retreat, learning from nature, and noninterference by the state

Confucianism: culture of literate elite (*rujia*) informed by Confucius and his disciples

Confucius and the Literati Tradition

Although one of the most influential figures in world history, **Master K'ung** (551–479 BCE) failed to realize his own goal of securing an influential position as a state minister. He was a most gifted, inspired teacher, and because his students collected and passed down his oral teachings to their own students, his ideas took hold. Confucius developed the concepts of righteousness and of **ren**, a term that has many shades of meaning but captures the sense of "being fully human." The chief means to ren was **li**, which consisted of ethical propriety, good manners, and the cultivation of traditional ritual performances on musical instruments, in sacrifices, and in ancestor veneration. The early Confucians imagined a male-led world, and their ideal was the *jun-zi*, a cultivated gentleman who learns from his teacher in youth and then continues to study constantly, both to develop his virtue and to serve others.

Master K'ung: given name of sage later known as Confucius

ren: Confucian ideal of "being fully human"

li: Confucian ethic of correct behavior, which leads to ren

The most important aspect of the li is the individual's conduct within the family. Here the central principle is filial conduct (**xiao**). The key domain for xiao is the bond between child and parent, a relationship that implies mutual obligations on both parties within a hierarchical framework. Protection and nurturing by a superior were rendered in return for selfless service and obedience. Classical Confucianism conceived of this bond as the fundamental human connection and identified four

xiao: Confucian ideal of filial conduct; respect for one's parents, elders, and ruler

Image of Master K'ung, whose Western name, Confucius, was coined by early Jesuit missionaries.

other bonds as extensions of it. These are the ties between husband and wife, between elder and younger brother, between friend and friend, and between ruler and minister. The entire set comprised the Five Hierarchical Relationships, which, properly served, were to lead the entire society toward harmony and "human flourishing." If xiao began with serving one's parents, it was to continue with serving one's ruler, thus bringing to maturity one's own character.

In East Asia, family metaphors are likewise applied to community, state, and heaven based on this idea. Confucius' theory was that if those who ruled and ministered both followed and encouraged the society's adherence to maintaining these ideals, all would benefit and the state's harmony would be ensured. As set forth in the *Analects*, the compilation of the master's teachings, anecdotes, and sayings, Confucius became a model for emulation for subsequent generations. The cultured human should be at ease while always showing careful respect; he is firm but kindhearted, an advocate for the practice of moderation who finds a natural balance in all endeavors. One passage in the *Analects* describes Confucius' own search for the ideal:

> At 15 I set my heart on learning; at 30, I firmly took my stand; at 40 I came to be free from doubts; at 50 I understood the decree of Heaven; at 60 my ear was attuned; at 70 I follow my heart's desire without overstepping the line.[1]

Although he is described as being unsure of the reality of the spirits, Confucius was emphatic on the need for individuals to develop a deep respect for others as well as to establish harmony in the personalities of their immediate kin by their careful performance of funeral rituals and the rites of ancestor veneration.

The success of Confucius' teachings was largely due to their systematic and forceful advocacy by several great disciples, notably Master Meng (or **Mencius**, 371–289 BCE) and **Master Xun** (298–238 BCE). The sayings of Mencius argue that human nature is essentially good, that humans are naturally compassionate, dutiful, courteous, and inclined toward learning. Mencius also developed the Confucian view that the well-being of society depends on the virtue of the rulers and that it is the state's responsibility to ensure the flourishing of its citizens. Another especially influential theory of Mencius applied Confucian thought to the destiny of a state: If a dynasty rules by virtue, then it receives the **Mandate of Heaven**, an authorization that can be revoked if rulers cease to be virtuous.

Master Xun, the third of the classical Confucian sages, proposed a more pessimistic, mechanistic, and authoritarian application of Master K'ung's ideas. In his view, humans are inherently antisocial and the universe turns on impersonal forces. But since people can be trained, once shown the good, they will inherently adopt practices that lead in that direction. Hence, Xun turned Confucians toward the careful study of the past, its ancient sages, and the texts that record the human history.

By the late Han (100 CE), the two interrelated elements of the Confucian tradition were established: *inner sagehood* and *outer nobility*. Dynasties recorded their histories, officials and the discontented argued about the Mandate of Heaven, scholars looked

---

Analects: collection of sayings attributed to Confucius

"Behave when away from home as though you were in the presence of an important guest. Deal with commoners as though you were officiating at an important ceremony."

—Confucius

Mencius: first major disciple of Confucius; systemized Master's thought

Master Xun: influential early Confucian exponent with emphasis on authoritarian rule

Mandate of Heaven: theory that the forces of the universe favor a ruler to the earliest sages to model their own lives. We must also note that the notion of Confucius as merely a human, this-worldly sage had already given way to a popular portrayal of him as a demigod.

Early Daoist Philosophy

The formative era in China saw many other teachers who proposed alternative philosophies to meet the needs of organizing society harmoniously. Yet the most important and long-enduring critique of Confucian doctrine came from those who argued that social relations would be harmonious only after humanity had synchronized itself with nature and with the **Dao**, the mystical reality underlying it. In today's English, the name of this school is rendered *Daoist*.

Dao: mysterious power that moves the universe and is the source of life for all beings

Daoist ideas were being expressed in antiquity at roughly the same time as those of Confucius, and the first great expression of Daoism is the terse and poetic *Daodejing* (*Tao Te Ching*). This often-translated work, traditionally attributed to an anonymous "Old Baby," or **Lao Zi** (Lao Tzu), aims to express the nature of the Dao while paradoxically beginning with the proviso that "the true Dao" cannot be spoken or adequately defined. Various cryptic passages suggest that the Dao that pervades all reality can be truly known only through silence and through experiences that transcend words. (The sage's odd name implies the goal of attaining a pristine spiritual state, forever young.)

Lao Zi: "Old Sage;" author of *Daodejing* and founder of Daoism

In this philosophical system, Dao is the prime source of creation, from which the yin and yang forces emerge in ever-shifting harmonies. Dao determines all things and flows naturally as the mysterious and spontaneous energy (**de**) of the universe, functioning without the will or purpose of a divine creator. To experience the Dao, one must let go and pursue the path of noninterference (**wu-wei**) as in Lao Zi's dictum "Do nothing and nothing will be left undone." The best teacher is (to use the example of the *Daodejing*) water that flows freely with the natural forces and in all circumstances yet can overcome all obstacles.

de: mysterious, spontaneous energy of the universe

wu-wei: Daoist ideal of "noninterference"

The Daoists felt that the Confucians harmed society through imposing rules and artificial practices that interfered with humanity's natural inclinations. Their political message was to return to primal simplicity, with the state interfering as little as possible with the lives of the people. The

Lao Zi on an ox. The sage of Daoism depicted in a Ming-era painting.

Defining Terms

Our treatment of multiple East Asian religions in the same chapter calls for a brief explanation of the central terms. Each topic highlighted here is developed in the chapter.

For convenience, we use Confucianism, a Western term originating in eighteenth-century Europe, instead of the corresponding Chinese term, *rujia*, meaning "literati tradition." The tradition of the literati (or intellectuals) is rooted in the system of moral observance and ritual performance praised in the sixth century BCE by Master K'ung (or, in English rendering, Confucius), whose teachings were commented on and extended by subsequent sages. The Confucian tradition was made China's state ideology over two millennia ago, and it became noted for its wisdom books, political institutions, social teachings, and attention to self-cultivation. In this cumulative form and as adapted by medieval scholars influenced by Buddhism, the *rujia* tradition became the most common shared spiritual and ethical culture of China, Korea, and Japan. The scholars who edited the foundational texts and established the expressions of this tradition are known by Westerners as neo-Confucians. A mastery of the tradition's classical texts and central doctrines was at the center of the educational system and government bureaucracy until well into the modern era (1905 in China, 1867 in Japan, 1910 in Korea). Reflecting this diversity, we use *Confucianism* without imputing to the tradition a singular creed, ritual, or institution.

Daoism can refer to loosely connected philosophical and religious traditions and so always needs further specification. Philosophical Daoism aims to cultivate an immediate sense of personal connection with the primal force or reality of the universe, one that its sages labeled "the Dao," using a character that means "way" or "path." The sages of religious Daoism themselves are revered as humans who had realized supernatural physical powers or spiritual immortality and have become divine. Through meditation or

alchemy, this strand of Daoism advocated the sages' path to immortality, and eventually monastic traditions (on the model of Buddhism, imported centuries later) were developed to sustain communities of seekers. Many aspects of "applied" Daoism were developed to manage worldly life in East Asia: acupuncture to adjust the flow of the life force flowing in the human body, *feng shui* to help humans live their lives in harmony with the natural energy flowing in the natural and built environment, *Yi-Jing* and other forms of prognostication to determine the proper moment to perform important tasks (marriage, travel, etc.), *wu-shu*, or the martial arts, to focus human powers in order to overcome enemies.

Deity cults in traditional East Asia were universal. Springs, rivers, remarkable geographic features—particularly mountain peaks—are still thought to have extraordinary divine inhabitants whose spiritual force, or *ling*, is immanent. The same ling is evident and personified in wind, rain, the stars, and legendary figures whose souls endured and who became deities. Each sector of the earth, in fact, is thought to have a resident deity who serves as the counterpart of the government official in charge of the village, the town, the province, and the state itself, with a hierarchy of gods mirroring the human civil service. Across East Asia, the common popular perception is that the deities exist and that they can be contacted at temples. A person will question a god and then, through ancient divination rituals, attempt to discern an answer. In the popular conception, deities, like local officials, can be paid to provide favors; the big gods may be induced to discipline lesser gods (or demons) who cause troubles. Humans out of mutual respect are obliged to show the gods thanksgiving regularly for life, health, and prosperity. Gods who fail to provide assistance are reviled and abandoned.

Diffuse religion is the useful term that indicates what for most East Asians consists of a spiritual life that is centered within the family unit and immediate locality. It has its roots in the ancestor veneration and spirit worship of earliest antiquity but incorporates general and basic elements of Confucianism, Daoism, and Buddhism. The unity of a region's diffuse religion derives from the long-established state bureaucracy practice of promulgating full expressions of the common traditions; at times, scholars were assigned to codify the myriad texts and practices to give them coherence. From medieval times until now, traditional printed almanacs have been important texts that record such teachings and orchestrate yearly practices for families and localities. Among the major elements of the diffuse religion is belief in deities and in rituals relating to them. There is also a sense that the universe has fundamental forces and powers, requiring humans to seek harmony with them to achieve health and long life. Further, the world is believed to have certain natural hierarchies that must be acknowledged and respected, in forms prescribed by the ancient traditions. This requirement of hierarchical respect extends to one's departed kin. Finally, the strength of the diffuse religions comes from the conviction that the ways of the past should be revered and studied to discern the proper path to the future. At least since Confucius, Chinese people have accorded great respect to past traditions, resulting in a very long period in which states disseminated the core elements of East Asian religion across the entire region.

The *sectarian religions* in East Asia were institutional Buddhism and Daoism and the sects that arose periodically, often with the goal of overthrowing the state. Such separate religions were meaningful primarily for the very small elites who joined an order, adopted a singular discipline within one tradition, or sought individualistic sectarian goals. But over time, many sects ceased to advocate the singularity of their approach alone.

Thus it is hard to find firm boundaries separating the spiritual traditions of East Asia. The Dao is a concept shared by all schools, for example; indeed,

the Buddhists used the term to define the Buddha's teaching (Dharma) in early translations. The goal of harmony is also common in each spiritual path. We are able to treat East Asia's religions under a single heading precisely because of the commonality of this "diffuse borrowing," the nexus of the diffuse religion in the home and among kin rather than in large institutions, and the pertinent attempts by elites and commoners alike to harmonize these rich traditions. In each nation, the inclusive harmonizing trait has been expressed with only slight variation: in Japan, "Shintoist in youth, Confucian as an adult, Buddhist in old age"; in Korea, "Confucian by obligation, shamanist at heart"; in China, "Confucian in the office, Daoist outside."

Yin	Yang
Dark	Bright
Earth	Heaven
Female	Male
Autumn	Spring
Valley	Mountain
West	East
Po Soul (grave)	*Hun* Soul (heaven)

The symbolism of the *Yi-Jing* was the main system for East Asians conceptualizing the incessantly changing universe, much as math equations are used to express the essential truths underlying the discoveries of modern science. The most common *yin-yang* symbol should be viewed as ever in motion, with the circles in each sector expanding until black becomes white and white black.

highest calling for humans, argued the Daoists, is not state service but retreat into the mountains, where the reality of the Dao can be felt most clearly.

The second Daoist classic, the **Zhuang Zi**, is attributed to and named after a sage who lived several centuries later, Zhuang Zi (Chuang Tzu, 365–290 BCE). Through lively parables and mind-boggling paradoxes, his sayings explore the mysterious reality of the Dao in everyday human experiences. The most famous example perhaps is his meditation on waking from a dream of being a butterfly. He asks: Which is "real"? Was Zhuang Zi dreaming of being a butterfly, or is the human Zhuang Zi instead merely that butterfly's dream? This text also explores death and advocates accepting the changes the mysterious Dao brings, including the naturalness of death's transforming us into other life forms. Such acceptance is the necessary step toward experiencing transcendent freedom.

Daoist mysticism provided a balance against the bounded rules and regulations of strict Confucianism, offering a rich lore of parables as well as spiritual guidance to those who retreated from government service or active social life. Daoist refuge is found in nature, and the natural world inspired subsequent Chinese artists, including poets and painters.

"Religious Daoism" (Dao Jiao)

As Daoism developed into various religious traditions, its schools included the philosophical ideas we have just discussed, but they differed according to the spiritual disciplines each followed for individuals to become immortals seeking a way for individuals to achieve immortality. Their texts urge the emulation of sages who now ride the clouds like dragons and reside in paradises on islands in the eastern seas. There were two main avenues to reach this goal. The first required meditation aimed at strengthening and multiplying the life force (**qi**), typically through breathing exercises, fasting, and sexual practices. This inner alchemy (*nei-tan*) creates a subtle but undying spiritual essence that can survive the gross body's death.

A second path involved the study of alchemy, the art of transforming

---

Zhuang Zi: the second Daoist classic text, named after a sage of this name

"Standing by the deep valley makes you think deep; Scaling the heights makes you aim high."
—*Book of Yi Xun*

Deity from a Daoist temple, where immortals are worshipped to secure blessings.

qi: vital life force in individuals and in nature

such substances as mercury and gold into an outer elixir (*wai-tan*) that can, when ingested, give birth to an "inner child" whose body and soul are invincible to decay or death. Doubtless the Daoist mystics and alchemists who lived in secluded retreats contributed to the development of Chinese science and medicine as well as to the martial arts traditions, all of which applied Daoist terms and theories to specific and more worldly endeavors. **Religious Daoism** also focused on temples dedicated to the divine immortals, who were called upon to help in practical matters such as making the rain fall and helping with the harvest or in vanquishing troublesome spirits.

religious Daoism: tradition devoted to attaining individual immortality through alchemical infusions or meditative practices

Daoism Traditions: Basic Beliefs

Philosophical Daoism evolved from the *Daodejing* and through subsequent thinkers, and, indeed, certain basic ideas from this elite tradition remain important across East Asia. First, there is in Daoism the "organic" notion that humanity is interconnected in a web of interacting natural forces, some visible, some unseen, all shifting and reversing direction when they reach their apex. The opposing yet complementary yin-yang forces became the means of comprehending and analyzing the universe and its effect on human destiny. Reality is best perceived through this interconnection, for in this movement the dynamic power of the mysterious and determining Dao can be discerned from moment to moment. The classic text describing "the state of the moment" is the *Yi-Jing*, and it has helped East Asians determine the various combinations of yin and yang forces at work in a given setting. Perhaps Song-era landscape paintings influenced by Daoism best convey to outsiders this sense of human beings finding their proper place in the vast natural world: Amid the great mountains and flowing waters, humans—inevitably dwarfed by the landscape—can find transcendent harmony.

philosophical Daoism: tradition articulating path to harmony for individuals and society based on understanding and flowing with natural forces

The second central Daoist notion is that some individuals can attain a state of ultimate transformation, transcending mortality via alchemical, dietary, or meditative practices that impart the power to know and control unseen forces. The human condition is thus one of great positive potential; the human body is a potentially perfectible vessel, even though those who attain immortality are few. Here, Daoists join with Confucians in seeing the world as redeemable through human agency, with nature occupying a dual role as humanity's true home and teacher. In China, then, what many other religions refer to as secular is seen as sacred.

The third Daoist conviction is that the pursuit of simplicity is essential for spiritual development as well as for the betterment of society. Only the "natural person" who "goes with the flow" (wu-wei), avoiding unnatural action, can find the truth, and only a society whose citizens live in a simple manner can find true peace and justice. Daoism thus, with Buddhism,

A recluse in the mountains. Hermits like the one in this fourteenth-century Chinese painting looked to nature for inspiration and as a source of primal energy (qi).

Path to Spiritual Transformation in Religious Daoism

MYRIAD THINGS

to the

↓↓↓

THREE

essence (*jing*), life energy (*qi*)
(*each "fixed" through alchemical practices*)

to the

↓↓

TWO

yin and yang in perfect harmony
(*through taming the thought processes via meditation*)

to the

ONE

a state of eternal union with the Dao

provided a counterculture to the Confucian establishment, one that served those who wished to withdraw from society or to critique the excesses of those in power, and even, at times, bolstering a rebel group's intention to overthrow the regime.

State Religion: The First Confucian Epoch (220 BCE–200 CE)

The first full unification of China—from central Asia to the eastern coast—was brought about by the first Qin emperor, who instituted a central bureaucracy and state religion, both designed to promote social unity by harmonizing the forces of nature with imperial rule. China's first emperor, though making good on many of his lofty ambitions, obsessively sought personal immortality through Daoist alchemy and ruthlessly suppressed viewpoints he considered deviant. His Mandate of Heaven lasted only fifteen years (221–206 BCE). Many later Chinese emperors would act as though, and even assert, they were divine.

The next unification of China occurred under the Han, who established an imperial university and examination system (121 BCE) that was based exclusively on Confucian teachings and texts. By the later Han (ca. 175 CE) the content of the Five Confucian Classics had been officially established for the first time. Synthesizing

TEACHINGS OF RELIGIOUS WISDOM: Daoist

The need for individuals who seek to understand the universe to travel to mountains and rivers to discuss ultimate principles is conveyed in this parable by the great Daoist sage Zhuang Zi.

A frog in a well, restricted in his environment, is unable to talk about the ocean. A summer insect, confined to its season, cannot talk about ice. A poor village scholar, restricted by his learning, cannot discuss the Dao. A person can find spiritual truth only by leaving his home cliffs and riverbanks and gazing upon the mighty ocean. Only then can the seeker perceive his own place and begin to understand the Great Dao.

—Zhuang Zi

Source: Adapted from D. Howard Smith, ed., *The Wisdom of the Taoists* (New York: New Directions, 1980), pp. 82–83.

---

treatises drawing on them guided the spiritual cultivation of Chinese life thereafter. Once fixed in literary form and connected with the authority of Confucius, the **Five Classics** provided the literati of subsequent centuries with a multidisciplinary and holistic perspective on humanity. The canon comprises the *Yi-Jing* (*Book of Changes*), *Shu Jing* (*Book of Documents*), *Shi Jing* (*Book of Poetry*), and *Li Jing* (*Book of Rites*) and a historical work that records events in early Chinese states for the purpose of assessing blame and praise. The classics promoted a tradition of learning from the past to guide future governance, and they supported the view that for full development, a human must integrate historical, social, political, and metaphysical awareness.

> **Five Classics:** Confucian canon of five works attributed to Master K'ung

The state religion developed in the Han placed the emperor as chief priest, advised by Confucian experts on ritual performance. The integration of Daoist thought in imperial religion was done by specialists who used Daoist techniques to interpret omens in the natural world. On behalf of the kingdom, the emperor alone could sacrifice to the spirits of the departed imperial ancestors; as the Son of Heaven, he revered heaven and earth as his symbolic parents and worshipped the primary cosmic spirits. The emperor held the Confucian Mandate of Heaven as long as he acted for the well-being of the empire; earthquakes, eclipses, and unusual weather were interpreted as signs that heaven might be withdrawing its mandate.

Being Human: The Individual, the Family, and the Ancestors

The Confucian worldview fostered a sense of the person as at the center of multiple relationships, the most fundamental determined by the individual's gender, generational location in the family, and status in the empire. The individualism that dominates the West and has spread across the globe through modernization is quite the opposite from this East Asian understanding. According to the norms of filial piety, the young owe obedience to parents, women to men, citizens to rulers.

The Confucian vision is that society will be in maximum harmony if individuals mute their individualistic desires to conform to the dictates of the Five Hierarchical Relationships, listed earlier. The ideal was for all the family to benefit in old age from the reciprocities that required their deference earlier in life and to have their political obedience rewarded by heaven's blessings. To support this understanding, Daoism contributed the belief that since human beings are a combination of heaven (*yang*) and earth (*yin*), which in their exact balance determine gender, personality, and health, they must pursue harmony in their social relations and so respect these primary relations.

All persons are also seen as benefiting after death from the Confucian ordering of life, since the living descendants are expected to attend to all the necessary rites to ensure their best possible destiny in the afterlife. Indigenous beliefs going back to the Shang era (1500 BCE) later merged with Buddhist notions to create a composite (and not completely integrated) understanding of the individual's fate after death. What emerged in classical China (and was accepted in Korea and Japan, too) was a belief in the concept of *karma* as known from Buddhism and an understanding that after death all souls undergo processing in a netherworld. Here divine magistrates carefully calculate karma by means of rigorous bookkeeping methods and then send the soul on to its proper destiny. In this way indigenous Chinese and Buddhist ideas coexisted in harmony.

Buddhist rituals for manipulating the death passage were developed throughout East Asia; in China, institutional Daoism created these rites, as well. In Japan, the great Buddhist monasteries included within their vast estates sites for family graves where the burial remains are kept and where ritual offerings can be made for departed kin.

In conception and in practice, then, ancestors live on in the East Asian family's presence and receive ongoing ritual attention: in the grave, in an ancestral tablet

Modern Chinese family grave site in Singapore, sited and designed in accordance with the principles of feng shui. Here family members gather twice yearly to feast and make offerings to their ancestors.

(located in the home altar or clan temple), and potentially in the underworld, especially in the first years after death. The Korean and Chinese practice of burning paper replicas of items considered useful in the underworld is thought to send relief to loved ones who are waiting out an intermediate state before reincarnation.

By the end of the Han, after centuries of state support, Confucian ethics centered on hierarchy and mutual obligation had thoroughly permeated Chinese society through proverbs, storytelling, theater, and songs. The key elements of the "diffuse religion" were widely shared and had come to include the notions of yin-yang theory, geomancy (*feng shui*), the major deities of the pantheon, and the understanding of souls going to an afterlife. The Confucian literati were also convinced that they could unite the society around a common ritual discipline, with ancestor rites the universal and civilizing norm. The early Confucian sage Master Xun explicitly recognized that people had different views of these rites when he wrote:

> Among gentlemen, rites for the dead are taken as the way of man;
> Among the common people, they are taken as matters involving demons.[2]

Development of the Multiple Traditions in Post-Han China, Korea, and Japan

We now move into the fractured China of the post-Han centuries (220–617), a time when the Confucian tradition so tied to Han rule fell out of power, and at just the time when Buddhist missionaries arrived and secured a permanent place in China for their faith. It is in this period, as well, that Japan and Korea enter the region's religious history.

Arrival of Buddhism

The transplantation of Buddhism from India into East Asia is one of the greatest cultural conquests in world history, matched in importance only by the conversion to Christianity of the peoples of Europe and the Americas and the conversion to Islam by many peoples of Eurasia. Buddhist monks reached China on the Silk Road through central Asia by 120 CE and later over the sea routes. Once established in China's major urban and cultural centers, Buddhism spread to Korea by 372 and then to Japan from Korea by 552.

Mahayana Buddhism entered Asia through merchants and missionary monks but became firmly established everywhere owing to the patronage of emperors

With a sacred mushroom in his pocket, a Daoist immortal plays his flute in paradise.

and aristocracy. Most East Asians came to believe in karma and worshipped the Buddha and celestial bodhisattvas. Many eventually accepted enlightenment as the highest spiritual goal.

Chinese literati from the beginning recognized Buddhism's deviance from Confucian values and criticized it on several grounds, including its rejection of family life and service to one's kin and the worship of deities who originated from "barbarian" peoples outside China. The Buddhist ideal of monastic retreat for personal enlightenment was construed as an antisocial behavior. But in splintered China after the fall of the Han, the Confucian literati had little state backing or power. In Korea and Japan, the literati tradition itself was newly introduced; Buddhist monks and nuns, however, still had to win over supporters of the local gods, whose priests attributed national misfortune and natural disasters at this time to the nation's acceptance of Buddhism.

These Confucian anti-Buddhist arguments would be recycled at various times, but for almost all of its first 500 years in East Asia, Buddhism was widely and deeply incorporated into the region's religious life, finding support in the imperial courts and eventually among all segments of society, from philosophers to farmers. As time went on, Chinese, Korean, and Japanese monks would formulate their own interpretations of the many Buddhist teachings, creating distinctive East Asian schools of textual interpretation and ritual practices.

The Institutional Development of Daoism

Another effect of Buddhism's rise to prominence was to motivate the hitherto-disparate adherents of Daoism to systematize their texts and teachings and to create institutions modeled after Buddhist monasteries. The regularized meditative regimes and elaborate rituals that eventually developed in the Daoist monasteries gave individuals many avenues for being Daoist in their spiritual development and for propitiating local gods.

By 300, there were several branches of religious Daoism that had formalized early practices. Guo Hong (283–363) was the most prominent figure, known for his seeking to harmonize the tradition with Confucianism. Beginning with the notion that heaven's greatest creation is life itself, he argued that pursuing longevity and immortality must be the greatest human goal. Guo prescribed a very specific path to that goal, based on moral goodness, social service, and alchemy utilizing two metals: gold (which neither corrodes nor diminishes if buried or melted) and cinnabar (a red mercury ore that keeps changing as long as it is heated). This "inner alchemy" culminated in the practitioner's ingesting the perfectly refined substances, reversing Lao Zi's formula of creation, ending in oneness with the cosmos, as in the nearby box.

Revived Daoism competed with Buddhism for favor at the imperial courts, and devotees among the emperors spread the reformed and newly organized tradition across China. The new monastic orders strengthened Daoist traditions. In 471, Master Lu Xinjing (406–77) completed the first cataloging and organization of the

Daoist scriptures. He found 1,226 texts for inclusion in this canon, which he called *The Three Caves.* Later commentaries expanded the tradition's literature by thousands of additional works. Organized Daoism never penetrated Korea or Japan through monasticism, but organized Buddhism did. We now turn to this important cultural export from China.

Early Korean Buddhism

For the first millennium of the Korean state, Buddhism dominated the spiritual formation of the nation. Mahayana Buddhism entered the Korean peninsula through missions by Chinese monks. The Chinese monk Shundao ordained the first Korean monks in 384, and by 554 its monks and artisans had brought Buddhism to Japan along with a wave of Korean immigrants.

From roughly 700 onward, the Korean version of the classical Buddhist formula of "state-protected Buddhism" was in place. That is, the state protected the tradition in return for monks performing rituals designed to benefit the state. Lavish patronage enabled Buddhism to flourish; all the Chinese scholastic schools were introduced, and Koreans journeyed to China, where some became influential monks. In Korea, the scholarly assimilation of the faith led not to competition but to attempts to find common ground. As a result, under the Silla dynasty, Korean Mahayana Buddhism became the most ecumenical in Asia.

Religion Under the Early Japanese Imperial State: Buddhism and Shinto

In Japan, as elsewhere, Buddhism began among the elite, who saw in it a means to unite a fragmented land. Indeed, it was under the royal sponsorship of Prince Shotoku (d. 622) that Buddhism became the state religion. By 741, an edict called for officials to establish a Buddhist monastery and temple in many Japanese provinces, enroll at least twenty monks and ten nuns, and recite texts and perform rituals for the benefit of emperor and state.

But Buddhism was not the only foreign belief system to shape the development of Japan: Confucian texts and teachers from China and Korea were also influential in the early courts. A seventh-century reform established a Confucian bureaucracy modeled after that of China. Daoist ideas of natural harmony and energy flow, both in the environment and within the person, along with

The eight immortals of Daoism, depicted in a Qing dynasty hanging scroll, with the Three Stars and the Queen Mother of the West. These were the chief divinities enshrined in Daoist temples from the Ming period onward.

yin-yang analysis, were part of this broad cultural influence. Neither Daoist monasteries nor Daoist monks ever existed. Moreover, the Japanese never ceased to worship their own distinct divinities, believing the islands themselves to have been established by these native deities, the *kami*, who remain eternally present. This religious tradition is called **Shinto**.

Shinto: indigenous religion of Japan that reveres native deities, including the Emperor

The Shinto Pantheon of Japan

In many respects, the Shinto tradition in Japan shares basic assumptions and practices regarding deities found throughout East Asia. Shamanism also developed in Japan, because its mediums gave the community access to the gods as well as to their departed ancestors. Pilgrimages to mountains thought to be divine abodes were common. However, as Shinto mythology developed, it was adapted, systematized, and disseminated by the early state. These accounts portrayed Japan as a unique spiritual territory filled with the distinctive deities called **kami**. The existence of an extensive set of legends focused on the kami enabled the Shinto priests to enshrine and relate to a unique pantheon. This helps explain why the Japanese, despite the importation of many other aspects of the country's religious life from China and Korea, were less ready to adopt Chinese deities and folk traditions.

kami: Japanese deity associated with places, certain animals, and the emperor

The Shinto pantheon is headed by **Amaterasu**, the kami of the sun, credited in Japanese myth with having aided in the creation of the country and with being a progenitor of the royal family. Other kami exist in profusion. Some are associated with the natural forces of wind, thunder, lightning, and rain; some are thought to dwell in natural objects, such as mountains, rivers, trees, and rocks; some are ancestral spirits; and some dwell in certain animals, such as cows and foxes. Exponents of Shinto emphasize the "this-worldly" and positive perception of life, society, and nature that their indigenous faith has imparted. Shinto shrines often display mirrors as symbols of Amaterasu and for their symbolic meaning: Free from dust and capable of reflecting

Amaterasu: kami of the sun; progenitor of Japanese imperial line

Wood-block print of the sun goddess Amaterasu, legendary progenitor of the Japanese people.

Amaterasu: Kami of the Sun

In Shinto mythology, a primordial couple creates the physical world and the numerous deities who inhabit it. Most important among them were the moon goddess, a male earth god, and his sister the sun goddess, Amaterasu. In the earliest myths, distressed by her brother's impertinence and rudeness, Amaterasu hid in a cave, darkening the world. Only after the other kami gathered offerings, put on entertainments, and attracted her with a mirror did she restore light to the world. The reformed earth god and his ally, the kami of Izumo prefecture, then blessed the people of the islands of Japan. A grandson of Amaterasu, having received training from the gods and blessings from the Izumo kami, was designated the divine ruler of the nation, and he established the chief shrine for Amaterasu on the seashore at Ise, with a mirror as her symbol. Most Shinto shrines include a mirror, where devotees can honor the sun goddess.

images with natural clarity, these symbolize the Shinto ideals of purity and brilliance. In the modern period, the state regulated and reformed Shinto for it to become, as we shall see, a vehicle for modernization.

East Asian Religions in the Classical Era (645–1800 CE)

Classical Imperial China (645–1271 CE)

With the great unification of the T'ang Dynasty (618–907), when China ended four centuries of fragmentation, Buddhism enjoyed extraordinary development in East Asia. At first, Buddhism in northern China appealed to the non-Han conquerors and in the south succeeded through popular and charismatic monastic preachers. But in the T'ang era, more unified, panregional monastic networks developed into seven doctrinal schools; each school took as its highest authoritative source a different text that was thought to contain the Buddha's highest teachings. Chinese Buddhists organized the confusing welter of texts from India.

T'ang China, with its capital in Chang'an (modern Xi'an), was the world's most advanced civilization. Living within the high city walls were merchants from across the Eurasian world; distributed in neighborhoods were Nestorian Christians, Hindus, Manicheans, Zoroastrians, and Muslims. These resident aliens mixed with Buddhists and Daoists, who had their own numerous monasteries and temples. The wealth from trade, efficient taxation, and imperial patronage underwrote a golden age that found expression in all the fine arts while spreading Buddhist influences and

"The belief is that the new year is given to us by . . . the kami of years. What comes from the realm of the kami is inherently good. . . . So we look out upon the possibilities of the new year, and we want to purify our blunders and cast off whatever evil influences we may have accumulated in the old year."

—Shinto priest Uesugi Guji (1987)

SOURCE: John K. Nelson, *A Year in the Life of a Shinto Shrine* (Seattle: University of Washington Press, 1996), p. 207.

religious practices across the empire and into both Korea and Japan. Adventurous Chinese monks, such as the renowned Xuan Zang (d. 664), even traveled to India for fourteen years in search of additional texts and teachers; Chinese emperors likewise lavished patronage on brahmins from India, who were reputed to be masters of longevity medicine.

This pluralistic, tolerant world was disrupted in 845, when edicts by Emperor Wu-zong forced 250,000 Buddhist monastics to return to lay life and confiscated all but forty-nine monasteries throughout the empire. Officials destroyed sacred texts by the tens of thousands and melted down Buddha images for the imperial mint. This emperor was partly motivated by considerations of manpower and finances: With the success of Buddhism, more lands were being donated to the monastic community, thereby losing their taxable status; and ever more men and women were joining Buddhist orders, exempting themselves both from taxation and, in the case of the men, from military service. Wu-zong's second motivation was religious. He was an ardent Daoist eager to advance the tradition's popularity.

Although this aggressively anti-Buddhist policy was reversed by the next emperor, the damage was quite severe: Buddhism's predominance was drastically reduced, and Buddhism was never again to dominate China's religious landscape.

The later T'ang was a time of resurgent Confucianism. This tradition had continued to guide the familial life of commoners, and Confucius himself was used as a symbol of national unity. The groundwork was being laid for a brilliant assimilation of Buddhism and Daoism.

Song Dynasty: The Second Epoch of Confucianism (960–1279)

The so-called Second Epoch of Confucianism erected for the literati a philosophical tradition that rivaled Buddhism and Daoism, reinvigorating the older ideology of human relatedness based on hierarchy, age, and gender. Neo-Confucianism moved to the center of Chinese religious life, later influencing Korea and Japan, as well.

Song dynasty administrators restored mastery of Confucian learning as the basis for winning a position in its burgeoning civil service. This measure, coupled with relative neglect of Buddhism by the authorities, provided a strong inducement for a return to the Confucian classics as a subject for study, further scholarship, and teaching. As the best minds of the day once again were drawn into reinterpreting the indigenous tradition, private academies that instilled virtue and erudition flowered.

Zhu Xi: great Neo-Confucian master who integrated elements of Buddhism and Daoism into Confucianism

neo-Confucianism: tradition seeking to harmonize early Confucian humanism with elements of Daoism and Buddhism

The Confucian tradition's great "Second Master" was **Zhu Xi** (also written Chu Hsi) (1130–1200). The works compiled and commented on by him, entitled *Jinsi Lu* ("Reflections of Things at Hand"), were immensely influential. Zhu Xi gave students a curricular order in which to study the classics and powerfully articulated long-standing polemics against Buddhism and Daoism. Zhu Xi also added brilliant reinterpretations of Confucian doctrines, thus codifying the thoroughgoing system of thought that has been labeled **neo-Confucianism** in Western parlance.

Core Confucianism: The Five Relationships According to Mencius

Mencius developed Confucian social theory to imagine the human community living in sustained harmony when these central relationships were established and nurtured.

Relationship	Principles of the Relationship
son and father	filial piety ↔ paternal example
minister and ruler	obedience ↔ righteousness
wife and husband	obedience ↔ faithful dominance
young and old	respect ↔ precedence and example
friend and friend	mutuality and trust (*hsin*)

Despite its apparent criticism directed against Daoism and Buddhism, the neo-Confucians in fact were strongly influenced by both. Of equal importance in securing the success of neo-Confucianism was Zhu Xi's compilation of a ritual manual that imparted Confucian procedures and cogent rationales for all life-cycle rites, clearly giving non-Buddhist and non-Daoist practices around which the majority of Chinese ordered their lives. This ritual text, like the *Jinsi Lu*, was influential across East Asia.

Neo-Confucianism's strength was that it provided both the individual and the state with a convincing philosophy for understanding the world. Song thinkers argued that Confucianism was built on the interconnected unity of humanity with the natural world. They tried to understand perceived phenomena through a series of polarities that associated yin-yang forces within the triad of heaven, earth, and humanity. The neo-Confucian philosophers emphasized that education was needed to perfect human awareness of li and that inner meditative cultivation (a borrowing from Buddhism), which Zhu Xi called "investigating the nature of things," was needed to perfect the qi. Almost all the neo-Confucians assumed the reality of karma as one of life's causal agents.

Neo-Confucian Theories of Order, Hierarchy, and Relatedness

The Confucian notion of the self that became reinforced in family norms and in state law is decidedly not that of the isolated individual but of the person as "a center of relatedness." This concept can be understood as a series of concentric circles, with the assumption that to reach their highest potential, persons must act harmoniously within their families, local communities, and states and with heaven beyond. This scheme clearly implies that engagement in culture and community is necessary for both the person and humanity overall to flourish. As the Confucian classic, the *Great Learning*, states:

> The ancients who wished to bring order to their states would first regulate their families. Those who wished to regulate their families would first cultivate

"The ideal sage is one who is first in worrying about the world's troubles and last in enjoying its pleasures."

—Fan-Chung-Yen (989–1052)

SOURCE: Arthur Wright, *Buddhism in Chinese History* (Stanford, CA: Stanford University Press, 1959), p. 43.

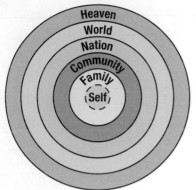

Two-dimensional representation of Confucian model of the individual integrated in expanding realms of connection.

their personal lives. Those who wished to cultivate their personal lives would first rectify their minds. Those who wished to rectify their minds would first make their intentions sincere.

Those who wished to make their intentions sincere would first extend their knowledge. The extension of knowledge consists of the investigation of things. . . . Only when the personal life is cultivated, the family will be regulated; when the family is regulated, the state will be in order; and when the state is in order, there will be peace throughout the world.[3]

The elaboration of meditative practices and multidisciplinary studies by the neo-Confucian masters established a rich tradition designed to develop the individual's integral relations with each circle (see illustration). Such later figures as Zhang Zai (1020–77) went on to combine this concentric conception with the Daoist ideal of finding "full humanity" by merging with the cosmos:

Heaven is my father and Earth is my mother, and even such a small creature as I finds an intimate place in their midst. Therefore that which fills the universe I regard as my body and that which directs the universe I consider as my nature. All people are my brothers and sisters, and all things are my companions.[4]

The popular convergence of the classical traditions in late traditional China was inspired by Zhu Xi, Zhang Zai, and other figures who sought harmony by learning from all orientations. The "diffuse religion" still extant in contemporary East Asia stems from their brilliant syntheses of ancient sources.

The Development of Buddhism, Daoism, and Confucianism in Korea and Japan

In Korea, Buddhism flourished under imperial support once the country had been united under the Silla dynasty (668–918). Ties to Chinese Buddhism were strong, and almost all of the Chinese schools had Korean counterparts. Korean monks were notable in China, and their commentaries on major texts were studied in both Japan and Tibet. Yet over time, Korean monks were most successful at finding harmony rather than division in their development of the tradition from the various schools and teachings.

Religion in the Koryo dynasty (918–1392) continued in this mode. Uniquely Korean was the centrality of Son (Ch'an/Zen) Buddhism, which was to become the most influential school in subsequent Korean Buddhist history. It assimilated the scholastic schools introduced from China and closely adapted Buddhism to Korean culture.

In Japan, the assimilation of Buddhism had ecumenical aspects as well. It had continued strongly when the capital was moved to Kyoto in 800 CE, as various elements

Buddhism and Neo-Confucianism in a Still-Popular Ming Tale

The *Journey to the West* (or "monkey story"), written by the Confucian scholar Wu Cheng-en (1500–1582), is a prime example of the Ming-era harmonization of the "three faiths." It recounts the journey of the great Buddhist monk Xuan Zang (d. 664) to search for texts in India. In this dangerous quest, he is assisted by the Monkey King, Sun Wukong, a figure from the Chinese folk pantheon. While ostensibly the account of the great Buddhist monk's journey, recurring incidents in the long tale (spanning four hefty volumes in English translation) are employed to teach self-discipline—a personal trait valued by both traditions—to the Monkey King and Confucian wisdom to the monk. In many episodes, the success of Xuan Zang's mission depends on the Monkey King's aid and on the monk's timely learning how common people think about the ways of the world. Translated into opera and folk ballads, the monkey story became one of China's most popular narratives, its major characters defining important personality stereotypes while conveying the pattern of Confucianism dominating the literati culture of the Ming dynasty.

The Monkey King leads the monk Xuan Zang and other companions, illustrating a scene from *Journey to the West*.

of Mahayana Buddhism and Daoist theories of yin-yang imported from China were effectively integrated with Shinto practices.

The later Kamakura era (1185–1333) ushered in almost 700 years of rule by military leaders who usurped the power of the emperor and established a social system closely akin to that of European feudalism. This period was one of widespread contact with China, as trade grew and Buddhist monks were instrumental in bringing the two schools that had survived the persecutions in post-T'ang China: Pure Land and Ch'an/Zen. Notable monks of this era also brought neo-Confucian learning, literature, and the arts to Japan.

The disorder and suffering in the Kamakura also led to dramatic changes in Japanese religions, especially Buddhism. It was widely believed that the world had entered into a period of **mappo**, or decline, in which human capacity for spiritual

mappo: Buddhist doctrine of world in decline

pursuit had become degraded. This perception was used to justify new interpretations of Buddhism appropriate for this degraded age. Thus, the Kamakura religious leaders in Japan established the framework for subsequent schools that remained relatively stable until the early modern era.

The most popular Buddhist school was Pure Land, and in Chapter 7 we encountered its polemical advocate, Shinran (1173–1262). Shinran and other Pure Land exponents taught that an individual's salvation was completely in the hands of the Buddha of the Pure Land, whom they called Amida, from the Sanskrit name Amitabha. They emphasized the practice of repeating Amida's name and the belief that faith alone could achieve nirvana realization in the mappo era. Shinran ended the requirement of monastic celibacy, and Pure Land remains the largest Buddhist school in Japan today.

The second new school established during the Kamakura era was Zen, and it, too, was brought from China, by two Japanese monks, Eisai (1141–1215) and Dogen (1200–1253). In adopting sitting meditation, mind puzzles (koans), and unusual teaching methods, Zen masters created an innovative lineage of Buddhist practice. It also was very traditionalist, however, in rejecting the concept of mappo and resisting the other schools' radical simplification of Buddhism into mere ritual repetition and reliance on faith. Zen teachers insisted that each individual had to win his or her own salvation on the meditation mat through persistence and self-power alone.

Another remarkable Buddhist leader of this era was **Nichiren** (1222–82), a monk who opposed the Pure Land schools and in fact all the other Buddhist orders. He attributed the decline in Japanese life to the neglect of the *Lotus Sutra*, which he viewed as containing the supreme teaching. The Nichiren-shu advocated chanting the name of this text as the means for personal transformation as well as national renewal. (It is a practice continued to the present day in the **Soka Gakkai**, a modern Nichiren-derived school that now spans the globe.)

In the Kamakura era, ideas regarding Shinto-Buddhist accommodation were heard from both sides: Shinto exponents argued that the Buddhas and bodhisattvas were really indigenous gods, and the Buddhists built Shinto shrines in their monastic courtyards, consistent with the view that the kami were in fact protectors or bodhisattvas. This urge to harmonize the various spiritual traditions was one that Japan shared with Korea.

Nichiren: monk who founded new Buddhist school based on primacy of the *Lotus Sutra*

Soka Gakkai: twentieth-century offshoot from Nichiren school, now a global Buddhist organization seeking world peace

East Asian Religions in the Late Classical Era (1400–1800)

The four centuries preceding the modern era show few religious innovations across East Asia. It was a time when philosophies of interest to the literati were more fully commented on, printed, and disseminated, as in the case of neo-Confucianism in Japan. For Buddhism, this era is characterized by elaborations of traditional practices (as illustrated in the box titled "Selections from a Chinese Buddhist Merit Account Sheet" in Chapter 7), and the modest growth of monastic networks. Due to the unsteadiness in both state support and spiritual vitality, Chinese Buddhism produced no special developments; in Korea there were prominent attempts to reduce the political power of Buddhism.

Across East Asia, the diffuse religion remained central, as ancestor ritualism, local cults to important deities, and the role of the spirit mediums defined the religious field in cities and villages alike. For Ming-era China (1368–1644), the popular text *Feng Shen Yan-yi* ("*The Canonization of the Gods*") was especially influential in promulgating the idea of an orderly pantheon of Chinese divinities in a hierarchy that included Buddhas, immortals, gods, and local spirits. Throughout China, a standard organization for the state's official religion was fixed in each province. There would be a Confucian temple with major disciples, a military temple featuring the war god Guan Yu and other notable heroes, and a **city god**, who supervises all the village earth gods.

> **city god:** Chinese deity who oversees a city's spirits and to whom every family's kitchen god reports at year's end

"The Unity of the Three Traditions": Late Ming to Early Qing Eras in China

The Chinese emphasis on harmony was also extended to "the unity of the **three faiths**" (*san-jiao heyi*, still a widely used phrase), meaning Confucianism, Daoism, and Buddhism. Many philosophers who were exclusively committed to one of these faiths still argued that their tradition was superior in answering the fundamental spiritual questions. But more popular were teachers such as Jiao Hong (1540–1620), who regarded all three teachings as in fact "a single teaching," stating that each merely uses separate language to articulate its truth and that all three could and should be believed. There were also other expressions of this era's delicate balance of combination and compartmentalization between these faiths:

> **three faiths:** Chinese grouping of the three great traditions (Confucianism, Daoism, and Buddhism)

> Use Buddhism to rule the mind, Daoism to rule the body, Confucianism to rule the world.[5]
>
> —*Emperor Xiao Zong (1163–1189)*

> Although the Three Teachings are different, in the arguments they put forward, they are One.[6]
>
> —*Liu Mi (active 1324)*

> If someone is a Confucian, give him Confucius; if he is a Daoist, give him Lao Zi; if he is a Buddhist, give him Shakyamuni; if he isn't any of them, give him their unity.[7]
>
> —*Lin Zhao'en (1517–98)*

Among Confucians who most powerfully conveyed this ecumenical ethos was Wang Yangming (1472–1529), whose view of the "true gentleman" was based on the assumption that everyone can know the good and that "self-perfection" means knowing this goodness to the maximum. Wang argued, in language mirroring the "all beings have the Buddha nature" doctrine of Mahayana Buddhism, that all humans have the potential to achieve self-perfection, since all share a primordial awareness:

> Forming one body with Heaven, Earth, and the myriad things is not only true of the great man. Even the heart-mind of the small man is no different. . . . Therefore when he sees a child about to fall into the well, he cannot help feeling alarm and commiseration.[8]

Buddhism by the end of the Ming dynasty (1368–1644) had worked out its permanent place in Chinese civilization, as its monastic leaders taught Buddhist doctrine in ways to ensure that there would never be another imperial persecution. We thus find influential teachers such as Chu-hong (1535–1615) preaching that the essence of Buddhism was social activism as expressed through charity and moral action. He also emphasized that to be a filial child and a loyal subject was to be a "good Buddhist." This view was expressed by many subsequent Chinese Buddhists.

The Ming dynasty also saw the beginning of regular contact with Europe, first with the Portuguese in 1514. With these traders and then with growing numbers of missionaries, the Chinese found little to admire and much resented the "barbaric manners" of most of their guests. In this early era of small-scale contact, failure to institute good relations with the Europeans or to attempt to understand the world beyond China set up the problematic and confrontational geopolitical environment of the colonial era.

One scene from the *Shengzhi tu*, carved in marble in a Beijing temple, here depicting how a son should show filial piety (xiao) to his ailing mother.

The Qing dynasty (1644–1912) brought outsiders again in control of China, this time in the form of the Manchurians, who continued most traditional state administration. Confucian imperial ritual remained central to the state, and mastery of the classics was the basis for the selection of the literati who ran it.

Confucian ideas and practices throughout China were strengthened by the *Sheng-zhi tu* ("*Pictures of the Sage's Traces*"), captioned accounts of Confucius' life and exemplary tales of ethical practices. The stories appeared on stone tablets installed in temples (Daoist as well as Buddhist), on silk paintings, and in inexpensive and widely disseminated block-printed books. Many versions of the great teacher appeared, some with Confucius as a human being living an exemplary ethical life, others described miracles and magic, while still others emphasized the sage's commending great ritual exertions. Many of these publications were also exported to Japan, where they influenced the efflorescence of Confucian studies and related arts in the Tokugawa era (1600–1868).

Zen and the Shoguns (Twelfth to Nineteenth Centuries)

In Japan during medieval and early modern times, there were no Daoist temples competing with institutional Buddhism or Shinto shrines, nor did the deities of "diffuse Chinese popular religion" find their way across the waters. Instead, Shinto theologians presented the nation's deities in a uniquely Japanese pantheon, although the relationships between them varied by region and were not thoroughly systematized nationwide until the modern era.

Zen Buddhism, however, also exerted a strong ecumenical influence in this period. The Zen school's strong relationship with China fostered studies in both the texts of Daoism and the Confucian classics. It also promoted the acceptance of the idea that Daoist concepts and Confucian morality could be combined. Zen, the vehicle for Japan's cultural elite, adopted art forms derived from China, but Japanese masters soon took them to new levels of originality in such fields as ink painting, poetry, and tea ceremony.

Zen and the other Buddhist schools were closely tied to the ruling elites, who were a source of protection and patronage for their favorite monasteries and teachers. This relationship also led Buddhists then in Japan to vie for support among the factions at the top ranks in society, which most of them tended to view uncritically. The habit of overlooking discrepancies between Buddhist teachings and rulers' practices continued right into the modern period, when most monks were more concerned about accommodation with the elite than with reforming Japanese society or preventing war.

The Shoguns Persecute Christians and Promote Buddhism

Although Buddhism enjoyed official support during most of the shogunate, Nobunaga (1534–82) waged an anti-Buddhist campaign, going so far as to burn the great monastery center on Mount Hiei, outside Kyoto, where Japanese Buddhism was first established. It was dislike of Buddhism that probably led Nobunaga to be receptive to the first Jesuit missionaries, giving Christianity more early support than it received anywhere else in East Asia. Much to the chagrin of the European missionaries, however, most Japanese had trouble seeing in Christianity anything but an obscure form of Buddhism. Catholic rituals appeared to be similar to certain monastic rites, and the concept of a heavenly Lord whose son became incarnate to serve humanity was not unlike Mahayana Buddhism's doctrine of the cosmic Buddha whose sons, the compassionate bodhisattvas, also served humanity.

But squabbles that developed among European Franciscans, Jesuits, and later Protestants, as well as some missionary attempts to manipulate Japanese politics in the name of their home countries, convinced Iyesu, the first Tokugawa shogun, to outlaw Christianity in 1606. When in 1616 he expelled all remaining missionaries, there were already an estimated 300,000 Japanese converts. The next decades saw attempts by the Japanese state to extirpate Christianity. Officials penned vigorous attacks against Christian beliefs. Some pointed out how it clashed with the region's "commonsense" spiritual understandings; others questioned the logic of a theology in which a reputedly omnipotent, benevolent God would allow "original sin"; still other tracts objected to biblical passages that undermine loyalty to kin and ruler.

Other efforts at removing Christianity were gruesome, and many converts who would not recant their faith were tortured. A Christian-government conflict in 1637–38 that resulted in over 37,000 deaths confirmed for its Japanese opponents the disruptive potential of the foreign faith. From this time onward, too, every Japanese family was required by law to be registered with a Buddhist temple, in an effort to regularize ties with Buddhism and to emphasize that in Tokugawa times being Buddhist was inherently part of being Japanese. (We will see, however, that in the post-Tokugawa era, nationalists argued the reverse, that is, that Buddhism was a "foreign religion" in Japan!)

The Regional Spread of Neo-Confucianism

Neo-Confucian thought spread under the Tokugawa shoguns. Confucianism—long present among scholars, in state ritualism, and as part of Buddhist moral teachings from China—finally found its own strong supporters in a succession of prominent Japanese philosophers, many of whom were not part of the samurai elite. For some, Confucian teachings gave those of lower birth ideals to uphold against the hierarchical system instituted by Japan's hereditary nobility. Unlike in China, the ideals of Confucianism spread among both the merchant class and the samurai as Japanese intellectuals throughout the Tokugawa era studied and defended the positions of all the major neo-Confucian sages. Efforts were also made to rationalize Shinto beliefs with Confucian doctrines.

Spiritual Training for the Religious Elites

By 1600 CE, all the religious traditions of East Asia had developed institutions and courses of training for those wishing to become scholars, ritual masters, or meditative adepts. Although a very small percentage of the entire populations actually were initiated into such disciplines, it is useful to understand something of the spiritual training that the region's different religious leaders (priests, monks, and nuns) had to undertake to fulfill their roles.

Confucianism. Only under the guidelines set forth by the neo-Confucian masters did the literati (*rujia*) tradition acquire its own systematic regime. The first stage of training was "disciplining the body" (*shen-jiao*) by means of the zealous study of the six arts of Confucian education: ritual, music, archery, calligraphy, horsemanship, and mathematics. All were defined very broadly. For example, *ritual* means conducting religious rites as well as mastering the proper ways of eating, walking, and asking questions. The *Analects* provide many instances of seemingly trivial events associated with Confucius, but those events had their use in just this context of providing the sage's life as a model for disciplined training.

Beyond foundational training, all the neo-Confucian subschools called for the "rectification of the heart-mind" and prescribed new practices: discipline manifested by outward zeal in investigating the external world as well as the personal goal of knowing oneself. The aim was to become a perfected person, a *sheng-ren*, who has achieved fully his or her complete human nature. A common practice to realize this is called *quiet sitting*, one that its proponents were adamant on distinguishing from forms of Buddhist or Daoist meditation. This neo-Confucian meditation was not based on stopping discursive thought but on calming the mind from the flow of events, perceiving the goodness of the in-dwelling primal human nature, and becoming aware of selfish desires.

Daoism. Like the Buddhists, Daoists sought a more individualistic "ultimate transformation" through practices that originated in antiquity. For philosophers such as Zhuang Zi, only through the practice of detaching from the mind (*wai-wu*) and ceasing to distinguish separated things could one find union with the Dao. In Zhuang Zi's writings, one also finds cryptic references to a "heart-fast" (*xin-zhai*) that starved the mind of all externalities, allowing one proficient in the practice to forget his senses, ideas, feelings, and wishes and so experience only the primordial and mys-

TALES OF SPIRITUAL TRANSFORMATION: Confucian

The Sage ideal of the Confucian tradition is indicated in a text that prescribes total commitment to truthfulness which, if fully put in practice, can be a path to cosmic harmony.

Only one who is perfectly truthful can give full realization to his human nature; able to give full realization to his human nature, he is then able to give full realization to the human nature of others; able to give full realization to the human nature of others, he is then able to give full realization to the nature of other creatures; able to give this, he can then assist in the transformative and nourishing processes of heaven and earth. If he can assist in the transformative and nourishing powers of heaven and earth, he can then form a triad with heaven and earth.

Source: *Maintaining Perfect Balance*, a neo-Confucian classic, in Daniel Gardiner, *The Four Books* (Indianapolis: Hackett, 2007), p. 124.

terious Dao. When the spiritual adept has reached this stage, the practice of "free and easy wandering" in nature can be fully undertaken. In the traditional poetic expression, one then ascends the cloud vapors, rides the flying dragon, and travels to the infinite. Facing death involves no travail and only blissful transformation.

Shintoism. Until the modern era, Shinto priests of major shrines inherited their positions and learned the rituals from their fathers; thus they were always males from aristocratic families. Over the last 150 years, priests have had to pass a state-prescribed course of training at an institution such as Kokugakuin University, founded for this purpose. The role of the *shinshoku*, as the priests are usually called, involves mastery of the daily gestures of respect offered to the kami, the annual rituals of the shrine, calligraphy, and complex forms of ritual purification. Shinto has never developed any "inner" spiritual practices. For its modern exponents, however, the artful rituals oriented to the deities throughout the seasons offer a means of achieving refined sensitivity and moral transformation.

East Asian Religions in the Early Modern Era

Disruptive European Intrusions

Attired in white robes that symbolize purity, a Shinto priest kneels in the Meiji temple in Tokyo.

Post-Enlightenment colonialism, also called *imperialism*, represents the first modern attempt to establish a global world order. Europeans forced Asian societies to change on European terms, abruptly imposing new ideas, technologies, and institutions that had evolved naturally over many years in Europe. European imperialism caused chaos and crises that undermined most institutions in premodern East Asia, with the organized religions especially subject to disruption and decline. Imperialism's impact in Asia can be likened to that of a strong earthquake, one that levels many structures, leaving only the strongest foundations on which to rebuild.

Understanding the world's religions today requires an awareness of this legacy, for East Asian religions and cultures were decisively altered over this period as never before. Though the effects of colonialism were overwhelmingly destructive, the fusion of older traditions with modern changes led to a number of religious innovations that were compelling and original.

By the beginning of the nineteenth century, European civilization had ascended as the supreme force on the global stage. The Renaissance had transformed Europe with powerful innovations in the intellectual, political, economic, and military spheres. The West's unprecedented sociopolitical dynamism accelerated up through

TEACHINGS OF RELIGIOUS WISDOM: Confucian

The following is the text of a message of Emperor T'ai Tsung to a Korean ruler, returning his thank offering of two young and surpassingly beautiful women, showing his Confucian integrity, intelligence, and grace.

"Go back and say to your master that although beauty and a fair appearance are made much of by men—and truly his gifts are voluptuously beautiful—I pity them, separated from father, mother, and brothers older and younger in their own country. To detain their persons while forgetting their families—to love their fairness while wounding their hearts—this I cannot do."

the eighteenth century, when the major states (Great Britain, Netherlands, Portugal, Spain, Germany) vied, often militarily, to exert their newfound political and economic power around the globe. Internally, of course, Europe was diverse, transformed by its own class and ethnic conflicts, and facing newly arising problems; new ideologies competed with old to provide solutions to these crises. Some of these ideas, too, were exported to Asia.

The emerging nations of Europe were above all self-assured regarding their sense of superiority over Asians in every aspect of life, from morality and intellectual understanding to religion and technology. For many this included belief in the primacy of the white race, and many, too, saw in the march of colonialism a confirmation that Christianity would ultimately triumph on the world stage. Thus, some European leaders felt they were the vehicles of triumphant Christianity, and their merchants were dedicated to making their fortunes through overseas trade, ready to pursue often-risky ventures, and to do so quite ruthlessly.

Colonialism was a brutal enterprise at times. It forcibly changed every regional economy, promoted trafficking in narcotics when the opium trade was profitable, challenged East Asians' fundamental understandings regarding humanity and cosmos through science and Christian missions, and undermined the long-held view of Asia's ruling classes that their civilizations were the world's greatest.

The crisis of colonial encroachment and imperial challenge led the national elites away from their own indigenous traditions and on a forced march directed toward understanding the Western world and its technologies. From about 1850, across the region, the best minds in East Asia chose to learn about the West first and about their own traditions hardly at all, with the result that the Enlightenment mentality, with its revolutionary terms of analysis, entered powerfully into the cultural heritage of modern East Asia. Among a large portion of this Western-influenced elite, agnosticism or atheism replaced belief in their own indigenous spiritual traditions.

It would be wrong, however, to see the history of East Asia as dictated solely by European actors and external forces. There were important internal dynamics at work in Korea, China, and Japan, and the different processes already under way in each shaped their emphatically different destinies under colonialism.

Traumatic Transitions of the Modern Era

The era of colonialism was perceived across Asia as a time of repeated crises. The common terms used to express the peoples' sense of inundation and powerlessness across East Asia convey this: *humiliation* (*chi*) in Chinese, *bitterness* (*hahn*) in Korean, and *patient endurance* (*nin*) in Japanese. For most East Asians, the modern era was a time of trial, though each nation had slightly differing reactions to the experience of modernization. It is essential to appreciate the magnitude of these disruptions to understand the changes in religious life across East Asia.

The Decline of Confucian Ideology and Exponents

The crisis and rapid changes brought by the onslaught of imperialism ended the unchallenged influence of the Confucian elite in China, Korea, and Japan. The Confucian worldview and social ideology were subjected to scathing critiques by the native-born reformers of each nation, who took up the task of saving state sovereignty and attempting to match the wealth, knowledge, and power put on display by the Western imperialists. In addition, many young people abandoned the traditional curriculum to pursue "Western learning," honing their intellectual development by critiquing what they perceived as the disabilities imposed on society under the Confucian tradition. Finally, the fall of the Korean and Chinese states, whose political and economic resources supported Confucianism in many domains, made it certain that this tradition would lose its central place in the region's early modernization.

Confucianism was blamed for every ill visible in the region. The failure to develop modern trade was blamed on the classical ranking of social classes by occupation, which in the Confucian view of the good society placed at the top scholar-officials who administered the bureaucracy and taught in schools; below them were the farmers, followed by artisans, and finally the merchants. Confucius had no respect for merchants, whom he called "parasites," describing them as ever ready to take advantage of others, motivated by greed, and inclined to dishonesty.

The traditional Confucian educational system was also blamed for stifling the nation's technical development, inasmuch as it valued generalists over specialists and rewarded rote memorization and imitation, not independent thinking. Moreover, for the critics, the Confucian view of history as cyclical had made the elite prone to stagnation and disinclined to pursue innovation or progress.

The strongest terms of rejection were directed toward Confucian social norms and, at their center, family relations. The classical formula for social harmony that East Asians had incorporated from the ancient period, as we have discussed, was framed in two triads: the three bonds (between ruler and minister, father and son, and husband and wife) and the three principles (hierarchy, age, gender). Reformers found each of these principles to be an obstacle to modernization in many respects. Individuals who placed loyalty to family first, for example, were unable to extend trust to others as needed in the more impersonal workings of a modern economy. Similarly, filial deference to elders made individuals dependent on the collective family, thwarting the creative thrust toward individuality and encouraging a "Confucian personality" that either (in the young) followed authority blindly or (in the elders) gave too much power to those who were merely of senior rank. All such relationships were seen as stifling innovation. On the national level, reformers saw the "three bonds" as merely serving authoritarian political control. Both East Asian reformers and Western social scientists until the 1970s agreed that Confucianism was the key obstacle to the region's modernization.

A reconsideration of the characteristics fostered by Confucian humanism, however, has revealed that these Confucian elements also played a role in the region's ultimately successful response to the challenges of the postcolonial era. These include, for example, the high emphasis on education, the practice of carefully studying problems before taking action, the expectation that state officials will act for the good of the whole, and the intellectual elite's acceptance of responsibility for the nation's well-being. But what is certain is that the imperial system that supported the Confucian literati tradition was overthrown completely in China and Korea. By contrast, in neighboring Japan, the emperor-led state after 1868 melded nationalism and Confucianism with its own form of colonialism. Whatever Confucianism means exactly in the present day, a break with the past had irrevocably occurred. We must first turn to the important exception of Japan and its distinctive fusion of belief systems: melding modernization with Confucianism in the form of nationalist **neo-Shintoism**.

neo-Shintoism/state Shinto: reformation of Japan's indigenous religion after 1869, with the divine emperor at its center

State and Civil Religion in Japan: Neo-Shintoism

By 1882, a decade and a half after the demise of the shogunate and the restoration of the Japanese monarchy in the person of the Meiji emperor, the Shinto tradition was officially adopted as the state religion. To bring this about, most shrines and temples were integrated into a single system under government supervision. The emperor was revered as a divinity on earth, whose presence was a blessing to the nation. This idea was expressed at the national shrines in the capital and then in rituals regularly conducted in every local shrine as well; Japanese were directed to worship daily facing the emperor in Tokyo, just as Muslims to worship Allah face Mecca. The reformed educational system also centered its curriculum on the sanctity of the emperor, and all citizens were expected to honor him by working for the good of the nation. This was one of the Confucian elements in Japan's modernization.

A constitution adopted in 1889 limited Japanese citizens' freedom to express any opinions critical of Shinto doctrines and practices, especially the imperial ties to the indigenous deities, but it guaranteed religious freedom to followers of other religions as long as they did not undermine Shinto and were loyal to the nation. Those affected included the Buddhist schools and the Christian denominations, which were legalized again in 1863, as well as the "new religion" sects that multiplied throughout the modern era and are discussed later.

Procession bearing the local god (kami) through Kamakura, Japan, during the Spring Festival.

The Meiji state religion, or state-Shinto, can be labeled neo-Shintoist, for it was associated with the religious tradition of ancient origins that reveres the indigenous deities of the Japanese islands. It is also fundamental to see, however, that the "civil religion" constructed around Shintoism by the Meiji elite was thoroughly Confucian in character. It emphasized loyalty to the state, the norm of filial piety, self-sacrifice, and dedication. Moreover, it heralded the contributions of individuals that would be needed to make the modernization of Japan a success. Finally, a Confucian vocabulary was used to define the emperor's and the nation's mission, with special emphasis on the emperor's Mandate of Heaven. Thus, Meiji Japan was the first political entity in East Asia to harness reformed Confucian values to meet the challenges of modernizing and adopting the technologies pioneered in the West.

Institutional Buddhism

As we noted in Chapter 7, institutional Buddhism took root in Asia by way of a monastic system in which monasteries became landlords reliant on lay believers to till the lands and on charitable donations from the faithful. At times of economic hardship or when the state could not extend customary protections, Buddhism declined. In general, the crises of the modern era across East Asia also deprived Buddhism of economic support, of donations, and of individuals who in other eras might have joined a monastic order and contributed to its vitality. Now the most gifted people wanted to learn about the West and to lead their countries in modernizing national industries, governments, and military establishments.

In nineteenth-century China, there were few signs of innovation and few Buddhists who rose to contribute to the national struggles. In Japan's long Tokugawa era (1600–1867), on the other hand, the military leaders supported Buddhism strongly, including the promotion of Buddhist pilgrimage as a means of having the Japanese acquire a sense of national integration. But the Meiji reformers felt it essential to reverse course, both to weaken pro-Buddhist foes and because they believed that Buddhist influences were inimical to Japan's Shinto-centered revitalization.

Zealous attempts in the first Meiji years to prohibit Buddhism outright were abandoned, but the Buddhist tradition sustained considerable damage: From 1871 to 1876, the number of temples throughout Japan was reduced from an estimated 465,000 to 71,000. In 1872, the government decreed that Buddhist monks were free to marry and follow nonvegetarian diets, a move that undermined discipline and popular regard for renunciants in the sangha. The Buddhists successfully rallied support against further acts directed against them, but the Shinto-based nationalism and the state-encouraged challenges to institutional Buddhism forced followers to shift their emphases and re-think their doctrines in light of the changes under way in their society.

The Buddhist establishment after 1876 strove mightily to prove its patriotism and relevance, as a host of writers and lay organizations arose to explain why charges of dis-loyalty and obsolescence were unfounded. Major schools competed to implement Meiji social and national programs, and they, too, fanned the rising flame of anti-Western feelings, supported the successive war efforts (in public statements and with funds), and translated into positive doctrinal terms rationales for imperial expansion.

Compared with elsewhere in Asia, early movements led by Japanese householders to reinterpret Buddhism in terms of modern philosophy were few. Instead, religious reformers were more likely to found their own sects, drawing on doctrines as they liked, without trying to work through the Buddhist establishment.

In Korea, Confucianism was strongly supported in the nineteenth century and Buddhism was increasingly marginalized, as the government also tried to limit the economic power of monastic estates by consolidating schools and seizing lands. State decrees went so far as to prohibit Buddhist monks from setting foot in major cities. Early Western accounts of Korea describe monastic buildings as falling down and the Buddhist monks as ignorant and undisciplined.

The same remarks about Chinese monastic Buddhism in the modern era apply to Daoist monasticism as well. The institutions carried on, but they brought little to the discussion about creating the new China in the radical intellectual climate of the early twentieth century. Daoism, too, was attacked from the standpoints of science and democracy. One reformer, Liang Qichao, described this religion as "a great hu-miliation whose activities have not benefited the nation at all."[9]

Later Christian Missions in China, Japan, Korea

The Jesuits, the first Christians to proselytize in Ming China, followed their uni-versal strategy of focusing on the elite, not the masses, for conversion. Unlike their counterparts in Japan, who were expelled after an era of toleration, they did succeed at winning imperial approval for their residence. Acceptance was far less ready for their religious teachings, however, than for their cogent introduction into China of European sciences, particularly astronomy, mathematics, and ballistics. The failure of early Catholic missionaries can be attributed to an inability to explain their theology in terms of traditional Chinese language or logic. For example, they never were able to find a satisfactory way of translating *God* into Chinese. No less a drag on prose-lytizing efforts were the very bitter controversies that broke out between the Jesuit and Dominican Catholics, particularly on the issue of whether to tolerate Confucian morality or ancestor veneration. An imperial edict proscribed Christianity in 1724, but the censure was not as extreme or as thoroughly enforced as in Japan.

Scenes from missionary life in China: a missionary family resident in China ca. 1898 shown in formal Chinese dress; a classroom in a Methodist boarding school for girls; a group of Chinese converts and Western missionaries with shipments of Bibles and evangelical publications.

Taiping Rebellion: violent revolt led by Chinese converts to Christianity, who established a separate state with its capital in Nanjing

The Protestant presence was significant only after 1800, as Americans and Europeans fanned out from Guangdong Province, on the South China Sea. Their missionary efforts were directed to the masses, and a Chinese translation of the complete Bible appeared in 1815. As elsewhere, the missionaries were less successful at mass proselytizing than at transmitting Western medicine, schooling, and new technologies, such as printing by means of movable type. By 1877, there were 347 missionary schools and an estimated 400,000 Chinese converts.

In addition to the earlier issues of Chinese receptivity, Christianity was associated with the bullying of colonialists and the horrific violence of the nineteenth-century **Taiping Rebellion**, which we will discuss shortly. Christianity did, however, appeal to those interested in finding a religious framework for protest against the weight of traditionalism. In addition, those needing charity or wishing to do business with Westerners often benefited from having themselves baptized.

Outlawed in Japan in 1606, its missionaries expelled in 1616, and its followers violently persecuted, Christianity survived there underground among remarkably faithful converts. Once granted religious freedom in 1863, Japanese Christians built churches and asserted their faith in the public domain. Soon, however, like the Buddhists, the Christians began to feel the need to prove their religion's this-worldly relevance and nationalistic credentials. They joined the jingoistic chorus supporting the war efforts launched by the state and proclaimed that Christianity strengthened Japan by supporting ethics in national life, resisting radicalism, and combating communism.

Korea remained closed to Christian missionaries until the late nineteenth century, when representatives primarily from American Methodist and Presbyterian denominations settled and attracted converts while building schools and hospitals. Korean Christians, like those in Japan, also had to prove their patriotism by emphasizing their independence from Western churches. Scholars are still uncertain as to why Korea embraced Christianity so much more readily than other Asian countries. (Latest surveys have found that 32 percent of South Koreans are converts.)

The Appearance of New Religious Movements and Religions

From the imperial era until the present, **"new religions"** have emerged across Asia, underscoring this period as one of social dislocation, dissatisfaction, and cross-traditional synthesis. It also signals the extent to which the "established religions" of the region (Confucianism, Daoism, Buddhism) had lost their allure for some who were increasingly drawn to ideas from the West.

For the majority of peasants and artisans, the crises that resulted from foreign domination undermined many local subsistence economies, with disastrous effects. Peasants continued to have faith in their own deities, shamans, and ancestors and indeed turned to them in times of trouble. Yet given the turmoil of the modern era, it is not hard to imagine that countless rituals failed and a great many prayers went unanswered. For all these reasons, the modern era in East Asia is marked by the unprecedented flowering of "new religious movements" that did not rely on old deities, institutions, or rituals. Most often, they arose from the lower classes through sects entirely independent of the traditional institutions of Daoism, Buddhism, and (premodern) Shinto.

> **"new religions":** new sects formed since the nineteenth century combining elements of Buddhism, Daoism, and Confucianism with ideas imported from the West

Taiping Rebellion in China (1850–1864)

Beyond the challenges provoked by the foreigners in their midst, a rebellion led by a Chinese convert to Christianity nearly ended Manchu rule a half century before their Qing dynasty was overthrown by revolutionaries led by Sun Yat-sen. The nineteenth-century rebellion began with a humble and failed village scholar, **Hong Xiuquan** (1814–64).

After an illness during which he was delirious for several weeks, Hong, with the help of an American Southern Baptist missionary, interpreted his fevered visions as Christian revelations. Despite limited knowledge of the Bible, Hong proceeded to found his own form of Christianity, convinced that he had seen God, who had charged him with saving humanity and destroying demons, and that he had met Jesus, who was revealed to be Hong's "older brother." A charismatic preacher whose apocalyptic predictions captured the imagination of many, Hong organized his followers into a militant sect called the *Taipings*. Although the Western missionaries rejected his teachings, to some Chinese they offered a prophetic, utopian vision of a future "Heavenly Kingdom of Great Peace" based on egalitarianism, shared property, and gender equality. One of his Old Testament–inspired proclamations was that all idols

> **Hong Xiuquan:** charismatic instigator of the Taiping Rebellion; claimed to be younger brother of Jesus

be destroyed, be they Buddhist, Daoist, or even Confucian ancestor tablets. He also insisted that those joining his group adopt a puritanical moral code, abstaining from alcohol, tobacco, and opium.

Hong vilified the Manchu elite as demons standing in the way of the sect's radical transformation of China. The Qing state, in turn, persecuted the group, stepping up its efforts after 1850, by which time the Taipings had over 10,000 members. Thus provoked, Hong gathered an army whose bloody campaigns likely comprised the most destructive civil war in world history. Most of China was affected, and an estimated 20 million people perished.

China had already been humiliated and weakened by the European powers, which offered many reasons for discontent in addition to those initially proposed by Hong, and the forces of rebellion mushroomed. The Taiping army captured Nanjing in 1853 and occupied it for ten years, establishing a separate regional state ruled by Hong and his neo-Christian ministers.

Ultimately, however, the movement fell apart, owing to internal divisions, refusal to cooperate with potential allies, the leadership's ruthless brutality and paranoia in governing the Taiping community, and their hostility to the Confucian elements deeply embedded in China's population. Nanjing was retaken in 1864, all Taiping leaders not killed in battle were executed, and the first Asian-Christian "new religion" was utterly eradicated.

"Religion of the Heavenly Way": Ch'ondogyo in Korea

Ch'ondogyo: Korean movement reaffirming the truth of human dignity and the vitality of Daoism and Confucianism

The **Ch'ondogyo**, which merges elements of Confucianism, Daoism, shamanism, and Roman Catholicism, was founded by Ch'oe Suun (1824–64) in 1860. Its original name, *Tonghak* ("Eastern learning"), signals its origins as an indigenous response to the challenge of newly imported Christianity (called "Western learning" in Korean). According to the sect's scriptures, Suun received a direct revelation of a new "Heavenly Way" (*Ch'ondo*) designed to awaken each person to the totality of life in the universe and the divinity immanent in each person and all creation. Sunn was inspired to reverence the Ultimate Reality, called *Hanullim,* an impersonal force with whom each person can have an intimate, impersonal connection.

The essential path to individual realization is through repetitive private and communal chanting. To invoke Hanullim to enter into personal awareness, this "21-syllable Incantation" is intoned:

> Ultimate Energy being all around me, I pray that I feel that Energy within me here and now. Recognizing that Hanullim is within me, I will be transformed. Constantly aware of that divine presence within, I will become attuned to all that is going on around me.[10]

Drawing on Confucianism for ethical principles and on Korea's folk religion for the communal rituals, Suun organized his movement on the notion that those who shared belief in that one God constituted a separate and distinct community within

Korean society. Suun attracted a large following but was martyred by the government. The Ch'ondogyo continued to grow under Suun's successors, becoming one of the major religions of the Korean peninsula. Like Korean Christians, Ch'ondogyo members were active in resisting Japanese rule. Although banned in North Korea since 1949, recent reports mention its survival there; the group remains very popular in the south. There is an institutional center in Seoul, and in 2005 its membership, governed by an elected body, was reported to number over 3 million.

The collected writings of the first three leaders became the sect's chief scriptures. Ch'ondogyo's theology is expressed in one simple phrase: "Humans bear divinity." The ethics of the sect emphasize respecting this universal divinity in others. The injunction "Treat others as divine" seems tame today but was revolutionarily democratic in the status-conscious Korea of the late nineteenth century. Ch'ondogyo appealed especially to the lower classes, who were told that they, along with scholars and high officials, could achieve salvation through disciplined effort. There is reason to believe that Ch'ondogyo had an important role in the development of democratic and anti-authoritarian thought in Korea. The group's goal is to achieve a heavenlike earthly existence marked by widespread social cooperation.

The Older "New Religions" Arising in Pre-Meiji Japan

By the end of the Tokugawa era, the medieval social order in Japan had begun to break down, and for some the vitality of Buddhism and traditional Confucianism had waned. Of the several dozen spiritual movements that arose in this period, three grew to become denominations among the postmodern "new religions" of the early twenty-first century.

Each of these movements began with a charismatic individual who experienced extraordinary revelations after a serious illness. Having shared their discoveries with others, these leaders began building communities of followers who felt the teachings helped them reorder their lives on new spiritual principles. Almost every "new religion" thus offered a singular path to salvation out of the maze of choices that had developed along the way of Japanese religious history: Buddhism, neo-Confucianism, elements of Daoism, Shinto. All later were harmonized with the Meiji state's neo-Shintoism, eventually becoming regarded as "Shinto sects."

Kurozumikyo. Kurozumikyo ("Kurozumi's religion") was founded by Kurozumi Munetada, a charismatic teacher who in 1815 was possessed by the central Shinto deity, the sun goddess, Amaterasu, whom he asserted really to be the single Lord of the Universe. Although Kurozumi did not register his group until 1842, soon after his initial experience he began preaching and attracting disciples, who spread his revelations across Japan.

Followers of Kurozumikyo believe that all humans are emanations of the kami and that individual believers may become kami, or become one with them, securing eternal life, by adopting the moral and spiritual practices of these Japanese deities. The

"True Sincerity is the one thing
we must be most thankful for;
with sincerity alone
the Earth can be a family.

In this world of ours
we have come together to form a circle;
let us pray to be joined by
the Heart of all our hearts."

—Munetada, founder of Kurozumikyo

potential for all to realize the divine state explains the Kurozumikyo emphasis on the equality of all people, a radical idea in pre-Meiji Japan, where class completely determined individual destiny. Kurozumikyo grew dramatically after winning Meiji recognition. Its leaders had a central shrine established in Okayama City, and the group numbered perhaps 700,000 by 1880. In 2010, 361 centers were counted in Japan, and its membership had dropped to just more than 200,000.

Tenrikyo: *"Religion of Heavenly Wisdom"*; Shinto sect focused on social service founded in the nineteenth century

Tenrikyo. Tenrikyo ("Religion of Heavenly Wisdom") began with messages its founder, Nakayama Miki (1798–1887), received while in a trance. The source of these communications, he reported, was a spirit Nakayama called "God the Parent" (Oyagami). Regarded by followers as the one true god of the universe, Oyagami commanded Nakayama to be his medium and to further his mission through healing and preaching. Tenrikyo claimed that its newly released universal doctrine of harmonious living would usher in a new world order, a divine kingdom in which humanity would enjoy blissful union with God the Parent. In the sect's view, the "one, true kami" in the universe had created humanity to see it find harmonious life and then entered into creation in the form of ten other kami. Tenrikyo adherents believe that Oyagami made his new revelation to Nakayama to rectify growing human selfishness, a shortcoming that has undermined the original divine intent.

The Tenrikyo belief system accepts reincarnation until the heart is purified of the "eight dusts" (grudges, covetousness, hatred, selfish love, enmity, fury, greed, arrogance). Essential for salvation are a dance ritual, an initiation ("receiving the holy grant"), and performance of daily social service for others. Tenrikyo became a recognized Shinto sect in 1838 and rapidly spread throughout Japan. Its members carried missions to the United States in 1896, Taiwan in 1897, Korea in 1898, and China in 1901. Like the other Shinto-related sects, after the Second World War the group made efforts to "purify" Tenrikyo of its Shinto and nationalist associations. By 2013, there were over 3.75 million members, who had established over 16,000 centers in Japan, with an additional 20,000 mission centers worldwide.

Nichiren-Related Sects of the Meiji Era

As the Meiji reforms opened and transformed Japanese society after 1867 and government calls to modernize Japan multiplied, the spirit of renewal found religious expression as well. In some cases, the sects arising passed beyond what the state found tolerable, and thus followers were persecuted and pressured to modify their teachings. Other groups became vehicles of resistance to the state's militarism and nationalism. Numerous laity-led groups arose because the Buddhist "establishment" gave few openings for those wishing to reinterpret the doctrines or apply them in the context of modern scientific discoveries from the West.

Many modern groups formed in association with Nichiren-shu, a Kamakura-era Buddhist school created by the charismatic thirteenth-century monk and introduced in Chapter 7. Directly stemming from this school is the largest new religion of modern Japan, the lay organization called *Soka Gakkai* ("Value Creation Society"). Established in 1930 by the Nichiren disciple and educator Makiguchi Tsunesaburo (1877–1944), the Soka Gakkai aims to foster a "Third Civilization" based on Nichiren's teachings, one in which the true Buddhism would spread throughout the world. Its members believe that repeatedly chanting the *Nam-Myoho-renge-kyo* (the name of the great Buddhist text, the *Lotus Sutra*) is "medicine for the soul" and a means for changing the world. The Soka Gakkai also considers its mission to work for world peace and human welfare, and after 1960 it established a political party in Japan (the Komeito) to implement specific government programs to achieve this goal in Japan. It has also sent missionaries to every major country of the world. By 2013, the Soka Gakkai had registered 12 million Japanese members and claimed 1.4 million international adherents.

Also originated by and for Nichiren laity, *Reiyukai Kyodan* ("Spiritual Friends Association") was intended to support the school's regular practices and to exert beneficial influences on Japanese society. Founded in 1925 by Kubo Kakutaro (1890–1944) and Kotani Kimi (1901–71), the group stressed the need for ancestor worship by the laity and attributed the upheavals of the era to ancestral distress over the ineffectiveness of the contemporary Buddhist leaders. Only when ancestors achieve peace and salvation through lay rituals utilizing the *Lotus Sutra* can the living really find spiritual grace. The Reiyukai also emphasizes conservative social values and expects its members to work hard to strengthen the Confucian "three bonds" (between ruler and minister, father and son, and husband and wife). The Reiyukai are also strong supporters of imperial veneration and other conservative causes in Japanese society. One of the most active proselytizing new religions, the Reiyukai by 2013 had 5 million members and centers abroad in twenty-six countries.

East Asian Religions and Postmodern Trends in a Postcolonial World

Practitioners have pushed back at every religious barrier that the states of East Asia erected in the modern era. In Korea and Japan, this return to religious freedom opened the way for reformers of ancient traditions as well as charismatic innovators founding "new religions." The coming of the Marxist state to mainland China in 1949 and the imposition of totalitarian rule by the officially atheistic Communist Party began an era of sustained religious repression. Chinese religions suffered the destruction of properties and religious institutions through concerted governmental attempts—unprecedented in world history—to exterminate any vestige of traditional religious teaching or spiritual training. In China, this lasted for almost two generations, until 1976.

But as we discussed in Chapter 1, such repression and persecution have not led to the end of religion in China. Far from it. State-sponsored substitution of modernist

TALES OF SPIRITUAL TRANSFORMATION: Daoist

This Daoist tale describes how Zhuang Zi learned from his wife's death and explained his spiritual realization to a friend who discovered him drumming and singing instead of maintaining the expected Confucian decorum of solemnity.

I pondered over her beginning before she was born; not merely before she was born but when there was as yet no body; not merely when there was no body but not even a vital spirit. Within an inchoate confusion there took forth a transformation and there was vital spirit. The vital spirit was transformed and there came forth form, and with the transformation there was life. Now once again there is a transformation and she died. What happened may be compared to the four seasons. . . . Now she is lying in peace in a small room. For me to follow after her weeping and wailing would be an indication that I have no thorough understanding of human destiny.

Source: Smith, *The Wisdom of the Taoists*, p. 88.

Marxist ideologies, utopian mythology, and the orchestration of a personality cult centered on Mao Zedong represented attempts to substitute a communist Chinese civil religion for Confucianism, Daoism, and Buddhism. The effort failed, though it did weaken the bond between most mainland Chinese and their traditional organized religions.

Since the reform era that began soon after the death of Mao in 1976, the restoration of religion in China has been very gradual and has proceeded under the supervision of the state. A popular upsurge of practice at Daoist temples, family graves, Buddhist monasteries, Christian churches, and mosques is evident, however. Despite reverses, over the last decades, as the door has been cracked open, countless Chinese have rushed through to make pilgrimages, reopen shrines, and resume the ritual practices of their ancestors. We discuss here both the surviving traditions and new religions that have even further multiplied the pluralism characteristic of the postcolonial era.

Continuities and Transformations in the East Asian Religions

Having traced the "rush hour" of new religions and the transformations of the older faiths in modern East Asia, we need to convey how religion exists now, in the twenty-first century. A knowledgeable visitor to Osaka, Seoul, or Shanghai today would be intrigued to see how traditions endure amid signs of extraordinary changes: Shinto shrines tucked into spaces between skyscrapers, new Confucius Institutes being built by the Chinese governments, Buddhist television stations broadcasting from corporate headquarters in Korea. The ways of balancing modern lifestyles with millennia-old religious traditions continue to evolve; new religions are being formed, and old ritual practices are being applied to new human problems. As global awareness is further influencing East Asian religions, they are also expanding to Asian communities across the globe. These trends now merit our attention, country by country.

The Reality of Gods and Spirits in China

Chinese myths dating back to the Zhou era (700 BCE) mention deities of mountains, rivers, rain, and the earth that have remained part of the diffuse Chinese religion. Interestingly, most deities appearing later in East Asia have human origins, as heroic ancestral spirits have become gods who have won renown beyond their own kin. This is true of **Guan Yu**, the god of war (in life, a Han general), various deified statesmen, Confucius, and even, in recent years, Mao Zedong. Most other important deities have been Buddhist in origin.

In regional and local contexts, the East Asian pantheon has always been in flux as new heroes arise and the deities are obliged continuously to show their power (***ling***), perhaps through healing or in dramatic shamanic displays of possessions, to prove themselves worthy of the investment of further offerings. Those manifesting strong healing powers or success in responding to popular appeals win devotees, patrons, new temples. Alternatively, other deities have lost favor and efficacy and so have faded from popularity. Thus, the East Asian understanding of and experience with divinities has not been based so much on faith as on dramatic experiential encounters and proven long-term potency at providing cures and other beneficial results.

Who are the most common deities found on the typical altars in a Chinese community? Ubiquitous in Chinese homes and temples are icons of the *triple gods*: *Longevity*, in the form of a vigorous old man; *Wealth*, embodied by a Confucian official; and *Blessings*, symbolized by a male god holding male progeny.

Another prominent deity, Tian Shang Sheng-mu ("Holy Mother in Heaven"), is popularly known as *Mazu* ("Grandmother"). Her origins can be traced to a girl born in the ninth century, in coastal Fujian, who saved her father and brothers at sea by exercising magical powers acquired via Daoist practice. She died young, and soon apparitions and miracles attributed to her were reported. By the mid-twelfth century, the state had recognized Tian Shang Sheng-mu and Mazu cult and temples that spread along the eastern coast of China, where the goddess remains popular today.

In every traditional Chinese and Korean home (but not in Japan) will be another deity, Zao Wangye, the "**kitchen god**." From the kitchen hearth, he records the household goings on and composes a yearly report right before New Year's Day. Folk belief is that Zao Wangye can even determine the length of every household member's life. As early as the Ming era, this popular notion was part of a more systematic articulation of the pantheon (reflecting China's urban centers and government bureaucracy), by which the kitchen gods and earth gods of each locality were viewed as reporting to the nearby city gods, who in turn informed the celestial Jade Emperor on New Year's Day. This notion of a divine, hierarchical officialdom shaped the popular understanding in China of what happens when a person dies: The earth god of the locality

Guan Yu: Chinese god of war, worshipped for protection today

ling: spiritual force possessed by geographic places, deities, and sages

kitchen god: in China and Korea, deity residing in every household

Image of Mazu, the protective deity worshipped along the Chinese seacoast.

Representations of the "triple gods" Blessings, Wealth, and Longevity, found on many altars in Chinese homes and temples.

reports to the city god, who then escorts the soul to the underworld to appear before ten judges who determine punishments and karmic destiny. It is to these divine "magistrates" that the family addresses prayers and sends bribes ("spirit money"), the latter consisting of specially purchased paper "currency" that is burned to expedite its magical, otherworld delivery.

Ritual Practices

In many respects, East Asia derives its unity as a religious and cultural area less from a common set of beliefs than from the shared ritualism within its temples and at family graves. These core rituals are simply an extension of the human custom of feasting an honored guest, in these cases an ancestral spirit or a deity. The foods offered in temples, which are those humans consume, including alcoholic drinks, are not wasted: Once the deities are thought to have consumed their essence, the humans eat the material leavings. Other items presented in East Asian rituals include candles, flowers, oil lamps, and incense. In keeping with the idea that the deities are senior but essentially human is the practice of full prostration (*ketou*, or "kowtow") before icons or tablets, an obeisance that junior kin also make before their living elders at festival times.

For most occasions in daily life, priests (be they Daoist, Buddhist, or shamans) are not needed. This is because senior householders and state officials, even at the highest level, have ritual tasks to perform according to their status. Such tasks are especially well defined at the time of death. In particular, Confucian filial piety is shown at a parent's death through careful carrying out of the appropriate rituals. The reward is

Items for burning to be sent to the dead by the affluent Chinese of Shanghai and Singapore.

the soul spirit's blessings and the promise of a reunion with kin after the children's own demise.

Death is indeed a crisis, and at funerals people show their loyalty and love to the departed. In East Asia, a long period of time is traditionally set aside to honor the dead. Further, participation in a funeral is one of the key events binding families and transmitting family values: All the relatives of the deceased remove jewelry, wear rough mourning garments, and wail ritually during specific times until actual burial. Burial will be after two days, with a longer wait in well-to-do families. The funeral itself involves the largest and most ostentatious procession that can be afforded, with musicians and mourners carrying large paper replicas of items the deceased is expected to need in the afterlife.

The traditional death rituals end with the priests ritually transferring the soul in two places for future worship, inviting it to reside in the same places where those who long ago expired are thought to dwell. The cremation remains are taken out in a procession to the family grave or clan temple. Here they are left in an urn, and a grave tablet with the deceased's name is fixed. The yin (earthly) soul stays with these remains. The yang (heavenly) soul is carried to the family's home placed on a sword-shaped paper brought from the graveside. It is then ritually installed on the family altar as a permanent tablet inscribed with the person's name set in place. Placed near other senior kin and the various images of the deities, this spirit receives all the offerings made to the gods. Moreover, any important event in the family is announced to the tablets as if the ancestors resided there.

Although not all families can afford family grave sites, all wish to have them, since with such a burial the family can most directly ensure the happiness of the earthbound

GENDER FOCUS: Women and East Asian Religions

We have seen repeatedly in this study of world religions that as the religions of the world arose and became dominant forces in societies across the globe, this world of states and empires was almost exclusively a man's world. Just as men ruled in the political realm, so too did they control the religious institutions of every tradition. The conception of "God" in the Abrahamic faiths, while regarded by some theologians as beyond human categories, was predominantly represented in language and art as of male gender. And in the Quran and Bible, stories recount why men should rule all creation, including women, to conform to divine law.

Likewise in the Asian traditions, the great sages are all male, as are the preponderance of major gods. The great monastic traditions that were formed by Christians, Buddhists, and Daoists all rendered nuns as secondary figures who exerted little control of the central religious institutions. In East Asia, this pattern of religious traditions providing legitimation for gender inequality is also clearly seen in Confucian thought. As we have seen, the control of women by men is deemed natural and necessary for the establishment of a good, harmonious society. The fact that men are instructed to act in ways to deserve this power by ensuring the flourishing of women and girls does not alter the reality of male control. Nor did the doctrines of the Daoists, seeing harmony in the universe based on a balancing of yin and yang, including male and female, exert any counterforce to the gender hierarchy found across East Asia.

In China, the subjugation of women found extraordinary expression in the practice of women "binding their feet." Widespread in Chinese society from 1000 CE until the mid-twentieth century, this custom involved the excruciatingly painful process of young girls (ages five through seven) having the bones of their toes and arches broken, then bound in place inward, creating an incapacitating deformity. Scholars have naturally interpreted foot binding as an expression of gender relations in conformity with the dominant neo-Confucian tradition. Although this contradicts a central ethical principle of this tradition that prohibits individuals from mutilating their bodies, this ideal seems to have been applied to men alone. Instead, foot binding was part of the male-regulated family, in which bound feet rendered women dependent on their families, particularly their men, and, therefore, became an alluring symbol of chastity and male ownership.

Attention to gender and the male control of Confucianism, Daoism, and Buddhism makes it especially understandable that women were drawn to the hundreds of "new religions" established across East Asia. Many were founded by, supported by, and to a greater extent than in the older faiths, run by women. Under conditions of modernity, women seeking power, prestige, and careers outside the traditional boundaries of family life found many new options in these new religions that cultivated their membership. The changing familial, educational, and economic conditions for women in 2014 seen across Asia today are also forcing the long-established religions to re-form their institutions to attract females as devotees.

souls. Families possessing graveyards go to them on two occasions each year to tidy them, make sacrifices, and then eat and drink among the family's ancestral graves. The cemeteries in East Asia are not dreaded locales but places one can go to feel close to one's deceased parents and grandparents as well as to conform to the basic Confucian requirement of caring for them after death.

The Religious Institutions: Monasteries, Temples, Shrines

The religious institutions that sustain the three traditions in East Asia vary widely. For their surrounding householder communities, Buddhist monasteries have temples with images of compassionate bodhisattvas and include monks who specialize in healing and death rituals. The temple in all these religions is considered as simply a house for humanlike divinities. They can be modest roadside boxes where humble images or cheap lithographic prints are kept, or they can be massive palaces with halls and side buildings, housing gilded images flanked by hosts of attending demigods.

Some deities, such as the earth god (*Tudi*) found in most agricultural settlements, can be worshipped in a simple manner outdoors on a raised mound of decorated earth. Small temples are merely rooms made of wood or cement, housing a simple tablet with the name of the deity inscribed on it. Traditional Chinese towns had a profusion of such shrines and larger temples, making it hard to understand the assertion by Westernized Chinese that "Chinese have no religion!"

The larger temples share certain characteristics. The greatest temples contain all the major deities of the pantheon, giving devotees "one-stop" access to the supernatural world. The entrance always opens to the south, an auspicious direction, and is guarded by statues of protectors in fierce poses. In larger establishments these guardians are lodged in a gatehouse through which all visitors must pass. The areas devoted to multistory pagoda temples in many cases reflect attention to geomancy calculations, complete with artificial mountains to channel positive energy to the site. In larger compounds, the main deity will be in the last hall on the same axis as the entrance, with halls containing lesser deities arrayed on the same line and separated by courtyards. Before each icon is an altar for receiving offerings, most commonly candles or incense sticks that go into large braziers. Kneeling cushions are supplied as well as a means of divination for the use of those posing questions to a deity: Two half-moon wooden blocks are thrown to derive a "yes" or "no" answer, based on their resting alignment.

The aesthetic in contemporary Chinese temples can be described as highly baroque. The temples, with their curving roof lines, eaves, and finials, are full of bright colors, from roof beams to columns to the decorated vestments adorning the deities.

The larger Daoist temples are usually served by a resident priesthood and by *fa-shi*, mediums who serve in temples. The mediums specialize in exorcisms and help private clients make simple offerings. Resident priests, called *dao-shi*, may assist in rituals such as exorcisms but have also mastered complex Daoist death liturgies and wear more formal attire.

Shinto Shrines: Jinja

Equipped and arrayed in keeping with norms similar to those of the Chinese temple but in sharp decorative contrast are the Japanese Shinto shrines, *jinja*. They are notable for their natural wood, plain roof tiles, and restrained aesthetic. Every jinja is also marked by a gateway called a *torii*. Given the high emphasis on purification in Shintoism, water (left) Chinese temple, the home of the gods, featuring the ornate pillars and roof tiles of the palace style. (right) Main gate, or torii, of the Fushimi Inari Shrine in Kyoto, Japan.

sources for rinsing the face and mouth are always present where devotees approach the main shrine. These distinctive features of Japan's Shinto architecture delineate a transition from the ordinary world into sacred space.

After purification, devotees proceed to the main and subsidiary shrines. Facing the main icon, they go before it to present their petitions. Before making a request, a visitor can pull on long, thick ropes to ring a shrine bell. Ending the ritual by clapping shows respect.

The Diffuse Religion in Practice: The Major Religious Festivals

In our collective discussion of the religious practices of China, Korea, and Japan, we have pointed to the "diffuse religion" that gives the region a characteristic unity, drawing on elements of the three traditions. The festivals express this diffuse religion most clearly, since Confucian, Daoist, and Buddhist elements have clearly been woven into the yearly cycle of life. Only continued reliance on the ancient Chinese calendars in some areas of these countries has led to complications. Officially, all East Asian nations have adopted Western calendar days and selected celebrations: China from its connections with international communism, Korea and Japan through Christian influences. Yet the Chinese system of twelve-year cycles, lunar days, and solar seasons is still used in many areas and has been intermixed with the Western calendar. Since Japan shifted many of its holidays away from the Chinese calendar and to fixed "Western" days, Japan's dates for the festivals it shares with the East Asian region are most often not on the same calendar day observed elsewhere.

A small Shinto shrine (jinja) dedicated to the protector of cows, the cow kami.

National holidays have grown out of a variety of origins: mythic events or deities indigenous to the particular nation, days accentuating Confucian values, or relatively recent events that the nation's leaders wish to mark in the country's "civil religion." For example, Japan celebrates the Cherry Blossom Festival (April 1–8) to thank the kami of the forests for the renewal of life seen in the blossoming of the trees.

Every major deity in every locality is thought to have a "birthday" each year either a day celebrated nationally or the day a more local deity's temple was first established. On these annual occasions, which usually last for two or three days, the priests and temple supporters arrange for elaborate ritual performances, local devotees come to make their most elaborate yearly offerings (and petitions), merchants and artisans set up their wares to create a temporary fair, and in the evenings theatrical performances are staged to entertain deity and devotees alike.

Most common festivals of East Asia have Chinese or Buddhist origins and can be mentioned only in passing. New Year's Day (by either calendar) is a time for gathering family and friends, settling debts, and seeking blessings and divine protection for the year ahead. The day in China and Korea is called *Spring Festival*, although it falls usually just after the middle of winter. In traditional preholiday rites, householders send the Kitchen God (Zao Wangye) off to heaven by burning his paper icon and installing a new paper icon; they also post ancient characters on doorways to invite prosperity for the year ahead. The essentials of Confucian family life are

Daoist New Year celebrations in Beijing.

Qing-Ming: annual spring festival when Chinese tend to family graves and make offerings to the ancestors

marked in sacrifices offered to ancestors at their tablets. It is customary for junior family members to kowtow to seniors, who then in turn receive gifts of money in special red envelopes.

Ancestor's Day, or **Qing-Ming** ("Pure Brightness Festival"), is the first of two dates over the year when families must visit the ancestral graves to maintain them, make sacrifices, and feast together there with the departed spirits, usually in early April. In Japan, this festival has been fixed as the vernal equinox (March 21) and is called *Higan* ("Further Shore"), with a second Higan on the autumnal equinox. In the Chinese manner, families visit family graves together. Buddhist priests are also expected to come to the home on a short visit, during which they recite sacred scriptures. The merit earned for this good deed is dedicated to the dead.

Japanese Buddhists mark the Buddha's birthday on April 8, when people anoint images of baby Buddha with flowers and scented water, just as the texts describe the local deities doing at the actual birth of Siddhartha. Chinese and Korean Buddhists do the same on the eighth day of the fourth lunar month. Confucius' birthday is celebrated today only in Korea and always on September 28. In Taiwan, on Teacher's Day, Confucius is honored with colorful rituals and elaborate sacrifices laid out before the sage's temple tablets.

All Souls Festival: summer event when families perform rituals to connect the living with their ancestors and ensure ancestors' comfort in the afterlife

All Souls Festival is a summer event when the gates of purgatory are thought to be momentarily held open. On this occasion, families integrate practices from all three traditions to connect the living members with their departed kin. Buddhist and Daoist priests perform rituals to aid families in their effort to ensure their ancestors' comfort in the afterlife.

Full Moon Festival: fall festival to feast with kin and celebrate the harvest moon

The early fall **Full Moon Festival** is a time to worship the harvest moon with special sweet "moon cakes." All are urged to take sight of the "full rabbit moon," an

Scene in Chengudu, China from the Qing-Ming festival, the yearly family ritual for feasting and honoring the ancestors.

association derived from both Buddhist and Daoist traditions: In the popular Buddhist scriptures, the Buddha was once born as a rabbit who rendered such extraordinary service to his fellow animals that the gods placed his image on the moon's surface; in the Daoist perception, a rabbit can be seen on the moon, using a pestle to pound the herbs of immortality in a mortar. Across East Asia, people view the rising moon on this night to ask for blessings that in rural communities include a good rice harvest in the month ahead.

The Return of Religion to China: Case Studies

Between 1949 and 1976, the heavy hand of the Communist Party–led government succeeded in disestablishing almost every public religious institution that anchored the "three faiths." It dispersed the religious specialists (monks, nuns, and priests) and destroyed much of the formal infrastructure of the organized religions of China, demolishing Buddhist and Daoist monasteries and image shrines as well as the nearly countless deity temples that before 1949 could be found in every community. The party also pushed the devout underground, since in the most active phase of the **Cultural Revolution** (1966–69), any attempt to pray, meditate, or read religious literature was a serious offense, a sign of being "reactionary" or an "enemy of the revolution," a potentially capital crime. We now examine a few examples in pursuit of understanding the extraordinary phenomenon of religion's return to the People's Republic of China.

Cultural Revolution: period in Communist China under Mao Zedong when religious traditions and practitioners were persecuted

Mao in the Rearview Mirror

Suppose you arrive in Beijing on your first visit to China and decide to go to the former imperial palace, the Forbidden City, the immense, walled complex from which the Yuan, Ming, and Qing emperors ruled all of China. It was at the top of the palace's southern gateway, called the Gate of Heavenly Peace (Tian'anmen), that Mao Zedong proclaimed the establishment of the People's Republic of China in 1949. Despite all the changes that have swept China since Mao's death in 1976, you would easily see from your taxi window the immense painted portrait that hangs over that gateway. The image commemorates the "new beginning" of China then and serves as a constant reminder of Mao's heroic and determined role in leading the Communist Party's triumphant success.

The style of the Tian'anmen Square portrait suggests that Mao is the ascetic servant of the people, a true communist leader whose deeds are legendary. He bravely fought the Japanese, and in the Long March of 1934 he led the troops in strategic retreat halfway across China. Later he exposed the internal enemies that had kept China backward, poor, and subjugated. Inspired by Marx, Engels, and Lenin, Mao identified these enemies as the landlords who oppressed the peasant masses, religious ideas and institutions, and Western capitalism, all of which kept the people from rising up and forcing China to become a just society. For Mao and so for the early Chinese Communist Party leaders, religion and religious institutions were "enemies of the people." Mao was a rationalist who critiqued "superstitious" religious ideas that allegedly blocked the people's attempts to understand the world; he never ceased to highlight the classic modernist goal of setting the world free from the wrong thinking stemming from belief in supernatural "magic."

Like Marx, Engels, and Lenin, Mao believed a true communist utopia was not obtainable in a society with strong religious traditions. Although official Chinese historians have by now admitted that Mao's own blind faith in communist ideology led to blunders causing the death of millions (especially in the 1958–62 famine), the massive Tian'anmen portrait still hangs today as an icon of communist China. (Occasionally iconoclasts are caught defacing this portrait. Even in recent incidents, offenders have typically received multiyear prison terms.)

People who grew up during the decades of Mao's dictatorship later painfully realized how full of "superstition" they had been in uncritically following the Communist Party and especially in showing reverence for Chairman Mao. Yet today, nearly thirty years after his death, for many Chinese, party members and nonparty members alike, Mao retains his standing as a sincere and uncorrupted champion of China's renewal who tried (however erringly) to seek justice and the common good. But regard for Mao endures in ways that even he did not anticipate.

As your taxi driver turns the corner on the great square near the stolid mausoleum where Mao's remains lie embalmed in a glass-enclosed tomb, you notice on the windshield mirror a gold-colored frame, decorated with red and yellow tassels. You immediately recognize the back-to-back portraits of Mao, a youthful one and one from middle age (similar to that overlooking Tian'anmen Square). You ask your interpreter

Contemporary Mao amulet, inscribed with prayers for good fortune and safe travel, of the kind found widely in China today adorning rearview mirrors in cars.

what the object is and what it means. The answer, from the thirty-something driver of a government-owned vehicle, takes a few moments to register: "*Ta shi shen*" ("He is a deity"). The driver then adds with unconcealed fervor that with so many more cars on the road, his work is quite dangerous, but this deity's amulet makes him feel safe. His income as a driver in fact has multiplied since he put it up, just as his fellow drivers in the work unit had promised. On later outings, you question other drivers who display similar icons, you learn that many believe that the icon—and Mao's spirit—have helped them in business. The transformations under way in China today and the restoration of religion among the Chinese people are embedded in this striking turn of fate: The most powerful man in East Asia, while alive an atheist who suppressed religion, is in death a powerful spirit.

While his transformation to a revered protective spirit and god of wealth would doubtless have dismayed Chairman Mao, it does demonstrate the global pattern of religious traditions responding to the exigencies of local life. As the state and party have moved since the early 1990s away from collectivist policies to emphasize individual and private enterprise, leaders have exhorted the Chinese people that "to get rich is glorious." At the same time, the government has retreated from promises of guaranteed state employment, pensions, and universal medical care. So is it really surprising that an unassailable icon would be adopted as the very needed god of personal protection and wealth?

The Force of Feng Shui

Ideas about what constitutes "religion" in China not only fascinate modern scholars but have been repeatedly debated by officials of the Communist Party. In the reform era, as pressure has been exerted to reintroduce almost every sort of former spiritual practice, the East Asian organized religions, with their potential for reestablishing nationwide institutional networks, have had to deal with deliberate governmental attempts aimed at controlling and regulating them. A few ancient practices, however, were left almost entirely unmolested. One of these is *feng shui*, the school of applied religious Daoism that seeks to maximize human flourishing in natural and man-made environments. (The name, which means literally "wind-water," refers to the principal bearers of environmental energy used in geomancy.)

Feng shui consultants are today found everywhere across mainland China. Masters from overseas Chinese communities have returned to advise those building the myriad new hotels, residences, and factories rising so quickly across the PRC. The goal of feng shui is to determine the best sites, architectural designs, and living arrangements. Both private concerns and state ventures with party approval now take the "science" of mapping the qi, the inherent energy of a place, quite seriously. In mainland China today one can hear both success and disaster stories pointing to the advisability of consulting a feng shui expert before embarking on any construction project.

The state's support of the return of feng shui has given credence to the classical religious worldview regarding humanity and the environment. It is based on Daoist

A feng shui master holds a compass, or lopan, used to determine auspicious environments.

principles of balancing yin and yang, channeling the subterranean and atmospheric flow of their qi, and pursuing health and prosperity through expert arrangement of harmonious design features. The government's policy reflects the perennial Chinese emphasis on religion's practical, this-worldly benefits, which is visible elsewhere in society, too. Throughout the modern and postmodern eras, for example, doctors have had unobstructed leeway to practice acupuncture and other healing arts based on Daoist principles applied to the human body.

Nor is mainland China the only area to see the effect of this revival of the ancient worldview: As significant numbers of Chinese people have migrated overseas, real estate brokers from London to San Francisco are having to take account of feng shui analysis in marketing their properties. Feng shui's ideas about interior decorating have likewise entered into the ken of new age religion, where concern for fixing "the wealth corner" in one's house, situating decorations recognized for their "harmonious vibrations," and the plotting of energy flow from front door to back have been loosely borrowed from this Chinese system of thought.

Nationalism and Confucianism Revived

Perhaps even more striking than the abandonment of attempts to stamp out long-favored cultural practices is the return of Confucius to an honored position in modern China. In the retreat from socialist collectivism and having tacitly recognized the failure to convert the Chinese masses to the worldview of Marxist-Maoist communism, China has been beset by corruption accompanying its hastily instituted market reforms. Many

Chinese writers have pointed out the crisis in faith and values that has gripped China as the profit-seeking motive has been unleashed over the last three decades. As one of China's first rock stars, Cui Jian, sings in a popular album entitled *Eggs Under the Red Flag*, "Money is fluttering in the wind. We have no ideals." Recent reports of onlookers in major cities lending no assistance to injured elders and children led the Communist Party newspaper *The China Daily* to declare that the country was experiencing "our moral decline."

The Communist Party, in apparent recognition of this potential source of chaos, recently embarked on another great reversal: It has turned back to Confucius. While the party publicly ignores its failure to make communist ideology the common foundation of postwar China, the restoration of Confucius to respectability is part of its promotion of a more primordial Chinese tradition on which to anchor its permanent power base: staunch nationalism.

Regardless of whether they support the communist government, Chinese people widely share a certain pride in their civilization and its culture. Party strategists see the world economy as developing in a direction leading to eventual domination by China. Thus, in the interest of guiding the country to reach this pinnacle, they have all but ended any demands that the people accept ideologies counter to millennia of Chinese traditions.

The PRC has readmitted Confucianism to the ideological stage in order to evoke nationalistic pride, another complete reversal by the Communist Party leadership. During the Cultural Revolution, Mao required Red Guards to denounce Confucius and his sons specifically as "villainous slave owners," tarring the master as an apologist for feudalism and exploitation, a symbol for all the traditions that the Communist Party was out to replace.

Yet the hated excesses of the Cultural Revolution may have sparked renewed interest in Confucian thought in China. In 1994, to mark the 2,545th birthday of the great sage, the party launched an initiative to revive Confucian thought. An international conference was convened, the Confucian temple in Beijing was restored and reopened to the public, and Confucius' home temple in Qufu was celebrated as a place to visit. By the year 2000, China's president, Jiang Zemin, was frequently quoting from Confucius in his public

With the allowance for religious freedom after the Cultural Revolution, traditional Daoist priests have enjoyed their restoration to temple service across China.

RITUALS AND RITES: Ancestor Veneration

Then: Traditional Funerals

In its zeal to end wasteful expenditures on the rituals of death and ancestor veneration, which for some traditional families meant going into nearly inescapable debt for extravagant funerals, the Communist Party in 1956 issued strict regulations limiting funeral observances and—a radical break from the past—required secular cremation while also prohibiting rituals at ancestral graves. This attempt to break with the Confucian tradition went even further during the periods of greatest excess in the Cultural Revolution, when the young revolutionaries called Red Guards ransacked and destroyed grave sites throughout China, including parts of the great imperial tombs. By unleashing these energetic young zealots on the countryside, Mao was trying to destroy the familial tradition, which he saw as dividing "the people" and so undermining the party's quest to promote the collective good.

Beginning in the early 1990s, the practices of traditional funeral processions and burial of the dead in family graves slowly began to return, largely in villages and smaller towns, but hardly at all around major cities such as Beijing, where until 1996 the government posted signs threatening punishment for those burning paper money or artificial gold ingots at gravesides. Since 2008, when the Chinese government reinstated Ching Ming as a national holiday, old cemeteries have been restored and new ones established to accommodate the wishes of families to re-establish the old family traditions. Ideal sites near Beijing and Shanghai now command high prices and one sees burial places of elaborate design, including permanent brick structures with nameplates affixed. Now, even government-owned shops can be found selling the paper currency used in this exceedingly popular observance.

Now: Online Memorial Rituals

Across Asia, during the Ching Ming Festival, virtual possibilities exist if the individuals can't take time off, are allergic to incense smoke, or the family grave is too far away. Now, one can simply go online. There are a growing number of websites in China and Taiwan dedicated to ancestor worship on the Internet, as well as thousands of online memorial halls. These prayer websites offer users the convenience of paying one's respects from the comfort of one's home, with many featuring a special form they can fill in to send good wishes, messages, and even presents to heaven (or hell).

For example, the Chinese website Xinzheng .gov.cn features a virtual altar table with an incense burner, candles, offerings of flowers and rice wine. Visitors can click on the different pictures to light the sticks of incense and candles, put flowers in the vase, or pour the rice wine in a ceremonial offering container. At the bottom of the page, there is a form to send virtual gifts with a personalized message to the dead. Another site allows the mourner to create a personal avatar, and click to make it light candles and kowtow in front of a virtual family memorial.

Some Netizens find this a meaningful innovation. One is quoted as saying on the online forum QBAR, "This is a very good idea. It feels like this is the first time someone came up with this idea." But others expressed the opposite view, that such virtual ancestor worship just cultivates laziness and insincerity. "This is too unrealistic. It doesn't mean that once we've sent the message, the prayer would reach the intended persons." Sites such as BuddhistSpace (http://www.buddhistspace.com/) have created the same service for East Asian Buddhists.

Core Confucianism: "The Three Bonds" (San-kang)

The Three Bonds emerged as principles of state administration several centuries after Mencius, who argued that if they are followed, the world will be in peace; if the three are ignored, society will be in chaos. Later Confucian reformers taught that it was wrong to use the Three Bonds as a fixed hierarchy if they lacked the notion of mutuality and reciprocity.

Ruler over the Minister
Father over the Son
Husband over the Wife

speeches; in 2006, one of the best-selling books in China was an introduction to Confucian thought and its applications to contemporary life.

Qi Gong

Another area in which the spiritual has returned to mainland China in the guise of applied therapy is in the practice of **qi gong**. This healing art, like feng shui, draws on Daoist theories of vital energy in the body and on techniques of awakening its force in practitioners, both of which have their origins in religious Daoism's ancient paths to achieve immortality. It is now quite common in major cities for qi gong practitioners

qi gong: discipline of cultivating the vital individual life force

Sales clerk at an ancestor worship shop, Shanghai. Government shops across China now sell the paper money, candles, and incense needed for this ancient practice, once prohibited by official regulations. Recent additions available in upscale memorial supply shops include paper replicas of ipads, android phones, and computers.

Women performing a qi gong ritual in Shanghai, with gestures designed to cultivate and concentrate the qi energy in the body.

to open shops in the precincts of Buddhist or Daoist monasteries, with banners and posters unfurled outside their entranceways explaining the theory and practice as well as testimonials from people cured of various maladies. In most instances, a qi gong master uses his own body to concentrate healing energy and project it outwardly (through the hands) to affect the flow of energy in the patient. In the famous Great Goose Pagoda in Xi'an, the Buddhist committee since 1993 has rented a side assembly hall to a qi gong practitioner. These masters draw a steady stream of interested people who can listen to an introductory lecture and, for a modest fee, take their first treatment.

In some governmental circles, there is ambivalence about such applied spirituality. Although the modern official press features an occasional article, often by a prominent scientist, that denounces "phony qi gong" as "harmful" and criticizes individual practitioners for "feudal and superstitious activities which use the flag of qi gong as a cover for swindling others," it continues to allow the practice to flourish, even in state-controlled temple precincts. Thus, while this medically oriented practice is mixed with other therapies (Chinese and Western), qi gong, like feng shui, now affirms the credibility of the most elemental ideas of classical Daoism.

Falun Gong and Eastern Lightning: The Limits of Religious Freedom

In general, there were fewer "new religions" in the PRC under communist rule than in Korea or Japan; but barely a quarter century after Mao's death, the party leadership discovered that its relaxation of earlier repressive policies had allowed the formation of powerful new Chinese religions called Buddhist Law Power (*Falun Gong* or *Falun Dafa*) and Eastern Lightning (Dongfang Shǎndiàn).

Founded in 1990, Eastern Lightning emerged into public awareness near the end of 2012, when it widely publicized that the end of the world was about to begin. Leaders announced that on December 21, three days of darkness would be followed by seventy-two days of natural disasters, after which the earth would be devastated. The group would be led by a woman from central China, "Lightning Deng," who has been identified as "Jesus Christ incarnated"; her mission is to "slay the great red dragon," the Communist Party. Her most widely distributed book, *Lightning from the Orient*, proclaims itself the Word of God. It claims the first coming of Christ was to redeem humanity, while hers as the second is "to conquer men's hearts and defeat Satan." Recruiting with aggressive means, Eastern Lightning leaders have attracted over a million followers. Anticipating these last days, many withdrew all their money from banks and sold their property. The Chinese government has launched a campaign of arrests against members, declaring it a dangerous cult and "a social cancer and a plague on humankind."

Quickly after its founding in 1992, Falun Gong attracted millions across China—young and old, Communist Party members and poor migrating laborers alike—and built an organization across the nation, its leaders began to attract government criticism, and its members suffered episodes of forceful intimidation. In late April 1999, the group staged a protest against these actions, with 10,000 members surrounding the Communist Party leadership compound in central Beijing. Arriving undetected, Falun Gong followers sat in silent, nonviolent protest throughout the day and then dispersed without incident. The massive sit in provoked an all-out propaganda offensive, capped by the arrest of Falun Gong leaders, who were charged with antigovernment subversion. Within months, the group had been outlawed as a "pernicious superstition." Thousands of members in small groups still stage protests against the Chinese government across the world, calling attention to how adherents have been imprisoned, tortured, or killed.

Falun Gong and Eastern Lightning resemble the new religions we have described in Korea and Japan: Their doctrines comprise an original recombination of Buddhist, Daoist, and Christian millennial doctrines, and their founders, the charismatic leaders Li Hongzhi of Falun Gong, and Lightning Deng of Eastern Lightning, both claim supernormal status, "on a level the same as Buddha and Jesus." Falun Gong's principal practice of qi gong exercises promises to promote individual health and spiritual transformation through the generation of extraordinary energy, in line with Daoist traditions at least two millennia old. Claiming 100 million followers in China and thirty other countries, Master Li from his exile in the United States has written texts and used mass media (videos, CDs, and websites) to maintain connections between himself and his disciples. Falun Gong is an apt example of a new East Asian religion in the age of media technology, when so many regional faiths are becoming global.

Shrines in Chinese Village Squares, Shops, and Front Doors

Across mainland China since 1976, there has been the slow, hesitant, but unmistakable movement by devotees to reestablish shrines, temples, and the ritual practices

Rituals performed at a Daoist temple in Xi'an.

destroyed or prohibited under government orders dating back to 1949. Exactly where the Communist Party's line of toleration lies has varied according to the region and its succession of officials. Tensions still exist over what is "superstition" (*mixin*), which is strongly discouraged by the government, versus what is considered "religion" (*zongjiao*). Individuals have a constitutional right to practice a religion, but the state reserves the right to grant or withhold this designation for a given belief system.

Even so, the return of temples to the public domain for ritual use is in evidence everywhere. Daoist and Buddhist shrines are surrounded by flourishing votive markets, usually owned by or rented from the temple itself. Incense, candles, printed texts and scrolls with spiritual exhortations, souvenirs, and amulets are among the items sold. Devotional traditions are flourishing, in forms that were popular centuries earlier.

Accounts of village life cite the near-universal attempt of rural peasants to use part of their new earnings to build (or rebuild) the public temples that house the local and regional gods. None is more telling than the practice of making offerings to the local earth gods (*tu-di*). In pre-PRC China, the humble earth god shrines were found in every locality, possessing in fact a multiple presence according to the settlement: Tudi shrines were found in homes, in neighborhoods, in villages, in government offices (where they received offerings from state officials), and even in Buddhist monasteries. All deaths, births, and troubles were reported to them, and the simple icon or tablet was taken out of the temple to "inspect" sites suffering from severe problems. People believe that, if petitioned properly and sincerely, the earth gods protect against locusts, mildew, disease, and other obstacles to a rich harvest as well as solve any other difficulties in their domain. These shrines and this cult have returned everywhere.

The restoration of shrine and ritual has gone ahead even in restaurants and homes. After several attempted crackdowns by the government, restaurants have succeeded in reinstalling small altars to the local gods of wealth and protection. In private homes, the Chinese New Year has been increasingly observed with the traditional pasting of calligraphic good-luck icons, including the word for good fortune (*Fu*) placed upside down to indicate the sound of good fortune's arrival. Clearly, the Chinese government has accepted the return of China's diffuse religion, as long as the new organizations do not threaten the Community Party's ruling power. By being sensitive to the importance and meaning of religion, we can comprehend how it is changing to meet the needs of the common people: As the party expands economic opportunity but ends the social safety-net protection programs (guaranteed employment, medical insurance, housing) people increasingly feel that to prosper, they need all the luck, and divine assistance, they can attract. Accordingly, the quest to satisfy the perceived need for good fortune is so intense that the official proponents of communist doctrine are reluctant to suppress practices many old Communist Party members consider "an opiate of the masses."

Japan's Creative Diversity: Old Traditions and New

Whereas in China the Cultural Revolution postponed the expression of religious awakening until after Mao's death in 1976, in Japan this era of innovation commenced in 1945, with the necessity of rebuilding the war-ravaged country both physically and spiritually. For seven years occupied and ruled by the Allied powers (principally the United States), Japan had to reinvent a form of government, redesign its economic system, and rebuild its major cities without reference to the emperor as their divine leader. Japan's surrender in 1945 was spoken by Emperor Hirohito in his own voice, and during the occupation he was compelled to renounce his divinity (as a Shinto kami) explicitly and to underscore his purely ceremonial presence in Japan's political future.

The state system of neo-Shintoism, which was integral to the modernizations that had begun in 1867, was also discredited and discarded. Shinto then survived largely in its myriad shrines dedicated to divinities in neighborhoods, villages, and regions and attended to by hereditary priests. Establishment Buddhism, like the rest of Japan's cultural institutions, also had to rebuild its physical and social presence, overcoming the stigma of having uncritically supported the fascist state. As the economic system flourished, the country's wealth eventually was used to rebuild these institutions, accelerating the traditional religion's material recovery and, in some cases, expansion.

The Claim of "Having No Religion" and the Reality of New Year's Rituals

Educated Japanese and oftentimes their friends in intellectual Western circles are fond of proclaiming that the Japanese are "lacking in religion," an Enlightenment attitude common among educated East Asians. Some try to project an image of Japan as a modern society comparable to Europe or North America in its scientific sophistication. While few Japanese today care to learn much in depth about Shinto mythology or Buddhist doctrine, widespread indifference does not prove that Japan "lacks religion."

Beyond the unprecedented growth of the new religions, one has only to know where and when to seek a wealth of examples that dispel this widespread stereotype about a Japanese people somehow being different from everyone else. While it is foolish to ignore the force of skepticism, scientific theory, and cynicism in any modern society, it is also naive to judge "religiousness" by formal institutional measures alone. Contemporary New Year's Day observances provide an example of the strength of "diffuse popular religion" in modern Japan.

During the Meiji era, Japan had legislated a shift away from the Chinese lunar calendar's determining the date of the "new year" festival and adopted the Western (or Gregorian) system that has the year begin on January 1. On this day and days around it, Japan shuts down its industrial economy. Families begin the process of renewal through a special cleaning of the house (*susuharae*, "soot and cobweb clearing"). On New Year's Eve or early New Year's morning, a visitor to any Shinto shrine—even in the most modern Tokyo urban neighborhood—will see long lines of family members coming for *hatsu-mode*, a formal visit to pay their respects to their neighborhood's kami. The people then consign to the carefully laid bonfires all the family amulets accumulated over the past year. That evening or the next day, a family member will purchase new amulets that will be carefully set up on the newly purified family altar. Many temples plan their annual festival for this period, when crowds throng to temple precincts to buy amulets and attend the priestly rituals empowering them. In nearly every shop and house are decorations dedicated to the kami residing in the neighborhood. On New Year's morning, too, families gather at their household altars to worship the Buddhas, Kannon, and local gods. Thus, in the renewal of the family shrine at the year's turning, by "being careful" with local divinities, in sacralizing family ties, and by suspending the profane activities of markets and business activities, contemporary New Year's Day traditions in Japan fit perfectly into the "religion" framework we introduced in Chapter 1. Since 2006, due to the discomforts of joining the usual crowd of 4 million people who traditionally visit the Meiji Shrine on New Year's Day, this shrine, like many across Japan, has a website. Without leaving home, a virtual visit can be made: Cyber-visitors can click onto the site, bow twice, clap their hands, and bow again, after which they can express their request to the shrine's kami and order auspicious amulets online. (For an online index, see, for example, http://www.japan-guide.com/e/e2059.html.)

Another indication of enduring religiosity of the Japanese was seen in the aftermath of the 2011 earthquake and tsunami that struck eastern Japan, a catastrophe that claimed several thousand lives. As the world watched, it was quite evident how the rituals of Shinto and Buddhism still permeate Japanese life. Prominent monks in the months following pointed out that the community's response is indicative of the Buddhist tradition's enduring place there: showing patience, resilience, and self-sacrifice in the face of tragedy. The absence of looting, acts of self-sacrifice, and workers facing dangerous radiation for the common good epitomized the Buddhist bodhisattva ideal. And there was the memorializing of the dead by priests reading scripture and chanting sutras before bodies were cremated. Doing so, citizens followed the traditional norm of taking great care to help the passage of the consciousness from the realm of the living to the dead. And for bodies washed out to sea, there were prominent and nationally televised mass memorials for the dead. Then, as people began rebuilding their homes and lives until the present, Shinto moved to center stage. People turned to Shinto rituals performed by priests to restore the balance between the human and the divine, bless the construction sites, and pacify the local kami. At the Otsuchi shrine that stood undamaged in a small town devastated by the waves, throngs of survivors stopped by daily in the first months to bow and ring the bell at the main shrine. As one CNN report noted, "Their prayers to this local kami in the first months were heart breaking, as residents asked for help in finding missing relatives before continuing the grim task of searching for their bodies. Others asked for strength in the face of the horrific post-tsunami reality."

Continuing Support for Shinto Shrines

Most Japanese—housewives, salaried workers, artisans—still widely believe that wherever one lives and certainly wherever one's family still has an ancestral residence, one has loose ties to the shrine that houses the deity of that locality, the *uji-kami*. We've seen that on New Year's Day at least, paying respects to that kami remains a very popular observance. Almost equally popular in most parts of Japan is the ritual of bringing newborn babies to "meet" the kami and to pay their own respects, requesting protection. There is also a yearly Shinto festival dedicated to the well-being of children.

A man strolls with his dog past the *tori* of a Shinto shrine damaged by the 2011 earthquake and tsunami in Yamamoto, Japan.

When we try to understand the typical individual today visiting a Shinto shrine, it is nearly impossible to separate the spiritual from the habitual or the recreational. In a recent survey of those who visited shrines, 65 percent of men and 75 percent of women reported experiencing *aratamatta kimochi*, "a feeling of inner peace," afterward.[11] The observer at the shrine finds many ritual activities that seem to indicate religious conviction—clapping the hands together, bowing before an image, making an offering, buying an amulet.

A modern exponent of Shinto's relevance in contemporary Japan would certainly note that, although some Shinto shrines may be neglected, there are over 100,000 such holy places, and none of them is in ruins.

The Zen of Daruma-san

Daruma-san:
Japanese name of legendary Indian sage who brought Zen tradition to East Asia; a folk icon in Japan

If any single religious icon could be said to embody all the mind-boggling complexities and paradoxes of religion in Japan today, it might be **Daruma-san**. The name and identity of this figure derive from Bodhidharma, the sage renowned as the transmitter of the Buddhist meditation tradition from India (around 600 CE) that became Ch'an in China and Zen in Japan. Daruma-san became a Zen saint, and legends about him are part of the scriptural lore of this school. They celebrate his unbending commitment to meditation retreats and his terse, no-nonsense replies to students and patrons. From the Kamakura period in Japan, when Zen schools were imported from China, Daruma-san became a favorite subject for painters and sculptors. Images of Daruma-san came to be popular in Japanese folk traditions as well: His visage adorns kites, toys, knockdown dolls, sake cups. Several dozen major Buddhist temples feature his icon and offer a full range of amulets.

Today, the most widely used images of Daruma-san are limbless round papier-mâché icons called *okiagari* that are employed for making vows or proclaiming formal wishes. The standard ritual consists of making a wish and coloring in one eye of the statue, which is then placed on the family altar. When there is success in the matter wished for, the other eye is colored in and the doll (like all other amulets) is eventually discarded, fueling the next New Year's temple bonfire. The Daruma-san icon is used in the same manner by businesspeople undertaking new ventures and politicians beginning election campaigns.

Thus with Daruma-san we witness the domestication into popular Japanese ritual life of the founding saint of Zen Buddhism, a fiercely ascetic meditation master who has become transmuted into an ostensibly comic figure, who nonetheless commands a following of millions. The subtle meanings of Daruma-san stand in stark contrast to the extreme teachings of a recent Japanese cult, one that attempted to use the Buddha's Four Noble Truths to rationalize a premeditated attack with nerve gas on innocent citizens.

The Rise and Fall of the Aum Cult

In March 1995, as government investigators were about to arrest its leaders, at least ten determined members of the Aum Shinrikyo sect executed a terrorist attack in the centrally located Kasumigaseki Station of the Tokyo subway. Twelve people were killed, and 5,500 were injured. The terrorist disciples were acting on the orders of the sect's guru, Shoko Asahara, a semiblind forty-year-old who claimed to be an incarnation of Jesus and a spiritual master who had distilled the final truths of tantric Buddhism, Hindu yoga, the LSD psychedelic experience, New Age astrology, and the self-proclaimed sixteenth-century seer Nostradamus. In 1989, Asahara applied for and received registration as a tax-exempt religious organization for Aum Shinrikyo ("the True Teaching of Aum"). Then he set about building his sect around a core of commune-living disciples, many of whom were highly educated, successful people who commanded considerable wealth. Devotion to Asahara himself reached fanatical cultic proportions, with Aum members buying bottles of his bathwater.

In the aftermath of the attack, the Japanese cultural elite and the media questioned what this group's success says about the moral and cultural state of the nation. How large was the young population that was so alienated from tradition that they could accept such an unlikely collection of ideas and blindly follow a pudgy dropout who made the bizarre claim to be both Buddha and Jesus? Most disturbingly, what led followers to express murderous hatred against innocent fellow citizens? And why have followers kept the organization going until today, under its new name, Aleph?

The Aum tragedy also brought to popular attention the thousands of post–World War II "new religions" that claim the loyalty of an estimated 20 percent of modern Japanese; our survey of religion in Japan today concludes with a sampling of them.

Shinto shrines remain reference points for many modern Japanese today. These rocks conjoined by sacred hemp rope are located near Ise, symbolizing the union of the first kami.

Zen painting depicting Bodhidharma, founder of the Ch'an/Zen Buddhist school.

The Newer "New Religions" in Japan

A generation of Japanese spiritual leaders has arisen to form independent groups that have met the new yearnings, none bearing deadly fruit like the Aum attack. Still, the attraction of "new religions" must be kept in perspective: Most Japanese today have not joined them. The majority find the older traditions or being nonreligious more to their liking.

Some of the new "new religions" were synthesized by charismatic founders from Japan's long-extant traditions along with aspects of modern nationalism, elements of Christianity, or scientific principles. Many of the "new religions" began in some measure as responses to the dislocations that shook Japanese society during its sudden opening to the outside world in the late nineteenth century and the headlong modernization and Westernization of the Meiji era. Almost every older "new religion" splintered with the passing of its founder and the struggles of interpretation and succession that followed, adding to the number of groups. But most of the popular "new religions" today are more recent in origin, attracting followers who find themselves disconnected from the old pattern of melding Shintoism and Buddhism that satisfied their ancestors.

The lives of the Japanese people are changing in many dimensions—through migration from rural homesteads to burgeoning cities, with the concomitant separation from extended families and loss of community in newly built urban enclaves, and as travel and media have engendered an awareness of every portion of the world. In this new and often-chaotic environment, many individuals have been drawn to the "new religions" to find original answers to life's perennial questions.

In 2013 there were over 25,000 "new religion" organizations officially registered with the Japanese government. The great majority are exceedingly small in size, inconsequential, and for the most part rarely active. Many are hard to distinguish from poetry circles, philosophy clubs, or groups formed around health practitioners. The major new religions, however, are an important part of today's spiritual landscape; roughly 20 percent of Japanese people surveyed in recent years reported that their predominant religious affiliation is with one of the "new religions."[12]

While Aum's mass murder plot is completely atypical of the new religions, other aspects of this cult are not. Most form around a charismatic leader whose personal struggle to find the truth becomes paradigmatic for disciples drawn to the movement. Some sort of shamanic experience or performance is the most common ritual. In addition, members of most are taught to reject the diffuse eclecticism of Shintoism or Buddhism, and their gurus insist that one practice and one singular revelation are definitive. Yet many of the "new religion" worldviews draw on ancient traditions such as Buddhist karma and reincarnation doctrines, Confucian moral teachings and ancestor rites, or Shinto styles of worship. Some also import practices from the West (e.g., older psychologies like "new thought" or Norman Vincent Peale's "power of positive thinking") or from India (e.g., Hindu yoga). Each new religion also tends to be this-worldly in its goals (especially emphasizing healing) and imbued with the mission of ushering in a new divine era.

The most successful sects are built around a new "sacred center," a shrine that expresses the sect's mission and a priestly-bureaucratic administration that manages the organization. Membership in most new religions is quite open, but there is typically an initiation that requires individuals to make a personal commitment to the group, following what in the Abrahamic faiths would be called a "conversion experience."

Japan's new religions can be conveniently arranged according to their chronological emergence. The earliest, which are "new" only in relation to Japan's long history, are those that began in the nineteenth century and were eventually aligned with Shintoism. The most popular among them, the Kurozumikyo and the Tenrikyo, discussed earlier, have survived into the present. The most prominent of the second-tier group, which arose during the Meiji era (post-1867), remain among the largest new religions today: the Buddhist-derived Soka Gakkai and Reiyukai Kyodan and the Seicho no Ie, a group we have not mentioned, which teaches the unity of all religions. These older but now-established "new religions" have followed a standard pattern: The religions that began in prewar Japan have evolved through tumultuous times, and the survivors long ago abandoned their rebellious teachings to fit into the mainstream society. Each now allows families to participate in once-prohibited rituals to the Shinto gods and at Buddhist temples.

The most successful new religions have built schools, colleges, and hospitals; some offer residential communities and athletic facilities to sustain their members from cradle to grave. These resources are also useful for proselytizing purposes and for demonstrating the power and success of the new path itself. The Tenrikyo, for example, one of the most successful new religions, has centers in every urban area of Japan; its headquarters, called Tenri City (near Nara), is a center for pilgrimage comparable to Salt Lake City for Mormons.

Sociological surveys have shown that devotees of the new religions are most commonly those excluded from dominant avenues to prestige in modern Japan. That is, with certain exceptions, members do not typically have prestigious jobs in the large corporations but run small family businesses. Within the group there are characteristically hierarchies and internal ranks to which individuals can aspire. Women typically outnumber men in membership and serve as leaders; their proselytizing is notable for its distinctly maternal style.

The new religions assume a common outlook (hence social posture) in presenting themselves as experts at solving human problems. Whatever their supernatural beliefs, all hold that sickness, economic failure, and all interpersonal relations can be fully under individual control. Life will improve, they assert, if devotees will only discipline themselves in realizing the core values of Japanese culture: harmony, loyalty, filial piety, selflessness, diligence, ritual service. Problems can be solved by making a concerted effort to practice these virtues, to perfect the self, and to harmonize it with all levels of life (from personality integration to reconciliation with one's family, society, nature, ancestors, and the supernatural). The sects differ astoundingly in the prescriptions for accomplishing these goals, and we can give here only a representative sampling of the "new, new religions," groups formed in the postmodern era.

Rissho Koseikai ("Society Establishing Righteousness and Harmony").
Rissho Koseikai was founded by Reiyukai member Niwano Nikkyo (1906–99), who retained the Nichiren Buddhist school's focus on the *Lotus Sutra*. After 1969, the group's focus shifted to the individual's personality development through special counseling sessions (*hoza*) led by trained lay "teachers" and the goal of world peace. In them, hoza members sit together in a circle, creating a warm, intimate atmosphere for open discussion. The range of problems and questions raised in the hoza varies from personal problems at home or office, through problems of human relationships, to questions of religion and ethics. Rissho Koseikai teachers are trained to bring the Mahayana teachings, particularly those highlighting the universal Buddha-nature within all beings, to bear on all problems. The member's vow, repeated daily, shows its Buddhist center and its commitment to bring the teachings to life in the modern world:

> We, members of Rissho Koseikai,
> Take refuge in the Eternal Buddha Shakyamuni,
> And recognize in Buddhism the true way of salvation,
> Under the guidance of our revered founder, Nikkyo Niwano.
> In the spirit of lay Buddhists,
> We vow to perfect ourselves
> Through personal discipline and leading others
> And by improving our knowledge and practice of the faith,
> And we pledge ourselves to follow the bodhisattva way
> To bring peace to our families, communities, and countries and to the world.[13]

The group does not forbid members to join other religious groups or to participate in their rituals. International missionary movements have brought Rissho Koseikai to Korea, Brazil, and the United States. As of 2011, the Koseikai was Japan's second-largest new religion, organized uniquely according to government unit lines and claiming over 6.5 million members in twenty countries, the great majority in Japan.

Perfect Liberty Kyodan. Another among the most popular groups is the Perfect Liberty Kyodan (P. L. Kyodan, or PL), whose primary slogan, "religion is art," indicates its emphasis on the spiritual value of practicing the fine arts in everyday life. Its focal practice is liturgical, that is, prayers choreographed with stylized prostrations, gestures, and offerings. The theology is monotheistic, but there is a strong emphasis on the human mind's central role in discerning divine warnings (*mishirase*) and receiving divine instruction (*mioshie*) through the sect's training. PL claims 500 churches in ten different countries, with more than 1 million members; its official aim is, according to its website, "to make true world peace a reality by inspiring people to understand and appreciate their power to create and plan, judge and decide, and make the world a true utopia."

Agonshu. A new religion founded in 1971, Agonshu also has a Buddhist identity. The group was founded by Kiriyama Seiyu (b. 1921–), a charismatic spiritualist who declared that he had "cut off" his own karma and that through visits by Buddhas and deities, the true and original teachings of Shakyamuni Buddha were revealed to him. Kiriyama's distilled "essence of Buddhism" is that the ancestors must be properly "turned into realized Buddhas" through performing special rituals for them in the afterlife, a belief that would be disputed by traditional Buddhist monks and scholars. Agonshu teachings attribute the world's current troubles to the influence of the restless dead, who afflict the living to protest neglect. In the group's view, Kiriyama has rescued for the good of the entire world esoteric practices to pacify and enlighten the dead, particularly through fire rituals kept secret for centuries by the tantric Buddhist school in Japan called *Shingon*. The greatest yearly practice of this Agonshu rite, called *hoshi matsuri*, or "star festival," has become one of the most spectacular events in modern Japanese religion, attracting a half-million pilgrims to the site, while millions watch the spectacle on television. Each year Agonshu priests set massive twin fires, one to benefit the ancestors, the other to promote the personal welfare of all participants, who contribute millions of small boards to fuel the flaming blazes.

The goal of world peace has also in the last decade been featured as part of the sect's mission; Kiriyama has been photographed with Pope John Paul II and with the Dalai Lama to highlight Agonshu's intention of acting on the world stage for that end. Even with its outward missionizing, like many other new religions the group does not neglect fostering benefits for its individual disciples. Members are urged to chant the following five lines daily, the same words used to conclude Agonshu rallies:

Let's do it!
I will certainly succeed!
I am blessed with very good luck!
I will certainly do well!
I will definitely win![14]

Sukyo Mahikari. The group called Sukyo Mahikari, founded in 1963, provides an example of a more ethnocentric new religion that affirms fascist prewar values and presents a more narrow, sectarian view of salvation. It teaches that the postwar occupation unnaturally imposed democracy and materialism on the Japanese people, causing them to be possessed by evil spirits angry over the corruption of the country. Then communism was sent by the gods to warn humanity of a coming ordeal, or "baptism by fire," that will claim all but the elect, who must restore patriotic ties to the emperor and demonstrate their loyalty to other Confucian relationships (between parents and children, husbands and wives). Those who follow this vision set forth by the founder, Okada Kotama, will be the "seed people" to restart the world in its proper order, as set forth in a myth that foretells the leadership of Okada. This group's social programs without subtlety evoke a religious expression of prewar fascism by sponsoring military-style parades during which troops of disciples honor their founder with extended arms, a replica of the Nazi salute. Since the founder's death and the succession of his daughter to leader, the group has established branches in seventy-five countries and its aims have become more global. As its website proclaims: "Sukyo Mahikari strives to manifest a heavenly world: a civilization of peace, abundant health, and material well-being. It endeavors to reestablish a pristine and pollution-free world."

Korea's Strong Confucian Tradition Accommodates Diversity

With the strong living tradition of Confucianism entrenched in family rituals, marriage arrangements, and the moral education programs in the public school curriculum, South Korea today is by all accounts the "most Confucian" nation in East Asia. Institutions dedicated to Confucian studies thrive in Korea, and exponents use the mass media to preach Confucian values. A common message is that by being true to its Confucian identity, Korea has a key role to play in achieving a harmonious "meeting of West and East."

Some among the Korean political elite (like many others in East Asia) believed Confucianism to be harmful to the nation, hindering its progress in the modern world. For those espousing this viewpoint, Westernization, agnosticism, and/or Christianity served as an antidote. However, Confucianism as the cultural center of Korea has endured even among Christian converts, most of whom openly observe their family's older rituals in honor of ancestors. South Korea adopted national economic goals in a Confucian framework: The central government takes responsibility for the citizenry's education and economic well-being, supports the family as the basis for social stability, accepts the intelligentsia as the conscience of the nation, and invests in education as the essential foundation for both material and cultural progress. The government has likewise supported major institutions dedicated to Confucian studies.

In the nation of North Korea, a strong if archaic emphasis on communist civil religion remains. Much as in the Maoist era, citizens are expected to renounce the culture of the past, sacrifice themselves for the common good, and participate in the "cult of personality" centered on the modern nation's ruling patriarch, Kim Jong Il.

As with Japan, we highlight groups that are shaping the diverse religious environment in modern South Korea.

Confucian Revival: The T'oegyehak Movement

Since learning the lessons of history is a strong Confucian value, it is not surprising that an important South Korean group emphasizes a prominent figure in its own historical tradition, the philosopher Yi T'oegye (1501–70). Master T'oegye developed the ideas of the most famous neo-Confucian Chinese thinker, Zhu Xi, whose Second Epoch leadership we have discussed, and T'oegye was responsible for making his system of thought prominent in Korea. To this end, he wrote treatises on the works of Zhu Xi and other neo-Confucians; all these texts were especially influential in the realm of state law and in focusing on ancestor ritualism.

The extraordinary industrial leader Lee Dong-choon (1919–89) started the traditionalist **T'oegyehak** movement group by publishing the prolific writings of Master T'oegye. The T'oegyehak, which is a presence not only across East Asia but among East Asians living in the West, has tapped Lee's personal fortune to promote detailed studies of the Confucian values as interpreted by Chinese and Korean masters. The organization has sponsored numerous conferences and made low-cost copies of the Confucian classics available across the globe.

T'oegyehak: modern Korean Confucian group based on teachings of master Yi T'oegye

Buddhist Revival

Despite many setbacks over the last century, the surviving Korean Buddhist institutions remain well endowed with landed income. As a result the major schools have established an important niche in Korean society through the monastery schools and lay institutions they founded. The Son Buddhist school, the Korean version of Zen, has sent several prominent teachers to the West, winning international support and renown.

A new school calling itself Won-bul-gyo, styled **Won Buddhism** in English, arose in 1924, founded by Soe-Tae San (1891–1943), a teacher who claimed to have been enlightened through his own independent ascetic practices. He and his disciples sought to revive Buddhism by simplifying its doctrines and combining Pure Land and Zen teachings. The only Won ritual involves the worship of a picture of a black circle in a white background, symbolizing the *dharmakaya*, the cosmic body of the Buddha.

Won Buddhism: Korean school of Buddhism that combines Zen and Pure Land teachings

Only after the death of San and the end of Japanese occupation did the group find popular acceptance across Korea. Typical of reformist "Protestant Buddhist" groups elsewhere in Asia (see Chapter 7), Won Buddhism has been especially popular in major urban areas and emphasizes that Buddhist doctrines are compatible with modern thought. It also makes Buddhism attractive to the laity by translating classical texts into vernacular Korean and through weekly congregational worship involving chanting, simple rituals, and sermons. The group encourages women to be leaders and active participants. Won Buddhist monks or nuns, who lead the ritual services, can marry.

Another aspect of Won Buddhism that resembles reform Buddhism as practiced outside Korea is the encouragement of lay meditation and social service. For the former, members try to cultivate the "Buddha nature in all things" and bring this awareness to all work done in everyday life, an exercise known as *Zen without time or place*. For Won social engagement, the Buddhist ideal of nonself (*anatman*) is sought through service offered to the public, and these activities are also seen in classical terms as a means to address the universality of suffering. The primary form of service by Won Buddhists has been in building schools, from kindergartens to universities. Its moral emphasis is also quite Confucian, emphasizing filial relations as the proper vehicle for Buddhist ethical aspiration.

By 2013, this school claimed 450 temples and 960,000 followers; it had built a grand central headquarters in Iri in southwest Korea and a convention center in Seoul. The group has also spread to fourteen countries and the United States by way of immigrants, who have built many branch temples. Won Buddhists have shown increasing interest in ecumenical relations with other faiths, both in Korea and with Japanese Buddhist groups.

Christianity in Korea

An alert observer of religion living in North America will be aware that significant numbers of native Koreans are Christians; signs with Korean characters dotting the landscape of many U.S. and Canadian cities announce that these congregations exist and sometimes share church sanctuaries with English-speaking Christians. As of 2013, approximately 32 percent of the South Korean population was Christian, with Protestants outnumbering Catholics by 4 to 1.

What makes Korea a unique stronghold of Christianity in Asia? Similarities between emotional Protestant rituals and the *mudang* tradition have been suggested as well as several elements unique to the recent Korean historical experience, such as the Buddhist cooperation with Japan's imperial rulers, churches' prominent involvement in the struggle against Japanese occupation (1910–45), and Korean Christians' subsequent leadership in human rights activism. With the exception of some churches tolerating shamanism and reinterpreting ancestor ritualism within a Christian framework, there has been little doctrinal innovation outside the traditional denominational frameworks.

Persistence of the Shaman's Drum

mudang: Korean shaman

Amid a rising number of Christian converts and modest revivals under way among the various Buddhist schools, old and new, one finds a steady and unmistakable reliance on shamans, or **mudang**, in South Korea. As discussed in Chapter 2, shamans

---

TALES OF SPIRITUAL TRANSFORMATION: Buddhist Satori

The greatest experience in Buddhism is the realization of ultimate truth of a reality "beyond words." Zen masters preserved stories of the conditions existing at the pivotal moments when disciples broke through to deeper, transformative realization. Like this one, for example.

Late one night a female Zen adept was carrying water in an old wooden bucket when she happened to glance across the surface of the water and saw the reflection of the moon. As she walked the bucket began to come apart and the bottom of the pail

broke through, with the water suddenly disappearing into the soil beneath her feet and the moon's reflection disappearing along with it. In that instant the young woman realized that the moon she had been looking at was just a reflection of the real thing . . . just as her whole life had been. She turned to look at the moon in all its silent glory, her mind was ripe, and that was it . . . satori ("Enlightenment").

Source: Zen Master Chiyono, *No Moon, No Water.*

Shamans have thrived in modern Korea through dramatic rituals such as this one, in which the mudang subdues a troublesome local spirit.

in Korea enjoy uniquely high status and popularity in the East Asian region. Once demonized by Christian missionaries and denounced as charlatans by the early post–World War II South Korean governments, in 2013 shamans are lauded as bearers of "intangible cultural assets" and now have a growing following. An estimated 300,000 shamans exist in South Korea, and many now have commercial websites. Scholars speculate that it is shamanic traditions that have helped foster Korea's harmonious and richly pluralistic religious culture.

Korean "New Religions"

As in Japan, the collapse of the traditional order in the nineteenth century precipitated a host of religious responses, and the one major avenue was the "new religions," formed to meet a three-part challenge: rebuilding the nation, restoring its spiritual center, and supporting individuals who were coping with rapid and often-traumatic changes.

Peak times of sociopolitical turmoil—for example, the years immediately following World War II—saw an especially great upsurge in these movements. Also conforming to the pattern seen in Japan's new religions, most Korean groups have been founded around men who claim a new supernatural revelation, usually a reassemblage of traditional doctrines from Buddhism, Daoism, Confucianism, or Christianity. Korean new religions likewise focus on this-worldly problems rather than the afterlife; some also imagine their playing a leading role in establishing Korea as humanity's global leader and/or creating a utopia on earth. Most have developed their doctrinal teachings into a comprehensive worldview and have created supportive social institutions. The total number of new religion adherents was last determined in 2003 by the government to number about 1 million, or 5 percent of the South Korean population. (We discuss the most prominent Korean new religion, the Unification Church, in the next chapter.)

Conclusion: Have We Entered a Third Confucian Age?

The vibrant religious and philosophical ferment felt by many Chinese is clearly visible in the new art being produced by artists such as Zhang Huan. This installation, called *Peace Bell II* (2001), is intended to suggest, in the artist's comments, "The act of ringing the bell—slamming the figure of the artist into the record of his ancestry to produce a beautiful and powerful sound—suggests that artistic struggle with the circumstances of and inheritance from family is both necessarily violent and richly generative."

Our study of the religions of East Asia, past and present, has shown conclusively that contrary to assertions of many among the modern elites of China and Japan as well as numerous Western scholars, religious beliefs and practices are central to the life and culture of the region. East Asians are by no means an exception to the human condition, namely, that in every known society there are religious traditions at the center of its cultural life. Moreover, only by understanding the religious dimensions of Shintoism and Confucianism can one comprehend the nationalism and cultural foundations of Japan's and China's post-WWII rise to create two of the world's leading economies. Likewise, only by recognizing the religious dimensions of Maoist communism is it possible to fathom how in China the Communist Party has sustained its place of power since 1949, a topic we'll return to in Chapter 9.

Nevertheless, Confucianism and Daoism present a challenge to the Western monotheistic model of "being religious," with some scholars claiming that these belief systems are not "religions" at all. Of course, in no manner is either monotheistic. Rather, their diverse aspects, as we illustrated, suggest another way for humans to be religious: not centering the sacred on a single God above but seeing as sacred this world "below," in which humans live together and within nature. Respect and reverence are the central religious emotions here. Confucianism and the diffuse religions of East Asia have both cultural and supernatural dimensions. They create in each society circles of reciprocal relatedness, making social relations sacred, harmonizing human existence with vital energies of nature, and respecting the creative power of the universe. In the supernatural dimension, they envision a world affected by deities and reverence the survival of ancestors as spirits with whom relations can endure forever.

Both attributes of religion outlined in Chapter 1—"being bound to others" and "being careful"—are abundantly highlighted across the diverse landscape of East Asian religions. The general ethos promoted by all East Asian religions, old and new, can be characterized as optimistic toward human life and human potential, seeing the improvement of the individual and improvement of society as sacred goals.

Respect for the multiple threads of the past serves to uphold acceptance of pluralism and the tolerance of religious diversity. The "diffuse religion" supports family cohesion as the center of a moral society, and the Confucian core of East Asia supports education for its role in cultivating character and in the acquisition of practical knowledge. This sort of "pragmatic idealism" calls for improving the world for the sake of this-worldly concerns, not as the dictate of a transcendent deity. The success in the modern global marketplace of this complex of religion and culture has given the lie to Western scholars who had argued that East Asian religions were obstacles to modern economic development. New syncretistic religious understandings, informed by growing global connections, seem destined to develop further in China, as seen in new artistic movements.

The reemergence of religion in China is powerful proof that Marx and Mao erred when they consigned religion to the "dustbin of history." Moreover, religion is gaining importance in the country, including underground Christian church movements, even as modern science, technology, and nationalism advance. The census figures in Table 8.1 reveal the official reckoning of the scale and variation of organized religions in China today.

If the Confucian system of family/ancestral devotion is regarded as the central pillar of Chinese tradition, then it is clear that it, too, has survived the criticisms and persecutions and that it has done so strongly. What is remarkable is that this has happened largely independent of any formal institutions and simply through the family relations that continued even amid fierce totalitarian attempts to suppress Confucianism.

It is remarkable, however, to note that in 2013 there were signs that the "Confucian family revival" in China was not as vibrant as originally thought. The market economy made extended family living as difficult as it had become elsewhere in the world, so the elderly were left behind as jobs required moves; the Party's "one-child policy" resulted in many millions of single-child families, which naturally unfolded to place the burden for elder care on one individual adult child; and the Party's suppression of children's literature promoting filial piety until recent years deprived today's adults

Table 8.1 Five Permitted Religions in the People's Republic of China

Religion	Adherents (millions)	Clergy (thousands)	Places of Worship
Buddhism	200	200	22,500
Islam	25	40	30,000
Daoism	100	38	5,800
Christianity: Protestantism	30	18	55,000
Christianity: Catholicism	15	4	4,600

SOURCE: "Religious Believers Thrice the Official Estimate Poll." *China Daily*, 7 February 2007. Chinadaily.com.cn of that teaching during their childhood. These effects of earlier government policies became clear as a groundswell of press reports in 2012–2013 exposed adults who had been scandalously unfilial: parents forced to live in unheated rooms, eat only gruel, and survive on their own in abject rural poverty. Shocked and dismayed, the Communist Party passed a law in 2013 requiring children to call parents regularly and act on their filial piety. Can a law change the press of the market economy to restore Confucian virtue?

It is possible that the future revival of religion in China will threaten regional stability. A large state trying to hold together diverse groups and disparate regions faces certain inherent problems, and difficulties loom large in the present relationship between communist China and its principal minorities. In particular, it is across religious issues that major fault lines affecting modern China are to be found—with Muslims in Xinjiang Province and with Buddhists in the Tibetan cultural region.

Ascribing East Asia's economic revival mainly to its Confucian roots remains, for some, a contested position. According to "Third Epoch" proponents, the traumas of the modern era succeeded in liberating the Confucian worldview from the trappings of power that had developed in the imperial systems of China, Korea, and Japan. Under them, the application of the highest Confucian ideals had been corrupted by government officials and the organized religious academies that turned "mastery" of the classics into a mere exercise in memorization needed to pass imperial examinations.

Confucian schools promoting the classical Confucian humanities are being reinvented in China in the twenty-first century.

Now the Confucian revival movement seeks to return to the basic teachings of the early sages (Confucius and Mencius, of the First Epoch) and do what Master Zhu Xi and other reformers did in their time (Song Dynasty, 960–1279), when they revived, reinterpreted, and adapted the tradition to the challenges of their era posed by Daoism and Buddhism (the Second Epoch of neo-Confucianism). Believers in "Third Epoch" Confucianism, working in the states on the periphery of China and finding growing supporters in mainland China as well, are now addressing the challenges of economic and cultural globalization.

Such efforts to revive this spiritual tradition have made "Third Epoch" Confucians critical of the global modernizing process, especially insofar as it has caused the extreme fragmentation of society, promoted the vulgarization of social life, disregarded the public good, or overglorified wealth. The vast majority of modernist Confucians adopt this critical stance while also being committed to empirical science, democratic politics, gender equality, and the economic development in their own countries. In early twenty-first-century China, interest in promoting Confucianism as a means of forming the character of citizens is winning widespread support among intellectuals and parents and even within the Communist Party itself. A host of newly approved schools include in their curriculum the study of traditional Confucianism; "Harmonious Society," the 2002 slogan for the nation's future that has been adopted by Xi Jinping, the new Communist Party president, has Confucian overtones. In 2007, a book on Confucian thought published in China became a best seller: *Yu Dan's Reflections on "The Analects"* sold over 10.2 million copies in the first year, and the author became a media celebrity starring in a show covering the basic

In 2010, the Chinese government placed an image of Confucius in Tian'anmen Square, Beijing, forty-one years after the sage was reviled by Communist Party Red Guards during the Cultural Revolution. Early in 2011, it was removed without comment, an indication of the persistence of ambivalence in the Chinese Communist Party leadership.

teachings. Though some traditional scholars have criticized her simplified, selective interpretations of how the *Analects* provide advice for "stress reduction, forgiveness, simple living, friendship, and achieving one's dreams,"[15] the success of this book signals how far the culture of China has shifted again toward its great classical heritage. The theme of the 2008 Beijing Olympics, "One world, one dream," also projected the early Confucian ideal of a world led by ethical ideals.

The global vision of "Third Epoch" exponents is to bring the Confucian tradition into the debate about how the twenty-first century's global order should be conceived. They aim to foster dialogue between the Confucian worldview and the ideologies of sociopolitical modernization and consumerism prominent in the Euro-American world. One "Third Epoch" Confucian summarized this goal as follows:

> Copernicus decentered the earth, Darwin relativized the godlike image of man, Marx exploded the ideology of social harmony, and Freud complicated our conscious life. They have redefined humanity for the modern age. Yet they have also empowered us with communal, critical self-awareness, to renew our faith in the ancient Confucian wisdom that the globe is the center of our universe and the only home for us and that we are the guardians of the good earth, the trustees of the Mandate of Heaven that enjoins us to make our bodies healthy, our hearts sensitive, our minds alert, our souls refined, and our spirits brilliant. . . . We are Heaven's partners, indeed co-creators. . . . Since we help Heaven to realize itself through our self-discovery and self-understanding in day-to-day living, the ultimate meaning of life is found in our ordinary human existence.[16]

Informed by very different notions of religious truth and by ethnocentric visions of their own central places in the cosmos, will the world's people outside East Asia be interested in such a dialogue?

Discussion Questions

1. In terms of the discussion in Chapter 1, is ancestor veneration really a "religious tradition"? Why?

2. What beliefs from each of the three religious traditions of the region might explain the East Asian peoples' unique capacity for sustaining the three without choosing just one?

3. Why do purity and brightness sum up the ethos of Shintoism?

4. Why, from the Daoist perspective, are disasters in the natural world taken so seriously by Chinese emperors?

5. How is the cult of ancestor veneration related to the norms of Confucian character formation and family morality?

6. A Chinese novelist in the colonial period described the Chinese family as "a prison ward" that denies basic rights to the individual, exploits women, and wastes the energy of the young. How would you defend Confucian ideals against these criticisms?

7. What features of East Asia's "diffuse religion" would a Christian missionary find most important to resist? What features would be compatible?

8. How might neo-Confucianism be seen as an attempt to harmonize Buddhism, Daoism, and early Confucianism?

9. In Korea, does shamanism reinforce ancestor veneration or undermine its practice?

10. Critique the following proposition: China's religious revival was postponed by the Chinese communists, who imposed a "forced conversion" of the nation to Marxism-Leninism, the "new religion" it had imported from Europe.

11. For all the nations of East Asia, the colonial era was very destructive. But certain individuals fused ideas from global culture with older beliefs, creating new and original religious understandings. Cite an example of this process in China, in Korea, and in Japan.

12. What influences from the West might have influenced elites in East Asia to claim that the Chinese (or the Japanese) are "not religious"?

Key Terms

All Souls Festival	"kitchen god"	Qing-Ming
Amaterasu	Lao Zi	religious Daoism
Analects	li	ren
ancestor veneration	ling	*Shang-di*
Ch'ondogyo	Mandate of Heaven	Shinto
city god	mappo	Soka Gakkai
Confucianism	Master K'ung	Taiping Rebellion
Cultural Revolution	Master Xun	Tenrikyo
Dao	Mencius	three faiths
Daoist	mudang	Tian di
Daruma-san	neo-Confucianism	T'oegyehak
de	neo-Shintoism/state	Tu-di gong
diffuse religion	Shinto	Won Buddhism
Five Classics	"new religions"	wu-wei
Full Moon Festival	Nichiren	xiao
Guan Yu	philosophical Daoism	yin-yang theory
Hong Xiuquan	qi	Zhu Xi
kami	qi gong	*Zhuang Zi*

Suggested Readings

Ashiwa, Yoshiko, and David L. Want, eds. *Making Religion, Making the State: The Politics of Religion in Modern China* (Stanford, CA: Stanford University Press, 2009).

Bell, Daniel A., and Hahm Chaibong, eds. *Confucianism for the Modern World* (Cambridge: Cambridge University Press, 2003).

Buswell, Robert E. *Religions of Korea in Practice* (Princeton, NJ: Princeton University Press, 2007).

Chau, Adam Yuet. *Miraculous Response: Doing Popular Religion in Contemporary China* (Stanford, CA: Stanford University Press, 2006).

Earhart, H. Byron. *Japanese Religion: Unity and Diversity*, 4th ed. (Belmont, CA: Wadsworth, 2003).

Gardner, Daniel. *The Four Books* (Indianapolis: Hackett, 2007).

Kendall, Laurel. *Shamans, Housewives, and Other Restless Spirits: Women in Korean Ritual Life* (Honolulu: University of Hawaii Press, 1985).

Lee, Peter H., ed. *Sources of Korean Tradition: From Early Times to the 16th Century* (New York: Columbia University Press, 1996).

Lopez, Donald S., Jr., ed. *Religions of China in Practice* (Princeton, NJ: Princeton University Press, 1996).

Nelson, John K. *Experimental Buddhism: Innovation and Activism in Contemporary Japan.* (Honolulu: University of Hawaii Press, 2013).

————. *A Year in the Life of a Shinto Shrine* (Seattle: University of Washington Press, 1996).

Park, Jin Y. *Makers of Modern Korean Buddhism* (Albany: State University of New York Press, 2010).

Picken, S. D. B. *Shinto: Japan's Spiritual Roots* (Tokyo: Kodansha, 1980).

Reader, Ian. *Religion in Contemporary Japan* (Honolulu: University of Hawaii Press, 1991).

Reader, Ian, and George J. Tanabe Jr. *Practically Religious: Worldly Benefits and the Common Religion of Japan* (Honolulu: University of Hawaii Press, 1998).

Reid, T. R. *Confucius Lives Next Door: What Living in the East Teaches Us About Living in the West* (New York: Vintage Books, 1999).

Sommer, Deborah. *Chinese Religion: An Anthology of Sources* (New York: Oxford University Press, 1995).

Swanson, Paul, and Clark Chilson, eds. *The Nanzan Guide to Japanese Religions.* (Honolulu: University of Hawaii Press, 2006).

Thompson, Laurence G. *Chinese Religion: An Introduction*, 5th ed. (Belmont, CA: Wadsworth, 1996).

Notes

1. In D. C. Lau, *Confucius: The Analects* (New York: Penguin, 1979), p. 63.
2. In D. C. Lau, *Mencius* (New York: Penguin, 1970), p. 191.
3. Quoted in Stephen Teiser, "Popular Religion," *Journal of Asian Studies* 54, no. 2 (1995), p. 378.
4. In Wing-sit Chan, *A Sourcebook of Chinese Philosophy* (Princeton, NJ: Princeton University Press, 1973), pp. 86–87.
5. Ibid., pp. 497–98.

6. Timothy Brook, "Rethinking Syncretism: The Unity of the Three Teachings and Their Joint Worship in Late-Imperial China," *Journal of Chinese Religions* 21 (1993), 17.

7. Ibid., 18.

8. Ibid., 22.

9. Quoted in Wing-tsit Chan, *Instructions for Practical Living and Other Neo-Confucian Writings by Wang Yang-ming* (New York: Columbia University Press, 1962), p. 272.

10. Robert Buswell Jr., ed., *Religions of Korea in Practice* (Princeton, NJ: Princeton University Press, 2007), p. 450.

11. In Donald E. MacInnis, *Religion in China Today* (New York: Orbis, 1989), p. 206.

12. S. D. B. Picken, *Shinto: Japan's Spiritual Roots* (Tokyo: Kodansha International, 1980), p. 56.

13. http://www.rk-world.org/ (November 10, 2007).

14. Ian Reader, *Religion in Contemporary Japan* (Honolulu: University of Hawaii Press, 1991), p. 100.

15. "Modern Gloss on China's Golden Age," *New York Times*, September 3, 2007.

16. Ian Reader, "The Rise of a Japanese 'New New Religion,'" *Japanese Journal of Religious Studies* 15, no. 4 (1988), p. 244.

Additional Resources

Marukoto: The Teaching of Roundness (http://www.kurozumikyo.com/marukoto_e.html). An introduction to the Japanese "New Religion," Kurozumikyo.

Reiyukai (http://www.reiyukai.org/). Website for this Nichiren-related sect.

Rissho Kosei-kai (http://www.rk-world.org). Worldwide Buddhist organization founded in Japan that combines the wisdom of both the *Lotus Sutra* and the foundational teachings of Shakyamuni Buddha.

Agon Shu (http://www.agon.org/en/). Website for this new Buddhist group that emphasizes relic veneration and rituals for ancestors.

Jodo Shu (http://www.jodo.org/about_js/history.html). Website for the oldest Pure Land Buddhist lineage in Japan.

International Association of Shinto Shrine (http://www.jinjahoncho.or.jp/en/index.html). Information on shrines, rituals, and festivals.

GLOBALIZATION

From New to New Age Religions

9

ebbie belongs to a Baptist church in Atlanta and regularly attends services on Sunday mornings and Wednesday evenings. However, she has other religious interests as well. Indeed, she regularly checks her astrological chart in the newspaper to see what kind of day she can expect to have. And on Tuesday nights she practices Zen Buddhist meditation with a small Zen group that meets at the house of her friend Sherry. Indeed, Sherry, who happens to be Jewish, is in fact the organizer and leader of the group, or "sangha," as Buddhists call it. Moreover, next week, she and her friend are going for a three-day Zen meditation retreat that she hopes will help deepen her spirituality both as a Christian and as a practitioner of Zen. Last week, Debbie's friend Michael talked her into going to a program led by a psychic medium who offers to put people in touch with their dead relatives. She is not sure what she thinks about this but is open to giving it a try. Likewise, Debbie has been reading *Dianetics*, by Scientology founder L. Ron Hubbard, just to see what it is all about.

All these activities mark Debbie as one of countless individuals who are on a personal quest that is typical of new age religion: They are eager to explore the mystery of the "self" and its perfection. Debbie has another friend, Marcus, who thinks she is too self-absorbed and needs to pay more attention to issues of social justice in a global culture dominated by mass media and multinational corporations, and marred by racial and economic exploitation. Marcus is trying to get her involved in a small interracial activist group inspired by the life and teachings of Martin Luther King Jr.

"The New Age is partially an offshoot of the Age of Science. . . . Children of the Age of Science, myself included, prefer to arrive firsthand, experimentally, at their own conclusions as to the nature and limits of reality. Shamanism provides a way to conduct these personal experiments, for it is a methodology, not a religion."

—Michael Harner, *The Way of the Shaman*

The group meets at Ebenezer Baptist Church in Atlanta, where Martin Luther King Jr.'s father was once the pastor and Martin the co-pastor. These activities of Debbie and her friends, as we shall see, could all be grouped together under the heading of *new age religion*.

In this chapter we will first explore what we mean by "new" religions and then focus primarily on "new age religions"—the distinctive forms that new religions and new ways of being religious have taken in response to globalization. New religions represent the integration of influences from multiple religions and cultures, resulting in the creation of new variations and expressions of known religious practices. In one familiar pattern, a new prophet or sage reveals new understandings of an existing tradition, given to him or her in religious experiences or revelations.

In the past the messages of prophets and sages reflected primarily local situations—typically the incursion of elements imported from nearby religions and cultures. Today, however, many new religious movements reflect not just a response to local diversity—to this or that movement that has entered the environment of a relatively stable culture. Rather, they are indicative of an awareness of global religious diversity as a whole, past and present. This awareness is fostered by mass communications, especially the Internet and cable television, and widespread access to international transportation, made possible by modern science and technology.

It is in this new environment of the awareness of the diversity of human religious experience that the "new age" religions are emerging, both accommodating and integrating diverse elements of varying, often quite dissimilar, existing traditions. Some movements, however, represent the attempt to reassert particular forms of past

A Pagan outdoor ceremony with a flaming pentagram at a stone circle in England. The ceremony is held on the full moon closest to the summer solstice.

religious expression that adherents believe have been neglected but should be operative in the new age of global interdependence. Contemporary interest in shamanism and goddess worship would be examples of this. What these movements typically have in common is the belief that humanity is indeed entering a "new age" in which global harmony must be achieved, not only with other religions and cultures but also with the natural environment.

Encounter with Modernity: The Challenge of Global Diversity to the "Purity" of Tradition

In the twenty-first century, Christianity, like all other religious traditions, seeks to communicate its understanding of truth on a variety of websites. Many of these websites address the concerns of those who hold fundamentalist beliefs and seek to educate their believers against the dangers of "new age religion." Such websites often contain warnings such as "'New Age' Religions and Why Christians Can't Participate." Such websites warn a Christian like "Debbie" (described above) that she is in danger of worshipping false gods. She is warned that she is failing to be faithful to the Gospel of Jesus Christ, who offers the one and only path to God and salvation. In postmodern societies, Christianity is not alone in facing the problem of keeping its followers "true to the tradition." Other traditions, especially the monotheistic traditions of Judaism and Islam, also warn their "faithful" to "be faithful" and keep to the way of Torah or the way of the Quran, as the case may be.

Globalization presents challenges to believers of all traditions. These challenges come from intimate exposure to the beliefs of other cultures and traditions, which are now commonly found in everyone's hometown. The challenge of new age religions is a challenge to the purity of tradition. Persons involved in postmodern spirituality do not see themselves in an "either/or" situation. They do not see themselves as having to choose one spiritual practice or path to the exclusion of others. In fact, they see themselves in a "both/and" situation. For the new age believer, one can be a Jew and still engage in Buddhist rituals and meditation; one can be a Catholic and still practice Hindu meditation and ritual; and so on.

The problem of keeping the tradition "pure" may be more challenging for monotheistic religions than it is for the religious traditions of India and China, where different religious paths have often interpenetrated. Nevertheless, people of all religions and cultures often have reservations when they see their children departing from strict adherence to the "sacred traditions" as they have known and practiced them. In every tradition this can seem quite threatening. The issue presented by globalization is whether it shall lead to greater understanding and cooperation among religions and cultures or greater defensiveness, prejudice, and even violence. The answer, as we shall see, is that globalization can lead to both.

New Religions

Old Religions and New Religions in the History of Religions

From a historical perspective, as this book has amply indicated, no religion has ever managed to remain unchanged. Indeed, while every chapter in this book began with an "overview" description of the religious beliefs and practices of the tradition, in every case we went on to say that such a snapshot was no more than a broad generalization that did not accurately reflect the tremendous diversity found among practitioners, yesterday or today. There is not one Judaism but many, not one Buddhism but many—likewise there are many Christianities, many Islams and Hinduisms, many Daoisms and Confucianisms.

New religions test and transform boundaries. Every tradition tolerates a tremendous amount of diversity. An emerging movement that at first is treated as a form of error may finally be accepted into the fold or at least tolerated as a distant cousin. It may, for example, be seen as a reform within the tradition to bring it back to its original purity. But then there are other movements, perhaps brought about by new religious experiences and extraordinary revelations, whose "errors" seem too great. Changes that had started out as reforms may present such a dramatic break with past beliefs and practices that they come to be perceived not as a continuation of the old tradition but as a fatal error—a deviation from the true path. The new tradition, of course, sees the error lying not in itself but in the old tradition, which had somehow lost its way.

Although before the common era there was more than one form of Judaism, Christianity, which began as a Jewish sect called the *Nazarenes*, came to be seen, and to see itself, as crossing a boundary that made it no longer a Jewish alternative but a "new religion." And while Christianity also encompasses tremendous diversity, when Islam emerged in Arabia in the seventh century it was seen by Christians as a new and heretical religion, even though Muslims recounted many of the same biblical stories and saw their faith as the continuation and culmination of God's revelations handed down through Moses and Jesus. Moreover, Islam developed two major branches, Sunni and Shiah, as well as many schools of theology and law. However, in nineteenth-century Persia, when the Baha'i movement claimed to bring a final revelation that included all the religions, East and West, it came to be viewed as "not true Islam," but a new belief system.

When we look at Asian religions we find the same pattern. Hinduism encompasses great diversity, yet as Buddhism grew and developed it was seen, and came to see itself, as a "new religion." Buddhism, too, splintered into many Buddhisms, some claiming to be more advanced than others.

In every tradition, some movements emerged and then disappeared. Even so, in century after century, many of "today's" new religions become tomorrow's old and established religions. We can illustrate the character of new religions with a few examples before turning to our primary concern, examples of "new age" religions that have appeared in our emerging global civilization. The relatively recent history of Christianity in North American culture presents an interesting illustration of how a new religion comes to be.

In the 1800s, Christian denominationalism began to emerge as a way of moving beyond the hostile sectarianism that had divided Christians, and by the late twentieth century there was a broad spectrum of "acceptable" religious diversity in America. Nevertheless, a number of very distinctive religious movements that originated in the nineteenth century tested the limits of denominationalism. As a rule, contemporary mainline Christian denominations (i.e., those representing widely established, long-accepted church traditions in America, such as the Methodists, Presbyterians, and Episcopalians) tend to regard these unique movements as having strayed beyond the boundaries of Christianity. Mormonism provides us with a good example; Jehovah's Witnesses provides another.

The Church of Jesus Christ of Latter-day Saints: A New American Christianity

The Church of Jesus Christ of Latter-day Saints, or Mormonism, was established on April 6, 1830, by Joseph Smith Jr. It appears to have arisen in response to the confusion and conflict created by the incredible sectarian diversity of nineteenth-century Christianity. Joseph Smith believed he had been led by angels to discover a revelation that would overcome this confusion. The new revelation, contained in the Book of Mormon, was understood by Smith and his followers as a continuation of the revelation given in the Bible. It was a revelation that had been given first to Native Americans, as descendants of the lost tribes of ancient Israel. Mormons believe that these tribes had migrated to the North American continent, where the risen Christ visited them and gave them new revelations. Eventually the book containing these pronouncements was buried by a Native American named Mormon, who was killed by tribesmen who rejected the new message and wanted to suppress it. It was these "pagan" natives who met Columbus in 1492. But the revelation could not be suppressed forever, and so Joseph Smith was guided by angels to find the Book of Mormon so that it could flourish once more.

Earlier, in Chapter 4, we noted the incorporation into Christianity of traditions specific to Africa and Asia. Similarly, Mormonism links biblical religion to the history of an indigenous population—in this case producing a distinctively

Joseph Smith Jr. receiving the sacred plates of the Book of Mormon from the Angel Moroni.

American Christianity, one that includes visits of the risen Christ and several of the risen apostles to a new land, to guarantee the purity of Mormon revelation and so set it apart from existing "human interpretations" of Christianity. The capstone of the message was the promise that at the end of time, in the "latter days," Christ would return to establish a "New Jerusalem" in America. The growing stature of Mormonism in America is illustrated by Mitt Romney as the first Mormon candidate for President of the United States in 2012. Mormonism, with its emphasis on family, community, and healthy, wholesome living, flourishes today, with well over 10 million members worldwide.

Jehovah's Witnesses—Another American Vision of the End Time

The nineteenth century saw the emergence of other apocalyptic movements looking for the coming of a New Jerusalem in America. William Miller (1782–1849), a farmer in upstate New York, considered the founder of the Seventh Day Adventists, predicted the second coming of Christ would occur on March 21, 1843. When that did not happen, he recalculated and predicted March 21 a year later. Another, Charles Taze Russell (1852–1916) was swept up in the apocalyptic fervor of movements similar to the Millerites. Charles Taze Russell may have learned from the failure of those predictions, for he embraced an interesting twist on the apocalyptic belief that Christ was coming soon, suggesting that Christ had already spiritually returned as an invisible presence in 1874, initiating a 40-year period for the ingathering of true believers, culminating in 1914, the beginning of World War I as the beginning of the time of apocalyptic sufferings that would announce the second coming.

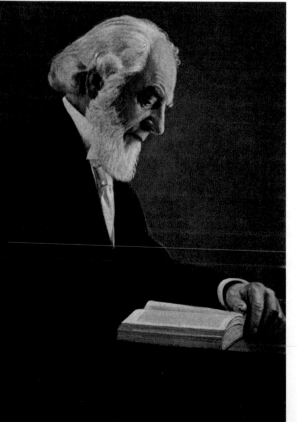

Charles Taze Russell, founder of the original Watchtower Bible and Tract Society.

Russell began publishing his beliefs in a journal called *Zion's Watch Tower and Herald of Christ's Presence* in 1879. Small congregations following his teachings began holding annual conventions in 1891. Beginning in Allegheny, Pennsylvania, the movement established headquarters in Brooklyn, New York, by 1909. After Russell's death the movement was led by Joseph Franklin Rutherford (1869–1942). In the twentieth century Jehovah's Witnesses grew into a significant international movement with a presence in Europe, Asia, Latin America, and the Middle East. In the year 2000, the Watch Tower Society separated out from the Watch Tower Bible and Tract Society and the new Watch Tower Society's governing board assumed leadership authority in the global movement.

The Jehovah's Witnesses take their name from the Hebrew name for God, the four letters of the tetragrammerton—YHWH. There are no vowels in biblical Hebrew, so they adopted the practice of pronouncing this as "Yehovah." They refer to themselves as Yehovah's Witnesses, those who are called to champion the oneness of God. Although they consider themselves Christians, they do not adhere to the teachings of the ancient church councils that affirmed the trinitarian theology accepted by both the Catholic and mainline Protestant Reformation traditions, which consider God to be one, yet three—Father, Son, and Holy Spirit, all equal in status. For Jehovah's Witnesses, "trinity" is not found in the Bible. In the New Testament, they argue, Jesus is not equal to God but is "first born of all creation" (St Paul's Letter to the Colossians, 1:15) and the "Holy Spirit" simply refers to the active power of God at work in the world. For similar reasons they do not celebrate traditional Christian holidays like Christmas and Easter, which they see as later pagan nonbiblical additions to Christianity.

Like the Millerites or Seventh Day Adventists, Jehovah's Witnesses are distant inheritors of the traditions of the Anabaptist wing of the sixteenth-century Protestant Reformation, who were known for their distrust of government as the work of the devil. Indeed, the Jehovah's Witnesses have a reputation as "conscientious objectors" who refuse to cooperate with any government's conscription into military service. They have also been responsible for several U.S. Supreme Court decisions protecting the separation of church and state. Perhaps most well known among these was securing the right to refuse blood transfusions, which they believe are forbidden by the Bible.

Also, like the Adventists, Jehovah's Witnesses strongly identify with the Jewishness of early Christianity, before its explicit doctrinal move into Trinitarianism. Russell saw 1914, the beginning of World War I, as a spiritually pivotal time which marked the end of the gentile domination over Israel and the beginning of the difficult end times predicted in the Bible. Indeed, Adventists present in Nazi Germany during World War II were courageous in their resistance to the Nazis and Nazi anti-Semitism. Like Jews, they became targets for imprisonment in the death camps.

Civil Religion in China—A Blend of Confucianism and Marx's Secular Apocalyptic Vision

Civil religions represent yet another form in which new religious traditions can play very traditional roles in a society. In most times and most places throughout the history of civilization, religion and politics permeated all of culture and were like two sides of the same coin. It was, as we have seen, modernity that introduced secular nation-states and the idea that government should not impose on citizens the obligation to join or practice any particular religion. But having removed religion as a legitimizer of their own authority, these modern states faced a new problem—winning loyalty from their citizens without the traditional appeal to religion. The result has been the creation of a distinct entity we shall call *civil religion*. Civil religion reintroduces religion under the disguise of "indigenous cultural history and tradition" to reinforce the authority of new and more secular political social orders.

Thus a civil religion is based on a sacred narrative of the state's founding, in which the development of the state is portrayed as a just, moral enterprise, in harmony with

Mao Zedong, founder
of the People's Republic
of China.

ideals of the religious traditions shared by most citizens. Typically, the state's leaders developed a set of national rituals and yearly holidays (holy days) that celebrate and allow the regular, solemn reliving of key events in the nation's history. Such civil religions come to expression in national anthems and patriotic songs, school textbooks that emphasize the righteousness of the country's founders, and war memorials honoring those who sacrificed their lives for the nation.

In many cases, the cultural pattern from one tradition (Christianity, Islam, Confucianism, etc.) clearly comes to underlie the nation's civil religion, though seldom to the extent of specific endorsement. What is striking is how nearly all the great ideas in the history of religions (e.g., sacrifice, sage, prophet, martyrdom, sacred center, "chosen people," rebirth, *millennialism*—the belief in an age of peace and perfection at the end of time) have been adopted across the world in the service of creating and sustaining the civil religions that support modern nations. Chinese communist civil religion provides a helpful example of this.

When the Red Army gained control of the mainland of China in 1949, Communist Party leader Mao Zedong ascended the southern gateway to the emperor's old palace (the Forbidden City) to proclaim the creation of the People's Republic of China. This moment was later pictured on currency and in popular prints, and soon thereafter an immense portrait of Chairman Mao was mounted over the ancient gateway. Over the next twenty-five years, the Communist Party drew on a variety of religious conceptions to legitimate its position in China and to wield power. Essential to this was the communist millennial doctrine imported from Russian revolutionaries. They in turn drew upon Karl Marx's modernist grand narrative derived from Joachim of Fiore's apocalyptic-biblical vision of the three ages of the human race as a story of progress ending in a final new age. Paradise on earth was inevitable if the people changed their ways and lived in thoroughgoing cooperation. Citizens who sacrificed themselves for the common good were immortalized as "heroes of the people," and their dying was said to hasten the arrival of the new age.

Early on, the government integrated this with ancient Confucian imperial doctrine to promote the cult of Mao himself as the sage-philosopher leader of the nation. His words and teachings were pivotal for national salvation, and his character radiated the morality of communist truth. Statues of Mao were put up in public spaces around the nation, his portrait replaced images of family ancestors in home shrines, and during the Cultural Revolution (1966–76) his "Little Red Book" became a sacred text to be memorized, followed, and always possessed. Officially, the Communist Party disavowed religion as superstition and railed at long-dead Chinese emperors as feudal exploiters of the masses. Nevertheless, it is not hard to see how party strategists adapted powerful religious ideas from both European and Chinese traditions to create a civil religion to confirm the legitimacy of its dictatorship.

The New Age and New Age Religions

Postmodernism and the New Age

The collapse of colonialism, especially after World War II, was followed by the emergence of globalization. This globalization was fostered by the development of international corporations, global mass transportation, and global mass media, carrying modern science and technology around the world. Logically enough, then, since the 1960s and 1970s new patterns of religion have appeared that reflect a global consciousness. These religions shaped by science and technology as well as by the traditional considerations, although incredibly diverse, are often grouped together under the title *new age religions*. Not all new age religions are postmodern as we have defined that term. Indeed, many are content to continue the modernist pattern of privatization rather than seek a new public role for religion. But global consciousness has been a significant factor in the emergence of all new age religions. In this section and the next, we will look at examples of modernist and postmodernist new age religions.

In the first chapter we cited Jean-François Lyotard's definition of *postmodernism* as the collapse of metanarratives, the grand stories or myths that gave each civilization a sense of meaning, purpose, and identity. The great metanarratives created a relationship of identity between religion and culture, giving us Hindu civilization, Christian civilization, Islamic civilization, and so on. Each civilization was centered in its own grand stories and the social practices that came from the vision of life the stories promoted. Modernism, with its myth of scientific progress, was a relatively recent addition.

The resurgence of religions around the globe since the 1970s may well represent the need to fill the vacuum created by the tendency of secularization to purge events of meaning. The problem with a secular understanding of time, history, and society is that the significance and drama provided by the grand narratives of religions are missing. Pluralism may have collapsed the grand metanarratives into smaller stories, but there is still a great hunger for such stories, and new age religions help people discover the meaning and significance of time and their place in it. New age religions provide a rich feast for the religious imagination as seekers attempt to penetrate the mysteries of their time and to explore the wonders they offer.

Postmodern culture represents the loss of a normative center in every culture that has been touched by global mass media, international corporations, and global mass transportation. Postmodern culture is pluralistic, relativistic, and eclectic—seemingly without any public norms or standards. The choice between "truths" is said to be intellectually "undecidable" and so is decided pragmatically, in terms of "what works for me." Truth, goodness, and beauty are in the eye of the beholder. People mix and match beliefs, practices, and aesthetic choices to their own taste in all areas of life—whether music, clothing, architecture, intellectual beliefs, or religion.

Globalization provides the social context of postmodernism. Globalization "marbleizes" all cultures so that the world's religions are accessible in everyone's hometown.

A young Buddhist monk at a school in Burma looks at his photo on a laptop.

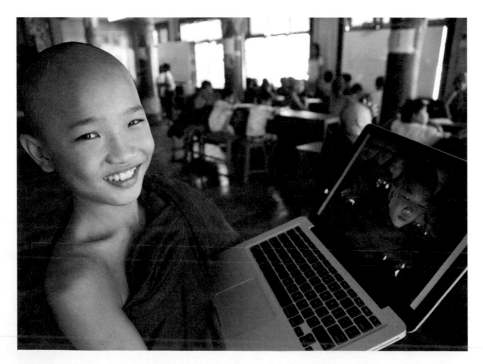

Today, much more than in the past, in the same community you will find Jews, Christians, Muslims, Hindus, Buddhists, and many others. Such pluralism is a powerful social force inducing the collapse of metanarrative, whereby a story that was once embraced by almost all people in a given culture is now simply one of many stories. In this situation religions are challenged first to relinquish their position of being identical with the culture and then to accommodate an existing cultural pluralism. In this context, almost all religious communities have had to embrace denominational type identities, accepting the existence of other beliefs and practices, although fundamentalist communities strive mightily to resist such an accommodation. This denominational accommodation, we said, was what sociologist Peter Berger meant by saying that all religions have become "Protestant." But for most new age groups their religious practices have gone a step further, moving from organizational pluralism (denominationalism) to eclecticism.

Many of the "new age" religions, like older "new religions," represent the integration of the diverse influences from different traditions. The new age religions are not based solely on the great world religions; often they incorporate elements of primal religions, exhibiting a special interest in shamanism. Moreover, today these eclectic belief systems typically reflect not only global religious diversity but the global influence of science and technology as well.

A group in the Netherlands performs a ritual based on the Thirteen Moon calendar of the Maya.

The New Age—Modern and Postmodern?

New age religious movements can be divided into modernist forms, which continue to privatize religion, and postmodernist public forms of religious practice, which seek an active role, socially and politically, in transforming society. Most modernist new age religions are highly diverse in their practices and beliefs, with minimal organizational structure. Nevertheless, there are some very important instances of highly structured new age movements; as we shall see, Scientology is one and Baha'i is another. What unites new age seekers, despite their diversity, however, is the quest for the perfection of the self. Their goal is to realize a "higher self" through intense personal experiences of transformation.

Many new age seekers are not interested in joining religious organizations. They typically integrate a variety of interests into their personal style of spiritual practice. Many read "spiritual" books and go to workshops and seminars intended to guide them to self-realization. Modernist "new agers" are interested in such shamanistic practices as channeling information from other-worldly spiritual beings, contacting the dead through mediums, spiritual healing, and the cultivation of ecstatic out-of-body experiences (sometimes referred to as *astral projection*). They are also interested in the mystical traditions and meditation practices of all religions as well as the ancient divination practice of astrology. Some combine these interests with the teachings and practices of transpersonal psychologists such as Abraham Maslow (1908–70) and Fritz Perls (1894–1970); others embrace speculative visions that combine the "new physics" with religion, believing that science itself is finally coming to discover and affirm ancient religious and metaphysical insights. The final test of each seeker's synthesis is personal experience and pragmatically evaluated usefulness.

Modernity, we learned in Chapter 4, on Christianity, emerged out of the splitting of the medieval unity of faith and reason into the *via moderna* of empirical rationality and the *devotio moderna* of personal emotional experiences of transformation (mysticism, pietism, and the experience of being "born again"). The first path became dominant in the Enlightenment and the second in the Romantic movement, as a reaction to the Enlightenment. The growth of new age religiousness is deeply rooted in this Romantic reaction to the rationalism of the Enlightenment.

The Enlightenment emphasized universal rationality (i.e., the sameness of human nature everywhere), science, and progress. Its philosophers rejected the ancient, the archaic, the traditional, the idiosyncratic, and the nonrational. The Romantic reaction, a stage we are still in, did just the opposite, embracing in all their diversity the emotional, the experientially transformational, the historically unique and particular, as well as the "primitive" and traditional aspects of human history.

Like fundamentalist forms of evangelical Christianity, modernist forms of new age religions are expressions of the human need for transformative experience, a need as old as shamanism and as recent as the Romantic reaction to Enlightenment rationalism and its expression in evangelical pietism. Both deemphasize rationality and focus on the experiential transformation and perfection of the self through deeply emotional experiences of the kind we have called religious. And both share the conviction that all social change begins by changing the self (i.e., by being born again).

The Age of Apocalypse or the Age of Aquarius?

Two new age models of religious meaning are playing a role in our emerging global civilization—the apocalyptic and the astrological. These models share a vision of the conflict and discord of the past and present giving way to a future era of global peace and harmony. Among Christian evangelicals the popularity of the belief that the end of time is near is evidenced by sales of tens of millions of books such as Hal Lindsey's *The Late Great Planet Earth* and the *Left Behind* series of novels. As indicated by the popularity of biblical prophecies of the end times among evangelical Christians, there are still many heirs to the apocalyptic religious vision of the medieval monk Joachim of Fiore, who anticipated a "third age" (the age of the Spirit) as a time of global peace and harmony. However, the third age will be preceded by the biblical apocalypse, which in turn will bring the cataclysmic end of time. The belief that there will be a cataclysmic end to time followed by a new age of peace and harmony is also illustrated in such late-twentieth-century movements such as Aum Shinrikyo (to be reviewed shortly). But first we will turn to the alternative vision—the astrological vision of the age of Aquarius.

A gentler vision of the new age, the age of Aquarius, has been offered by some astrologers in recent decades:

> We are passing out of 2,000 years of Piscean astrological influence into the influence of Aquarius, which will affect all aspects of our culture as we move from Piscean structures of hierarchical devotion to more fluid and spontaneous relationships that dance to an Aquarian rhythm.[1]

Predictions of the coming of a new age by others not of the apocalyptic tradition include the writings of José Argüelles. In his book *The Mayan Factor*, this new age author used ancient Mayan and Aztec astrology to calculate that the age of Aquarius would begin in 1987, on August 16 or 17.[2] When that did not happen, new interpretations or perhaps misinterpretations of Mayan texts emerged predicting a more traditional apocalyptic view of the end of the world which would occur when the Mayan calendar ends (according to some) on December 21, 2012. As of 2013, that has not happened either. In these Aquarian times, many forms of new age religion tap into a very ancient type of religious experience found in primal animistic and early urban polytheistic religious practices—that of the shaman. As we saw in Chapter 2, in his or her ecstatic or out-of-body experiences, the shaman explores the spirit world, the realm of contact with spiritual beings and dead ancestors.

Everywhere in the world, shamanism appears to be the earliest form of religious experience. And everywhere, the great world religions emerge with the discovery that the realm that a shaman visits when he or she leaves her physical body to travel to the domains of the spirits and of dead ancestors is really an intermediate spiritual realm between the earthly physical world and a higher unitary reality. For example, in the Vedas of Hinduism the highest realities are the many gods and goddesses of nature, but in the Upanishads the discovery is made that the gods are part of the order of this world of samsara and that there is a higher power beyond their realm, the reality of Brahman.

The emergence of monotheism out of polytheism in the Mediterranean world (in Judaism, Christianity, and Islam) provides another example. The polytheistic realm of the gods was not denied. It could not be denied because many people continued to have shamanistic-type experiences of another realm inhabited by spiritual beings. So this realm of the deities was reassigned to a different kind of spiritual being and renamed the realm of angels and demons. Like the devas or gods of Hinduism, angels were recognized as spiritual beings, yet they were part of the cosmic order created by a higher reality, God. In China this concept of a higher unitary reality was given the impersonal name of Dao.

For all the differences between ancient urban religious cultures and religions in postmodern society, there is at least one profound similarity between them: Both premodern urban society, as typified, for instance, by the polytheistic culture of ancient Rome, and postmodern society, with its myriad eclectic religious practices, lack an integrating center. In both, being religious is not so much about belonging to "a religion" as it is about selecting from the chaotic variety of available beliefs and practices, a mix that will serve the pragmatic purposes of finding health, happiness, and meaning, that is, of having the unseen powers that govern your destiny on your side.

Wicca and the Resurgence of Goddess Worship

Determining how many people "practice new age religion" is next to impossible. This is because it is quite common for nominal adherents to one of these belief systems to practice several different forms in their private life while perhaps also belonging to a traditional church or synagogue. One form this eclectic spirituality can take is sometimes called *neopaganism*, which is vividly exemplified in a return to the practice of witchcraft, or attunement to the sacred powers of nature, a pattern found in all premodern societies. The most prominent such practice today is Wicca, which appears to be a self-conscious reconstruction of ancient pagan religious practices. The Wiccan movement can be traced back to England in the 1940s and the writings of Gerald Gardener, who claimed to be an initiate of a Wiccan coven, authorized to reveal its teachings and practices to the public. Two students of Gardener's brought the practice to America in the 1960s. By 1965 a church of Wicca was established in Mississippi, and by 1978 the handbook for U.S. military chaplains included Wicca in its list of religions.

Wiccans see the world ordered by sacred forces that can be accessed through ritual magic. These powers are personified as gods and goddesses. Wiccan rituals involve the

High priestess and priest Gypsy and Richard Ravish sit at a Wiccan altar dedicated to magick in Salem, Massachusetts.

elaborate use of chant, dance, drumming, and meditation. By following the ancient Celtic agricultural cycle of festivals for the seasons of the year, these rituals enable Wiccans to reconnect with the rhythms of nature and to experience its hidden unity. Many tend to see their ritual practice as an outward expression of the fundamental truth of the interconnectivity of all things, a view that they believe modern science also affirms. One particular strand of Wicca, Dianic Wicca, presents itself as a feminist religion that rejects references to gods in favor of goddess worship and has radicalized its practice by banning male membership.

J. Z. Knight and the Ramtha School of Enlightenment

The Ramtha movement begun by J. Z. Knight provides another example of new age religion that appeals to pre-Christian shamanistic practices. It is a very good example of what is called "channeling," in which a spiritual being takes over and speaks through the body of a person. Knight is considered by her followers to be the psychic medium who channels Ramtha, a 35,000-year-old warrior, who speaks through her, revealing an ancient wisdom. It is said that when Ramtha possesses her, Knight's entire personality, her voice quality, and all her mannerisms change, as if she is another person altogether. Like the shamans of tribal cultures, she is revered by her followers as one who communicates between two worlds, the physical and the spiritual. Ramtha is an ancient warrior who supposedly lived in the city of Lemuria and defeated the armies of the ancient city of Atlantis. Ramtha was wounded in battle, and during the seven years of his recovery he had profound out-of-body spiritual and enlightenment experiences and finally transcended human form to become a being of light. The teachings of Ramtha are embodied in a text known as *The White Book*.

The vision of Ramtha appears to have much in common with the teachings of Gnosticism from ancient Greece and Rome. The highest spiritual reality, for instance, is said to be both male and female; the spiritual realm is said to be made up of seven levels; and Ramtha is said to be a being of light. All of these are characteristic teachings of ancient Gnosticism. Ramtha's revelation to Knight is intended to help people realize their true divine nature. Once upon a time people had divine powers to create objects in the world simply by thinking them. However, humans lost their awareness of the divine core of their being and became imprisoned in the material world. Ramtha has come to help them rediscover their true spiritual nature and their true powers and so overcome "the ditch of limitation."

J. Z. Knight was born in Roswell, New Mexico, a city famed for the belief among flying saucer enthusiasts that in 1947 an alien spaceship crashed and was examined by the military, which has kept the findings secret. Knight's mother is said to have had the power to foretell the future through dreams. Furthermore, the stories of Knight's childhood include one that says an elderly Yaqui Indian woman predicted that the infant Knight would grow up to be one who sees "what no one else sees." In addition, a psychic predicted that Knight would move to a mountainous area covered in pine trees, which Knight saw fulfilled when she was offered a job in the Tacoma, Washington, area. It was there that Knight experienced the manifestation of Ramtha for the first time in 1973. Five years later she made her first public appearance as the medium or channeler of Ramtha. Knight has become famous, publishing books, making TV appearances, and so on. Eventually, she established a kind of Ramtha retreat or teaching center on her ranch in Yelm, Washington. There she teaches Ramtha's followers that they can perfect themselves. There is no need to be trapped in their limitations. Everyone should realize their true divine powers.

Madame Helena Petrovna Blavatsky, founder of the theosophy movement.

Theosophy, Christian Science, and the Unity School of Christianity

The precedents for the Ramtha school and many other forms of new age religion go back to the interest in esoteric religious beliefs and practices that flourished in the nineteenth century, when historical and ethnographic researchers were just beginning to catalog the diverse practices of primal (tribal) and archaic (early urban) religions. From Europe, the teachings of Emanuel Swedenborg (1688–1772) and Franz Anton Mesmer (1734–1815) spread belief in the validity of the shamanistic experience of other worlds and in the animistic unity of all things, which made spiritual healing possible. In America, Ralph Waldo Emerson (1803–82) and others popularized a school of thought called *transcendentalism*, which integrated certain Asian religious beliefs (especially Hinduism) with American philosophy, affirming the existence of a "world soul" that all beings shared. In this context the practice of spiritualism also flourished, with psychic mediums performing in private séances the ancient shamanistic rituals for contacting spirit beings and dead relatives.

One of the most important movements to emerge at this time was theosophy, founded in New York by Helena Petrovna Blavatsky (1831–91) in 1875. Like the transcendentalists, theosophists found great spiritual wisdom in esoteric teachings, especially in the ancient teachings of Hinduism, with their focus on the interconnectedness of all beings through the universal Brahman. In the theosophical view, all world religions have a hidden unity of message and metaphysical reality, which could be sought through the truths of esoteric texts as well as through the help of leaders who claimed to receive guidance from "living masters," residing in the Himalayas. As we saw in Chapter 7, the theosophists had considerable influence among Asian reformers who were trying to modernize Buddhism. This growing interest in global religious wisdom is illustrated by the first Parliament of World Religions in Chicago in 1893, at which representatives of all the world's religions convened to share their views.

Emma Curtis Hopkins, founder of the Unity School of Christianity.

This historical milieu gave birth to two important nineteenth-century precursors of new age religion, both with roots in the New Thought movement: the Church of Christ, Scientist (Christian Science) and the Unity School of Christianity. Women were leaders in both movements. Mary Baker Eddy was the founder of the Christian Science movement, and Emma Curtis Hopkins, a former disciple, broke with Eddy to form the Unity School. The two movements drew on popular forms of philosophical idealism, and the Unity School emphasized Hindu teachings, as well. These influences were integrated with an aura of "science" to affirm the higher reality of mind over matter and therefore the possibility of spiritual healing and spiritual control over the events of one's life.

Scientology

As the new age religions began to appear in the twentieth century, the religious fascination with the authority of "science" broke free of its earlier linkage to Christianity in movements of the "Christian Science" type. One result was the emergence of *Scientology*, founded by L. Ron Hubbard (1911–86). In 1950 Hubbard published *Dianetics: The Modern Science of Mental Healing*, in which he claimed to have discovered a cure for all human psychological and psychosomatic ills through the realization of a state of mind he called "Clear." Hubbard went on to establish the Hubbard Dianetic Research Foundation in Elizabeth, New Jersey. Later he moved the organization to

"The lofty reasonings of Science are the sunshine of the Spirit. They are the works of Truth. Truth is in us. Let it shine. Truth performs great tasks. Let it shine on miracles of health, cheering, enlightening the nations."

—Emma Curtis Hopkins

Phoenix, Arizona, where the Hubbard Association of Scientologists was founded in 1952.

Although born in Tilden, Nebraska, Hubbard was exposed to Asian religion and culture as a child because he traveled with his father, who was in the navy. As a young man with an adventurous spirit, Hubbard was involved in three Central American ethnological expeditions. He received a commission in the navy during World War II, during which service he was pronounced dead twice. In one instance he apparently had something like a shamanistic out-of-body experience in which he acquired spiritual knowledge that gave him his life's mission.

In *Dianetics: The Modern Science of Mental Healing*, which became the foundation for Scientology, we learn that the mind is made up of two parts, the analytic and the reactive. Traumatic experiences in early life or even in the womb are said to imprint themselves on the reactive mind as *engrams*, which cause psychological and psychosomatic problems if they are not dissolved. The way to dissolve these traumatic impressions is to work with a counselor called an *auditor*, who leads the individual into reenacting the events that caused the trauma, thus releasing or liberating the individual from the engrams' negative effects. Hubbard called this state of release "Clear," and devotees of Scientology work hard to attain it.

Mary Baker Eddy, founder of the Church of Christ, Scientist (Christian Science).

Scientology, however, went beyond the psychological orientation of Dianetics to develop an elaborate mythology according to which all humans were once advanced beings Hubbard called *Thetans*. These are all-powerful, eternal, and omniscient beings. The first Thetans relieved their boredom by playing mind games in which they used imagination to create different physical worlds. However, they soon forgot their true identity as creators and found themselves trapped in these worlds, living as mortals who died, only to be reincarnated again and again. At each reincarnation, people accumulated more psychological baggage, or engrams. To be liberated from this pattern and realize one's true identity, it is necessary to gain insight into one's engrams. Upon finally achieving the "Clear" state of mind, a person gains control over both mind and life. The auditing process that leads to this liberation came to involve the use of a machine that works somewhat like a lie detector. This device, the E-meter, it is believed, measures reactions of resistance to words and other symbols that reveal undissolved engrams. After achieving "Clear," one can go on to higher states that involve out-of-body experiences.

In 1954 Hubbard established the first Church of Scientology in Washington, DC, and in 1959 he started the Hubbard College of Scientology in England. Whereas many new age religious movements stress individualism and are quite loosely organized, Scientology has an elaborate bureaucratic global organization, similar to that of Roman

TALES OF SPIRITUAL TRANSFORMATION: A Scientologist's Account of Achieving "Clear"

As with other religious movements throughout history, Scientologists seek to undergo spiritual death and rebirth, or being "born again." In such rebirth experiences the old way of experiencing the world is replaced by a dramatically new one. The following example is taken from a publication of the Church of Scientology of California dated 1970.

There is no name to describe the way I feel. At last I am at cause. I am Clear—I can do anything I want to do. I feel like a child with a new life—everything

is so wonderful and beautiful. Clear is Clear! It's unlike anything I could have imagined. The colors, the clarity, the brightness of everything is beyond belief. Everything is so new, I feel newborn. I am filled with the wonder of everything.

Source: Quoted in Robert S. Ellwood and Harry Partin, eds., *Religious and Spiritual Groups in America*, 2nd ed. (Upper Saddle River, NJ: Prentice Hall, 1988), p. 140.

Catholicism or Mormonism. Perhaps an even better analogy is to the modern international business corporation, with its penchant for technical language, efficient organization, and the dissemination of polished communications to interface with the world. And yet all this organization and efficiency is focused on bringing about a powerful experience of enlightenment or rebirth that perfects the self and opens it to the spiritual world that shamans have traversed throughout the ages. Scientologists have also shown a keen interest in Buddhist teachings, there may be Taoist influences as well, and of course the parallels of the auditing practices to depth psychology are obvious. The achievement of "Clear" shows the movement's affinity with both Western experiences of being "born again" and Eastern experiences of enlightenment.

Scientology is, in many ways, the perfect illustration of the global eclectic integration of the elements that make up new age religions: science (especially psychology), technology (corporate and technical structure), Asian religions (reincarnation and the quest for liberation), and shamanism (out-of-body spiritual explorations). A Thetan, according to Hubbard, goes "through walls, barriers, vanishes space, appears anywhere at will and does other remarkable things."[3]

L. Ron Hubbard, founder of Scientology

"Philosophic knowledge is only valuable if it is true or if it works. . . . A philosophy can only be a *route* to knowledge. It cannot be crammed down one's throat. If one has a route, he can then find what is true for him. And that is Scientology."

—L. Ron Hubbard

The Baha'i Global Religious Vision

As we transition from the nineteenth through the twentieth and into the twenty-first century, the Baha'i tradition presents us with a powerful example of the embrace of globalization in a new religious movement that links the biblical religions of Judaism, Christianity, and Islam in a sweeping vision that comes to embrace the religions of Asia as well.

The Baha'i tradition emerged in nineteenth-century Persia (Iran today) in a world dominated by Islam. There is a kind of logical development that goes on among the biblical religions. Arising out of the religious traditions of an ancient Israel, Judaism began to emerge after the Babylonian Exile as the first biblical witness to the oneness of God through its Torah and eventually Talmud. In the first century, Christianity, starting as a Jewish sect, broke off from Judaism to become a new religion. Christians claimed that Jews had failed to recognize Jesus as Messiah and Son of God, who fulfills the ancient Jewish prophecies which Christians believe are contained in the Torah. For Christians, Jesus is the final fulfillment of the Bible; nothing and no one else is needed after him. So Christians added the New Testament to the Torah to make a new Bible in two parts: Old Testament (an adaptation of the Torah) and New Testament.

Then in the seventh century, in Arabia, Muhammad emerged as a new prophet, who teaches that both Jews and Christians have strayed from the straight path God had laid out in his revelations in history. Muslims believe God sent the "seal of the prophets," Muhammad, as the last and final prophet to reveal the truth of God's will. Just as Christianity did not deny that God revealed himself to Jews first, but asserted Jesus completed God's revelation in Christianity, so Muslims argue that revelation is only completed by God's revelation through the "seal of the prophets," Muhammad. The Quran, like the New Testament, embraced the great figures of biblical revelation, such as Adam, Abraham, Isaac, Jacob, Moses, David, and Jesus and even recognizes Jesus as the Messiah who will return at the end of time, but it does not call him, as Christians do, Son of God.

In the nineteenth century in Persia, a new religious movement, Baha'i, emerged and claimed to be founded on a new revelation to the Bab in 1844. The Baha'i emerge out of Shiite Islam, which emphasizes the primacy of political leadership by divinely inspired Imams rather than the Sunni Ulama or scholars sharing authority with political leaders or Caliphs. One Shiite branch, The Twelvers, held that there would be twelve such Immams. The twelfth disappeared and is said to have gone into occulatation, a state of being not unlike Jesus' ascension into heaven, to come again at the end of time. In fact, some teach that Jesus and the twelfth Imam—the Madhi—will appear together at the end of time. Around this time this messianic expectation for the reappearance of the twelfth Imam—Mohammad al Madhi—was heating up, leading to the expectation that since it was one thousand years since the disappearance of the "hidden Imam" his promised return was eminent.

Shirazi Sayid Ali Muhammad, who came to be known as the Bab, was the first Shiite Muslim messianic leader to break away from Islam to forge a new religious movement and was seen by some as the hoped-for revelation of the hidden Imam. He was executed for his attempt in 1850. The followers of the Bab (a word meaning "gate") were initially known as the Babis. The Bab, who came to play a role similar to John the Baptist in the Christian story of Jesus, is said to have prophesied that his disciple, Mirza Husayn ali Nuri (1817–1892), was to be the promised one—*He Who God Will Manifest*—a new messenger of God. Mirza Husayn ali Nuri was imprisoned in Tehran during a persecution of the Babis in 1852. While in prison he came to believe he was indeed called to be a divine messenger. He became known as

Bahaaullah—"the splendor or glory of God." He authored the *Kitab al-aqdas* or the "Most Holy Book" of the Baha'i faith. In 1863, while in exile in Baghdad, he publicly embraced his role as God's promised messenger. He was imprisoned in Acre for nine years and later settled in Haifa in what is now Israel. He died in 1892. Haifa is now the site of the Baha'i World Center.

Baha'i teaching claims that God's revelation did not end with Jesus, nor with Muhammad, nor even with Bahaaullah, but God provides a new messenger or "Manifestation" for each new age of humanity. Naturally, Muslims take exceptions to the idea that Muhammad is not the seal of the prophets, just as Christians reject the Muslim view that Islam corrects and supersedes Christian teachings, and just as Jews take exception to Christian and Muslim claims to have superseded Judaism. The teachings of the Baha'i complicate this picture further by arguing that God has provided other revelations in Asian religions, like Hinduism and Buddhism through

The Baha'i Gardens and the Shrine of the Bab in Haifa, Israel.

Krishna and Buddha, that are a part of God's "Great Covenant" of continuing revelations to all humanity. Baha'i is just the most recent example. According to Baha'i teaching, all these prophets or "mirrors" of God are part of God's continuing manifestations leading the whole human race into a new global unity. The global vision of the Baha'i teaches the oneness of God, the oneness of all God's prophets around the world, and the oneness of humanity. Baha'i calls on all to establish this oneness as a fact in a global harmony beyond all divisions of nationality, religion, race, or gender.

Baha'i teaching offers a parallel to the vision of history of progress through the three ages of the human race. This view, rooted in Joachim of Fiore's account of the Book of Revelation in Christianity, was adopted in Western Enlightenment philosophical thought by figures like Immanuel Kant, G. W. F. Hegel, and Karl Marx. The great Enlightenment philosopher Immanuel Kant was perhaps the first philosopher to see the ethical significance of an emerging global consciousness. At the end of the eighteenth century, in his "Idea for a Universal History from a Cosmopolitan Point of View" (1784) and in his essay on "Perpetual Peace" (1795), Kant argued that living on a round earth we cannot escape from each other. Rather, we are forced to recognize our equality and interdependence with each other as human beings. Kant was a severe critic of Western colonialism and called for the creation of a "league of nations" to promote our common human rights and bring an end to all war. He brought together the Stoic dream of cosmopolitan citizenship with the Christian millennial hope that at the end of time all the tribes of the earth would live together in perpetual peace. Kant's ideals came to be embodied in the experiment with the League of Nations from 1920 to 1946 and the birth of the United Nations in 1945.

Parallel commitments are expressed in Baha'i teachings that have established a global "House of Justice" and Spiritual Assemblies to provide a model for—and encouragement of—the global unification of the human race in peace and universal harmony. Baha'i teachings do not see the teachings of Bahaaullah as competing with these other trends toward globalization but rather see in them the multiple instances in which God is working to unify the human race in confirmation of the Baha'i vision. It was, Abdul-Baha, Bahaaullah's son and successor in spiritual teaching, who appointed his grandson, Shoghi Effendi, as the Guardian of the Baha'i Community and it was Effendi who established the Universal House of Justice. Under his guidance the laws and institutions needed to promote the unity of the human race became organized into "the Administrative Order" of the Baha'i community. This institution exists at the local, national, and finally the international level through which Baha'i's work promotes the establishment of world harmony and God's kingdom on earth. This emerging kingdom, they believe, will pass from a stage of crisis through a lesser peace gradually established by agreements among the nations, to the "Most Great Peace," which results from finally realizing the truth of Bahaaullah's teaching by the masses as a "coming of age" of the whole human race. Baha'i teaching and practice provides global leadership through The World Centre of Baha'i Faith and its "International Teaching Center" in Haifa in Israel. The estimated population of Baha'i's in the world today is over 5 million.

East Goes West: Zen in America

Yogic meditation, whether in its Hindu or Buddhist forms, has made surprising inroads into American religious life in the "new age." Transcendental Meditation is an example of the first, while Zen Buddhism is an example of the second. Both are examples of a new "methodism" in American culture. As we learned in Chapter 4, Methodism was one of the most successful evangelical forms of Christianity transplanted from England to America. Evangelical Christianity originated as a rebellion against religious dogmatism and the religious wars that dogmatism had caused in Europe. It emphasized the spiritual practices of piety and prayer (praying regularly or "methodically") and the religious experience of being "born again" as more important than religious dogma. And evangelicals saw the test of true faith as demonstrating the fruit of that experience by exercising ethical compassion toward all others. In this way Methodism prepared the way for new forms of methodism in an age of globalization in America. Zen is one way in which the "methodist impulse" of pragmatic Americans looking for experiential religion finds expression in the new age. Like Methodism, it minimizes belief and maximizes spiritual practice leading to transformative experience and ethical compassion.

As we learned in Chapter 7, "Zen" is a Japanese translation of the word *Ch'an*, which is the Chinese translation of the Sanskrit *dhyana*, meaning "meditation." Zen is rooted in the practice of yogic meditation that has its origins in India. The core of this spiritual practice is emptying the mind of all thoughts, which begins by simply focusing one's mind on following one's breathing. Unlike the Hindu tradition, however, Zen Buddhist practice requires meditating with your eyes open, emphasizing that Zen is about transforming how you see and experience the world around you. Zen emphasizes the spiritual practice of sitting cross-legged (in the "lotus position") with an empty mind free of all emotional attachments so as to remain "mindful" or open to every new experience as you engage in your everyday activities.

Bodhidharma is said to have brought Buddhism from India to China in the fifth century CE as the first patriarch of the Chinese tradition of Ch'an. He defined Zen as a transformative experience rather than a religion of doctrines to be believed. The goal of meditation was to lead one to experience "no self," or "emptiness of all self." He emphasized that the self could not be defined, only experienced in its emptiness and immediacy or "suchness." So he said that Zen was

A special tradition outside the scriptures;
No dependence upon words or letters;
Direct pointing at the soul of man;
Seeing into one's own nature, and the attainment of Buddhahood.

The "enlightened" person is one who is "born again" (to use an evangelical phrase)— one who experiences his or her interdependence with all beings. Such a person sees everything with astonishment and wonder, as if for the first time, and knows that no one has an independent self. This experience is said to lead one to embrace all beings with compassion.

A famous Zen *koan* is "What is the sound of one hand clapping?" A Zen master gives this koan or spiritual puzzle to Zen disciples and asks them to meditate on it until they have an answer. Then the disciples are to come back to have their answers tested. The problem is that there is no "rational" answer. This spiritual puzzle is meant to defeat the rational mind and its abstract conventional beliefs in order to startle each disciple into a direct experience of reality. According to Zen teaching, you cannot know who you are and what reality is by "believing" some doctrines or truths. You can only know your true nature and the true nature of all reality by experiencing a breakthrough (called *kensho* or "enlightenment") that forces you to abandon all conventional beliefs and experiences for a direct experience of reality that cannot be put into words.

Zen Buddhism began to establish itself in America in the 1930s, at first to serve immigrant Japanese communities in California. But Buddhism did not become an American phenomenon until the 1950s and 1960s. The stories of Zen as a spiritual practice that challenges conventional religion and conventional forms of experience

Buddhist scholar and writer D. T. Suzuki at work.

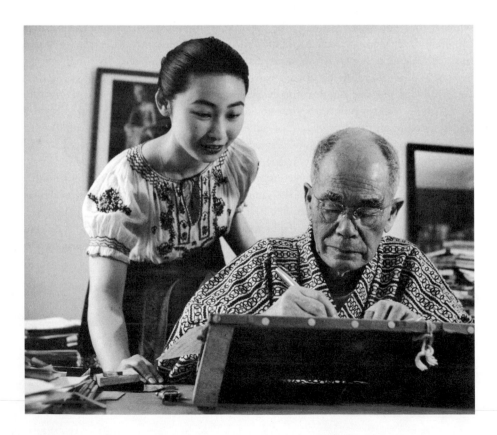

and authority appealed to the "Beat generation" or "beatniks" of the 1950s (novelists and poets such as Jack Kerouac and Gary Snyder) and the "counterculture" of the "hippies," who carried their irreverent attitude toward "conventional" middle-class life in America into the 1960s and beyond. Authors such as Alan Watts and D. T. Suzuki played a major role in bringing Zen to popular attention in the 1960s and 1970s. Almost a half century later Zen communities can be found in most large cities around the world. Zen in America tends to be less monastic and far more open to the leadership of women than would be the case in Japan. It is not unusual, in the spirit of the "new age," for American Zen communities or sanghas to have many members who continue to practice their Judaism or Christianity as well. Also, many atheists and agnostics are attracted to it as a way to be religious without having to be theistic. These communities seem to have integrated Zen into the middle-class lifestyle of a now-postmodern culture that encourages diversity and experimentation in a way that the conformist America of the 1950s, protested by "beatniks," did not.

West Goes East: The Aum Shinrikyo Movement

The new age religions we have looked at so far have been more Aquarian than apocalyptic. They have been rooted in the nature-oriented religions deeply attuned to the cycles of nature, like the astrological tradition that posits the Aquarian age. But other new age religions reflect the pattern of the eastward migration of biblical apocalyptic traditions, leading to some interesting integrations of West and East. The Japanese religion Aum Shinrikyo is a good example. An apocalyptic new age vision has taken root in this new religion, which achieved global notoriety and terrorist status when some members released deadly sarin gas into the Tokyo subway system in 1995. As a child in a school for the blind, Aum Shinrikyo founder Chizuo Matsumoto boasted that he would one day be prime minister of Japan. Yet the early years of the severely sight-impaired youth were not promising. After two failures to enter the Japanese university system, he joined a new religious movement called *Agonshu*, which mixed Buddhist, Daoist, and Hindu teachings. In 1984 he broke with Agonshu and developed a personal religious vision, integrating elements of Hindu yoga, Buddhist meditation, and Christian apocalyptic beliefs. He visited India in 1986 and had what he believed to be a powerful enlightenment experience. Convinced that he was destined to be a great spiritual master, Chizuo Matsumoto, then the leader of his own small movement, took on the name Shoko Asahara and named his group Aum Shinrikyo.

In 1986 Shoko Asahara registered the Aum Shinrikyo ("Supreme Truth") movement as a religion with the Japanese government. Having done this, he attracted additional followers by writing extensively in his country's new age religious publications, promising to teach seekers out-of-body shamanistic skills such as clairvoyance and teleportation. He had a charismatic personality, and his movement, which has had an extraordinary appeal among the university-educated professional class, quickly became one of the fastest-growing new religions in Japan.

Cult of Doom

A poison-gas attack triggers fears about extremists using homemade weapons of mass death

Shoko Asahara, leader of the apocalyptic cult Aum Shinrikyo

Shoko Asahara, founder of Aum Shinrikyo

Through a well-developed bureaucracy, with Asahara at the top, Aum Shinrikyo established monastic-like separatist communities throughout Japan, where the most devoted followers congregated, having left their families and given all their earthly belongings to the movement. Descriptions of the initiation rituals have mentioned the heavy use of hallucinogens, the drinking of vials of Asahara's blood, and a total surrender to Asahara as the spiritual master.

In the beginning Asahara taught that the world would end soon and that it was the task of his followers to save humanity through their hard work in Aum business ventures and through purification by personal spiritual practices. After Asahara and some of his handpicked leaders were decisively defeated in an attempt to win seats in Japan's parliament in 1990, Asahara's teachings took a darker turn, seeking to destroy what he believed were the demonic forces that opposed his movement.

By 1993 Aum Shinrikyo had plants producing automatic weapons as well as chemical and biological weapons, ostensibly to protect Japan against its enemies. Believing that the United States was about to trigger an apocalyptic nuclear war, Aum scientists traveled to Russia and Africa in search of biological and nuclear weapons. Aum Shinrikyo's following in Russia by 1995 was estimated at 30,000, roughly three times its membership in Japan. The group's terrorist plans, however, were known only to a small, mostly Japanese, elite.

Asahara came under legal scrutiny for his varied activities, especially after authorities learned that the worth of Aum's assets exceeded $1 billion. In 1994, convinced that the Japanese government's special police force had set out to destroy him, Asahara ordered the assassination of three judges by releasing poison gas in their neighborhoods. The judges survived, but some innocent bystanders were killed. The next year, after the Tokyo subway gassing, he was arrested.

Asahara integrated Japanese Shinto beliefs with Hinduism and Tibetan Buddhism in a way that appealed to many young Japanese professionals (including scientists) by calling into question modern materialism as well as the stress and decadence of modern life. Indeed, influenced by the science fiction of Isaac Asimov, Asahara developed a vision of the role of scientists in building an elite secret society that would save civilization from cataclysmic wars. To this he added a strong dose of Christian apocalyptic expectations (mixed with the predictions of Nostradamus) about the imminent end of the world in a battle between good and evil. He justified his murderous assaults on his fellow citizens by pronouncing that killing those who are creating bad karma was actually doing them a spiritual favor, since it stopped them before they produced even more negative karma.

To his followers, Asahara declared himself to be Jesus Christ, come to bring judgment on the world. In preparation for the global nuclear war he believed the United States was plotting, he bought land in Australia. There his followers could start to build a new civilization as they waited out the years of lethal radiation in a devastated Northern Hemisphere. Ultimately, Asahara was convicted for having masterminded the Tokyo sarin gas attack. He was sentenced to death in 2004, and the movement, which regrouped under the name *Aleph* ("the beginning"), still reveres him as its spiritual leader.

Like Scientology, Aum Shinrikyo illustrates the integration of shamanism and Eastern mysticism with scientific research and technological applications organized by a highly efficient globally oriented bureaucratic organization. The difference between them is equally important, for Asahara's eclectic religious vision adds elements of Western apocalyptic thought colored by his own paranoid vision of himself as the rejected prophet and spiritual master. The result was dangerously violent.

Conclusion: The Postmodern Challenge— Can There Be a Global Ethic in a World of Religious Diversity?

In 2010 various atheist groups in the United States and Britain began an advertising campaign, affirming on billboards and other media that you can be "Good Without God." This, of course, was shocking to many pious people in both countries. However, from the perspective of the comparative study of religions, atheism appears to be a culturally relative phenomenon. It seems to depend on the versions of monotheistic belief generated by the biblical religions of Judaism, Christianity, and Islam. Many Buddhists, it is often noted, have no belief in God yet are deeply religious and morally courageous. One of the attractions of Buddhism in a world shaped by modern science is to offer educated persons a way to be religious without believing in God. The real question for the global future of religions is this: Can there be a shared global ethic in a world of diverse worldviews, whether theistic or nontheistic?

Beyond Atheism: The Challenge of Postmodern Secular Relativism

As we noted in the first chapter, religion is about what people hold sacred, and what they hold sacred is their way of life. God, gods, or spirits are often introduced in sacred stories to explain why a group's way of life is sacred, but that way of life may be considered sacred even if such beings are not appealed to. A good example of this, noted in Chapter 4, is the Russian revolution under Stalin, which declared itself an atheist state whose idea of good was the mass extermination of its own citizens that rivaled the devastation of the Holocaust. The Soviet Union was an atheist state that considered its way of life sacred and so executed countless numbers who threatened the new communist way of life.

The interesting question is not whether one can be good without God but whether one can be good without being religious—and here the answer seems to be no. For even those who champion a secular humanist morality hold some things sacred, especially human dignity and human rights. In the United States, atheists have sometimes embraced a kind of fundamentalism. Some have challenged whether a city council, a state government, or even the U.S. Senate violates the First Amendment to the U.S. Constitution by beginning proceedings with a prayer. Many championing atheism have argued that no prayer should ever be said as part of a government proceeding. The First Amendment, however, forbids two opposing things in one sentence—(1) "the establishment of religion" (where the government gives official preference to one religion over all others) and (2) any attempt to restrict the "free exercise of religion" by the government. According to the Constitution, the state should show no preference but should support religious diversity. If we understand that even atheists hold their values and way of life sacred, then they are religious and should be neither forbidden nor favored by government. Globalization relativizes all worldviews, including atheistic ones. The true challenge to religion in a global civilization is not atheism but relativism. If all views, whether theistic or atheistic, are relative, then who can say how human beings ought to live? If good is in the eye of the beholder, then even Hitler and Stalin can be made to seem good. To affirm human dignity against the brutality of such figures is to reject relativism and affirm the sacredness of human dignity.

Among religious modernists a different solution was sought to the challenge of scientific rationality and theistic belief. As explained in Chapter 4, on Christianity, the difference between fundamentalists and modernists stems from an argument about the impact of science on traditional religious beliefs. Theistic fundamentalists often seem to believe they must oppose science to reaffirm traditional religious beliefs, while atheistic fundamentalists seem to believe that they must oppose religion in order to affirm scientific beliefs. Modernists attempt to embrace science, preferring to find a rational balance between science and religious beliefs.

Traditional theistic fundamentalists generally had no objection to the use of science to invent things like the automobile or for the creation of better medications. When science impinged on religious beliefs concerning the origins of humanity and the right way to order society, however, many drew a line. If the human self and society do not have sacred origins but are the result of biological evolution and human decisions, then the human self and society seem to be set adrift in a relativistic world without meaning, purpose, or ethical norms.

As modern science and technology—and the worldview they foster—were carried around the world by colonialism, the impact of modernity was felt in different ways in different societies and cultures. Not every religious tradition emphasizes orthodoxy ("right beliefs") the way Christianity does. For example, Hinduism, Judaism, and

Islam place far more emphasis on orthopraxy ("right actions"), the maintenance of a sacred way of life. Thus the most common feature of the fundamentalist reaction to modernity across religions and cultures is the desire to preserve the premodern sacred "way of life" against the threat of secularization and the normless relativism it seems to engender.

The social sciences of the nineteenth century promoted a technological understanding of society. According to this understanding, society itself can be redesigned through public policy decisions, just as engineers periodically redesign cars. While the use of scientific and technological inventions per se was relatively uncontroversial, many rejected the way social science treated the social order in a secular and technological fashion, as if society could or should be shaped and reshaped by human choices, without regard to the sacred ways of one's ancestors. In our chapter on Christianity (Chapter 4), we pointed to the emergence of existentialism as a watershed moment in the history of modernization, opening the door to postmodern relativism by calling into question the idea of *human nature*. For many, this seeming disappearance of human nature is terrifying, suggesting that we as human beings know neither who we are nor what we ought to do. This is the mindset Nietzsche was addressing when he said that "modern man" had murdered God and so now wandered the universe without a sense of direction. In fact, as we noted in the chapter on Christianity, the one thing Christian fundamentalists and Nietzschean atheists have in common (unlike Christian modernists) is that both see science and the Bible as incompatible. Depending on which camp you are in, either God or science has to be rejected. For many theistic fundamentalists today, it seems that the secular "technologized" understandings of self and society can only lead to moral decadence—a decadence in which the family and the fabric of society will be destroyed. Those who believe that secularization is robbing humanity of an understanding of its sacred origins and destiny reject scientific-technologized understandings of self and society. As an antidote, they favor a return to the sacred fundamental truths about human nature that governed life in premodern times.

Modernization is often presented in terms of a story about the secularization of society, that is, the liberation of the various dimensions of cultural life from the authority of religion. Since religion in premodern societies preserves the sacred by governing every aspect of life, modernization and secularization are threats to traditional societies everywhere. Nevertheless, sacralizing society to protect a divinely ordered way of life is not the only role religion has played in history. Moreover, as we have noted, secular ways of life that appeal to the rationality of science have also become sacred. Paradoxically, the most successful critiques of the sacralization of society have come from religions. The great sociologist Max Weber pointed out that religion not only sacralizes and reinforces the unchanging "routine" order of society (as the French sociologist Émile Durkheim held); sometimes it also "charismatically" desacralizes and transforms society. Religion, like reason, sometimes criticizes and transforms sacred order rather than functioning as its defender. Brahmanic Hinduism sacralized caste society in ancient India, but Buddhism began as a movement to desacralize the priestly elite and see all persons in the caste system as equal and capable of achieving spiritual deliverance. Sacralization readily accommodates hierarchies (e.g., a caste system, or hierarchical social order), whereas desacralizing breaks with caste, inviting pluralism and equality.

Because religions (even in the same traditions) often manifest dramatically opposing values and orientations, the sociologist Jacques Ellul has argued that it is helpful in understanding the role of religion in society to distinguish between two terms that are typically used interchangeably: sacred and holy. In his view, the experience of the sacred leads to a view of society as an order that is itself sacred and must be protected from all profane attempts to change it. The experience of the holy, on the other hand, calls into question the very idea of a sacred order. It desacralizes (or secularizes) society and seeks to introduce change in the name of a higher truth and/or justice. According to this view, the same religious tradition can express itself in opposite ways in different times and places. In India, early Buddhism called into question the sacred order of Hindu caste society, but later Buddhist societies developed their own sacred orders. Early Daoists in China called into question the sacred hierarchical order of Confucianism but later also integrated themselves into the sacred order of Confucian society by means of a neo-Confucian synthesis.

In the West, early Christianity, sharing a common ethos with Judaism, called the sacred order of Roman civilization into question, but medieval Christianity resacralized Europe. Then later, Protestantism desacralized the medieval European social order and unleashed the dynamics of modernism, which is also in danger of sacralization. From this perspective, the struggle between fundamentalism and modernism in the modern world that we have surveyed in this textbook is an example of the conflict between the sacralizing and desacralizing (secularizing) roles of religion.

Traditional religious fundamentalists express the desire to preserve the sacredness of human identity in a rightly ordered society against what they perceive as the chaos of today's decadent, normless secular relativism. Secular fundamentalists express a desire to preserve the sacredness of the scientific and rational way of life against the chaos introduced into society by diverse forms of religious absolutism. To restore the sacred normative order, religious fundamentalists tend to affirm the desirability of achieving the premodern ideal of one society, one religion. In the case of secular fundamentalism, what is to be preserved is the sacredness of the way of life made possible by scientific rationality in an age of progress. Both religious and secular or atheistic fundamentalists remain uncomfortable with the religious diversity that thrives in a secular society.

Religious modernism as it emerged in the West rejected the fundamentalist ideal, adopted from premodern societies, of identity between religion and society. Instead of dangerous absolutism, modernists looked for an accommodation between religion and modern secular society. They argued that it is possible to desacralize one's way of life and identity in a way that creates a new identity that preserves the essential values or norms of the past tradition, but in harmony with a new modern way of life. Modernists secularize society and privatize their religious practices, hoping by their encouragement of denominational forms of religion to ensure an environment that supports religious diversity.

What we are calling religious postmodernism, like religious modernism, accepts secularization and religious pluralism. But religious postmodernism, like fundamentalism, rejects the modernist solution of privatizing religious belief and practice and seeks a public role for religion. It differs from fundamentalism, however, in that it rejects the domination of society by a single religion. Religious postmodernists insist that there is a way for religious communities in all their diversity to shape the public order and so rescue society from secular relativism. The chief example of this option is the model established by Mohandas K. Gandhi. Because his disciples rejected the privatization of religion while affirming religious diversity, Gandhi's movement must be defined as a postmodern new age religious movement rather than a modernist one.

"Passing Over": A Postmodern Spiritual Adventure That Responds to the Challenge of Globalization

All the great world religions date back a millennium or more, and each provided a grand metanarrative for the premodern civilization in which it emerged—in the Middle East, in India, and in China. In the past these world religions were relatively isolated from one another. There were many histories in the world, each shaped by a great metanarrative, but no global history.

The perspective of religious postmodernism arises from a dramatically different situation. We are at the beginning of a new millennium, which is marked by the development of a global civilization. The diverse spiritual heritages of the human race have become the common inheritance of all. Modern changes have ended the isolation of the past, and people following one great tradition are now very likely to live in proximity to adherents of other faiths. New age religion has tapped this condition of globalization but in two different ways. In its modernist forms it has privatized the religious quest as a quest for the perfection of the self. In its postmodern forms, without rejecting self-transformation, it has turned that goal outward in forms of social organization committed to bettering society, bringing personal and social transformation into balance.

The time when a new world religion could be founded has passed, argues John Dunne in his book *The Way of All the Earth*. What is required today is not the conquest of the world by any one religion or culture but a meeting and sharing of religious and cultural insight. "The holy man of our time, it seems, is not a figure like Gautama [Buddha] or Jesus or Mohammed, a man who could found a world religion, but a figure like Gandhi, a man who passes over by sympathetic understanding from his own religion to other religions and comes back again with new insight to his own. Passing over and coming back, it seems, is the spiritual adventure of our time."[4]

This postmodern spiritual adventure occurs when we pass over into another's religion and culture and come to see the world through another's eyes. When we do this, we "come back" to our own religion and culture enriched with new insight not only into the other's religion and culture but also into our own—insight that builds bridges of understanding, a unity in diversity between people of diverse religions and cultures. The model for this spiritual adventure is found in the lives of Leo Tolstoy (1828–1910), Mohandas K. Gandhi (1869–1948), and Martin Luther King Jr. (1929–68).

Two of the most inspiring religious figures of the twentieth century were Mahatma Gandhi and Dr. King. They are the great champions of the fight for the dignity and rights of all human beings, from all religions and cultures. Moreover, they are models for a different kind of new age religious practice, one that absorbs the global wisdom of diverse religions, but does so without indiscriminately mixing elements to create a new religion, as is typical of the eclectic syncretism of most new age religions. Yet clearly these religious leaders initiated a new way of being religious that could occur only in an age of globalization.

Martin Luther King Jr. often noted that his commitment to nonviolent resistance, or civil disobedience, as a strategy for protecting human dignity had its roots in two sources: Jesus' Sermon on the Mount and Gandhi's teachings of nonviolence derived from his interpretation of the Hindu sacred story called the *Bhagavad Gita*. Gandhi died when King was a teenager, but Dr. King did travel to India to study the effects of Gandhi's teachings of nonviolence on Indian society. In this he showed a remarkable openness to the insights of another religion and culture. In Gandhi and his spiritual heirs, King found kindred spirits, and he came back to his own religion and culture enriched by the new insights that came to him in the process of passing over and coming back. Martin Luther King Jr. never became a Hindu, but his Christianity was profoundly transformed by his encounter with Gandhi's Hinduism.

Just as important, however, is the spiritual passing over of Gandhi himself. As a young man, Gandhi went to England to study law. His journey led him not away from Hinduism but more deeply into it, for it was in England that Gandhi discovered the *Bhagavad Gita* and began to fully appreciate the spiritual and ethical power of Hinduism.

Having promised his mother that he would remain a vegetarian, Gandhi took to eating his meals with British citizens who had developed similar commitments to vegetarianism through their fascination with India and its religions. It is in this context that Gandhi was brought into direct contact with the nineteenth-century theosophical roots of new age globalization. In these circles he met Madame Blavatsky and her disciple Annie Besant, both of whom had a profound influence on him. His associates also included Christian followers of the Russian novelist Leo Tolstoy, who, after his midlife conversion, had embraced an ethic of nonviolence based on Jesus' Sermon on the Mount (Matthew 5–7).

At the invitation of his theosophist friends, Gandhi read the *Bhagavad Gita* for the first time, in an English translation by Sir Edwin Arnold, entitled *The Song Celestial*. It was only much later that he took to a serious study of the Hindu text in Sanskrit. He was also deeply impressed by Arnold's *The Light of Asia*, recounting the life of the

Buddha. Thus, through the eyes of Western friends, he was first moved to discover the spiritual riches of his own Hindu heritage. The seeds were planted in England, nourished by more serious study during his years in South Africa, and brought to fruition on his return to India in 1915.

From his theosophist friends, Gandhi not only learned to appreciate his own religious tradition but came to see Christianity in a new way. For unlike the evangelical missionaries he had met in his childhood, the theosophists had a deeply allegorical way of reading the Christian scriptures. This approach to Bible study allowed people to find in the teachings of Jesus a universal path toward spiritual truth that was in harmony with the wisdom of Asia. The power of allegory lay in opening the literal stories of the scripture to reveal a deeper symbolic meaning based on what the theosophists believed was profound universal religious experience and wisdom. From the theosophists, Gandhi took an interpretive principle that has its roots in the New Testament writings of St. Paul: "The letter killeth, but the spirit giveth life" (2 Corinthians 3:6). This insight would enable him to read the *Bhagavad Gita* in the light of his own deep religious experience and find in it the justification for nonviolent civil disobedience.

Gandhi was likewise profoundly influenced by Tolstoy's understanding of the Sermon on the Mount. The message of nonviolence—love your enemy, turn the other cheek—took hold of Gandhi. And yet Gandhi did not become a Christian. Rather, he returned to his parents' religion and culture, finding parallels to Jesus' teachings in the Hindu tradition. And so he read Hindu scriptures with new insight, interpreting the *Bhagavad Gita* allegorically, as a call to resist evil by nonviolent means. And just as King would later use the ideas of Gandhi in the nonviolent struggle for the dignity of black citizens in North America, so Gandhi was inspired by Tolstoy as he led the fight for the dignity of the lower castes and outcasts within Hindu society and for the liberation of India from British colonial rule.

Gandhi never became a Christian and King never became a Hindu. Nevertheless, Gandhi's Hindu faith was profoundly transformed by his encounter with the Christianity of Tolstoy, just as King's Christian faith was profoundly transformed by his encounter with Gandhi's Hinduism. In the lives of these twentieth-century religious activists we have examples of "passing over" as a transformative postmodern spiritual adventure. Whereas in the secular forms of postmodernism all knowledge is relative, and therefore the choice between interpretations of any claim to truth is "undecidable," Gandhi and King opened up an alternate path. While agreeing that in matters of religion, truth is undecidable, they showed that acceptance of diversity does not have to lead to the kind of ethical relativism that so deeply troubles fundamentalists. For in the cases of Gandhi and King, passing over led to a sharing of wisdom among traditions that gave birth to an ethical coalition in defense of human dignity across religions and cultures—a global ethic for a new age.

Mohandas K. Gandhi, whose techniques of non-violent civil disobedience led to the liberation of India from British colonial rule in 1947.

By their lives, Gandhi and King demonstrated that, contrary to the fears raised by fundamentalism, the sharing of a common ethic and of spiritual wisdom across traditions does not require any practitioners to abandon their religious identity. Instead, Gandhi and King offered a model of unity in diversity. Finally, both Gandhi and King rejected the privatization of religion, insisting that religion in all its diversity plays a decisive role in shaping the public order of society. And both were convinced that only a firm commitment to nonviolence on the part of religious communities would allow society to avoid a return to the kind of religious wars that accompanied the Protestant Reformation and the emergence of modernity.

The spiritual adventure initiated by Gandhi and King involves passing over (through imagination, through travel and cultural exchange, through a common commitment to social action to promote social justice, etc.) into the life and stories and traditions of others, sharing in them and, in the process, coming to see one's own tradition through them. Such encounters enlarge our sense of human identity to include the other. The religious metanarratives of the world's civilizations may have become "smaller narratives" in an age of global diversity, but they have not lost their power. Indeed, in this Gandhian model, it is the sharing of the wisdom from another tradition's metanarratives that gives the stories of a person's own tradition their power. Each person remains on familiar religious and cultural ground, yet each is profoundly influenced by the other.

Tolstoy, Jesus, and "Saint Buddha": An Ancient Tale with a Thousand Faces

Although at first glance the religious worlds of humankind seem to have grown up largely independent of one another, a closer look will reveal that hidden threads from different religions and cultures have for centuries been woven together to form a new tapestry, one that contributes to the sharing of religious insight in an age of globalization. In *Toward a World Theology*, Wilfred Cantwell Smith traces the threads of this new tapestry, and the story he tells is quite surprising.[5] Smith notes, for example, that to fully appreciate the influence on Gandhi of Tolstoy's understanding of the Sermon on the Mount, it is important to know that Tolstoy's own conversion to Christianity, which occurred in a period of midlife crisis, was deeply influenced not only by the Sermon on the Mount but also by the life of the Buddha.

Tolstoy was a member of the Russian nobility, rich and famous because of his novels, which included *War and Peace* and *Anna Karenina*. Yet in his fifties, Tolstoy went through a period of great despair that resolved itself in a powerful religious conversion experience. Although nominally a member of the (Russian) Orthodox Church, Tolstoy had not taken his faith seriously until he came to the point of making the Sermon on the Mount a blueprint for his life. After his conversion, Tolstoy freed his serfs, gave away all his wealth, and spent the rest of his life serving the poor.

As Wilfred Cantwell Smith tells it, a key factor in Tolstoy's conversion was his reading of a story from the lives of the saints. The story was that of Barlaam and

Josaphat. It is the story of a wealthy young Indian prince by the name of Josaphat who gave up all his wealth and power and abandoned his family to embark on an urgent quest for an answer to the problems of old age, sickness, and death. During his search, the prince comes across a Christian monk by the name of Barlaam, who tells him a story. It seems that once there was a man who fell into a very deep well and was hanging onto two vines for dear life. As he was trapped in this precarious situation, two mice, one white and one black, came along and began to chew on the vines. The man knew that in short order the vines would be severed and he would plunge to his death.

The story was an allegorical parable of the prince's spiritual situation. Barlaam points out that the two mice represent the cycle of day and night, the passing of time that brings us ever closer to death. The paradox is that like the man in the well, Josaphat cannot save his life by clinging to it. He must let go of the vines, so to speak. He can save his life only by losing it. That is, if he lets go of his life now, no longer clinging to it but surrendering himself completely to the divine will, his spiritual death will lead

Leo Tolstoy, the famous Russian novelist, whose writings on Jesus' Sermon on the Mount inspired Gandhi.

to a new life that transcends death. This story and its parable touched the deeply depressed writer and led him to a spiritual surrender that brought about his rebirth. Out of this rebirth then came a new Tolstoy, the author of *The Kingdom of God Is Within You*, which advocates a life of nonviolent resistance to evil based on the Sermon on the Mount.

The story of the Indian prince who abandons a life of wealth and power and responds to a parable of a man about to fall into an abyss is of course a thinly disguised version of the life story of the Buddha. Versions of the story and the parable can be found in almost all the world's great religions, recorded in a variety of languages (Greek, Latin, Czech, Polish, Italian, Spanish, French, German, Swedish, Norwegian, Arabic, Hebrew, Yiddish, Persian, Sanskrit, Chinese, Japanese, etc.). The Greek version came into Christianity from an Islamic Arabic version, which was passed on to Judaism as well. The Muslims apparently got it from members of a Gnostic cult in Persia, who got it from Buddhists in India. The Latinate name *Josaphat* is a translation of the Greek *Loasaf*, which is translated from the Arabic *Yudasaf*, which comes from the Persian *Bodisaf*, which is a translation of *Bodhisattva*, a Sanskrit title for the Buddha.

The parable of the man clinging to the vine may be even older than the story of the prince (Buddha) who renounces his wealth. It may well go back to early Indic sources at the beginnings of civilization. It is one of the oldest and most universal stories in the history of religions and civilizations. Tolstoy's conversion was brought about in large part by the story of a Christian saint, Josaphat, who was, so to speak, really the Buddha in disguise.

The history of the story of a great sage's first steps toward enlightenment suggests that the process leading to globalization goes back to the very beginnings of civilization.

Therefore the line between new religions and new age (globalized) religions may not be as sharp as previously assumed. We can see that the practice of passing over and coming back, of being open to the stories of others, and of coming to understand one's own tradition through these stories is in fact very ancient. Therefore, when Martin Luther King Jr. embraced the teachings of Gandhi, he embraced not only Gandhi but also Tolstoy and, through Tolstoy, two of the greatest religious teachers of nonviolence: Jesus of Nazareth, whose committed follower King already was, and Siddhartha the Buddha. Thus from the teachings of Gandhi, King actually assimilated important teachings from at least four religious traditions—Hinduism, Buddhism, Judaism, and Christianity. This rich spiritual debt to other religions and cultures never in any way diminished King's faith. On the contrary, the Baptist pastor's Christian beliefs were deeply enriched, in turn enriching the world in which we live. The same could be said about Gandhi and Hinduism.

Gandhi's transformation of the *Bhagavad Gita*—a Hindu story that literally advocates the duty of going to war and killing one's enemies—into a story of nonviolence is instructive of the transforming power of the allegorical method that he learned from his theosophist friends. The *Bhagavad Gita* is a story about a warrior named Arjuna, who argues with his chariot driver, Krishna, over whether it is right to go to war if it means having to kill one's own relatives. Krishna's answer is yes—Arjuna must do his duty as a warrior in the cause of justice, but he is morally obliged to do it selflessly, with no thought of personal loss or gain. Gandhi, however, transformed the story of Arjuna and Krishna from a story of war as physical violence into a story of war as active but nonviolent resistance to injustice through civil disobedience.

If the message of spiritual realization in the *Gita* is that all beings share the same self (as Brahman or Purusha), how could the *Gita* be literally advocating violence, for to do violence against another would be to do violence against oneself? The self-contradiction of a literal interpretation, in Gandhi's way of thinking, forces the mind into an allegorical mode, where it can grasp the *Gita*'s true spiritual meaning. Reading the *Gita* allegorically, Gandhi insisted that the impending battle described in the Hindu classic is really about the battle between good and evil going on within every self.

Krishna's command to Arjuna to stand up and fight is thus a "spiritual" command. But for Gandhi this does not mean, as it usually does in "modern" terms, that the struggle is purely inner (private) and personal. On the contrary, the spiritual person will see the need to practice nonviolent civil disobedience: that is, to replace "body force" (i.e., violence) with "soul force." As the *Gita* suggests, there really is injustice in the world, and therefore there really is an obligation to fight, even to go to war, to reestablish justice. One must be prepared to exert Gandhian soul force by putting one's body on the line, but in a nonviolent way, through civil disobedience. In so doing, one leaves open the opportunity to gain the respect, understanding, and perhaps transformation of one's enemy.

The lesson Gandhi derived from the *Gita* is that the encounter with the other need not lead to conquest. It can lead, instead, to mutual understanding and mutual respect. King's relationship to Gandhi and Gandhi's relationship to Tolstoy are models of a postmodern spirituality and ethics that transform postmodern relativism and eclecticism into the opportunity to follow a new spiritual and ethical path—"the way of all the earth"—the sharing of spiritual insight and ethical wisdom across religions and cultures in an age of globalization.

On this path, people of diverse religions and cultures find themselves sharing an ethical commitment to protect human dignity beyond the postmodern interest in personal transformation fostered by the modernist ideal of privatization. Gandhi and King were not engaged in a private quest to perfect the self (although neither neglected the need for personal transformation). Rather, each man embarked on a public quest to transform human communities, socially and politically, by invoking a global ethical commitment to protect the dignity of all persons. The religious movements associated with both men fit the pattern of the holy that affirms the secularization of society in order to embrace religious pluralism. Gandhi and King recovered the premodern ideal of religion shaping the public order but now in a postmodern mode, committed to religious pluralism.

The Children of Gandhi: An Experiment in Postmodern Global Ethics

In April 1968, Martin Luther King Jr., sometimes referred to as "the American Gandhi," went to Memphis to support black municipal workers in the midst of a strike. The Baptist minister was looking forward to spending the approaching Passover with Rabbi Abraham Joshua Heschel. Heschel, who had marched with King during the voter registration drive in Selma, Alabama, three years earlier, had become a close friend and supporter. Unfortunately, King was not able to keep that engagement. On April 4, 1968, like Gandhi before him, Martin Luther King Jr., a man of nonviolence, was shot to death by an assassin.

The Buddhist monk and anti–Vietnam War activist Thich Nhat Hanh, whom King had nominated for a Nobel Peace Prize, received the news of his friend's death while at an interreligious conference in New York City. Only the previous spring, King had expressed his opposition to the Vietnam War, largely at the urging of Thich Nhat Hanh and Rabbi Heschel. King spoke out at an event sponsored by Clergy and Laymen Concerned about Vietnam, a group founded by Heschel, Protestant cleric John Bennett, and Richard Neuhaus, then a Lutheran minister. Now another champion in the

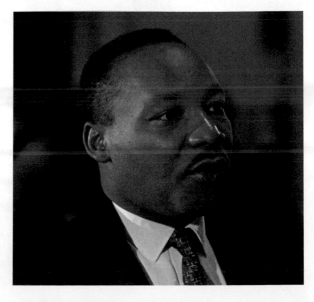

Martin Luther King Jr., who led the civil rights movement for racial equality in the United States, using the techniques of nonviolent civil disobedience inspired by Gandhi.

struggle against hatred, violence, and war was dead. But the spiritual and ethical vision he shared with his friends, across religions and cultures, has continued to inspire followers throughout the world.

These religious activists—a Baptist minister who won the Noble Peace Prize for his leadership in the American civil rights movement, a Hasidic rabbi and scholar who narrowly escaped the death camps of the Holocaust, and a Buddhist monk who had been targeted for assassination in Vietnam but survived to lead the Buddhist peace delegation to the Paris peace negotiations in 1973—are the spiritual children of Gandhi. By working together to protest racial injustice and the violence of war, they demonstrated that religious and cultural pluralism do not have to end in ethical relativism and, given a commitment to nonviolence, can play a role in shaping public life in an age of globalization. The goal, Martin Luther King Jr. insisted, is not to humiliate and defeat your enemy but to win him or her over, bringing about not only justice but also reconciliation. The goal, he said, was to attack the evil in systems, not to attack persons. The goal was to love one's enemy, not in the sense of sentimental affection or in the reciprocal sense of friendship, but in the constructive sense of seeking the opponent's well-being.

Nonviolence, King argued, is more than just a remedy for this or that social injustice. It is, he was convinced, essential to the survival of humanity in an age of nuclear weapons. The choice, he said, was "no longer between violence and nonviolence. It is either nonviolence or nonexistence."

Truth is to be found in all religions, King said many times, and "injustice anywhere is a threat to justice everywhere. We are caught in an inescapable network of mutuality, tied in a single garment of destiny. Whatever affects one directly affects all

A Buddhist monk meditates during a moment of silence near the finish line of the Boston Marathon bombings on the one-week anniversary of the April 22, 2013 attack.

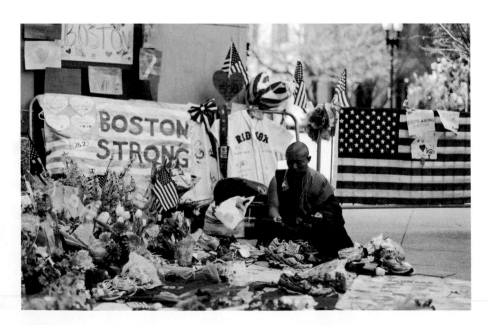

TEACHINGS OF RELIGIOUS WISDOM: Thich Nhat Hanh on the Shared Wisdom of Buddhism and Christianity

Thich Nhat Hanh was nominated by Martin Luther King Jr. for the Nobel Peace Prize for his nonviolent struggle to establish peace between North Vietnam and South Vietnam during the Vietnam War in the 1960s. During this time Thich Nhat Hanh also engaged in dialogue with the famous Catholic Christian monk Thomas Merton about the similarities and differences between Buddhist and Christian monastic spirituality. Since then Hanh's influence has become global. In his writings, especially *Living Buddha, Living Christ,* he insists that religious language is about direct religious experience, not about abstract metaphysical beliefs. On this, he says, both Buddhist and Christian contemplative monks agree.

Once the ultimate is touched, all notions are transcended: birth, death, being, non-being, before, after, one, many and so forth. Questions like "Does God exist?" or "Does nirvana exist" are no longer valid. God and nirvana as concepts have been transcended. . . . For the one who has had an experience of God or nirvana, the question "does God exist?" is an indication of the lack of insight. (p. 189)

Buddhists and Christians know that nirvana or the Kingdom of God is within their hearts. Buddhist sutras speak of Buddha nature as the seed of enlightenment that is already in everyone's consciousness. The Gospels speak of the Kingdom of God as a mustard seed planted in the soil of consciousness. The practices of prayer and meditation help us touch the most valuable seeds that are within us and they put us in contact with the ground of our being. . . . When the energy of mindfulness is present, transformation takes place. When the energy of the Holy Spirit is within you, understanding, love, peace, and stability are possible. God is within. You are, yet you are not, but God is in you. This is interbeing. This is non-self. (p. 167–68)

Source: Thich Nhat Hanh, *Living Buddha, Living Christ* (New York: G. P. Putnam and Sons, Riverhead Books), 1995.

---

indirectly."[6] The scandal of our age, said Abraham Joshua Heschel, is that in a world of diplomacy "only religions are not on speaking terms." But, he also said, no religion is an island, and all must realize that "holiness is not the monopoly of any particular religion or tradition."[7]

"Buddhism today," writes Thich Nhat Hanh, "is made up of non–Buddhist elements, including Jewish and Christian ones." And likewise with every tradition. "We have to allow what is good, beautiful, and meaningful in the other's tradition to transform us," the Vietnamese monk continues. The purpose of such passing over into the other's tradition is to allow each to return to his or her own tradition transformed. What is astonishing, says Thich Nhat Hanh, is that we will find kindred spirits in other traditions with whom we share more than we do with many in our own tradition.[8]

The Future of Religion in an Age of Globalization

Will the global future of religion and civilization be shaped by this Gandhian model of new age spiritual practice? It clearly offers an alternative to both traditional denominational modernist religions and the more privatistic modernist forms of new age religion. The Gandhian model also offers an alternative to the fundamentalist rejection of modernization and secularization by showing that religious pluralism does not have to lead to relativism. On the contrary, it can lead to the sanctification of life and the promotion of an ethic of human dignity across religions and cultures. The challenge is that the sharing of spiritual wisdom does require seeing the religions and cultures of others as having wisdom to share, and not all will accept this presupposition. Nevertheless, the emergence of religious postmodernism means that in the future, the struggle among religions will most likely be not so much between fundamentalism and modernism, nor between theists and atheists, but between religious fundamentalist exclusivism and postmodern religious pluralism—both as forms of religion that shape not only private but also public life.

Discussion Questions

1. What is the difference between a "new religion" and a "new age religion"?

2. How do modernist new age religious belief and practice differ from postmodernist new age religious belief and practice? Give an example of each.

3. How does new age religion relate to the split between faith and reason (the *via moderna* and the *devotio moderna*) that shaped the emergence of the modern world through the Enlightenment and the Romantic reaction it provoked?

4. In what sense is "civil religion" a new way of being religious, and in what sense is it a very old way of being religious?

5. What do the authors mean by suggesting that in a postmodern society, atheism can itself become a form of fundamentalism?

6. In what way is the postmodern path of religious ethics opened up by M. K. Gandhi and Martin Luther King Jr. similar to fundamentalist ideals for society, and in what way is it different?

Suggested Readings

Bruce, Steve. *Religion in the Modern World* (New York: Oxford University Press, 1996).

Dunne, John S. *The Way of All the Earth* (1972; rpt., Notre Dame, IN: University of Notre Dame Press, 1978).

Ellwood, Robert S., and Harry B. Partin, eds. *Religious and Spiritual Groups in Modern America*, 2nd ed. (Upper Saddle River, NJ: Prentice Hall, 1973, 1988).

Fasching, Darrell J. *The Coming of the Millennium* (San Jose, CA: Authors Choice Press, 1996, 2000).

———. "Stories of War and Peace: Sacred, Secular and Holy," in Sarah Deets and Merry Kerry, eds., *War and Words* (Lanham, MD: Rowman and Littlefield, 2004).

Fasching, Darrell J., Dell deChant, and David Lantigua. *Comparative Religious Ethics: A Narrative Approach to Global Ethics*, 2nd ed. (Oxford: Blackwell, 2011).

Jones, Lindsay, ed. *Encyclopedia of Religion*, 2nd ed., 15 vols. (Detroit: Macmillan Reference USA, 2005).

Juergensmeyer, Mark. *Terror in the Mind of God* (Berkeley: University of California Press, 2000).

Laderman, Gary, and Luis Leon, eds. *Religion and American Cultures*, vol. 1 (Santa Barbara, CA: ABC Clio, 2003).

Lewis, James R., ed. *The Oxford Handbook of New Religious Movements* (New York: Oxford University Press, 2004).

Melton, J. Gordon. *Finding Enlightenment* (Hillsboro, OR: Beyond Words Publishing, 1998).

Rothstein, Mikael, ed. *New Age Religion and Globalization* (Aarhus, Denmark: Aarhus University Press, 2001).

Notes

1. William Bloom, *The New Age: An Anthology of Essential Writings* (London: Rider/Channel 4, 1991), p. xviii. Quoted in Steve Bruce, *Religion in the Modern World* (Oxford: Oxford University Press, 1996).

2. Sarah Pike, "New Age," quoted in Robert S. Ellwood and Harry B. Partin, eds., *Religious and Spiritual Groups in Modern America*, 2nd ed. (Upper Saddle River, NJ: Prentice Hall, 1988), p. 140.

3. L. Ron Hubbard, *Scientology: The Fundamentals of Thought* (Edinburgh: Publications Organization Worldwide, 1968); originally published 1950. Quoted in Ellwood and Partin, *Religions and Spiritual Groups in Modern America*, p. 147.

4. John Dunne, *The Way of All the Earth* (Notre Dame, IN: University of Notre Dame Press, 1978), p. ix.

5. Wilfred Cantwell Smith, *Toward a World Theology* (Philadelphia: Westminster Press, 1981), chap. 1.

6. Martin Luther King Jr., "Letter from Birmingham Jail," in King, *I Have a Dream: Writings and Speeches That Changed the World*, ed. James M. Washington (San Francisco: HarperSanFrancisco, 1992), p. 85.

7. Abraham Joshua Heschel, *Moral Grandeur and Spiritual Audacity: Essays [of] Abraham Joshua Heschel*, ed. Susannah Heschel (New York: Farrar, Straus & Giroux, 1996), pp. 241, 247.

8. Thich Nhat Hanh, *Living Buddha, Living Christ* (New York: G. P. Putnam and Sons, Riverhead Books, 1995), pp. 9, 11.

Additional Resources

Cults a.k.a. New Religious Movements, Ontario Consultants on Religious Tolerance (http://www.religioustolerance.org/cultmenu.htm)

This site devoted to religious tolerance offers comprehensive, balanced information on new religions, "cults," and the anti-cult and counter-cult movements. Principal new religions are profiled, including their history, beliefs, practices, publications, and conflicts with government or other groups. Offers an overview of the conflicts, including references supporting the various sides of the conflicts.

Religious Movements, University of Virginia (http://cti.itc.virginia.edu/~jkh8x/soc257/)

This archive provides detailed profiles of more than 200 different religious groups and movements. The founding editor of the Religious Movements Homepage Project, Jeff Hadden, passed away in 2003. The new editor-in-chef is Douglas E. Cowan, who is at the University of Waterloo in Ontario Canada (http://artsweb.uwaterloo.ca/~decowan/). Through the work of an advisory board of internationally recognized scholars of new religious movements, the data are being expanded and updated.

GLOSSARY

Adi Granth: the scripture worshipped by Sikhs

Aggadah: the stories of the Tanak and the Talmud that communicate spiritual truths

ahimsa: nonviolence, the ideal of doing no killing, especially for its karmic effects

al-haram al-sharif: the noble sanctuary

All Souls Festival: a summer event when the gates of purgatory are thought to be held open; families perform rituals to connect the living members with their departed kin and ensure their ancestors' comfort in the afterlife

Allah: God

al-Quds: the holy city (i.e., Jerusalem)

Amaterasu: the kami of the sun and progenitor of the Japanese imperial line

Amitabha/Amida: the most important and highly developed of the Pure Land schools created by a Chinese Buddha named Amitabha in Sanskrit (Amitofo in Chinese, Amida in Japanese), featured chanting Amitabha's name (*Namo A-mi-t'o Fo*) as a meditative act and communal ritual

amoraim: the generation of sages that created the Gemara

Analects: collection of sayings attributed to Confucius

anatman: "nonself," the doctrine denying the reality of a permanent, immortal soul as the spiritual center of the human being

ancestor veneration: worship, feeding, and petitioning of the souls of dead ancestors at family graves, temples, or home altars

animism: religious tradition whose basic perception entails belief in an inner soul that gives life and ultimate identity to humans, animals, and plants and that places primary emphasis on experiential rituals in which humans interact with other souls

arhat: an enlightened disciple, according to the Theravada school; an advanced disciple, according to the Mahayana

Arya Samaj: religious organization that redefined and defended reformed Hindu traditions

Ashkenazi: Jews whose traditions originated in central and eastern Europe

Ashoka: (273–232 BCE), ruler whose patronage spread Buddhist institutions and teachings across his empire, and likely beyond

ashram: center of religious practice following a guru

atman: in Hindu thought, the soul that resides in the heart, is the source of both life energy and spiritual awareness, and transmigrates after death

Augustinian: refers to views of St. Augustine, for example, his view of the separation of church and state, in which the state is answerable to the church in religious matters while the church is answerable to the state in secular matters—yet both exist to promote the spread of the Gospel

Avalokiteshvara: *see* Guanyin

avatara: "incarnation" of a god that descends to earth; avataras assume life forms that aid creation, usually to defeat demons and overcome evil

ayatollah: literally, "sign of God"; title used by certain Shiah religious leaders who are widely reputed for their learning and piety

bar/bat mitzvah: the rite of passage for boys (bar mitzvah) whereby they become full members of the religion of Judaism who are able to read and interpret Torah; in modern times a parallel rite for girls (bat mitzvah) has been established in some forms of Judaism

Bhagavad Gita: Hindu scripture inserted into the great epic, the *Mahabharata*, extolling the divinity of Krishna as the ultimately real deity

bhakti: devotionalism to a divinity, a means to reach salvation from the world of rebirth

Bharatiya Janata Party (BJP): Hindu nationalism party that rose meteorically in popularity in the 1990s and assumed national rule in 1998

bhikku/bhikkhuni: nuns

Bodh Gaya: the site of Shakyamuni Buddha's enlightenment, under a tree

bodhisattva: a Buddha to be, either in the present life or in a future life. In the Mahayana tradition, all individuals should aspire to be Buddhas; hence, the bodhisattva is the highest human role. Some future Buddhas can be reborn as deities; hence, in Mahayana Buddhism there are also bodhisattvas who can assist humans

Brahman: world spirit that arises at creation, which Hindus hold is either in impersonal form, nirguna Brahman, or human form, saguna Brahman

brahmin: member of the highest caste, innately possessing the highest natural purity; the men traditionally specialize in ritual performance, textual memorization and study, and theology

Buddha: literally, one who has "awakened," ended karmic bondage, and will no longer be reborn; one who will enter nirvana

Buddhaghosa: (fifth century CE), great Theravadin monk-scholar

Buddha-nature school: a Mahayana Buddhist belief that all beings have a portion of nirvana and so possess the latent potential for its realization; a reversion to belief in the soul that also reinforced the need for traditional meditation practices

Bwiti: a West Central African religion that incorporates animism, ancestor worship, and Christianity into its belief system, along with a specially cultivated hallucinogen

caitya: a term that can also signify any Buddha shrine; *see also* stupa

caliph (khalifah): successor of Muhammad as the political and military head of the Muslim community

Catholic: those churches that define their Christian authenticity through apostolic succession

Ch'an: a Mahayana Buddha-nature tradition in East Asia called *Ch'an* in China, *Sön* in Korea, and *Zen* in Japan

Ch'ondogyo: Korean movement reaffirming the truth of human dignity and the vitality of Daoism and Confucianism

Christ: from Greek translation of the Hebrew word meaning "messiah" or "anointed one," the title Christians apply to Jesus of Nazareth

circular time: the awareness, more prevalent in hunter-gather than in industrial societies, that life is governed by the rising and the setting of the sun, the phases of the moon, and the seasons of the year

circumcision: the cutting of the foreskin of the penis as a sign of the covenant of Abraham

Cittamatra: Mahayana philosophical school that focuses on consciousness as the center of spiritual realization

city god: Chinese deity with influence on spirits living within city precincts, to whom every family's kitchen god reported at year's end

civil religions: the beliefs and rituals of modern "secular" societies that treat their social order as sacred due to the "cultural" influence of the religions that shaped their origin and development

Confucianism: culture of the literate elite (rujia) informed by Confucius and his disciples, who mastered the classics and rituals; the moral tradition upholding the "three bonds" and the "three principles" as the basis of social life; the spiritual tradition of revering ancestors as part of the family bond

Confucius: *see* Master K'ung

Constantinian/Constantinianism: view of the unity of church and state attributed to the first Christian Roman Emperor, Constantine, in which the state exists to rule over and protect the church as the official religion of the empire

cosmogony: mythological account of the creation

covenant: the agreement between God and the people of Israel whereby they are chosen to be God's people; God agrees to guide and protect them; the people agree to follow God's commandments (*halakhah*)

Cultural Revolution: period from 1966 to 1976 when China's Communist Party, under the leadership of Mao Zedong, attacked religious traditions and practitioners

dana: one of the four merit-making activities in Buddhist culture, "self-less giving" to diminish desire

Dao: mysterious power that moves the universe and all beings

Daoism, philosophical: Chinese tradition advocating the way to harmony for individuals and society based on understanding natural forces and flowing with life naturally

Daoism, religious: Chinese tradition that cultivates individual immortality through either alchemical infusions or meditative practices

Daoist: East Asian visionaries who advocated individualistic retreat, learning from the natural world, and noninterference by the state as the best way to ensure humanity's flourishing

dar al-Islam: the house or abode of Islam, as opposed to the house of war; territory controlled and ruled by Muslims

darshan: seeing the divine; making eye contact with a god, holy site, or guru

Daruma-san: Japanese name for the monk Bodhidharma, who brought a meditation-centered Buddhist tradition to China, which would be called Zen in Japan

dawah: call, missionary work, proselytization

de: mysterious and spontaneous energy of the universe

deism: Enlightenment view that God created the world the way a watchmaker creates a clock and leaves it to run on its own without interference

dependent origination: a twelve-part formula explaining how individuals are bound to future rebirth until they extirpate desire and ignorance

dharma: "duty" determined by one's caste and gender

Dharma: the Buddha's teaching, one of the three refuges; more broadly, the truth at the center of Buddhism, the basis for realizing enlightenment

dhimmi: literally, protected non-Muslim peoples; refers to Jews and Christians (later extended to others) who were granted "protected" status and religious freedom under Muslim rule in exchange for payment of a special tax

Diaspora: the dispersion of a religious people outside their geographic homeland, where they must live as a minority among others

diffuse religion: spiritual tradition centered on family and locality, informed by common ideas from Confucianism, Daoism, and Buddhism

divine: representative of the gods

Dogen: (1200–1253), Japanese monk; founder of Soto Zen school

Dreamtime: in Aboriginal legend, the time when the world was being created

dual Torah: the scriptures of Rabbinic Judaism, composed of the written Torah (Tanak) and the oral Torah (Talmud)

Eightfold Path: the eight qualities needed to reach nirvana, concerning morality, meditation, and salvific wisdom

Eisai: (1141–1215), Japanese monk; founder of Rinzai Zen school

engaged Buddhism: a reformist movement among global Buddhists seeking to relate the teachings to contemporary suffering

enlightenment: *see* nirvana

evangelical: refers to pietistic Christian movements that arose in response to the Enlightenment and also dogmatic divisions within Protestantism; emphasizes the unifying power of conversion as an emotional transformation rather than a rational/dogmatic one

fana: in Sufi usage, annihilation of the ego-centered self

faqih (pl. fuqaha): jurist, legal scholar; one who elaborates *fiqh*

faqir: ascetic mendicant mystic ideal; Sufi *shaykh*

fatwa: legal opinion or interpretation issued on request by legal expert (*mufti*) to either judges or private individuals

fiqh: understanding; science of Islamic law; jurisprudence; human interpretation and application of divine law

Five Classics: Confucian canon attributed to Master K'ung: *Book of Changes (Yi-Jing), Book of Documents (Shu Jing), Book of Poetry (Shi Jing),* and *Book of Rites (Li Jing),* and a historical work that uses events in the early Chinese state to show how to assess praise and blame

Four Good Deeds: a doctrinal formula guiding the laity on the uses of wealth, advising the pursuit of happiness, security, philanthropy, and ritual

Four Noble Truths: a doctrinal formula focusing on diagnosing the human condition as marked by suffering and distorted by desire and then prescribing the Eightfold Path as a solution

Full Moon Festival: an early fall festival to worship the harvest moon with special sweet "moon cakes"; across East Asia, people view the rising moon on this night to ask for blessings; rural communities request a good rice harvest in the month ahead

fundamentalist: term first emerged to refer to evangelical Protestants who believed that certain fundamental truths of the Gospel were threatened by modern interpreters; in general, fundamentalist movements in all religions see modernity as corrupting the fundamental truths and practices of a society as they were expressed in the premodern stage of their respective traditions

Gandhara: area of Indo-Greek interaction, influential in the creation of Buddhist art

Gandhi, Mohandas K.: (1869–1948), iconic leader who inspired mass support and led India to independence combining religious and political reforms

Gelugpa: monastic school that came to dominate all others, whose head, the Dalai Lama, ruled Tibet until 1959

Gemara: *see* Talmud

gentile: anyone not Jewish

Ghost Dance: a shaman-led nationwide movement aimed at reviving the indigenous nations of North America; ended in 1890 when the U.S. Cavalry massacred up to 300 of the men, women, and children gathered for the Ghost Dance at Wounded Knee, South Dakota

globalization: for the purposes of world religions, the idea that all the world's religions have members in every country or society; anyone using the Internet can view the major temples, shrines, churches, mosques, or monasteries from around the world and offer ritual prayers or make monetary offerings to them

Gospel: literally, "good news"; usually refers to the four Gospels of the New Testament, which retell the words and deeds of Jesus of Nazareth; can also refer to other, similar ancient writings not included in the Christian scriptures

grace: expresses the idea of unmerited divine love and assistance given to humans

Guan Yu: Chinese god of war, regarded as protector of merchants

Guanyin: the most popular and universal celestial bodhisattva was Avalokiteshvara, known as Guanyin in China, Kannon in Japan, Chenrizi in Tibet, and Karunamaya in Nepal

guru: a teacher in matters spiritual and cultural, whom disciples regard as semidivine

*gurudwara***:** Sikh temple

*hadith***:** narrative report of Muhammad's sayings and actions

*hajj***:** annual pilgrimage to Mecca; all Muslims should make the *hajj* at least once in their lifetime, but it is recognized that individual circumstances may make compliance impossible

*halakhah***:** the commandments of God revealed in the Tanak and commented on in the Talmud; the word means "to walk in the way of God" by obeying his commands or laws

Hare Krishna/(ISKON): Global devotional movement focused on Krishna founded by Swami Prabhupada (1896–1977)

haredim: Jewish ultra-Orthodox movements that reject all modernist forms of Judaism

Hasidism: a form of Judaism emerging in the eighteenth century, focused on piety and joy, with strong roots in Jewish mysticism

heresy: comes from the Greek term that means "choice"; came to be used as a negative term for choosing to believe doctrines viewed as erroneous by those who considered themselves to be "more orthodox"

heretic: from the ancient Greek, meaning "to choose"; in our postmodern world every religious person becomes a heretic, that is, one who is not simply born into a given religion or identity but must choose it, even if it is only to choose to retain the identity offered by the circumstances of his or her birth

hijab: Arabic word for veil or external covering; can consist of headscarf alone or full body covering; also known as *chador* (in Iran) or *burqa* (in Afghanistan)

hijra: migration; Muhammad's *hijra* from Mecca to Medina in 622 marks the first year of the Muslim lunar calendar

Hindutva: Hindu-ness

Holocaust: meaning "burnt sacrifice," one name given to the attempt by Nazi Germany to eliminate the Jewish people

Homo religiosus: religious humanity; a term coined by comparative religions scholar Mircea Eliade to indicate that religious practice was universal to all humans

homoousios/homoiousios: first term was used to assert that the Word of God through which all things were created is "the same as" God; second term was used to assert that this Word was "like God"; Council of Nicaea (325 CE) affirmed the first and rejected the second

Hong Xiuquan: (1814–64), charismatic instigator of the Taiping Rebellion, whose trance experiences led him to believe that he was the "younger brother" of Jesus, charged with establishing a new state in China

Huang-di: "Yellow Emperor," first immortal in religious Daoism

hudud: Quranically prescribed crimes and punishments for consumption of alcohol, theft, fornication, adultery, and false witnessing; some countries have adopted these punishments as evidence of the "Islamic" nature of their political rule and law

ibadat: worship, ritual obligations

ijma: consensus; in Islamic law, refers to agreement of scholars on interpretation of legal questions; some have reinterpreted this principle to justify the right of a parliament to enact legislation

ijtihad: human interpretation or independent reasoning in Islamic law

imam: in Sunni Islam, the prayer leader and the one who delivers the Friday sermon; in Shiah Islam, refers to Muhammad's descendants as legitimate successors, not prophets, but divinely inspired, sinless, infallible, and the final authoritative interpreter of God's will as formulated in Islamic law

incarnation: the eternal Word of God is embodied in the flesh of Jesus during his earthly life; there were two basic formulations of this: "the Word became flesh" and "the Word bodily dwells in the flesh" of Jesus

ISKON: *see* Hare Krishna

Islam: submission or surrender to God

Israel: either Jews as a religious people or the land and state of Israel, depending on the context

jahiliyya: the period of ignorance in which justice is guaranteed and administered not by God but by threat of retaliation by family or tribe

Janam Sakhis: traditional stories about life and teachings of Guru Nanak *jihad*: to strive or struggle; exerting oneself to realize God's will, lead a virtuous life, fulfill the universal mission of Islam, and spread Islam through preaching and/or writing; defense of Islam and Muslim community; currently often used to refer to the struggle for educational and social reform and social justice as well as armed struggle, holy war

jun-zi: a Confucian gentleman who has cultivated character and learning

justification by faith: Protestant Reformation doctrine formulated by Martin Luther, asserting that humans are saved by faith as a gift rather than through works of obedience to the law

Kabbalah: Jewish mysticism; the most important Kabbalistic work is the *Zohar*; for Kabbalists, God is the *En Sof*, the limitless or infinite, who manifests himself in the world through his *Shekinah*, or "divine presence" in all things; the reunion of all with the infinite through mystical contemplation will bring about nothing less than the messianic kingdom

Kali Yuga: the dark age the world has now entered, when human spiritual capacity is thought to be diminished; a view shared by some Hindus and Buddhists

kami: deity of Japan associated with places, certain animals, and the emperor

karma: literally "action" but also meaning the effects of actions that, through a hidden natural causality, condition a being's future; Hindus fix karma as acting on the inborn soul, and Buddhists define its effects on the consciousness and habits

karuna: compassion, the quality that motivated the Buddha to preach and the principal Buddhist social virtue

Khalsa: Sikh organization for the defense of the faith, marked by their uncut hair (covered with a turban), short trousers, steel wristlet, comb, and sword

khatam: seal or last of the prophets; Muhammad

khutba: sermon delivered at Friday prayer session in the mosque

Kingdom of God: the kingdom occurs whenever humans live in accord with the will of God and especially at the end of time, when God will be all in all

"kitchen god" (Zao Wangye): deity residing in every household, thought to observe and report on family events to his celestial superiors yearly

koan: a Buddhist spiritual riddle designed to foster spiritual growth, posed by monastic teacher to junior monks, such as "What is the sound of one hand clapping?" or "Does a dog have Buddha nature?"

kosher: what is *halal,* suitable or fit, used especially in reference to foods permitted by Jewish dietary laws

Lao Zi (Lao Tzu): "Old Sage," reputed author of *Daodejing* and founder of Daoism

li: in Confucian thought, individual performances needed for personal development, including manners, service to others, and rituals

liberation theology: liberation theology emerged in Latin America in the twentieth century; the goal was to show that the Gospel was more radical than Marxism in its promotion of justice for the poor

lila: term reflecting theology of this world as a sphere of divine play

ling: spiritual force possessed by geographic places, such as rivers, mountains, and caves, as well as by deities and charismatic sages

literati tradition: *see* Confucianism

Lotus Sutra: one of the earliest and most influential Mahayana Buddhist texts, which reveals the cosmological nature of a Buddha and the universal character of Buddhist truth

Madhyamaka: a Mahayana philosophical school that posits the provisional and incomplete nature of all assertions; its goal is to clear away attachment even to words, making realization possible

Maharishi Mahesh Yogi: (1917–2008), founder of the Transcendental Meditation movement

Mahayana: the "Great Vehicle" that was the dominant school of Buddhism in Tibet and East Asia; the Mahayana philosophical schools developed cosmological theories of Buddhahood and envisioned the universe as permeated by bodhisattvas, some of whom were like deities and the focus of ritual veneration

Mahdi: expected or awaited one; divinely guided one who is expected to appear at the end of time to vindicate and restore the faithful Muslim community and usher in the perfect Islamic society of truth and justice

Maitreya: the next historical Buddha uniquely depicted in China as corpulent and happy

maitri: loving-kindness, a Buddhist ethical virtue and topic of meditation

Mandate of Heaven: theory that the forces of the universe favor the ruler

mappo: Buddhist doctrine of the world in decline, especially that humans cannot practice meditation as well as in the time of the Buddha

Marranos: the Jews of Spain who were forced to convert to Christianity during the Inquisition but secretly continued to practice their Jewish faith

Master K'ung: given name of sage (551–479 BCE) to whom Catholic missionaries later gave the Latinate name Confucius

Master Xun: (298–238 BCE), influential early Confucian exponent with emphasis on authoritarian rule

matha: monastery

Mencius: first major disciple of Master K'ung; a systematizer of Confucian ideals who lived 371–289 BCE

merit: *see* punya

metanarrative: a grand cosmic and/or historical story accepted by the majority of a society as expressing its beliefs about origin, destiny, and identity

millennialism: beliefs about an age of peace (1,000 years) at the end of time that have their origin in the New Testament Book of Revelation

Mi-lo Fo: *see* Maitreya

minbar: pulpit in the mosque from which the Friday sermon (*khutba*) is preached

Mishnah: *see* Talmud

mitzvot: the commandments of God requiring deeds of loving kindness

mizuko cult: a new form of Kannon devotionalism in Japan organized to seek the forgiveness of the spirits of aborted fetuses and transfer merit to them until they fulfill their destiny and continue on to another human rebirth

modern: a civilization that separates its citizens' lives into public and private spheres, assigning politics to public life while restricting religion to personal and family life; a dominant scientific metanarrative provides the most certain public truths people believe they know; society and politics are governed by secular, rational, and scientific norms rather than religion

moksha: "release" from samsara, freedom from future rebirth and redeath (i.e., salvation)

morality: the rightness of any human action

mosque (*masjid*): Islamic temple, from *masjid*, "place of prostration"

muamalat: social interactions

mudang: Korean shamans, predominantly women, drawn into the role through either troubling personal experiences or inheritance

muezzin: one who issues the call to prayer from the top of the *minaret*

mufti: legal expert, adviser, or consultant; one who issues *fatwas* to judges and litigants

mujaddid: renewer; one who comes to restore and revitalize the Islamic community; one who purifies and restores true Islamic practice; one *mujaddid* is to be sent at the beginning of each century

mujtahid: expert in Islamic law; one who exercises *ijtihad*, or independent reasoning, in legal matters; one capable of interpreting Islamic law

Muslim: one who submits or surrenders himself or herself to God and his will; one who follows Islam

myth: from the Greek *mythos*, meaning "story"; a symbolic story about the origins and destiny of human beings and their world; myth relates human beings to whatever powers they believe ultimately govern their destiny and explains to them what the powers expect of them

n/um kausi: shamans of the Kung people

Nagarjuna: (born c. 150 CE), influential analytical philosopher of the early Mahayana school

Native American Church: a "Pan-American" movement among American Native peoples that has factions related in varying ways to Christianity but that are united in their ceremonial use of the cactus peyote as the group's own communal sacrament

nembutsu: repetition of the name of the Buddha Amitabha, for the purpose of making merit and gaining rebirth in the Pure Land

neo-Confucianism: tradition originating in the Song dynasty and developed subsequently by masters such as Zhu Xi who sought to harmonize early Confucian humanism with more cosmological theories of Daoism and karma doctrine of Buddhism, adopting meditation techniques from both

neopaganism: modern adaptations of ancient pagan (polytheistic and animistic) beliefs

neo-Shintoism (or state Shinto): Meiji state's adoption of Shinto as state religion, with emperor as focal divinity, which lasted from 1868 to 1945

new age religions: religions that emerge by breaking with traditional beliefs and practices, typically through the influence of other religious practices around the globe due to the influence of modern science, global media, and global travel

new religions: religions that arise as new revelations within a tradition that change it in ways that traditional adherents do not accept, often through the influence of new religious prophets and the influence of other religions in their local environment

"new religions": sects arising in Japan from the early nineteenth century combining elements of Buddhism, Daoism, and Confucianism with ideas imported from abroad; term may also be applied outside Japan

Nichiren: (1222–1282), Japanese monk who taught that the *Lotus Sutra* is the only true Buddhist text and that chanting its title was an essential salvation practice; founded new school based on these ideas

nirguna Brahman: *see* Brahman

nirvana: a blissful state achieved by individuals who have cut off their karma by ending desire, attachment, and ignorance; after death, they enter the final transpersonal state for eternity, free from future rebirth

nonviolence: a strategy for dealing with the violence of others through nonviolent acts of civil disobedience

numinous: the human perception of the sacred

OM: also written in full phonetic rendition as AUM, one of the most prominent symbols of Hinduism; repeated as part of almost every mantra for offerings and meditation as well as written calligraphically on icons and other symbols

Om-kara ("Divine One") and Sat Guru ("True Teacher"): Sikh terms for the impersonal ultimate reality

original sin: the sin of Adam and Eve, who disobeyed the command of God not to eat the fruit of the tree of knowledge of good and evil; said to have affected all human beings by corrupting their will so that they are often unable to do the good they intend

orthodoxy: acceptance of "right beliefs" or "doctrines" based on sacred texts as formulated by religious authorities

orthopraxy: the practice of "right actions" or rituals as prescribed by sacred traditions

Pali Canon: the only complete canon among the early collection of Buddha's teachings, in this case in the Pali language derived from Sanskrit; it is split into three divisions: *Vinaya* (monastic code), *Sutras* (sermons), and *Abhidhamma* (advanced teaching formula)

pap: "demerit"; bad karma earned by breaking the precepts

passing over: the act of imagination whereby one sees the world through the eyes of another's religion and thereby gains new insight into one's own religion

Pentecostal: refers to churches that emphasize possession by the Holy Spirit and speaking in tongues

People of the Book (*ahl al-kitab*): those possessing a revelation or scripture from God; typically refers to Jews and Christians, Muslims, and sometimes includes Zoroastrians

philosophical Daoism: tradition articulating path to harmony for individuals and society based on understanding and flowing with natural forces

postmodern: a society typified by diversity in both beliefs and social practices that has no single dominant metanarrative (other than the narrative of diversity) and is skeptical of finding either certain knowledge or norms in any public form of truth, whether religious, ethical, or scientific

prajna: the "insight" or "wisdom" necessary for enlightenment in Buddhism, comprising the ability to "see clearly" into the nature of existence as marked by suffering, impermanence, and absence of a soul

prasad: the remains of any substance (food, flowers, incense, etc.) used in a ritual offering, thought to be medicinal because it has been in contact with the divinity

premodern: a civilization in which there is no separation between religion and society; a dominant religious metanarrative provides the most certain truths people believe they know; by being a member of that culture, one automatically participates in its religious vision and lives by its religious norms

Protestant: the churches, beginning at the time of Martin Luther, that teach salvation by faith rather than works and also reject the mediation of the church through apostolic succession as necessary for salvation in favor of a direct personal relationship with God in Christ

Protestant Buddhism: a term signifying a pattern of reform in which Buddhists protested colonial rule yet adopted perspectives and missionary techniques of Protestant Christianity

Protestant ethic: term coined by sociologist Max Weber, who noted that the Calvinist branch of the Reformation fostered a belief in working hard and living simply for the glory of God and as proof that one was among those destined to be saved; such an attitude, Weber said, contributed to the accumulation of wealth needed for investment and fueled the Industrial Revolution and the flourishing of capitalist societies

puja: a ritual offering to a Hindu or bodhisattva deity, Buddha, or bodhisattva

punya: merit, or the good karma that enters into the content of an individual's life, earned in Buddhist doctrine by moral practices, learning, and meditation

puranas: texts extolling the histories, theologies, and necessary rituals for expressing the Bhakti faith for the different Hindu deities

purdah: seclusion of women from men who are not relatives; segregation of the sexes

Pure Land: in Mahayana Buddhism, the belief that Buddhas and advanced bodhisattvas can through their inexhaustible merit create rebirth realms where humans can easily engage in Buddhist practices conducive to enlightenment

qi: vital force of life within individuals and in nature

qi gong: discipline of cultivating the vital individual life force that can be used for worldly goals such as healing or to reach immortality

Qing Ming: yearly spring festival when Chinese visit and clean family graves and then feast after making offerings to the ancestors

qiyas: legal term for analogical reasoning

Quran: revelation, recitation, message; Muslim scripture

Rabbinic: a rabbi is a teacher; the name came to designate the Judaism of the *dual Torah* introduced by the Pharisees, which came to be normative in the premodern period

Ramadan: month of fasting; ninth month of the Muslim calendar

Ramakrishna Mission: founded by Swami Vivekananda to further the teachings of his guru, Ramakrishna; an influential Hindu missionary and reform organization that today runs hospitals, schools, and temples and has centers in over a dozen countries

Ramanuja: an influential theologian (1025–1137) who argued that the ultimate reality humans could relate to was saguna Brahman

Rammohan Roy: pioneering religious figure who called for the reform of Hindu beliefs and practices

Rashtriya Svayamsevak Sangh (RSS): "National Union of [Hindu] Volunteers"; group advocating "Hinduism" as devotion to "Mother India"

redemption: root meaning is "to be rescued or freed," especially from slavery; used in both a literal and a metaphorical sense: God redeemed Israel from slavery in Egypt and exile in Babylonia; God redeems sinners from punishment and death due to sin

religion: from the Latin *religare*, meaning "to tie or bind," and the root *religere*, which has the connotation of "acting with care"; expresses a sense of being "tied and bound" by obligations to whatever powers are believed to govern one's destiny—whether those powers be natural or supernatural, personal or impersonal, one or many; ancient peoples everywhere believed that the powers governing their destiny were the forces of nature

religious Daoisim: tradition devoted to attaining individual immortality through alchemical infusions or meditative practices

ren: Confucian ideal of being "fully human" in ethics, manners, and cultivation

ritual: actions that connect the individual and the community to each other, through the sacred

sacraments: ritual actions, such as baptism and holy communion, said to impart the grace of God to Christians, usually through the mediation of ordained clergy

saguna Brahman: *see* Brahman

salat: official prayer or worship performed five times each day

samsara: "the world" of rebirth subject to the law of karma and the inevitable reality of death, a religious understanding shared by Hinduism, Buddhism, Jainism, and Sikhism

sangha: the Buddhist monastic community of monks and nuns

Sat Guru: "true teacher"; Sikh term indicating the active mode of Om-kara

satyagraha: Gandhi's central principle of "grasping the truth"; with roots in the Hindu and Jain doctrine of nonviolence (ahimsa) and in Christianity's injunctions to love one's enemy and turn the other cheek (as a reaction to being struck in the face), Gandhi required those opposing the government to confine their protests to nonviolent acts, to accept suffering for the cause, to love the opponent, and to be disciplined in personal life

Second Coming: belief that Jesus, who died on the cross, arose from the dead, and ascended into heaven, will return at the end of time to raise the dead and establish a new heaven and a new earth

secular: sociologically used to mean "nonreligious"

Sephardic: Jews whose traditions originated in Spain and Portugal

shahadah: declaration of faith, witness, testimony; refers to the declaration of Muslim faith: "There is no god but God and Muhammad is His Messenger"

Shaivite: devotee of Shiva

shaktas: devotees of Devi

shakti: innate, creative force of this universe, understood as feminine

shaman: *see* spirit medium

shamanism: the traditions focused on individuals who can leave their bodies to enter the realm of the afterlife and spirits where they can learn higher spiritual truths and the arts of healing to bring back to one's people; has its roots in ancient animistic and polytheistic cultures

Shang-di: Heavenly Lord, thought to preside over early Chinese pantheon; term Christians used as translation for *God*

Shankara: Hindu philosopher (788–820) and monastic organizer, whose monistic interpretation of the *Upanishads* became the most influential expression of nirguna Brahman doctrine

sharia: Islamic law; straight path

Shema: the essential declaration of monotheistic faith as found in Judaism: "Hear O Israel, the Lord our God, the Lord is One"

shen: usual term in Chinese for a kindly god or goddess

Shiah or Shii: follower(s), partisan(s); refers to those who followed the leadership of Ali, the nephew and son-in-law of Muhammad, as Muhammad's successor; those who believe that leadership of the Muslim community should belong to Muhammad's descendants

Shinto: indigenous religion of Japan that reveres the deities of the islands, including the emperor

shirk: polytheism, idolatry, association of anyone or anything with God; the most serious sin in Islam

shramana: wandering ascetic known at the time of the Buddha

shunyata: "zero-ness"; the term used to designate the emptiness of all constructs

siddha: tantric saint

skandha: an aggregate, used in Buddhist thought to identify each of the five components that define a human being: the physical body (*rupa*), feelings (*vedana*), perceptions (*samjna*), habitual mental dispositions (*samskaras*), and consciousness (*vijnana*)

Soka Gakkai: Nichiren Buddhist offshoot, now global religion seeking world peace through Mahayana Buddhist teachings

Son of God: title applied to Jesus of Nazareth

sorcerers: mediums who manipulate the spirit world and coerce the supernaturals without their consent, often for their own benefit and against community values

spirit flight: "soul journey"; a shaman's attempt to locate another person's soul, perhaps because it has wandered off in this world or needs assistance to reach the afterlife of the clan's ancestors

spirit medium: person who communicates with deities and spirits through ritually induced trance

State Shinto: *see* neo-Shintoism

Sthaviravadins: the traditionalists among the early Buddhist monastic schools, the only surviving school today being the Theravadins

stupa: the distinctive Buddhist shrine, a raised mound surmounted by a ceremonial pole and umbrella; contains the relics of a Buddha or enlightened saint, either the literal bodily relics or other items left behind, such as words in textual form or clothing items worn

Sufi: literally "one who wears wool"; Muslim mystic or ascetic

Sufism: Islamic mysticism or asceticism

Sunnah: example; typically refers to Muhammad's example, which is believed by Muslims to be the living out of the principles of the Quran; *Sunni* is derived from this word

Sunni: those who accept the *sunna* and the historic succession of the Caliphs; the majority of the Muslim community

*surah***:** chapter, particularly of the Quran

Swami Vivekananda: Ramakrishna's foremost disciple

sympathetic imagination: empathy; necessary to understand the religious languages and messages of different times and places

synagogue: a community centered on the study of Torah and prayer to God; the buildings used to house these activities also came to be known as synagogues

syncretism: the weaving together of alien and indigenous religious beliefs and practices; or the combining of elements from different practices to create a new religion

syncretistic: the identification of the gods of one religion with the gods of another so that one's own gods are seen as the same as those of the other's religion but under different names

t'i: affection for siblings, in Confucianism a marker of character

T'oegyehak: modern Korean Confucian group based on teachings of master Yi T'oegye (1501–70)

taboo: forbidden

Taiping Rebellion: nineteenth-century revolt in China led by converts to Christianity, who established a separate state in the city of Nanjing; resulting civil war was bloodiest in world history

Talmud: the oral Torah, recorded in the *Mishnah*, and the commentary on the *Mishnah* called the *Gemara*; there are two Talmuds: the Bavli (Talmud of Babylonia) and the Yerushalmi (the Jerusalem Talmud); the former is considered the more comprehensive and authoritative

Tanak: the written Torah, or Hebrew Bible, made up of Torah (the first five books, from Genesis to Deuteronomy), Neviim (the prophets and historical writings such as Jeremiah and 1 and 2 Kings), and Ketuvim (the wisdom writings, such as Proverbs, Job, etc.)

Tannaim: the generation of sages, beginning with Hillel and Shammai, that created the *Mishnah*

tantra: the esoteric tradition common to both Hinduism and Buddhism that employs unorthodox practices including sexual yoga to transform the body and lead individuals quickly to experience moksha/nirvana

Tattvabodhini Sabha: a colonial Hindu sect, powerful around Calcutta, that promoted the "modern Hindu's" adaptation to India's new economic and political realities; merged the values of working hard, living honestly, saving rationally, and promoting altruism with the individual controlling personal desires; along with Rammohan Roy (1772–1833), they saw reformed Hinduism now being led by the "godly householder," not the premodern elite of world-renouncing ascetics

*tawhid***:** oneness, unity, and uniqueness of God; absolute monotheism

temple: a place to worship God or the gods in diverse religions; in Judaism only one temple was allowed for the worship of God in Jerusalem, whereas each Jewish community would have a synagogue for study and prayers

Tenrikyo: Tenrikyo ("Religion of Heavenly Wisdom") was founded by Nakayama Miki (1798–1887) and became a recognized Shinto sect in 1838; essential for salvation are a dance ritual, an initiation ("receiving the holy grant"), and performance of daily social service for others

Theravada: traditionalists, the last surviving Buddhist school of elders (Sthaviravadins) that is now dominant in South and Southeast Asia

three faiths: Chinese grouping of the three great traditions: Confucianism, Daoism, and Buddhism

Three Marks of Existence: the Buddhist terms for analyzing human reality as marked by impermanence, suffering, and no soul

Three Refuges: *see* Triratna

Thunderbolt Vehicle: *see* Vajrayana

Tian: "heaven," understood as impersonal yet responsive to human actions

Tian di: a supreme overlord believed to keep records on each individual soul, according to texts found in Han-era tombs in China

*tirtha***:** a holy space defined by a river confluence

Tisha B'Av: a day of mourning to commemorate tragedies affecting the Jewish people, particularly the fall of the First and Second Temples in Jerusalem

totem: symbol taken from the natural world that stands for a social group possessing a common origin and essence

transcendent: beyond all finite things

Transcendental Meditation (TM): a movement founded by Maharishi Mahesh Yogi that brought mystical Hindu teachings to the West through mantra-centered meditation

Trinity: God as Father, Son, and Holy Spirit; meant to suggest that the transcendent God can be immanent in the world without losing his transcendence—when

God acts in the world (as Son or Spirit), God does not cease to be father and Creator of the universe; therefore, God is not many gods but one God in three persons

Triratna: the "Three Jewels" that every Buddhist takes refuge in for all rituals: the Buddha, the Dharma, and the Sangha

Tu-di: "Earth Ruler," local god who is worshipped across modern China to control the earth's fertility

Tu-di (or Tu Chu): Gong: the cult of the "earth ruler" who controls fertility, widespread among farmers in China during the millennium from the Zhou dynasty (1122–221 BCE) until the fall of the Han (206 BCE–220 CE)

tutelary spirit: a supernatural agent, often an ancestral spirit, whose help is required by a shaman to perform the difficult soul journeys, negotiate with evil spirits, compel a soul to return, or increase the shaman's healing powers

two natures, one person: doctrine affirmed by Council of Chalcedon (451 CE); in the one person of Jesus are two natures (divine and human) said to coexist in unity but without confusion or mixture, so Jesus is fully human in everything except sin, and yet the fullness of God is also present in him and united to him

Tzaddik: in the Hasidic tradition, a "righteous man," as powerful as the rabbi in a traditional Talmudic community but revered for mystical piety and devotion, not Talmudic scholarship; for the Hasidim, the Tzaddik was especially chosen by God as a direct link between heaven and earth, whose holiness was so powerful that, like Moses (Exodus 32:11–14), he could intervene on behalf of the faithful and change the mind of God

ulama **(sing.** *alim***):** religious scholars

ultimate reality: that which is the highest in value and meaning for the group

*ummah***:** Muslim community of believers

Upanishads: appendices to the Vedas that record early Hindu speculations on Brahman, atman, the means to realize their identity, and moksha

Vaishnavite: devotee of Vishnu or his incarnations

Vajrayana: the Mahayana-derived Buddhist tantric "vehicle" of belief and practice that uses unorthodox means, including sexual experience, to propel individuals quickly toward enlightenment

Vedas: the collection of the earliest Hindu hymns directed to the pantheon of deities, including ritual directions and chanting notations for their use

"Venus" figurines: prehistoric Eurasian small stone sculptures of females with large breasts and hips, often with their genitalia emphasized, thought to indicate a worship of fertility in small communities

*via analogia***:** a way of knowing spiritual reality through the use of analogy, for example, "God is my shepherd" *via negativa:* the mystical way of knowing the highest spiritual reality (God, Brahman, etc.) by negating all finite qualities and characteristics; Hindus, for instance, say Brahman is "neti . . . neti"—not this and not that (i.e., Brahman is not a thing, Brahman is no-thing and therefore is pure nothingness, Brahman is beyond imagination and cannot be imaged, Brahman can only be known by a mystical experience of unknowing)

vihara: a Buddhist monastery

vipassana **meditation:** the widespread Buddhist meditation practice focusing on calming the mind and discerning the truly real

Vishva Hindu Parishad (VHP): an organization of religious leaders founded in 1964 to promote the interests of Hindus and advocate for India to be recognized as a "Hindu state"

wali: friend or protégé of God; Sufi term referring to saint; one reputed to have the power to bilocate, cure the sick, multiply food, and read minds

white shamans: Westerners who create global organizations propagating a purported "universal" shamanic tradition, charging high fees for tours, courses, initiations, and healing services, some pledging to use some of the proceeds to assist indigenous shamans

Won Buddhism: a new Korean school of Buddhism founded in 1924 by Soe-Tae San (1891–1943); it ritualizes worship of a picture of a black circle in a white background, symbolizing the *dharmakaya,* the cosmic body of the Buddha; the group is named *Won* from the Korean reading of the Chinese character "round"

Wu Tai Shan: sacred mountain in China refered as home of the bodhisattva Manjushri

wu-wei: "noninterference" or "non-[forced] action," an ideal in Daoism

xiao: Confucian ideal of children honoring their parents, attitude that extends to the ruler

yin-yang theory: twin forces by which the Dao is known, each complementing the other (female/male, valley/mountain, etc.)

yoga: a term meaning "union" that refers to the various means of realizing union with the divine; earliest use of yoga refers to ascetic practices but expands to include the path of philosophical inquiry, bhakti, and tantra

Yoga Sutras: codification of yoga practices, attributed to Patanjali

zakat: almsgiving, one of the Five Pillars of Islam: 2.5 percent tithe of one's net worth to help the poor is required of all Muslims

Zen: the Japanese Mahayana Buddhist school focused on meditation practice, as transmitted from and organized in China as the Ch'an

Zhu Xi: (1130–1200), great Chinese master of neo-Confucian thought who integrated into Confucianism elements of Buddhism and Daoism and established core rituals of subsequent tradition

Zhuang Zi: second great Daoist classic, named after a mystical sage of the same name

Zionism: the desire to return to the land of Israel as a homeland; in modern times, the secular movement started by Theodor Herzl that led to the formation of the state of Israel

Zohar: major book of Jewish Kabbalism: *The Book of Splendor*

ART CREDITS

INDEX